Accounting
An Introduction

Companion Website resources

Visit the Companion Website at
www.pearsoned.co.uk/atrillmclaney

For students
- Learning objectives for each chapter
- Multiple choice questions to help test your learning
- Additional exercises and review questions
- Solutions to end of chapter review questions
- Links to relevant sites on the web
- An online glossary to explain key terms

For lecturers
- Complete, downloadable Instructor's Manual
- PowerPoint slides that can be downloaded and used as OHTs
- Case study material with solutions
- Progress tests, consisting of various questions and exercise material with solutions
- Tutorial/seminar questions and solutions
- Solutions to end of chapter review questions

Also: This website has a Syllabus and Profile Manager, online help, search functions, and email results functions.

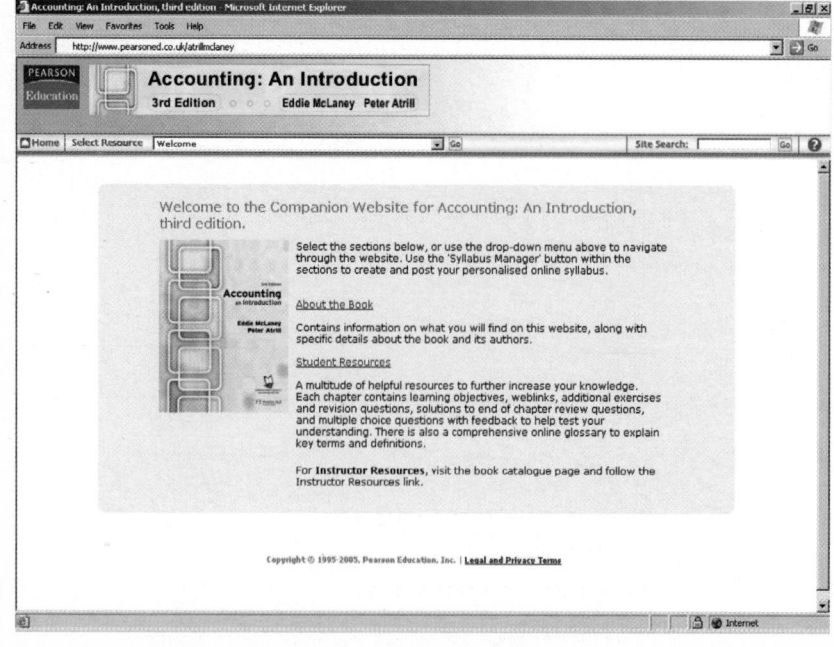

THIRD
EDITION

Accounting
An Introduction

Eddie McLaney
and
Peter Atrill

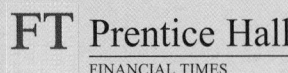

FT Prentice Hall
FINANCIAL TIMES

An imprint of **Pearson Education**
Harlow, England • London • New York • Boston • San Francisco • Toronto
Sydney • Tokyo • Singapore • Hong Kong • Seoul • Taipei • New Delhi
Cape Town • Madrid • Mexico City • Amsterdam • Munich • Paris • Milan

Pearson Education Limited

Edinburgh Gate
Harlow
Essex CM20 2JE
England

and Associated Companies throughout the world

Visit us on the World Wide Web at:
www.pearsoned.co.uk

———————————

First published 1999 by Prentice Hall Europe
Second edition published 2002
Third edition published 2005

ISBN 0 273 68822 7

British Library Cataloguing-in-Publication Data
A catalogue record for this book is available from the British Library

Library of Congress Cataloging-in-Publication Data
A catalog record for this book is available from the Library of Congress

10 9 8 7 6 5 4 3 2 1
09 08 07 06 05

Typeset in 9.5/12.5pt Stone by 35
Printed and bound by Mateu Cromo Artes Graficas, Madrid, Spain

The publisher's policy is to use paper manufactured from sustainable forests.

Brief contents

Detailed contents

Part 1   Financial accounting

5 Accounting for limited companies (2)   145

Part 2   Management accounting

Part 3 Financial management

15 Financing a business 514

Part 4   Supplementary information

Preface

This text provides a comprehensive introduction to financial accounting, management accounting and core elements of financial management. It is aimed both at students who are not majoring in accounting or finance and those who are. Those studying introductory-level accounting and/or financial management as part of their course in business, economics, hospitality management, tourism, engineering or some other area should find that the book provides complete coverage of the material at the level required. Students who are majoring in either accounting or finance should find the book useful as an introduction to the main principles, which can serve as a foundation for further study. The text does not focus on the technical aspects, but rather examines the basic principles and underlying concepts. The ways in which financial statements and information can be used to improve the quality of management decision making are the main focus of the book. To reinforce this practical emphasis, there are, through-out the text, numerous illustrative extracts with commentary from company reports, survey data and other sources.

In this third edition, we have taken the opportunity to make improvements that have been suggested by students and lecturers who used the previous edition. We have also brought up to date and expanded the number of examples from real life. We have also introduced 'bullet-point' chapter summaries. These should help to remind you of the key issues in each chapter. From 2005, most of the larger UK companies will have to adopt a new set of international rules relating to their preparation of the main financial statements. These new rules form the basis of the section of the book that deals specifically with accounting for limited companies.

The text is written in an 'open-learning' style. This means that there are numerous integrated activities, worked examples and questions throughout the text to help you to understand the subject fully. You are encouraged to interact with the material and to check your progress continually. Irrespective of whether you are using the book as part of a taught course or for personal study, we have found that this approach is more 'user-friendly' and makes it easier for you to learn.

We recognise that most of you will not have studied accounting or finance before, and we have therefore tried to write in a concise and accessible style, minimising the use of technical jargon. We have also tried to introduce topics gradually, explaining everything as we go. Where technical terminology is unavoidable we try to provide clear explanations. In addition, you will find all the key terms highlighted in the text. These are then listed at the end of each chapter with a page reference. All of these key terms are also listed alphabetically, with a concise definition, in the glossary given in Appendix B towards the end of the book. This should provide a convenient point of reference from which to revise.

A further important consideration in helping you to understand and absorb the topics covered is the design of the text itself. The page layout and colour scheme have been carefully considered to allow for the easy navigation and digestion of material.

The layout features a large page format, an open design, and clear signposting of the various features and assessment material.

More detail about the nature and use of these features is given in the 'How to use this book' section below; and the main points are also summarised, using example pages from the text, in the Guided tour on pages xxiv–xxv hereafter.

We hope that you will find the book readable and helpful.

Eddie McLaney
Peter Atrill

How to use this book

We have organised the chapters to reflect what we consider to be a logical sequence and, for this reason, we suggest that you work through the text in the order in which it is presented. We have tried to ensure that earlier chapters do not refer to concepts or terms that are not explained until a later chapter. If you work through the chapters in the 'wrong' order, you will probably encounter concepts and terms that were explained previously.

Irrespective of whether you are using the book as part of a lecture/tutorial-based course or as the basis for a more independent mode of study, we advocate following broadly the same approach.

Integrated assessment material

Interspersed throughout each chapter are numerous **Activities**. You are strongly advised to attempt all of these questions. They are designed to simulate the sort of quick-fire questions that your lecturer might throw at you during a lecture or tutorial. Activities serve two purposes:

- To give you the opportunity to check that you understand what has been covered so far.
- To encourage you to think about the topic just covered, either to see a link between that topic and others with which you are already familiar, or to link the topic just covered to the next.

The answer to each Activity is provided immediately after the question. This answer should be covered up until you have deduced your solution, which can then be compared with the one given.

Towards the middle/end of each chapter there is a **Self-assessment question**. This is more comprehensive and demanding than any of the Activities, and is designed to give you an opportunity to check and apply your understanding of the core coverage of the chapter. The solution to each of these questions is provided in Appendix C at the end of the book. As with the Activities, it is important that you attempt each question thoroughly before referring to the solution. If you have difficulty with a self-assessment question, you should go over the relevant chapter again.

End-of-chapter assessment material

At the end of each chapter there are four **Review questions**. These are short questions requiring a narrative answer or discussion within a tutorial group. They are intended to help you assess how well you can recall and critically evaluate the core terms and concepts covered in each chapter. Answers to these questions are provided in the student access Companion Website. At the end of each chapter, except for Chapter 1, there are eight **Exercises**. These are mostly computational and are designed to reinforce your knowledge and understanding. Exercises are graded as 'basic' and 'more advanced', according to their level of difficulty. The basic-level questions are fairly straightforward; the more advanced ones can be quite demanding but are capable of being successfully completed if you have worked conscientiously through the chapter and have attempted the basic exercises. Solutions to five of the exercises in each chapter are provided in Appendix D at the end of the book. A coloured exercise number identifies these five questions. Here, too, a thorough attempt should be made to answer each exercise before referring to the solution. Solutions to the other three exercises and to the review questions in each chapter are provided in a separate Instructors' Manual.

To familiarise yourself with the main features and how they will benefit your study from this text, an illustrated Guided tour is provided on pages xxiv–xxv.

Content and structure

The text comprises 16 chapters organised into three core parts: financial accounting, management accounting and financial management. A brief introductory outline of the coverage of each part and its component chapters is given in the opening double-page spread which precedes each part.

The market research for this text revealed a divergence of opinions, given the target market, on whether or not to include material on double-entry bookkeeping techniques. So as to not interrupt the flow and approach of the financial accounting chapters, Appendix A on recording financial transactions (including Activities and three Exercise questions) has been placed in Part 4.

Supplements and website

A comprehensive range of supplementary materials is available to lecturers adopting this text at www.pearsoned.co.uk/atrillmclaney.

- **Solutions Manual**
  - Solutions to all the exercises not provided in the text.
- **OHP masters**
  - Over 150 A4 sheets comprising all the Figures from the text, as well as other material, including the bullet-point chapter summaries.
- **PowerPoint**
  - Over 150 A4 sheets comprising all the Figures from the text, as well as other material, including the bullet-point chapter summaries.
- **Teaching material**
  - Case studies with solutions
  - Progress tests with solutions
  - Tutorial questions with outline solutions

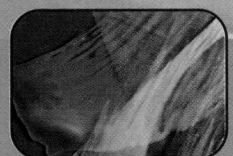

Guided tour of the book

Learning objectives Bullet points at the start of each chapter show what you can expect to learn from that chapter, and highlight the core coverage

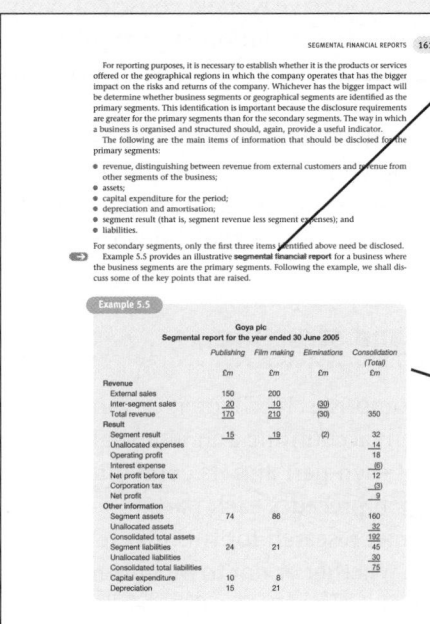

Key terms The key concepts and techniques in each chapter are highlighted in colour where they are first introduced, with an adjacent icon in the margin to help you refer back to the most important points.

Examples At frequent intervals throughout most chapters, there are numerical examples that give you step-by-step workings to follow through to the solution.

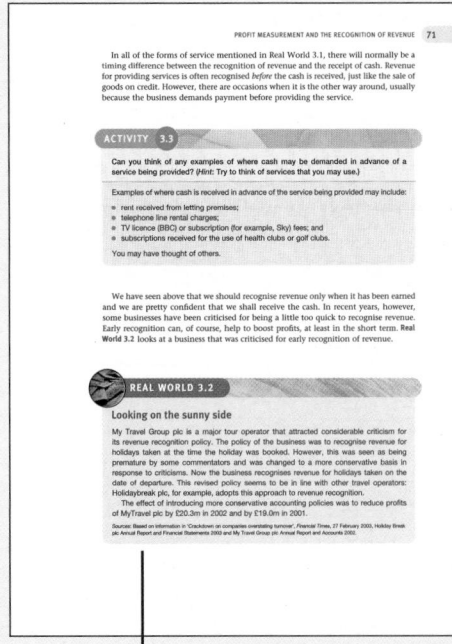

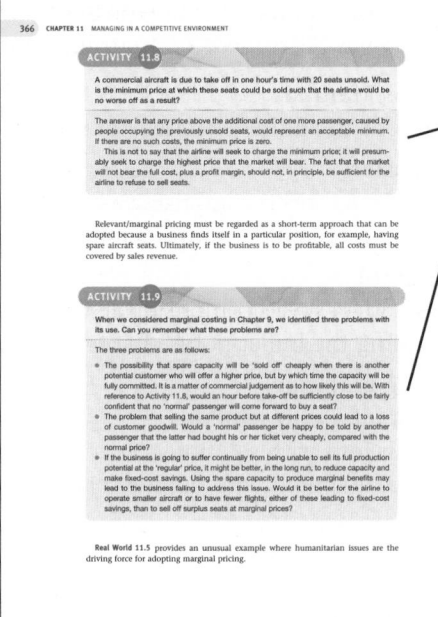

Activities These short questions, integrated throughout each chapter, allow you to check your understanding as you progress through the text. They comprise either a narrative question requiring you to review or critically consider topics, or a numerical problem requiring you to deduce a solution. A suggested answer is given immediately after each activity.

'Real World' illustrations Integrated throughout the text, these illustrative examples highlight the practical application of accounting concepts and techniques by real businesses, including extracts from company reports and financial statements, survey data and other interesting insights from business.

Self-assessment questions   Towards the end of most chapters you will encounter one of these questions, allowing you to attempt a comprehensive question before tackling the end-of-chapter assessment material. To check your understanding and progress, solutions are provided in Appendix C.

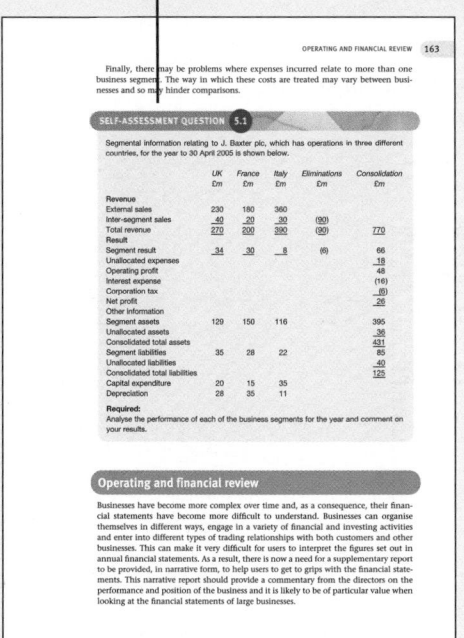

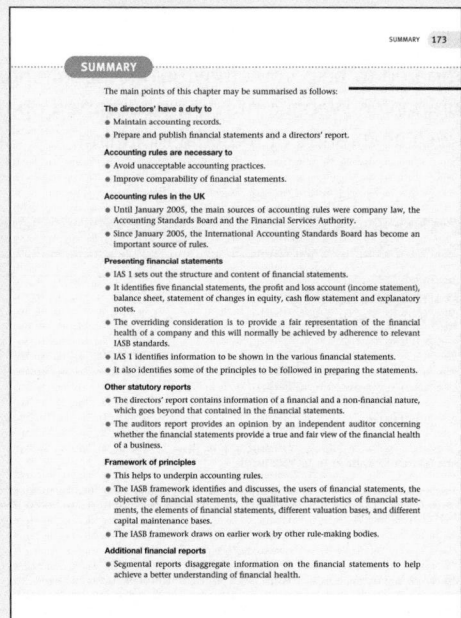

Bullet point chapter summary   Each chapter ends with a 'bullet-point' summary. This highlights the material covered in the chapter and can be used as a quick reminder of the main issues.

Key terms summary   At the end of each chapter, there is a listing (with page reference) of all the key terms, allowing you to refer back easily to the most important points.

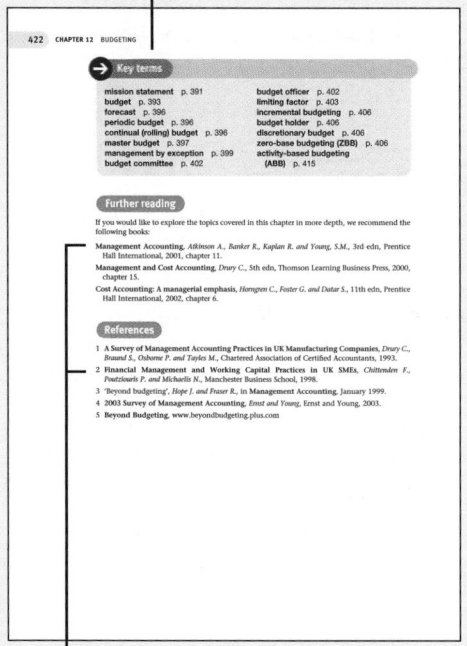

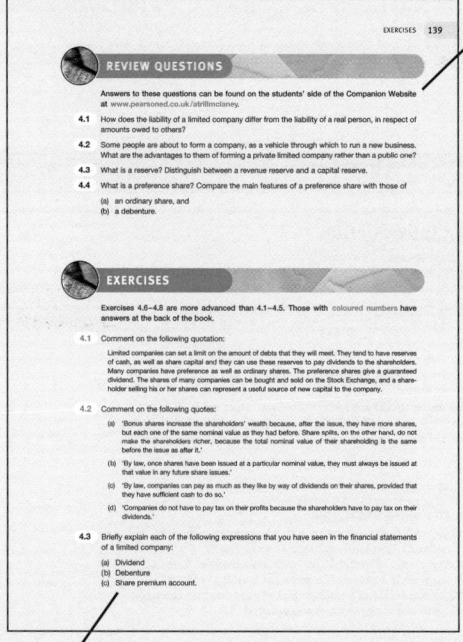

Review questions   These short questions encourage you to review and/or critically discuss your understanding of the main topics covered in each chapter, either individually or in a group. Solutions to these questions can be found on the Companion Website at **www.pearsoned.co.uk/atrillmclaney**.

Further reading   This section comprises a listing of relevant chapters in other textbooks that you might refer to in order to pursue a topic in more depth or gain an alternative perspective.

References   Provides full details of sources of information referred to in the chapter.

Exercises   There are eight of these comprehensive questions at the end of most chapters. The more advanced questions are separately identified. Solutions to five of the questions (those with coloured numbers) are provided in Appendix D, enabling you to assess your progress. Solutions to the remaining questions are available for lecturers only. An additional exercise for each chapter can be found on the Companion Website at **www.pearsoned.co.uk/atrillmclaney**.

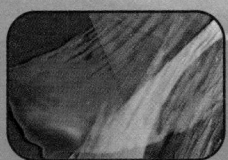

Extra material has been prepared to help you study using *Accounting: An Introduction*. This material can be found on the book's Companion Website at **www.pearsoned.co.uk/atrillmclaney**. You will find links to websites of interest, as well as a range of material including:

Interactive quizzes

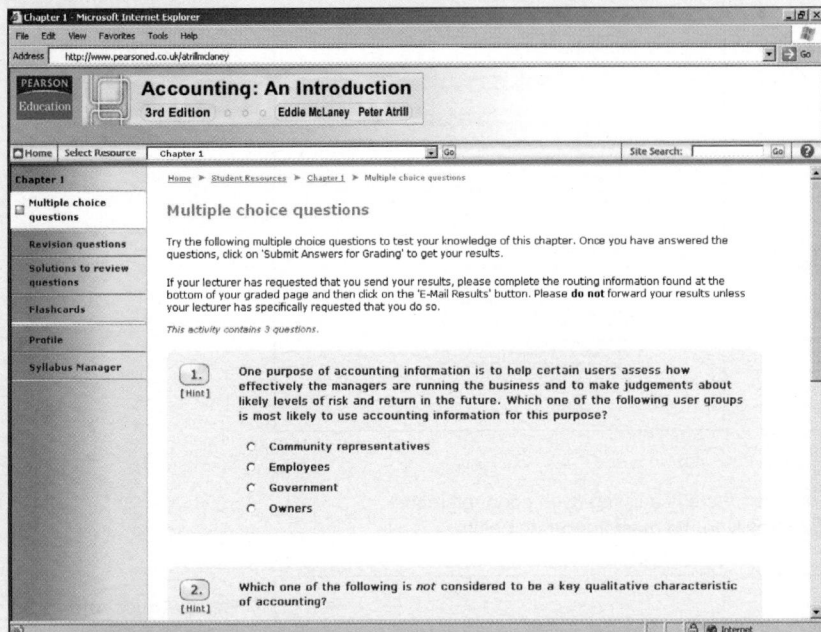

For each chapter there is a set of interactive multiple choice questions, plus a set of fill-in-the blanks questions and an extra exercise. Test your learning and get automatic grading on your answers.

Revision questions

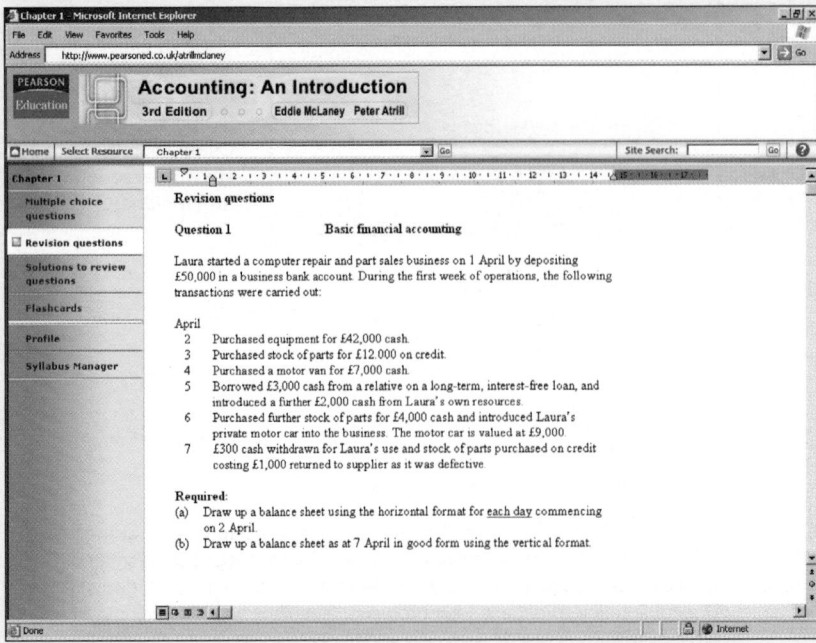

Sets of questions covering the whole book are designed to help you check your overall learning whilst you are revising.

Review questions solutions

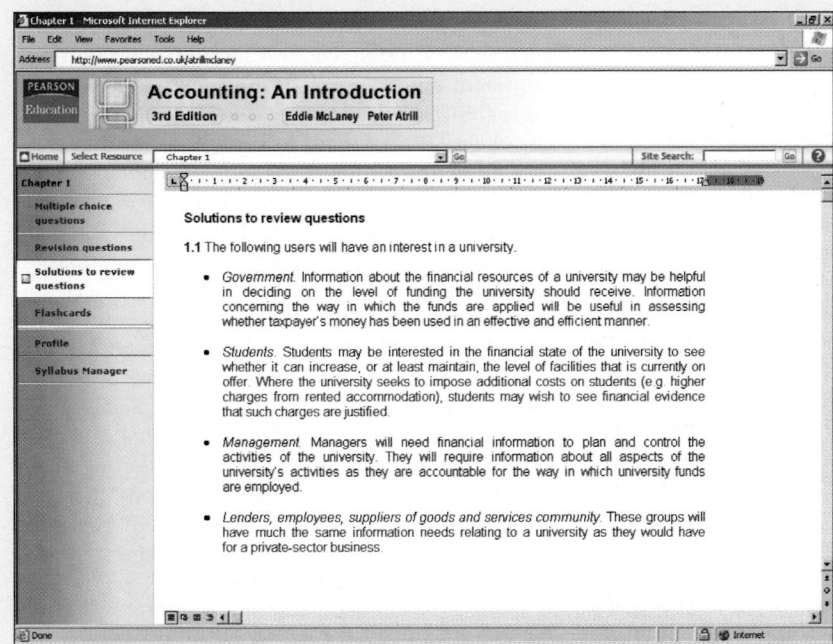

Answers to the end-of-chapter review questions that appear in the book are to be found on the website, so you can check your progress.

Glossary and flashcards

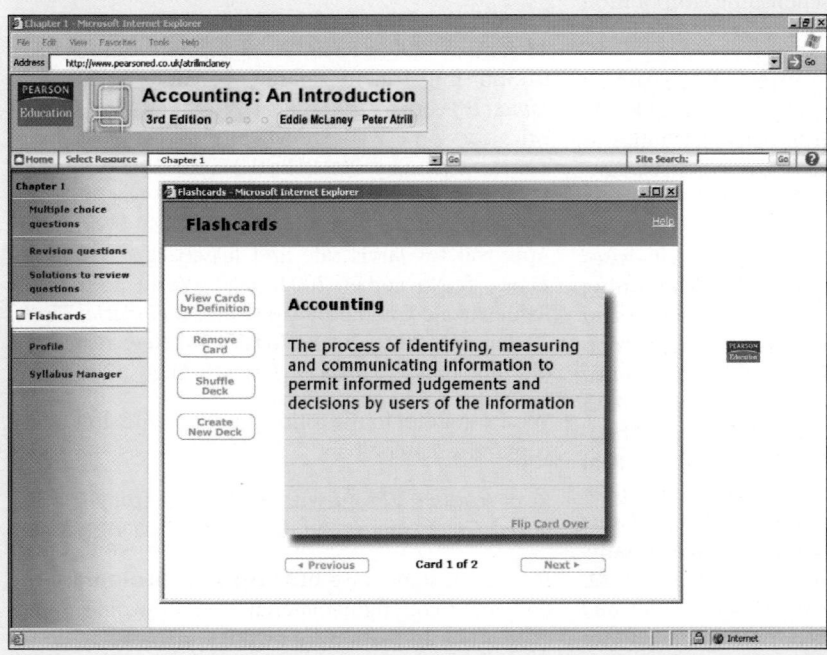

Full version of the book's glossary to help you check definitions while you are online. Flashcards help you to learn and test yourself on definitions of key terms. A term is displayed on each card: 'flip over' for the definition. 'Shuffle' the cards to randomly test your knowledge.

Acknowledgements

We are grateful to the following for permissions to reproduce copyright material:

Times Newspapers Limited for an extract (Real World 1.2) adapted from the article 'Margin of success for clothing retailers' published in *The Times* 20 November 2002 © The Times 2002; Thorntons plc for an extract (Real World 3.3) from the 2003 Thorntons plc Annual Report and Accounts; Kingfisher plc for an extract (Real World 4.4) from the 2003 Annual Review of Kingfisher plc; Tesco Stores Ltd for extracts (various) from the 2003 Tesco Annual Report and Financial Statements; Rolls-Royce International Ltd for an extract (Real World 4.9) from the 2002 Annual Financial Statements of Rolls-Royce; Today's CPA, a publication of the Texas Society of Certified Public Accountants for an extract (Real World 5.11) from the article 'The rise and fall of Enron' by C.W. Thomas published in *Journal of Accountancy* Vol. 194 Issue 3, April 2002; Unilever plc for an extract (Exercise 5.8) from a segmental report for 2002 of Unilever plc; and Harvard Business School Publishing Corporation for an extract (Real World 11.16) from the article 'The Balanced Scorecard' by R. Kaplan and D. Norton © The Harvard Business School Publishing Corporation 1996.

Real World 7.6 from Marks and Spencer plc, Annual Report 2003 – reproduced by kind permission of Marks and Spencer plc; Figure 7.7 from Financial ratios as predictors of failure in *Empirical Research in Accounting: Selected Studies*, Institute of Professional Accounting, University of Chicago, Blackwell Publishers (Beaver, W.H. 1966); Figure 11.1 reprinted from *Activity-based Costing-A Review With Case Studies*, CIMA Publishing (Innes, J. and Mitchell, F. 1990) with permission from Elsevier; Figure 11.9 reprinted by permission of Harvard Business School Press from *The Balanced Scorecard* by Kaplan, R. and Norton, D., Boston, M.A., 1996. Copyright © 1996 by Harvard Business School Publishing Corporation, all rights reserved; Real World 12.2, 12.5, 13.2 and 13.3 from *A Survey of Management Accounting Practices in UK Manufacturing Companies*, Chartered Association of Accountants (Drury, C., Braund, S., Osbourne, P. and Tayles, M. 1993); Figure 12.5 from *Financial Management and Working Capital Practices in UK SMEs*, Manchester Business School (Chittenden, F., Poutziouris, P. and Michaelas, N. 1998); Figure 12.6 from www.bbrt.org. Copyright and source Beyond Budgeting Round Table (BBRT) – www.bbrt.org; Real World 14.4 from The theory-practice gap in capital budgeting: evidence from the United Kingdom in *Journal of Business Finance and Accounting*, June/July, Blackwell Publishing (Arnold, G.C. and Hatzopoulos, P. 2000); Figures 15.5 and 15.7 compiled from information kindly provided by the Finance and Leasing Association (www.fla.org.uk) with thanks; Figures 15.9 and 15.10 compiled from BVCA Report on Investment Activity, British Venture Capital Association with thanks; Figure 15.11 from ESRC reprinted in *Accountancy Age*, 19 June 2003, www.accountancyage.com; Real World 15.14 from *Angel Investing: Matching start-up Funds With Start-up Companies*, John Wiley & Sons, Inc. (Van Osnabrugge, M. and Robinson, R.J. 2000), reprinted in *Financial Times* 6 November 2000, reprinted with permission of John Wiley & Sons, Inc.

We are grateful to the Financial Times Limited for permission to reprint the following material:

Real World 4.1 Monotub industries in a spin as founder gets Titan for £1, FT.com, © *Financial Times*, 23 January 2003; Real World 6.1 Eurotunnel takes £1.3bn impairment charge, FT.com, © *Financial Times*, 9 February 2004; Real World 7.4 Market statistics for some well known businesses, © *Financial Times*, 3 January 2004; Real World 11.2 Sony and Microsoft in European console price war, FT.com, © *Financial Times*, 28 August 2002; Real World 15.5 Approval for Jarvis sale and leaseback, © *Financial Times*, 8 November 2002; Real World 15.6 Laura Ashley to close 35 European stores, © *Financial Times*, 23 January 2003; Real World 15.7 New issues but old problems, © *Financial Times*, 8 August 2003.

We are grateful to the following for permission to use copyright material:

Real World 1.3 Profit without honour from *The Financial Times Limited*, 29/30 June 2002, © John Kay.

In some instances we have been unable to trace the owners of copyright material, and we would appreciate any information that would enable us to do so.

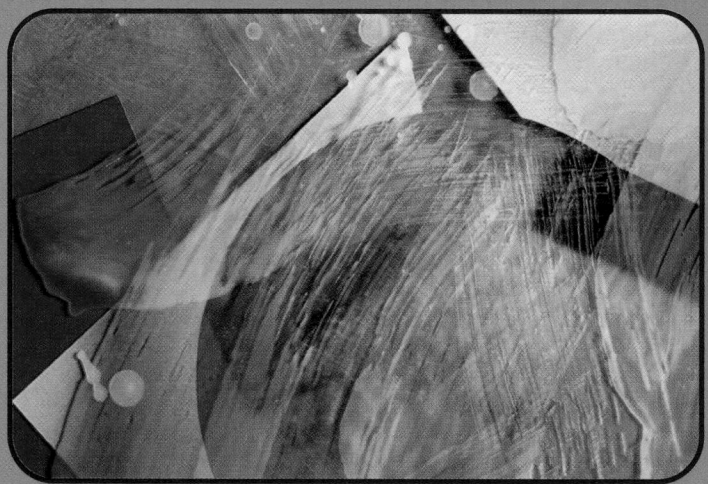

CHAPTER 1

Introduction to accounting and finance

OBJECTIVES

When you have completed this chapter, you should be able to:

- Explain the nature and roles of accounting and finance.

- Identify the main users of financial information and discuss their needs.

- Identify and discuss the main forms of business enterprise.

- Discuss the key financial objective of a business.

INTRODUCTION

In this opening chapter, we begin by considering the roles of accounting and finance. We shall identify the main users of accounting information and discuss the ways in which accounting can improve the quality of the decisions that they make. In subsequent chapters, we develop this decision-making theme by considering in some detail the kinds of financial reports and methods used to aid decision-making.

As this book is concerned with accounting and financial decision making for private sector businesses, we shall also examine the main forms of business enterprise and consider what the key objective of a business is likely to be. The particular objective chosen will exert an important influence on what is reported and how it is reported.

What are accounting and finance?

Let us start our study of accounting and finance by trying to understand the purpose of each. **Accounting** is concerned with collecting, analysing and communicating financial information. This information is useful for those who need to make decisions and plans about businesses, and for those who need to control those businesses. For example, the managers of businesses may need accounting information to decide whether to:

- develop new products or services (such as a computer manufacturer developing a new range of computers);
- increase or decrease the price or quantity of existing products or services (such as a telecommunications business changing its mobile phone call and text charges);
- borrow money to help finance the business (such as a supermarket wishing to increase the number of stores it owns);
- increase or decrease the operating capacity of the business (such as a beef farming business reviewing the size of its herd); and
- change the methods of purchasing, production or distribution (such as a clothes retailer switching from UK to overseas suppliers).

The information provided should help in identifying and assessing the financial consequences of such decisions.

Though managers working within a particular business are likely to be significant users of accounting information about that particular business, they are by no means the only ones. There are those outside the business (whom we shall identify later) who may need information to decide whether to:

- invest or disinvest in the ownership of the business;
- lend money to the business;
- offer credit facilities;
- enter into contracts for the purchase of products or services.

Sometimes the impression is given that the purpose of accounting is simply to prepare financial reports on a regular basis. While it is true that accountants undertake this kind of work, the preparation of financial reports does not represent an end in itself. The ultimate purpose of the accountant's work is to give people better information on which to base their decisions. This decision-making perspective of accounting fits in with the theme of this book and shapes the way in which we deal with each topic.

 Finance, like accounting, exists to help decision makers. It is concerned with the ways in which funds for a business are raised and invested. This lies at the very heart of what a business is about. In essence, a business exists to raise funds from investors (owners and lenders) and then to use those funds to make investments (equipment, premises, stocks and so on) in an attempt to make the business, and its owners, wealthier. It is important that funds are raised in a way that is appropriate to the particular needs of the business and an understanding of finance should help in identifying:

● the main forms of finance available;
● the costs and benefits of each form of finance;
● the risks associated with each form of finance; and
● the role of financial markets in supplying finance.

Once the funds are raised, they must be invested in a way that will provide the business with a worthwhile return. An understanding of finance should help in evaluating:

● the returns from an investment; and
● the risks associated with an investment.

Businesses tend to raise and invest funds in large amounts for long periods of time. The quality of the investment decisions made can, therefore, have a profound impact on the fortunes of the business.

There is little point in trying to make a sharp distinction between accounting and finance. We have already seen that both are concerned with the financial aspects of decision making. There is considerable overlap between the two subjects and, in this book, we shall not emphasise the distinctions.

Accounting and user needs

For accounting information to be useful, the accountant must be clear *for whom* the information is being prepared and *for what purpose* the information will be used. There are likely to be various groups of people (known as 'user groups') with an interest in a particular organisation, in the sense of needing to make decisions about it. For the typical private sector business, the most important of these groups are shown in Figure 1.1.

The conflicting interests of users

Conflicts of interest may arise between the various user groups over the ways in which the wealth of the business is generated and/or distributed. For example, a conflict of interest may arise between the managers and the owners of the business. Although managers are appointed to act on behalf of the owners, there is always a risk that they will put their own interests first. They may use the wealth of the business to, for example, furnish large offices or buy expensive cars. Accounting information has an important role to play in reporting the extent to which various groups have benefited from the business. Thus, owners may rely on accounting information to check whether

ACTIVITY 1.1

Ptarmigan Insurance plc (PI) is a large motor insurance business. Taking the user groups identified above, suggest what sort of decisions each one is likely to make about PI.

Your answer may be as follows:

User group	Decision
Customers	Whether to take further motor policies with PI. This would probably involve an assessment of PI's ability to continue in business and to supply customers' needs.
Competitors	How best to compete against PI or, perhaps, whether to leave the market on the grounds that it is not possible to compete profitably with PI. This might involve using PI's performance in various aspects as a 'benchmark' when evaluating their own performance. They might also try to assess PI's competitive strength and to identify significant changes that may signal PI's future actions (for example, expanding its ability to provide its service as a prelude to market expansion).
Employees	Whether to take up or to continue in employment with PI. Employees might assess this by considering the ability of the business to continue to provide employment and to reward employees adequately for their labour.
Government	Whether PI should pay tax and, if so, how much, whether it complies with agreed pricing policies, whether financial support is needed and so on. In making these decisions an assessment of its profits, sales and financial strength would be made.
Community representatives	Whether to allow PI to expand its premises or whether to provide economic support for PI. To assess these, PI's ability to continue to provide employment for the community, to use community resources and to help fund environmental improvements might be considered.
Investment analysts	Whether or not to advise clients to buy shares in PI. This would involve an assessment of the likely risks and returns associated with PI.
Suppliers	Whether to continue to supply PI and, if so, whether to supply on credit. This would involve an assessment of PI's ability to pay for any goods and services supplied.
Lenders	Whether to lend money to PI and/or whether to require repayment of any existing loans. To assess this, PI's ability to meet its obligations to pay interest and to repay the principal would be considered.
Managers	Whether the performance of the business requires improvement. Here performance to date would be compared with earlier plans or some other 'benchmark' to decide whether action needs to be taken. Whether there should be a change in PI's future direction. In making such decisions, management will need to look at PI's ability to perform and at the opportunities available to it.
Owners (shareholders)	Whether to buy additional shares in PI or to sell some or all of those presently held. This would involve an assessment of the likely risks and returns associated with PI. Owners would also be involved with decisions on the employment of senior managers. Here past performance of the business would be assessed.

You may have thought of other reasons why each group would find accounting information useful.

| Figure 1.1 | Main users of financial information relating to a business |

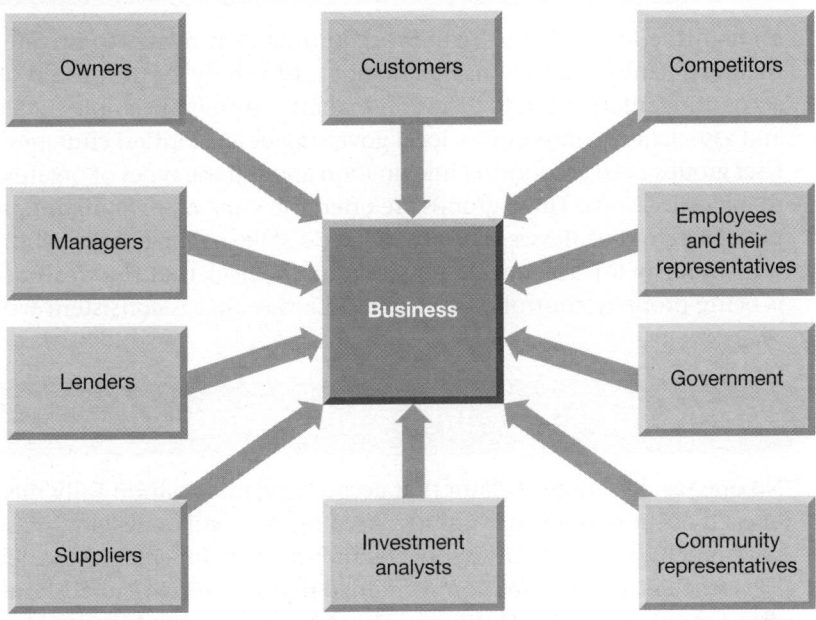

There are several user groups with an interest in the accounting information relating to a business. The majority of these are outside the business but, nevertheless, they have a stake in it. This is not meant to be an exhaustive list of potential users; however, the groups identified are normally the most important.

the pay and benefits of managers are in line with agreed policy. A further example of potential conflict is between lenders and owners. There is a risk that the funds loaned to a business will not be used for purposes that have been agreed. Lenders may, therefore, rely on accounting information to check that the funds have been applied in an appropriate manner and that the terms of the loan agreement are being adhered to.

ACTIVITY 1.2

Can you think of other examples where accounting information may be used to monitor potential conflicts of interest between the various user groups identified?

Two possible examples that spring to mind are:

- Employees (or their representatives) wishing to check that they are receiving a 'fair share' of the wealth created by the business and that agreed profit-sharing schemes are being adhered to.
- Government wishing to check that the profits made from a contract that it has given to a business are not excessive.

You may have thought of other examples.

Not-for-profit organisations

Though the focus of this book is accounting as it relates to private sector businesses, there are many organisations that do not exist mainly for the pursuit of profit yet produce accounting information for decision-making purposes. Examples include: charities, clubs and associations, universities, local government authorities, churches and trades unions. User groups need accounting information about these types of organisation to help them to make decisions. These groups are often the same as, or similar to, those identified for private sector businesses. They may have a stake in the future viability of the organisation and may use accounting information to check that the wealth of the organisation is being properly controlled and used in a way that is consistent with its objectives.

How useful is accounting information?

No one would seriously claim that accounting information fully meets all of the needs of each of the various user groups. Accounting is still a developing subject and we still have much to learn about user needs and the ways in which these needs should be met. Nevertheless, the information contained in accounting reports should help users make decisions relating to the business. The information should reduce uncertainty over the financial position and performance of the business. It should help to answer questions concerning the availability of cash to pay owners a return for their investment or to repay loans and so on. Typically, there is no close substitute for the information that is provided by financial statements. This is to say that if users are not to get the information from the financial statements, they will not get it at all. Other sources of information concerning the financial health of a business are normally regarded as less useful than the financial statements.

ACTIVITY 1.3

What other sources of information might users employ to gain an impression of the financial position and performance of a business? What kind of information might be gleaned from these sources?

Other sources of information available include:

- Meetings with managers of the business
- Public announcements made by the business
- Newspaper and magazine articles
- Radio and TV reports
- Information-gathering agencies (for example, Dun and Bradstreet)
- Industry reports
- Economy-wide reports.

These sources can provide information on various aspects of the business, such as new products or services being offered, management changes, new contracts offered or awarded, the competitive environment within which the business operates, the impact of new technology, changes in legislation, changes in interest rates and future levels of inflation. However, the various sources of information identified are not really substitutes for accounting reports. Rather, they should be used in conjunction with the reports in order to obtain a clearer picture of the financial health of a business.

The evidence on the usefulness of accounting

There are arguments and convincing evidence that accounting information is at least *perceived* as being useful to users. There have been numerous research surveys that asked users to rank the importance of accounting information, in relation to other sources of information, for decision-making purposes. Generally speaking, these studies have found that users rank accounting information very highly. There is also considerable evidence that businesses choose to produce accounting information that exceeds the minimum requirements imposed by accounting regulations. (For example, businesses often produce a considerable amount of accounting information for managers, which is not required by any regulations.) Presumably, the cost of producing this additional accounting information is justified on the grounds that users believe it to be useful to them. Such arguments and evidence, however, leave unanswered the question as to whether the information produced is actually being used for decision-making purposes, that is: does it affect people's behaviour?

It is normally very difficult to assess the impact of accounting on decision-making. One situation arises, however, where the impact of accounting information can be observed and measured. This is where the **shares** (portions of ownership of a business) are traded on a stock exchange. The evidence reveals that, when a business makes an announcement concerning its accounting profits, the prices at which shares are traded and the volume of shares traded often change significantly. This suggests that investors are changing their views about the future prospects of the business as a result of this new information available to them and that this, in turn, leads them to make a decision either to buy or sell shares in the business.

Thus, we can see that there is evidence that accounting reports are perceived as being useful and are used for decision-making purposes. It is impossible, however, to measure just how useful accounting reports are to users and whether the cost of producing those reports represents value for money. Accounting information will usually represent only one input to a particular decision and the precise weight attached to the accounting information by the decision maker and the benefits which flow as a result cannot be accurately assessed. We shall see below, however, that it is at least possible to identify the kinds of qualities which accounting information must possess in order to be useful. Where these qualities are lacking, the usefulness of the information will be diminished.

Accounting as a service function

One way of viewing accounting is as a form of service. Accountants provide economic information to their 'clients', who are the various users identified in Figure 1.1. The quality of the service provided would be determined by the extent to which the information needs of the various user groups have been met. It can be argued that, to be useful, accounting information should possess certain key qualities, or characteristics. These are:

- **Relevance**. Accounting information must have the ability to influence decisions. Unless this characteristic is present, there is really no point in producing the information. The information may be relevant to the prediction of future events (for example, in predicting how much profit is likely to be earned next year) or relevant in helping confirm past events (for example, in establishing how much profit was earned last year). The role of accounting in confirming past events is important because users often wish to check on the accuracy of earlier predictions that they have made. The accuracy (or inaccuracy) of earlier predictions may enable users to judge the likely accuracy of current predictions.

● **Reliability**. Accounting should be free from significant errors or bias. It should be capable of being relied upon by users to represent what it is supposed to represent. Though both relevance and reliability are very important, the problem that we often face in accounting is that information that is highly relevant may not be very reliable, and that which is reliable may not be very relevant.

ACTIVITY 1.4

To illustrate this last point, let us assume that a manager has to sell a custom-built machine owned by the business and has recently received a bid for it. What information would be relevant to the manager when deciding whether to accept the bid? How reliable would that information be?

The manager would probably like to know the current market value of the machine before deciding whether or not to accept the bid. The current market value would be highly relevant to the final decision, but it might not be very reliable because the machine is unique and there is likely to be little information concerning market values.

Where a choice has to be made between providing information that has either more relevance or more reliability, the maximisation of relevance tends to be the guiding rule.

● **Comparability**. This quality will enable users to identify changes in the business over time (for example, the trend in sales over the past five years). It will also help users to evaluate the performance of the business in relation to other similar businesses. Comparability is achieved by treating items that are basically the same in the same manner for accounting purposes. Comparability tends also to be enhanced by making clear the policies that have been adopted in measuring and presenting the information.

● **Understandability**. Accounting reports should be expressed as clearly as possible and should be understood by those at whom the information is aimed.

ACTIVITY 1.5

Do you think that accounting reports should be understandable to those who have not studied accounting?

It would be useful if anyone could understand accounting reports, but realistically, this is not likely to be the case. Complex financial events and transactions cannot always be reported easily. It is probably best that we regard accounting reports in the same way as we regard a report written in a foreign language. To understand either of these, we need to have had some preparation. Generally speaking, accounting reports assume that the user not only has a reasonable knowledge of business and accounting, but is also prepared to invest some time in studying the reports.

The threshold of materiality

The qualities, or characteristics, that have just been described will help us to decide if a particular piece of financial information is potentially useful. However, in order to make a final decision, we also have to consider whether the information is material, or significant. This means that we should ask whether its omission or misrepresentation in the financial reports would really alter the decisions that users make. Thus, in addition to possessing the characteristics mentioned above, financial information must also achieve a threshold of **materiality**. If the information is not regarded as material, it should not be included within the reports as it will merely clutter them up and, perhaps, interfere with the users ability to interpret the financial results. The type of information and amounts involved will normally determine whether it is material.

Costs and benefits of accounting information

Having read the previous sections you may feel that, when considering a piece of financial information, provided the four main qualities identified are present, and it is material, it should be included in the financial reports. Unfortunately, there is one more hurdle to jump. A piece of financial information may still be excluded from the financial reports even when it is considered to be useful. Consider Activity 1.6 below.

ACTIVITY 1.6

Suppose an item of information is capable of being provided. It is relevant to a particular decision, it is also reliable, comparable and can be understood by the decision maker concerned and is material.

Can you think of a reason why, in practice, you might choose not to produce the information?

The reason that you may decide not to produce, or discover, the information is that you judge the cost of doing so to be greater than the potential benefit of having the information. This cost–benefit issue will place limits on the extent to which accounting information is provided.

In theory, financial information should only be produced if the costs of providing a particular item of information are less than the benefits, or value, to be derived from its use. Figure 1.2 shows the relationship between the costs and value of providing additional financial information. The figure shows how the value of information received by the decision maker eventually begins to decline. This is, perhaps, because additional information becomes less relevant, or because of the problems that a decision maker may have in processing the sheer quantity of information provided. The costs of providing the information, however, will increase with each additional piece of information. The broken line indicates the point at which the gap between the value of information and the cost of providing that information is at its greatest. This represents the optimal amount of information that can be provided. This theoretical model, however, poses a number of problems in practice, as discussed below.

Figure 1.2	Relationship between costs and the value of providing additional financial information

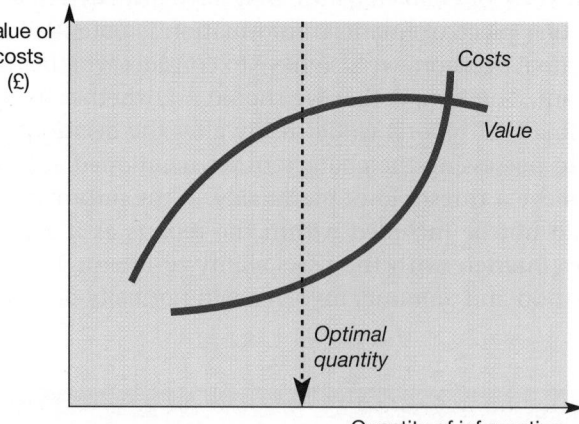

The benefits of each additional item of financial information eventually decline. The cost of providing information, however, will rise with each additional piece of information. The optimal level of information provision is where the gap between the value of the information and the costs of providing it is at its greatest.

To illustrate the practical problems of establishing the value of information, suppose that we wish to buy a particular DVD system that we have seen in a local shop for sale at £250. We believe that other local shops may have the same system on offer for a lower price. The only way of finding out the prices at other shops are either to telephone them or to visit them. Telephone calls cost money and involve some of our time. Visiting the shops may not involve the outlay of money, but more of our time will be involved. Is it worth the cost of finding out the price of the system at various shops? The answer, as we have seen, is that if the cost of discovering the price is less than the potential benefit, it is worth having that information.

To identify the various selling prices of the DVD system, there are various points to be considered including:

● How many shops shall we telephone or visit?
● What is the cost of each telephone call?
● How long will it take to make all the telephone calls or visits?
● How much do we value our time?

The economic benefit of having the information on the price of the system is probably even harder to assess and the following points need to be considered:

● What is the cheapest price that we might be quoted for the DVD system?
● How likely is it that we shall be quoted prices cheaper than £250?

The answers to these questions may be far from clear. When assessing the value of accounting information we are confronted with similar problems.

The provision of accounting information can be very costly; however, the costs are often difficult to quantify. The direct, out-of-pocket, costs such as salaries of accounting staff are not really a problem, but these are only part of the total costs involved. There are also less direct costs, such as the cost of the manager's time spent on analysing and interpreting the information contained in reports. In addition, costs will also be incurred if users employ the accounting information to the disadvantage of the business. For example, if suppliers discovered from the accounting reports that the business was in a poor financial state, they might decide to refuse to supply further goods or to impose strict conditions.

The economic benefit of having accounting information is even harder to assess. It is possible to apply some 'science' to the problem of weighing the costs and benefits, but a lot of subjective judgement is likely to be involved. Whilst no one would seriously advocate that a typical business should not produce accounting information, at the same time, no one would advocate that every item of information which could be seen as possessing one or more of the key characteristics should be produced, irrespective of the cost of producing it.

When weighing the costs of providing additional financial information against the benefits, there is also the problem that those who bear the burden of the costs may not be the ones who benefit from the additional information. The costs of providing accounting information are usually borne by the owners, but other user groups may be the beneficiaries.

The characteristics that influence the usefulness of accounting information and which have been discussed in this section and the preceding section are set out in Figure 1.3.

Figure 1.3	The characteristics that influence the usefulness of accounting information

There are four main qualitative characteristics that influence the usefulness of accounting information. In addition, however, accounting information should be material and the benefits of providing the information should outweigh the costs.

Accounting as an information system

We have already seen that accounting can be seen as the provision of a service to 'clients'. Another way of viewing accounting is as a part of the business's total information system. Users, both inside and outside the business, have to make decisions concerning the allocation of scarce economic resources. To try to ensure that these resources are allocated in an efficient manner, users require economic information on which to base decisions. It is the role of the accounting system to provide that information and this will involve information gathering and communication.

 The **accounting information system** has certain features that are common to all information systems within a business. These are:

● identifying and capturing relevant information (in this case economic information);
● recording in a systematic manner the information collected;
● analysing and interpreting the information collected;
● reporting the information in a manner that suits the needs of users.

The relationship between these features is set out in Figure 1.4.

Given the decision-making emphasis of this book, we shall be concerned primarily with the final two elements of the process – the analysis and reporting of financial information. We shall consider the way in which information is used by, and is useful to, managers rather than the way in which it is identified and recorded. In this context, information technology is playing an increasingly important role. It has created opportunities for analysis and reporting that were not possible before.

Figure 1.4	The accounting information system

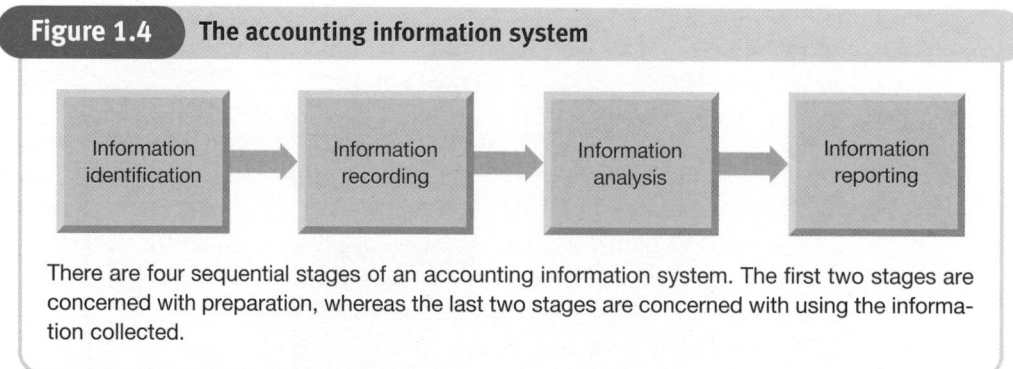

There are four sequential stages of an accounting information system. The first two stages are concerned with preparation, whereas the last two stages are concerned with using the information collected.

Management and financial accounting

Accounting is usually seen as having two distinct strands. These are:

 ● **Management accounting**, which seeks to meet the needs of managers; and
● **Financial accounting**, which seeks to meet the accounting needs of all of the other users that were identified in Figure 1.1, earlier in the chapter.

The differences between the two types of accounting reflect the different user groups that they address. Briefly, the major differences are as follows:

● *Nature of the reports produced*. Financial accounting reports tend to be general-purpose. That is, they contain financial information that will be useful for a broad range of users and decisions rather than being specifically designed for the needs of a particular group or set of decisions. Management accounting reports, on the other hand, are often specific-purpose reports. They are designed either with a particular decision in mind or for a particular manager.

● *Level of detail*. Financial accounting reports provide users with a broad overview of the performance and position of the business for a period. As a result, information is aggregated and detail is often lost. Management accounting reports, however, often provide managers with considerable detail to help them with a particular operational decision.

● *Regulations*. Financial reports, for many businesses, are subject to accounting regulations that try to ensure they are produced with standard content and in a standard format. Law and the accounting profession impose these regulations. Since management accounting reports are for internal use only, there are no regulations from external sources concerning the form and content of the reports. They can be designed to meet the needs of particular managers.

● *Reporting interval*. For most businesses, financial accounting reports are produced on an annual basis, though large businesses may produce half-yearly reports and a few produce quarterly ones. Management accounting reports may be produced as frequently as required by managers. In many businesses, managers are provided with certain reports on a weekly or monthly basis, which allows them to check progress frequently. In addition, special-purpose reports will be prepared when required (for example, to evaluate a proposal to purchase a piece of machinery).

● *Time horizon*. Financial accounting reports reflect the performance and position of the business for the past period. In essence, they are backward looking. Management accounting reports, on the other hand, often provide information concerning future performance as well as past performance. It is an oversimplification, however, to suggest that financial accounting reports never incorporate expectations concerning the future. Occasionally, businesses will release projected information to other users in an attempt to raise capital or to fight off unwanted takeover bids.

● *Range and quality of information*. Financial accounting reports concentrate on information that can be quantified in monetary terms. Management accounting also produces such reports, but is also more likely to produce reports that contain information of a non-financial nature such as measures of physical quantities of stocks and output. Financial accounting places greater emphasis on the use of objective, verifiable evidence when preparing reports. Management accounting reports may use information that is less objective and verifiable, but they provide managers with the information they need.

We can see from this that management accounting is less constrained than financial accounting. It may draw on a variety of sources and use information that has varying degrees of reliability. The only real test to be applied when assessing the value of the information produced for managers is whether or not it improves the quality of the decisions made.

The distinction between the two areas reflects, to some extent, the differences in access to financial information. Managers have much more control over the form and content of information they receive. Other users have to rely on what managers are prepared to provide or what the financial reporting regulations state must be provided. Though the scope of financial accounting reports has increased over time, fears concerning loss of competitive advantage and user ignorance concerning the reliability of forecast data have led businesses to resist providing other users with the detailed and wide-ranging information that is available to managers.

ACTIVITY 1.7

Are the information needs of managers and those of other users so very different?
Is there any overlap between the information needs of managers and the needs of other users?

The distinction between management and financial accounting suggests that there are differences between the information needs of managers and those of other users. Whilst differences undoubtedly exist, there is also a good deal of overlap between these needs. For example, managers will, at times, be interested in receiving an historical overview of business operations of the sort provided to other users. Equally, the other users would be interested in receiving information relating to the future, such as the planned level of profits and non-financial information such as the state of the sales order book and the extent of product innovations.

Scope of this book

This book covers both financial accounting and management accounting topics. Broadly speaking, the next six chapters (Part 1, Chapters 2–7) are concerned with financial accounting topics, and the six thereafter (Part 2, Chapters 8–13) with management accounting topics. Part 3 of this book, comprising Chapters 14–16, is concerned with the **financial management** of the business. That is, the chapters examine issues relating to the financing and investing activities of the business. Accounting information is usually vitally important for these kinds of decisions.

Has accounting become too interesting?

In recent years, accounting has become front-page news both in the US and Europe and has become a major talking point among those connected with the world of business. Unfortunately, the attention that accounting has attracted has been for all the wrong reasons. We have seen that investors rely on financial reports to help to keep an eye on both their investment and the managers. However, what if the managers provide misleading financial reports to investors? Recent revelations suggest that the managers of some large companies have been doing just this.

Two of the most notorious cases have been those of Enron, an energy-trading business based in Texas, which was accused of entering into complicated financial arrangements in order to obscure losses and to inflate profits, and Worldcom, a major long-distance telephone operator in the US, which was accused of reclassifying $3.9 billion of expenses so as to falsely inflate the profit figure that the business reported to its owners (shareholders) and to others. In the wake of these scandals, there was much closer scrutiny by investment analysts and investors of the financial reports that businesses produce. This has led to further businesses, in both the US and Europe, being accused of using dubious accounting practices to bolster profits.

Various reasons have been put forward to explain this spate of scandals. Some may have been caused by the pressures on managers to meet unrealistic expectations of investors for continually rising profits, others by the greed of unscrupulous executives whose pay is linked to financial performance. However, they may all reflect a particular economic environment.

Real World 1.1 gives some comments suggesting that when all appears to be going well with a business, people can be quite gullible and over-trusting.

REAL WORLD 1.1

The thoughts of Warren Buffett

Warren Buffett is one of the world's shrewdest and most successful investors. He believes that the accounting scandals mentioned above were perpetrated during the 'new economy boom' of the late 1990s when confidence was high and exaggerated predictions were being made concerning the future. He states that during that period:

> You had an erosion of accounting standards. You had an erosion, to some extent, of executive behaviour. But during a period when everybody 'believes', people who are inclined to take advantage of other people can get away with a lot.

He believes that the worst is now over and that the 'dirty laundry' created during this heady period is being washed away and that the washing machine is now in the 'rinse cycle'. However, he points out that: 'It's only in the rinse cycle that you find out how dirty the laundry has been.'

Source: *The Times*, Business Section, 26 September 2002, p. 25.

Whatever the causes, the result of these accounting scandals has been to undermine the credibility of financial statements and to introduce much stricter regulations concerning the quality of financial information. We shall return to this issue in later chapters when we consider the financial statements.

The changing nature of accounting

Over the past two decades, the environment in which business operates has become increasingly turbulent and competitive. Various reasons have been identified to explain these changes, including:

- the increasing sophistication of customers;
- the development of a global economy where national frontiers become less important;
- rapid changes in technology;
- the deregulation of domestic markets (for example, electricity, water and gas);
- increasing pressure from owners (shareholders) for competitive economic returns; and
- the increasing volatility of financial markets.

This new, more complex, environment has brought new challenges for both financial accounting and management accounting. To meet the changing needs of users there has been a radical review of what kind of information is reported and how it is reported.

In recent years, there have been various attempts to set out the principles upon which financial accounting is based. This is designed to help users to understand more clearly the nature and purpose of financial accounting reports and to provide a more solid foundation for the development of accounting rules. These principles try to address fundamental questions such as 'Who are the users of financial accounting information?', 'What kinds of financial accounting reports should be prepared and what should they contain?' and 'How should items be measured?'

In response to criticisms that the financial reports of some businesses are too opaque, accounting rule-makers have tried to improve the framework of rules to ensure that the accounting policies of businesses are more comparable, more transparent and portray economic reality more faithfully. The recent spate of accounting scandals, however, suggests that there is still work to be done.

The internationalisation of businesses has created a need for accounting rules to have an international reach. It can no longer be assumed that users of accounting information relating to a particular business are based in the country in which the business operates or are familiar with the accounting rules of that country. Thus, there has been increasing harmonisation of accounting rules across national frontiers. A more detailed review of these developments is included in Chapter 6.

Management accounting has also changed by becoming more outward looking in its focus. In the past, information provided to managers has been largely restricted to that collected within the business. However, the attitude and behaviour of customers and rival businesses have now become the object of much information gathering. Increasingly, successful businesses are those that are able to secure and maintain competitive advantage over their rivals.

To obtain this advantage, businesses have become more 'customer driven' (that is, concerned with satisfying customer needs). This has led to management accounting information that provides details of customers and the market, such as customer evaluation of services provided and market share. In addition, information about the costs and profits of rival businesses, which can be used as 'benchmarks' by which to gauge competitiveness, is gathered and reported.

To compete successfully, businesses must also find ways of managing costs. The cost base of modern businesses is under continual review and this, in turn, has led to the development of more sophisticated methods of measuring and controlling costs. These changes are considered in more detail in Chapter 11.

Why do I need to know anything about accounting and finance?

At this point you may be asking yourself 'Why do I need to study accounting and finance? I don't intend to become an accountant!' Well, from the explanation of what accounting and finance is about, which has broadly been the subject of this chapter so far, it should be clear that the accounting/finance function within an organisation is a central part of its management information system. On the basis of information provided by the system, managers make decisions concerning the allocation of resources. These decisions may concern whether to:

● continue with certain business operations;
● invest in particular projects; or
● sell particular products.

Such decisions can have a profound effect on all those connected with the organisation. It is important, therefore, that *all* those who intend to work in organisations should have a fairly clear idea of certain important aspects of accounting and finance. These aspects include:

● how financial reports should be read and interpreted;
● how financial plans are made;
● how investment decisions are made;
● how businesses are financed.

Many, perhaps most, students have a career goal of being a manager within an organisation – perhaps a personnel manager, production manager, marketing manager or IT manager. If you are one of these students, an understanding of accounting and finance is very important. When you become a manager, even a junior one, it is almost certain that you will have to use financial reports to help you to carry out your management tasks. It is equally certain that it is largely on the basis of financial information and reports that your performance as a manager will be judged.

As a manager, it is likely that you will be expected to help in forward planning for the organisation. This will often involve the preparation of projected financial statements and setting of financial targets.

If you do not understand what the financial statements really mean and the extent to which the financial information is reliable, you will find yourself at a distinct disadvantage to others who know their way round the system. As a manager, you will also be expected to help decide how the limited resources available to the business should be allocated between competing options. This will require an ability to evaluate the costs and benefits of the different options available. Once again, an understanding of accounting and finance is important to carrying out this management task.

This is not to say that you cannot be an effective and successful personnel, production, marketing or IT manager unless you are also a qualified accountant. It does mean, however, that you need to acquire a bit of 'street wisdom' in accounting and finance in order to succeed. This accounting and finance book aims to give you just that.

Forms of business unit

Businesses may be classified according to their form of ownership. The particular classification has important implications when accounting for businesses – as we shall see in later chapters – and so it is useful to be clear about the main forms of ownership that can arise.

There are basically three arrangements:

● Sole proprietorship
● Partnership
● Limited company.

Each of these is considered below.

Sole proprietorship

Sole proprietorship, as the name suggests, is where an individual is the sole owner of a business. This type of business is often quite small in terms of size (as measured, for example, by sales generated or number of staff employed), however, the number of such businesses is very large indeed. Examples of sole-proprietor businesses can be found in most industrial sectors but particularly within the service sector. Hence, services such as electrical repairs, picture framing, photography, driving instruction, retail shops and hotels have a large proportion of sole-proprietor businesses. The sole-proprietor business is easy to set up. No formal procedures are required and operations can often commence immediately (unless special permission is required because of the nature of the trade or service, such as running licensed premises). The owner can decide the way in which the business is to be conducted and has the flexibility to restructure or dissolve the business whenever it suits. The law does not recognise the sole-proprietor business as being separate from the owner, so the business will cease on the death of the owner.

Although the owner must produce accounting information to satisfy the taxation authorities, there is no legal requirement to produce accounting information relating to the business for other user groups. However, some user groups may demand accounting information about the business and may be in a position to have their demands met (for example, a bank requiring accounting information on a regular basis as a condition of a loan). The sole proprietor will have unlimited liability which means that no distinction will be made between the proprietor's personal wealth and that of the business if there are business debts that must be paid.

Partnership

 A **partnership** exists where at least two individuals carry on a business together with the intention of making a profit. Partnerships have much in common with sole-proprietor businesses. They are often quite small in size (although some, such as partnerships of accountants and solicitors, can be large). Partnerships are also easy to set up as no formal procedures are required (and it is not even necessary to have a written agreement between the partners). The partners can agree whatever arrangements suit them concerning the financial and management aspects of the business, and the partnership can be restructured or dissolved by agreement between the partners.

Partnerships are not recognised in law as separate entities and so contracts with third parties must be entered into in the name of individual partners. The partners of a business usually have unlimited liability.

ACTIVITY 1.8

What are the main advantages and disadvantages that should be considered when deciding between a sole proprietorship and a partnership?

The main advantages of a partnership over a sole-proprietor business are:

- Sharing the burden of ownership.
- The opportunity to specialise rather than cover the whole range of services (for example, a solicitors' practice, where each partner tends to specialise in a different aspect of the law).
- The ability to raise capital where this is beyond the capacity of a single individual.

The main disadvantages of a partnership compared with a sole proprietorship are:

- The risks of sharing ownership of a business with unsuitable individuals.
- The limits placed on individual decision making that a partnership will impose.

Limited company

Limited companies can range in size from quite small to very large. The number of individuals who subscribe capital and become the owners may be unlimited, which provides the opportunity to create a very large-scale business. The liability of owners, however, is limited (hence 'limited' company), which means that those individuals subscribing capital to the company are liable only for debts incurred by the company up to the amount that they have agreed to invest. This cap on the liability of the owners is designed to limit risk and to produce greater confidence to invest. Without such limits on owner liability, it is difficult to see how a modern capitalist economy could operate. In many cases, the owners of a limited company are not involved in the day-to-day running of the business and will only invest in a business if there is a clear limit set on the level of investment risk.

The benefit of limited liability, however, imposes certain obligations on such a company. To start up a limited company, documents of incorporation must be prepared that set out, amongst other things, the objectives of the business. Furthermore, a framework of regulations exists that places obligations on the way in which such a company conducts its affairs. Part of this regulatory framework requires annual financial reports to be made available to owners and lenders and an annual general meeting of the owners to be held to approve the reports. In addition, a copy of the annual financial reports must be lodged with the Registrar of Companies for public inspection. In this way, the financial affairs of a limited company enter the public domain. With the exception of small companies, there is also a requirement for the annual financial reports to be subject to an audit. This involves an independent firm of accountants examining the annual reports and underlying records to see whether the reports provide a true and fair view of the financial health of the company and whether they comply with the relevant accounting rules established by law and by the accounting profession.

Limited companies are considered in more detail in Chapters 4 and 5.

ACTIVITY 1.9

What are the main advantages and disadvantages that should be considered when deciding between a partnership business and a limited liability company?

The main advantages of a partnership over a limited company are:

- The ease of setting up the business.
- The degree of flexibility concerning the way in which the business is conducted.
- The degree of flexibility concerning restructuring and dissolution of the business.
- Freedom from administrative burdens imposed by law (for example, the annual general meeting and the need for an independent audit).

The main disadvantages of a partnership compared with a limited company are:

- The fact that it is not possible to limit the liability of partners.

This book concentrates on the accounting aspects of limited liability companies, because this type of business is by far the most important in economic terms. The early chapters will introduce accounting concepts through examples that do not draw a distinction between the different types of business. Once we have dealt with the basic accounting principles, which are the same for all three types of business, we can then go on to see how they are applied to limited companies. It must be emphasised that there are no differences in the way that all three of these forms of business keep their day-to-day accounting records. In preparing their periodic financial statements, there are certain differences that need to be considered. These differences are not ones of principle, however, but of detail.

Business objectives

A business seeks to enhance the wealth of its owners, and throughout this book we shall assume that this is its main objective. This may come as a surprise, as there are other objectives that a business may pursue that are related to the needs of others associated with the business. For example, a business may seek to provide good working conditions for its employees, or it may seek to conserve the environment for the local community. While a business may pursue these objectives, it is normally set up with a view to increasing the wealth of its owners, and in practice the behaviour of businesses over time appears to be consistent with this objective.

Real World 1.2 provides an example of how many clothes retailers pursue the search for profit.

REAL WORLD 1.2

From rags to riches

Progress in the search for profit is reported by the accounting information system. If managers find that the reported profits are inadequate, this can be an important driver for change within a business. This change can, in turn, have a profound effect on the working lives of those both inside and outside the business.

Many clothes retailers have been concerned with profit levels in recent years. This has led them to make radical changes to the ways in which they operate. Low inflation and increased competition in the high street have forced the retailers to keep costs under strict control in order to meet their profit objectives. This has been done in various ways, including:

● moving production to cheaper countries and closing inflexible manufacturing offshoots;
● using fewer manufacturers and working more closely with manufacturers in the design of clothes. This has enabled the retailers to add details, such as embroidery or unusual design features, and to command a higher price for relatively little cost;
● improving communication to suppliers of materials and to manufacturers so that design and sourcing decisions can be made faster and more accurately. This has meant that the time to make garments has been reduced from as much as nine months to just a few weeks;
● predicting more accurately what customers want in order to avoid being left with stocks of unwanted items.

The effect of implementing these changes has been to reduce costs, and thereby improve profits, and to have more flexibility in the cost structure so that the clothes retailers are more able to weather a downturn.

Source: Adapted from 'Margin of success for clothing retailers', *The Times*, 20 November 2002, p. 30.

Does this mean that the needs of other groups associated with the business (employees, customers, suppliers, the community and so on) are not really important? The answer to this question is almost certainly no, if the business wishes to survive and prosper over the longer term. Satisfying the needs of other groups will normally be consistent with the need to increase the wealth of the owners over the longer term. A dissatisfied workforce, for example, may result in low productivity, strikes and so forth, which will in turn have an adverse effect on the wealth of the owners. Similarly, a business that upsets the local community by polluting the environment may attract bad publicity, resulting in a loss of customers and heavy fines.

We should be clear that businesses need to do more than just maximise this year's profit if they are to generate as much wealth as possible for their owners. In the short term, corners can be cut and risks taken that will improve profit. Wealth is a longer-term concept, since it relates not only to this year's profit, but to that of future years as well. **Real World 1.3** gives some examples of how emphasis on short-term profits can damage wealth.

REAL WORLD 1.3

Short-term gains, long-term problems   FT

In recent years, many businesses have been criticised for failing to consider the long-term implications of their policies on the wealth of the owners. John Kay argues that some businesses have achieved growth in short-term increases in wealth by sacrificing their longer-term prosperity. He points out that:

> . . . The business of Marks and Spencer, the retailer, was unparalleled in reputation but mature. To achieve earnings growth consistent with a glamour rating the company squeezed suppliers, gave less value for money, spent less on stores. In 1998, it achieved the highest (profit) margin in sales in the history of the business. It had also compromised its position to the point where sales and profits plummeted.
>
> Banks and insurance companies have taken staff out of branches and retrained those that remain as sales people. The pharmaceuticals industry has taken advantage of mergers to consolidate its research and development facilities. Energy companies have cut back on exploration.
>
> We know that these actions increased corporate earnings. We do not know what effect they have on the long-run strength of the business – and this is the key point – do the companies themselves know? Some rationalisations will genuinely lead to more productive businesses. Other companies will suffer the fate of Marks and Spencer.

Source: 'Profit without honour', John Kay, *Financial Times Weekend*, 29/30 June 2002.

SUMMARY

The main points of this chapter may be summarised as follows:

What are accounting and finance?

● Accounting provides financial information for a range of users to help them make better judgements and decisions concerning a business.

● Finance also helps users to make better decisions and is concerned with the financing and investing activities of the business.

Accounting and user needs

- For accounting to be useful, there must be a clear understanding of *for whom* and *for what purpose* the information will be used.

- There may be conflicts of interest between different users over the ways in which the wealth of a business is generated or distributed.

- There is evidence that users find accounting information useful and use it to make decisions.

- Accounting can be viewed as a form of service as it involves providing financial information required by the various users.

- To provide a useful service, accounting must possess certain qualities, or characteristics. These are relevance, reliability, comparability and understandability. In addition, accounting information must be material.

- Providing a service to users can be costly and financial information should be produced only if the cost of providing the information is less than the benefits gained.

Accounting information

- Accounting is part of the total information system within a business. It shares the features that are common to all information systems within a business, which are the identification, recording, analysis and reporting of information.

Management and financial accounting

- Accounting has two main strands – management accounting and financial accounting.

- Management accounting seeks to meet the needs of the business's managers and financial accounting seeks to meet the needs of the other user groups.

- These two strands differ in terms of the types of reports produced, the level of reporting detail, the time horizon, the degree of standardisation and the range and quality of information provided.

Is accounting too interesting?

- In recent years, there has been a wave of accounting scandals in the US and Europe.

- This appears to reflect a particular economic environment, although other factors may also play a part.

Accounting change

- Changes in the economic environment have led to changes in the nature and scope of accounting.

- Financial accounting has improved its framework of rules and there has been greater international harmonisation of accounting rules.

- Management accounting has become more outward looking and new methods for managing costs have emerged.

Why study accounting?

- Everyone connected with business should be a little 'streetwise' about accounting and finance. Financial information and decisions exert an enormous influence over the ways in which a business operates.

Forms of business

There are three main forms of business unit:

● Sole proprietorship – easy to set up and flexible to operate but the owner has unlimited liability.

● Partnership – easy to set up and spreads the burdens of ownership, but partners usually have unlimited liability and there are ownership risks if the partners are unsuitable.

● Limited company – limited liability for owners but obligations imposed on the way a company conducts its affairs.

Accounting and business objectives

● A business may pursue a variety of objectives but the main objective for virtually all businesses is to enhance the wealth of its owners. This does not mean, however, that the needs of other groups connected with the business, such as employees, should be ignored.

→ Key terms

accounting p. 2
finance p. 3
shares p. 7
relevance p. 7
reliability p. 8
comparability p. 8
understandability p. 8
materiality p. 9

accounting information
  system p. 12
management accounting p. 12
financial accounting p. 12
financial management p. 14
sole proprietorship p. 17
partnership p. 18
limited company p. 19

Further reading

If you would like to explore the topics covered in this chapter in more depth, we recommend the following books:

Accounting Theory, *Riahi-Belkaoui A.*, 4th edn, Thomson Learning, 2000, chapters 1 and 2.

Management and Cost Accounting, *Horngren C., Bhimani A., Foster G. and Datar S.*, 2nd edn, Prentice Hall, 2002, chapter 1.

Business Finance: Theory and practice, *McLaney E.*, 6th edn, Prentice Hall, 2003, chapters 1 and 2.

REVIEW QUESTIONS

Answers to these questions can be found on the students' side of the Companion Website at www.pearsoned.co.uk/atrillmclaney.

1.1 What is the purpose of producing accounting information?

1.2 Identify the main users of accounting information for a university. Do these users differ very much from the users of accounting information for private-sector businesses? Is there a major difference in the ways in which accounting information for a university would be used compared with that of a private-sector business?

1.3 Management accounting has been described as 'the eyes and ears of management'. What do you think this expression means?

1.4 Financial accounting statements tend to reflect past events. In view of this, how can they be of any assistance to a user in making a decision when decisions, by their very nature, can only be made about future actions?

Financial accounting

Part 1 of this book deals with the area of accounting and finance usually referred to as 'financial accounting'. Here we shall introduce the three principal financial statements:

● Balance sheet
● Profit and loss account (also known as the income statement)
● Cash flow statement.

In Chapter 2, we provide an overview of these three statements and then go on to consider the first of these, the balance sheet, in some detail. Included in our consideration of the balance sheet will be an introduction to some of the conventions of accounting. These 'conventions' are generally-accepted rules that are used when preparing financial statements. In Chapter 3 we examine the second of the major financial statements, the profit and loss account. Here we shall be looking at such issues as how profit is measured and the point in time at which we recognise when a profit has been made. We shall also consider some accounting conventions that are used when preparing the profit and loss account.

The most important business form in the UK is the limited company and, in Chapters 4 and 5, we focus on accounting specifically for companies. There is nothing in essence that makes companies different from other types of private-sector business as far as accounting is concerned, but there some points of detail that we need to consider. Chapter 5 deals specifically with companies reporting to their shareholders and with public accountability. Here we shall consider the framework of principles that has been proposed to guide the preparation of financial reports. We shall also review some important regulations surrounding the preparation of company financial statements.

Chapter 6 deals with the last of the three principal financial statements, the cash flow statement. This document is viewed as an important supplement to the other two statements because it identifies from where the business obtained cash and how the cash was used during an accounting period.

Reading the three statements will provide information about the business's performance and position for the period concerned. It is possible, however, to gain even more helpful insights to the business by analysing these statements, using financial ratios and other techniques. Combining two figures from the financial statements in a ratio, and comparing this with a similar ratio for, say, another business, can often tell us much more than just reading the figures themselves. In Chapter 7 we consider some of the techniques for analysing financial statements.

CHAPTER 2

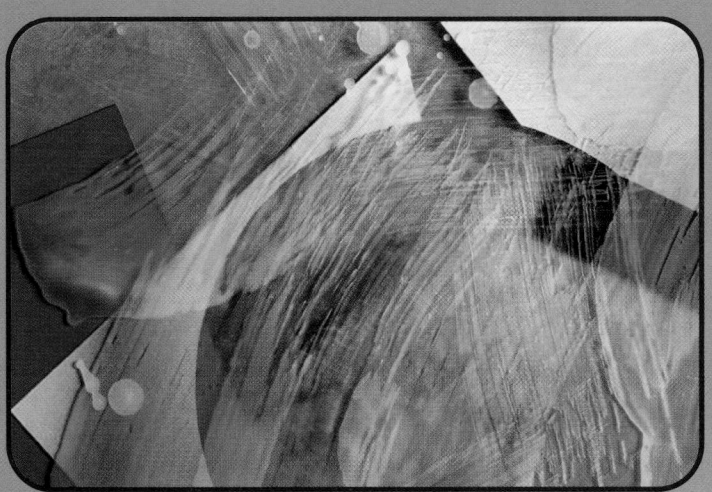

Measuring and reporting financial position

OBJECTIVES

When you have completed this chapter, you should be able to:

● Explain the nature and purpose of the three major financial statements.

● Prepare a simple balance sheet and interpret the information that it contains.

● Discuss the accounting conventions underpinning the balance sheet.

● Discuss the limitations of the balance sheet in portraying the financial position of a business.

INTRODUCTION

We saw in the previous chapter that accounting has two distinct strands – financial accounting and management accounting. This chapter, and Chapters 3 to 7 examine the three major financial statements that form the core of financial accounting. We begin our examination by providing an overview of these statements and we shall see how each contributes towards an assessment of the overall financial position and performance of a business.

Following this overview, we begin a more detailed examination by turning our attention towards one of these financial statements – the balance sheet. We shall see how it is prepared, and examine the principles underpinning this statement. We shall also consider its value for decision-making purposes.

The major financial statements – an overview

The objective of the major financial accounting statements is to provide a picture of the overall financial position and performance of the business. To achieve this objective, the business's accounting system will normally produce three particular statements on a regular, recurring basis. These three are concerned with answering the following questions:

● What cash movements (that is, cash in and cash out) took place over a particular period?
● How much wealth (that is, profit) was generated, or lost, by the business over that period?
● What is the accumulated wealth of the business at the end of that period?

These questions are addressed by the following three financial accounting statements, with each one addressing a particular question. The financial statements are:

- ● The **cash flow statement**
- ● The **profit and loss account** (also known as the **income statement**)
- ● The **balance sheet**.

Taken together, they provide an overall picture of the financial health of the business.

Perhaps the best way to introduce these financial statements is to look at an example of a very simple business. From this we shall be able to see the sort of information that each of the statements can usefully provide. It is, however, worth pointing out that, whilst a simple business is our starting point, the principles that we consider are also applied to more complex businesses. This means that we shall frequently encounter these principles again in later chapters.

Example 2.1

Paul was unemployed and unable to find a job. He therefore decided to embark on a business venture. Christmas was approaching, and so he decided to buy gift wrapping paper from a local supplier and to sell it on the corner of his local high street. He felt that the price of wrapping paper in the high street shops was excessive, and that this provided him with a useful business opportunity.

He began the venture with £40 in cash. On the first day of trading, he purchased wrapping paper for £40 and sold three-quarters of his stock for £45 cash.

● **What cash movements took place during the first day of trading?**
On the first day of trading, a *cash flow statement* showing the cash movements for the day can be prepared as follows:

Cash flow statement for day 1

	£
Opening balance (cash introduced)	40
Add Cash from sales of wrapping paper	45
	85
Less Cash paid to purchase wrapping paper	40
Closing balance of cash	45

● **How much wealth (that is, profit) was generated by the business during the first day of trading?**
A *profit and loss account* can be prepared to show the wealth (profit) generated on the first day. The wealth generated will represent the difference between the value of the sales made and the cost of the goods (that is, wrapping paper) sold:

Profit and loss account for day 1

	£
Sales revenue	45
Less Cost of goods sold ($^3/_4$ of £40)	30
Profit	15

Note that it is only the *cost* of the wrapping paper sold that is matched against the sales revenue in order to find the profit, and not the whole of the cost of wrapping paper acquired. Any unsold stock (in this case $^1/_4$ of £40 = £10) will be charged against the future sales revenue that it generates.

● **What is the accumulated wealth at the end of the first day?**
To establish the accumulated wealth at the end of the first day, we can draw up a *balance sheet*. This will list the resources held at the end of that day:

Balance sheet at the end of day 1

	£
Cash (closing balance)	45
Stock of goods for resale ($^1/_4$ of £40)	10
Total business wealth	55

We can see from the financial statements in Example 2.1 that each statement provides part of a picture that sets out the financial performance and position of the business. We begin by showing the cash movements. Cash is a vital resource that is necessary for any business to function effectively. Cash is required to meet debts that may become due and to acquire other resources (such as stock). Cash has been described as the 'lifeblood' of a business, and movements in cash are usually given close scrutiny by users of financial statements.

However, it is clear that reporting cash movements alone would not be enough to portray the financial health of the business. The changes in cash over time do not give an insight into the profit generated. The profit and loss account provides us with information concerning this aspect of performance. For day 1, for example, we saw that the cash balance increased by £5, but the profit generated, as shown in the profit and loss account, was £15. The cash balance did not increase by the amount of the profit made because part of the wealth generated (£10) was held in the form of stocks.

To gain an insight to the total wealth of the business, a balance sheet can be drawn up at the end of the day. Cash is only one form in which wealth can be held. In the case of this business, wealth is also held in the form of a stock of goods for resale (also known as inventories). Hence, when drawing up the balance sheet, both forms of wealth held will be listed. In the case of a large business, there may be many other forms in which wealth will be held, such as land and buildings, equipment, motor vehicles and so on.

Let us now continue with our example.

Example 2.1 continued

On the second day of trading, Paul purchased more wrapping paper for £20 cash. He managed to sell all of the new stock and all of the earlier stock, for a total of £48.

The cash flow statement on day 2 will be as follows:

Cash flow statement for day 2

	£
Opening balance (from the end of day 1)	45
Add Cash from sales of wrapping paper	48
	93
Less Cash paid to purchase wrapping paper	20
Closing balance	73

The profit and loss account for day 2 will be as follows:

Profit and loss account for day 2

	£
Sales revenue	48
Less Cost of goods sold (£20 + £10)	30
Profit	18

The balance sheet at the end of day 2 will be:

Balance sheet at the end of day 2

	£
Cash (closing balance)	73
Stock of goods for resale	–
Total business wealth	73

We can see that the total business wealth increased to £73 by the end of day 2. This represents an increase of £18 (that is, £73 – £55) over the previous day – which, of course, is the amount of profit made during day 2 as shown on the profit and loss account.

ACTIVITY 2.1

On the third day of his business venture, Paul purchased more stock for £46 cash. However, it was raining hard for much of the day and sales were slow. After Paul had sold half of his total stock for £32, he decided to stop trading until the following day.

Have a go at drawing up the three financial statements for day 3 of Paul's business venture.

Cash flow statement for day 3

	£
Opening balance (from the end of day 2)	73
Add Cash from sales of wrapping paper	32
	105
Less Cash paid to purchase wrapping paper	46
Closing balance	59

Profit and loss account for day 3

	£
Sales revenue	32
Less Cost of goods sold ($\frac{1}{2}$ of £46)	23
Profit	9

Balance sheet at the end of day 3

	£
Cash (closing balance)	59
Stock of goods for resale ($\frac{1}{2}$ of £46)	23
Total business wealth	82

Note that the total business wealth had increased by £9 (that is, the amount of the day's profit) even though the cash balance had declined. This is because the business is holding more of its wealth in the form of stock rather than cash, compared with the end of day 2.

We can see that the profit and loss account and cash flow statement are both concerned with measuring flows (of wealth and cash respectively) during a particular period (for example, a particular day, a particular month or a particular year). The balance sheet, however, is concerned with the financial position at a particular moment in time.

Figure 2.1 illustrates this point. The profit and loss account, cash flow statement and balance sheet, when taken together, are often referred to as the **final accounts** of the business.

For external users, these statements are normally backward looking because they are based on information concerning past events and transactions. This can be useful in

Figure 2.1	The relationship between the balance sheet, the profit and loss account and the cash flow statement

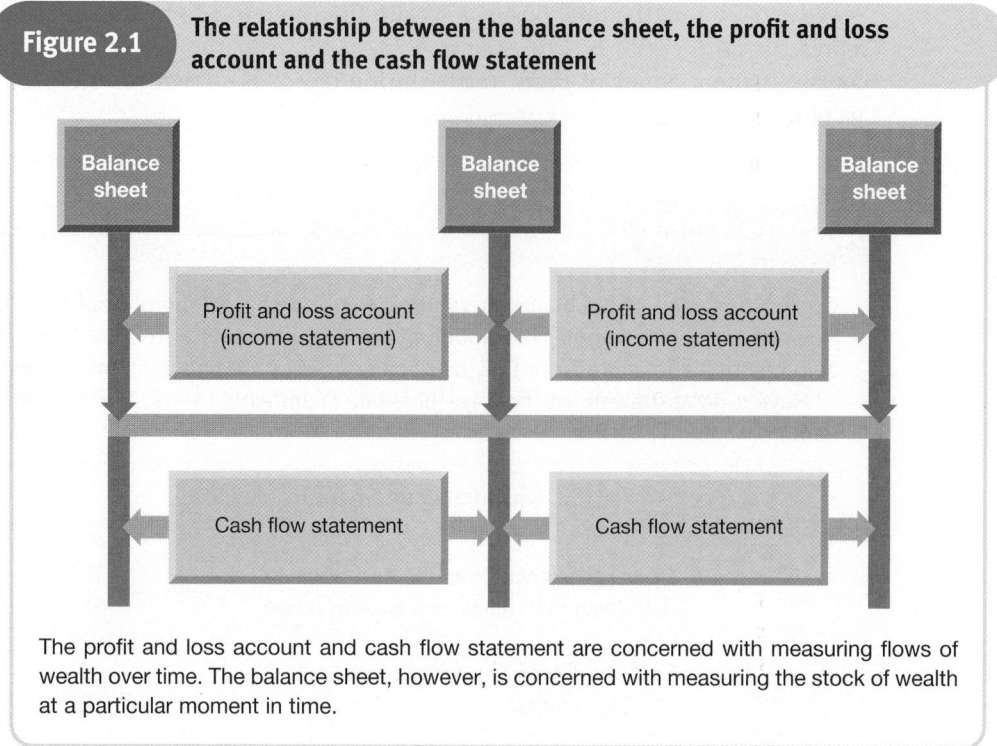

The profit and loss account and cash flow statement are concerned with measuring flows of wealth over time. The balance sheet, however, is concerned with measuring the stock of wealth at a particular moment in time.

providing feedback on past performance, and in identifying trends that provide clues to future performance. However, the statements can also be prepared using projected data to help assess likely future profits, cash flows and so on. The financial statements are normally prepared on a projected basis for internal decision-making purposes only. Managers are usually reluctant to publish these projected statements for external users, as they may reveal valuable information to competitors.

Now that we have an overview of the financial statements, we shall consider each statement in more detail. We shall go straight on to look at the balance sheet. Chapter 3 looks at the profit and loss account, Chapter 6 goes into more detail on the cash flow statement. (Chapters 4 and 5 consider the balance sheet and profit and loss accounts of limited companies.)

The balance sheet

The purpose of the balance sheet is simply to set out the financial position of a business at a particular moment in time. (The balance sheet is sometimes referred to as the *position statement*, because it seeks to provide the user with a picture of financial position.) We saw above that the balance sheet will reveal the forms in which the wealth of the business is held and how much wealth is held in each form. We can, however, be more specific about the nature of the balance sheet by saying that it sets out the **assets** of the business on the one hand, and the **claims** against the business on the other. Before looking at the balance sheet in more detail, we need to be clear about what these terms mean.

Assets

An asset is essentially a resource held by the business. For a particular item to be treated as an asset for accounting purposes:

- *A probable future benefit must exist.* This simply means that the item must be expected to have some future monetary value. This value can arise through its use within the business or through its hire or sale. Thus, an obsolete piece of equipment that could be sold for scrap would still be considered an asset, whereas an obsolete piece of equipment that could not be sold for scrap would not be regarded as one.
- *The business must have an exclusive right to control the benefit.* Unless the business has exclusive rights over the resource it cannot be regarded as an asset. Thus, for a business offering holidays on barges, the canal system may be a very valuable resource, but as the business will not be able to control the access of others to the canals, it cannot be regarded as an asset of the business. (However, the barges owned by the business would be regarded as assets.)
- *The benefit must arise from some past transaction or event.* This means that the transaction (or other event) giving rise to the business's right to the benefit must have already occurred, and will not arise at some future date. Thus an agreement by a business to purchase a piece of machinery at some future date would not mean the item is currently an asset of the business.
- *The asset must be capable of measurement in monetary terms.* Unless the item can be measured in monetary terms, with a reasonable degree of reliability, it will not be regarded as an asset for inclusion on the balance sheet. Thus, the title of a magazine (for example '*Hello!*' or '*Vogue*') that was created by its publisher may be extremely valuable to the business, but this value is usually impossible to quantify. It will not, therefore, be treated as an asset.

Note that all four of these conditions must apply. If one of them is missing, the item will not be treated as an asset, for accounting purposes, and will not appear on the balance sheet.

We can see that these conditions will strictly limit the kind of items that may be referred to as 'assets' in the balance sheet. Certainly not all resources exploited by a business will be assets of the business for accounting purposes. Some, like the canal system or the magazine title '*Hello!*', may well be assets in a broader sense, but not for accounting purposes. Once an asset has been acquired by a business, it will continue to be considered an asset until the benefits are exhausted or the business disposes of it in some way.

ACTIVITY 2.2

Indicate which of the following items could appear as an asset on the balance sheet of a business. Explain your reasoning in each case.

1 £1,000 owing to the business by a customer who is unable to pay.
2 The purchase of a patent from an inventor that gives the business the right to produce a new product. Production of the new product is expected to increase profits over the period during which the patent is held.
3 The business hiring a new marketing director who is confidently expected to increase profits by over 30 per cent over the next three years.
4 The purchase of a machine that will save the business £10,000 each year. It is currently being used by the business but it has been acquired on credit and is not yet paid for.

Activity 2.2 continued

Your answer to the above problems should be along the following lines:

1 Under normal circumstances a business would expect a customer to pay the amount owed. Such an amount is therefore typically shown as an asset under the heading 'debtors' or 'receivables'. However, in this particular case the debtor is unable to pay. Hence the item is incapable of providing future benefits, and the £1,000 owing would not be regarded as an asset. Debts that are not paid are referred to as 'bad debts'.

2 The purchase of the patent would meet all of the conditions set out above and would therefore be regarded as an asset.

3 The hiring of a new marketing director would not be considered as the acquisition of an asset. One argument against its classification as an asset is that the business does not have exclusive rights of control over the director. (Nevertheless, it may have an exclusive right to the services that the director provided.) Perhaps a stronger argument is that the value of the director cannot be measured in monetary terms with any degree of reliability.

4 The machine would be considered an asset even though it is not yet paid for. Once the business has agreed to purchase the machine, and has accepted it, the machine is legally owned by the business even though payment is still outstanding. (The amount outstanding would be shown as a claim, as we shall see below.)

The sorts of items that often appear as assets in the balance sheet of a business include:

● freehold premises
● machinery and equipment
● fixtures and fittings
● patents and trademarks
● debtors (receivables)
● investments.

ACTIVITY 2.3

Can you think of three additional items that might appear as assets in the balance sheet of a business?

You may be able to think of a number of other items. Some that you may have identified are:

● motor vehicles
● stock of goods (inventories)
● computer equipment
● cash at bank.

Note that an asset does not have to be a physical item – it may also be a non-physical right to certain benefits. Assets that have a physical substance and can be touched are referred to as **tangible assets**. Assets that have no physical substance but which, nevertheless, provide expected future benefits (such as patents) are referred to as **intangible assets**.

Claims

A claim is an obligation on the part of the business to provide cash, or some other form of benefit, to an outside party. A claim will normally arise as a result of the outside party providing funds in the form of assets for use by the business. There are essentially two types of claim against a business:

● **Capital**. This represents the claim of the owner(s) against the business. This claim is sometimes referred to as the *owner's equity*. Some find it hard to understand how the owner can have a claim against the business, particularly when we consider the example of a sole-proprietor-type business where the owner *is*, in effect, the business. However, for accounting purposes, a clear distinction is made between the business (whatever its size) and the owner(s). The business is viewed as being quite separate from the owner and this is equally true for a sole proprietor like Paul, the wrapping-paper seller, in Example 2.1, or a large company like Marks and Spencer plc. It is seen as a separate entity with its own separate existence and when financial statements are prepared, they are prepared for the business rather than for the owner(s). This means that the balance sheet should reflect the financial position of the business as a separate entity. Viewed from this perspective, any funds contributed by the owner will be seen as coming from outside the business and will appear as a claim against the business in its balance sheet.

As we have just seen, the business and the owner are separate for accounting purposes, irrespective of the type of business concerned. It is also true that the operation of the capital section of the balance sheet is broadly the same irrespective of the type of business concerned. As we shall see in Chapter 4, with limited companies the capital figure must be analysed according to how each part of the capital first arose. For example, companies must make a distinction between that part of the capital that arose from retained profits and that part that arose from the owners putting in cash to start up the business.

● **Liabilities**. Liabilities represent the claims of individuals and organisations, apart from the owner, that have arisen from past transactions or events such as supplying goods or lending money to the business.

Once a claim has been incurred by a business, it will remain as an obligation until it is settled.

Now that the meaning of the terms *assets* and *claims* has been established, we can go on and discuss the relationship between the two. This relationship is quite simple and straightforward. If a business wishes to acquire assets, it will have to raise the necessary funds from somewhere. It may raise the funds from the owner(s) or from other outside parties or from both. To illustrate the relationship let us take the example of a business, as set out in Example 2.2.

Example 2.2

Jerry and Co. deposits £20,000 in a bank account on 1 March in order to commence business. Let us assume that the cash is supplied by the owner (£6,000) and by a lender (£14,000) and paid into the business bank account. The raising of the funds in this way will give rise to a claim on the business by both the owner (capital) and the lender (liability). If a balance sheet of Jerry and Co. is prepared following the above transactions, the assets and claims of the business will appear as follows:

Jerry and Co.
Balance sheet as at 1 March

Assets	£	Claims	£
Cash at bank	20,000	Capital	6,000
		Liability – loan	14,000
	20,000		20,000

We can see from the balance sheet that has been prepared that the total claims are the same as the total assets. Thus:

$$\text{Assets} = \text{Capital} + \text{Liabilities}$$

This equation – which is often referred to as the *balance sheet equation* – will always hold true. Whatever changes may occur to the assets of the business or the claims against the business, there will be compensating changes elsewhere that will ensure that the balance sheet always 'balances'. By way of illustration, consider the following transactions for Jerry and Co.:

2 March Purchased a motor van for £5,000, paying by cheque.
3 March Purchased stock in trade (that is, goods to be sold) on one month's credit for £3,000.
4 March Repaid £2,000 of the loan from the lender.
6 March Owner introduced another £4,000 into the business bank account.

A balance sheet may be drawn up after each day in which transactions have taken place. In this way, the effect can be seen of each transaction on the assets and claims of the business. The balance sheet as at 2 March will be as follows:

Jerry and Co.
Balance sheet as at 2 March

Assets	£	Claims	£
Cash at bank (20,000 – 5,000)	15,000	Capital	6,000
Motor van	5,000	Liabilities – loan	14,000
	20,000		20,000

As can be seen, the effect of purchasing a motor van is to decrease the balance at the bank by £5,000 and to introduce a new asset – a motor van – to the balance sheet. The total assets remain unchanged. It is only the 'mix' of assets that will change. The claims against the business will remain the same because there has been no change in the way in which the business has been funded.

The balance sheet as at 3 March, following the purchase of stock, will be as follows:

Jerry and Co.
Balance sheet as at 3 March

Assets	£	Claims	£
Cash at bank	15,000	Capital	6,000
Motor van	5,000	Liabilities – loan	14,000
Stock (inventories)	3,000	Liabilities – trade creditor	3,000
	23,000		23,000

The effect of purchasing stock has been to introduce another new asset (stock) to the balance sheet. In addition, the fact that the goods have not yet been paid for means that the claims against the business will be increased by the £3,000 owed to the supplier, who is referred to as a *trade creditor* (or trade payable) on the balance sheet.

ACTIVITY 2.4

Try drawing up a balance sheet for Jerry and Co. as at 4 March.

The balance sheet as at 4 March, following the repayment of part of the loan, will be as follows:

Jerry and Co.
Balance sheet as at 4 March

Assets	£	Claims	£
Cash at bank (15,000 – 2,000)	13,000	Capital	6,000
Motor van	5,000	Liabilities – loan (14,000 – 2,000)	12,000
Stock (inventories)	3,000	Liabilities – trade creditor (payable)	3,000
	21,000		21,000

The repayment of £2,000 of the loan will result in a decrease in the balance at the bank of £2,000 and a decrease in the loan claim against the business by the same amount.

ACTIVITY 2.5

Try drawing up a balance sheet as at 6 March for Jerry and Co.

The balance sheet as at 6 March, following the introduction of more funds, will be as follows:

Jerry and Co.
Balance sheet as at 6 March

Assets	£	Claims	£
Cash at bank (13,000 + 4,000)	17,000	Capital (6,000 + 4,000)	10,000
Motor van	5,000	Liabilities – loan	12,000
Stock (inventories)	3,000	Liabilities – trade creditor (payable)	3,000
	25,000		25,000

The introduction of more funds by the owner will result in an increase in the capital of £4,000 and an increase in the cash at bank by the same amount.

Example 2.2 illustrates the point that the balance sheet equation (assets equals capital plus liabilities) will always hold true, because it reflects the fact that, if a business wishes to acquire assets, it must raise funds equal to the cost of those assets. The funds raised must be provided by the owners (capital), or by others (liabilities) or by both the owners and others. Hence the total cost of assets acquired should always equal the total capital plus liabilities.

It is worth pointing out that a business would not draw up a balance sheet after each day of transactions as shown in the example above. Such an approach is likely to be impractical, given even a relatively small number of transactions each day. A balance sheet for the business is usually prepared at the end of a defined reporting period.

Determining the length of the reporting interval will involve weighing up the costs of producing the information against the perceived benefits of the information for decision-making purposes. In practice, the reporting interval will vary between businesses, and could be monthly, quarterly, half-yearly or annually. For external reporting purposes, an annual reporting cycle is the norm (although certain businesses, typically larger ones, report more frequently than this). However, for internal reporting purposes to managers, many businesses produce monthly financial statements.

The effect of trading operations on the balance sheet

In the example we considered earlier, we dealt with the effect on the balance sheet of a number of different types of transactions that a business might undertake. These transactions covered the purchase of assets for cash and on credit, the repayment of a loan, and the injection of capital. However, one form of transaction, trading, has not yet been considered. To deal with the effect of trading transactions on the balance sheet, let us return to our earlier example.

Example 2.2 continued

The balance sheet that we drew up for Jerry and Co. as at 6 March was as follows:

Jerry and Co.
Balance sheet as at 6 March

Assets	£	Claims	£
Cash at bank	17,000	Capital	10,000
Motor van	5,000	Liabilities – loan	12,000
Stock (inventories)	3,000	Liabilities – trade creditor (payable)	3,000
	25,000		25,000

Let us assume that, on 7 March, the business managed to sell all of the stock for £5,000 and received a cheque immediately from the customer for this amount. The balance sheet on 7 March, after this transaction has taken place, will be as follows:

Jerry and Co.
Balance sheet as at 7 March

Assets	£	Claims	£
Cash at bank (17,000 + 5,000)	22,000	Capital [10,000 + (5,000 – 3,000)]	12,000
Motor van	5,000	Liabilities – loan	12,000
Stock (inventories) (3,000 – 3,000)	–	Liabilities – trade creditor (payable)	3,000
	27,000		27,000

We can see that the stock (£3,000) has now disappeared from the balance sheet, but the cash at bank has increased by the selling price of the stock (£5,000). The net effect has therefore been to increase assets by £2,000 (that is £5,000 – £3,000). This increase represents the net increase in wealth (the profit) that has arisen from trading. Also note that the capital of the business has increased by £2,000, in line with the increase in assets. This increase in capital reflects the fact that increases in wealth, as a result of trading or other operations, will be to the benefit of the owners and will increase their stake in the business.

ACTIVITY 2.6

What would have been the effect on the balance sheet if the stock had been sold on 7 March for £1,000 rather than £5,000?

The balance sheet on 7 March would be as follows:

Jerry and Co.
Balance sheet as at 7 March

Assets	£	Claims	£
Cash at bank (17,000 + 1,000)	18,000	Capital [10,000 + (1,000 – 3,000)]	8,000
Motor van	5,000	Liabilities – loan	12,000
Stock (inventories) (3,000 – 3,000)	–	Liabilities – trade creditor (payable)	3,000
	23,000		23,000

As we can see, the stock (£3,000) will disappear from the balance sheet, but the cash at bank will rise by only £1,000. This will mean a net reduction in assets of £2,000. This reduction represents a loss arising from trading and will be reflected in a reduction in the capital of the owner.

We can see that any decrease in wealth (loss) arising from trading or other transactions will lead to a reduction in the owner's stake in the business. If the business wished to maintain the level of assets as at 6 March, it would be necessary to obtain further funds from the owner or from lenders, or both.

What we have just seen means that the balance sheet equation can be extended as follows:

Assets = Capital + Profit (or – Loss) + Liabilities

As we have seen, the profit or loss for the period impacts on the balance sheet as an addition to capital. Any funds introduced or withdrawn by the owner for living expenses or other reasons also affect capital, but are shown separately. By doing this, we provide more comprehensive information for users of the financial statements. If we assume that the above business sold the stock for £5,000, as in the earlier example, and further assume that the owner withdrew £1,500 for his or her own use, the capital of the owner would appear as follows on the balance sheet:

	£
Capital (owner's equity)	
Opening balance	10,000
Add Profit	2,000
	12,000
Less Drawings	1,500
Closing balance	10,500

If the drawings were in cash, the balance of cash would decrease by £1,500 in the balance sheet.

Note that, like all balance sheet items, the amount of capital is cumulative. This means that any profit made that is not taken out as drawings by the owner(s) remains in the business. These retained profits have the effect of expanding the business.

The classification of assets

If the items on the balance sheet are listed haphazardly, with assets listed on one side and claims on the other, it can be confusing. To help users to understand more clearly the information that is presented, assets and claims are usually grouped into categories. Assets may be categorised as being either current or non-current.

Current assets
....

➡ **Current assets** are basically assets that are held for the short term. To be more precise, they are assets that meet any one of four criteria. These are:

● they are held for sale or consumption in the normal course of a business's operating cycle;
● they are for the short-term (that is, to be sold within the next year);
● they are held primarily for trading; and
● they are cash, or near cash such as easily marketable, short-term investments.

The most common current assets are stock (or inventories), customers who owe money for goods or services supplied on credit (known as trade debtors or receivables), and cash.

Perhaps it is worth making the point here that most sales made by most businesses are made on credit. This is to say that the goods pass to, or the service is rendered to, the customer at one point but the customer pays later. Retail sales are the only significant exception to this general point.

For businesses that sell goods, rather than render a service, the current assets of stock, trade debtors and cash are interrelated. They circulate within a business as

| Figure 2.2 | The circulating nature of current assets |

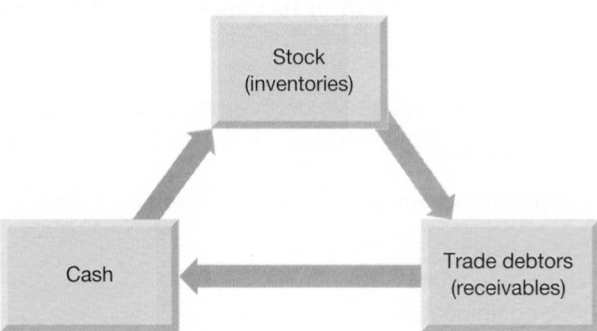

Stock may be sold on credit to customers. When the customers pay, the trade debts will be converted into cash, which can then be used to purchase more stock, and so the cycle begins again.

shown in Figure 2.2. We can see that cash can be used to purchase stock, which is then sold as credit. When the credit customers (trade debtors) pay, the business receives an injection of cash, and so on.

Non-current assets

Non-current assets (also called **fixed assets**) are assets that do not meet the above criteria. They are held for the long-term operations of the business. Essentially, they are the 'tools' of the business and are held with the objective of generating wealth.

This distinction between assets that are continuously circulating within the business and assets used for long-term operations may be helpful when trying to assess the appropriateness of the mix of assets held. A business will need a certain amount of both types of asset to operate effectively.

ACTIVITY 2.7

Can you think of two examples of assets that may be classified as non-current assets?

Examples of assets that may be defined as being non-current are:

- freehold premises
- plant and machinery
- motor vehicles
- patents.

This is not an exhaustive list. You may have thought of others.

It is important to appreciate that how a particular asset is classified (that is, between current and non-current) varies according to the nature of the business. This is because the *purpose* for which a particular type of asset may differ from business to business. For example, a motor vehicle manufacturer will normally hold a stock of the motor vehicles produced for resale, and would therefore classify them as part of the current assets. On the other hand, a business that uses motor vehicles for delivering its goods to customers (that is, as part of its long-term operations) would classify them as non-current assets.

ACTIVITY 2.8

The assets of Kunalun and Co., a large advertising agency, are:

- Cash at bank
- Fixtures and fittings
- Office equipment
- Motor vehicles
- Freehold office premises
- Computer equipment
- Work-in-progress (that is, partly completed work for clients).

Which of these do you think should be defined as non-current assets, and which should be defined as current assets?

Your answer should be as follows:

Non-current assets	Current assets
Fixtures and fittings	Cash at bank
Office equipment	Work-in-progress
Motor vehicles	
Freehold office premises	
Computer equipment	

The classification of claims

As we have already seen, claims are normally classified into capital (owner's claim) and liabilities (claims of outsiders). Liabilities are further classified into two groups:

- **Current liabilities** are basically amounts due for settlement in the short-term. To be more precise, they are liabilities that meet any one of four criteria:
  - they expect to be settled within the normal course of the business's operating cycle;
  - they are due to be settled within 12 months of the balance sheet date;
  - they are held primarily for trading purposes; and
  - the business does not have the right to defer settlement beyond 12 months after the balance sheet date.
- **Non-current liabilities** represent those amounts due to outside parties that are not current liabilities.

This classification of liabilities can help gain an insight to the ability of the business to meet its maturing obligations (that is, claims that must shortly be met). The current liabilities, which show the amounts that must be paid within the normal operating cycle, can be compared with the current assets, which show the assets to be sold within the same period. It should also help to highlight how the long-term finance of the business is raised. If a business relies on long-term loans to finance the business, the financial risks associated with the business will increase. This is because these loans will bring a commitment to make interest payments and capital repayments and the business may be forced to stop trading if this commitment is not fulfilled. Thus when raising long-term finance, a business must strike the right balance between non-current liabilities and owners capital. We shall consider this issue in more detail in Chapter 7.

ACTIVITY 2.9

Can you think of an example of each of a current liability and a non-current liability?

An example of a non-current liability would be a long-term loan. An example of a current liability would be amounts owing to suppliers for goods supplied on credit (known as trade creditors or trade payables) or a bank overdraft (a form of bank borrowing that is repayable on demand).

Balance sheet formats

Now that we have looked at the classification of assets and liabilities, it is possible to consider the format of the balance sheet. Although there is an almost infinite number of ways in which the same balance sheet information could be presented, we shall consider two basic formats. The first of these follows the style we adopted with Jerry and Co. earlier. A more comprehensive example of this style is shown in Example 2.3, below.

Example 2.3

Brie Manufacturing
Balance sheet as at 31 December 2005

	£		£
Non-current assets		**Capital**	
Freehold premises	45,000	Opening balance	50,000
Plant and machinery	30,000	*Add* Profit	14,000
Motor vans	19,000		64,000
	94,000	*Less* Drawings	4,000
			60,000
		Non-current liabilities	
		Loan	50,000
Current assets		**Current liabilities**	
Stock (inventories)	23,000	Trade creditors (payables)	37,000
Trade debtors (receivables)	18,000		
Cash at bank	12,000		
	53,000		
	147,000		147,000

Within each category of asset (non-current and current) shown in Example 2.3, the items are listed in reverse order of liquidity (nearness to cash). Thus, the assets that are furthest from cash are listed first and the assets that are closest to cash are listed last. In the case of non-current assets, freehold premises are listed first as these assets are usually the most difficult to turn into cash and motor vans are listed last as there is usually a ready market for them. In the case of current assets, we have already seen that stock is converted to debtors and then debtors are converted to cash. Hence, under the heading of current assets, stock is listed first, followed by debtors and finally cash itself.

This ordering of assets is a normal practice, which is followed irrespective of the format used. Note also that the current assets are listed individually in the first column, and a subtotal of current assets (£53,000) is carried out to the second column to be added to the subtotal of non-current assets (£94,000). This convention is designed to make the balance sheet easier to read.

An obvious change to the format illustrated in Example 2.3 is to show claims on the left and assets on the right. Some people prefer this approach because the claims can be seen as the source of finance for the business, and the assets show how that finance has been deployed. It could be seen as more logical to show sources first and uses second.

The format shown above is sometimes referred to as the *horizontal layout*. However, in recent years, a more common form of layout for the balance sheet is the *vertical* (or *narrative*) form of layout. This format is really based on a rearrangement of the balance sheet equation. With the horizontal format above, the balance sheet equation is set out as in Figure 2.3. The vertical format merely rearranges this equation as shown in Figure 2.4.

Figure 2.3 The horizontal balance sheet

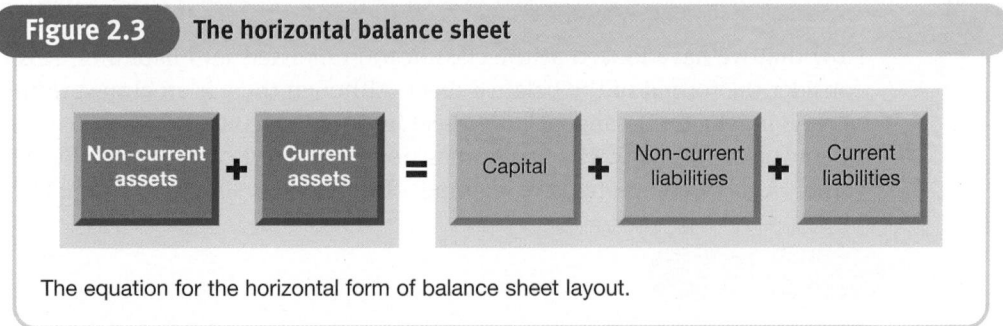

The equation for the horizontal form of balance sheet layout.

Figure 2.4 The vertical balance sheet

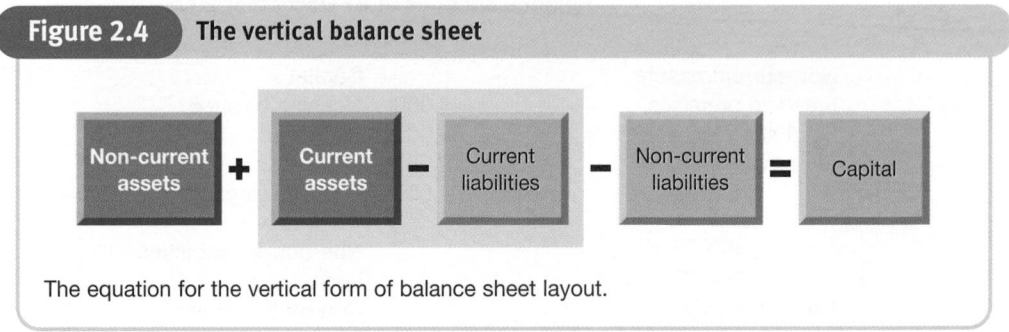

The equation for the vertical form of balance sheet layout.

The vertical layout not only rearranges the equation but, as the name suggests, presents the information vertically rather than horizontally. The balance sheet starts with non-current assets and works downwards towards capital at the end. The balance sheet of Brie Manufacturing which was arranged in horizontal format in Example 2.3 can be rearranged in vertical format as shown in Example 2.4.

Some people find the vertical format of Example 2.4 easier to read than the horizontal format as it usefully highlights the relationship between current assets and current liabilities. The figure derived from deducting current liabilities from the current assets is sometimes referred to as *net current assets* or *working capital*. We can see that for Brie Manufacturing this figure is £16,000, indicating that the short-term liquid assets more than cover the short-term claims against the business.

Example 2.4

Brie Manufacturing
Balance sheet as at 31 December 2005

	£	£
Non-current assets		
Freehold premises		45,000
Plant and machinery		30,000
Motor vans		19,000
		94,000
Current assets		
Stock (inventories)	23,000	
Trade debtors (receivables)	18,000	
Cash at bank	12,000	
	53,000	
Less **Current liabilities**		
Trade creditors (payables)	37,000	
		16,000
Total assets *less* current liabilities		110,000
Less **Non-current liabilities**		
Loan		50,000
Net assets		60,000
Capital		
Opening balance		50,000
Add Profit		14,000
		64,000
Less Drawings		4,000
		60,000

SELF-ASSESSMENT QUESTION 2.1

The following information relates to Simonson Engineering as at 30 September 2005:

	£
Plant and machinery	25,000
Trade creditors (payables)	18,000
Bank overdraft	26,000
Stock (inventories)	45,000
Freehold premises	72,000
Long-term loans	51,000
Trade debtors (receivables)	48,000
Capital at 1 October 2004	117,500
Cash in hand	1,500
Motor vehicles	15,000
Fixtures and fittings	9,000
Profit for the year to 30 September 2005	18,000
Drawings for the year to 30 September 2005	15,000

Required:

Prepare a balance sheet in the vertical format.

The balance sheet as a position at a point in time

As we have already seen, the balance sheet is a statement of the financial position of the business at *a specified point in time*. The balance sheet has been compared to a photograph. A photograph 'freezes' a particular moment in time and will represent the situation only at that moment. Hence, events may be quite different immediately before and immediately after the photograph was taken. Similarly, the balance sheet represents a 'snapshot' of the business at a particular moment. When examining a balance sheet, therefore, it is important to establish the date at which it has been drawn up. This information should be prominently displayed in the balance sheet heading, as shown above. The more recent the balance sheet date, the better when we are trying to assess the current financial position.

A business will normally prepare a balance sheet as at the close of business on the last day of its accounting year. In the UK, businesses are free to choose their accounting year. When making a decision on which year-end date to choose, commercial convenience can often be a deciding factor. Thus, a business operating in the retail trade may choose to have a year-end date early in the calendar year (for example 31 January) because trade tends to be slack during that period and more staff time is available to help with the tasks involved in the preparation of the annual financial statements (such as checking the amount of stock held). Since trade is slack, it is also a time when the amount of stock held by the retail business is likely to be atypically low as compared with other times of the year. Thus the balance sheet, though showing a fair view of what it purports to show, may not show a picture of what is more typically the position of the business over the rest of the year.

Accounting conventions and the balance sheet

Accounting is based on a number of rules or conventions that have evolved over time. They have evolved as attempts to deal with practical problems experienced by preparers and users, rather than to reflect some theoretical ideal. In preparing the balance sheets earlier, we have followed various **accounting conventions**, although they have not been explicitly mentioned. We shall now identify and discuss the major conventions that we have applied.

Business entity convention

For accounting purposes, the business and its owner(s) are treated as being quite separate and distinct. This is why owners are treated as being claimants against their own business in respect of their investment in the business. The **business entity convention** must be distinguished from the legal position that may exist between businesses and their owners. For sole proprietorships and partnerships, the law does not make any distinction between the business and its owner(s). For limited companies, on the other hand, there is a clear legal distinction between the business and its owners. (As we shall see in Chapter 4, the limited company is regarded as having a separate legal existence.) For accounting purposes these legal distinctions are irrelevant, and the business entity convention applies to all businesses.

Money measurement convention

Accounting normally deals with only those items that are capable of being expressed in monetary terms. Money has the advantage that it is a useful common denominator with which to express the wide variety of resources held by a business. However, not all such resources are capable of being measured in monetary terms and so will be excluded from a balance sheet. The **money measurement convention**, therefore, limits the scope of accounting reports.

ACTIVITY 2.10

Can you think of resources held by a business that cannot be quantified in monetary terms?

In answering this activity you may have thought of the following:

- the quality of the workforce
- the reputation of the business's products
- the location of the business
- the relationship with customers
- the ability of the managers.

Over the years, attempts have been made to measure, and then include on the balance sheet, resources of a business that have been previously excluded. For example, we have seen attempts to measure the 'human assets' of the business. It is often claimed that employees are the most valuable 'assets' of a business. By measuring these assets and putting the amount on the balance sheet, it is sometimes argued that we have a more complete picture of the financial position. However, these attempts are resisted because they involve softening the recognition criteria for an asset that we discussed earlier in the chapter. In particular, the ability to measure the value of the staff in monetary terms is an issue here.

Real World 2.1 shows how one business has succeeded in putting people on the balance sheet.

REAL WORLD 2.1

Rio's on the team sheet and the balance sheet

It may be surprising to learn that although human 'assets' are not shown on the balance sheet of a business as a general rule, there are exceptions to this rule. The most common exception arises with professional football clubs. Although football clubs cannot own players, they can own the rights to the players' services. Where these rights are acquired by compensating other clubs for releasing the players from their contracts, the amounts paid provide a reliable basis for measurement. This means that the rights to services can be regarded as an asset of the club for accounting purposes (assuming, of course, the player will also bring benefits to the club).

Real World 2.1 continued

Manchester United Football Club has acquired several key players in this way and reports the cost of acquiring those right to the players' services in its balance sheet. The balance sheet for 2003 shows the cost of registering its current squad of players as £89 million. The item of players' registrations is shown as an intangible asset in the balance sheet as it is the rights to services not the players that are the assets. The figure of £89 million includes the cost of bought-in players such as Rio Ferdinand but not 'home-grown' players such as Paul Scholes and the Neville brothers. The 'home-grown' players are not included because the club did not pay a transfer fee for them, so no clear-cut value can be placed on their services.

Source: Manchester United Annual Report 2003.

Historic cost convention

Assets are shown on the balance sheet at a value that is based on their **historic cost** (that is, acquisition cost). This method of measuring asset value has been adopted by accountants in preference to methods based on some form of current value. Many people find this particular convention difficult to support, as outdated historical costs are unlikely to help in the assessment of current financial position. It is often argued that recording assets at their current value would provide a more realistic view of financial position and would be relevant for a wide range of decisions. However, a system of measurement based on current values can present a number of problems.

ACTIVITY 2.11

Can you think of reasons why current value accounting may pose problems for both preparers and users of financial statements?

The term 'current value' can be defined in a number of ways. For example, it can be defined broadly as either the current replacement cost or the current realisable value (selling price) of an asset. These two types of valuation may result in quite different figures being produced to represent the current value of an item. (Think, for example, of second-hand car values: there is often quite a difference between buying and selling prices.) In addition, the broad terms 'replacement cost' and 'realisable value' can be defined in different ways. We must therefore be clear about what kind of current value accounting we wish to use. There are also practical problems associated with attempts to implement any system of current value accounting. For example, current values, however defined, are often difficult to establish with any real degree of objectivity. This may mean that the figures produced are heavily dependent on the opinion of managers. Unless the current value figures are capable of some form of independent verification, there is a danger that the financial statements will lose their credibility among users.

By reporting assets at their historic cost, it is argued that more reliable information is produced. Reporting in this way reduces the need for subjective opinion, as the amount paid for a particular asset is usually a matter of demonstrable fact. However, information based on past costs may not always be relevant to the needs of users.

Later in the chapter, we shall consider the valuation of assets in the balance sheet in more detail. We shall see that the historic cost convention is not always rigidly adhered to, and that departures from this convention often occur.

Going concern convention

→ The **going concern convention** holds that the financial statements should be prepared on the assumption that the business will continue operations for the foreseeable future, unless this is known not to be true. In other words, it is assumed that there is no intention, or need, to sell off the assets of the business. Such a sale may arise where the business is in financial difficulties and it needs to pay the creditors. This convention is important because the market (sale) value of non-current assets is often low in relation to the values at which they appear in the balance sheet, and an expectation of having to sell off the assets would mean that anticipated losses on sale should be fully recorded. However, where there is no expectation of a need to sell off the assets, the value of non-current assets can continue to be shown at their recorded values (that is, based on historic cost). This convention therefore provides some support for the historic cost convention under normal circumstances.

Dual aspect convention

Each transaction has two aspects, both of which will affect the balance sheet. Thus the purchase of a motor car for cash results in an increase in one asset (motor car) and a decrease in another (cash). The repayment of a loan results in the decrease in a liability (loan) and the decrease in an asset (cash/bank).

ACTIVITY 2.12

What are the two aspects of each of the following transactions?

- Purchase £1,000 stock on credit.
- Owner withdraws £2,000 in cash.
- Repayment of a loan of £3,000.

Your answer should be as follows:

- Stock increases by £1,000, creditors increase by £1,000.
- Capital reduces by £2,000, cash reduces by £2,000.
- Loan reduces by £3,000, cash reduces by £3,000.

→ Recording the **dual aspect** of each transaction ensures that the balance sheet will continue to balance.

Prudence convention

→ The **prudence convention** holds that financial statements should err on the side of caution. The convention represents an attempt to deal with the uncertainty surrounding many events reported in the financial statements, and evolved to counteract the excessive optimism of some managers and owners, which resulted in an overstatement of financial position. This convention requires the recording of all losses in full, and applies to both actual losses and expected losses. For example, if certain goods purchased for resale proved to be unpopular with customers and, as a result, the goods are to be sold below their original cost, the prudence convention requires that the expected loss from the future sales should be recognised immediately rather than when the goods are eventually sold. Profits, on the other hand, are not recognised until they are realised (that is, when the goods are actually sold). When the prudence convention conflicts with another convention, it is prudence that will normally prevail.

ACTIVITY 2.13

Can you think of a situation where certain users might find a prudent view of the financial position of a business will work to their disadvantage?

Applying the prudence convention can result in an understatement of financial position as unrealised profits are not recognised but expected losses are recognised in full. This may result in owners selling their stake in the business at a price that is lower than they would have received if a more balanced approach to valuation were employed.

The degree of bias towards understatement may be difficult to judge. It is likely to vary according to the views of the individual carrying out the valuation.

Stable monetary unit convention

The **stable monetary unit convention** holds that money, which is the unit of measurement in accounting, will not change in value over time. However, in the UK and throughout much of the world, inflation has been a persistent problem. This has meant that the value of money has declined in relation to other assets. In past years, high rates of inflation have resulted in balance sheets, which are drawn up on an historic cost basis, reflecting figures for assets that were much lower than if current values were employed. This sparked a big debate within the accounting profession and business community and there were calls to abandon historic costs in favour of current values in accounting. In more recent years, however, there have been lower rates of inflation and the debate has lost its intensity.

Objectivity convention

The **objectivity convention** seeks to reduce personal bias in financial statements. As far as possible, financial statements should be based on objective verifiable evidence rather than on matters of opinion.

ACTIVITY 2.14

Which of the above conventions does the objectivity convention support and which does it conflict with?

The objectivity convention provides further support (along with the going concern convention) for the use of historic cost as a basis of valuation. It can conflict, however, with the prudence convention, which requires the use of judgement in determining values.

Accounting for goodwill and product brands

Some intangible non-current assets are similar to tangible non-current assets, in so far as they have a clear and separate identity and the cost of the asset can be reliably determined. Patents, trademarks, copyrights and licences would normally fall into this category. Some intangible non-current assets, however, are quite different in nature. They lack a clear and separate identity and are really a hotch-potch of attributes that form part of the essence of the business. Goodwill and product brands fall into this category.

The term 'goodwill' is often used to cover various attributes of the business such as the quality of the products, the skill of the workforce and the relationship with customers. Product brands are similar to goodwill in that they are made up of various attributes, such as the brand image, the quality of the product, the trademark and so on. Although goodwill and product brands may be valuable to a business, this does not mean that they meet the recognition criteria for accounting assets that were discussed earlier in the chapter. Where they have been generated internally by the business it is often difficult to measure their cost or even to verify their existence. They are, therefore, excluded from the balance sheet.

When these items are acquired through an arm's-length transaction, however, the problems of verification and measurement are resolved. (An 'arm's-length' transaction is one that is undertaken between two unconnected parties.) If goodwill is acquired when taking over another business, or if a business acquires a particular product brand from another business, these items will be clearly identified and a price agreed for them. Under these circumstances, they should be reported as assets by the business that acquired them. **Real World 2.2** provides an example of a purchase of goodwill.

REAL WORLD 2.2

Where there's goodwill

CRH is a Dublin-based building materials business that has expanded its operations in recent years. In October 2003 it was reported that it had purchased Cementbouw, Handel and Industrie, a Dutch building materials business. CRH paid €646m for Cementbouw's distribution and building products operations. This was made up of €354m for the net assets (that is, assets less liabilities taken over) leaving a payment of €292m for goodwill. The payment for goodwill, which represents around 45 per cent of the total purchase price, will be recorded as an asset on the balance sheet of CRH.

Source: Based on information in 'CRH purchase of Cementbouw gets approval', *Financial Times*, 1 October 2003.

The basis of valuation of assets on the balance sheet

It was mentioned earlier that, when preparing the balance sheet, the historic cost convention is normally applied for the reporting of assets. However, this point requires further elaboration as, in practice, it is not simply a matter of recording each asset on the balance sheet at its original cost. We shall see that things are a little more complex than this. Before discussing the valuation rules in some detail, however, we should point out that these rules are based on international accounting standards. These are a set of rules that are generally accepted world-wide. The nature and role of accounting standards will be discussed in detail in Chapter 5.

Tangible non-current assets (property, plant and equipment)

Tangible non-current assets tend to be referred to as 'property, plant and equipment' and we shall use this terminology from now on. Property, plant and equipment should be measured initially at their historic cost. However, they will normally be used up over time as a result of wear and tear, obsolescence and so on. The amount used up, which is referred to as *depreciation*, must be measured for each accounting period that the assets are held. Although we shall leave a detailed examination of depreciation until Chapter 3, we need to know that when an asset has been depreciated, this fact should be reflected in the balance sheet. The total depreciation that has accumulated over the period since the asset was acquired must be deducted from its cost. This net figure (that is, the cost of the asset less the total depreciation to date) is referred to as the *net book value*, *written down value* or *carrying amount*. The procedure described is not really a contravention of the historic cost convention. It is simply recognition of the fact that a proportion of the cost of the non-current asset has been consumed in the process of generating benefits for the business.

Although using depreciated cost is the 'benchmark treatment' for these assets, an alternative is allowed. Property, plant and equipment can be measured using **fair values** provided that these values can be measured reliably. The 'fair values', in this case, are usually the current market values (that is, the exchange values in an arm's-length transaction). By using fair value, a more up-to-date figure than the depreciated cost figure is provided to users, which may be more relevant to their needs. It may also place the business in a better light, as assets such as freehold property may increase significantly in value over time. Of course, increasing the balance sheet value of an asset does not make that asset more valuable. However, perceptions of the business may be altered by such a move.

One consequence of revaluing the freehold premises is that the depreciation charge will be increased. This is because the depreciation charge is based on the increased value of the asset.

Real World 2.3 shows that one well-known business revalued its land and buildings and, by doing so, greatly improved the looks of its balance sheet.

REAL WORLD 2.3

Retailer marks up land and buildings

The balance sheet of Marks and Spencer plc, a major high street retailer, as at 29 March 2003 reveals land and buildings at a net book value, or carrying amount, of £2,148.4m. These land and buildings are shown at an open market value and were valued by a firm of independent surveyors. If the land and buildings of the business had not been valued in this way, the net book value at 29 March 2003 would have been £1,451.3m. The effect of using market values was, therefore, to increase the net book value of these assets by £697.1m. This represents approximately 20% of the net book value of all the tangible non-current assets of the business.

Source: Marks and Spencer plc Annual Report 2003, www.marksandspencer.com.

ACTIVITY 2.15

Refer to the vertical format balance sheet of Brie Manufacturing shown earlier (page 45). What would be the effect of revaluing the freehold land to a figure of £110,000 on the balance sheet?

The effect on the balance sheet would be to increase the freehold land to £110,000 and the gain on revaluation (that is, £110,000 – £45,000 = £65,000) would be added to the capital of the owner, as it is the owner who will benefit from the gain. The revised balance sheet would therefore be as follows:

Brie Manufacturing
Balance sheet as at 31 December 2004

	£	£
Non-current assets		
Freehold premises		110,000
Plant and machinery		30,000
Motor vans		19,000
		159,000
Current assets		
Stock (inventories)	23,000	
Trade debtors (receivables)	18,000	
Cash at bank	12,000	
	53,000	
Less **Current liabilities**		
Trade creditors (payables)	37,000	
		16,000
Total assets *less* current liabilities		175,000
Less **Non-current liabilities**		
Loan		50,000
Net assets		125,000
Capital		
Opening balance		50,000
Add Revaluation gain		65,000
Profit		14,000
		129,000
Less Drawings		4,000
		125,000

Once assets are revalued, the frequency of revaluation then becomes an important issue as assets recorded at out-of-date values can mislead users. Using out-of-date revaluations on the balance sheet is the worst of both worlds. It lacks the objectivity and verifiability of historic cost; it also lacks the realism of current values. Revaluations should therefore be frequent enough to ensure that the net book value, or carrying amount, of the revalued asset does not differ materially from its fair value at the balance sheet date.

When an item of property, or plant, or equipment is revalued on the basis of fair values, all assets within that particular group must be revalued. Thus, it is not acceptable to revalue some property but not others. Although this provides some degree of consistency within a particular group of assets, it does not, of course, prevent the balance sheet from containing a mixture of valuations.

Intangible non-current assets

For these assets, the balance sheet treatment used for tangible non-current assets broadly applies. The 'benchmark treatment' is that they are measured initially at historic cost and any depreciation (or *amortisation* as it is usually termed in this context) incurred following acquisition will be deducted to obtain a net book value. Once again, the alternative of revaluing intangible assets using fair values is available. However, this can only be used where fair values can be properly determined by reference to an active market. In practice, this is likely to be a rare occurrence.

The impairment of non-current assets

There is always a risk that both types of non-current asset may suffer a significant fall in value. This may be due to factors such as changes in market conditions, technological obsolescence and so on. In some cases, this fall in value may lead to the net book value, or carrying amount, of the asset being higher than the amount that could be recovered from the asset through its continued use or through its sale. When this situation arises, the asset figure on the balance sheet should be reduced to its recoverable amount. Unless this is done, the asset will be overstated on the balance sheet.

ACTIVITY 2.16

With which of the accounting conventions described earlier is this accounting treatment consistent?

The answer is the prudence convention, which states that actual or anticipated losses should be recognised in full.

We have seen that, under normal circumstances, a business may have a choice of using either depreciated cost or a value-based measure when reporting its non-current assets. However, under the circumstances just described, the business has no choice; the use of depreciated cost is not an option. **Real World 2.4** provides an example of where the

 ### REAL WORLD 2.4

Talking telephone numbers

mmO$_2$ plc is a major mobile phone operator. During the year to 31 March 2003, the business was badly affected by a downturn in market conditions, which led to a review of the carrying amounts of its non-current assets. Following this review, the business decided to reduce the value of its intangible non-current assets by a total of £8,300m on the year-end balance sheet. This amount included write-downs for licences and goodwill in its operations in the UK and Germany of £2,300m and £4,700m respectively, and a write-down of goodwill in its operations in Ireland of £1,300m.

Source: mmO$_2$ Annual Report 2003.

application of this 'impairment rule' as it is called, resulted in huge write-downs for a business.

Stocks (inventories)

It is not only non-current assets that run the risk of a significant fall in value. The stocks, or inventories, of a business could also suffer this fate, which could be caused by factors such as obsolescence, deterioration, damage and so on. Where a fall in value means that the amount likely to be recovered from the sale of the stocks will be lower than their cost, this loss must be reflected in the balance sheet. Thus, if the net realisable value (that is, selling price less any selling costs) falls below the cost of stocks held, the former should be used as the basis of valuation. Once again, this reflects the influence of the prudence convention on the balance sheet.

Real World 2.5 shows how stocks may be reported in the financial statements of large businesses.

REAL WORLD 2.5

Reporting the valuation basis of stocks

The published financial statements of large businesses normally show the basis on which the stocks of the business are valued. For example, Unilever plc, a large business selling food and home- and personal-care products, stated in its 2002 financial statements:

> Stocks are stated at the lower of cost and estimated net realisable value.

In some cases, the way in which the cost of stocks has been derived (usually when the goods are manufactured by the business rather than bought in) will be stated and, in a few cases, the basis for deriving net realisable value is stated. For example, the published financial statements of Thorntons plc, the chocolate makers, include the following statement:

> Cost includes materials, direct labour and an attributable part of the overheads according to the stage of production reached. Net realisable value is the estimated value which would be realised after deducting all costs of completion, marketing and selling.

Source: Unilever plc, Annual Report 2002; Thorntons plc, Annual Report 2003.

Interpreting the balance sheet

We have seen that the conventional balance sheet has a number of limitations. This has led some users of financial information to conclude that the balance sheet has little to offer in the way of useful information. However, this is not really the case. The balance sheet can provide useful insights into the financing and investing activities of a business. We shall consider this in detail in Chapter 7 when we deal with the analysis and interpretation of the financial statements.

SUMMARY

The main points of the chapter may be summarised as follows:

The major financial statements

● There are three major financial statements – the cash flow statement, the profit and loss account (income statement) and the balance sheet.
● The cash flow statement shows the cash movements over a particular period.
● The profit and loss account shows the wealth (profit) generated over a particular period.
● The balance sheet shows the accumulated wealth at a particular point in time.

The balance sheet

● This sets out the assets of the business, on the one hand, and the claims against those assets, on the other.
● Assets are resources of the business that have certain characteristics, such as the ability to provide future benefits.
● Claims are obligations on the part of the business to provide cash, or some other benefit, to outside parties.
● Claims are of two types – capital and liabilities.
● Capital represents the owner's claim and liabilities represent the claims of others, apart from the owner.

Classification of assets and liabilities

● Assets are normally categorised as being current or non-current (fixed).
● Current assets are held for sale or consumption in the normal course of business or are held for the short term.
● Non-current assets are held for use within the business for long-term operations.
● Liabilities are normally categorised as being current or non-current liabilities.
● Current liabilities represent amounts due in the normal course of the business's operating cycle or due for repayment within 12 months.
● Non-current liabilities represent amounts due that are not current liabilities.

Balance sheet formats

● The horizontal format sets out the assets on one side of the balance sheet and the capital and liabilities on the other side.
● The vertical format begins with the assets at the top of the balance sheet and deducts the liabilities. The resulting figure represents the net assets of the business. The capital of the business is shown at the bottom of the balance sheet.

Accounting conventions

● Accounting conventions have evolved to deal with practical problems experienced by those preparing financial statements.
● The main conventions relating to the balance sheet include business entity, money measurement, historic cost, going concern, dual aspect, prudence, stable monetary unit and objectivity.

Asset valuation

- Property, plant and equipment are shown at historic cost less any amounts written off for depreciation. However, fair values may be used rather than depreciated cost.
- Where the amount that can be recovered from the tangible non-current assets is below the net book value, this lower amount should be reflected in the balance sheet.
- Intangible non-current assets broadly follow the same valuation rules as just described.
- Current assets are shown at the lower of cost or net realisable value.

→ Key terms

cash flow statement p. 28
profit and loss account p. 28
income statement p. 28
balance sheet p. 28
final accounts p. 31
assets p. 32
claims p. 32
tangible assets p. 34
intangible assets p. 34
capital p. 35
liabilities p. 35
current assets p. 40
non-current (fixed) assets p. 41
current liabilities p. 42

non-current liabilities p. 42
accounting conventions p. 46
business entity convention p. 46
money measurement convention
  p. 47
historic cost convention p. 48
going concern convention p. 49
dual aspect convention p. 49
prudence convention p. 49
stable monetary unit convention
  p. 50
objectivity convention p. 50
fair value p. 52

Further reading

If you would like to explore the topics covered in this chapter in more depth, we recommend the following books:

Financial Reporting, *Alexander D. and Britton A.*, 6th edn, International Thomson Business Press, 2001, chapter 3.

Corporate Financial Accounting and Reporting, *Sutton T.*, 2nd edn, Financial Times Prentice Hall, 2004, chapters 2 and 8.

International Financial Reporting Standards (IFRSs) 2003, *International Accounting Standards Board*, IASCF, 2003, IAS 16, IAS 36 and IAS 38.

Accounting Theory and Practice, *Glautier M. and Underdown B.*, 7th edn, Financial Times Prentice Hall, 2001, chapter 12.

REVIEW QUESTIONS

Answers to these questions can be found on the students' side of the Companion Website at **www.pearsoned.co.uk/atrillmclaney**.

2.1 An accountant prepared a balance sheet for a business using the horizontal layout. In the balance sheet, the capital of the owner was shown next to the liabilities. This confused the owner, who argued: 'My capital is my major asset and so should be shown as an asset on the balance sheet.' How would you explain this misunderstanding to the owner?

2.2 'The balance sheet shows how much a business is worth.' Do you agree with this statement? Discuss.

2.3 What is meant by the balance sheet equation? How does the form of this equation differ between the horizontal and vertical balance sheet format?

2.4 In recent years there have been attempts to place a value on the 'human assets' of a business in order to derive a figure that can be included on the balance sheet. Do you think humans should be treated as assets? Would 'human assets' meet the conventional definition of an asset for inclusion on the balance sheet?

EXERCISES

Exercises 2.5 to 2.8 are more advanced than 2.1 to 2.4. Those with coloured numbers have answers at the back of the book.

2.1 On the fourth day of his business venture, Paul, the street trader in wrapping-paper (see earlier in the chapter), purchased more stock for £53 cash. During the day he sold stock that had cost £33 for a total of £47.

Required:
Draw up the three financial statements for day 4 of Paul's business venture.

2.2 The 'total business wealth' belongs to Paul because he is the sole owner of the business. Can you explain how the figure for total business wealth at the end of day 4 has arisen? You will need to look back at the events of days 1, 2 and 3 (in this chapter) to do this.

2.3 Whilst on holiday in Bridlington, Helen had her credit cards and purse stolen from the beach while she was swimming. She was left with only £40, which she had kept in her hotel room, but she had three days of her holiday remaining. She was determined to continue her holiday and decided to make some money to enable her to do so. She decided to sell orange juice to holidaymakers using the local beach. On day 1 she bought 80 cartons of orange juice at £0.50 each for cash and sold 70 of these at £0.80 each. On the following day she purchased 60 cartons for cash and sold 65 at £0.80 each. On the third and final day she purchased another 60 cartons for cash. However, it rained and, as a result, business was poor. She managed to sell 20 at £0.80 each but sold off the rest of her stock at £0.40 each.

Required:
Prepare a profit and loss account and cash flow statement for each day's trading and prepare a balance sheet at the end of each day's trading.

2.4 On 1 March, Joe Conday started a new business. During March he carried out the following transactions:

1 March Deposited £20,000 in a bank account
2 March Purchased fixtures and fittings for £6,000 cash, and stock £8,000 on credit
3 March Borrowed £5,000 from a relative and deposited it in the bank
4 March Purchased a motor car for £7,000 cash and withdrew £200 for own use
5 March A further motor car costing £9,000 was purchased. The motor car purchased on 4 March was given in part exchange at a value of £6,500. The balance of purchase price for the new car was paid in cash
6 March Conday won £2,000 in a lottery and paid the amount into the business bank account. He also repaid £1,000 of the loan

Required:
Draw up a balance sheet for the business at the end of each day.

2.5 The following is a list of the assets and claims of Crafty Engineering Ltd at 30 June last year:

	£000
Trade creditors (payables)	86
Motor vehicles	38
Loan from Industrial Finance Co. (long-term)	260
Machinery and tools	207
Bank overdraft	116
Stock (inventories)	153
Freehold premises	320
Trade debtors (receivables)	185

Required:
(a) Prepare the balance sheet of the business as at 30 June last year from the above information using the vertical format. *Hint*: There is a missing item that needs to be deduced and inserted.
(b) Discuss the significant features revealed by this financial statement.

2.6 The balance sheet of a business at the start of the week is as follows:

Assets	£	Claims	£
Freehold premises	145,000	Capital	203,000
Furniture and fittings	63,000	Bank overdraft	43,000
Stock in trade	28,000	Trade creditors (payables)	23,000
Trade debtors (receivables)	33,000		
	269,000		269,000

During the week the following transactions take place:

(a) Stock sold for £11,000 cash; this stock had cost £8,000.
(b) Sold stock for £23,000 on credit; this stock had cost £17,000.
(c) Received cash from trade debtors totalling £18,000.
(d) The owners of the business introduced £100,000 of their own money, which was placed in the business bank account.
(e) The owners brought a motor van, valued at £10,000, into the business.
(f) Bought stock in trade on credit for £14,000.
(g) Paid trade creditors £13,000.

Required:
Show the balance sheet after all of these transactions have been reflected.

2.7   The following is a list of assets and claims of a manufacturing business at a particular point in time:

	£
Bank overdraft	22,000
Freehold land and buildings	245,000
Stock (inventories) of raw materials	18,000
Trade creditors (payables)	23,000
Plant and machinery	127,000
Loan from Industrial Finance Co. (long-term)	100,000
Stock (inventories) of finished goods	28,000
Delivery vans	54,000
Trade debtors (receivables)	34,000

Required:

Write out a balance sheet in the standard vertical form incorporating these figures. *Hint*: There is a missing item that needs to be deduced and inserted.

2.8   You have been talking to someone who had read the first chapter of an accounting text some years ago. During your conversation the person made the following statements:

(a)   The profit and loss account (income statement) shows how much cash has come into and left the business during the accounting period and the resulting balance at the end of the period.

(b)   In order to be included in the balance sheet as an asset, an item needs to be worth something in the market, that is all.

(c)   The balance sheet equation is:

$$\text{Assets} + \text{Capital} = \text{Liabilities}$$

(d)   Non-current assets are things that cannot be moved.

(e)   Working capital is the name given to the sum of the current assets.

Required:

Comment critically on each of the above statements, going into as much detail as you can.

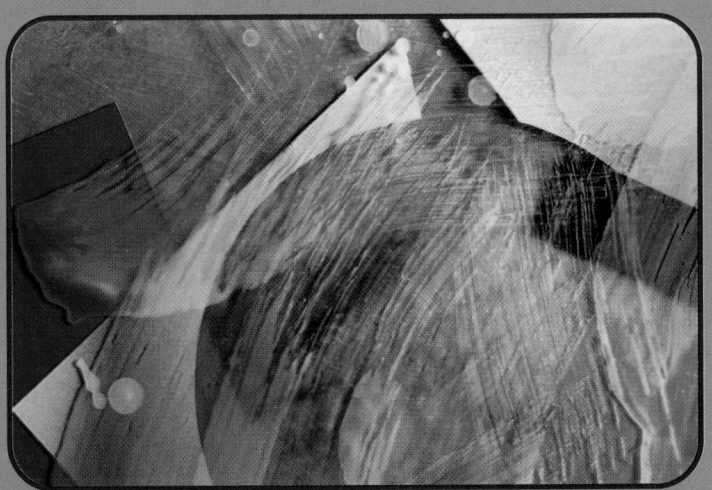

CHAPTER 3

Measuring and reporting financial performance

When you have completed this chapter, you should be able to:

● Discuss the nature and purpose of the profit and loss account.

● Prepare a profit and loss account from relevant financial information.

● Discuss the main recognition and measurement issues that must be considered when preparing the profit and loss account.

● Explain the main accounting conventions underpinning the profit and loss account.

INTRODUCTION

This chapter continues our examination of the major financial statements by looking at the profit and loss account (income statement). This statement was briefly considered in Chapter 2 and we shall now examine it in some detail. We shall see how this statement is prepared and how it links with the balance sheet. We shall also consider some of the key measurement problems to be faced when preparing this statement.

The profit and loss account (income statement)

The previous chapter examined the nature and purpose of the balance sheet. We saw that this statement was concerned with setting out the financial position of a business at a particular moment in time. However, it is not usually enough for users to have information relating only to the amount of wealth held by a business at one moment in time. Businesses exist for the primary purpose of generating wealth, or profit, and it is the profit generated *during a period* that is the main concern of many users of financial statements. Although the amount of profit generated is of particular interest to the owners of a business, other groups such as managers, employees and suppliers will also have an interest in the profit-making ability of the business. The purpose of the profit and loss account – or income statement, as it is sometimes called – is to measure and report how much **profit** (wealth) the business has generated over a period. As with the balance sheet that we examined in Chapter 2, the profit and loss account is prepared following the same principles, irrespective of whether the business is a sole proprietorship or a limited company.

The measurement of profit requires that the total revenue of the business, generated during a particular period, be identified. **Revenue** is simply a measure of the inflow of economic benefits arising from the ordinary activities of a business. These benefits, which accrue to the owners, will result in either an increase in assets (such as cash or amounts owed to the business by debtors) or a decrease in liabilities. Different forms of business enterprise will generate different forms of revenue. Some examples of the different forms that revenue can take are as follows:

● sales of goods (for example, of a manufacturer);
● fees for services (for example, of a solicitor);
● subscriptions (for example, of a club);
● interest received (for example, of an investment fund).

The total expenses relating to each accounting period must also be identified. **Expense** is really the opposite of revenue. It represents the outflow of economic benefits arising from the ordinary activities of a business. This loss of benefits will result in either a decrease in assets or an increase in liabilities. Expenses are incurred in the process of generating revenue, or attempting to generate them. The nature of the business will again determine the type of expenses that will be incurred. Examples of some of the more common types of expenses are:

● the cost of buying goods that are subsequently sold – known as *cost of sales* or *cost of goods sold*;

- salaries and wages;
- rent and rates;
- motor vehicle running expenses;
- insurances;
- printing and stationery;
- heat and light;
- telephone and postage, and so on.

The profit and loss account for a particular period simply shows the total revenue generated during that period and deducts from this the total expenses incurred in generating that revenue. The difference between the total revenue and total expenses will represent either profit (if sales revenue exceeds expenses) or loss (if expenses exceed revenue). Thus, we have:

> **Profit (loss) for the period = Total revenue for the period**
> ***less* Total expenses incurred**
> **in generating the revenue**

Relationship between the profit and loss account and the balance sheet

The profit and loss account and the balance sheet should not be viewed in any way as substitutes for one another. Rather they should be seen as performing different functions. The balance sheet is, as stated earlier, a statement of the financial position of a business at a single moment in time – a 'snapshot' of the stock of wealth held by the business. The profit and loss account, on the other hand, is concerned with the *flow* of wealth over a period of time. The two statements are closely related. The profit and loss account can be viewed as linking the balance sheet at the beginning of the period with the balance sheet at the end. Thus, at the start of a new business, a balance sheet will be produced to reveal the opening financial position. After an appropriate period, a profit and loss account will be prepared to show the wealth generated over the period. A balance sheet will also be prepared to reveal the new financial position at the end of the period covered by the profit and loss account. This balance sheet will incorporate the changes in wealth that have occurred since the previous balance sheet was drawn up.

We saw in the previous chapter (p. 40) that the effect on the balance sheet of making a profit (loss) means that the equation can be extended as follows:

> **Assets = Capital + Profit (or – Loss) + Liabilities**

The amount of profit or loss for the period affects the balance sheet as an adjustment to capital.

The above equation can be extended to:

> **Assets = Capital + (Sales revenue – Expenses) + Liabilities**

In theory, it would be possible to calculate profit and loss for the period by making all adjustments for revenue and expenses through the capital section of the balance sheet. However, this would be rather cumbersome. A better solution is to have an 'appendix' to capital, in the form of a profit and loss account. By deducting expenses from revenue for the period, the profit and loss account derives the profit (loss) for adjustment in the capital item in the balance sheet. This figure represents the net effect of trading for the period. Providing this 'appendix' means that a detailed and more informative view of performance is presented to users.

The format of the profit and loss account

The format of the **profit and loss account** will vary according to the type of business to which it relates. To illustrate a profit and loss account, let us consider the case of a retail business (that is, a business that purchases goods in their completed state and resells them). This type of business usually has straightforward operations and, as a result, the profit and loss account is relatively easy to understand.

Example 3.1 sets out a typical format for the profit and loss account of a retail business.

Example 3.1

Hi-Price Stores
Profit and loss account for the year ended 31 October 2005

	£	£
Sales revenue		232,000
Less Cost of sales		154,000
Gross profit		78,000
Add Interest received from investments		2,000
		80,000
Less Salaries and wages	24,500	
Rent and rates	14,200	
Heat and light	7,500	
Telephone and postage	1,200	
Insurance	1,000	
Motor vehicle running expenses	3,400	
Loan interest	1,100	
Depreciation – fixtures and fittings	1,000	
Depreciation – motor van	600	
	54,500	
Net profit		25,500

The first part of the statement is concerned with calculating the **gross profit** for the period. The trading revenue, which arises from selling the goods, is the first item that appears. Deducted from this item is the cost of sales, which is the cost of the goods sold during the period. The difference between the trading revenue and cost of sales is referred to as gross profit. This represents the profit from simply buying and selling goods without taking into account any other expenses or revenues associated with the business.

Having calculated the gross profit, any additional sources of revenue of the business are then added to this figure. In the above example, interest from investments represents an additional source of revenue. From this subtotal of gross profit and additional revenues, the other expenses (overheads) that have to be incurred in operating the business (salaries and wages, rent and rates and so on) are deducted. The final figure derived is the **net profit** for the period. This net profit figure represents the wealth generated during the period that is attributable to the owner(s) of the business and which will be added to their capital in the balance sheet. As can be seen, net profit is a residual – that is, the amount left over after deducting all expenses incurred in generating the sales for the period.

The profit and loss account – some further aspects

Having set out the main principles involved in preparing a profit and loss account, we need to consider some further points.

Cost of sales

The **cost of sales** figure for a period can be identified in different ways. In some businesses, the cost of sales is identified at the time a sale has been made. Sales are closely matched with the cost of those sales and so identifying the cost of sales figure for inclusion in the profit and loss account is not a problem. Many large retailers (for example, supermarkets) have point-of-sale (checkout) devices that not only record each sale but also simultaneously pick up the cost of the particular sale. Other businesses that sell a relatively small number of high-value items (for example, an engineering business that produces custom-made equipment) also tend to match sales revenue with the cost of the goods sold at the time of the sale. However, some businesses (for example, small retailers) do not usually find it practical to match each sale to a particular cost of sales figure as the accounting period progresses. They find it easier to identify the cost of sales figure at the end of the accounting period.

To understand how this is done, it is important to recognise that the cost of sales figure represents the cost of goods that were *sold* during the period rather than the cost of goods that were *purchased* during the period. Part of the goods purchased during a particular period may remain in stock and not be sold until a later period. To derive the cost of sales for a period, it is necessary to know the amount of opening and closing stocks (inventories) for the period and the cost of goods purchased during the period. Example 3.2 below illustrates how the cost of sales is derived.

Example 3.2

Hi-Price Stores, which we considered in Example 3.1 above, began the accounting year with unsold stock of £40,000 and during that year purchased stock at a cost of £189,000. At the end of the year, unsold stock of £75,000 was still held by the business.

The opening stock at the beginning of the year *plus* the goods purchased during the year will represent the total goods available for resale. Thus:

	£
Opening stock	40,000
Plus Goods purchased	189,000
Goods available for resale	229,000

→

The closing stock will represent that portion of the total goods available for resale that remains unsold at the end of the period. Thus, the cost of goods actually sold during the period must be the total goods available for resale *less* the stocks remaining at the end of the period. That is:

	£
Goods available for resale	229,000
Less Closing stock	75,000
Cost of goods sold (or cost of sales)	154,000

These calculations are sometimes shown on the face of the profit and loss account as in Example 3.3.

Example 3.3

	£	£
Sales revenue		232,000
Less Cost of sales		
Opening stock	40,000	
Plus Goods purchased	189,000	
	229,000	
Less Closing stock	75,000	154,000
Gross profit		78,000

The above is simply an expanded version of the first section of the profit and loss account for Hi-Price Stores, as set out in Example 3.1. We have simply included the additional information concerning stock balances and purchases for the year provided in Example 3.2.

Classification of expenses

The classifications for the revenue and expense items, as with the classifications of various assets and claims in the balance sheet, are often a matter of judgement by those who design the accounting system. In the profit and loss account in Example 3.1, the insurance expense could have been included with telephone and postage under a single heading – say, general expenses. Such decisions are normally based on how useful a particular classification will be to users. This will usually mean, however, that expense items of material size will be shown separately. For businesses that trade as limited companies, there are rules that dictate the classification of various items appearing in the accounts for external reporting purposes. These rules will be discussed in Chapter 5.

ACTIVITY 3.1

The following information relates to the activities of H & S Retailers for the year ended 30 April 2005:

	£
Motor vehicle running expenses	1,200
Rent received from subletting	2,000
Closing stock	3,000
Rent and rates payable	5,000
Motor vans	6,300
Annual depreciation – motor vans	1,500
Heat and light	900
Telephone and postage	450
Sales revenue	97,400
Goods purchased	68,350
Insurance	750
Loan interest payable	620
Balance at bank	4,780
Salaries and wages	10,400
Opening stock	4,000

Prepare a profit and loss account for the year ended 30 April 2005. (*Hint*: Not all items shown above should appear on this statement.)

Your answer to this activity should be as follows:

H & S Retailers
Profit and loss account for the year ended 30 April 2005

	£	£
Sales revenue		97,400
Less Cost of sales		
Opening stock	4,000	
Plus Purchases	68,350	
	72,350	
Less Closing stock	3,000	69,350
Gross profit		28,050
Rent received		2,000
		30,050
Less Salaries and wages	10,400	
Rent and rates	5,000	
Heat and light	900	
Telephone and postage	450	
Insurance	750	
Motor vehicle running expenses	1,200	
Loan interest	620	
Depreciation – motor van	1,500	
		20,820
Net profit		9,230

In the case of the balance sheet, we saw that the information could be presented in either a horizontal format or a vertical format. This is also true of the profit and loss account. Where a horizontal format is used, expenses are listed on the left-hand side and revenues on the right, the difference being either net profit or net loss. The vertical format has been used above as it is easier to understand and is now almost always used.

The reporting period

We have seen already that for reporting to those outside the business, a financial reporting cycle of one year is the norm, though some large businesses will produce a half-yearly, or interim, financial statement to provide more frequent feedback on progress. For those who manage a business, however, it is important to have much more frequent feedback on performance. Thus it is quite common for profit and loss accounts to be prepared on a quarterly, monthly, weekly or even daily basis in order to show how things are progressing.

Profit measurement and the recognition of revenue

A key issue in the measurement of profit concerns the point at which revenue is recognised. Where there is a sale of goods or provision of services, the revenue arising from a particular sale could be recognised at one of the different points in the process.

For example, a firm of solicitors undertakes to handle a house purchase for a client for which it will charge a fixed fee. In theory, the firm could recognise the revenue at any one of several different points in the process. The obvious possibilities seem to be

- at the time of agreement to do the work;
- at the time of completing the work; or
- at the time the client pays.

This particular point is not simply a matter of academic interest: it can have a profound impact on the total revenues, and therefore total profits, reported for a particular period. If the solicitors' case (above) straddled the end of an accounting period, the choice made between the three possible times for recognising the revenue could determine whether the revenue is included as a revenue of an earlier accounting period or a later one.

 The **realisation convention** in accounting states that a revenue should be recognised only when it has been realised. However, this begs the question, 'When is revenue considered to be realised?' When dealing with the sale of goods or the provision of services, there are three basic criteria that must be met. These are that:

- the amount of revenue can be measured reliably;
- it is probable that the economic benefits will be received; and
- the costs associated with the transaction can be measured reliably.

However, there is an additional criterion to be applied where the revenue comes from the sale of goods.

The sale of goods

Where there is a sale of goods, there is the additional criterion that ownership and control of the items should pass to the buyer before revenue is recognised. Activity 3.2

below provides an opportunity to apply the various criteria discussed to a practical problem.

ACTIVITY 3.2

A manufacturing business sells goods on credit (that is, the customer pays for the goods some time after they are received). Below are four points in the production/selling cycle at which revenue might be recognised by the business:

- when the goods are produced;
- when an order is received from a customer;
- when the goods are delivered to, and accepted by, the customer; and
- when the cash is received from the customer.

A significant amount of time may elapse between these different points. At what point do you think the business should recognise revenue?

....

The criteria will usually be fulfilled at point 3; when the goods are passed to, and accepted by, the customer. By this point the buyer and seller will have agreed both the selling price and the settlement terms and both parties will have legally enforceable rights. As a result, the revenue can be reliably measured, it is probable that the amounts due will be paid and ownership and control will have passed to the buyer. (At this point, the costs of the transaction can also normally be established.)

We can see that the effect of applying these criteria is that a sale on credit is usually recognised *before* the cash is received. Thus, the total sales revenue figure shown in the profit and loss account may include sales transactions for which the cash has yet to be received. The total sales revenue figure in the profit and loss account for a period will often, therefore, be different from the total cash received from sales during that period.

Where goods are sold for cash rather than on credit, the revenue will normally be recognised at the point of sale. It is at this point that all the criteria will usually be met. For cash sales, there will be no difference in timing between reporting sales revenue and cash received.

Some products (and services, as we shall see shortly), have long production cycles. One example is a new building. A customer may enter a contract with a builder to build a new house, with all of the conditions regarding the work specified in the contract. The contract may also break the building work into a number of stages. Stage 1 might be clearing and levelling the land and putting in the foundations. Stage 2 might be building the walls. Stage 3 might be putting on the roof and so on. Each stage would have a separate price, the total for all the stages equalling the contract total for building the house. As each stage is completed, the builder recognises the price for it as a revenue and bills the customer. Were the builder to wait until the house is completed before recognising the revenue, all of the profit would be recognised in the accounting year in which the house was completed. If the building work was started in one accounting year and completed in the following one, none of the revenue and profit would be recognised in the earlier year, when perhaps nearly all of the work was done. This could provide misleading information in the profit and loss account. Other business activities, like shipbuilding, where the time taken from the start of the work to completion is lengthy, adopt a similar approach to revenue recognition.

Providing services

Where a business provides a service, revenue may be recognised *before* the service is fully complete provided a particular stage of completion can be reliably measured. In some cases, a service may be carried out over a long period of time, such as a management consultancy service to help restructure a large business. The consultants may work for some years on the restructuring project but will not wait until it is complete before recognising any part of the revenue. Such a large project is usually undertaken in stages and a proportion of the total revenue may be recognised when an agreed stage of the service is complete: for example, when an identifiable division of the business has been restructured. The proportion of revenue recognised will normally reflect the proportion of work done or costs incurred. This is exactly the same approach as used by builders in long contracts.

Another example of recognising revenue before the service is complete is when a business provides an unspecified number of services over an agreed period of time. For example, an Internet business may provide open access to the Internet for those who pay a subscription fee. In this case, it is usually assumed that the economic benefits flow evenly over time and so revenue would normally be recognised evenly over the subscription period.

For many services, however, it is not possible to recognise revenue in stages, so recognition will take place when the service is fully completed: for example, the solicitor handling a house sale that we discussed above. **Real World 3.1** provides some examples of how different kinds of businesses recognise revenue in practice.

REAL WORLD 3.1

Recognising revenue in practice

Large businesses often disclose the way in which revenue appearing in the profit and loss account is recognised. Here are a few examples:

mmO$_2$, the mobile phone operator recognises:

- revenues from handsets at the point of sale;
- revenues from pre-pay call cards when the customer has used up the card to pay for calls;
- revenues from connection fees and subscriptions evenly over the period to which they relate.

Source: mmO$_2$ Annual Report 2003.

Brandon Hire plc operates tool and equipment hire services and recognises revenues from hiring over the period of the contract.

Source: Brandon Hire plc Annual Report and Accounts 2003.

Hyder Consulting plc is an engineering design, planning and management consultancy business, which generates revenue principally from long-term contracts. Revenue from contracts is recognised on the basis of the sales value of the work performed in relation to the total sales value of the contract and its stage of completion.

Source: Hyder Consulting plc Annual Report 2003.

In all of the forms of service mentioned in Real World 3.1, there will normally be a timing difference between the recognition of revenue and the receipt of cash. Revenue for providing services is often recognised *before* the cash is received, just like the sale of goods on credit. However, there are occasions when it is the other way around, usually because the business demands payment before providing the service.

ACTIVITY 3.3

Can you think of any examples of where cash may be demanded in advance of a service being provided? (*Hint*: Try to think of services that you may use.)

Examples of where cash is received in advance of the service being provided may include:

- rent received from letting premises;
- telephone line rental charges;
- TV licence (BBC) or subscription (for example, Sky) fees; and
- subscriptions received for the use of health clubs or golf clubs.

You may have thought of others.

We have seen above that we should recognise revenue only when it has been earned and we are pretty confident that we shall receive the cash. In recent years, however, some businesses have been criticised for being a little too quick to recognise revenue. Early recognition can, of course, help to boost profits, at least in the short term. **Real World 3.2** looks at a business that was criticised for early recognition of revenue.

REAL WORLD 3.2

Looking on the sunny side

My Travel Group plc is a major tour operator that attracted considerable criticism for its revenue recognition policy. The policy of the business was to recognise revenue for holidays taken at the time the holiday was booked. However, this was seen as being premature by some commentators and was changed to a more conservative basis in response to criticisms. Now the business recognises revenue for holidays taken on the date of departure. This revised policy seems to be in line with other travel operators: Holidaybreak plc, for example, adopts this approach to revenue recognition.

The effect of introducing more conservative accounting policies was to reduce profits of MyTravel plc by £20.3m in 2002 and by £19.0m in 2001.

Sources: Based on information in 'Crackdown on companies overstating turnover', *Financial Times*, 27 February 2003, Holiday Break plc Annual Report and Financial Statements 2003 and My Travel Group plc Annual Report and Accounts 2002.

Profit measurement and the recognition of expenses

→ Having decided on the point at which revenue is recognised, we must now turn to the issue of the recognition of expenses. The **matching convention** in accounting is designed to provide guidance concerning the recognition of expenses. This convention states that expenses should be matched to the revenue that they helped to generate. In other words, expenses must be taken into account in the same profit and loss account in which the associated sale is included in the total sales revenue figure. Applying this convention may mean that a particular expense reported in the profit and loss account for a period may not be the same figure as the cash paid for that item during the period. The expense reported may be either more or less than the cash paid during the period. Let us consider two examples that illustrate this point.

When the expense for the period is more than the cash paid during the period

Example 3.4

Domestic Ltd retails household electrical appliances. It pays its sales staff a commission of two per cent of sales revenue generated, and total sales revenue for the year amounted to £300,000. This will mean that the commission to be paid in respect of the sales for the period will be £6,000. However, by the end of the period, the sales commission paid to staff was £5,000. If the business reported only the amount paid, it would mean that the profit and loss account would not reflect the full expense for the year. This would contravene the *matching convention* because not all of the expenses associated with the revenue of the period would have been matched in the profit and loss account. This will be remedied as follows:

● Sales commission expense in the profit and loss account will include the amount paid *plus* the amount outstanding (that is, £6,000 = £5,000 + £1,000).
● The amount outstanding (£1,000) represents an outstanding liability at the
→ balance sheet date and will be included under the heading **accrued expenses**, or 'accruals', in the balance sheet. As this item will have to be paid within 12 months of the balance sheet date, it will be treated as a current liability.
● The cash will already have been reduced to reflect the commission paid (£5,000) during the period.

These points are illustrated in Figure 3.1.

In principle, all expenses should be matched to the period in which the sales revenue to which they relate is reported. However, it is sometimes difficult to match closely certain expenses to sales revenue in the same precise way that we have matched sales commission to sales revenue. It is unlikely, for example, that electricity charges incurred can be linked directly to particular sales in this way. As a result, the electricity charges incurred by, say, a retailer would be matched to the *period* to which they relate. Example 3.5 illustrates this.

Figure 3.1   **Accounting for sales commission**

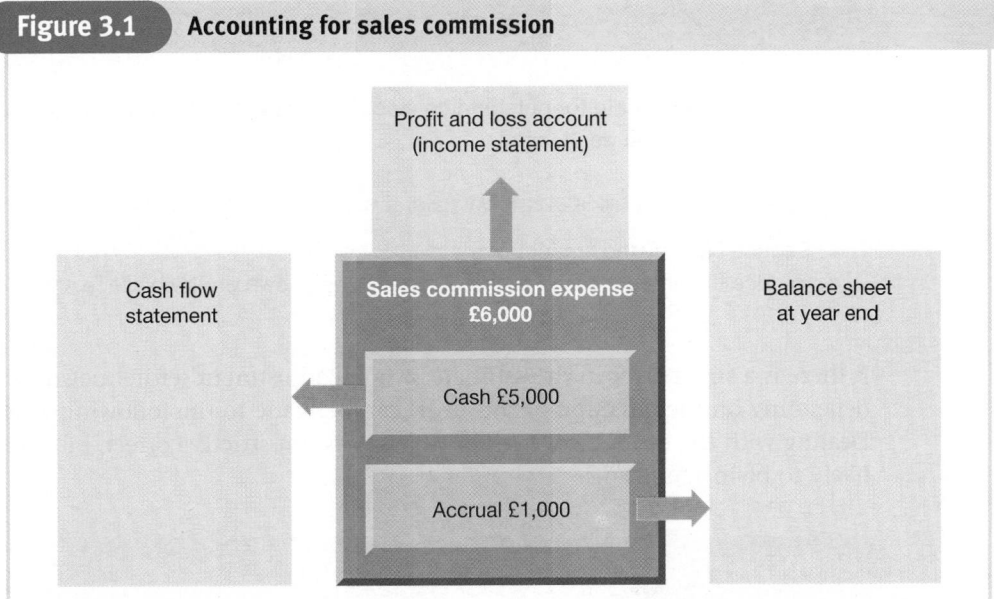

This illustrates the main points of Example 3.4. We can see that the sales commission expense of £6,000 (which appears in the profit and loss account) is made up of a cash element £5,000 and an accrued element £1,000. The cash element appears in the cash flow statement and the accrued element will appear as a year-end liability in the balance sheet.

Example 3.5

Domestic Ltd has reached the end of its accounting year and has only been charged electricity for the first three quarters of the year (amounting to £1,900). This is simply because the electricity company has yet to send out bills for the quarter that ends on the same date as Domestic Ltd's year end. In this situation, an estimate should be made of the electricity expense outstanding (that is, the bill for the last three months of the year is estimated). This figure (let us say the estimate is £500) is dealt with as follows:

● Electricity expense in the profit and loss account will include the amount paid, plus the amount of the estimate (that is, £1,900 + £500 = £2,400) in order to cover the whole year.
● The amount of the estimate (£500) represents an outstanding liability at the balance sheet date, and will be included under the heading 'accruals' or 'accrued expenses' in the balance sheet. As this item will have to be paid within 12 months of the balance sheet date, it will be treated as a current liability.
● The cash will already have been reduced to reflect the electricity paid (£1,900) during the period.

This treatment will have the desired effect of increasing the electricity expense to the 'correct' figure for the year in the profit and loss account, presuming that the estimate is reasonably accurate. It will also have the effect of showing that, at the end of the accounting year, Domestic Ltd owed the amount of the last quarter's electricity bill. Dealing with the outstanding amount in this way reflects the dual aspect of the item, and will ensure that the balance sheet equation is maintained.

ACTIVITY 3.4

Let us say the estimate for outstanding electricity was correct. How will the payment of the electricity bill be dealt with?

When the electricity bill is eventually paid, it will be dealt with as follows:

● Reduce cash by the amount of the bill.
● Reduce the amount of the accrued expense as shown on the balance sheet.

If there is a slight error in the estimate, a small adjustment (either negative or positive depending on the direction of the error) can be made to the following year's expense. Dealing with the estimation error in this way is not strictly correct, but the amount is likely to be insignificant.

ACTIVITY 3.5

Can you think of other expenses, apart from electricity charges, that cannot be linked directly to sales revenue and for which matching will therefore be done on a time basis?

You may have thought of the following examples:

● rent and rates
● insurance
● interest payments
● licences.

This is not an exhaustive list. You may have thought of others.

When the amount paid during the year is more than the full expense for the period

It is not unusual for a business to be in a situation where it has paid more during the year than the full expense for that year. Example 3.6 below illustrates how we deal with this.

Example 3.6

Images Ltd, an advertising agency, normally pays rent for its premises quarterly in advance (on 1 January, 1 April, 1 July and 1 October). On the last day of the last accounting year (31 December), it paid the next quarter's rent (£4,000) to the following 31 March, which was a day earlier than required. This would mean that a total of five quarters' rent was paid during the year. If Images Ltd reports all of the cash paid as an expense in the profit and loss account, this would be more than the full expense for the year. This would contravene the matching convention because a higher figure than the expenses associated with the revenue of the year would appear in the profit and loss account.

The problem is overcome by dealing with the rental payment as follows:

● Show the rent for four quarters as the appropriate expense in the profit and loss account (that is, 4 × £4,000 = £16,000).
● The cash (that is, 5 × £4,000 = £20,000) would already have been paid during the year.
● Show the quarter's rent paid in advance (£4,000) as a **prepaid expense** on the asset side of the balance sheet. (The prepaid expense will appear as a current asset in the balance sheet, under the heading 'prepaid expenses' or 'prepayments'.)

In the next accounting period, this prepayment will cease to be an asset and will become an expense in the profit and loss account of that period. This is because the rent prepaid relates to that period and will be 'used up' during that period.

These points are illustrated in Figure 3.2.

Figure 3.2   Accounting for rent payable

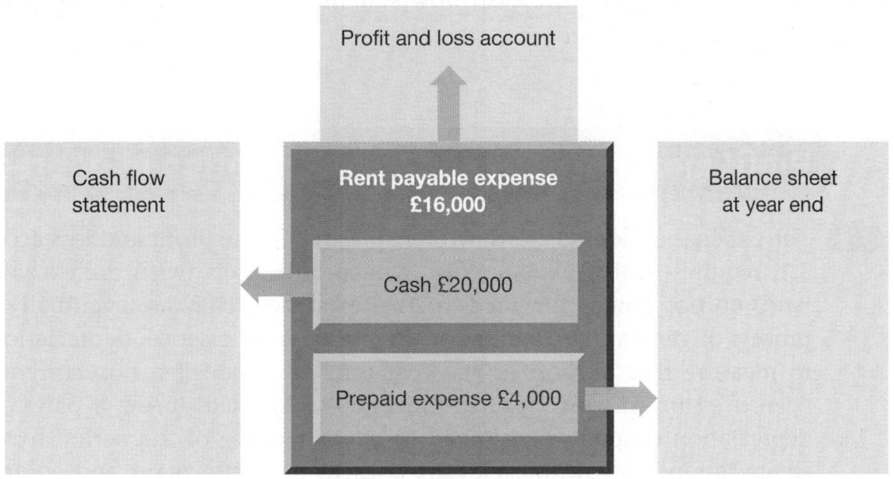

This illustrates the main points of Example 3.6. We can see that the rent expense of £16,000 (which appears in the profit and loss account) is made up of four quarters' rent at £4,000 per quarter. This is the amount that relates to the period and is 'used up' during the period. The cash paid of £20,000 (which appears in the cash flow statement) is made up of the cash paid during the period, which is five quarters at £4,000 per quarter. Finally, the prepayment of £4,000 (which appears on the balance sheet) represents the payment made on 31 December and relates to the next financial year.

In practice, the treatment of accruals and prepayments will be subject to the **materiality convention** of accounting. This convention states that, where the amounts involved are immaterial, we should consider only what is expedient. This may mean that an item will be treated as an expense in the period in which it is paid, rather than being strictly matched to the revenue to which it relates. For example, a business may find that, at the end of an accounting period, there is a bill of £5 owing for stationery used during the year. For a business of any size, the time and effort involved in recording this as an accrual would have little effect on the measurement of profit or financial position. It would, therefore, be ignored when preparing the profit and loss account for the period. The bill would, presumably, be paid in the following period and therefore be treated as an expense of that period.

Profit, cash and accruals accounting

As we have just seen, revenue does not usually represent cash received and expenses are not the same as cash paid. As a result, the net profit figure (that is, total revenue minus total expenses) will not normally represent the net cash generated during a period. It is therefore important to distinguish between profit and liquidity. Profit is a measure of achievement, or productive effort, rather than a measure of cash generated. Although making a profit will increase wealth, as we have already seen in Chapter 2, cash is only one form in which that wealth may be held. These points are summarised as the **accruals convention** of accounting. This asserts that profit is the excess of revenue over expenses for a period, not the excess of cash receipts over cash payments.

Leading on from this, the approach to accounting encompassed in the accruals convention is frequently referred to as **accruals accounting**. Thus the balance sheet and the profit and loss account are both prepared on the basis of accruals accounting. On the other hand, the cash flow statement is not. It deals with cash receipts and payments.

Profit measurement and the calculation of depreciation

The expense of **depreciation**, which appeared in the profit and loss account in Activity 3.1, requires further explanation. Non-current assets (with the exception of freehold land) do not usually have a perpetual existence. They are eventually used up in the process of generating revenue for the business. In essence, depreciation is an attempt to measure that portion of the cost (or fair value) of a non-current asset that has been used up in generating the revenue recognised during a particular period. The depreciation charge is considered to be an expense of the period to which it relates. Depreciation tends to be relevant both to property, plant and equipment (tangible non-current assets) and to intangible non-current assets.

To calculate a depreciation charge for a period, four factors have to be considered:

● the cost (or fair value) of the asset;
● the useful life of the asset;
● the residual value of the asset; and
● the depreciation method.

The cost (or fair value) of the asset

The cost of an asset will include all costs incurred by the business to bring the asset to its required location and to make it ready for use. Thus, in addition to the costs of acquiring the asset, any delivery costs, installation costs (for example, setting up a new machine) and legal costs incurred in the transfer of legal title (for example, in the case of freehold property) will be included as part of the total cost of the asset. Similarly, any costs incurred in improving or altering an asset in order to make it suitable for its intended use within the business will also be included as part of the total cost.

ACTIVITY 3.6

Andrew Wu (Engineering) Ltd purchased a new motor car for its marketing director. The invoice received from the motor car supplier revealed the following:

	£	£
New BMW 325i		26,350
Delivery charge	80	
Alloy wheels	660	
Sun roof	200	
Petrol	30	
Number plates	130	
Road fund licence	160	1,260
		27,610
Part exchange – Reliant Robin		1,000
Amount outstanding		26,610

What is the total cost of the new car that will be treated as part of the business's property, plant and equipment?

The cost of the new car will be as follows:

	£	£
New BMW 325i		26,350
Delivery charge	80	
Alloy wheels	660	
Sun roof	200	
Number plates	130	1,070
		27,420

These costs include delivery costs and number plates, as they are a necessary and integral part of the asset. Improvements (alloy wheels and sun roof) are also regarded as part of the total cost of the motor car. The petrol costs and road fund licence, however, represent a cost of operating the asset rather than a part of the total cost of acquiring the asset and making it ready for use: hence these amounts will be charged as an expense in the period incurred (although part of the cost of the licence may be regarded as a prepaid expense in the period incurred).

The part-exchange figure shown is part payment of the total amount outstanding, and is not relevant to a consideration of the total cost.

The fair value of an asset was defined in Chapter 2 as the exchange value that could be obtained in an arm's-length transaction. For land and buildings, this is normally the market value, as determined by professionally qualified valuers. For other types of property, plant and equipment, such as a motor vehicle, market values may also be used. However, where the asset is very specialised and this value is difficult to determine, replacement cost may be used instead. The problems of using current values were discussed in Chapter 2.

The useful life of the asset

An asset has both a *physical life* and an *economic life*. The physical life of an asset will be exhausted through the effects of wear and tear and/or the passage of time. It is possible, however, for the physical life to be extended considerably through careful maintenance, improvements and so on. The economic life of an asset is decided by the effects of technological progress and by changes in demand. After a while, the benefits of using the asset may be less than the costs involved. This may be because the asset is unable to compete with newer assets, or because it is no longer relevant to the needs of the business. The economic life of an asset may be much shorter than its physical life. For example, a computer may have a physical life of eight years and an economic life of three years.

It is the economic life of an asset that will determine the expected useful life for the purpose of calculating depreciation. Forecasting the economic life of an asset, however, may be extremely difficult in practice: both the rate at which technology progresses and shifts in consumer tastes can be swift and unpredictable.

Residual value (disposal value)

When a business disposes of a non-current asset that may still be of value to others, some payment may be received. This payment will represent the **residual value**, or *disposal value*, of the asset. To calculate the total amount to be depreciated with regard to an asset, the residual value must be deducted from the cost of the asset. The likely amount to be received on disposal is, once again, often difficult to predict.

Depreciation method

Once the amount to be depreciated (that is, the cost, or fair value, of the asset less the residual value) has been estimated, the business must select a method of allocating this depreciable amount over the asset's useful life. Although there are various ways in which the total depreciation may be allocated and, from this, a depreciation charge for a period derived, there are really only two methods that are commonly used in practice.

The first of these is known as the **straight-line method**. This method simply allocates the amount to be depreciated evenly over the useful life of the asset. In other words, an equal amount of depreciation will be charged for each year the asset is held.

Example 3.7

To illustrate this method, consider the following information:

Cost of machine	£40,000
Estimated residual value at the end of its useful life	£1,024
Estimated useful life	4 years

To calculate the depreciation charge for each year, the total amount to be depreciated must be calculated. This will be the total cost *less* the estimated residual value: that is, £40,000 − £1,024 = £38,976. Having done this, the annual depreciation charge can be derived by dividing the amount to be depreciated by the estimated useful life of the asset of four years. The calculation is therefore:

$$\frac{£38,976}{4} = £9,744$$

Thus, the annual depreciation charge that appears in the profit and loss account in relation to this asset will be £9,744 for each of the four years of the asset's life.

The amount of depreciation relating to the asset will be accumulated for as long as the asset continues to be owned by the business. This accumulated depreciation figure will increase each year as a result of the annual depreciation amount charged to the profit and loss account. This accumulated amount will be deducted from the cost of the asset on the balance sheet. Thus, for example, at the end of the second year the accumulated depreciation will be £9,744 × 2 = £19,488, and the asset details will appear on the balance sheet as follows:

	£	£
Machine at cost	40,000	
Less Accumulated depreciation	19,488	
		20,512

The balance of £20,512 shown above is referred to as the **written-down value**, *net book value* or *carrying amount* of the asset. It represents that portion of the cost (or fair value) of the asset that has still to be written off (that is treated as an expense). It must be emphasised that this figure does *not* represent the current market value, which may be quite different.

The straight-line method derives its name from the fact that the written-down value of the asset at the end of each year, when plotted against time, will result in a straight line, as shown in Figure 3.3.

The second approach to calculating depreciation for a period is referred to as the **reducing-balance method**. This method applies a fixed percentage rate of depreciation to the written-down value of an asset each year. The effect of this will be high annual depreciation charges in the early years and lower charges in the later years. To illustrate

Figure 3.3 Graph of written-down value against time using the straight-line method

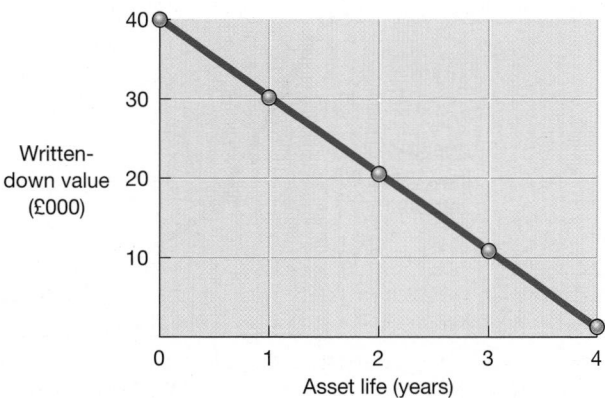

The written-down value of the asset declines by a constant amount each year. This is because the straight-line method provides a constant depreciation charge each year. The result, when plotted on a graph, is a straight line.

this method, let us take the same information used in Example 3.7. It can be shown that using a fixed percentage of 60 per cent of the written-down value to determine the annual depreciation charge will have the effect of reducing the written-down value to £1,024 after four years.

The calculations will be as follows:

	£
Cost of machine	40,000
Year 1 Depreciation charge (60%* of cost)	(24,000)
Written-down value (WDV)	16,000
Year 2 Depreciation charge (60% WDV)	(9,600)
Written-down value	6,400
Year 3 Depreciation charge (60% WDV)	(3,840)
Written-down value	2,560
Year 4 Depreciation charge (60% WDV)	(1,536)
Residual value	1,024

* Deriving the fixed percentage to be applied requires the use of the following formula:

$$P = (1 - \sqrt[n]{R/C} \times 100\%)$$

where: P = the depreciation percentage;
n = the useful life of the asset (in years);
R = the residual value of the asset;
C = the cost, or fair value, of the asset.

The fixed percentage rate will, however, be given in all examples used in this text.

We can see that the pattern of depreciation is quite different for the two methods. If we plot the written-down value of the asset, which has been derived using the reducing-balance method, against time, the result will be as shown in Figure 3.4.

Figure 3.4 **Graph of written-down value against time using the reducing-balance method**

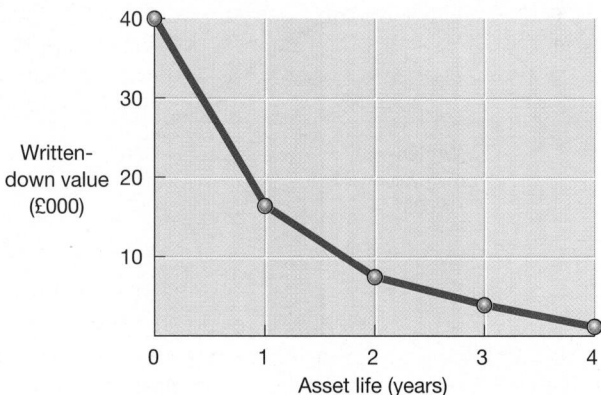

Under the reducing-balance method, the written-down value of an asset falls by a larger amount in the earlier years than in the later years. This is because the depreciation charge is based on a fixed-rate percentage of the written-down value.

ACTIVITY 3.7

Assume that the machine used in the example above was owned by a business that made a profit *before* depreciation of £20,000 for each of the four years in which the asset was held.

Calculate the net profit for the business for each year under each depreciation method, and comment on your findings.

Your answer should be as follows:

Straight-line method

	(a) Profit before depreciation £	(b) Depreciation £	(a–b) Net profit £
Year 1	20,000	9,744	10,256
Year 2	20,000	9,744	10,256
Year 3	20,000	9,744	10,256
Year 4	20,000	9,744	10,256

Reducing-balance method

	(a) Profit before depreciation £	(b) Depreciation £	(a–b) Net profit/ (loss) £
Year 1	20,000	24,000	(4,000)
Year 2	20,000	9,600	10,400
Year 3	20,000	3,840	16,160
Year 4	20,000	1,536	18,464

The straight-line method of depreciation results in a constant net profit figure over the four-year period. This is because both the profit before depreciation and the depreciation charge are constant over the period. The reducing-balance method, however, results in a changing profit figure over time, despite the fact that in this example the pre-depreciation profit is the same each year. In the first year a net loss is reported, and thereafter a rising net profit is reported.

Although the *pattern* of net profit over the four-year period will be quite different, depending on the depreciation method used, the *total* net profit for the period (£41,024) will remain the same. This is because both methods of depreciating will allocate the same amount of total depreciation (£38,976) over the four-year period. It is only the amount allocated *between years* that will differ.

In practice, the use of different depreciation methods may not have such a dramatic effect on profits as suggested in the activity above. Where a business replaces some of its assets each year, the total depreciation charge calculated under the reducing-balance method will reflect a range of charges (from high through to low), as assets will be at different points in the replacement cycle. This could mean that the total depreciation charge may not be significantly different from the total depreciation charge that would be derived under the straight-line method.

Selecting a depreciation method

How does a business choose which depreciation method to use for a particular asset? The most appropriate method should be the one that best matches the depreciation expense to the economic benefits that are consumed. The business may therefore decide to undertake an examination of the pattern of benefits consumed. Where the asset's benefits are likely to be consumed evenly over time (buildings, for example), the straight-line method may be considered appropriate. Where assets lose their efficiency and the benefits consumed decline over time as a result (for example, certain types of machinery), the reducing-balance method may be considered more appropriate. Where the pattern of economic benefits consumed is uncertain, the straight-line method is normally chosen.

There is an international accounting standard to deal with the problem of depreciation. As we shall see in Chapter 5, the purpose of accounting standards is to narrow areas of accounting difference and to ensure that information provided to users is transparent and comparable. The standard for handling depreciation endorses the view that the depreciation method chosen should reflect the pattern in which the asset's economic benefits are consumed. The standard also requires that businesses disclose a fair amount of detail concerning depreciation charges in their financial statements. Thus, information such as the methods of depreciation used, the accumulated amount of depreciation at the beginning and end of the financial period and either the depreciation rates applied or the useful lives of the assets must be disclosed.

Real World 3.3 sets out the depreciation policies of Thorntons plc.

REAL WORLD 3.3

Depreciation policies in practice

Thorntons plc, the manufacturer and retailer of confectionery, uses the straight-line method to depreciate its non-current assets. The financial statements for the year ended 30 June 2003 show the period over which different classes of tangible assets are depreciated as follows:

In equal annual instalments	
Factory freehold premises	50 years
Short leasehold land and buildings	Period of the lease
Retail fixtures and fittings	5 years
Retail equipment	4 to 5 years
Retail shop improvements	10 years
Other equipment and vehicles	3 to 7 years
Manufacturing plant and machinery	12 to 15 years

We can see that there are wide variations in the expected useful lives of the various non-current assets held.

Source: Thorntons plc Annual Report and Accounts 2003.

The approach taken for the depreciation (or amortisation as it is usually called in this context) of intangible non-current assets is broadly the same as that of property, plant and equipment (tangible non-current) assets. However, there is often much greater uncertainty surrounding the future economic benefits from intangible non-current assets. International accounting standards deal with this greater uncertainty by applying stricter rules. For example, there is a presumption that the depreciation (or amortisation) period for intangible assets is no more than twenty years. This presumption can only be rebutted if there is persuasive evidence to the contrary. International accounting standards also insist that a review of the depreciation period and depreciation method used must be carried out at least annually. For property, plant and equipment (tangible non-current assets), the review periods can be less frequent.

The approach taken to calculating depreciation is summarised in Figure 3.5.

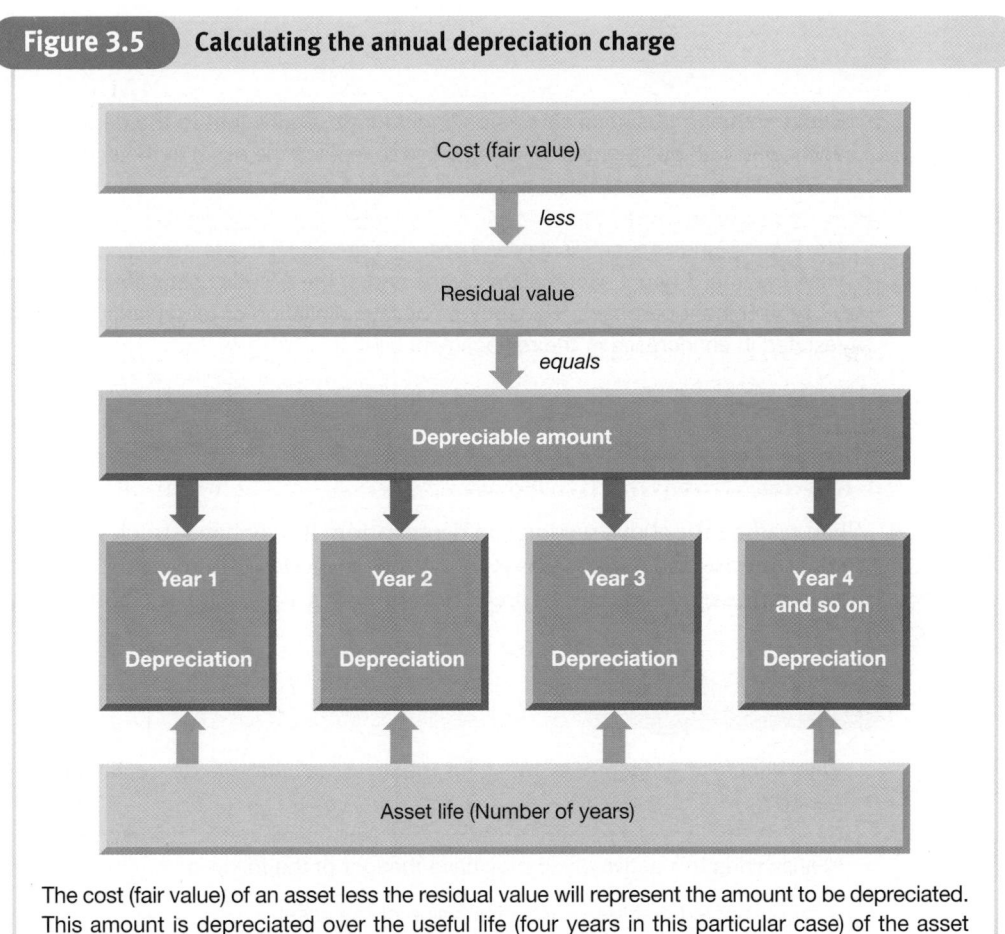

Figure 3.5 Calculating the annual depreciation charge

The cost (fair value) of an asset less the residual value will represent the amount to be depreciated. This amount is depreciated over the useful life (four years in this particular case) of the asset using an appropriate depreciation method.

Depreciation and the replacement of non-current assets

There seems to be a misunderstanding in the minds of some people that the purpose of depreciation is to provide the funds for the replacement of an asset when it reaches the end of its useful life. However, this is *not* the purpose of depreciation as conventionally defined. It was mentioned earlier that depreciation represents an attempt to allocate the cost, or fair value, (less any residual value) of an asset over its expected useful life. The resulting depreciation charge in each period represents an expense, which is then used in the calculation of net profit for the period. Calculating the depreciation charge for a period is therefore necessary for the proper measurement of financial performance, and must be done whether or not the business intends to replace the asset in the future. The principle is illustrated in Figure 3.5, on p. 83.

If there is an intention to replace the asset, the depreciation charge in the profit and loss account will not ensure that liquid funds are set aside by the business specifically for this purpose. Although the effect of a depreciation charge is to reduce net profit, and therefore to reduce the amount available for withdrawal by the owners, the amounts retained within the business as a result may be invested in ways that are unrelated to the replacement of the specific asset.

ACTIVITY 3.8

Suppose that a business sets aside liquid funds, equivalent to the depreciation charge each year, with the intention of using these to replace the asset at the end of its useful life. Will this ensure that there will be sufficient funds available for this purpose?

No. Even if funds are set aside each year that are equal to the depreciation charge for the year, the total amount accumulated at the end of the asset's useful life may be insufficient for replacement purposes. This may be because inflation or technological advances have resulted in an increase in the replacement cost.

Depreciation and judgement

When reading the above sections on depreciation, it may have struck you that accounting is not as precise and objective as is sometimes suggested. There are areas where subjective judgement is required, and depreciation provides a good illustration of this.

ACTIVITY 3.9

What kinds of judgements must be made to calculate a depreciation charge for a period?

In answering this activity, you may have thought of the following:

● the expected residual or disposal value of the asset
● the expected useful life of the asset
● the choice of depreciation method.

Making different judgements on these matters would result in a different pattern of depreciation charges over the life of the asset, and therefore in a different pattern of reported profits. However, underestimations or overestimations that are made in relation to the above will be adjusted for in the final year of an asset's life, and so the total depreciation charge (and total profit) over the asset's life will not be affected by estimation errors.

Real World 3.4 shows the effect of changing the useful life of assets on the annual profit of one large business.

REAL WORLD 3.4

Changing the useful life of assets

In 2002, Euro-Disney, the theme park and hotel operator, extended the estimated life of some of its non-current assets relating to infrastructure and buildings. The management argued that the revisions were designed to reflect more faithfully the useful lives of these assets in relation to their intended use and in relation to industry practice. The effect of doing this was to decrease the depreciation charge (and, therefore, increase profit) in 2002 by €5.7m. As the profit for the year, before exceptional items, was €4.9m, this change turned a loss for the period into a profit.

Source: Euro-Disney plc 2002 Financial Report.

ACTIVITY 3.10

Sally Dalton (Packaging) Ltd purchased a machine for £40,000. At the end of its useful life of four years, the amount received on sale was £4,000. When the asset was purchased the business received two estimates of the likely residual value of the asset, which were: (a) £8,000, and (b) zero.

Show the pattern of annual depreciation charges over the four years and the total depreciation charges for the asset under each of the two estimates. The straight-line method should be used to calculate the annual depreciation charges.

The depreciation charge, assuming estimate (a), will be £8,000 a year ((£40,000 − £8,000)/4). The depreciation charge, assuming estimate (b), will be £10,000 a year (£40,000/4). As the actual residual value is £4,000, estimate (a) will lead to underdepreciation of £4,000 (£8,000 − £4,000) over the life of the asset, and estimate (b) will lead to overdepreciation of £4,000 (£0 − £4,000). These under- and overestimations will be dealt with in year 4.

The pattern of depreciation and total depreciation charges will therefore be:

		Estimate	
		(a)	(b)
Year		£	£
1	Annual depreciation	8,000	10,000
2	Annual depreciation	8,000	10,000
3	Annual depreciation	8,000	10,000
4	Annual depreciation	8,000	10,000
		32,000	40,000
4	Under/(over)depreciation	4,000	(4,000)
	Total depreciation	36,000	36,000

The final adjustment for underdepreciation of an asset is often referred to as 'loss on sale of non-current asset', as the amount actually received is less than the residual value. Similarly, the adjustment for overdepreciation is often referred to as 'profit on sale of non-current asset'.

Profit measurement and stock (inventories) costing methods

The way in which we measure the cost of stock (or inventories) is important, because the cost of the stock sold during a period will affect the calculation of net profit, and the remaining stock held at the end of the period will affect the portrayal of the financial position. In the last chapter, we saw that historic cost is the basis for valuing assets, and so it is tempting to think that determining the cost of stocks held is not a difficult issue. However, in a period of *changing prices*, the costing of stock can be a problem.

A business must determine the cost of the stock sold during the period and the cost of the stock remaining at the end of the period. To do this, both of these costs are calculated as if it had been physically handled in a particular assumed manner. The assumption made has nothing to do with how the stock is *actually* handled; it is concerned only with which assumption is likely to lead to the most useful accounting information.

Two common assumptions used are:

- **first in, first out (FIFO)** – the earliest stocks held are the first to be sold;
- **last in, first out (LIFO)** – the latest stocks held are the first to be sold.

Another approach to deriving the cost of stocks is to assume that stocks entering the business lose their separate identity, and any issues of stock reflect the average cost of the stocks that are held. This is the **weighted average cost (AVCO)** method, where the weights used in deriving the average cost figures are the quantities of each batch of stock purchased. Example 3.8 below provides a simple illustration of the way in which each method is applied.

Example 3.8

A business that supplies coal to factories has the following transactions during a period:

		Tonnes	Cost/tonne
1 May	Opening stock	1,000	£10
2 May	Purchased	5,000	£11
3 May	Purchased	8,000	£12
		14,000	
6 May	Sold	(9,000)	
	Closing stock	5,000	

First in, first out (FIFO)

Using the first in, first out approach, the first 9,000 tonnes of coal are assumed to be those that are sold. This is the opening stock (1,000 tonnes), the stock bought on 2 May (5,000 tonnes) and 3,000 tonnes of the 3 May purchase. The remainder of the 3 May purchase (5,000 tonnes) will comprise the closing stock. Thus we have:

	Cost of sales			Closing stock		
	Tonnes	Cost/tonne £	Total £000	Tonnes	Cost/tonne £	Total £000
1 May	1,000	10	10.0			
2 May	5,000	11	55.0			
3 May	3,000	12	36.0	5,000	12	60.0
Cost of sales			101.0	Closing stock		60.0

Last in, first out (LIFO)

Using the last in, first out approach, the later purchases will be the first to be sold. This is the 3 May purchase (8,000 tonnes) and 1,000 tonnes of the 2 May purchase. The earlier purchases (the rest of the 2 May purchase and the opening stock) will comprise the closing stock. Thus we have:

	Cost of sales			Closing stock		
	Tonnes	Cost/tonne £	Total £000	Tonnes	Cost/tonne £	Total £000
3 May	8,000	12	96.0			
2 May	1,000	11	11.0	4,000	11	44.0
1 May				1,000	10	10.0
Cost of sales			107.0	Closing stock		54.0

Weighted average cost (AVCO)

Using this approach, a weighted average cost will be determined that will be used to derive both the cost of goods sold and the cost of the remaining stocks held. This simply means that the total cost of the opening stock, the 2 May and 3 May purchases are added together and divided by the total number of tonnes, to obtain the weighted average cost per tonne. Both the cost of sales and closing stock values are based on that average cost per tonne. Thus we have:

	Purchases		
	Tonnes	Cost/tonne £	Total £000
1 May	1,000	10	10.0
2 May	5,000	11	55.0
3 May	8,000	12	96.0
	14,000		161.0

Average cost = £161,000/14,000 = £11.5 per tonne.

Cost of sales			Closing stock		
Tonnes	Cost/tonne £	Total £000	Tonnes	Cost/tonne £	Total £000
9,000	11.5	103.5	5,000	11.5	57.5

ACTIVITY 3.11

Suppose the 9,000 tonnes of stock in Example 3.8 were sold for £15 per tonne.
(a) Calculate the gross profit for the period under each of the three methods.
(b) What observations concerning the portrayal of financial position and performance can you make about each method when prices are rising?

....

Your answer should be along the following lines:

(a) Gross profit calculation:

	FIFO £000	LIFO £000	AVCO £000
Sales revenue (9000@£15)	135.0	135.0	135.0
Cost of sales	101.0	107.0	103.5
Gross profit	34.0	28.0	31.5
	£000	£000	£000
Closing stock figure	60.0	54.0	57.5

(b) The above figures reveal that FIFO will give the highest gross profit during a period of rising prices. This is because sales revenue is matched with the earlier (and cheaper) purchases. LIFO will give the lowest gross profit because sales revenue is matched against the more recent (and dearer) purchases. The AVCO method will normally give a figure that is between these two extremes.

   The closing stock figure in the balance sheet will be highest with the FIFO method. This is because the cost of goods still held will be based on the more recent (and dearer) purchases. LIFO will give the lowest closing stock figure as the goods held in stock will be based on the earlier (and cheaper) stocks purchased. Once again, the AVCO method will normally give a figure that is between these two extremes.

ACTIVITY 3.12

Assume that prices in Activity 3.11 are falling rather than rising. How would your observations concerning the portrayal of financial performance and position be different for the various stock valuation methods?

When prices are falling, the position of FIFO and LIFO is reversed. FIFO will give the lowest gross profit as sales revenue is matched against the earlier (and dearer) goods purchased. LIFO will give the highest gross profit as sales revenue is matched against the more recent (and cheaper) goods purchased. AVCO will give a cost of sales figure between these two extremes. The closing stock figure in the balance sheet will be lowest under FIFO as the cost of stock will be based on the more recent (and cheaper) stocks purchased. LIFO will provide the highest closing stock figure and AVCO will provide a figure between the two extremes.

It is important to recognise that the different stock valuation methods will only have an effect on the reported profit *from one year to the next*. The figure derived for closing stock will be carried forward and matched with sales revenue in a later period. Thus, if the cheaper purchases of stocks are matched to sales revenue in the current period, it will mean that the dearer purchases will be matched to sales revenue in a later period. Over the life of the business, therefore, the total profit will be the same whichever valuation method has been used.

Stock valuation – some further issues

We saw in Chapter 2 that the closing stock figure will appear as part of the current assets of the business and that the convention of prudence requires current assets to be valued at the lower of cost and net realisable value. (The net realisable value of stocks is the estimated selling price less any further costs that may be necessary to complete the goods and any costs involved in selling and distributing the goods.) This rule may mean that the valuation method applied to stock will switch each year depending on which of cost and net realisable value is the lower. In practice, however, the cost of the stock held is usually below the current net realisable value – particularly during a period of rising prices. It is, therefore, the cost figure that will normally appear in the balance sheet.

ACTIVITY 3.13

Can you think of any circumstances where the net realisable value will be lower than the cost of stocks held, even during a period of generally rising prices?

The net realisable value may be lower where:

- Goods have deteriorated or become obsolete.
- There has been a fall in the market price of the goods.
- The goods are being used as a 'loss leader'.
- Bad purchasing decisions have been made.

There is an international accounting standard to deal with the issue of stock valuation. The 'benchmark treatment' is that the cost of stocks held should be determined using either FIFO or AVCO. The LIFO approach is not an acceptable method to use. The standard also supports the 'lower of cost or net realisable value' rule.

Real World 3.5 sets out the policies of two businesses with respect to their stock holdings.

REAL WORLD 3.5

Stock valuation in practice

Some businesses indicate the basis for establishing the cost of stocks held. For example, Tate and Lyle plc, the sugar and other starch-based food processor, reveals that stock is transferred to the profit and loss account on a 'first in, first out' basis whereas Euro-Disney uses weighted average cost.

Sources: Tate and Lyle plc Annual Report 2003, Euro-Disney 2002 Financial Report.

Stock valuation and depreciation provide two examples where the **consistency convention** must be applied. This convention holds that when a particular method of accounting is selected to deal with a transaction, this method should be applied consistently over time. Thus, it would not be acceptable to switch from, say, FIFO to AVCO between periods (unless there are exceptional circumstances that make this appropriate). The purpose of this convention is to try to ensure that users are able to make valid comparisons between periods.

ACTIVITY 3.14

Stock valuation provides a further example of where subjective judgement is required to derive the figures for inclusion in the financial statements. For a retail business, what are the main areas where judgement is required?

The main areas are:

- The choice of cost method (FIFO, LIFO, AVCO).
- Deriving the net realisable value figure for stocks held.

Profit measurement and the problem of bad and doubtful debts

Many businesses sell goods on credit. When credit sales are made, the revenue is usually recognised as soon as the goods are passed to, and accepted by, the customer. Recording the dual aspect of a credit sale will involve:

- increasing sales revenue;
- increasing debtors by the amount of the credit sale.

However, with this type of sale there is always the risk that the customer will not pay the amount due, however reliable they might have appeared to be at the time of the sale. When it becomes reasonably certain that the customer will never pay, the debt is considered to be 'bad' and this must be taken into account when preparing the financial statements.

ACTIVITY 3.15

When preparing the financial statements, what would be the effect on the profit and on the balance sheet, of not taking into account the fact that a debt is bad?

The effect would be to overstate the assets (debtors) on the balance sheet and to over-state profit in the profit and loss account, as the sale (which has been recognised) will not result in any future benefit arising.

To provide a more realistic picture of financial performance and position, the **bad debt** must be 'written off'. This will involve:

- reducing the debtors;
- increasing expenses (by creating an expense known as 'bad debts written off') by the amount of the bad debt.

The matching convention requires that the bad debt is written off in the same period as the sale, that gave rise to the debt, is recognised.

Note that, when a debt is bad, the accounting response is not simply to cancel the original sale. If this were done, the profit and loss account would not be so informative. Reporting the bad debts as an expense can be extremely useful in the evaluation of management performance.

At the end of the accounting period, it may not be possible to identify with reasonable certainty all the bad debts that have been incurred during the period. It may be that some debts appear doubtful, but only at some later point in time will the true position become clear. The uncertainty that exists does not mean that, when preparing the financial statements, we should ignore the possibility that some of the debtors outstanding will eventually prove to be bad. It would not be prudent to do so, nor would it comply with the need to match expenses to the period in which the associated sale is recognised. As a result, the business will normally try to identify all those debts that, at the end of the period, can be classified as doubtful (that is, there is a possibility that they may eventually prove to be bad). This can be done by examining individual accounts of debtors or by taking a proportion of the total debtors outstanding based on past experience.

Once a figure has been derived, a **provision for doubtful debts** can be created. This provision will be:

- shown as an expense in the profit and loss account, and
- deducted from the total debtors figure in the balance sheet.

By doing this, full account is taken, in the appropriate accounting period, of those debts where there is a risk of non-payment. This accounting treatment of doubtful debts will be in addition to the treatment of bad debts described above.

Example 3.9 illustrates the reporting of bad and doubtful debts.

Example 3.9

Desai Enterprises has debtors of £350,000 at the end of the accounting year to 30 June 2005. Investigation of these debtors revealed that £10,000 was likely to prove irrecoverable and that a further £30,000 was doubtful.

Extracts from the profit and loss account would have been as follows:

Profit and loss account (extracts) for the year ended 30 June 2005

	£
Bad debts written off	10,000
Provision for doubtful debts	30,000

Balance sheet (extracts) as at 30 June 2005

	£
Debtors	340,000*
Less Provision for doubtful debts	30,000
	310,000

* that is, £350,000 – £10,000 irrecoverable debts

The provision for doubtful debts is, of course, an estimate, and it is quite likely that the actual amount of debts that prove to be bad will be different from the estimate. Let us say that, during the next accounting period, it was discovered that £26,000 of the doubtful debts in fact proved to be irrecoverable. These debts must now be written off as follows:

● reduce debtors by £26,000, and
● reduce provision for doubtful debts by £26,000.

However, a provision for doubtful debts of £4,000 will remain. This amount represents an overestimate made when creating the provision in the profit and loss account for the year to 30 June 2005. As the provision is no longer needed, it should be eliminated. Remember that the provision was made by creating an expense in the profit and loss account for the year to 30 June 2005. As the expense was too high, the amount of the overestimate should be 'written back' in the next accounting period. In other words, it will be treated as revenue for the year to 30 June 2006. This will mean:

● reducing the provision for doubtful debts by £4,000, and
● increasing revenue by £4,000.

Ideally, of course, the amount should be written back to the 2005 profit and loss account; however, it is too late to do this. At the end of 2006, not only will 2005's over-provision be written back but a new provision should be created to allow for the debts, arising from 2006's sales that seem doubtful.

ACTIVITY 3.16

Clayton Conglomerates had debts of £870,000 outstanding at the end of the account-ing year to 31 March 2005. The chief accountant believed that £40,000 of those debts were irrecoverable and that a further £60,000 were doubtful. In the subsequent year, it was found that an overpessimistic estimate of doubtful debts had been made and that only a further £45,000 of debts had actually proved to be bad.

Show the relevant extracts in the profit and loss account for both 2005 and 2006 to report the bad debts written off and the provision for doubtful debts. Also show the relevant balance sheet extract as at 31 March 2005.

Your answer should be as follows:

Profit and loss account (extracts) for the year ended 31 March 2005

	£
Bad debts written off	40,000
Provision for doubtful debts	60,000

Profit and loss account (extracts) for the year ended 31 March 2006

	£
Provision for doubtful debts written back (revenue)	15,000

Note: This figure will usually be netted off against any provision created for doubtful debts in respect of 2006.

Balance sheet (extracts) as at 31 March 2005

	£
Debtors	830,000
Less Provision for doubtful debts	(60,000)
	770,000

ACTIVITY 3.17

Bad and doubtful debts represent further areas where judgement is required in deriving expenses figures for a particular period. What will be the effect of different judgements concerning the amount of bad and doubtful debts on the profit for a particular period and on the total profit reported over the life of the business?

Judgement is often required in deriving a figure for bad debts incurred during a period. There may be situations where views will differ concerning whether or not a debt is irrecoverable. The decision concerning whether or not to write off a bad debt will have an effect on the expenses for the period and, hence, the reported profit. However, over the life of the business the total reported profit would not be affected, as incorrect judgements in one period will be adjusted for in a later period.

Suppose, for example, that a debt of £100 was written off in a period and that, in a later period, the amount owing was actually received. The increase in expenses of £100 in the period in which the bad debt was written off would be compensated for by an increase in revenue of £100 when the amount outstanding was finally received (bad debt recoverable). If, on the other hand, the amount owing of £100 was never written off in the first place, the profit for the two periods would not be affected by the bad debt adjustment and would, therefore, be different – but the total profit for the two periods would be the same.

A similar situation would apply where there are differences in judgements concerning doubtful debts.

Real World 3.6 shows the effect of bad debt provisions on the profits of one well-known business

REAL WORLD 3.6

Making a dent in profits

The size of bad debt provisions can be high in relation to reported profits. In February 2003, Barclays Bank plc announced annual profits for the preceding year of £3.2bn. The profits were lower than expected because of the need to increase bad debt provisions by nearly a third to £1.48bn. The reasons for the increase included lending problems in Argentina and business collapses in the telecoms and energy sectors.

Source: Based on information in 'Barclays hit by bad debt provisions', FT.com, 13 February 2003.

Let us now try to bring together some of the points that we have raised in this chapter through a self-assessment question.

SELF-ASSESSMENT QUESTION   3.1

TT and Co is a new business that started trading on 1 January 2004. The following is a summary of transactions that occurred during the first year of trading:

1 The owners introduced £50,000 of capital, which was paid into a bank account opened in the name of the business.
2 Premises were rented from 1 January 2004 at an annual rental of £20,000. During the year, rent of £25,000 was paid to the owner of the premises.
3 Rates (a tax on business premises) were paid during the year as follows:

For the period 1 January 2004 to 31 March 2004	£500
For the period 1 April 2004 to 31 March 2005	£1,200

4 A delivery van was bought on 1 January 2004 for £12,000. This is expected to be used in the business for four years and then to be sold for £2,000.
5 Wages totalling £33,500 were paid during the year. At the end of the year, the business owed £630 of wages for the last week of the year.
6 Electricity bills for the first three quarters of the year were paid totalling £1,650. After 31 December 2004, but before the final statements had been finalised for the year, the bill for the last quarter arrived showing a charge of £620.
7 Stock-in-trade totalling £143,000 was bought on credit.
8 Stock-in-trade totalling £12,000 was bought for cash.
9 Sales revenue on credit totalled £152,000 (cost of sales £74,000).
10 Cash sales revenue totalled £35,000 (cost of sales £16,000).
11 Receipts from trade debtors totalled £132,000.
12 Payments to trade creditors totalled £121,000.
13 Van running expenses paid totalled £9,400.

At the end of the year it was clear that a trade debtor who owed £400 would not be able to pay any part of the debt. The business uses the straight-line method for depreciating non-current assets.

Required:
Prepare a balance sheet as at 31 December 2004 and a profit and loss account for the year to that date. (Use the outline financial statements produced below to help you.)

TT and Co
Balance sheet as at 31 December 2004

	£	£	£
Non-current assets			
Motor van			
Current assets			
Stock-in-trade			
Trade debtors			
Prepaid expenses			
Cash	___		
Less **Current liabilities**			
Trade creditors			
Accrued expenses	___	___	___
			___
Capital			
Original			
Add Profit			___
			___

Profit and loss account for the year ended 31 December 2004

	£	£
Sales revenue		
Less Cost of sales		___
Gross profit		
Less Rent		
Rates		
Wages		
Electricity		
Bad debts		
Van expenses		
Van depreciation		___
Net profit for the year		___

Interpreting the profit and loss account

When a profit and loss account is presented to users it is sometimes the case that the only item that will concern them will be the final net profit figure, or *bottom line* as it is sometimes called. Although the net profit figure is a primary measure of performance, and its importance is difficult to overstate, the profit and loss account contains other information that should also be of interest. To evaluate business performance effectively, it is important to find out how the final net profit figure was derived. Thus the level of sales revenue, the nature and amount of expenses incurred, and the profit in relation to sales revenue are important factors in understanding the performance of the business over a period. The analysis and interpretation of financial statements is considered in detail in Chapter 7.

SUMMARY

The main points of this chapter may be summarised as follows:

The profit and loss account (income statement)

- Measures and reports how much profit (loss) has been generated over a period.
- Profit (loss) for the period is the difference between the total revenue and total expenses for the period.
- Links the balance sheets at the beginning and end of a financial period.
- The profit and loss account of a retail business will first calculate gross profit, then add any additional revenue and then deduct any overheads for the period. The final figure derived is the net profit (loss) for the period.
- Gross profit represents the difference between the sales revenue for the period and the cost of sales.

Expenses and revenue

- Cost of sales may be identified by either matching the cost of each sale to the particular sale or by adjusting the goods purchased during the period to take account of opening and closing stocks.
- The classification of expenses is often a matter of judgement, although there are statutory rules for businesses that trade as limited companies.
- The realisation convention states that revenue is recognised when it has been realised.
- Realisation occurs when the amount of revenue can be measured reliably, it is probable that the economic benefits will be received and the costs of the transactions can be measured reliably.
- Where there is a sale of goods, there is an additional criterion that ownership and control must pass to the buyer before revenue can be recognised.
- Revenue can be recognised after partial completion provided a particular stage of completion can be measured reliably.
- The matching convention states that expenses should be matched to the revenue that they help generate.
- A particular expense reported in the profit and loss account may not be the same as the cash paid. This will result in some adjustment for accruals or prepayments.
- The materiality convention states that where the amounts are immaterial, we should consider only what is expedient.
- 'Accruals accounting' is preparing the profit and loss account and balance sheet following the accruals convention, which says that profit = revenue – expenses (not cash receipts – cash payments).

Depreciation of non-current assets

- Depreciation requires a consideration of the cost (or fair value), useful life and residual value of an asset. It also requires a consideration of the method of depreciation.
- The straight-line method of depreciation allocates the amount to be depreciated evenly over the useful life of the asset.

- The reducing-balance method applies a fixed percentage rate of depreciation to the written-down value of an asset each year.
- The depreciation method chosen should reflect the pattern of benefits associated with the asset.
- Depreciation is an attempt to allocate the cost (or fair value), less the residual value, of an asset over its useful life. It does not provide funds for replacement of the asset.

Stock (inventory) costing methods

- The way in which we derive the cost of stocks is important in the calculation of profit and the presentation of financial position.
- The first in, first out (FIFO) method assumes that the earliest stocks held are the first to be sold.
- The last in, first out (LIFO) method assumes that the latest stocks are the first to be sold.
- The weighted average cost (AVCO) method applies an average cost to all stocks sold.
- When prices are rising, FIFO gives the lowest cost of sales and highest closing stock figure and LIFO gives the highest cost of sales figure and the lowest closing stock figure. AVCO gives a figure for cost of sales and closing stock that lies between FIFO and LIFO.
- When prices are falling, the positions of FIFO and LIFO are reversed.
- Stocks are shown at the lower of cost and net realisable value.
- When a particular method of accounting, such as a stock costing method, is selected, it should be applied consistently over time.

Bad debts

- Where it is reasonably certain that a credit customer will not pay, the debt is regarded as 'bad' and written off.
- Where it is doubtful that a credit customer will pay, a provision for doubtful debts should be created.

→ Key terms

profit p. 62
revenue p. 62
expense p. 62
profit and loss account p. 64
gross profit p. 64
net profit p. 65
cost of sales p. 65
realisation convention p. 68
matching convention p. 72
accrued expenses p. 72
prepaid expense p. 75
materiality convention p. 75
accruals convention p. 76

accruals accounting p. 76
depreciation p. 76
residual value p. 78
straight-line method p. 78
written-down value p. 79
reducing-balance method p. 79
first in, first out (FIFO) p. 86
last in, first out (LIFO) p. 86
weighted average cost
  (AVCO) p. 86
consistency convention p. 90
bad debt p. 91
provision for doubtful debts p. 91

Further reading

If you would like to explore the topics covered in this chapter in more depth, we recommend the following books:

Financial Reporting, *Alexander D. and Britton A.*, 6th edn, International Thomson Business Press, 2001, chapter 4.

Financial Accounting and Reporting, *Elliott B. and Elliott J.*, 8th edn, Financial Times Prentice Hall, 2004, chapters 14 and 17.

Corporate Financial Accounting and Reporting, *Sutton T.*, 2nd edn, Financial Times Prentice Hall, 2004, chapters 2, 8, 9 and 10.

International Financial Reporting Standards (IFRSs) 2003, *International Accounting Standards Board*, IASCF, 2003, IAS 16 and IAS 38.

REVIEW QUESTIONS

Answers to these questions can be found on the students' side of the Companion Website at www.pearsoned.co.uk/atrillmclaney.

3.1 'Although the profit and loss account is a record of past achievement, the calculations required for certain expenses involve estimates of the future.' What is meant by this statement? Can you think of examples where estimates of the future are used?

3.2 'Depreciation is a process of allocation and not valuation.' What do you think is meant by this statement?

3.3 What is the convention of consistency? Does this convention help users in making a more valid comparison *between* businesses?

3.4 'An asset is similar to an expense.' Do you agree?

EXERCISES

Exercises 3.6 to 3.8 are more advanced than 3.1 to 3.5. Those with a coloured number have answers at the back of the book.

3.1 You have heard the following statements made. Comment critically on them.

  (a) 'Capital only increases or decreases as a result of the owners putting more cash into the business or taking some out.'
  (b) 'An accrued expense is one that relates to next year.'
  (c) 'Unless we depreciate this asset we shall be unable to provide for its replacement.'
  (d) 'There is no point in depreciating the factory building. It is appreciating in value each year.'

3.2 Singh Enterprises has an accounting year to 31 December. On 1 January 2002 the business purchased a machine for £10,000. The machine had an expected useful life of four years and an estimated residual value of £2,000. On 1 January 2003 the business purchased another machine for £15,000. This machine had an expected useful life of five years and an estimated residual value of £2,500. On 31 December 2004 the business sold the first machine purchased for £3,000.

Required:
Show the relevant profit and loss account extracts and balance sheet extracts for the years 2002, 2003 and 2004.

3.3 The owner of a business is confused, and comes to you for help. The financial statements for his business, prepared by an accountant, for the last accounting period revealed an increase in profit of £50,000. However, during the accounting period the bank balance declined by £30,000. What reasons might explain this apparent discrepancy?

3.4 Spratley Ltd is a builders' merchant. On 1 September the business had 20 tonnes of sand in stock at a cost of £18 per tonne and at a total cost of £360. During the first week in September, the business purchased the following amounts of sand:

September	Tonnes	Cost per tonne £
2	48	20
4	15	24
6	10	25

On 7 September the business sold 60 tonnes of sand to a local builder.

Required:
Calculate the cost of goods sold and the closing stock figures from the above information using the following stock costing methods:

(a) first in, first out
(b) last in, first out
(c) weighted average cost.

3.5 Fill in the values (a) to (f) in the following table on the assumption that there were no opening balances involved:

	Relating to period		At end of period	
	Paid/ received £	Expense/ revenue for period £	Prepaid £	Accruals/ deferred revenues £
Rent payable	10,000	a	1,000	
Rates and insurance	5,000	b		1,000
General expenses	c	6,000	1,000	
Loan interest payable	3,000	2,500	d	
Salaries	e	9,000		3,000
Rent receivable	f	1,500		1,500

3.6 The following is the balance sheet of TT and Co at the end of its first year of trading (from Self-assessment question 3.1):

TT and Co
Balance sheet as at 31 December 2004

	£	£	£
Non-current assets			
Motor van: Cost			12,000
Depreciation			2,500
			9,500
Current assets			
Stock-in-trade	65,000		
Trade debtors	19,600		
Prepaid expenses*	5,300		
Cash	750		
		90,650	
Less **Current liabilities**			
Trade creditors	22,000		
Accrued expenses†	1,250		
		23,250	
			67,400
			£76,900
Capital			
Original			50,000
Add Profit			26,900
			£76,900

* The prepaid expenses consisted of rates (£300) and rent (£5,000).
† The accrued expenses consisted of wages (£630) and electricity (£620).

During 2005, the following transactions took place:

1 The owners withdrew capital in the form of cash of £20,000.
2 Premises continued to be rented at an annual rental of £20,000. During the year, rent of £15,000 was paid to the owner of the premises.
3 Rates on the premises were paid during the year as follows: for the period 1 April 2005 to 31 March 2006 £1,300.
4 A second delivery van was bought on 1 January 2005 for £13,000. This is expected to be used in the business for four years and then to be sold for £3,000.
5 Wages totalling £36,700 were paid during the year. At the end of the year, the business owed £860 of wages for the last week of the year.
6 Electricity bills for the first three quarters of the year and £620 for the last quarter of the previous year were paid totalling £1,820. After 31 December 2005, but before the accounts had been finalised for the year, the bill for the last quarter arrived showing a charge of £690.
7 Stock-in-trade totalling £67,000 was bought on credit.
8 Stock-in-trade totalling £8,000 was bought for cash.
9 Sales revenue on credit totalled £179,000 (cost £89,000).
10 Cash sales revenue totalled £54,000 (cost £25,000).
11 Receipts from trade debtors totalled £178,000.
12 Payments to trade creditors totalled £71,000.
13 Van running expenses paid totalled £16,200.

The business uses the straight-line method for depreciating non-current assets.

Required:
Prepare a balance sheet as at 31 December 2005 and a profit and loss account for the year to that date.

3.7   The following is the balance sheet of WW Limited as at 31 December 2004:

Balance sheet as at 31 December 2004

	£	£	£
Non-current assets			
Machinery			25,300
Current assets			
Stock-in-trade	12,200		
Trade debtors	21,300		
Prepaid expenses (rates)	400		
Cash	8,300		
		42,200	
Less **Current liabilities**			
Trade creditors	16,900		
Accrued expenses (wages)	1,700		
		18,600	
			23,600
			48,900
Capital			
Original			25,000
Retained profit			23,900
			48,900

During 2005 the following transactions took place:

1   The owners withdrew capital in the form of cash of £23,000.
2   Premises were rented at an annual rental of £20,000. During the year, rent of £25,000 was paid to the owner of the premises.
3   Rates on the premises were paid during the year for the period 1 April 2005 to 31 March 2006 and amounted to £2,000.
4   Some machinery, which was bought on 1 January 2004 for £13,000, has proved to be unsatisfactory. It was part-exchanged for some new machinery on 1 January 2005, and WW Limited paid a cash amount of £6,000. The new machinery would have cost £15,000 had the business bought it without the trade-in.
5   Wages totalling £23,800 were paid during the year. At the end of the year, the business owed £860 of wages.
6   Electricity bills for the four quarters of the year were paid totalling £2,700.
7   Stock-in-trade totalling £143,000 was bought on credit.
8   Stock-in-trade totalling £12,000 was bought for cash.
9   Sales revenue on credit totalled £211,000 (cost £127,000).
10   Cash sales revenue totalled £42,000 (cost £25,000).
11   Receipts from trade debtors totalled £198,000.
12   Payments to trade creditors totalled £156,000.
13   Van running expenses paid totalled £17,500.

The business uses the reducing-balance method of depreciation for non-current assets at the rate of 30 per cent each year.

Required:
Prepare a balance sheet as at 31 December 2005 and a profit and loss account for the year to that date.

3.8 The following is the profit and loss account for Nikov and Co. for the year ended 31 December 2005, along with information relating to the preceding year.

Profit and loss account for the year ended 31 December

	2004		2005	
	£000	*£000*	*£000*	*£000*
Sales revenue		382.5		420.2
Less Cost of sales		114.8		126.1
Gross profit		267.7		294.1
Less				
Salaries and wages	86.4		92.6	
Selling and distribution costs	75.4		98.9	
Rent and rates	22.0		22.0	
Bad debts written off	4.0		19.7	
Telephone and postage	4.4		4.8	
Insurance	2.8		2.9	
Motor vehicle expenses	8.6		10.3	
Loan interest	5.4		4.6	
Depreciation – Motor van	3.3		3.1	
– Fixtures and fittings	4.5		4.3	
		216.8		263.2
Net profit (loss)		50.9		30.9

Required:

Analyse the performance of the business for the year to 31 December 2005 in so far as the information allows.

CHAPTER 4

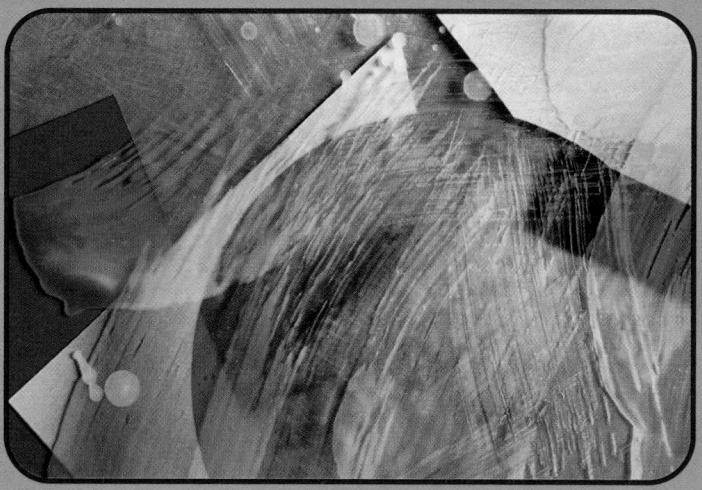

Accounting for limited companies (1)

OBJECTIVES

When you have completed this chapter, you should be able to:

- Discuss the nature of the limited company.

- Explain the role of directors of limited companies.

- Outline and explain the particular features and restrictions of the owners' claim, in the context of limited companies.

- Outline the nature and preparation of group financial statements.

INTRODUCTION

In the UK, most businesses, except the very smallest, trade in the form of limited companies. There are currently about 1.5 million limited companies in the UK. It is estimated that in the UK, 80 per cent of business activity and 60 per cent of all employment occurs in limited companies. This is probably fairly representative of many of the world's countries, particularly the more industrialised ones.

In this chapter we shall examine the nature of limited companies to see how they differ in practical terms from sole proprietorships and partnerships. This involves considering the ways in which the owners provide finance. It also requires an examination of the ways in which the financial statements which we disscussed in the last two chapters, relating to companies, differ from those of sole proprietors.

The following chapter, continues our examination of the financial statements of limited companies, by looking at the framework of regulations that surround their preparation.

Generating wealth through limited companies

The nature of limited companies

Let us begin our examination of limited companies by discussing their legal nature. A **limited company** has been described as an artificial person that has been created by law. This means that a company has many of the rights and obligations that 'real' people have. For example, it can sue or be sued by others and can enter into contracts in its own name. This contrasts sharply with other types of business, such as a sole proprietor, where it is the owner(s) rather than the business that must sue, enter into contracts and so on, because the business has no separate legal identity.

With the rare exceptions of those that are created by Act of Parliament or by Royal Charter, all UK companies are created by registration. To create a company the person or persons (usually known as *promoters*) wishing to create it, fill in a few simple forms and pay a modest registration fee. After having ensured that the necessary formalities have been met, the Registrar of Companies, a government official, enters the name of the new company on the Registry of Companies. Thus, in the UK, companies can be formed very easily and cheaply (for about £100).

Companies may be owned by just one person, but most have more than one owner and some have many owners. The owners are usually known as *members* or *shareholders*. The ownership of a company is normally divided into a number, frequently a large number, of **shares**, each of equal size. Each owner, or shareholder, owns one or more shares in the company. Large companies typically have a very large number of shareholders. For example at 31 March 2003, BT Group plc, the telecommunications business, had over 1.6 million different shareholders.

As a limited company has its own legal identity, it is regarded as being quite separate from those who own and manage it. This fact leads to two important features of the limited company: perpetual life and limited liability. These are now explained.

Perpetual life

A company is normally granted a perpetual existence and so will continue even where an owner of shares in the company dies. The shares of the deceased person will simply pass to the beneficiary of his or her estate. The granting of perpetual existence means that the life of a company is quite separate from the lives of those individuals who own or manage it. It is not, therefore, affected by changes in ownership that arise when individuals buy and sell shares in the company.

Though a company may be granted a perpetual existence when it is first formed, it is possible for either the shareholders or the courts to bring this existence to an end. When this is done, the assets of the company are sold off to meet outstanding liabilities. Any surplus arising from the sale will then be used to pay the shareholders. Shareholders may agree to end the life of a company where it has achieved the purpose for which it was formed or where they feel that the company has no real future. The courts may bring the life of a company to an end where creditors have applied to the courts for this to be done because they have not been paid amounts owing.

Where shareholders agree to end the life of a company, it is referred to as a 'voluntary liquidation'. **Real World 4.1** describes the demise of one company by this method.

REAL WORLD 4.1

Monotub Industries in a spin as founder gets Titan for £1 FT

Monotub Industries, maker of the Titan washing machine, yesterday passed into corporate history with very little ceremony and with only a whimper of protest from minority shareholders.

At an extraordinary meeting held in a basement room of the group's West End headquarters, shareholders voted to put the company into voluntary liquidation and sell its assets and intellectual property to founder Martin Myerscough for £1. (The shares in the company were at one time worth 650p each.)

The only significant opposition came from Giuliano Gnagnatti who, along with other shareholders, has seen his investment shrink faster than a wool twin-set on a boil wash.

The not-so-proud owner of 100,000 Monotub shares, Mr Gnagnatti, the managing director of an online retailer, . . . described the sale of Monotub as a 'free gift' to Mr Myerscough. This assessment was denied by Ian Green, the chairman of Monotub, who said the closest the beleaguered company had come to a sale was an offer for £60,000 that gave no guarantees against liabilities, which are thought to amount to £750,000.

The quiet passing of the washing machine, eventually dubbed the Titanic, was in strong contrast to its performance in many kitchens.

Originally touted as the 'great white goods hope' of the washing machine industry with its larger capacity and removable drum, the Titan ran into problems when it kept stopping during the spin cycle, causing it to emit a loud bang and leap into the air.

Summing up the demise of the Titan, Mr Green said: 'Clearly the machine had some revolutionary aspects, but you can't get away from the fact that the machine was faulty and should not have been launched with those defects.'

The usually vocal Mr Myerscough, who has promised to pump £250,000 into the company and give Monotub shareholders £4 for every machine sold, refused to comment on his plans for the Titan or reveal who his backers were. But . . . he did say that he intended to 'take the Titan forward'.

Source: 'Monotub Industries in a spin as founder gets Titan for £1', Lisa Urquhart, *Financial Times*, 23 January 2003, FT.com.

Limited liability

Since the company is a legal person in its own right, it must take responsibility for its own debts and losses. This means that once the shareholders have paid what they have agreed to pay for the shares, their obligation to the company, and to the company's creditors, is satisfied. Shareholders limit their losses to that which they have paid, or agreed to pay, for their shares. This is of great practical importance to potential shareholders, since they know that what they can lose, as part-owners of the business, is limited.

Contrast this with the position of sole proprietors or partners (that is the owners or part-owners of unincorporated businesses). They cannot 'ring fence' assets that they do not want to put into the business. If a sole proprietary business finds itself in a position where liabilities exceed the business assets, the law gives unsatisfied creditors the right to demand payment out of what the sole proprietor may have regarded as 'non-business' assets. Thus the sole proprietor could lose everything – house, car, the lot. This is because the law sees Jill, the sole proprietor, as being the same as Jill the private individual. The shareholder, by contrast, can lose only the amount committed to that company. Legally, the business operating as a limited company, in which Jack owns shares, is not the same as Jack himself. This is true even if Jack were to own all of the shares in the company.

Real World 4.2 gives an example of a well-known case where the shareholders of a particular company were able to avoid any liability to those that had lost money as a result of dealing with the company.

REAL WORLD 4.2

Carlton and Granada 1 – Nationwide Football League 0

A recent example of shareholders taking advantage of limited liability status is that of two television companies, Carlton and Granada, which each owned 50 per cent of ITV Digital (formerly ON Digital). ITV Digital collapsed because it was unable to meet its liabilities. Before its collapse, the company had signed a contract to pay the Nationwide Football League more than £89 million on both 1 August 2002 and 1 August 2003 for the rights to broadcast football matches over three seasons. However, the company was unable to meet this commitment and the shareholders could not be held legally liable for the amounts owing.

Carlton and Granada merged into one business in 2003, but at the time of ITV Digital were two independent companies.

ACTIVITY 4.1

We have just said that the fact that shareholders can limit their losses to that which they have paid, or have agreed to pay, for their shares is of great practical importance to potential shareholders.

Can you think of any practical benefit to a private-sector economy, in general, of this ability of shareholders to limit losses?

Business is a risky venture – in some cases very risky. People with money to invest will tend to be more content to do so where they know the limit of their liability. This means that more businesses will tend to be formed and that existing ones will find it easier to raise additional finance from existing and/or additional part-owners. This is good for the private-sector economy, since businesses will tend to form and expand more readily. Thus, the wants of society are more likely to be met where limited liability exists.

Though **limited liability** has this advantage to the providers of capital (the shareholders), it is not necessarily to the advantage of all others who have a stake in the business, like the Nationwide Football League clubs (see Real World 4.2). Limited liability is attractive to shareholders because they can, in effect, walk away from the unpaid debts of the company if their contribution has not been sufficient to meet those debts. This is likely to make any individual, or another business, that is considering advancing credit, wary of dealing with the limited company. This can be a real problem for smaller, less established companies. For example, suppliers may insist on cash payment before delivery of goods or the rendering of a service. Alternatively, a supplier may require a personal guarantee from a major shareholder that the debt will be paid before allowing a company trade credit. In the latter case, the supplier will circumvent the company's limited liability status by establishing the personal liability of an individual. However, larger, more established companies, tend to have built up the confidence of suppliers.

Legal safeguards

The fact that a company is limited must be indicated in the name of the company. This is mainly to warn individuals and other businesses contemplating dealing with a limited company that the liability of the owners (shareholders) is limited. As we shall see later in this chapter, there are other safeguards for those dealing with a limited company, in that the extent to which shareholders may withdraw their investment from the company is restricted.

Another important safeguard for those dealing with a limited company is that all limited companies must produce annual financial statements (profit and loss account (income statement), balance sheet and cash flow statement), and in effect make these available to the public. The rules surrounding the financial statements of limited companies will be discussed in Chapter 5.

Just before we leave the topic of the legal separateness of owners and the company, it is worth emphasising that this has no connection with the business entity convention of accounting, which we discussed in Chapter 2. This accounting convention applies equally well to all business types, including sole proprietorships where there is certainly no legal distinction between the owner and the business.

Public and private companies

When a company is registered with the Registrar of Companies, it must be registered either as a public or as a private company. The main practical difference between these is that a **public company** can offer its shares for sale to the general public, but a **private company** is restricted from doing so. A public limited company must signal its status to all interested parties by having the words 'public limited company', or its abbreviation 'plc' in its name. For a private limited company, the word 'limited' or 'Ltd' must appear as part of its name.

Private limited companies tend to be smaller businesses where the ownership is divided among relatively few shareholders who are usually fairly close to one another – for example, a family company. Numerically, there are vastly more private limited companies in the UK than there are public ones. Of the total of 1.5 million UK limited companies, about 99 per cent are private limited companies and just one per cent are public limited companies.

Since the public ones tend to be individually larger, they probably represent a much more important group economically. Many private limited companies are no more than the vehicle through which businesses, which are little more than sole proprietorships, operate.

Taxation

Another consequence of the legal separation of the limited company from its owners is that companies must be accountable to the Inland Revenue for tax on their profits and gains. This introduces the effects of tax into the accounting statements of limited companies. The charge for tax is shown in the profit and loss account (income statement). The tax charge for a particular year is based on that year's profit. Since only 50 per cent of a company's tax liability is due for payment during the year concerned, the other 50 per cent will appear on the end-of-year balance sheet as a short-term liability. This will be illustrated a little later in the chapter. The tax position of companies contrasts with that of sole proprietorships and partnerships, where tax is levied not on the business but on the owner(s). Thus tax does not impact on the financial statements of unincorporated businesses, but is an individual matter between the owner(s) and the Inland Revenue.

 Companies are charged **corporation tax** on their profits and gains. The percentage rates of tax tend to vary from year to year, but have recently been in the low thirties for larger companies and in the low twenties for smaller companies. These rates of tax are levied on the company's taxable profit, which is not necessarily the same as the profit shown on the profit and loss account (income statement). This is because tax law does not, in every respect, follow the normal accounting rules. Generally, however, the taxable profit and the company's accounting profit are pretty close to one another.

Transferring share ownership – the role of the Stock Exchange

The point has already been made that shares in a company may be transferred from one owner to another. The desire of some shareholders to sell their shares, coupled with the desire of others to buy those shares, has led to the existence of a formal market in which shares can be bought and sold. The London Stock Exchange, and similar organisations around the world, provides a market place in which shares in public companies may be bought and sold. Share prices are determined by the laws of supply and demand, which are, in turn, determined by investors' perceptions of the future economic prospects of the companies concerned. Only the shares of certain companies (*listed* companies) may be traded on the London Stock Exchange. About 2,700 UK companies are listed. This represents only one in about 550 of all UK companies (public and private) and about one in six public limited companies. On the other hand, many of these 2,700 listed companies are massive. Nearly all of the 'household name' UK businesses (for example Tesco, Boots, BT, Cadbury-Schweppes, JD Wetherspoon and so on) are listed companies.

ACTIVITY 4.2

If, as has been pointed out earlier, the change in ownership of shares does not directly affect the particular company, why do many public companies actively seek to have their shares traded in a recognised market?

The main reason is that investors are generally very reluctant to pledge their money unless they can see some way in which they can turn their investment back into cash. In theory, the shares of a particular company may be very valuable because it has bright prospects, However, unless this value is capable of being realised in cash, the benefit to the shareholders is dubious. After all, we cannot spend shares; we generally need cash.

This means that potential shareholders are much more likely to be prepared to buy new shares from the company (thereby providing the company with new finance) where they can see a way of liquidating their investment (turning it into cash), as and when they wish. Stock exchanges provide the means of liquidation.

Though the buying and selling of 'second-hand' shares does not provide the company with cash, the fact that the buying and selling facility exists will make it easier for the company to raise new share capital when it needs to do so.

Managing a company – corporate governance and the role of directors

A limited company may have legal personality, but it is not a human being capable of making decisions and plans about the business and exercising control over it. People must undertake these management tasks. The most senior level of management of a company is the board of directors.

→ The shareholders elect **directors** (by law there must be at least one director) to manage the company on a day-to-day basis on behalf of those shareholders. In a small company, the board may be the only level of management and consist of all of the shareholders. In larger companies, the board may consist of ten or so directors out of many thousands of shareholders. Indeed, directors are not even required to be shareholders. Below the board of directors of the typical large company could be several layers of management comprising thousands of people.

→ In recent years, the issue of **corporate governance** has generated much debate. The term is used to describe the ways in which companies are directed and controlled. The issue of corporate governance is important because, in companies of any size, those who own the company (that is, the shareholders) are usually divorced from the day-to-day control of the business. The shareholders employ the directors to manage the company for them. Given this position, it may seem reasonable to assume that the best interests of shareholders will guide the directors' decisions. However, in practice this does not always occur. The directors may be more concerned with pursuing their own interests, such as increasing their pay and 'perks' (such as expensive motor cars, overseas visits and so on) and improving their job security and status. As a result, a conflict can occur between the interests of shareholders and the interests of directors.

Where directors pursue their own interests at the expense of the shareholders, there is clearly a problem for the shareholders. However, it may also be a problem for society as a whole. If shareholders feel their funds are likely to be mismanaged, they will be reluctant to invest. A shortage of funds will mean fewer investments can be made and the costs of funds will increase as businesses compete for what funds are available. Thus, a lack of concern for shareholders can have a profound effect on the performance of the economy. To avoid these problems, most competitive market economies have a framework of rules to help monitor and control the behaviour of directors.

These rules are usually based around three guiding principles:

● *Disclosure*. This lies at the heart of good corporate governance. An OECD report (see reference at end of chapter for details) summed up the benefits of disclosure as follows:

> Adequate and timely information about corporate performance enables investors to make informed buy-and-sell decisions and thereby helps the market reflect the value of a corporation under present management. If the market determines that present management is not performing, a decrease in stock [share] price will sanction management's failure and open the way to management change.

● *Accountability*. This involves defining the roles and duties of the directors and establishing an adequate monitoring process. In the UK, company law requires that directors of a business act in the best interests of shareholders. This means, among other things, that they must not try to use their position and knowledge to make gains at the expense of the shareholders. The law also requires larger companies to have their annual financial statements independently audited. The purpose of an independent audit is to lend credibility to the financial statements prepared by the directors.
● *Fairness*. Directors should not be able to benefit from access to 'inside' information that is not available to shareholders. As a result, both the law and the Stock Exchange place restrictions on the ability of directors to deal in the shares of the business. One example of these restrictions is that the directors cannot buy or sell shares immediately before the announcement of the final results of the business for a year or before the announcement of a significant event such as a planned merger or the loss of the chief executive.

Strengthening the framework of rules

The number of rules designed to safeguard shareholders has increased considerably over the years. This has been in response to weaknesses in corporate governance procedures, which have been exposed through well-publicised business failures and frauds, excessive pay increases to directors and evidence that some financial reports were being 'massaged' so as to mislead shareholders. However, some believe that the shareholders must shoulder some of the blame for any weaknesses. Not all shareholders in large companies are private individuals owning just a few shares each. In fact, 80 per cent, by market value, of the shares listed on the London Stock Exchange are owned by the investing 'institutions'. These include insurance businesses, pension funds and so on. These are often massive operations, owning large quantities of the shares of the companies in which they invest. The institutional investors employ specialist staff to manage their portfolios of shares in other companies. It is often argued that these large institutional shareholders, despite their size and relative expertise, are not very active in corporate governance matters. Thus there has been little monitoring of directors. However, things are changing.

The codes of practice
· ·

During the 1990s there was a real effort by the accountancy profession and the London Stock Exchange to address the problems mentioned above. A Code of Best Practice on Corporate Governance emerged in 1992. This was concerned with accountability and financial reporting. In 1995, a separate code of practice emerged. This dealt with directors' pay and conditions. These two codes were revised, 'fine tuned' and amalgamated to produce the **Combined Code**, which was issued in 1998.

The Combined Code was revised in 2003, following the recommendations of the Higgs Report. These recommendations were mainly concerned with the roles of the company chairman (senior director) and the other directors. It was particularly concerned with the role of 'non-executive' directors. These are directors who do not work full time in the company, but act solely in the role of director. This contrasts with 'executive' directors who are salaried employees. For example, the finance director of most large companies is a full-time employee. This person is a member of the board of directors and, as such, takes part in the key decision making at board level. At the same time, s/he is also responsible for managing the departments of the company that act on those board decisions as far as finance is concerned.

The view reflected in the 2003 Combined Code is that executive directors can become too embroiled in the day-to-day management of the company to be able to take a broad view. It also reflects the view that, for executive directors, conflicts can arise between their own interests and those of the shareholders. The advantage of non-executive directors can be that they are much more independent of the company than their executive colleagues. Non-executive directors are remunerated by the company for their work, but this would normally form only a small proportion of their total income. This gives them an independence that the executive directors may not have. Non-executive directors are often senior managers in other businesses or people who have had good experience of such roles.

Both the 1998 and 2003 Combined Codes received the backing of the London Stock Exchange. This means that companies listed on the London Stock Exchange are expected to comply with the requirements of the Code or must give their shareholders good reason why they do not. Failure to do one or other of these can lead to the company's shares being suspended from listing. This is an important sanction against non-compliant directors.

The Combined Code sets out a number principles relating to such matters as the role of the directors, their relations with shareholders, and their accountability. **Real World 4.3** outlines some of the more important of these.

REAL WORLD 4.3

The Combined Code

Some of the key elements of the Combined Code are as follows:

● Every listed company should have a board of directors to lead and control the company.
● There should be a clear division of responsibilities between the chairman and the chief executive officer of the company to ensure that a single person does not have unbridled power.

- There should be a balance between executive and non-executive (who are often part-time and independent) members of the board, to ensure that small groups of individuals cannot dominate proceedings.
- The board should receive timely information that is of sufficient quality to enable them to carry out their duties.
- Appointments to the board should be the subject of rigorous, formal and transparent procedures. All directors should submit themselves for re-election by the shareholders within a maximum period of three years.
- Boards should use the annual general meeting to communicate with private investors and encourage their participation.
- The board should publish a balanced and understandable assessment of the company's position and performance.
- Internal controls should be in place to protect the shareholders' wealth.
- The board should set up an audit committee of non-executive directors to oversee the internal controls and financial reporting principles that are being applied, and to liaise with the external auditors.

Strengthening the framework of rules has improved the quality of information available to shareholders, resulted in better checks on the powers of directors, and provided greater transparency in corporate affairs. However, rules can only be a partial answer. A balance must be struck between the need to protect shareholders and the need to encourage the entrepreneurial spirit of directors – which could be stifled under a welter of rules. This implies that rules should not be too tight and so unscrupulous directors may still find ways around them.

ACTIVITY 4.3

Can you think of ways in which the shareholders themselves may try to ensure that the directors act on their behalf?

Two ways are commonly used in practice:

- The shareholders may insist on monitoring closely the actions of the directors and the way in which they use the resources of the company.
- The shareholders may introduce incentive plans for directors that link their pay to the share performance of the company. In this way, the interests of the directors and shareholders will become more closely aligned.

Real World 4.4 shows an extract from the statement on corporate governance made by the directors of Kingfisher plc, the retail business that owns B&Q and Comet, in the UK, and a number of other chains in various European countries, particularly in France. Note how much emphasis is placed on the distinction between executive and non-executive directors in the membership of the various committees. The committees operated by Kingfisher are broadly as recommended by the Combined Code. The last committee mentioned by Kingfisher, the Share Option Committee, arises because many senior managers and directors are awarded bonuses in the form of 'share options'. These are, in effect, the right to buy shares at a price that may well be below their current Stock Exchange price. This is an area where directors of some companies have been criticised for being over-generous to themselves.

REAL WORLD 4.4

Corporate governance at Kingfisher

The following extract from the 2003 annual review of Kingfisher plc starts with a general statement that the directors have complied with the Combined Code during the year in question. It then goes on to detail how they complied in the specific context of board meetings and the establishment of committees to deal with sensitive issues.

Corporate governance – Combined Code statement

Kingfisher recognises the importance of, and is committed to, high standards of corporate governance. The principles of good governance adopted by the Group have been applied in the following way:

Main board

The Kingfisher Board currently comprises the Chairman, the Chief Executive, the Deputy Chairman, five other non-executive directors and four other executive directors.

Their biographies illustrate the directors' range of experience, which ensures an effective Board to lead and control the Group. All directors have access to the Company Secretary and may take independent professional advice at the Group's expense. Non-executive directors are appointed for an initial term of three years and each director receives appropriate training as necessary. Since April 2002 the Company has complied with the Combined Code requirement to have an identified senior independent director, namely John Nelson.

During the year ended 1 February 2003, the Board met on 24 occasions: 12 of these meetings were held principally to deal with regular business and the remaining 12 meetings were convened to approve the periodic trading statements or in connection with Castorama transaction. The Board has adopted a schedule of matters reserved for its decision and is primarily responsible for the strategic direction of the Group. All directors have full and timely access to information. The Board has successfully completed a further independent evaluation of the performance through the service provided by the Institute of Chartered Secretaries and Administrators. These evaluations, the first of which was undertaken in 2001, examine the operation of the Board in practice including its corporate governance and the operation and content of its meetings.

The Board has established six standing committees with defined terms of reference as follows:

● The Audit Committee is chaired by Phillip Bentley and includes three other independent non-executive directors. This committee is responsible for providing an independent oversight of the Group's systems of internal control and financial reporting processes. Each of our major operating businesses has its own audit committee, meetings of which are attended by both Kingfisher's Head of Internal Audit and the external auditors.

● The Nomination Committee is chaired by Francis Mackay and includes two other independent non-executive directors and the Chief Executive. The committee is responsible for the consideration and recommendation of the appointment of new directors. It met on one occasion during 2002 to consider the selection of the new Chief Executive and the two new non-executive directors. Specialist recruitment consultants were engaged to assist with this process.

● The Remuneration Committee is chaired by John Nelson and includes three other independent non-executive directors. The committee is responsible for advising the Board on the Company's executive remuneration policy and its costs, and for the application of this policy to the remuneration and benefits of executive directors and certain senior executives. The Remuneration Report contains a more detailed description of the Group's policy and procedures in relation to directors' and officers' remuneration.

● The Social Responsibility Committee is chaired by Margaret Salmon and includes the Chief Executive, three other executive directors and representative of the operating companies. The committee is responsible for discussing and developing a general policy relating to environmental, community and equal opportunities matters. The main Board director with overall responsibility for environmental matters is Gerry Murphy.

● The Finance Committee comprises the Chairman of the Board, the Chief Executive and two executive directors. The committee is responsible for the approval and authorisation of financing documents within its terms of reference and the authority limits laid down by the Board. On behalf of the Board, it reviews borrowing arrangements and other financial transactions, and makes appropriate recommendations. It also allots new shares in the Company to Group employees following the exercise of share options.

● The Share Option Committee comprises any two directors or any one director and the Company Secretary. Its role is to consider the Group's share funding policy in respect of share incentive awards and to decide upon the level of contributions of ESOP and QUEST in respect of the dilution cost when new shares are issued. The Committee also considers the making of loans to the ESOP in respect of grants that are hedged with existing shares. It has no authority in respect of the making of awards which is a matter reserved to the Remuneration Committee.

Source: Kingfisher plc Annual Review 2003.

Financing limited companies

Capital (owners'claim) of limited companies

The owner's claim of a sole proprietorship is normally encompassed in one figure on the balance sheet, usually labelled 'capital'. With companies, this is usually a little more complicated, though in essence the same broad principles apply. With a company, the owners' claim is divided between shares – for example, the original investment – on the one hand and **reserves** – that is, profits and gains subsequently made – on the other. There is also the possibility that there will be more than one type of shares and of reserves. Thus, within the basic divisions of share capital and reserves, there might well be further subdivisions. This might seem quite complicated, but we shall shortly consider the reasons for these subdivisions and all should become clearer. The sum of share capital and reserves is commonly known as **equity**.

The basic division

When a company is first formed, those who take steps to form it (the promoters) will decide how much needs to be raised by the potential shareholders to set the company up with the necessary assets to operate. Example 4.1 acts as a basis for illustration.

Example 4.1

Let us imagine that several people get together and decide to form a company to operate a particular business. They estimate that the company will need £50,000 to obtain the necessary assets to operate. Between them, they raise the cash which they use to buy shares in the company, on 31 March 2004, with a **nominal (or par) value** of £1 each.

At this point the balance sheet of the company would be thus:

Balance sheet as at 31 March 2004

	£
Net assets (all in cash)	50,000
Equity	
Share capital	
50,000 shares of £1 each	50,000

→ The company now buys the necessary non-current assets and stock-in-trade (inventories) and starts to trade. During the first year, the company makes a profit of £10,000. This, by definition, means that the owners' claim expands by £10,000. During the year, the shareholders (owners) make no drawings of their capital, so at the end of the year the summarised balance sheet looks like this:

Balance sheet as at 31 March 2005

	£
Net assets (various assets less liabilities)	60,000
Equity	
Share capital	
50,000 shares of £1 each	50,000
Reserves (revenue reserve)	10,000
	60,000

→ The profit is shown in a reserve, known as a **revenue reserve**, because it arises from generating revenue (making sales). Note that we do not simply merge the profit with the share capital: we must keep the two amounts separate (to satisfy company law). The reason for this is that there is a legal restriction on the maximum drawings of capital → (or payment of a **dividend**) that the owners can make. This is defined by the amount of revenue reserves, and so it is helpful to show these separately. We shall look at why there is this restriction, and how it works, a little later in the chapter.

Share capital

Shares represent the basic units of ownership of a business. All companies issue → **ordinary shares**. Ordinary shares are often known as *equities*. The nominal value of such shares is at the discretion of the people that start up the company. For example, if the initial capital is to be £50,000, this could be two shares of £25,000 each, 5 million shares of one penny each or any other combination that gives a total of £50,000. Each share must have equal value.

ACTIVITY 4.4

The initial capital requirement for a new company is £50,000. There are to be two equal shareholders. Would you advise them to issue two shares of £25,000 each? Why?

Such large denomination shares tend to be unwieldy. Suppose that one of the shareholders wanted to sell his or her shares. S/he would have to find one buyer. If there were shares of smaller denomination, it would be possible to sell part of the shareholding to various potential buyers. Furthermore, it would be possible to sell just part of the holding and retain a part.

In practice, £1 is the normal maximum nominal value for shares. Shares of 25 pence each and 50 pence each are probably the most common.
→ Some companies also issue other classes of shares, **preference shares** being the most common. Preference shares guarantee that *if a dividend is paid*, the preference shareholders

will be entitled to the first part of it up to a maximum value. This maximum is normally defined as a fixed percentage of the nominal value of the preference shares. If, for example, a company issues 10,000 preference shares of £1 each with a dividend rate of 6 per cent, this means that the preference shareholders are entitled to receive the first £600 (that is, 6 per cent of £10,000) of any dividend that is paid by the company for a year. The excess over £600 goes to the ordinary shareholders. Normally, any undistributed profits and gains accrue to the ordinary shareholders.

The ordinary shareholders are the primary risk-takers as they are entitled to share in the profits of the company only after other claims have been satisfied, and their potential rewards reflect this risk. There are no upper limits, however, on the amount by which they may benefit. The potential rewards available to ordinary shareholders reflect the risks that they are prepared to take. Since ordinary shareholders take most of the risks, power normally resides in their hands. Usually, only the ordinary shareholders are able to vote on issues that affect the company, such as who the directors should be.

It is open to the company to issue shares of various classes – perhaps with some having unusual and exotic conditions – but in practice it is rare to find other than straightforward ordinary and preference shares. Though a company may have different classes of shares whose holders have different rights, within each class all shares must be treated equally. The rights of the various classes of shareholders, as well as other matters relating to a particular company, are contained in that company's set of rules, known as the 'articles and memorandum of association'. A copy of these rules must be lodged with the Registrar of Companies, who makes it available for inspection by the general public.

Reserves

Reserves are profits and gains that have been made by a company and that still form part of the shareholders' (owners') claim or equity because they have not been paid out to the shareholders. Profits and gains tend to lead to assets flowing into the company. In Example 4.1 we came across one type of reserve, the revenue reserve. We should recall that this reserve represents the company's retained trading profits and gains on the disposal of non-current assets.

It is worth mentioning that retained profits represent overwhelmingly the largest source of new finance for UK companies – amounting for most companies to more than share issues and borrowings combined. These ploughed-back profits create most of a typical company's reserves. The shareholders' claim normally consists of share capital and reserves.

ACTIVITY 4.5

Are reserves amounts of cash? Can you think of a reason why this is an odd question?

To deal with the second point first, it is an odd question because reserves are a claim, or part of one, on the assets of the company, whereas cash is an asset. So reserves cannot be cash.

Reserves are classified as either revenue reserves or capital reserves. As we have already seen, revenue reserves arise from trading profit. They also arise from gains made on the disposal of non-current assets.

→ **Capital reserves** arise for two main reasons:

● issuing shares at above their nominal value (for example, issuing £1 shares at £1.50); and
● revaluing (upwards) non-current assets.

Where a company issues shares at above their nominal value, UK law requires that the excess of the issue price over the nominal value be shown separately.

ACTIVITY 4.6

Can you think why shares might be issued at above their nominal value? *Hint*: This would not usually happen when a company is first formed and the initial shares are being issued.

Once a company has traded and has been successful, the shares would normally be worth more than the nominal value at which they were issued. If additional shares are to be issued to new shareholders to raise finance for further expansion, unless they are issued at a value higher than the nominal value, the new shareholders will be gaining at the expense of the original ones.

Now let us consider another example.

Example 4.2

Based on future prospects, the net assets of a company are worth £1.5m. There are currently 1m ordinary shares in the company, each with a face (nominal) value of £1. The company wishes to raise an additional £0.6m of cash for expansion and has decided to raise it by issuing new shares. If the shares are issued for £1 each (that is 600,000 shares), the total number of shares will be:

$$1.0m + 0.6m = 1.6m$$

and their total value will be the value of the existing net assets plus the new injection of cash:

$$£1.5m + £0.6m = £2.1m$$

This means that the value of each share after the new issue will be:

$$£2.1m/1.6m = £1.3125$$

The current value of each share is:

$$£1.5m/1.0m = £1.50$$

So the original shareholders will lose:

$$£1.50 - £1.3125 = £0.1875 \text{ a share}$$

and the new shareholders will have gained

$$£1.3125 - £1.0 = £0.3125 \text{ a share}$$

The new shareholders will, no doubt, be delighted with this outcome; the original ones will not.

Things could be made fair between the two sets of shareholders described in Example 4.2 by issuing the new shares at £1.50 each. In this case it would be necessary to issue 400,000 shares to raise the necessary £0.6m. £1 a share of the £1.50 is the nominal value and will be included with share capital in the balance sheet (£400,000 in total). The remaining £0.50 is a share premium, which will be shown as a capital reserve known as the **share premium account** (£200,000 in total).

It is not clear why UK company law insists on the distinction between nominal share values and the premium. Certainly, other countries (for example, the United States) with a similar set of laws governing the corporate sector do not see the necessity of distinguishing between share capital and share premium. Instead, the total value at which shares are issued is shown as one comprehensive figure on the company balance sheet.

Real World 4.5 shows the capital of one well-known business.

REAL WORLD 4.5

How Tesco is funded

Tesco plc, the UK and international supermarket business, had the following share capital and reserves as at 22 February 2003:

	£m
Share capital (5p ordinary shares)	362
Share premium account	2,465
Other reserves (capital)	40
Profit and loss account (income statement)	3,649
	6,516

Tesco is typical of many companies that refer to their retained profit as 'profit and loss account'.

Note how the nominal share capital is tiny compared with the share premium account figure. This implies that Tesco has issued shares at much higher prices than the 5p per share nominal value. This reflects Tesco's trading success since the company was first formed. Note also how, at balance sheet values, retained profit makes up more than half of the total for share capital and reserves.

Source: Tesco plc Annual Report and Financial Statements 2003.

Altering the nominal value of shares

The point has already been made that the promoters of a new company may make their own choice of the nominal or par value of the shares. This value need not be permanent. At a later date the shareholders can decide to change it.

For example, a company has at issue 1 million ordinary shares of £1 each. A decision is made to change the nominal value of the shares from £1 to £0.50, in other words to halve the value. As a result, the company would issue each shareholder with a new share certificate (the shareholders' evidence of ownership of their shareholding) for exactly twice as many shares, each with half the nominal value. This would leave each shareholder with a holding of the same total nominal value. This process is known, not surprisingly, as splitting the shares. The opposite, reducing the number of shares and increasing their nominal value per share to compensate, is known as **consolidating**.

Since each shareholder would be left, after a split or consolidation, with exactly the same proportion of ownership of the company's assets as before, the process should not increase the value of the total shares held.

ACTIVITY 4.7

Why might the shareholders want to split their shares in the manner described above?

The answer is probably to avoid individual shares becoming too valuable and making them a bit unwieldy, in the way discussed in the answer to Activity 4.4. If a company trades successfully, the value of each share is likely to rise, and in time could increase to a level that is considered unwieldy. Splitting would solve this problem.

Real World 4.6 gives an example of a share split by a well-known UK company.

REAL WORLD 4.6

Share split at Enterprise Inns

In January 2004, Enterprise Inns plc split its ordinary shares' nominal value of 10p per share to 5p per share. This meant that each ordinary shareholder became the owner of twice as many new shares, with each share having a market value of one half of each of the old ones. The reason given by the company was that it would increase the liquidity of the shares.
    Enterprise Inns plc is the UK's second largest operator of pubs.

Bonus shares

It is always open to a company to take reserves of any kind (capital or revenue) and turn them into share capital. This will involve transferring the desired amount from the reserve concerned to share capital and then distributing the appropriate number of new shares to the existing shareholders. New shares arising from such a conversion are known as **bonus shares**. Issues of bonus shares are quite frequently encountered in practice. Example 4.3 illustrates this aspect of share issues.

Example 4.3

The summary balance sheet of a company is as follows:

Balance sheet as at 31 March 2005

	£
Net assets (various assets less liabilities)	128,000
Equity	
Share capital	
50,000 shares of £1 each	50,000
Reserves	78,000
	128,000

The company decides that it will issue to existing shareholders one new share for every share owned by each shareholder. The balance sheet immediately following this will appear as follows:

Balance sheet as at 31 March 2005

	£
Net assets (various assets less liabilities)	128,000
Equity	
Share capital	
100,000 shares of £1 each (50,000 + 50,000)	100,000
Reserves (78,000 − 50,000)	28,000
	128,000

We can see that the reserves have decreased by £50,000 and share capital has increased by the same amount. Share certificates for the 50,000 ordinary shares of £1 each, that have been created from reserves, will be issued to the existing shareholders to complete the transaction.

ACTIVITY 4.8

A shareholder of the company in Example 4.3 owned 100 shares before the bonus issue. How will things change for this shareholder as regards the number of shares owned and the value of the shareholding?

The answer should be that the number of shares will double, from 100 to 200. Now the shareholder owns one five-hundredth of the company (that is, 200/100,000). Before the bonus issue, the shareholder also owned one five-hundredth of the company (that is, 100/50,000). The company's assets and liabilities have not changed as a result of the bonus issue and so, logically, one five-hundredth of the value of the company should be identical to what it was before. Thus each share is worth half as much.

A bonus issue simply takes one part of the owners' claim (part of a reserve) and puts it into another part of the owners' claim (share capital). The transaction has no effect on the company's assets or liabilities, so there is no effect on shareholders' wealth.

Note that a bonus issue is not the same as a share split. A split does not affect the reserves.

ACTIVITY 4.9

Can you think of any reasons why a company might want to make a bonus issue if it has no economic consequence?

We think that there are three possible reasons:

● *Share price.* To lower the value of each share without reducing the shareholders' collective or individual wealth. This is the same effect as splitting and may be seen as an alternative to splitting.
● *Shareholder confidence.* To provide the shareholders with a 'feel-good factor'. It is believed that shareholders like bonus issues because it seems to make them better off, though in practice it should not affect their wealth.

→

Activity 4.9 continued

- *Lender confidence.* Where reserves arising from operating profits and/or realised gains on the sale of non-current assets are used to make the bonus issue, it has the effect of taking part of that portion of the owners' claim that could be drawn by the share-holders, as drawings (or dividends), and locking it up. The amount transferred becomes part of the permanent capital base of the company. (We shall see, a little later in this chapter, that there are severe restrictions on the extent to which shareholders may make drawings from their capital.) An individual or organisation contemplating lending money to the company may insist that the dividend payment possibilities are restricted as a condition of making the loan. This point will be explained shortly.

Real World 4.7 is an example of a bonus share issue by a well-known UK retailer.

REAL WORLD 4.7

Bonus on the cards

In October 2003, Clinton Cards plc announced a one-for-two bonus issue. The company said that the objective of this was to increase the liquidity/marketability of the shares, by reducing the market price per share. This is the first of the three reasons mentioned above for making bonus issues. The company's share price had increased strongly on the back of strong past, and expected future, profit growth.

Clinton Cards plc is the UK's largest specialist greetings card retailer.

Source: Based on information in FT Money – Markets week world: Clinton Cards, *Financial Times*, 4 October 2003, FT.com.

Share capital – some expressions used in company law

Before leaving our detailed discussion of share capital, it might be helpful to clarify some of the jargon relating to shares that is used in company financial statements.

When a company is first formed, the shareholders give the directors an upper limit on the amount of nominal value of the shares that can be issued. This is known as the **authorised share capital**. This value can easily be revised upwards, but only if the shareholders agree. That part of the authorised share capital that has been issued to shareholders is known as the **issued** (or **allotted**) **share capital**.

Sometimes, but not very often, a company may not require shareholders to pay the whole amount that is due to be paid for the shares at the time of issue. This may happen where the company does not need the money all at once. Some money would normally be paid at the time of issue and the company would 'call' for further instalments until the shares were **fully paid**. That part of the total issue price that has been 'called' is known as the **called-up share capital**. That part that has been called and paid is known as the **paid-up share capital**.

Real World 4.8 shows the share capital of a well-known UK business.

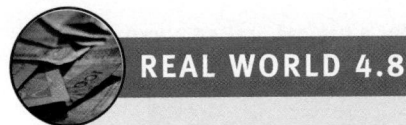

REAL WORLD 4.8

Glass maker's capital

The following extract shows the called up share capital section of the balance sheet of Pilkington plc as at 31 March 2003. Pilkington is a major UK glass manufacturer. Note that the company has just one class of share.

	2003
Share capital	£m
Authorised: 1,670,000,000 (2002 – 1,500,000,000) ordinary 50p shares	835
Allotted, called up and paid: 1,260,220,500 (2002 – 1,253,801,444) ordinary 50p shares	630

Source: Pilkington plc Annual Report, 2003.

Raising share capital

Once the company has made its initial share issue to start business, usually soon after the company is first formed, it may decide to make further issues of new shares. These may be:

- Rights issues, that is issues made to existing shareholders, in proportion to their existing shareholding.
- Public issues, that is issues made to the general investing public.
- Private placings, that is issues made to selected individuals who are usually approached and asked if they would be interested in taking up new shares.

During its lifetime a company may use all three of these approaches to raising funds through issuing new shares (although only public companies can make appeals to the general public). These approaches will be discussed in detail in Chapter 15.

Loans and other sources of finance

Many companies borrow money to supplement that raised from share issues and ploughed-back profits. Company borrowing is often on a long-term basis, perhaps on a ten-year contract. Lenders may be banks and other professional providers of loan finance. Many companies raise loan finance in such a way that small investors, including private individuals, are able to lend small amounts. This is particularly the case with the larger, Stock-Exchange-listed, companies and involves their making a **loan stock** or **debenture** issue, which, though large in total, can be taken up in small slices by individual investors, both private individuals and investing institutions, such as pension funds and insurance companies. In some cases, these slices of loans can be bought and sold through the Stock Exchange. This means that investors do not have to wait the full term of the loan to obtain repayment, but can sell their slice of the loan to another would-be lender at intermediate points in the term of the loan.

Some of the features of loan-stock financing, particularly the possibility that the loan stock may be traded on the Stock Exchange, can lead to a confusion that loan stock are shares by another name. We should be clear that this is not the case. It is the

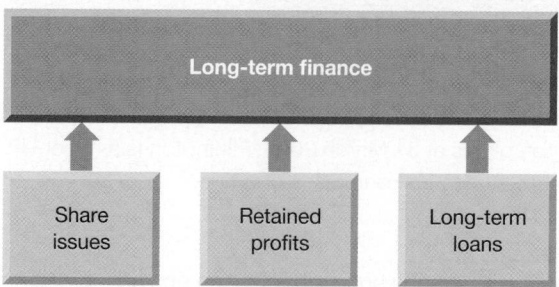

Figure 4.1 **Sources of long-term finance for a typical limited company**

Companies derive their long-term financing needs from three sources: new share issues, retained profit and long-term borrowings. For a typical company, the sum of the first two (jointly known as 'equity finance') exceeds the third. Retained profit usually exceeds either of the other two in terms of the amount of finance raised in most years.

shareholders who own the company and, therefore, who share in its losses and profits. Loan stockholders lend money to the company under a legally binding contract that normally specifies the rate of interest, the interest payment dates and the date of repayment of the loan itself. Usually, long-term loans are secured on assets of the company.

Long-term financing of companies can be depicted as in Figure 4.1.

Companies may also borrow finance on a short-term basis, perhaps from a bank as an overdraft. Most companies buy goods and services on a month or two's credit, as is normal in business-to-business transactions. This is, in effect, an interest-free loan.

It is important to the prosperity and stability of a company that it strikes a suitable balance between finance provided by the shareholders (equity) and loan financing. This topic will be explored in Chapter 7.

Real World 4.9 shows the long-term borrowings of Rolls-Royce plc, the engine-building business, at 31 December 2002. Note the large number of sources from which the company borrows. This is typical of most large companies and probably reflects a desire to exploit all available means of raising finance, each of which may have some advantages and disadvantages. 'Secured' in this context means that the lender would have the right, should Rolls-Royce fail to meet its interest and/or capital repayment obligations, to seize a specified asset of the business (probably some land) and use it to raise the sums involved. Normally, a lender would accept a lower rate of interest where the loan is secured in this way as there is less risk involved. It should be said that whether a loan to a company like Rolls-Royce is secured or unsecured is usually pretty academic. It is unlikely that such a large and profitable company would fail to meet its obligations.

'Finance leases' are, in effect, arrangements where Rolls-Royce needs the use of a non-current asset (such as an item of machinery) and, instead of buying the asset itself, it arranges for a financier to buy the asset. The financier then leases it to the business, probably for the entire economic life of the asset. Though legally it is the financier who owns the asset, from an accounting point of view the essence of the arrangement is that, in effect, Rolls-Royce has borrowed cash from the financier to buy the asset. Thus, the asset appears among the business's non-current assets and the financial obligation to the financier is shown here as a long-term loan. This is a good example of how accounting tries to report the economic *substance* of a transaction, rather than its strict legal *form*. Finance leasing is a fairly popular means of raising long-term funds.

Chapter 15 goes into more detail on the important factors that a business must consider in the context of how to finance its operations.

REAL WORLD 4.9

Borrowing at Rolls-Royce

The following extract from the annual financial statements of Rolls-Royce plc sets out the sources of the company's long-term borrowing as at 31 December 2002.

	2002 £m
Unsecured	
Bank loans	213
4$\frac{1}{2}$% Notes 2005	177
6$\frac{3}{8}$% Notes 2007	310
7$\frac{3}{8}$% Notes 2016	200
Other loans 2009 (interest rates nil)	4
Secured	
Bank loans	14
Obligations under finance leases payable:	
Between one and two years	7
Between two and five years	70
Zero-coupon bonds 2005/2007 (including 9.0% interest accretion)	43
	1,038
Repayable	
Between one and two years – by instalments	92
– otherwise	59
Between two and five years – by instalments	121
– otherwise	546
After five years – by instalments	20
– otherwise	200
	1,038

Source: Rolls-Royce plc Annual Financial Statements, 2002.

Restriction on the right of shareholders to make drawings of capital

Limited companies are required by law to distinguish between that part of their capital (shareholders' claim) or equity which may be withdrawn by the shareholders and that part which may not. The withdrawable part is that which has arisen from trading profits and from realised profits on the disposal of non-current assets (to the extent that tax payments on these profits and gains, as well as previous drawings, have not extinguished this part of the capital). This withdrawable element of the capital is *revenue reserves*.

The non-withdrawable part normally consists of that which has arisen from funds injected by shareholders buying shares in the company and that which came from upward revaluations of company assets that still remain in the company – that is, *share capital and capital reserves*.

The law does not specify how large the non-withdrawable part of a particular company's capital should be, but simply that anyone dealing with the company should be

ACTIVITY 4.10

Can you think of the reason why limited companies are required to distinguish different parts of their capital, whereas sole proprietorship businesses are not required to do so?

The reason for this situation is the limited liability, which company shareholders enjoy but which owners of unincorporated businesses do not. If a sole proprietor withdraws all of the owner's claim, or even an amount in excess of this, the position of the creditors of the business is not weakened since they can legally enforce their claims against the sole proprietor as an individual. With a limited company, where the business and the owners are legally separated, such a legal right to enforce claims against individuals does not exist. To protect the company's creditors, however, the law insists that a specific part of the company's capital cannot legally be withdrawn by the shareholders.

able to tell from looking at the company's balance sheet how large it is. In the light of this, a particular prospective lender, or supplier of goods or services on credit, can make a commercial judgement as to whether to deal with the company or not. The larger it is, however, the easier the company is likely to find it to persuade potential lenders to lend and suppliers to supply goods and services on credit.

Let us now look at another example.

Example 4.4

The summary balance sheet of a company at a particular date is as follows:

Balance sheet

	£
Total assets less current liabilities	43,000
Equity	
Share capital	
20,000 shares of £1 each	20,000
Reserves (revenue)	23,000
	43,000

A bank has been asked to make a £25,000 long-term loan to the company. If the loan were to be made, the balance sheet immediately following would appear as follows:

Balance sheet (after the loan)

	£
Total assets less current liabilities (£43,000 + £25,000)	68,000
Less Non-current liability	
Long-term loan	25,000
	43,000
Equity	
Share capital	
20,000 shares of £1 each	20,000
Reserves (revenue)	23,000
	43,000

As things stand, there are total assets less current liabilities to a total balance sheet value of £68,000 to meet the bank's claim of £25,000. It would be possible and perfectly legal, however, for the company to pay a dividend (withdraw capital) of £23,000. The balance sheet would then appear as follows:

Balance sheet

	£
Total assets *less* current liabilities (£68,000 – £23,000)	45,000
Less Non-current liabilities	
Long-term loan	25,000
	20,000
Equity	
Share capital	
20,000 shares of £1 each	20,000
Reserves (revenue (£23,000 – £23,000))	–
	20,000

This leaves the bank in a very much weaker position, in that there are now total assets less current liabilities with a balance sheet value of £45,000 to meet a claim of £25,000. Note that the difference between the amount of the bank loan and the total assets less current liabilities always equals the capital and reserves total. Thus, the capital and reserves represent a **margin of safety** for creditors. The larger the amount of the owners' claim withdrawable by the shareholders, the smaller is the potential margin of safety for creditors.

As we have already seen, company law says nothing about how large the margin of safety must be. It is up the company concerned to do what is desirable.

Perhaps it is worth noting, as a practical footnote to Example 4.4, that most potential long-term lenders would seek to have the loan secured against a particular asset of the company, particularly an asset such as freehold property. This, as we have seen, would give the lender the right to seize the asset concerned, sell it and satisfy the repayment obligation, should the company default.

ACTIVITY 4.11

Would you expect a company to pay all of its revenue reserves as a dividend? What factors might be involved with a dividend decision?

It would be rare for a company to pay all of its revenue reserves as a dividend: a legal right to do so does not necessarily make it a good idea. Most companies see ploughed-back profits as a major – usually *the* major – source of new finance.

The factors that influence the dividend decision are likely to include:

● the availability of cash to pay a dividend. It would not be illegal to borrow to pay a dividend, but it would be unusual and, possibly, imprudent;
● the needs of the business for finance for new investment; and
● the expectations of shareholders concerning the amount of dividends to be paid.

You might have thought of others.

The law is adamant, however, that it is illegal, under normal circumstances, for shareholders to withdraw that part of their claim that is represented by shares and capital reserves. This means that potential creditors of the company know the maximum amount of the shareholders' claim that can be drawn by the shareholders. Figure 4.2 shows the important division between that part of the shareholders' claim that can be withdrawn as a dividend and that part that cannot.

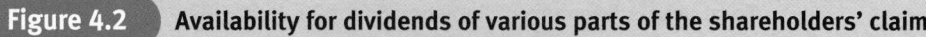

Figure 4.2 **Availability for dividends of various parts of the shareholders' claim**

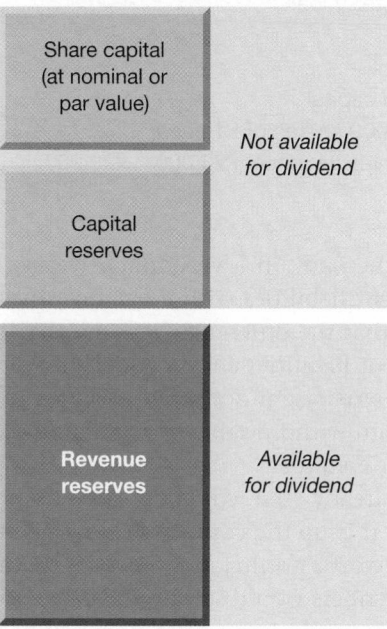

Total equity finance of limited companies consists of share capital, capital reserves and revenue reserves. Only the revenue reserves (which arise from realised profits and gains) can be used to fund a dividend. In other words, the maximum legal dividend is the amount of the revenue reserves.

Earlier in this chapter, the point was made that a potential creditor may insist that some revenue reserves are converted to bonus shares (or capitalised) to increase the margin of safety as a condition of granting the loan.

If we refer back to Real World 4.5, we can see that Tesco plc could legally have paid a dividend of £3,649m on 22 February 2003, which is the amount of its revenue reserves. For several reasons, including the fact that this represented over half of the balance sheet value of the company's net assets, no such dividend was paid.

ACTIVITY 4.12

Can you think of any circumstances where the non-withdrawable part of a company's capital could be reduced, without contravening the law?

It can be reduced, but only as a result of the company sustaining trading losses, or losses on disposal of non-current assets, that exceed the amount of the withdrawable portion of the company's capital. It cannot be reduced by shareholders making drawings.

Drawings are usually made in the form of a dividend paid by the company to the shareholders, in proportion to the number of shares owned by each one.

Accounting for limited companies

The main financial statements

As we might expect, the financial statements of a limited company are, in essence, identical to those of a sole proprietor. There are, however, some differences of detail, and we shall now consider these. Example 4.5 sets out are the profit and loss account (income statement) and balance sheet of a limited company:

Example 4.5

Da Silva plc
Profit and loss account for the year ended 31 December 2005

	£m	£m
Revenue		840
Less Cost of sales		520
Gross profit		320
Less Operating expenses		
Wages and salaries	98	
Heat and light	18	
Rent and rates	24	
Motor-vehicle expenses	20	
Insurance	4	
Printing and stationery	12	
Depreciation	45	
Audit fee	4	
		225
Operating profit		95
Less Interest payable		10
Profit before tax		85
Tax on profit		24
Profit after tax		61
Less: Transfer to general reserve	20	
Dividend paid	25	
		45
Unappropriated profit carried forward		16

Balance sheet as at 31 December 2005

	£m	£m
Non-current assets		
Property, plant and equipment		303
Current assets		
Stock (inventories)	65	
Trade debtors (receivables)	112	
Cash	36	
	213	
Less Current liabilities		
Trade creditors (payables)	99	
Corporation tax	12	
	111	
Net current assets (working capital)		102
Total assets less current liabilities		405
Less Non-current liabilities		
10% debentures		100
Net assets		305
Equity		
Share capital		
Ordinary shares of £0.50 each		200
Reserves		
Share premium account	30	
General reserve	50	
Profit and loss account	25	
		105
		305

Perhaps the most striking thing about these statements is the extent to which they look exactly the same as those that we have been used to with sole proprietors. This is correct; the differences are small. Let us go through and pick up these differences.

The profit and loss account (income statement)

There are several features in the profit and loss account that need consideration.

Profit

We can see that, following the calculation of gross profit, four further measures of profit are shown.

- The first of these is **operating profit**. This represents the profit achieved for the year before any financing expenses are taken into account. By excluding the financing expenses from the calculation of profit, a better idea of the operating performance for the year may be achieved.
- The second measure of profit is the net profit for the year (profit before tax). Interest charges are deducted from the operating profit to derive this figure. This measure is already familiar to us, and in the case of a sole proprietor business, the profit and loss account (income statement) would end here.
- The third measure of profit is the net profit after tax. As the company is a separate legal entity, it is liable to pay tax (known as corporation tax) on the profits generated. (This contrasts with the sole proprietor business where it is the owner rather than

the business that is liable for the tax on profits, as we saw earlier in the chapter.) This measure of profit represents the amount that is available for the shareholders.

- The final measure of profit is the unappropriated, or retained, profit for the year. We can see that most of the net profit after tax is appropriated, or allocated, to pay a dividend and to transfer to a general reserve (see below). Once these appropriations have been made we are left with the fourth measure of profit, which represents the unallocated profits. It is probably worth pointing out that the last part of the profit and loss account (income statement) dealing with appropriations for taxation, dividends and transfers to reserves is known as the 'appropriation account'.

Audit fee

As we shall see in Chapter 5, companies greater than a particular size are required to have their financial statements audited by an independent firm of auditors, for which a fee is charged. Though it is also open to sole proprietors to have their financial statements audited, very few do, so this is an expense that will normally be present in the profit and loss account of a company but not that of a sole proprietor.

Dividend

This represents the drawings of capital by the shareholders of the company. Only those dividends paid during the year and those approved by the shareholders before the year end, whether paid or not, appear in the profit and loss account. Sometimes shareholders receive a dividend before the end of the year. Companies may pay their shareholders an 'interim' dividend, part way through the year, and a 'final' dividend shortly after the year end. Had a dividend been approved before the year end, but was not yet paid at the year end, it would appear on the balance sheet as a current liability. Where a dividend has been recommended by the directors, but not approved by the shareholders, it should be mentioned in a note to the financial statements.

Transfer to general reserve

After dividends have been deducted from the net profit after tax figure, the remaining profit is normally reinvested ('ploughed back') into the operations of the company. For this company, the amount reinvested is £36 million (that is, £61 million less £25 million). This amount could all have been unallocated and simply gone to increase the unappropriated profit figure. We can see, however, that an amount (£20 million for this company) has been transferred to a separate general reserve, which is quite common in practice.

It is not entirely clear why directors decide to make transfers to general reserves, since the funds concerned remain part of the revenue reserves, and are, therefore, still available for dividend. The most plausible explanation seems to be that directors feel that taking amounts out of the profit and loss account and placing them in a 'reserve' indicates an intention to retain the funds permanently in the company and not to use them to pay a dividend. Of course, the unappropriated profit is also a reserve, but that fact is not indicated in its title.

The balance sheet

The main points for consideration in the balance sheet are:

- *Corporation tax*. The amount that appears as part of the short-term liabilities represents 50 per cent of the tax on the profit for the year 2005. It is, therefore, 50 per cent of the charge that appears in the profit and loss account; the other 50 per cent will already have been paid. The unpaid 50 per cent will be paid shortly after the balance sheet date. These payment dates are set down by law.

● *Equity*. We have already discussed this area earlier in the chapter. The general reserve balance must have stood at £30 million before the year end as it was increased to its final level of £50 million by the transfer of £20 million of the year 2005 profit. Similarly, the profit and loss account balance must have been £9 million, just before the year end. As was mentioned above, the general reserve and the profit and loss account balance are identical in all respects; they both arise from retained profits, and are both available for dividend.

Accounting for groups of companies

Most large businesses, including nearly all of the well known ones, operate not as a single company but as a group of companies. In these circumstances, one company (the **parent** or **holding company**) owns sufficient of the shares of various subsidiary companies to control them. In the case of many larger businesses, there are numerous subsidiary companies. Each of the subsidiaries operates some aspect of the group's activities. The reasons why many businesses operate in the form of groups include:

● A desire for each part of the business to have its own limited liability, so that financial problems in one part of a business cannot have an adverse effect on other parts.
● An attempt to make each part of the business have some sense of independence and autonomy and, perhaps, to create or perpetuate a market image of a smaller independent business.

From an accounting point of view, each company prepares its own independent annual financial statements. Company law also requires that the parent company of the group prepares **consolidated** or **group financial statements**. These group financial statements amalgamate the financial statements of all of the group members. Thus, for example, the group profit and loss account includes the total revenue figure for all group companies and the balance sheet includes the stock in trade (inventory) figure for all group members added together. As we might expect, the group financial statements would look exactly like the financial statements of the parent company had it owned and operated all of the assets of the business directly, instead of through subsidiary companies.

From what has just been said, if we look at a set of group financial statements, we might not be able to say whether the business operates through a single company or through a large number of subsidiaries. Only by referring to the heading at the top of each statement, which would mention the word 'consolidated' or 'group', might we know. In some cases, however, there might be one or two items in the group financial statements that tend to occur only there. These items are:

● *Goodwill arising on consolidation*. This occurs when a parent acquires a subsidiary from previous owners and pays more for the subsidiary than the values of the individual assets, net of liabilities, of the new subsidiary than they appear to be worth. This excess might represent such things as the value of a good reputation that the new subsidiary already has in the market, or the value of it having a loyal and skilled workforce.

    Goodwill arising on consolidation will appear as an intangible non-current asset on the group balance sheet.

● *Minority or outsiders' interests.* One of the principles followed when preparing group financial statements is that all of the revenue, expenses, assets, liabilities and cash flows of each subsidiary are reflected to their full extent in the group financial statements. This is true whether or not the parent owns all of the shares in each subsidiary, provided that the parent has control. Control normally means owning more than 50 per cent of the subsidiary's ordinary shares. Where not all of the shares are owned by the parent, this fact is reflected in the group balance sheet in that the investment of those shareholders in the subsidiary other than the parent company appears as part of the owners' claim (share capital and reserves). This indicates that the net assets of the group are being financed mainly by the parent company's shareholders, but that 'outside' shareholders finance a part of them. Similarly, the group profit and loss account reflects the fact that not all of the net profit of the group is attributable to the shareholders of the parent company; a part of it is attributable to the 'outside' shareholders.

Example 4.6 shows how the balance sheet of Major plc and its subsidiary is drawn up. Note that the group balance sheet closely resembles that of an individual company.

Example 4.6

Major plc has just bought, from the previous shareholders, 45m (out of 60m) ordinary shares in Minor plc, paying £75m for them. The other 15m Minor plc shares are owned by other shareholders. These shareholders are now referred to by Major plc as the 'minority'. Minor plc is thus now a subsidiary of Major plc and, as is clear from Major plc's balance sheet, the latter's only subsiduary company.

 The balance sheets of the two companies immediately following the **takeover** of Minor plc by Major plc were as follows:

	Major plc		Minor plc	
	£m	£m	£m	£m
Non-current assets				
Property, plant and equipment		63		67
Intangible – 45 million shares in Minor plc		75		–
		138		67
Current assets				
Stock (inventories)	37		21	
Trade debtors (receivables)	22		12	
Cash	16		2	
	75		35	
Current liabilities				
Trade creditors (payables)	(18)		(9)	
		57		26
		195		93
Non-current liabilities				
Loan stocks		(35)		(13)
		160		80
Equity				
Ordinary shares of £1 each		100		60
Reserves		60		20
		160		80

As would be normal practice, the balance sheet of the subsidiary (Minor plc) has been revised so that the values of the individual assets is based on *fair values*, rather than what Minor plc originally paid for them. Fair values are those that would be agreed as the selling price between a buyer and a seller, both of whom are knowledgeable and willing. In this particuar context, they probably equate to the values that Major plc would have placed on the individual tangible assets when assessing Minor plc's value.

If a balance sheet were to be drawn up immediately following the takeover, it would be as follows:

	Major plc and its subsidiary	
	£m	£m
Non-current assets		
Property, plant and equipment (63 + 67)		130
Intangible – goodwill (75 − ($^{45}/_{60}$ × 80))		15
		145
Current assets		
Stock (37 + 21)	58	
Trade debtors (22 + 12)	34	
Cash (16 + 2)	18	
	110	
Current liabilities		
Trade creditors (18 + 9)	(27)	
		83
		228
Non-current liabilities		
Loan stocks (35 + 13)		(48)
		180
Equity		
Ordinary shares of £1 each		100
Reserves		60
		160
Minority interests ($^{15}/_{60}$ × 80)		20
		180

Note that all of the items, except two, in the group balance sheet are simply the two figures for the item concerned added together. This is despite the fact that Major plc only owns three-quarters of the shares of Minor plc. The logic of group financial statements is that if the parent owns enough shares to control its subsidiary, all of the subsidiary's assets and claims should be reflected on the group balance sheet.

As we have seen, there are two exceptions to this approach: goodwill and minority interests.

Goodwill is simply the excess of what Major paid for the shares over their fair value, based on tangible assets. Major plc bought 45 million of 60 million shares, paying £75 million. According to Minor plc's balance sheet, this was net assets (non-current and current assets, less current and non-current liabilities) of £80 million. So Major plc paid £75 million for £60 million (that is, $^{45}/_{60}$ × £80m) of net assets – an excess of £15 million usually referred to as 'goodwill arising on consolidation'. This asset is seen as being the value of a loyal workforce, a regular and profitable customer base and so on, that a new business setting up would not have. The appropriate International Financial Reporting Standard (IFRS 23) asserts that the value of this goodwill needs to be revalued at the end of each accounting year. If its value has been impaired, it must written down to the lower value.

Minority interests take account of the fact that, although Major plc may control all of the assets and liabilities of Minor plc, it only provides the equity finance for three-quarters of them. The other quarter, £20 million (that is, $^{15}/_{60} \times £80m$), is still provided by shareholders in Minor plc, other than Major plc.

Example 4.7 shows the profit and loss account of Major plc and its subsidiary (Minor plc) for the first year following the takeover. As with the balance sheet, the various revenue and expense figures are simply the individual figures for each company added together. The minority interest figure (£2m) represents $^{15}/_{60} \times$ the after-tax profit of Minor plc.

Example 4.7

Profit and loss account of Major plc and its subsidiary

	£m	£m
Revenue		123
Cost of sales		(56)
Gross profit		67
Administration expenses	(28)	
Distribution expenses	(9)	(37)
Profit before tax		30
Taxation		(12)
Profit after tax		18
Attributable to minorities		(2)
Profit after tax attributable to Major plc shareholders		16
Profit and loss account balance brought forward from previous year		37
		53
Dividend paid on ordinary shares		(6)
Profit and loss account balance carried forward to following year		47

SELF-ASSESSMENT QUESTION   4.1

The summarised balance sheet of Dev Ltd is as follows:

Balance sheet as at 31 December 2005

	£
Net assets (various assets less liabilities)	235,000
Equity	
Share capital: 100,000 shares of £1 each	100,000
Share premium account	30,000
Revaluation reserve	37,000
Profit and loss account balance	68,000
	235,000

→

Self-assessment question 4.1 continued

Required:

(a) Without any other transactions occurring at the same time, the company made a one-for-five rights share issue at £2 per share payable in cash. This means that each shareholder was offered one share for every five already held. All shareholders took up their rights. Immediately afterwards, the company made a one-for-two bonus issue. Show the balance sheet immediately following the bonus issue, assuming that the directors wanted to retain the maximum dividend payment potential for the future.

(b) Explain what external influence might cause the directors to choose not to retain the maximum dividend payment possibilities.

(c) Show the balance sheet immediately following the bonus issue, assuming that the directors wanted to retain the *minimum* dividend payment potential for the future.

(d) What is the maximum dividend that could be paid before and after the events described in (a) if the minimum dividend payment potential is achieved?

(e) Lee owns 100 shares in Dev Ltd before the events described in (a). Assuming that the net assets of the company have a value equal to their balance sheet value, show how these events will affect Lee's wealth.

(f) Looking at the original balance sheet of Dev Ltd, shown above, what four things do we know about the company's status and history that are not specifically stated on the balance sheet?

SUMMARY

The main points of this chapter may be summarised as follows:

The main features of a limited company

- It is an artificial person that has been created by law.
- It has a separate life to its owners and is granted a perpetual existence.
- It must take responsibility for its own debts and losses but its owners are granted limited liability.
- A public company can offer its shares for sale to the public; a private company cannot.
- It is governed by a board of directors, which is elected by the shareholders.
- Corporate governance is a major issue, various scandals have led to the emergence of the Combined Code.

Financing the limited company

- The share capital of a company can be of two main types – ordinary shares and preference shares.
- Ordinary shares (equities) are the main risk-takers and are given voting rights; they form the backbone of the company.
- Preference shares are given a right to a fixed dividend before ordinary shareholders receive a dividend.
- Reserves are profits and gains made by the company and form part of the ordinary shareholders' claim.
- Loan capital provides another major source of finance.

Share issues

- Bonus shares are issued to existing shareholders when part of the reserves of the company are converted into share capital.
- Rights shares give existing shareholders the right to buy new shares in proportion to their existing holding.
- The shares of public companies may be bought and sold on a recognised stock exchange.

Reserves

- Reserves are of two types – revenue reserves and capital reserves.
- Revenue reserves arise from trading profits and from realised profits on the sale of non-current assets.
- Capital reserves arise from the issue of shares above their nominal value or from the upward revaluation of non-current assets.
- Revenue reserves can be withdrawn as dividends by the shareholders whereas capital reserves cannot.

Financial statements of limited companies

- The financial statements of limited companies are based on the same principles as those of sole proprietorship businesses. However, there are some differences in detail.
- The profit and loss account has four measures of profit displayed: operating profit, net profit for the year (profit before tax), net profit after tax and unappropriated profit.
- The profit and loss account also shows audit fees, transfers to reserves, corporation tax on profits for the year and dividends for the year.
- Any unpaid tax and unpaid, but authorised, dividends will appear in the balance sheet as current liabilities.
- The share capital plus the reserves will be shown as 'equity'.

Groups of companies

- Parent companies are required to produce group financial statements incorporating the results of all companies controlled by the parent.
- A group balance sheet is prepared by adding like items of assets and liabilities based on 'fair values' together, as if all of the trading is undertaken through the parent company.
- A goodwill arising on consolidation figure often emerges in the group balance sheet.
- Where the parent does not own all of the shares of each subsidiary, a minority interest figure will appear in the balance sheet, representing the outside shareholders' investment.
- A group profit and loss account is drawn up following similar logic to that applied to the group balance sheet.
- The group profit and loss account will contain a minority interest figure if not all subsidiaries are fully owned by the parent, which represents the outside shareholders' share of the group profit.

Key terms

limited company p. 105	capital reserves p. 118
shares p. 105	share premium account p. 119
limited liability p. 108	consolidating p. 119
public company p. 108	bonus shares p. 120
private company p. 108	authorised share capital p. 122
corporation tax p. 109	issued share capital p. 122
director p. 110	fully paid shares p. 122
corporate governance p. 110	called-up share capital p. 122
Combined Code p. 112	paid-up share capital p. 122
reserves p. 115	loan stock/debenture p. 123
equity p. 115	margin of safety p. 127
nominal value p. 115	operating profit p. 130
revenue reserve p. 116	parent/holding company p. 132
dividend p. 116	consolidated/group financial
ordinary shares p. 116	statements p. 132
preference shares p. 116	takeover p. 133

Further reading

If you would like to explore the topics covered in this chapter in more depth, we recommend the following books:

Financial Reporting, *Alexander D. and Britton A.*, 6th edn, International Thomson Business Press, 2001, chapter 12.

Financial Accounting and Reporting, *Elliott B. and Elliott J.*, 8th edn, Financial Times Prentice Hall, 2004, chapters 10 and 19.

Accounting Theory and Practice, *Glautier M. and Underdown B.*, 7th edn, Financial Times Prentice Hall, 2001, chapter 13.

Reference

Corporate Governance: Improving competitiveness and access to capital in global markets, an OECD report by Business Sector Advisory Group on Corporate Governance, Organisation for Economic Co-operation and Development, 1998, p. 14.

REVIEW QUESTIONS

Answers to these questions can be found on the students' side of the Companion Website at www.pearsoned.co.uk/atrillmclaney.

4.1 How does the liability of a limited company differ from the liability of a real person, in respect of amounts owed to others?

4.2 Some people are about to form a company, as a vehicle through which to run a new business. What are the advantages to them of forming a private limited company rather than a public one?

4.3 What is a reserve? Distinguish between a revenue reserve and a capital reserve.

4.4 What is a preference share? Compare the main features of a preference share with those of

    (a) an ordinary share, and
    (b) a debenture.

EXERCISES

Exercises 4.6–4.8 are more advanced than 4.1–4.5. Those with coloured numbers have answers at the back of the book.

4.1 Comment on the following quotation:

> Limited companies can set a limit on the amount of debts that they will meet. They tend to have reserves of cash, as well as share capital and they can use these reserves to pay dividends to the shareholders. Many companies have preference as well as ordinary shares. The preference shares give a guaranteed dividend. The shares of many companies can be bought and sold on the Stock Exchange, and a shareholder selling his or her shares can represent a useful source of new capital to the company.

4.2 Comment on the following quotes:

    (a) 'Bonus shares increase the shareholders' wealth because, after the issue, they have more shares, but each one of the same nominal value as they had before. Share splits, on the other hand, do not make the shareholders richer, because the total nominal value of their shareholding is the same before the issue as after it.'

    (b) 'By law, once shares have been issued at a particular nominal value, they must always be issued at that value in any future share issues.'

    (c) 'By law, companies can pay as much as they like by way of dividends on their shares, provided that they have sufficient cash to do so.'

    (d) 'Companies do not have to pay tax on their profits because the shareholders have to pay tax on their dividends.'

4.3 Briefly explain each of the following expressions that you have seen in the financial statements of a limited company:

    (a) Dividend
    (b) Debenture
    (c) Share premium account.

4.4 Iqbal Ltd started trading on 1 January 2002. During the first five years of trading, the following occurred:

Year ended 31 December	Trading profit (loss) £	Profit (loss) on sale of non-current assets £	Upward revaluation of non-current assets £
2002	(15,000)	–	–
2003	8,000	–	10,000
2004	15,000	5,000	–
2005	20,000	(6,000)	–
2006	22,000	–	–

Required:
Assuming that the company paid the maximum legal dividend each year, how much would each year's dividend be?

4.5 Da Silva plc's outline balance sheet as at a particular date was as follows:

	£m
Net assets	72
Equity:	
£1 ordinary shares	40
General reserve	32
	72

The directors made a one-for-four bonus issue, immediately followed by a one-for-four rights issue at a price of £1.80 per share.

Required:
Show the balance sheet of Da Silva plc immediately following the two share issues.

4.6 Presented below is a draft set of simplified financial statements for Pear Limited for the year ended 30 September 2005.

Profit and loss account for the year ended 30 September 2005

	£000	£000
Revenue		1,456
Costs of sales		(768)
Gross profit		688
Less Expenses:		
Salaries	220	
Depreciation	249	
Other operating costs	131	(600)
Operating profit		88
Interest payable		(15)
Profit before taxation		73
Taxation at 30%		(22)
Profit after taxation		51

Balance sheet as at 30 September 2005

	£000	£000
Non-current assets		
Property, plant and equipment		
Cost	1,570	
Depreciation	(690)	880
Current assets		
Stock (inventories)	207	
Trade debtors (receivables)	182	
Cash at bank	21	
	410	
Less **Current liabilities**		
Trade creditors (payables)	88	
Other creditors (payables)	20	
Taxation	22	
Bank overdraft	105	
	235	
Net current assets		175
Less **Non-current liabilities**		
10% debenture – repayable 2012		(300)
		755
Equity		
Share capital		300
Share premium account	300	
Retained profit at beginning of year	104	
Profit for year	51	455
		755

The following information is available:

(i) Depreciation has not been charged on office equipment with a written-down value of £100,000. This class of assets is depreciated at 12 per cent a year using the reducing-balance method.

(ii) A new machine was purchased, on credit, for £30,000 and delivered on 29 September 2005 but has not been included in the financial statements. (Ignore depreciation.)

(iii) A sales invoice to the value of £18,000 for September 2005 has been omitted from the financial statements. (The cost of sales figure is stated correctly.)

(iv) A dividend of £25,000 had been approved by the shareholders before 30 September 2005, but was unpaid at that date. This is not reflected in the financial statements.

(v) The interest payable on the debenture for the second half-year was not paid until 1 October 2005 and has not been included in the financial statements.

(vi) A general provision against bad debts is to be made at the level of 2 per cent of debtors (receivables).

(vii) An invoice for electricity to the value of £2,000 for the quarter ended 30 September 2005 arrived on 4 October and has not been included in the financial statements.

(viii) The charge for taxation will have to be amended to take account of the above information. Make the simplifying assumption that tax is payable shortly after the end of the year, at the rate of 30 per cent of the profit before tax.

Required:
Prepare a revised set of financial statements for the year ended 30 September 2005 incorporating the additional information in (i)–(viii) above. Note: work to the nearest £1,000.

4.7   Presented below is a draft set of financial statements for Chips Limited.

Chips Limited
Profit and loss account for the year ended 30 June 2005

	£000	£000
Revenue		1,850
Cost of sales		(1,040)
Gross profit		810
Less Depreciation	(220)	
Other operating costs	(375)	(595)
Operating profit		215
Interest payable		(35)
Profit before taxation		180
Taxation		(60)
Profit after taxation		120

Balance sheet as at 30 June 2005

Non-current assets	Cost	Depreciation	
Property, plant and equipment	£000	£000	£000
Buildings	800	(112)	688
Plant and equipment	650	(367)	283
Motor vehicles	102	(53)	49
	1,552	(532)	1,020
Current assets			
Stock (inventories)		950	
Trade debtors (receivables)		420	
Cash at bank		16	
		1,386	
Less **Current liabilities**			
Trade creditors (payables)		(361)	
Other creditors (payables)		(117)	
Taxation		(60)	
		(538)	
Net current assets			848
Less **Non-current liabilities**			
Secured 10% loan			(700)
			1,168
Equity			
Ordinary shares of £1, fully paid			800
Reserves at 1 July 2004		248	
Profit for the year		120	368
			1,168

The following additional information is available:

(i)   Purchase invoices for goods received on 29 June 2005 amounting to £23,000 have not been included. This means that the cost of sales figure in the profit and loss account has been understated.

(ii)   A motor vehicle costing £8,000 with depreciation amounting to £5,000 was sold on 30 June 2005 for £2,100, paid by cheque. This transaction has not been included in the company's records.

(iii) No depreciation on motor vehicles has been charged. The annual rate is 20 per cent of cost at the year end.

(iv) A sale on credit for £16,000 made on 1 July 2005 has been included in the financial statements in error. The cost of sales figure is correct in respect of this item.

(v) A half-yearly payment of interest on the secured loan due on 30 June 2005 has not been paid.

(vi) The tax charge should be 30 per cent of the reported profit before taxation. Assume that it is payable, in full, shortly after the year-end.

Required:

Prepare a revised set of financial statements incorporating the additional information in (i)–(vi) above. *Note*: Work to the nearest £1,000.

4.8   Rose Limited operates a small chain of retail shops that sell high-quality teas and coffees. Approximately half of sales are on credit. Abbreviated and unaudited financial statements are given below:

Profit and loss account for the year ended 31 March 2005

	£000	£000
Revenue		12,080
Cost of sales		(6,282)
Gross profit		5,798
Labour costs	(2,658)	
Depreciation	(625)	
Other operating costs	(1,003)	
		(4,286)
Net profit before interest		1,512
Interest payable		(66)
Net profit before tax		1,446
Tax payable		(434)
Net profit after tax		1,012
Dividend paid		(300)
Retained profit for year		712
Retained profit brought forward		756
Retained profit carried forward		1,468

(continued over)

Balance sheet as at 31 March 2005

	£000	£000
Non-current assets		2,728
Current assets		
Stock (inventories)	1,583	
Debtors (receivables)	996	
Cash	26	
	2,605	
Current liabilities		
Trade creditors (payables)	(1,118)	
Other creditors (payables)	(417)	
Tax	(434)	
Overdraft	(596)	
	(2,565)	
Net current assets		40
Non-current liabilities		
Secured loan (2010)		(300)
		2,468
Equity		
Share capital		
(50p shares, fully paid)		750
Share premium		250
Retained profit		1,468
		2,468

Since the unaudited financial statements for Rose Limited were prepared, the following information has become available:

(i)   An additional £74,000 of depreciation should have been charged on fixtures and fittings.
(ii) Invoices for credit sales on 31 March 2005 amounting to £34,000 have not been included; costs of sales is not affected.
(iii) Bad debts should be provided at a level of 2 per cent of debtors at the year end.
(iv) Stocks, which had been purchased for £2,000, have been damaged and are unsaleable. This is not reflected in the financial statements.
(v)   Fixtures and fittings to the value of £16,000 were delivered just before 31 March 2005, but these assets were not included in the financial statements and the purchase invoice had not been processed.
(vi) Wages for Saturday-only staff, amounting to £1,000, have not been paid for the final Saturday of the year. This is not reflected in the financial statements.
(vii) Tax is payable at 30% of net profit after tax. Assume that it is payable shortly after the year-end.

Required:
Prepare revised financial statements for Rose Limited for the year ended 31 March 2005, incorporating the information in (i)–(vii) above. Note: work to the nearest £1,000.

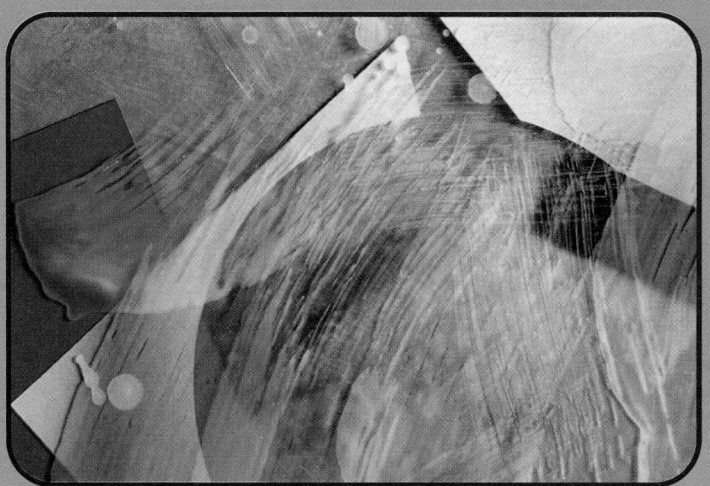

CHAPTER 5

Accounting for limited companies (2)

OBJECTIVES

When you have completed this chapter, you should be able to:

● Describe the responsibilities of directors and auditors concerning the annual financial statements provided to external users.

● Identify the main sources of regulation affecting the financial statements of limited companies.

● Discuss the framework of principles for accounting.

● Prepare a profit and loss account, balance sheet and statement of changes in equity for a limited company in accordance with international accounting standards.

● Explain the purpose of segmental reports and the operating and financial review and discuss the contents of these reports.

● Discuss the problem of creative accounting.

INTRODUCTION

This chapter continues our examination of the financial statements of limited companies. It identifies the legal responsibilities of directors and then goes on to discuss the main sources of accounting rules that govern the published financial statements. Although a detailed consideration of these accounting rules is beyond the scope of this book, the key rules that shape the form and content of the published financial statements are discussed along with the efforts that have been made to develop a framework of principles to underpin the accounting rules.

The increasing complexity of business and the increasing demands for information by users have led to the publication of a number of additional financial statements. This chapter considers two of the more important, namely the segmental financial report and the operating and financial review. The aim of both these reports is to provide users with a more complete picture of financial performance and position.

Despite the proliferation of accounting rules, there are still concerns over the quality of published financial statements. The chapter ends by considering the problem of creative accounting and its impact on financial reporting.

The directors' duty to account

It is not usually possible for all of the shareholders to be involved in the general management of the company, nor do most of them wish to be involved. Instead, they elect directors to act on their behalf. It is both logical, and required by UK company law, that directors are accountable for their actions in respect of their stewardship (management) of the company's assets. In this context, directors are required by law:

- to maintain appropriate accounting records;
- to prepare annual financial statements and a directors' report, and to make these available to all shareholders and to the public at large.

The financial statements are made available to the general public by the company submitting a copy to the Companies Registry (Department of Trade and Industry), which allows any one who wishes to do so to inspect these financial statements.

ACTIVITY 5.1

Can you think of any reasons why the law has decreed that companies must account in this way? We think there are broadly three reasons.

We thought of the following:

- *To inform and protect shareholders.* If shareholders do not receive a reasonable supply of information about the performance and position of their company, they will have problems in appraising their investment. Under these circumstances, they would probably be reluctant to invest and this, in turn, would affect the functioning of the private sector. Any society with a significant private sector needs to encourage equity investment.

● *To inform and protect suppliers of labour, goods, services and finance, particularly those supplying credit (loans) or goods and services on credit.* People and organisations would be reluctant to engage in commercial relationships, such as supplying goods or lending money, where a company does not provide information about its financial health. The fact that a company has limited liability increases the risks involved in dealing with the company. An unwillingness to engage in commercial relationships with limited companies will, once again, affect the functioning of the private sector.

● *To inform and protect society more generally.* Some companies exercise enormous power and influence in society generally, particularly on a geographically local basis. For example, a particular company may be the dominant employer and purchaser of commercial goods and services in a particular town or city. Legislators have tended to take the view that society has the right to information about the company and its activities.

The need for accounting rules

If we accept the need for directors of limited companies to prepare and publish financial statements, we must also accept the need for a framework of rules concerning how these statements are prepared and presented. A lack of regulation increases the risk that unscrupulous directors will use 'unacceptable' accounting practices when preparing the financial statements in order to portray a view of company performance that is not actually warranted. It also increases the risk that the financial statements of different companies will not be comparable, thereby making investment decisions difficult. These risks will, in turn, damage the integrity of the financial statements in the eyes of users.

Though the need for regulating the financial statements is widely accepted, users must be realistic about what can be achieved through regulation. Problems of manipulation and concealment can still occur, even in a highly regulated environment. However, regulation should reduce the scale of these problems. There are also limits to comparability between the financial statements of different companies. We have already seen that accounting is not a precise science and it will always be necessary for judgements and estimates to be made. In some cases, there may also be valid reasons for different companies to adopt different accounting methods.

The main sources of accounting rules

Before considering the particular rules to be followed by limited companies, we first need to be aware of the main sources of accounting rules. In the UK, we are currently going through a period of transition and the main sources of accounting rules are changing. The following sections provide some background to the changes.

The situation up until January 2005

In the UK, company law has been the primary source of authority when preparing and presenting financial statements. The main body of law is set out in the Companies

Act 1985, as amended by the Companies Act 1989. Company law incorporates the overriding requirement that the financial statements of limited companies show a true and fair view of the financial performance and position of the company. It also provides rules concerning the format (layout) of the financial statements as well as detailed disclosure requirements and valuation rules.

 To support the law, **financial reporting standards** (previously called **accounting standards**) have been issued by the Accounting Standards Board (ASB). The ASB was established by the UK accounting profession and the standards issued by the Board aim to improve the quality of the financial statements. These standards cover various aspects of preparing the financial statements including:

● what information should be disclosed;
● how information should be presented;
● how assets should be valued; and
● how profit should be measured.

Normally, companies must comply with ASB standards to ensure the financial statements provide a true and fair view. In essence, the law states that the financial statements should reflect a true and fair view, and the standards help to define what is meant by this expression. This gives accounting standards an important role in financial reporting.

Companies that are listed on the London Stock Exchange must adhere to further rules as a condition of having their shares traded there. These additional rules are imposed by the Financial Services Authority (FSA), in its role as the UK listing authority. These rules include publication of summarised interim (half-year) financial statements, in addition to the annual financial statements, and disclosure of details of holdings of more than 20 per cent of the shares of other companies.

Figure 5.1 illustrates the sources of accounting rules with which larger UK companies must comply.

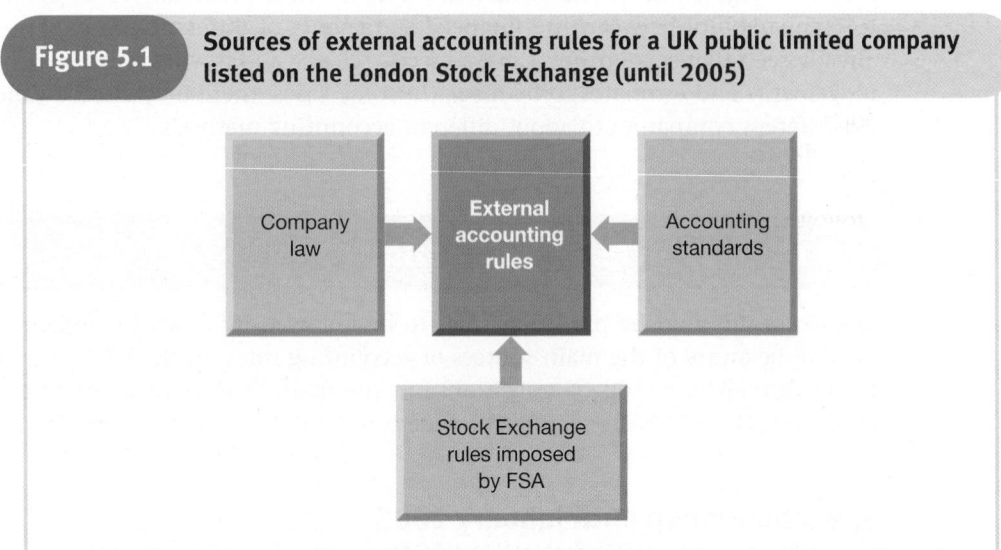

Figure 5.1   **Sources of external accounting rules for a UK public limited company listed on the London Stock Exchange (until 2005)**

Company law and accounting standards are the most important sources of accounting rules, but the FSA imposes additional rules.

The situation as from January 2005

There are significant changes to the sources of rules as from January 2005. This reflects the growing momentum towards international harmonisation. Business has become more international in nature and so, it is argued, accounting has to become more international in nature in order to keep pace. If the accounting rules of different countries are harmonised, companies with an international reach should find it easier to make investment decisions and to raise capital. It can also help them to reduce the time and cost of producing financial statements as different sets of financial statements will no longer have to be prepared for the different countries in which they have a presence.

The potential benefits of internationalising accounting practice led to the creation of the International Accounting Standards Committee (IASC) in 1973. The IASC was set up with the aim of achieving improvement and harmonisation of accounting standards and during its life issued a number of **international accounting standards** (IASs). The IASC was restructured and renamed the International Accounting Standards Board (IASB) in 2001. The objectives of the IASB, which is an independent body funded by voluntary contributions, are to:

- develop a single set of high quality, global accounting standards that require transparent and comparable information in financial statements;
- promote the use and application of these standards; and
- work towards the convergence of national accounting standards

The IASB's pronouncements are called **international financial reporting standards** (IFRSs) but the board has also adopted the international accounting standards (IASs) issued by the IASC. There are strong similarities between the standards issued, or adopted, by the IASB and those issued by the UK standard-setting body, the ASB. However, there are also important differences. The relationship between the two sets of standards has been described as that of 'cousins rather than siblings'. **Real World 5.1** provides a list of standards that have been issued, or adopted, by the IASB to give an idea of the range of topics that are covered.

The authority of the IASB was given a huge boost when the European Commission adopted a regulation requiring listed companies of EU Member States, to prepare their consolidated financial statements according to IASB standards as from January 2005. EU Member States have the power to extend this requirement to other companies and, in July 2003 the UK government announced that all companies would be allowed the option to adopt IASB standards. Non-listed companies can choose not to follow IASB standards, certainly for the immediate future. Many informed observers believe that once listed companies start to apply IASB standards, other companies will quickly follow, particularly larger and better-known non-listed companies. It seems likely that applying IASB standards will quickly become the norm.

The EU regulation overrides any laws in force in Member States that could either hinder or restrict compliance with IASB standards. However, those national laws that embody EU directives concerning the publication and audit of financial statements remain in force. The ultimate aim is to achieve a single framework of accounting rules for companies from all member countries. The EU recognises that this will only be achieved if governments of member countries do not add to the requirements imposed by the various IASB standards. Thus, it seems that accounting rules developed within individual EU member countries will eventually disappear.

For the time being, however, the EU accepts that the governments of Member States may need to impose additional disclosures for some corporate governance matters and regulatory requirements. In the UK, company law requires disclosure relating to various

REAL WORLD 5.1

International standards

The following is a list of the international accounting standards in force at the end of May 2004. Several standards have been issued and subsequently withdrawn, which explains the numerical gaps in sequence. In addition, many of them have been revised and re-issued.

IAS 1	Presentation of Financial Statements
IAS 2	Inventories
IAS 7	Cash Flow Statements
IAS 8	Net Profit or Loss for the Period, Fundamental Errors and Changes in Accounting Policies
IAS 10	Events After the Balance Sheet Date
IAS 11	Construction Contracts
IAS 12	Income Taxes
IAS 14	Segment Reporting
IAS 15	Information Reflecting the Effects of Changing Prices
IAS 16	Property, Plant and Equipment
IAS 17	Leases
IAS 18	Revenue
IAS 19	Employee Benefits
IAS 20	Accounting for Government Grants and Disclosure of Government Assistance
IAS 21	The Effects of Changes in Foreign Exchange Rates
IAS 23	Borrowing Costs
IAS 24	Related Party Transactions
IAS 26	Accounting and Reporting by Retirement Benefit Plans
IAS 27	Consolidated Financial Statements
IAS 28	Investments in Associates
IAS 29	Financial Reporting in Hyperinflationary Economies
IAS 30	Disclosures in the Financial Statements of Banks and Similar Financial Institutions
IAS 31	Financial Reporting of Interests in Joint Ventures
IAS 32	Financial Investments: Disclosure and Presentation
IAS 33	Earnings per Share
IAS 34	Interim Financial Reporting
IAS 35	Discontinuing Operations
IAS 36	Impairment of Assets
IAS 37	Provisions, Contingent Liabilities and Contingent Assets
IAS 38	Intangible Assets
IAS 39	Financial Instruments: Recognition and Measurement
IAS 40	Investment Property
IAS 41	Agriculture
IFRS 1	First-time Adoption of International Financial Reporting Standards
IFRS 2	Share-based Payments
IFRS 3	Business Combinations
IFRS 4	Insurance Contracts

Key:
IAS = International accounting standard
IFRS = International financial reporting standard

Gaps in the numerical sequence relate to statements that have been withdrawn.

Source: www.iasb.org.

corporate governance issues. For example, there is a requirement to disclose details of directors' remuneration in the published financial statements. This requirement goes beyond that required by IASB standards.

This means that, from 2005, the position shown in Figure 5.1 (p. 148) remains valid except that it is IASB, rather than UK, standards that provide that element. Company law and the FSA still play their part. It seems likely, that in the longer term, IASB standards will replace both company law and the FSA to become the sole source of company accounting requirements.

Presenting financial statements

Now that we have gained an insight to the sources of rules affecting limited companies, let us turn our attention to the main rules to be followed in the presentation of financial statements. We shall focus on the IASB rules and, in particular, those contained in IAS 1 *Presentation of Financial Statements*. This standard is very important as it sets out the structure and content of financial statements and the principles to be followed in preparing these statements.

According to IAS 1, the financial statements consist of:

- a profit and loss account (income statement)
- a balance sheet
- a statement of changes in equity
- a cash flow statement
- notes on accounting policies and other explanatory notes.

We shall discuss each of these below but, before doing so, we should be clear as to what is the main consideration when preparing these statements.

Fair representation

The overriding requirement is for the financial statements to provide a fair representation of the company's financial position, financial performance and cash flows. There is a presumption that this will be achieved where the financial statements are drawn up in accordance with the various IASB standards that have been issued. It is only in very rare circumstances that compliance with a standard would not result in a fair representation of the financial health of a company.

ACTIVITY 5.2

IAS 1 does not say that the overriding requirement is for the financial statements to show a 'correct' or an 'accurate' presentation of financial health. Why, in your opinion, does it not use those words? (*Hint*: Think of depreciation of fixed assets.)

Accounting can never really be said to be 'correct' or 'accurate' as these words imply that there is a precise value that any asset, claim, revenue or expense could have. This is simply not true in many, if not most, cases.

Depreciation provides a good example. The annual depreciation expense is based on judgements about the future concerning the expected useful life and residual value. If all relevant factors are taken into account and reasonable judgements are applied, it may be possible to achieve a fair representation of the amount of the asset that is consumed for a particular period. However, a precise figure for depreciation for a period cannot be achieved.

The profit and loss account (income statement)

IAS 1 sets out the *minimum* information to be presented on the face of the profit and loss account, or income statement. These items include:

- revenue
- finance costs
- gains or losses on the sale of assets or settlement of liabilities arising from discontinued operations
- tax expense and
- profit or loss.

The standard makes it clear, however, that further items should be shown on the face of the profit and loss account where they are relevant to an understanding of performance. For example, if a business is badly affected by flooding, and stocks (inventories) are destroyed as a result, the cost of the flood damage should be shown.

As a further aid to understanding, all material expenses must be separately disclosed. However, they need not be shown on the face of the profit and loss account: they can appear in the notes to the financial statements. The sort of material items that may require separate disclosure include:

- write down of stocks to net realisable value
- write down or disposal of property, plant and equipment
- disposal of investments
- restructuring costs
- discontinuing operations and
- litigation settlements.

This is not an exhaustive list and, in practice, other material expenses may require separate disclosure.

The standard suggests two possible ways in which expenses can be presented on the face of the profit and loss account. The first is to analyse the expenses according to their nature, such as depreciation, employee expenses and so on. Example 5.1 below sets out how a profit and loss account analyses expenses in this way.

Example 5.1

Turner plc
Profit and loss account for the year ended 31 December 2005

	£000	£000
Revenue		576
Other income		107
		683
Changes in stocks	65	
Raw material and consumables used	100	
Employee expenses	91	
Depreciation and amortisation	22	
Impairment of property, plant and equipment	25	
Other expenses	10	
Finance costs	8	
Total expenses		321
Profit before tax		362
Corporation tax		120
Profit for the period		242

The second way to analyse expenses is according to business functions, such administrative activities, distribution and finance. Example 5.2 below sets out a profit and loss account that analyses expenses in this way.

Example 5.2

Degas plc
Profit and loss account for the year ended 31 May 2005

	£000	£000
Revenue		690
Cost of sales		350
		340
Other income		20
		360
Distribution costs	102	
Administrative expenses	115	
Other expenses	14	
Finance costs	20	
Total expenses		251
Profit before tax		109
Corporation tax		24
Profit for the period		85

The choice between the two approaches will depend on which the directors believe will provide the more relevant and reliable information. This second form of presentation is potentially more relevant to users. It reveals how much of the revenue generated was absorbed by particular functions, which may provide a better insight to the efficiency of the business. However, it is not always easy to attribute costs to particular functional areas, particularly where facilities and other resources are being shared. If this second approach is adopted, additional information concerning the nature of the expenses, including depreciation charges and employee costs, must also be shown. This is because this kind of information can be useful in predicting future cash flows.

The balance sheet

IAS 1 prescribes the minimum information that should be presented on the face of the balance sheet. This includes the following:

- property, plant and equipment
- investment property
- intangible assets
- financial assets (such as shares and loans held)
- stocks (inventories)
- trade debtors and other receivables
- cash and cash equivalents
- trade creditors and other payables
- provisions
- financial liabilities (excluding payables and provisions shown above)
- tax liabilities and
- issued capital and reserves (equity).

Additional information should be also shown where it is relevant to an understanding of the financial position of the business.

The standard normally requires a distinction to be made on the balance sheet between current assets and non-current assets and between current liabilities and non-current liabilities. However, where a company considers that more reliable and relevant information will be presented by ordering the items according to their liquidity, it is permitted to do this. The standard does not prescribe a format for the balance sheet. Thus, the vertical format that we have been using so far in the book, and which has been almost universally adopted by UK companies to date, is acceptable. Example 5.3 below illustrates a balance sheet drawn up in accordance with IAS 1.

Example 5.3

Jhamna plc
Balance sheet as at 31 December 2005

	£m	£m	£m
Non-current assets:			
Property, plant and equipment		420	
Goodwill		125	
Other intangible assets		40	585
Current assets:			
Stocks (inventories)	41		
Trade debtors (receivables)	139		
Cash and cash equivalents	20	200	
Less Current liabilities			
Trade creditors (payables)	36		
Short-term borrowings	50		
Current portion of long-term borrowings	43		
Current corporation tax payable	12	141	
Net current assets			59
Total assets less current liabilities			644
Less Non-current liabilities			
Long-term borrowings	250		
Long-term provisions	83		
Total non-current liabilities			333
			311
Equity			
Share capital			150
Retained earnings			70
Other reserves			91
			311

The sub-classification of some of the items shown above may be necessary, either to comply with particular standards or because of their size or nature. For example, sub-classifications are required for certain assets such as property, plant and equipment and stocks as well as for provisions and reserves. In addition, details of share capital, such as the number of authorised and issued shares, and their par value must also be shown. However, to avoid cluttering up the balance sheet, this additional information can be shown in the notes.

Statement of changes to equity

The **statement of changes to equity** aims to help users to understand the changes in share capital and reserves that took place during the period. It reconciles the capital and reserves figures at the beginning of the period with those at the end of the period. This is achieved by showing the effect on the capital and reserves of all revenue and expenses, including gains and losses, as well as the effect of share issues and purchases during the period.

To show the effect on capital and reserves of gains and losses, we first need to understand how they are reported in the financial statements. The general rule is that the profit and loss account (income statement) should show all income and expenses, including gains and losses, for the period, that have already been realised. This contrasts with gains arising from an upward valuation of an asset that remains with the company. These do not affect the profit and loss account, but go directly to a revaluation reserve. We have seen in an earlier chapter, one example of where a gain, or loss, arising is not passed through the profit and loss account.

ACTIVITY 5.3

Can you think of this example?

It is where a business revalues its land and buildings, the gain, or loss, arising is not shown in the profit and loss account. It is transferred to a revaluation reserve, which forms part of the equity (capital and reserves). The rule does not just relate to land and buildings, but these types of asset are, in practice, far and away the most common examples of such unrealised gains.

Another exception to the general rule, which has not been mentioned so far, is exchange differences that arise when the results of foreign operations are translated into UK currency. Once again, any gain, or loss, bypasses the profit and loss account and is taken directly to a currency translation reserve. In the statement of changes in equity, we need to take account of *all* gains and losses that have arisen during the period. Thus, movements in the revaluation reserve and translation reserve must be identified in addition to profits (or losses) reported in the profit and loss account.

To see how a statement of changes in equity for a company may be prepared, let us consider Example 5.4 below.

Example 5.4

At 1 January 2005 Miro plc had the following share capital and reserves:

Miro plc

	£m
Share capital (£1 ordinary shares)	100
Revaluation reserve	20
Translation reserve	40
Retained earnings	150
	310

During 2005, the company made a profit after tax from normal business operations of £42m and reported a revaluation gain on freehold land and buildings of £120m. A loss on exchange differences on translating the results of foreign operations of £10m was also reported. To strengthen its balance sheet, the company issued 50m new shares during the year at a premium of £0.40. The dividends for the year were £27m.

The above information for 2005 can be set out in a statement of changes in equity as follows:

Statement of changes in equity for the year ended 31 December 2005

	Share capital	Share premium	Revaluation reserve	Translation reserve	Retained earnings	Total
	£m	£m	£m	£m	£m	£m
Balance as at 1 January 2005	100	–	20	40	150	310
Changes in equity for 2005						
Gain on revaluation of properties	–	–	120	–	–	120
Exchange differences on translation of foreign operations	–	–	–	(10)	–	(10)
Net income recognised directly to equity	–	–	120	(10)	–	110
Profit for the period	–	–	–	–	42	42
Total recognised income and expense for the period	–	–	120	(10)	42	152
Dividends	–	–	–	–	(27)	(27)
Issue of share capital	50	20	–	–	–	70
Balance at 31 December 2005	150	20	140	30	165	505

It is probably worth mentioning the treatment of dividends at this point. We can see that, in the example above, dividends are shown separately in the statement of changes in equity. However, we may recall that, in Chapter 4, dividends were shown on the face of the profit and loss account when illustrating the format of this statement for limited companies. In fact, both approaches are equally acceptable. IAS 1 allows a choice as to the way is which the dividends for distribution are disclosed. They can be shown:

- on the face of the profit and loss account (income statement); or
- in the statement of changes in equity; or
- in the notes.

Dividends that are proposed during the year, but which are not recognised for distribution, must only be disclosed in the notes.

Cash flow statement

The cash flow statement tries to help users to assess the ability of a company to generate cash flows, and also to assess the requirements for these cash flows. The presentation requirements for this statement are set out in IAS 7 *Cash Flow Statements*, which we shall consider in some detail in Chapter 6.

Explanatory notes

The notes play an important role in helping users to understand the financial statements. They will normally contain the following information:

- a statement that the financial statements comply with relevant IFRSs;
- a summary of the measurement bases used and other significant accounting policies applied (for example, the basis of stock valuation);
- supporting information relating to items appearing on the profit and loss account, balance sheet, statement of changes in equity or cash flow statement (as mentioned above); and
- other disclosures such as future contractual commitments that have not been recognised and management's objectives and policies.

General points

The standard requires that the financial statements be prepared annually, as a minimum, and that comparative figures be provided for the previous period. The standard provides support for three key accounting conventions when preparing the financial statements. These are:

- going concern
- accruals (except for the cash flow statement)
- consistency.

These conventions were covered in Chapters 2 and 3.

To improve the transparency of financial statements, the standard states that:

- offsetting liabilities against assets, or expenses against income, is not allowed. Thus, it is not acceptable, for example, to offset a bank overdraft against a positive bank balance; and
- material items must be shown separately.

Directors' report

In addition to preparing the financial statements discussed above, the law requires the directors to prepare an annual report to shareholders and other interested parties. This report contains information of both a financial and a non-financial nature and goes beyond that which is contained in the financial statements. The information disclosed covers a variety of topics including details of share ownership, details of directors and their financial interests in the company, employment policies, and charitable and political donations. The auditors do not carry out an audit of the **directors' report**. However, they will check to see that the information in the report is consistent with that contained within the audited financial statements.

Auditors

Shareholders are required to elect a qualified and independent person or, more usually, a firm to act as **auditors**. The auditors' main duty is to make a report as to whether, in their opinion, the financial statements do what they are supposed to do, namely show a true and fair view of the financial performance, position and cash flows of the company by complying with relevant accounting standards and statutory requirements. To be in a position to form such an opinion, auditors must scrutinise both the annual financial statements prepared by the directors and the evidence on which they are

| Figure 5.2 | The relationship between the shareholders, the directors and the auditors |

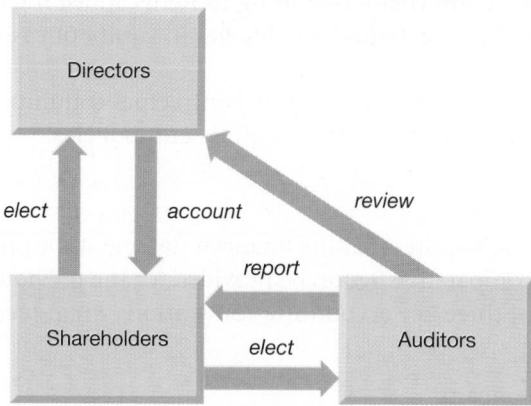

The directors are appointed by the shareholders to manage the company on the shareholders' behalf. The directors are required to report each year to the shareholders, principally by means of accounting statements, on the company's performance, position and cash flows. To give greater confidence in the statements, the shareholders also appoint auditors to investigate the reports and to express an opinion on their reliability.

based. The auditors' opinion must be included with the accounting statements that are sent to the shareholders and to the Registrar of Companies.

The relationship between the shareholders, the directors and the auditors is illustrated in Figure 5.2. This shows that the shareholders elect the directors to act on their behalf, in the day-to-day running of the company. The directors are required to 'account' to the shareholders on the performance, position and cash flows of the company, on an annual basis. The shareholders also elect auditors, whose role it is to give the shareholders an impression of the extent to which they can regard as reliable the accounting statements prepared by the directors.

The framework of principles

In Chapters 2 and 3, we came across various accounting conventions such as prudence, historic cost, going concern and so on. These conventions were developed as a practical response to particular problems that were confronted when preparing financial statements. They have stood the test of time and are still of value to preparers today. However, they do not provide, and were never designed to provide, a framework of principles to guide the development of financial statements. As we grapple with increasingly complex financial reporting problems, the need to have a sound understanding of *why* we account for things in a particular way becomes more and more pressing. Knowing *why* we account, rather than simply *how* we account, is vitally important if we are to improve the quality of financial statements.

In recent years, much effort has been expended in various countries, including the UK, to develop a clear **framework of principles** that will guide us in the development of accounting. Such a framework should provide clear answers to such fundamental questions as:

- Who are the main users of financial statements?
- What is the purpose of financial statements?
- What qualities should financial information possess?
- What are the main elements of financial statements?
- How should these elements be defined, recognised and measured?

If these questions can be answered, accounting rule makers (including the IASB) will be in a stronger position to identify best practice and to develop more coherent rules. This should, in turn, increase the credibility of financial reports in the eyes of users. It may even help reduce the possible number of rules, because some issues may be resolved by reference to the application of general principles rather than the generation of further rules.

The IASB framework

The quest for a framework of accounting principles began in earnest in the 1970s when the Financial Accounting Standards Board (FASB) in the US devoted a very large amount of time and resources to this endeavour. The FASB's efforts resulted in a broad framework of principles that other rule-making bodies, including the IASB, have drawn upon when developing their own frameworks.

The IASB has produced a 'Framework for the Preparation and Presentation of Financial Statements', which begins by discussing the main user groups and their needs. This is well-trodden territory and the various groups and needs identified are broadly in line with those set out in the sections on this topic in Chapter 1. The frame-work goes on to identify the objective of financial statements, which is:

> to provide information about the financial position, performance and changes in financial position of an enterprise that is useful to a wide range of users in making economic decisions.

This reflects the mainstream view and is very similar to the objective of financial statements that others have developed in recent years.

The IASB framework sets out the qualitative characteristics that make financial statements useful. The main characteristics identified are relevance, reliability, comparability, and understandability, all of which were discussed in Chapter 1. The framework also identifies the main elements of financial statements. These are assets, liabilities, equity, income and expense, and definitions for each element are provided. The definitions adopted hold no surprises and are very similar to those adopted by other rule-making bodies and to those discussed earlier, in Chapters 2 and 3.

The IASB framework identifies different valuation bases in use but does not indicate a preference for a particular valuation method. It simply notes that historic cost is the most widely-used method of valuation. Finally, the framework discusses the type of capital base that a business should try to maintain. It includes a discussion of the two main types of capital base – financial capital and physical capital – but, again, expresses no preference as to which should be maintained. The IASB framework does not have the same legal status as an IASB standard. Nevertheless, it should provide a basis for deciding on how to deal with accounting issues, particularly where there is no relevant accounting standard that can be used.

Overall, the IASB framework has provoked little debate and the principles and definitions adopted enjoy widespread acceptance. There has been some criticism, mainly from academics, that the framework is really a descriptive document and does not provide theoretical underpinning to the financial statements. There has also been some criticism of the definitions of the elements of the financial statements. However, these criticisms have not sparked a major controversy.

Segmental financial reports

Most large businesses are engaged in a number of different activities, with each activity having different levels of risk, growth and profitability. The problem for users of financial statements is that information relating to each type of activity will normally be aggregated in the financial statements to provide an overall picture of financial performance and position. This aggregation of information makes it difficult to undertake comparisons between businesses. The activities undertaken by a large business are likely to differ in range and/or scale from those of other businesses.

Where a business operates in different geographical markets, the same sort of arguments apply. The markets of different countries may well have different levels of risk, profitability and growth associated with them, and aggregation will obscure these differences. It will not be possible, for example, to assess the impact on a business of political changes, or changes in inflation or exchange rates that relate to a particular country, or geographical region, unless the degree of exposure to the country, or region, is known.

To undertake any meaningful analysis of financial performance and position, it is usually necessary to disaggregate the information contained within the financial statements. By breaking down the financial information according to business activities and/or geographical markets, we can evaluate the relative risks and profitability of each segment and make useful comparisons with other businesses or other business segments. We can also see the trend of performance for each segment over time and so determine more accurately the likely growth prospects for the business as a whole. We should also be able to assess more easily the impact on the overall business, of changes in market conditions relating to particular activities.

Disclosure of information relating to the performance of each segment may also help to improve the efficiency of the business by keeping managers on their toes. Business segments that are performing poorly will be revealed and this should put pressure on managers to take corrective action. In addition, where a business segment has been sold, the shareholders will be better placed to assess the wisdom of the managers' decision.

Segmental reporting: regulations and practice

An IASB standard (IAS 14 *Segment Reporting*) requires that large listed companies disclose segmental information according to each business segment *and* to each geographical region. Both forms of segmentation are regarded as important to users. A business segment, for the purposes of the standard, is a part of the business that can be separately identified and which provides an individual product or service, or a group of related products or services. A geographical segment is a part of the business that can be separately identified and which provides products or services within a particular economic environment. The environment may comprise a region within a country, a country or a group of countries. One problem that must be confronted when identifying geographical segments is whether the business should be segmented according to where the *operations* are located or where the *markets* are located. The relevant standard allows either approach to be used but states that the choice should be based on the way in which the business is organised and structured.

For reporting purposes, it is necessary to establish whether it is the products or services offered or the geographical regions in which the company operates that has the bigger impact on the risks and returns of the company. Whichever has the bigger impact will be determine whether business segments or geographical segments are identified as the primary segments. This identification is important because the disclosure requirements are greater for the primary segments than for the secondary segments. The way in which a business is organised and structured should, again, provide a useful indicator.

The following are the main items of information that should be disclosed for the primary segments:

- revenue, distinguishing between revenue from external customers and revenue from other segments of the business;
- assets;
- capital expenditure for the period;
- depreciation and amortisation;
- segment result (that is, segment revenue less segment expenses); and
- liabilities.

For secondary segments, only the first three items identified above need be disclosed.

Example 5.5 provides an illustrative **segmental financial report** for a business where the business segments are the primary segments. Following the example, we shall discuss some of the key points that are raised.

Example 5.5

Goya plc
Segmental report for the year ended 30 June 2005

	Publishing	Film making	Eliminations	Consolidation (Total)
	£m	£m	£m	£m
Revenue				
External sales	150	200		
Inter-segment sales	20	10	(30)	
Total revenue	170	210	(30)	350
Result				
Segment result	15	19	(2)	32
Unallocated expenses				14
Operating profit				18
Interest expense				(6)
Net profit before tax				12
Corporation tax				(3)
Net profit				9
Other information				
Segment assets	74	86		160
Unallocated assets				32
Consolidated total assets				192
Segment liabilities	24	21		45
Unallocated liabilities				30
Consolidated total liabilities				75
Capital expenditure	10	8		
Depreciation	15	21		

We can see that information relating to each segment is shown as well as information relating to the business as a whole. External sales and inter-segment sales for each segment appear separately, however, only the combined external sales for the segments appear in the far right-hand column. This is because the inter-segment sales will cancel one another out when calculating the sales for the business as a whole. Similarly, the combined operating profit of each segment *less* the inter-segment profit will appear as the operating profit for the business as a whole.

Unallocated expenses appearing in the above report are those which are not attributable to a particular segment or which cannot be allocated to a segment on any reasonable basis. Note that these expenses have not been apportioned between the two segments but have been deducted from the results of the business as a whole.

ACTIVITY 5.4

What kind of items do you think may appear as unallocated expenses?

These items may include:

- head office expenses
- research and development costs
- marketing expenses
- finance charges.

You may have thought of others.

Unallocated assets and liabilities are those which are not attributable to a particular segment or which cannot be allocated to a particular segment on any reasonable basis. Head office buildings may provide an example of such an unallocated asset and loan capital may provide an example of an unallocated liability.

A similar layout to the report shown above can be used to show geographical segments, where they are regarded as the primary segments.

Problems of segmental reporting

There are various problems associated with preparing segmental reports, not least of which is the problem of identifying a segment. The relevant standard mentions some of the factors that should be taken into account when identifying segments; however, a fair amount of judgement by the directors will often be required. Although this may be the only sensible course of action, it does mean that comparisons between businesses may still be difficult because of different judgements being applied within different companies.

Many segments do not operate in a completely independent manner and there may be a significant amount of sales between segments. If this is the case, the **transfer price** of the goods or services between segments can have a substantial impact on the reported profits of each segment. Indeed, it may be possible to manipulate profit figures for each segment through the use of particular transfer pricing policies. For this reason, the international accounting standard requires that the basis for inter-segment transfers must be disclosed.

Finally, there may be problems where expenses incurred relate to more than one business segment. The way in which these costs are treated may vary between businesses and so may hinder comparisons.

SELF-ASSESSMENT QUESTION 5.1

Segmental information relating to J. Baxter plc, which has operations in three different countries, for the year to 30 April 2005 is shown below.

	UK £m	France £m	Italy £m	Eliminations £m	Consolidation £m
Revenue					
External sales	230	180	360		
Inter-segment sales	40	20	30	(90)	
Total revenue	270	200	390	(90)	770
Result					
Segment result	34	30	8	(6)	66
Unallocated expenses					18
Operating profit					48
Interest expense					(16)
Corporation tax					(6)
Net profit					26
Other information					
Segment assets	129	150	116		395
Unallocated assets					36
Consolidated total assets					431
Segment liabilities	35	28	22		85
Unallocated liabilities					40
Consolidated total liabilities					125
Capital expenditure	20	15	35		
Depreciation	28	35	11		

Required:
Analyse the performance of each of the business segments for the year and comment on your results.

Operating and financial review

Businesses have become more complex over time and, as a consequence, their financial statements have become more difficult to understand. Businesses can organise themselves in different ways, engage in a variety of financial and investing activities and enter into different types of trading relationships with both customers and other businesses. This can make it very difficult for users to interpret the figures set out in annual financial statements. As a result, there is now a need for a supplementary report to be provided, in narrative form, to help users to get to grips with the financial statements. This narrative report should provide a commentary from the directors on the performance and position of the business and it is likely to be of particular value when looking at the financial statements of large businesses.

In the UK, the Accounting Standards Board (ASB) has recognised the need for such a report and has recommended that large businesses prepare an **operating and financial review** (OFR) each year. This report should contain a discussion of the:

- nature of the business, its objectives and how it seeks to achieve those objectives;
- performance of the business during the period under review and the factors affecting performance, including risks facing the business; and
- financial position of the business and the factors that affect it or are likely to affect it.

Each of these elements are discussed in more detail below.

ACTIVITY 5.5

What characteristics should the information contained within the OFR possess?

To be useful, the information should contain the characteristics for accounting information in general, which we identified in Chapter 1. Thus, the information should be relevant, understandable, reliable and comparable. The fact that we are dealing with a narrative report does not alter the need for these characteristics to be present.

We shall now look at the main elements of the OFR.

The business, its objectives and strategy

The OFR should identify and discuss the nature of the business to help set the context within which the financial statements are considered. This may include a discussion of the industries in which it operates, the products or services provided, the structure of the business and so on. The OFR should also discuss the financial and non-financial objectives of the business, how these objectives will be achieved and how this achievement will be measured. **Real World 5.2** provides an example of how one well-known company discussed its objectives.

The operating review

The operating review is designed to help explain to the user the main influences on the performance of the business. It should discuss the main factors that underlie the business and any changes that have occurred, or are likely to occur, to these factors. The following areas have been identified as providing a framework for the operating review.

Performance in the period

This section should discuss the significant features of the performance of the various business segments in relation to the business as a whole. It should cover all relevant aspects of performance and should include an analysis of the effect on current and future performance of significant changes within the industry or in the environment, such as changes in market conditions, new products, fluctuations in exchange rates, and so on.

REAL WORLD 5.2

What's brewing at S&N?

Scottish and Newcastle plc (S and N) is a large brewer. In its OFR for 2003, the company states its objective as follows:

> S and N's ultimate objective is sustained value creation. We shall focus on driving value from our existing business, maximising growth and operational efficiencies. We shall apply rigorous criteria to possible developments into carefully selected markets.

The company then goes on to state how this objective will be measured.

> In a business environment where capital is rationed, the level of return on invested capital is the key measurement. S and N monitors its return on capital rigorously and evaluates all budget and capital expenditure against the cost of capital with the aim of maximising economic profit.

Finally, the company indicates how this objective will be achieved.

> The key value drivers in the brewing industry are organic sales growth, brand development and operational excellence in brewing and distribution. We will focus more aggressively on these through sales growth and improved margins.

Source: Scottish and Newcastle plc Annual Report and Accounts 2003.

Real World 5.3 provides an example of how one company discussed its performance.

REAL WORLD 5.3

Brandon Hire not much higher

Brandon Hire plc operates tool hire and lifting equipment branches in England and Wales. In its operating review for 2002, the company discussed its performance for the year as follows:

> Brandon Tool Hire had a mildly disappointing year. Turnover increased by 10% but this was largely attributable to new and acquired branches. In 2001 we achieved organic growth of 14%. In 2002 we anticipated organic growth of 6% but realised a much smaller increase and were too slow in adjusting our cost base. This was the primary contributor to our fall in operating profits.
>
> Trading reflected our usual seasonality with a stronger second half. We experienced two particularly poor months during the year: June was exceptionally weak due to the Jubilee and the World Cup which disrupted many of our customers' work patterns, while December was also poor with many customers starting their Christmas break much earlier than usual. Encouragingly, there was a return to organic growth of year-on-year turnover in the second half.

Source: Brandon Hire plc Annual Report and Accounts 2002.

Returns to shareholders

This section should include a discussion of earnings per share, profits for the year and dividends. It should also indicate the dividend policy that has been adopted. Where a discussion of changes in the share price is included, a comparison of these changes in relation to those of similar businesses should be provided.

Dynamics of the business

This section should include a discussion of the main factors that are likely to influence future results. It will also consider the main risks facing the business and indicate how they are managed. These risks and uncertainties may cover a wide range of matters and could include inflation, skills shortages, product liability, scarcity of raw materials, and so on. There should also be some discussion of the strengths and resources of the business that are not shown in the balance sheet such as market position, customer relationships, business reputation, research and development, and so on.

Real World 5.4 continues with the example of Brandon Hire plc by showing how the company discussed its customer strengths.

REAL WORLD 5.4

Brandon Hire customer strengths

In its operating review for 2002, Brandon Hire plc, outlines its customer strengths as follows:

Our proposition for our customers is strong:

- we have a good reputation for service
- we have a full range of well-maintained equipment
- we have high density of coverage in the areas where we operate
- we have invested heavily in reducing our customers' administration costs.

Like many businesses we have a lot of customer data and we are now in a position to use that data to generate more business from existing customers, to target specific areas for new customers, and to assess the profitability to us of individual customers.

Source: Brandon Hire plc Annual Report and Accounts 2002.

Investment for the future

This section should include commentary on how the directors plan to maintain or improve the business through investment. This investment may take various forms such as building brands through marketing and advertising campaigns, staff development, research, and so on. Current and planned levels of capital expenditure should also be discussed. The benefits from these investments should be explained in relation to the objectives of the business.

Real World 5.5 reveals how Brandon Hire plc seeks to expand its business in the future.

REAL WORLD 5.5

Expanding the business

In its operating review for 2002, Brandon Hire plc includes a section on the expansion of its network of branches and states:

We expect to continue our strategy of using a combination of acquisitions and new branches to strengthen our position in areas where we currently operate and to increase the geographical area that we cover.

Source: Brandon Hire plc Annual Report and Accounts 2002.

The financial review

The second part of the OFR, the financial review, is concerned with explaining the capital structure of the business, its treasury policy and the influences on its financial position. The following areas have been identified as providing a framework for the review.

Capital structure and treasury policy

This should involve a discussion of the capital structure policies of the business (that is, the mix of share capital, reserves and long-term borrowing) along with any relevant ratios. Treasury policy is concerned with such matters as managing cash, obtaining finance and managing relationships with financial institutions. Possible areas for discussion in the financial review include the ways in which treasury activities are managed, the currencies in which borrowings are made and the way in which currency risk and interest rate risk is managed.

Real World 5.6 reveals how Brandon Hire plc disclosed information relating to interest rate risk.

REAL WORLD 5.6

Interest rate risk

Brandon Hire plc included the following statement on interest rate risk in its 2002 financial review:

> The company finances its operations through a mixture of retained profits, bank borrowings and hire purchase borrowings. . . . The Board considers that these arrangements provide an appropriate blend of certainty and flexibility in respect of interest rate risk. At the year end, 48% of the gross borrowings were at fixed rates and 52% at variable rates.

Source: Brandon Hire plc Annual Report and Accounts 2002.

Cash flows

This section should include a discussion of the cash inflows either from customers or from other sources and the special factors, if any, that influenced these. The main cash outflows for the period should also be identified and discussed. Real World 5.7 reveals how one major company disclosed information concerning cash flows for the period.

Current liquidity

The liquidity at the end of the accounting period should be discussed, along with comments on the level of borrowing at the end of the period. The amounts required to meet future investment commitments should be mentioned. Furthermore, any loan conditions or restrictions on the ability to transfer funds within the business should be mentioned.

Going concern

The OFR should contain a confirmation, if appropriate, that the business is a going concern.

We can see from the list of headings so far in this section that the OFR can be quite a long report – often between five and ten pages in length. However, for many large

REAL WORLD 5.7

Cash flows at GUS

GUS plc, which owns a number of major businesses including Argos and Homebase, included the following statement on cash flows in its 2003 financial review:

> Cash flow before acquisitions, disposals and dividends amounted to £616m compared to £478m in the previous year. Cash flow benefited from the growth in profits in the year and from tight control over working capital which was £201m lower despite the growth in the Argos store card loan book. Capital expenditure grew by £7m to £329m and was equivalent to 134% of the depreciation charge in 2003.
>
> With the £902m purchase of Homebase, there was a net cash outflow of £802m for the year after the payment of dividends, the repayment of securitised loans and acquisitions and disposals.

Source: GUS plc Annual Report 2003.

businesses, the OFR is really an incremental rather than a radical change in reporting practice. The OFR builds on best practice, as many of the topics identified were previously contained within the chairman's report or directors' report.

Summary financial statements

Though directors of all companies are required to make a set of the company financial statements available to each shareholder, these statements can be a summarised version of the full version that follows the complete legal requirements. The reasons for not requiring that the full version be sent to all shareholders are broadly that:

- many shareholders do not wish to receive the full version, because they may not have the time, interest or skill necessary to be able to gain much from it;
- directors could improve their communication with their shareholders by providing something closer to the needs of many shareholders;
- reproducing and posting copies of the full version is expensive and a waste of resources where particular shareholders do not wish to receive it.

 Many companies send all of their private shareholders a copy of the **summary financial statements**, with a clear message that the full versions are available on request. Each full version is, however, required for filing with the Registrar of Companies.

Accounting rules and creative accounting

Despite the proliferation of accounting rules and the independent checks that are imposed, there are still concerns over the quality of company financial statements. There is evidence that the directors of some companies have employed particular accounting policies or structured particular transactions in such a way that portrays a picture of financial health that is in line with what they would like users to see rather than what is a true and fair view of financial position and performance. This practice

→ is referred to as **creative accounting** and it poses a major problem for accounting rule-makers and for society generally.

ACTIVITY 5.6

Why might the directors of a company engage in creative accounting?

There are many reasons and these include:

- to get around restrictions (for example, to report sufficient profit to pay a dividend);
- to avoid government action (for example, the taxation of excessive profits);
- to hide poor management decisions;
- to achieve sales or profit targets, thereby ensuring that performance bonuses are paid to the directors;
- to attract new share capital or loan capital by showing a healthy financial position; and
- to satisfy the demands of major investors concerning levels of return.

Creative accounting methods

The particular methods that unscrupulous directors use to manipulate the financial statements are many and varied. Some of these methods concern the overstatement of revenue. These methods often involve the early recognition of sales income or the reporting of sales transactions that have no real substance. **Real World 5.8** provides examples of both types of revenue manipulation.

REAL WORLD 5.8

Overstating revenue

Hollow swaps: telecoms companies sell useless fibre optic capacity to each other in order to generate revenues on their income statements.

Channel stuffing: a company floods the market with more products than its distributors can sell, artificially boosting its sales. An international condom maker, shifted £60 million in excess stock on to trade customers. Also known as 'trade loading'.

Round tripping: also known as 'in-and-out trading'. Used to notorious effect by Enron. Two or more traders buy and sell energy among themselves for the same price and at the same time. Inflates trading volumes and makes participants appear to be doing more business than they really are.

Pre-dispatching: goods such as carpets are marked as 'sold' as soon as an order is placed. . . . This inflates sales and profits.

Note that some of the techniques used, such as round tripping, may inflate the sales for a period but do not inflate reported profits. Nevertheless, this may still benefit the company. Sales growth has become an important yardstick of performance for some investors and can affect the value they place on the company.

The revenue figure in the profit and loss account seems to be a popular target for creative accounting practices. It has been claimed that more than half the accounting irregularities investigated have been concerned with the overstatement of revenue. **Real World 5.9** provides an example of the impact of the early recognition of revenue on the measurement of performance.

REAL WORLD 5.9

Not to be copied

One case of overstating revenue is alleged to have been carried out by the Xerox Corporation, a large US company and a leading player in the photocopying business. It is alleged that the company brought forward revenues in order to improve profits as its fortunes declined in the late 1990s. These revenues related to copier equipment sales, particularly in Latin America. To correct for the overstatement of revenues, Xerox had to restate its equipment sales figures for a five-year period. The result was a reversal in reported revenues of a staggering $6.4 billion, although $5.1 billion was reallocated to other revenues as a result. This restatement was one of the largest in US corporate history.

In June 2002 the company paid a fine of $10m but denied any wrongdoing.

Sources: Based on information in 'Can't tell the scandals without a scorecard', *The Wall Street Journal Europe*, October 2003, p. A5. 'Xerox acts to put itself on a firmer footing', FT.com, 28 June 2002.

Some creative accounting methods focus on the manipulation of expenses, and certain types of expenses are particularly vulnerable. These are expenses that rely heavily on the judgement of directors concerning estimates of the future or concerning the most suitable accounting policy to adopt.

ACTIVITY 5.7

Can you identify the kind of expenses where the directors must use judgement in the ways described?

....

These include certain expenses that we discussed in Chapter 3, such as:

- depreciation of property, plant and equipment;
- amortisation of intangible assets, such as goodwill;
- stock costing methods; and
- provisions for doubtful debts.

By changing estimates about the future (for example, the useful life or residual value of an asset), or by changing accounting policies (for example, switching from FIFO to AVCO) it may be possible to derive an expense figure, and consequently a profit figure, that suits the directors.

The incorrect capitalisation of expenses may also be used as a means of manipulation. Expenses may be treated as if they were amounts incurred to acquire or develop non-current assets, rather than amounts consumed during the period. Companies that build their own assets are often best placed to undertake this form of malpractice.

ACTIVITY 5.8

What would be the effect on the profits and total assets of a business of incorrectly capitalising expenses?

Both would be artificially inflated. Reported profits would increase because expenses would be reduced. Total assets would be increased because the expenses would be incorrectly treated as non-current assets.

REAL WORLD 5.10

Sorry – wrong numbers

One particularly notorious case of capitalising expenses is alleged to have occurred in the financial statements of WorldCom (now renamed MCI). This company, which is a large US telecommunications business, is alleged to have overstated profits by treating certain operating expenses, such as basic network maintenance, as capital expenditure. This happened over a fifteen-month period during 2001 and 2002. To correct for this over-statement, net profits had to be reduced by a massive $3.8bn.

Source: Based on two personal views on WorldCom, FT.com site, 27 June 2002.

Some creative accounting methods focus on the concealment of losses or liabilities. The financial statements can look much healthier if these can somehow be eliminated. One way of doing this is to create a 'separate' entity that will take over the losses or liabilities.

REAL WORLD 5.11

For a very special purpose

Perhaps the most well-known case of concealment of losses and liabilities concerned the Enron Corporation. This was a large US energy business that used 'special purpose entities' (SPEs) as a means of concealment. SPEs were used by Enron to rid itself of problem assets that were falling in value, such as its broadband operations. In addition, liabilities were trans-ferred to these entities to help Enron's balance sheet look healthier. The company had to keep its gearing ratios (the relationship between borrowing and equity) within particular limits to satisfy credit-rating agencies and SPEs were used to achieve this. The SPEs used for concealment purposes were not independent of the company and should have been consolidated in the balance sheet of Enron, along with their losses and liabilities.

When these, and other accounting irregularities, were discovered in 2001, there was a restatement of Enron's financial performance and position to reflect the consolidation of the SPEs, which had previously been omitted. As a result of this restatement, the com-pany recognised $591m in losses over the preceding four years and an additional $628m worth of liabilities at the end of 2000.

The company collapsed at the end of 2001.

Source: 'The rise and fall of Enron', C.W. Thomas, *Journal of Accountancy*, Vol. 194 no. 3, April 2002. This article represents the opinion of the author(s) and are not necessarily those of the Texas Society of Certified Public Accountants.

Finally, creative accounting may involve the overstatement of asset values. This may involve revaluing the assets, using figures that do not correspond to their fair market values. It may also involve the capitalising of costs that should have been written off as expenses, as described earlier.

Checking for creative accounting

When examining the financial statements of a business, a number of checks may be carried out on the financial statements to help gain a 'feel' for their reliability. These can include checks to see whether:

- the reported profits are significantly higher than the operating cash flows for the period, which may suggest that profits have been overstated;
- the corporation tax charge is low in relation to reported profits, which may suggest, again, that profits are overstated, although there may be other, more innocent explanations;
- the valuation methods used for assets held are based on historic cost or current values, and if the latter approach has been used why and how the current values were determined;
- there have been any changes in accounting policies over the period, particular in key areas such as revenue recognition, stock valuation and depreciation;
- the accounting policies adopted are in line with those adopted by the rest of the industry;
- the auditors' report gives a 'clean bill of health' to the financial statements; and
- the 'small print', that is the notes to the financial statements, is not being used to hide significant events or changes.

Although such checks are useful, they are not guaranteed to identify creative accounting practices, some of which may be very deeply seated.

Creative accounting and economic growth

A few years ago, there was a wave of creative accounting scandals in both the US and Europe but this now appears to have subsided. It seems that accounting scandals are becoming less frequent and that the quality of financial statements is improving. It is to be hoped that trust among users in the integrity of financial statements will soon be restored. As a result of the actions taken by various regulatory bodies and by accounting rule makers, creative accounting has become a more risky and difficult process for those who attempt it. However, it will never disappear completely and a further wave of creative accounting scandals may occur in the future. The recent wave coincided with a period of strong economic growth, and during good economic times, investors and auditors become less vigilant. Thus, the opportunity to manipulate the figures becomes easier. We must not, therefore, become too complacent. Things may change again when we next experience a period of strong growth.

SUMMARY

The main points of this chapter may be summarised as follows:

The directors' have a duty to

- Maintain accounting records.
- Prepare and publish financial statements and a directors' report.

Accounting rules are necessary to

- Avoid unacceptable accounting practices.
- Improve comparability of financial statements.

Accounting rules in the UK

- Until January 2005, the main sources of accounting rules were company law, the Accounting Standards Board and the Financial Services Authority.
- Since January 2005, the International Accounting Standards Board has become an important source of rules.

Presenting financial statements

- IAS 1 sets out the structure and content of financial statements.
- It identifies five financial statements, the profit and loss account (income statement), balance sheet, statement of changes in equity, cash flow statement and explanatory notes.
- The overriding consideration is to provide a fair representation of the financial health of a company and this will normally be achieved by adherence to relevant IASB standards.
- IAS 1 identifies information to be shown in the various financial statements.
- It also identifies some of the principles to be followed in preparing the statements.

Other statutory reports

- The directors' report contains information of a financial and a non-financial nature, which goes beyond that contained in the financial statements.
- The auditors report provides an opinion by an independent auditor concerning whether the financial statements provide a true and fair view of the financial health of a business.

Framework of principles

- This helps to underpin accounting rules.
- The IASB framework identifies and discusses, the users of financial statements, the objective of financial statements, the qualitative characteristics of financial statements, the elements of financial statements, different valuation bases, and different capital maintenance bases.
- The IASB framework draws on earlier work by other rule-making bodies.

Additional financial reports

- Segmental reports disaggregate information on the financial statements to help achieve a better understanding of financial health.

- Companies can be segmented according to products or services and according to geographical operations.
- An IASB standard requires certain information relating to each segment to be shown.
- Identifying a segment and allocating costs between segments can raise problems.
- An operating and financial review (OFR) discusses the nature of the business and its objectives, the performance of the business for the period and the financial position of the business.
- In the UK, the ASB has produced guidelines on the preparation of an OFR.
- Summary financial statements are available to investors who do not require the full set of financial statements.

Creative accounting

- Despite the accounting rules in place there have been recent examples of creative accounting by directors.
- This involves using accounting practices to show what the directors would like users to see rather than what is a fair representation of reality.
- There are various checks that can be carried out to the financial statements to see whether creative accounting practices may have been used.

→ Key terms

Accounting (financial reporting) p. 148	**framework of principles** p. 158
international accounting (financial reporting) standards p. 149	**segmental financial report** p. 161
statement of changes to equity p. 155	**transfer price** p. 162
directors' report p. 157	**operating and financial review (OFR)** p. 164
auditor p. 157	**summary financial statement** p. 168
	creative accounting p. 169

Further reading

If you would like to explore the topics covered in this chapter in more depth, we recommend the following books:

Corporate Financial Accounting and Reporting, *Sutton T.*, 2nd edn, Financial Times Prentice Hall, 2004, chapters 6 and 7.

International Accounting, *Walton P., Haller A. and Raffournier B.* (eds), 2nd edn, Thomson, 2003, chapter 19.

Improvements to International Accounting Standards, *International Accounting Standards Board*, IASB, 2003.

Operating and Financial Review, *Accounting Standards Board*, ASB, January 2003.

REVIEW QUESTIONS

Answers to these questions can be found on the students' side of the Companion Website at www.pearsoned.co.uk/atrillmclaney.

5.1 'Searching for an agreed framework of principles for accounting rules is likely to be a journey without an ending'. Discuss

5.2 The size of annual financial reports published by limited companies has increased steadily over the years. Can you think of any reasons, apart from the increasing volume of accounting regulation, why this has occurred?

5.3 What problems does a user of segmental financial statements face when seeking to make comparisons between businesses?

5.4 'An OFR should not be prepared by accountants but should be prepared by the board of directors.' Why should this be the case?

EXERCISES

Exercises 5.6 to 5.8 are more advanced than 5.1 to 5.5. Those with coloured numbers have answers at the back of the book.

5.1 It has been suggested that too much information might be as bad as too little information for users of annual reports. Explain.

5.2 What problems are likely to be encountered when preparing summary financial statements for shareholders?

5.3 The following information was extracted from the financial statements of I. Ching (Booksellers) plc for the year to 31 December 2005:

	£m
Interest payable	40
Cost of sales	460
Distribution costs	110
Income from investments	42
Revenue	943
Administration expenses	314
Other expenses	25

Note: Corporation tax is calculated at 25% of the profit on ordinary activities.

Required:
Prepare a profit and loss account for the year ended 31 December 2005 that is set out in accordance with the requirements of IAS 1 *Presentation of Financial Statements*.

5.4 Manet plc had the following share capital and reserves as at 30 June 2004:

	£m
Share capital (£0.25 ordinary shares)	250
Share premium account	50
Revaluation reserve	120
Currency translation reserve	15
Retained earnings	380
	815

During the year to 30 June 2005, the company revalued it freehold land upwards by £30m and made a loss on foreign exchange translation of £5m. The company made a profit after tax from operations of £160m during the year and the dividend payout ratio was 50%.

Required:

Prepare a statement of changes in equity in accordance with the requirements of IAS 1 *Presentation of Financial Statements*.

5.5   Professor Myddleton argues that accounting standards should be limited to disclosure require-ments and should not impose rules on companies as to how to measure particular items in the financial statements. He states:

> The volume of accounting instructions is already high. If things go on like this, where will we be in 20 or 30 years time? On balance I conclude we would be better off without any standards on accounting measurement. There could still be some disclosure requirements for listed companies, though probably less than now.

Do you agree with this idea? Discuss. (*Note:* This issue has not been directly covered in the chapter, but you should be able to use your knowledge to try to come up with some points on both sides of the argument.)

5.6   The following is the segment reports of Tora plc, which manufactures and sells three main classes of product, for the year ended 31 December 2005.

	Paper £m	Plastic £m	Metal £m	Eliminations £m	Consolidation £m
Revenue					
External sales	420	280	140		
Inter-segment sales	20	10	15	(45)	
Total revenue	440	290	155	(45)	840
Result					
Segment result	80	65	45	(6)	184
Unallocated expenses					38
					146
Interest expense					(14)
Corporation tax					(26)
Net profit					106
Other information					
Segment assets	350	650	226		1,226
Unallocated assets					146
Consolidated total assets					1,372
Segment liabilities	55	150	42		247
Unallocated liabilities					60
Consolidated total liabilities					307
Capital expenditure	10	–	15		25
Depreciation	72	130	70		272

Required:

Analyse the performance of each of the business segments for the year and comment on your results.

5.7   Obtain a copy of an operating and financial review of two companies within the same industry. Compare the usefulness of each. In answering this question, you should consider the extent to which the OFRs incorporate the recommendations made by the Accounting Standards Board.

5.8 The following information has been extracted from the segmental report for 2002 of Unilever plc, a large Anglo-Dutch company that sells a variety of foods, home- and personal-care products under a variety of well-known brand names such as Flora, Ben & Jerry's, Surf, Comfort, Sunsilk, Dove and Calvin Klein.

Segment (see key below)	A €m	B €m	C €m	D €m	E €m	F €m	G €m	Total €m
Analysis by operation 2002								
Group turnover	9,272	6,145	4,064	7,456	8,565	12,236	532	48,270
Trading result	1,362	834	504	704	725	1,976	27	6,132
Amortisation of goodwill and intangibles								(1,245)
Other adjustments								154
Group operating profit								5,041
Depreciation and amortisation	1,291	204	220	315	437	252	83	2,802
Capital expenditure	202	166	167	270	215	251	27	1,298
Total assets by operation	19,717	3,610	4,095	3,851	3,581	4,066	2,662	41,582
Corporate assets								3,778
Other adjustments								(762)
Total assets								44,598

	€m United Kingdom & Netherlands	€m United States	€m Other	€m Total
Additional geographic analysis 2002				
Group turnover	5,406	11,421	31,443	48,270
Property, plant and equipment	979	1,564	4,893	7,436

Key to segments
A = Savoury and dressings
C = Health and wellness and beverages
E = Home care and professional cleaning
G = Other operations

B = Spreads and cooking products
D = Ice cream and frozen foods
F = Personal care

Source: Unilever plc.

Required:
(a) Analyse the performance of each of the major segments in so far as the information allows.
(b) State what additional information would be useful to help in your analysis of segmental performance.

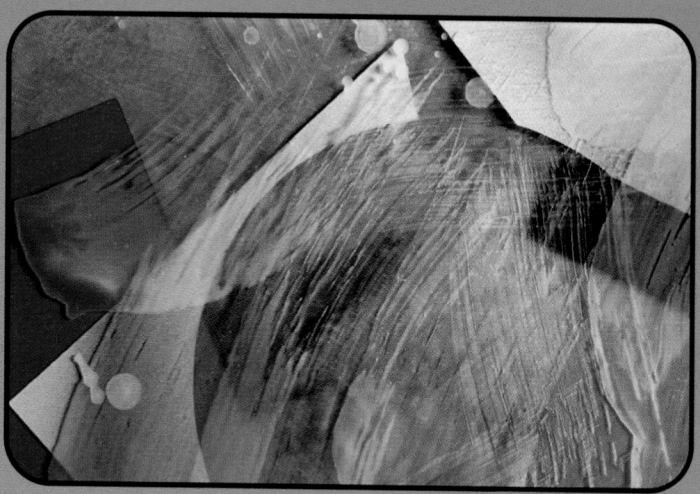

Measuring and reporting cash flows

INTRODUCTION

This chapter is devoted to the third major financial statement identified in Chapter 2 – the cash flow statement. This statement reveals the movements of cash over a period and the effect of these movements on the cash position of the business. It is an important financial statement because cash is important to the survival of a business. Without cash, no business can operate.

In this chapter, we shall see how the cash flow statement is prepared and how the information that it contains may be interpreted. We shall also see why the deficiencies of the profit and loss account (income statement) in revealing cash flows over time make a separate cash flow statement necessary.

The cash flow statement is being considered after the chapters on limited companies because the format of the statement requires an understanding of this type of business. Limited companies are required to provide a cash flow statement, as well as the more traditional profit and loss account and balance sheet, for share-holders and other interested parties.

The cash flow statement

The cash flow statement is a fairly recent addition to the set of financial statements sent to shareholders and to others. There used to be no regulation requiring companies to produce more than a profit and loss account (income statement) and balance sheet. The prevailing view seemed to have been that any financial information required would be contained within these two statements. This view may have been based partly on the assumption that if a business were profitable, it would also have plenty of cash. Though in the very long run this is likely to be true, it is not necessarily true in the short to medium term.

We have already seen in Chapter 3 that the profit and loss account sets out the revenue and expenses, rather than the cash receipts and cash payments, for the period. Thus, profit (loss), which represents the difference between the revenue and expenses for the period, may have little or no relation to the cash generated for the period. To illustrate this point, let us take the example of a business making a sale (a revenue). This may well lead to an increase in wealth and will be reflected in the profit and loss account. However, if the sale is made on credit, no cash changes hands – not at the time of sale at least. Instead, the increase in wealth is reflected in another asset – an increase in trade debtors (receivables). Furthermore, if an item of stock (inventory) is the subject of the sale, wealth is lost to the business through the reduction in the stock. This means an expense is incurred in making the sale, which will be shown in the profit and loss account. Once again, however, no cash has changed hands at the time of sale. For such reasons, the profit and the cash generated for a period will rarely go hand in hand.

The following activity helps to underline how profit and cash for a period may be affected differently by particular transactions or events.

ACTIVITY 6.1

The following is a list of business/accounting events. In each case, state the effect (increase, decrease or no effect) on both cash and profit:

	Effect on profit	on cash
1 Repayment of a loan	_____	_____
2 Making a sale on credit	_____	_____
3 Buying a non-current asset for cash	_____	_____
4 Receiving cash from a trade debtor (receivable)	_____	_____
5 Depreciating a non-current asset	_____	_____
6 Buying some stock (inventory) for cash	_____	_____
7 Making a share issue for cash	_____	_____

You should have come up with the following:

	Effect on profit	on cash
1 Repayment of a loan	none	decrease
2 Making a sale on credit	increase	none
3 Buying a non-current asset for cash	none	decrease
4 Receiving cash from a trade debtor (receivable)	none	increase
5 Depreciating a non-current asset	decrease	none
6 Buying some stock (inventory) for cash	none	decrease
7 Making a share issue for cash	none	increase

The reasons for these answers are as follows:

1 Repaying the loan requires that cash be paid to the lender. Thus two figures in the balance sheet will be affected, but not the profit and loss account.
2 Making a sale on credit will increase the sales figure and probably profit or loss (unless the sale was made for a price that precisely equalled the expenses involved). No cash will change hands, however, at this point.
3 Buying a non-current asset for cash obviously reduces the cash balance of the business, but the profit figure is not affected.
4 Receiving cash from a debtor increases the cash balance and reduces the debtor's balance. Both of these figures are on the balance sheet. The profit and loss account is unaffected.
5 Depreciating a non-current asset means that an expense is recognised. This causes the value of the asset, as it is recorded on the balance sheet, to fall by an amount equal to the amount of the expense. No cash is paid or received.
6 Buying some stock for cash means that the value of the stock will increase and the cash balance will decrease by a similar amount. Profit is not affected.
7 Making a share issue for cash increases the owners' claim and increases the cash balance; profit is unaffected.

It is clear from the above that if we are to gain an insight to cash movements over time, the profit and loss account is not the answer. Instead we need a separate financial statement. This fact has become widely recognised in recent years and in 1991 a UK financial reporting standard, FRS 1, emerged that requires all but the smallest companies to produce and publish a cash flow statement. This standard has been superseded for many companies from 2005 by the international accounting standard IAS 7. The two standards have broadly similar requirements. This chapter, follows the provisions of IAS 7.

Why is cash so important?

It is worth asking why is cash so important? After all, cash is just an asset that a business needs to help it to function. In that sense, it is no different from stock (inventory) or non-current assets.

The reason for the importance of cash is that people and organisations will not normally accept other than cash in settlement of their claims against the business. If a business wants to employ people it must pay them in cash. If it wants to buy a new non-current asset to exploit a business opportunity, the seller of the asset will normally insist on being paid in cash, probably after a short period of credit. When businesses fail, it is their inability to find the cash to pay the amounts owed that really pushes them under.

These factors lead to cash being the pre-eminent business asset. It is the one that analysts tend to watch most carefully when trying to assess the ability of businesses to survive and/or to take advantage of commercial opportunities as they arise. The fact that cash and profits do not always go hand in hand is illustrated in **Real World 6.1**. This explains how Eurotunnel, the cross-channel business between England and France continues to struggle to achieve profit, yet generates positive cash flows.

REAL WORLD 6.1

Cash flows under the channel   **FT**

'Richard Shirrefs [Eurotunnel's chief executive] called for a shift from "a stable equilibrium of failure to a stable equilibrium of success".'

'The company, which last restructured its long term debt in 2003, proposes to shift to a lower price, higher volume model for tunnel usage. Access rates for train operators would be reduced to entice them to introduce more services to more destinations, such as Amsterdam, and to encourage greater freight traffic.'

'Eurotunnel progressed its own plans for freight on Monday, announcing it expected to start a traction business in 2005 and that a platform designed to accept continental gauge freight trains would begin operations at Folkestone in the same next.'

'Mr Shirrefs said taxpayers had invested £10bn and industry £15bn in the tunnel and associated infrastructure and: 'We need to get all that infrastructure working . . . neither investor nor taxpayer is getting value".'

'Last year was a difficult one for Eurotunnel with reduced cross channel passenger flows bringing fare competition from ferry operators.'

'The company's operating revenue was down 5 per cent at £566m and its operating profit down 18 per cent at £170m. With interest payments of £318m, the underlying loss was up 40 per cent at £148m. However, it maintained a positive cash flow of £290m, down from £307m in 2002.'

Source: Extracts from 'Eurotunnel takes £1.3bn impairment charge' by Toby Shelley, FT.com, 9 February 2004.

The main features of the cash flow statement

The cash flow statement is, in essence, a summary of the cash receipts and payments over the period concerned. All payments of a particular type, for example cash payments to acquire additional non-current assets or other investments, are added together to give just one figure that appears in the statement. The net total of the statement is the net increase or decrease of the cash (and cash equivalents) of the business over the period. The statement is basically an analysis of the business's cash movements for the period.

A definition of cash and cash equivalents

IAS 7 defines cash as notes and coins in hand and deposits in banks and similar institutions that are accessible to the business on demand. Cash equivalents are short-term highly liquid investments that are readily convertible to known amounts of cash and which are subject to an insignificant risk of changes of value. Cash equivalents are held for the purpose of meeting short-term cash commitments rather than for investment or other purposes.

Activity 6.2 should clarify the types of items that fall within the definition of 'cash equivalents'.

ACTIVITY 6.2

At the end of its accounting period, Zeneb plc's balance sheet included the following items:

1 *A bank deposit account where one month's notice of withdrawal is required.* This deposit was made because the business has a temporary cash surplus that it will need to use in the short term for operating purposes;
2 *Ordinary shares in Jones plc (a Stock Exchange listed business).* These were acquired because the business has a temporary cash surplus and Zeneb plc's directors believed that the share represented a good short-term investment. The funds invested will need to be used in the short term for operating purposes.
3 *A bank deposit account that is withdrawable instantly.* This represents an investment of surplus funds that are not seen as being needed in the short term.
4 *An overdraft on the business's bank current account.*

Which (if any) of these four items would be included in the figure for cash and cash equivalents?

Your response should have been as follows:

1 A cash equivalent, because the deposit is part of the business's normal cash management activities and there is little doubt about how much cash will be obtained when the deposit is withdrawn.
2 Not a cash equivalent. Although the investment was made as part of normal cash management, there is a significant risk that the amount expected (hoped for!) when the shares are sold may not actually be forthcoming.
3 Not a cash equivalent, because this represents an investment, rather than a short-term surplus amount of cash.
4 This is cash itself, though a negative amount of it. The only exception to this classification would be where the business is financed in the longer term by an overdraft, when it would be part of the financing of the business.

As can be seen from the responses to Activity 6.2, whether a particular item falls within the definition of cash and cash equivalent depends on two factors:

● the nature of the item
● why it has arisen.

In practice, it is not usually difficult to decide whether an item is a cash equivalent.

The cash flow statement, the profit and loss account (income statement) and the balance sheet

The cash flow statement is now accepted, along with the profit and loss account and balance sheet, as a primary financial statement. The relationship between the three statements is shown in Figure 6.1. The balance sheet reflects the combination of assets (including cash) and claims (including the owners' capital) of the business *at a particular point in time*. Both the cash flow statement and the profit and loss account explain the *changes over a period* to two of the items in the balance sheet, namely cash and owners' claim respectively. In practice, this period is typically the business's accounting year.

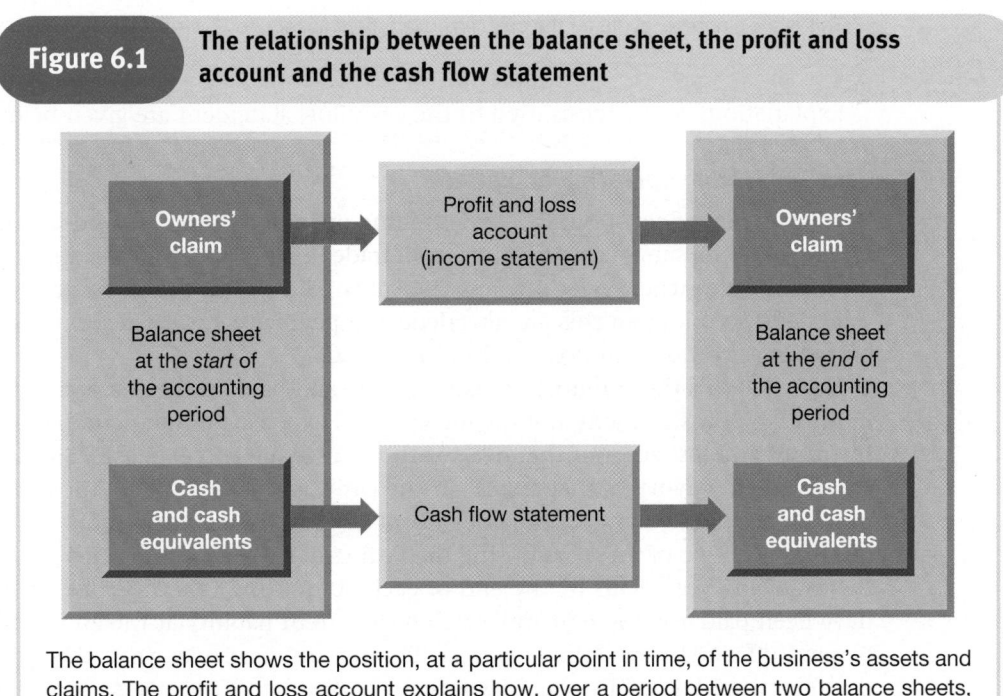

Figure 6.1   **The relationship between the balance sheet, the profit and loss account and the cash flow statement**

The balance sheet shows the position, at a particular point in time, of the business's assets and claims. The profit and loss account explains how, over a period between two balance sheets, the owners' claim figure in the first balance sheet has altered as a result of trading operations to become the figure in the second balance sheet. The cash flow statement also looks at changes over the accounting period, but this statement explains the alteration in the cash (and cash equivalent) balances shown in the two consecutive balance sheets.

The form of the cash flow statement

The standard layout of the cash flow statement is summarised in Figure 6.2.

> **Figure 6.2**   **Standard layout of the cash flow statement**
>
>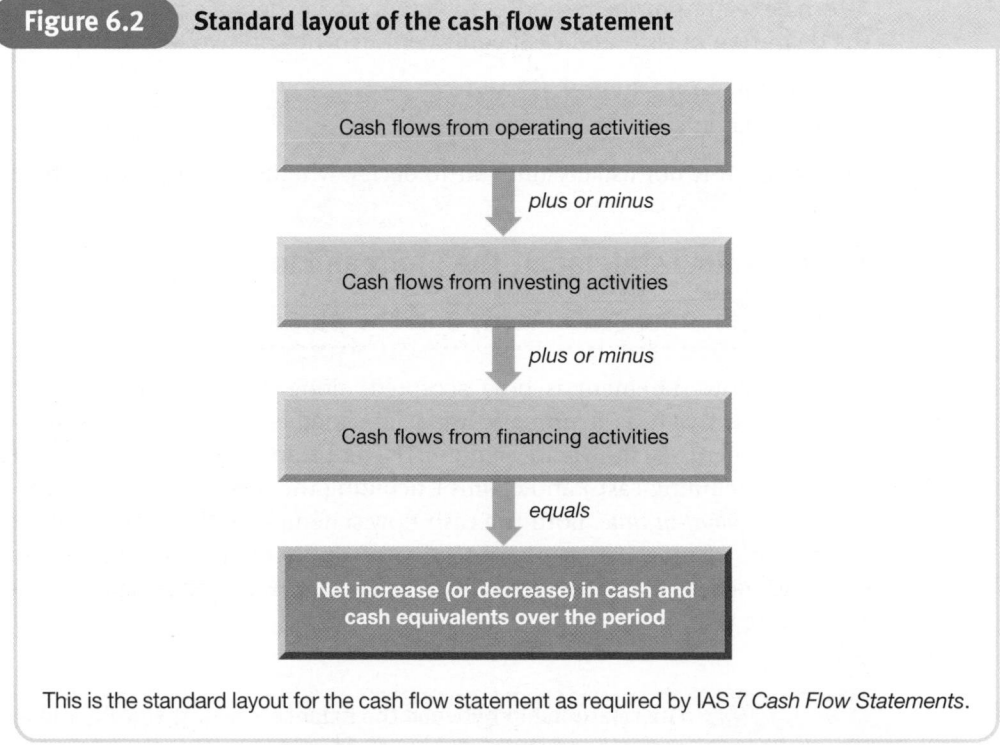
>
> This is the standard layout for the cash flow statement as required by IAS 7 *Cash Flow Statements*.

Explanations of the terms used in the cash flow statement are given below.

Cash flows from operating activities

This is the net inflow or outflow from trading operations, after tax and financing costs. It is equal to the sum of cash receipts from trade debtors (receivables), and cash receipts from cash sales where relevant, less the sums paid to buy stock, to pay rent, to pay wages and so on. From this are also deducted payments for interest on the business's borrowings, corporation tax and dividends paid.

Note that it is the amounts of cash received and paid during the period that feature in the cash flow statement, not the revenue and expense for that period. It is, of course, the profit and loss account that deals with the revenue and expenses. Similarly the tax and dividend payments that appear in the cash flow statement are those made in the period of the statement. Companies normally pay tax on their profits in four equal instalments. Two of these are during the year concerned, and the other two are during the following year. Thus by the end of each accounting year, one half of the tax will have been paid and the remainder will be a current liability at the end of the year, to be paid off during the following year. During any particular year, therefore, the tax payment would normally equal 50 per cent of the previous year's tax charge and 50 per cent of that of the current year.

The net figure for this section is intended to indicate the net cash flows for the period that arose from normal day-to-day trading activities after taking account of the tax that has to be paid on them and the cost of servicing the finance (equity and loans) needed to support them.

Cash flows from investing activities

This section of the statement is concerned with cash payments made to acquire additional non-current assets and with cash receipts from the disposal of non-current assets. These non-current assets could be loans made by the business or shares in

Figure 6.3   **Diagrammatical representation of the cash flow statement**

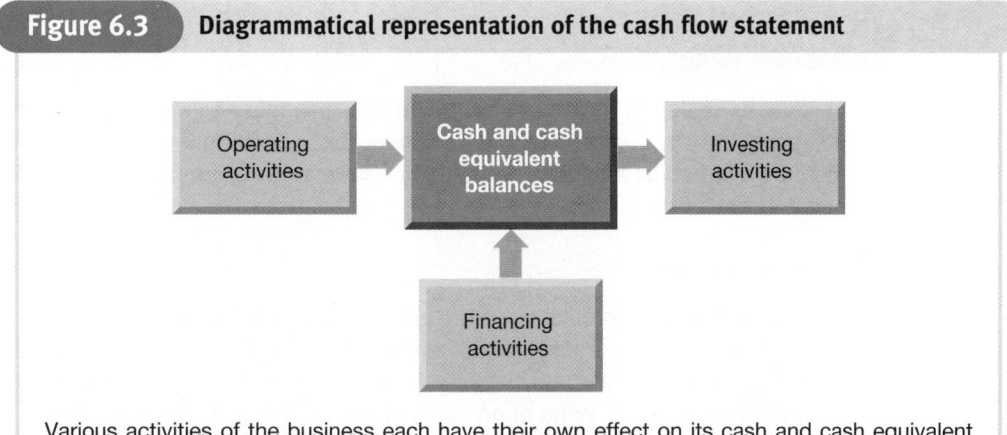

Various activities of the business each have their own effect on its cash and cash equivalent balances, either positive (increasing them) or negative (reducing them). The net increase or decrease in the cash and cash equivalent balances over a period will be the sum of these individual effects, taking account of the direction (cash in or cash out) of each activity.

Note that the direction of the arrow shows the *normal* direction of the cash flow in respect of each activity. In certain circumstances, each of these arrows could be reversed in direction.

another business bought by the business, as well as the more usual non-current assets such as buildings, machinery and so on.

This section also includes receipts from investments (loans and equity investments) made outside the business. These receipts are interest on loans made by the business and dividends from shares in other businesses that are owned by the business.

This section shows the net cash flows from making new investments and/or disposing of existing ones.

Cash flows from financing activities

This part of the statement is concerned with the long-term financing of the business. So we are considering borrowings (other than very short term) and finance from share issues. This category is concerned with repayment/redemption of finance as well as with the raising of it. It is permissible under IAS 7 to include dividend payments made by the business here, as an alternative to including them in 'Cash flows from operating activities' (above).

This section shows the net cash flows from raising and/or paying back long-term finance.

Net increase or decrease in cash and cash equivalents

The total of the statement must, of course, be the net increase or decrease in cash and cash equivalents over the period covered by the statement.

The effect on a business's cash and cash equivalents of its various activities is shown in Figure 6.3. The activities that affect cash are analysed in the same way as is required by IAS 7. As explained below, the arrows in the figure show the *normal* direction of cash flow for the typical healthy, profitable business in a typical year.

The normal direction of cash flows

Normally 'operating activities' provide positive cash flows: that is, they help to increase the business's cash resources. In fact, for UK businesses, cash generated from day-to-day trading, even after deducting tax, interest and dividends, is overwhelmingly the most important source of new finance for most businesses in most time periods.

ACTIVITY 6.3

Last year's cash flow statement for Angus plc showed a negative cash flow from operating activities. What could be the reason for this, and should the business's management be alarmed by it? (*Hint*: We think that there are two broad possible reasons for a negative cash flow.)

The two reasons are:

- The business is unprofitable. This leads to more cash being paid out to employees, suppliers of goods and services, interest and so on, than is received from debtors in respect of sales. This would be particularly alarming, because a major expense for most businesses is depreciation of non-current assets. Since depreciation does not lead to a cash flow, it is not considered in 'net cash inflows' from operating activities. Thus, a negative operating cash flow might well indicate a very much larger trading loss – in other words, a significant loss of the business's wealth.
- The other reason might be less alarming. A business that is expanding its activities (level of sales) would tend to spend quite a lot of cash, relative to the amount of cash coming in from sales. This is because it will probably be expanding its assets (non-current and current) to accommodate the increased demand. In the first instance, it would not necessarily benefit, in cash flow terms, from all of the additional sales. For example, a business may well have to have stock-in-trade (inventory) in place before additional sales can be made. Even when the additional sales are made, the sales would normally be made on credit, with the cash inflow lagging behind the sale. This would be particularly likely to be true of a new business, which would be expanding stocks and other assets from zero. Expansion typically causes cash flow strains for the reasons just explained. This can be a particular problem because the business's increased profitability might encourage a feeling of optimism, which could lead to lack of concern for the cash flow problem.

Investing activities can give rise to positive cash flows when a business sells some non-current assets. Because most types of non-current asset wear out, and because businesses tend to seek to expand their asset base, the normal direction of cash in this area is out of the business: that is, negative.

Financing can go in either direction, depending on the financing strategy at the time. Since businesses seek to expand, there is a general tendency for this area to lead to cash coming into the business rather than leaving it.

Preparing the cash flow statement

Deducing net cash flows from operating activities

The first category of cash flow statement, and the one that is typically the most important for most businesses, is the cash flow from operations. There are two methods that can be used to derive the figure in the statement: the direct method and the indirect method.

The direct method

The **direct method** involves an analysis of the cash records of the business for the period, picking out all payments and receipts relating to operating activities. These are summarised to give the total figures for inclusion in the cash flow statement. This could be a time-consuming and laborious activity, though a computer could do it. Not many businesses adopt this approach.

The indirect method

→ The **indirect method** is the more popular method. It relies on the fact that, broadly, sales give rise to cash inflows, and expenses give rise to outflows. Broadly, therefore, the net profit figure will be closely linked to the net cash inflows from operating activities. Since businesses have to produce a profit and loss account (income statement) in any case, information from it can be used as a starting point to deduce the cash inflows from operating activities.

Of course, within a particular accounting period, net profit will not normally equal the net cash inflows from operating activities. We saw in Chapter 3 that, when sales are made on credit, the cash receipt occurs some time after the sale. This means that sales made towards the end of an accounting year will be included in that year's profit and loss account, but most of the cash from those sales will flow into the business, and should be included in the cash flow statement, in the following year. Fortunately it is easy to deduce the cash received from sales if we have the relevant profit and loss account and balance sheets, as we shall see in Activity 6.4.

ACTIVITY 6.4

How can we deduce the cash inflows from sales using the profit and loss account and balance sheet for the business?

The balance sheet will tell us how much was owed in respect of credit sales at the beginning and end of the year (trade debtors (trade accounts receivable)). The profit and loss account tells us the sales figure. If we adjust the sales figure by the increase or decrease in trade debtors over the year, we deduce the cash from sales for the year.

Example 6.1

The sales figure for a business for the year was £34m. The trade debtors were £4m at the beginning of the year, but had increased to £5m by the end of the year.

Basically, the debtors figure is affected by sales and cash receipts. It is increased when a sale is made and decreased when cash is received from a debtor. If, over the year, the sales and the cash receipts had been equal, the beginning-of-year and end-of-year debtors figures would have been equal. Since the debtors figure increased, it must mean that less cash was received than sales were made. Thus the cash receipts from sales must be £33m (34 − (5 − 4)).

Put slightly differently, we can say that as a result of sales, assets of £34m flowed into the business during the year. If £1m of this went to increasing the asset of trade debtors, this leaves only £33m that went to increase cash.

The same general point is true in respect of nearly all of the other items that are taken into account in deducing the operating profit figure. The exception is depreciation. This is not necessarily associated with any movement in cash during the accounting period.

All of this means we can take the operating profit (that is, the profit after interest but before tax) for the year, add back the depreciation and interest expense charged in arriving at that profit, and adjust this total by movements in stock (inventories), trade debtors and creditors (trade accounts payable). If we then go on to deduct payments made during the accounting period for corporation tax, loan interest and dividends, we have the net cash from operating activities.

Example 6.2

The relevant information from the financial statements of Dido plc for last year is as follows:

	£m
Net profit, after interest, before taxation	122
Depreciation charged in arriving at net operating profit	34
Interest expense	6
At the beginning of the year	
Stock	15
Trade debtors	24
Trade creditors	18
At the end of the year	
Stock	17
Trade debtors	21
Trade creditors	19

The following further information is available about payments during last year:

	£m
Corporation tax paid	32
Interest paid	5
Dividends paid	9

The cash flow from operating activities is derived as follows:

		£m
Net profit, after interest, before taxation		122
Add Depreciation	34	
Interest expense	6	40
		162
Less Increase in stock (17 − 15)		(2)
Add Decrease in trade debtors (21 − 24)	3	
Increase in trade creditors (19 − 18)	1	4
Cash generated from operations		164
Less Interest paid	5	
Corporation tax paid	32	
Dividends paid	9	46
Net cash from operating activities		118

Thus the net increase in working capital, as a result of trading, was £162 million. Of this, £2 million went into increased stocks. More cash was received from trade debtors than sales were made, and less cash was paid to trade creditors than purchases of goods and services on credit. Both of these had a favourable effect on cash, which increased by £164 million. When account was taken of the payments for interest, tax and dividends, the net cash flow from operating activities was £118m (inflow).

Note that we needed to adjust the net profit, after interest, before taxation by the depreciation and interest expenses to derive the profit before depreciation and interest.

The indirect method of deducing the net cash flow from operating activities is summarised in Figure 6.4 on p. 190.

ACTIVITY 6.5

The relevant information from the financial statements of Pluto plc for last year is as follows:

	£m
Net profit, after interest, before tax	165
Depreciation charged in arriving at net operating profit	41
Interest expense	21
At the beginning of the year:	
Stock	22
Trade debtors	18
Trade creditors	15
At the end of the year	
Stock	23
Trade debtors	21
Trade creditors	17

The following further information is available about payments during last year:

	£m
Corporation tax paid	49
Interest paid	25
Dividends paid	28

What figure should appear in the cash flow statement for 'Cash flows from operating activities'?

Net cash inflows from operating activities:

	£m	£m
Net profit (after interest, before tax)		165
Add Depreciation	41	
Interest expense	21	62
		227
Less Increase in stock (23 – 22)	1	
Increase in trade debtors (21 – 18)	3	(4)
Add Increase in trade creditors (17 – 15)		2
Cash generated from operations		225
Less Interest paid	25	
Corporation tax paid	49	
Dividends paid	28	(102)
Net cash from operating activities		123

We can now go on to take a look at the preparation of a complete cash flow statement – see Example 6.3.

Figure 6.4   The indirect method of deducing the net cash flows from the operating activities

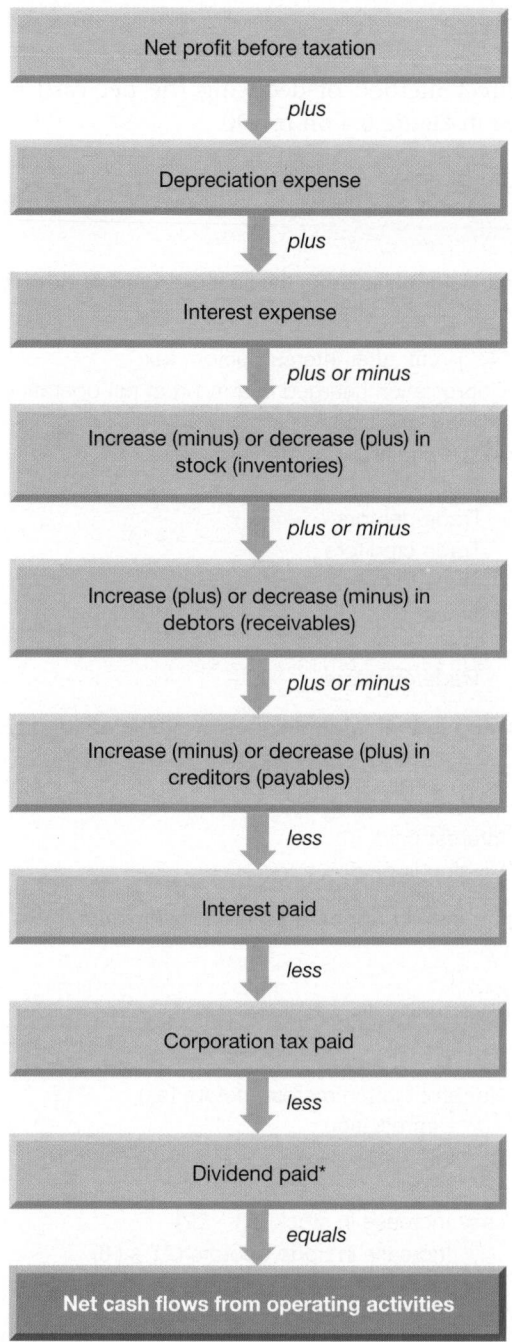

Determining the net cash from operating activities firstly involves adding back the depreciation and the interest expense to the net profit for the period. Next, adjustment is made for increases or decreases in stock, debtors and creditors. Lastly, cash paid for interest, tax and dividends is deducted.

*Note that dividends could alternatively be included under the heading 'Cash flows from financing activities'.

Example 6.3

Torbryan plc's profit and loss account for the year ended 31 December 2005 and the balance sheets as at 31 December 2004 and 2005 are as follows:

Profit and loss account for the year ended 31 December 2005

	£m	£m
Revenue		576
Less Cost of sales		307
Gross profit		269
Less Distribution costs	65	
Administrative expenses	26	91
		178
Other operating income		21
Operating profit		199
Interest receivable		17
		216
Less Interest payable		23
Profit on ordinary activities before taxation		193
Less Tax on profit (or loss) on ordinary activities		46
Profit on ordinary activities after taxation		147
Retained profit brought forward from last year		26
		173
Less Dividend paid on ordinary shares		50
Retained profit carried forward		123

Balance sheets as at 31 December 2004 and 2005

	2004 £m	2005 £m
Non-current assets		
Property, plant and equipment		
Land and buildings	241	241
Plant and machinery	309	325
	550	566
Current assets		
Stock	44	41
Trade debtors	121	139
	165	180
Less **Current liabilities**		
Bank overdraft	68	56
Trade creditors	55	54
Corporation tax	16	23
	139	133
Net current assets	26	47
Total assets less current liabilities	576	613
Less **Non-current liabilities**		
Debenture loans	400	250
	176	363
Equity		
Called-up ordinary share capital	150	200
Share premium account	–	40
Profit and loss account	26	123
	176	363

→

During 2005, the business spent £95m on additional plant and machinery. There were no other non-current-asset acquisitions or disposals. The interest receivable revenue and the interest payable expenses for the year were equal to the cash inflow and outflow respectively.

The cash flow statement would be as follows:

Torbryan plc
Cash flow statement for the year ended 31 December 2005

	£m	£m
Cash flows from operating activities		
Net profit, after interest, before taxation (see Note 1 below)		193
Adjustments for:		
Depreciation (Note 2)		79
Investment income (Note 3)		(17)
Interest expense (Note 4)		23
		278
Increase in trade debtors (139 – 121)		(18)
Decrease in trade creditors (55 – 54)		(1)
Decrease in stocks (44 – 41)		3
Cash generated from operations		262
Interest paid		(23)
Corporation tax paid (Note 5)		(39)
Dividend paid		(50)
Net cash from operating activities		150
Cash flows from investing activities		
Payments to acquire tangible non-current assets	(95)	
Interest received (Note 3)	17	
Net cash used in investing activities		(78)
Cash flows from financing activities		
Repayments of debenture stock (Note 7)	(150)	
Issue of ordinary shares (Note 8)	90	
Net cash used in financing activities		(60)
Net increase in cash and cash equivalents		12
Cash and cash equivalents at 1 January 2005 (Note 9)		(68)
Cash and cash equivalents at 31 December 2005		(56)

To see how this relates to the cash of the business at the beginning and end of the year it can be useful to provide a reconciliation as follows:

Analysis of cash and cash equivalents during the year ended 31 December 2005

	£m
Overdraft balance at 1 January 2005	(68)
Net cash inflow	12
Overdraft balance at 31 December 2005	(56)

Notes

1 This is simply taken from the profit and loss account for the year.

2 Since there were no disposals, the depreciation charges must be the difference between the start and end of the year's plant and machinery (non-current assets) values, adjusted by the cost of any additions.

	£m
Book value, at 1 January 2005	309
Add Additions	95
	404
Less Depreciation (balancing figure)	79
Book value, at 31 December 2005	325

3 Investment income (interest receivable) must be taken away to work towards the profit before crediting it, because it is not part of operations, but of investing activities. The cash inflow from this source appears under the 'Cash flows from investing activities' heading.

4 Interest payable expense must be taken out, by adding it back to the profit figure. We subsequently deduct the cash paid for interest payable during the year. In this case the two figures are identical.

5 Tax is paid by companies 50 per cent during their accounting year and the other 50 per cent in the following year. Thus the 2005 payment would have been half the tax on the 2004 profit (that is, the figure that would have appeared in the current liabilities at the end of 2004), plus half of the 2005 tax charge (that is, $16 + (\frac{1}{2} \times 46) = 39$). Probably the easiest way to deduce the amount paid during the year to 31 December 2005 is by following this approach:

	£m
Tax owed at start of the year (from the balance sheet as at 31 December 2004)	16
Add Tax charge for the year (from the profit and loss account)	46
	62
Less Tax owed at the end of the year (from the balance sheet as at 31 December 2005)	23
Tax paid during the year	39

This follows the logic that if we start with what the business owed at the beginning of the year, add on the increase in what was owed as a result of the current year's tax and then deduct what was owed at the end, the resulting figure must be what was paid during the year.

7 It has been assumed that the debentures were redeemed for their balance sheet value. This is not, however, always the case.

8 The share issue raised £90m, of which £50m went into the share capital total on the balance sheet and £40m into share premium.

9 There were no 'cash equivalents', just cash (though negative).

What does the cash flow statement tell us?

The cash flow statement tells us how the business has generated cash during the period and where that cash has gone. Since cash is properly regarded as the lifeblood of just about any business, this is potentially very useful information.

Tracking the sources and uses of cash over several years could show financing trends that a reader of the statements could use to help to make predictions about the likely future behaviour of the company.

Looking specifically at the cash flow statement for Torbryan plc, in Example 6.3, we can see the following:

● Net cash flow from operations was strong, much larger than the profit figure, after taking account of the dividend paid. This would be expected because depreciation is deducted in arriving at profit. There was a general tendency for working capital to absorb some cash. This would not be surprising had there been an expansion of activity (sales output) over the year. From the information supplied, we do not know whether there was an expansion or not. (We have only one year's profit and loss account.)

● There were net outflows of cash for investing activities, but this would not be unusual. Many items of property, plant and equipment have limited lives and need to be replaced with new ones. The expenditure during the year was not out of line with the depreciation expense for the year, which is what we might expect.

● There was a fairly major outflow of cash to redeem some debt finance, partly offset by the proceeds of a share issue. This presumably represents a change of financing strategy. Together with the ploughed-back profit from trading, there has been a significant shift in the equity/debt balance.

SELF-ASSESSMENT QUESTION 6.1

Touchstone plc's profit and loss accounts for the years ended 31 December 2004 and 2005 and the balance sheets as at 31 December 2004 and 2005 are as follows:

Profit and loss accounts for the years ended 2004 and 2005

	2004	2005
	£m	£m
Revenue	173	207
Cost of sales	(96)	(101)
Gross profit	77	106
Distribution costs	(18)	(20)
Administrative expenses	(24)	(26)
	35	60
Other operating income	3	4
Operating profit	38	64
Interest payable	(2)	(4)
Profit on ordinary activities before taxation	36	60
Tax on profit on ordinary activities	(8)	(16)
Profit on ordinary activities after taxation	28	44
Retained profit brought forward from last year	16	30
	44	74
Less Dividend paid on ordinary shares	14	18
Retained profit carried forward	30	56

Balance sheets as at 31 December 2004 and 2005

	2004	2005
Non-current assets	£m	£m
Property, plant and equipment:		
Land and buildings	94	110
Plant and machinery	53	62
	147	172
Current assets		
Stock	25	24
Treasury bills (short-term investments)	–	15
Trade debtors	16	26
Cash at bank and in hand	4	4
	45	69
Less **Current liabilities**		
Trade creditors (payables)	38	37
Corporation tax	4	8
	42	45
Net current assets	3	24
Total assets less current liabilities	150	196

	2004 £m	2005 £m
Less **Non-current liabilities**		
Debenture loans (10%)	20	40
	130	156
Equity		
Called-up ordinary share capital	100	100
Profit and loss account	30	56
	130	156

Included in 'cost of sales', 'distribution costs' and 'administration expenses', depreciation was as follows:

	2004 £m	2005 £m
Land and buildings	5	6
Plant and machinery	6	10

There were no non-current asset disposals in either year.

In the cases of both interest payable and receivable, the cash outflow/inflow equalled the expense/revenue.

The Treasury bills represent a short-term investment of funds that will be used shortly in operations. There is insignificant risk that this investment will lose value.

Required:

Prepare a cash flow statement for the business for 2005.

SUMMARY

The main points of this chapter may be summarised as follows:

The need for a cash flow statement

● Cash is important because no business can operate without it.

● The cash flow statement is specifically designed to reveal movements in cash over a period.

● Cash movements cannot be readily detected from the profit and loss account, which focuses on revenue and expenses rather than on cash receipts and cash payments.

● Profit (loss) and cash generated for the period are rarely equal.

● The cash flow statement is a primary financial statement, along with the profit and loss account and the balance sheet.

Preparing the cash flow statement

● The layout of the statement contains three categories of cash movement:
  – cash flows from operating activities;
  – cash flows from investing activities; and
  – cash flows from financing activities.

● The total of the cash movements under these three categories will provide the net increase or decrease in cash and cash equivalents for the period.

● A reconciliation can be undertaken to check that the opening balance of cash and cash equivalents plus the net increase (decrease) for the period equals the closing balance.

Calculating the cash generated from operations

● The net cash flows from operating activities can be derived from either the direct method or the indirect method.

● The direct method is based on an analysis of the cash records for the period, whereas the indirect method uses information contained within the profit and loss account and balance sheets of the business.

● The indirect method takes the net operating profit for the period, adds back any depreciation charge and then adjusts for changes in stocks, debtors and creditors during the period.

Interpreting the cash flow statement

● The cash flow statement shows the main sources and uses of cash.

● Tracking the cash movements over several periods may reveal financing and investing patterns and may help predict future management action.

 **Key terms**

direct method p. 186	**indirect method** p. 187

Further reading

If you would like to explore the topics covered in this chapter in more depth, we recommend the following books:

Financial Accounting and Reporting, *Elliott B. and Elliott J.*, 8th edn, Financial Times Prentice Hall, 2004, chapter 24.

Financial Reporting, *Alexander D. and Britton A.*, 6th edn, International Thomson Business Press, 2001, chapter 27.

Students' Guide to Accounting and Financial Reporting Standards, *Black G.*, 9th edn, Financial Times Prentice Hall, 2003, chapter 12.

REVIEW QUESTIONS

Answers to these questions can be found on the students' side of the Companion Website at **www.pearsoned.co.uk/atrillmclaney**.

6.1 The typical business outside the service sector has about 50 per cent more of its resources tied up in stock (inventories) than in cash, yet there is no call for a 'stock flow statement' to be prepared. Why is cash regarded as more important than stock?

6.2 What is the difference between the direct and indirect methods of deducing cash generated from operations?

6.3 Taking each of the categories of the cash flow statement in turn, in which direction would you normally expect the cash flow to be? Explain your answer.

(a) Cash flows from operating activities.
(b) Cash flows from investing activities.
(c) Cash flows from financing activities.

6.4 What causes the net profit for the year not to equal the net cash inflow?

EXERCISES

Exercises 6.3 to 6.8 are more advanced than 6.1 and 6.2. Those with coloured numbers have answers at the back of the book.

6.1 How will each of the following events ultimately affect the amount of cash?

(a) An increase in the level of stock-in-trade (inventories).
(b) A rights issue of ordinary shares.
(c) A bonus issue of ordinary shares.
(d) Writing off the value of some stock-in-trade.
(e) The disposal of a large number of the business's shares by a major shareholder.
(f) Depreciating a non-current asset.

6.2 The following information has been taken from the financial statements of Juno plc for last year and the year before last:

	Year before last £m	Last year £m
Net operating profit	156	187
Depreciation charged in arriving at net operating profit	47	55
Stock held at the end of:	27	31
Debtors at the end of:	24	23
Creditors at the end of:	15	17

Required:
What is the cash generated from operations figure for Juno plc for last year?

6.3 Torrent plc's profit and loss account for the year ended 31 December 2005 and the balance sheets as at 31 December 2004 and 2005 are as follows:

Profit and loss account

	£m	£m
Revenue		623
Less Cost of sales		353
Gross profit		270
Less Distribution costs	71	
Administrative expenses	30	101
		169
Rental income		27
Operating profit		196
Less Interest payable		26
Profit on ordinary activities before taxation		170
Less Tax on profit on ordinary activities		36
Profit on ordinary activities after taxation		134
Retained profit brought forward from last year		123
		257
Less Dividend paid on ordinary shares		60
Retained profit carried forward		197

Balance sheets as at 31 December 2004 and 2005

	2004 £m	2005 £m
Non-current assets		
Property, plant and equipment		
Land and buildings	310	310
Plant and machinery	325	314
	635	624
Current assets		
Stock	41	35
Trade debtors	139	145
	180	180
Current liabilities		
Bank overdraft	56	89
Trade creditors	54	41
Corporation tax	23	18
	133	148
Net current assets	47	32
Total assets less current liabilities	682	656
Less **Non-current liabilities**		
Debenture loans	250	150
	432	506
Equity		
Called-up ordinary share capital	200	300
Share premium account	40	–
Revaluation reserve	69	9
Profit and loss account	123	197
	432	506

During 2005, the business spent £67 million on additional plant and machinery. There were no other non-current asset acquisitions or disposals.

There was no share issue for cash during the year.

The interest payable expense was equal in amount to the cash outflow.

Required:
Prepare the cash flow statement for Torrent plc for the year ended 31 December 2005.

6.4 Chen plc's profit and loss accounts for the years ended 31 December 2004 and 2005 and the balance sheets as at 31 December 2004 and 2005 are as follows:

Profit and loss account

	2004 £m	2005 £m
Revenue	207	153
Cost of sales	(101)	(76)
Gross profit	106	77
Distribution costs	(22)	(20)
Administrative expenses	(20)	(28)
Operating profit	64	29
Interest payable	(4)	(4)
Profit on ordinary activities before taxation	60	25
Tax on profit (or loss) on ordinary activities	(16)	(6)
Profit on ordinary activities after taxation	44	19
Retained profit brought forward from last year	30	56
	74	75
Dividends paid on ordinary shares	(18)	(18)
Retained profit carried forward	56	57

Balance sheets as at 31 December 2004 and 2005

	2004 £m	2005 £m
Non-current assets		
Property, plant and equipment		
Land and buildings	110	130
Plant and machinery	62	56
	172	186
Current assets		
Stock	24	25
Trade debtors	26	25
Cash at bank and in hand	19	–
	69	50
Less **Current liabilities**		
Bank overdraft	–	2
Trade creditors	37	34
Corporation tax	8	3
	45	39
Net current assets	24	11
Total assets less current liabilities	196	197
Less **Non-current liabilities**		
Debenture loans (10%)	40	40
	156	157
Equity		
Called-up ordinary share capital	100	100
Profit and loss account	56	57
	156	157

Included in 'cost of sales', 'distribution costs' and 'administrative expenses', depreciation was as follows:

	2004	2005
	£m	£m
Land and buildings	6	10
Plant and machinery	10	12

There were no non-current asset disposals in either year.

The amount of cash paid for interest equalled the expense in both years.

Required:

Prepare a cash flow statement for the business for 2005.

6.5 The following are the financial statements for Nailsea plc for the years ended 30 June 2004 and 2005:

Profit and loss accounts for years ended 30 June

	2004		2005	
	£m	£m	£m	£m
Revenue		1,230		2,280
Less Operating costs	722		1,618	
Depreciation	270	992	320	1,938
Operating profit		238		342
Less Interest payable		–		27
Profit before tax		238		315
Less Tax		110		140
Profit after tax		128		175
Less Dividend paid		40		45
Retained profit for year		88		130

Balance sheets as at 30 June

	2004		2005	
	£m	£m	£m	£m
Non-current assets				
Property, plant and equipment (at net book value)				
Land and buildings		1,500		1,900
Plant and machinery		810		740
		2,310		2,640
Current assets				
Stock	275		450	
Trade debtors	100		250	
Bank	–		118	
	375		818	
Less **Current liabilities**				
Bank overdraft	32		–	
Trade creditors	170		230	
Taxation	55		70	
	257		300	
Net current assets		118		518
		2,428		3,158
Less **Non-current liabilities**				
9% debentures (repayable 2009)		–		300
		2,428		2,858
Equity				
Share capital (fully paid £1 shares)		1,400		1,600
Share premium account		200		300
Retained profits		828		958
		2,428		2,858

There were no disposals of non-current assets in either year.

Required:
Prepare a cash flow statement for Nailsea plc for the year ended 30 June 2005.

6.6 The following financial statements for Blackstone plc are a slightly simplified set of published accounts. Blackstone plc is an engineering firm that developed a new range of products in 2003; these now account for 60% of its turnover.

Profit and loss account for the years ended 31 March

	notes	2004 £m	2005 £m
Revenue		7,003	11,205
Cost of sales		(3,748)	(5,809)
Gross profit		3,255	5,396
Operating costs	1	(2,205)	(3,087)
Operating profit		1,050	2,309
Interest payable	2	(216)	(456)
Profit before taxation		834	1,853
Taxation		(210)	(390)
Profit after taxation		624	1,463
Dividend paid		(300)	(400)
Retained profit for the year		324	1,063
Retained profit brought forward		361	685
Retained profit carried forward		685	1,748

Balance sheets as at 31 March

	notes	2004 £m	2004 £m	2005 £m	2005 £m
Non-current assets					
Intangible assets	3		–		700
Property, plant and equipment	4		4,300		7,535
			4,300		8,235
Current assets					
Stock		1,209		2,410	
Trade debtors		641		1,173	
Cash at bank		123		–	
		1,973		3,583	
Current liabilities					
Trade creditors		(931)		(1,507)	
Taxation		(105)		(195)	
Bank overdraft		–		(1,816)	
		(1,036)		(3,518)	
Net current assets			937		65
Non-current liabilities					
Bank loan (repayable 2010)			(1,800)		(3,800)
			3,437		4,500
Equity					
Share capital			1,800		1,800
Share premium			600		600
Capital reserves			352		352
Retained profits			685		1,748
			3,437		4,500

Notes to the accounts

1 Operating costs include the following items:

	£m
Exceptional items	203
Depreciation	1,251
Administrative expenses	427
Marketing expenses	385

2 The expense and the cash outflow for interest payable are equal.

3 Intangible assets represent the amounts paid for the goodwill of another engineering business acquired during the year.

4 The movements in property, plant and equipment during the year are set out below.

	Land and buildings £m	Plant and machinery £m	Fixtures and fittings £m	Total £m
Cost				
At 1 April 2004	4,500	3,850	2,120	10,470
Additions	–	2,970	1,608	4,578
Disposals	–	(365)	(216)	(581)
At 31 March 2005	4,500	6,455	3,512	14,467
Depreciation				
At 1 April 2004	1,275	3,080	1,815	6,170
Charge for year	225	745	281	1,251
Disposals	–	(305)	(184)	(489)
At 31 March 2005	1,500	3,520	1,912	6,932
Net book value				
At 31 March 2005	3,000	2,935	1,600	7,535

Proceeds from the sale of non-current assets in the year ended 31 March 2005 amounted to £54 million.

Required:

Prepare a cash flow statement for Blackstone plc for the year ended 31 March 2005. (*Hint*: A loss (deficit) on disposal of non-current assets is simply an additional amount of depreciation and should be dealt with as such in preparing the cash flow statement.)

6.7 Simplified financial statements for York plc are set out below.

York plc
Profit and loss account for the year ended 30 September 2005

	£m
Revenue	290.0
Cost of sales	(215.0)
Gross profit	75.0
Less Operating expenses (note 1)	(62.0)
Operating profit	13.0
Interest payable (note 2)	(3.0)
Profit before taxation	10.0
Taxation	(2.6)
Profit after taxation	7.4
Dividends paid	(3.5)
Retained profit	3.9

Balance sheet at 30 September

	2004 £m	2004 £m	2005 £m	2005 £m
Non-current assets (note 3)		80.0		85.0
Current assets				
Stock and debtors	119.8		122.1	
Cash at bank	9.2		16.6	
	129.0		138.7	
Current liabilities				
Trade creditors	(80.0)		(82.5)	
Taxation	(1.0)		(1.3)	
	(81.0)		(83.8)	
Net current assets		48.0		54.9
Non-current liabilities		(32.0)		(35.0)
		96.0		104.9
Equity				
Share capital		35.0		40.0
Share premium account		30.0		30.0
Reserves		31.0		34.9
		96.0		104.9

Notes to the accounts

1 Operating expenses include depreciation of £13m and a surplus of £3.2m on the sale of non-current assets.
2 The expense and the cash outflow for interest payable are equal.
3 Non-current asset costs and depreciation:

	Cost £m	Accumulated depreciation £m	Net book value £m
At 1 October 2004	120.0	40.0	80.0
Disposals	(10.0)	(8.0)	(2.0)
Additions	20.0		20.0
Depreciation		13.0	(13.0)
At 30 September 2005	130.0	45.0	85.0

Required:

Prepare a cash flow statement for York plc for the year ended 30 September 2005 using the data above.

6.8 The balance sheets of Axis plc as at 31 December 2004 and 2005 and the summary profit and loss account for the year ended 31 December 2005 were as follows:

(continued over)

Balance sheet as at 31 December

	2004 £m	2004 £m	2005 £m	2005 £m
Non-current assets				
Property, plant and equipment				
Land and building at cost	130		130	
Less Accumulated depreciation	30	100	32	98
Plant and machinery at cost	70		80	
Less Accumulated depreciation	17	53	23	57
		153		155
Current assets				
Stock	25		24	
Trade debtors	16		26	
Short-term investments	–		12	
Cash at bank and in hand	–		7	
	41		69	
Current liabilities				
Trade creditors	31		36	
Taxation	7		8	
	38		44	
Net current assets		3		25
		156		180
Non-current liabilities				
10% debentures		(20)		(40)
		136		140
Equity				
Share capital		100		100
Revenue reserves		36		40
		136		140

Profit and loss account for the year ended 31 December 2005

	£m	£m
Revenue		173
Less Cost of sales		(96)
Gross profit		77
Interest receivable		2
		79
Less		
Sundry expenses	24	
Interest payable	2	
Deficit on sale of non-current asset	1	
Depreciation – buildings	2	
– plant	16	(45)
Net profit before tax		34
Corporation tax		(16)
Net profit after tax		18
Dividend paid		(14)
Unappropriated profit added to revenue reserves		4

During the year, plant (a non-current asset) costing £15m and with accumulated depreciation of £10m was sold.

The short-term investments were government securities, where there was little or no risk of loss of value.

The expense and the cash outflow for interest payable were equal.

Required:
Prepare a cash flow statement for Axis plc for the year ended 31 December 2005.

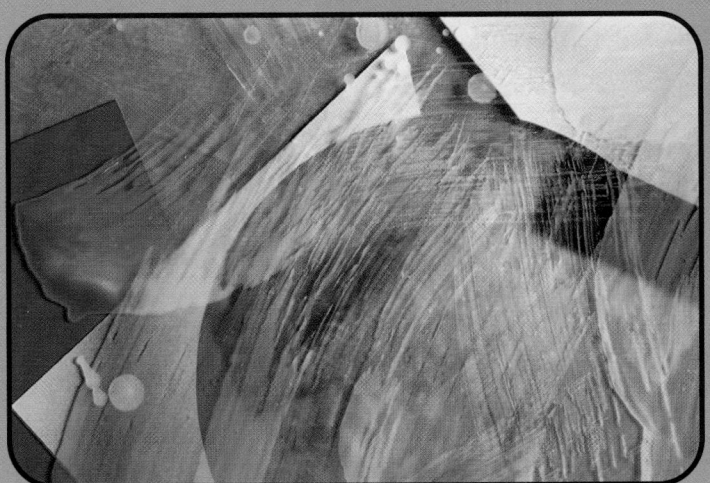

CHAPTER 7

Analysing and interpreting financial statements

INTRODUCTION

This chapter considers the analysis and interpretation of the financial statements discussed in Chapters 2, 3 and 6. We shall see how financial (or accounting) ratios can help in assessing the financial health of a business. We shall also consider the problems that are encountered when applying this technique.

Financial ratios can be used to examine various aspects of financial position and performance and are widely used for planning and control purposes. As we shall see in later chapters, they can be very helpful to managers in a wide variety of decision areas, such as profit planning, pricing, working-capital management, financial structure and dividend policy.

Financial ratios

Financial ratios provide a quick and relatively simple means of assessing the financial health of a business. A ratio simply relates one figure appearing in the financial statements to some other figure appearing there (for example, net profit in relation to capital employed) or, perhaps, to some resource of the business (for example, net profit per employee, sales revenue per square metre of counter space and so on).

Ratios can be very helpful when comparing the financial health of different businesses. Differences may exist between businesses in the scale of operations, and so a direct comparison of, say, the profits generated by each business may be misleading. By expressing profit in relation to some other measure (for example, sales revenue), the problem of scale is eliminated. A business with a profit of, say, £10,000 and sales revenue of £100,000 can be compared with a much larger business with a profit of, say, £80,000 and sales revenue of £1,000,000 by the use of a simple ratio. The net profit to sales revenue ratio for the smaller business is 10 per cent ([10,000/100,000] × 100%) and the same ratio for the larger business is 8 per cent ([80,000/1,000,000] × 100%). These ratios can be directly compared whereas comparison of the absolute profit figures would be less meaningful. The need to eliminate differences in scale through the use of ratios can also apply when comparing the performance of the same business over time.

By calculating a relatively small number of ratios, it is often possible to build up a good picture of the position and performance of a business. Thus, it is not surprising that ratios are widely used by those who have an interest in businesses and business performance. Though ratios are not difficult to calculate, they can be difficult to interpret and so it is important to appreciate that they are really only the starting point for further analysis.

Ratios help to highlight the financial strengths and weaknesses of a business, but they cannot, by themselves, explain why certain strengths or weaknesses exist, or why certain changes have occurred. Only a detailed investigation will reveal these underlying reasons.

Ratios can be expressed in various forms, for example as a percentage or as a proportion. The way that a particular ratio is presented will depend on the needs of those who will use the information. Though it is possible to calculate a large number of ratios, only a relatively few based on key relationships tend to be helpful to a particular user. Many ratios that could be calculated from the financial statements (for example, rent payable in relation to current assets) may not be considered because there is no clear or meaningful relationship between the two items.

There is no generally accepted list of ratios that can be applied to the financial statements, nor is there a standard method of calculating many ratios. Variations in both the choice of ratios and their calculation will be found in practice. However, it is important to be consistent in the way in which ratios are calculated for comparison purposes. The ratios discussed below are those that are widely used because many consider them to be among the more important for decision-making purposes.

Financial ratio classification

Ratios can be grouped into categories, each of which relates to a particular aspect of financial performance or position. The following broad categories provide a useful basis for explaining the nature of the financial ratios to be dealt with. There are five of them:

- *Profitability*. Businesses generally exist with the primary purpose of creating wealth for their owners. Profitability ratios provide an insight to the degree of success in achieving this purpose. They express the profits made (or figures bearing on profit, such as overheads) in relation to other key figures in the financial statements or to some business resource.
- *Efficiency*. Ratios may be used to measure the efficiency with which particular resources have been used within the business. These ratios are also referred to as *activity* ratios.
- *Liquidity*. It is vital to the survival of a business for there to be sufficient liquid resources available to meet maturing obligations (that is, debts that must be paid in the relatively near future). Some liquidity ratios examine the relationship between liquid resources held and creditors (payables) due for payment in the near future.
- *Financial gearing*. This is the relationship between the contribution to financing the business made by the owners of the business and the amount contributed by others, in the form of loans. The level of gearing has an important effect on the degree of risk associated with a business, as we shall see. Gearing is, therefore, something that managers must consider when making financing decisions. Gearing ratios tend to highlight the extent to which the business uses loan finance.
- *Investment*. Certain ratios are concerned with assessing the returns and performance of shares held in a particular business from the perspective of shareholders who are not involved with the management of the business.

The analyst must be clear *who* the target users are and *why* they need the information.

Different users of financial information are likely to have different information needs, which will in turn determine the ratios that they find useful. For example, shareholders are likely to be interested in their returns in relation to the level of risk associated with their investment. Thus profitability, investment and gearing ratios will be of particular interest. Long-term lenders are concerned with the long-term viability of the business and to help them to assess this, the profitability and gearing ratios of the business are also likely to be of particular interest. Short-term lenders, such as suppliers of goods and services on credit, may be interested in the ability of the business to repay the amounts owing in the short term. As a result, the liquidity ratios should be of interest.

We shall consider ratios falling into each of the five categories (profitability, efficiency, liquidity, gearing and investment) a little later in the chapter.

The need for comparison

Merely calculating a ratio will not tell us very much about the position or performance of a business. For example, if a ratio revealed that the business was generating £100 in sales revenue per square metre of counter space, it would not be possible to deduce from this information alone whether this particular level of performance was good, bad or indifferent. It is only when we compare this ratio with some 'benchmark' that the information can be interpreted and evaluated.

ACTIVITY 7.1

Can you think of any bases that could be used to compare a ratio you have calculated from the financial statements of a particular period?

In answering this activity you may have thought of the following bases:

- *Past periods*. By comparing the ratio we have calculated with the same ratio, but for a previous period, it is possible to detect whether there has been an improvement or deterioration in performance. Indeed, it is often useful to track particular ratios over time (say, five or ten years) to see whether it is possible to detect trends. The comparison of ratios from different time periods brings certain problems, however. In particular, there is always the possibility that trading conditions may have been quite different in the periods being compared. There is the further problem that, when comparing the performance of a single business over time, operating inefficiencies may not be clearly exposed. For example, the fact that net profit per employee has risen by 10 per cent over the previous period may at first sight appear to be satisfactory. This may not be the case, however, if similar businesses have shown an improvement of 50 per cent for the same period. Finally, there is the problem that inflation may have distorted the figures on which the ratios are based. Inflation can lead to an overstatement of profit and an understatement of asset values.

- *Similar businesses*. In a competitive environment, a business must consider its performance in relation to that of other businesses operating in the same industry. Survival may depend on the ability to achieve comparable levels of performance. Thus a very useful basis for comparing a particular ratio is the ratio achieved by similar businesses during the same period. This basis is not, however, without its problems. Competitors may have different year ends, and therefore trading conditions may not be identical. They may also have different accounting policies, which can have a significant effect on reported profits and asset values (for example, different methods of calculating depreciation or valuing stock (inventory)). Finally, it may be difficult to obtain the financial statements of competitor businesses. Sole proprietorships and partnerships, for example, are not obliged to make their financial statements available to the public. In the case of limited companies, there is a legal obligation to do so. However, a diversified business may not provide a breakdown of activities that is sufficiently detailed that analysts can compare the activities with those of other businesses.

- *Planned performance*. Ratios may be compared with the targets that management developed before the start of the period under review. The comparison of planned performance with actual performance may therefore be a useful way of revealing the level of achievement attained. However, the planned levels of performance must be based on realistic assumptions if they are to be useful for comparison purposes.

Planned performance is likely to be the most valuable benchmark for the managers to assess their own business. Businesses tend to develop planned ratios for each aspect of their activities. When formulating its plans, a business may usefully take account of its own past performance and that of other businesses. There is no reason, however, why a particular business should seek to achieve either its own previous performance or that of other businesses. Neither of these may be seen as an appropriate target.

Analysts outside the business do not normally have access to the business's plans. For these people, past performance and the performances of other, similar, businesses may be the only practical benchmarks.

Key steps in financial ratio analysis

When undertaking a ratio analysis, analysts follow a sequence of steps. The first step involves identifying the key indicators and relationships that require examination. In carrying out this step, the analyst must be clear *who* the target users are and *why* they need the information. We saw earlier that different types of users of financial information are likely to have different information needs that will, in turn, determine the ratios that they find useful.

The next step in the process is to calculate ratios that are considered appropriate for the particular users and the purpose for which they require the information.

The final step is interpretation and evaluation of the ratios. Interpretation involves examining the ratios in conjunction with an appropriate basis for comparison and any other information that may be relevant. The significance of the ratios calculated can then be established. Evaluation involves forming a judgement concerning the value of the information uncovered in the calculation and interpretation of the ratios. Whilst calculation is usually straightforward, and can be easily carried out by computer, the interpretation and evaluation are more difficult and often require high levels of skill. This skill can only really be acquired through much practice. The three steps described are shown in Figure 7.1.

Figure 7.1	The key steps of financial ratio analysis

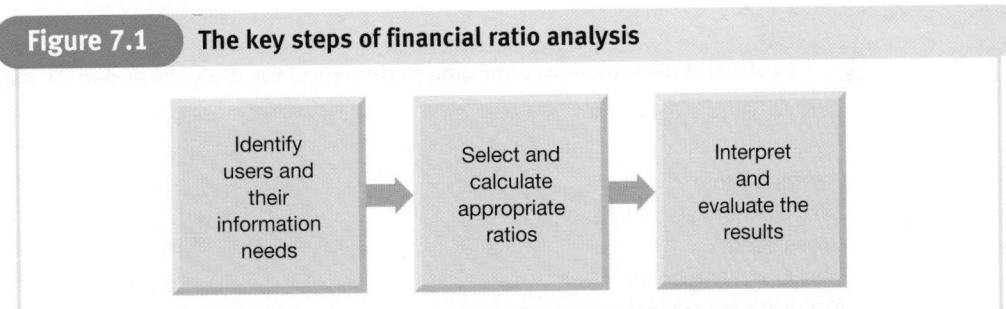

The three steps involve: firstly, identifying for whom and for what purpose the analysis and interpretation are required; secondly, selecting appropriate ratios and calculating them; and, finally, forming a judgement on the information produced.

Calculating the ratios

Probably the best way to explain financial ratios is through an example. Example 7.1 provides a set of financial statements from which we can calculate important ratios.

Example 7.1

The following financial statements relate to Alexis plc, which operates a whole-sale carpet business:

Balance sheets as at 31 March

	2004		2005	
	£m	£m	£m	£m
Non-current assets				
Property, plant and equipment (at cost less depreciation)				
Freehold land and buildings	381		427	
Fixtures and fittings	129		160	
		510		587
Current assets				
Stock at cost	300		406	
Trade debtors	240		273	
Bank	4		–	
	544		679	
Current liabilities				
Trade creditors	(221)		(314)	
Dividends approved, but unpaid	(40)		(40)	
Corporation tax due	(30)		(2)	
Bank overdraft	–		(76)	
	(291)	253	(432)	247
		763		834
Non-current liabilities				
9% debentures (secured)		(200)		(300)
		563		534
Equity				
£0.50 ordinary shares (Note 1)		300		300
Retained profit		263		234
		563		534

Profit and loss accounts (income statements) for the year ended 31 March

	2004	2005
	£m	£m
Revenue (Note 2)	2,240	2,681
Less Cost of sales (Note 3)	1,745	2,272
Gross profit	495	409
Less Operating costs	252	362
Net profit before interest and tax	243	47
Less Interest payable	18	32
Net profit before tax	225	15
Less Corporation tax	60	4
Net profit after tax	165	11
Add Retained profit brought forward	138	263
	303	274
Less Dividends aproved, but unpaid (Note 4)	40	40
Retained profit carried forward	263	234

Cash flow statement for the year ended 31 March

	2004 £m	2004 £m	2005 £m	2005 £m
Cash flows from operating activities				
Net profit, after interest, before taxation	225		15	
Adjustments for:				
Depreciation	26		33	
Interest expense	18		32	
	269		80	
Increase in stocks	(22)		(106)	
Increase in trade debtors	(17)		(33)	
Increase in trade creditors	21		93	
Cash generated from operations	251		34	
Interest paid	(18)		(32)	
Corporation tax paid	(63)		(32)	
Dividend paid	(40)		(40)	
Net cash from/(used in) operating activities		130		(70)
Cash flows from investing activities				
Payments to acquire property, plant and equipment	(77)		(110)	
Net cash used in investing activities		(77)		(110)
Cash flows from financing activities				
Issue of debenture stock	–		100	
Net cash from financing activities		–		100
Net increase in cash and cash equivalents		53		(80)
Cash and cash equivalents at start of year				
Cash/(overdraft)		(49)		4
Cash and cash equivalents at start of year				
Cash/(overdraft)		4		(76)

Notes:
1 The market value of the shares of the business at the end of the year was £2.50 for 2004 and £1.50 for 2005.
2 All sales and purchases are made on credit.
3 The cost of sales figure can be analysed as follows:

	2004 £m	2005 £m
Opening stock	241	300
Purchases (Note 2)	1,804	2,378
	2,045	2,678
Less Closing stock	300	406
Cost of sales	1,745	2,272

4 The dividend had been approved by the shareholders before the end of the accounting year (in both years), but not paid until after then.
5 The business employed 13,995 staff at 31 March 2004 and 18,623 at 31 March 2005.
6 The business expanded its capacity during 2005 by setting up a new warehouse and distribution centre in the north of England.
7 At 1 April 2003, the total of equity stood at £438m and the total of equity and non-current liabilities stood at £638m.

A brief overview

Before we start our detailed look at the ratios for Alexis plc (in Example 7.1), it is helpful to take a quick look at what information is obvious from the financial statements. This will usually pick up some issues that the ratios may not be able to identify. It may also highlight some points that could help us in our interpretation of the ratios. Starting at the top of the balance sheet, the following points can be noted:

- *Expansion of non-current assets.* These have increased by about 15 per cent (from £510m to £587m). This would appear not entirely (if at all) to be from any upward revaluation in assets existing in 2004, because the cash flow statement makes clear that £110m was spent on new non-current assets during 2005. The reason that the non-current assets in 2005 did not total £620m (that is, £510m plus £110m) is presumably that depreciation will have been charged. Note 5 mentions a new warehouse and distribution centre, which may account for much of the additional investment in non-current assets. We are not told when this new facility was established, but it is quite possible that it was well into the year. This could mean that not much benefit was reflected in terms of additional sales revenue or cost saving during 2005. Sales revenue, in fact, expanded by about 20 per cent (from £2,240m to £2,681m), greater than the expansion in non-current assets.

- *Major expansion in the elements of working capital.* Stock (inventory) increased by about 35 per cent, trade debtors (receivables) by about 14 per cent and trade creditors (payables) by about 33 per cent between 2004 and 2005. These are major increases, particularly in stock and creditors (which are linked because the stock is all bought on credit – see Note 2).

- *Reduction in the cash balance.* The cash balance fell from £4m (in funds) to a £76m overdraft, between 2004 and 2005. The bank may be putting the business under pressure to reverse this, which could raise difficulties.

- *Apparent debt capacity.* Comparing either the non-current assets or the net assets with the long-term borrowings implies that the business may well be able to offer security on further borrowing. This is because potential lenders usually look at the value of assets that can be offered as security when assessing loan requests. Lenders seem particularly attracted to freeholds as security. For example, at 31 March 2005, non-current assets had a balance sheet value of £587m, but long-term borrowing was only £300m (though there was also an overdraft of £74m). Balance sheet values are not normally, of course, market values. On the other hand, freeholds tend to have a market value higher than their balance sheet value due to inflation in land values.

- *Lower profit.* Though sales revenue expanded by 20 per cent between 2004 and 2005, both cost of sales and operating costs rose by a greater percentage, leaving both gross profit and, particularly, net profit massively reduced. The level of staffing, which increased by about 33 per cent (from 13,995 to 18,623), may have greatly affected the operating costs. (Without knowing when the additional employees were recruited during 2005, we cannot be sure of the effect on operating costs.) Increasing staffing by 33 per cent must put an enormous strain on management, at least in the short term. It is not surprising, therefore that 2005 was not successful for the business.

Having had a quick look at what is fairly obvious without calculating the normal ratios, we shall now go on to do so.

Profitability

The following ratios may be used to evaluate the profitability of the business:

- return on ordinary shareholders' funds;
- return on capital employed;
- net profit margin; and
- gross profit margin.

We shall now look at each of these in turn.

Return on ordinary shareholders' funds (ROSF)

The **return on ordinary shareholders' funds** compares the amount of profit for the period available to the owners, with the owners' average stake in the business during that same period. The ratio (which is normally expressed in percentage terms) is as follows:

$$\text{ROSF} = \frac{\text{Net profit after taxation and preference dividend (if any)}}{\text{Ordinary share capital plus reserves}} \times 100$$

The net profit after taxation and any preference dividend is used in calculating the ratio, as this figure represents the amount of profit that is left for the owners.

In the case of Alexis plc, the ratio for the year ended 31 March 2004 is:

$$\text{ROSF} = \frac{165}{(438 + 563)/2} \times 100 = 33.0\%$$

Note that, when calculating the ROSF, the average of the figures for ordinary shareholders' funds as at the beginning and at the end of the year has been used. It is preferable to use an average figure, as this might be more representative. This is, because the shareholders' funds did not have the same total throughout the year, yet we want to compare it with the profit earned during the whole period. We know, from Note 7, that the total of the shareholders' funds at 1 April 2003 was £438m. By a year later, however, it had risen to £563m, according to the balance sheet as at 31 March 2004.

The easiest approach to calculating the average amount of shareholders' funds is to take a simple average based on the opening and closing figures for the year. This is often the only information available, as is the case with Example 7.1. Where not even the beginning-of-year figure is available, it is usually acceptable to use just the year-end figure, provided that this approach is consistently adopted. This is generally valid for all ratios that combine a figure for a period (such as net profit) with one taken at a point in time (such as shareholders' funds).

ACTIVITY 7.2

Calculate the ROSF for Alexis plc for the year to 31 March 2005.

The ROSF for 2005 is:

$$\text{ROSF} = \frac{11}{(563 + 534)/2} \times 100 = 2.0\%$$

Broadly, businesses seek to generate as high a value as possible for this ratio, provided that it is not achieved at the expense of potential future returns by, for example, taking on more risky activities. In view of this, the 2005 ratio is very poor by any standards; a bank deposit account will yield a better return than this. We need to try to find out why things went so badly wrong in 2005. As we look at other ratios, we should find some clues.

Return on capital employed (ROCE)

The **return on capital employed** is a fundamental measure of business performance. This ratio expresses the relationship between the net profit generated during a period and the average long-term capital invested in the business during that period.

The ratio is expressed in percentage terms and is as follows:

$$ROCE = \frac{\text{Net profit before interest and taxation}}{\text{Share capital + Reserves + Long-term loans}} \times 100$$

Note, in this case, that the profit figure used is the net profit *before* interest and taxation, because the ratio attempts to measure the returns to all suppliers of long-term finance before any deductions for interest payable to lenders, or payments of dividends to shareholders, are made.

For the year to 31 March 2004, the ratio for Alexis plc is:

$$ROCE = \frac{243}{(638 + 763)/2} \times 100 = 34.7\%$$

ROCE is considered by many to be a primary measure of profitability. It compares inputs (capital invested) with outputs (profit). This comparison is vital in assessing the effectiveness with which funds have been deployed. Once again, an average figure for capital employed may be used where the information is available.

ACTIVITY 7.3

Calculate the ROCE for Alexis plc for the year to 31 March 2005.

For 2005, the ratio is:

$$ROCE = \frac{47}{(763 + 834)/2} \times 100 = 5.9\%$$

This ratio tells much the same story as ROSF; namely a poor performance, with the return on the assets being less than the rate that the business has to pay for most of its borrowed funds (that is, 9% for the debentures). See **Real World 7.2** (p. 231) for how Tesco plc, the well-known supermarket chain has been able to use loan financing to increase its ROSF ratios, despite a decline in ROCE.

Net profit margin

→ The **net profit margin ratio** relates the net profit for the period to the sales revenue during that period. The ratio is expressed as follows:

$$\text{Net profit margin} = \frac{\text{Net profit before interest and taxation}}{\text{Sales revenue}} \times 100$$

The net profit before interest and taxation is used in this ratio as it represents the profit from trading operations before the interest costs are taken into account. This is often regarded as the most appropriate measure of operational performance, when used as a basis of comparison, because differences arising from the way in which the business is financed will not influence the measure.

For the year ended 31 March 2004, Alexis plc's net profit margin ratio is:

$$\text{Net profit margin} = \frac{243}{2,240} \times 100 = 10.8\%$$

This ratio compares one output of the business (profit) with another output (sales revenue). The ratio can vary considerably between types of business. For example, supermarkets tend to operate on low prices and, therefore, low profit margins to stimulate sales and thereby increase the total amount of profit generated. Jewellers, on the other hand, tend to have high net profit margins, but have much lower levels of sales volume. Factors such as the degree of competition, the type of customer, the economic climate and industry characteristics (such as the level of risk) will influence the net profit margin of a business.

ACTIVITY 7.4

Calculate the net profit margin for Alexis plc for the year to 31 March 2005.

The net profit margin for 2005 is:

$$\text{Net profit margin} = \frac{47}{2,681} \times 100 = 1.8\%$$

Once again a very weak performance compared with that of 2004. Whereas in 2004 for every £1 of sales revenue an average of 10.8p (that is, 10.8%) was left as profit, after paying the cost of the carpets sold and other expenses of operating the business, for 2005 this had fallen to only 1.8p for every £1. Thus the reason for the poor ROSF and ROCE ratios was partially, perhaps wholly, a high level of expenses relative to sales revenue. The next ratio should provide us with a clue as to how the sharp decline in this ratio occurred.

Gross profit margin

→ The **gross profit margin ratio** relates the gross profit of the business to the sales revenue generated for the same period. Gross profit represents the difference between sales revenue and the cost of sales. The ratio is therefore a measure of profitability in buying (or producing) and selling goods before any other expenses are taken into account. As cost of sales represents a major expense for many businesses, a change in this ratio can have a significant effect on the 'bottom line' (that is, the net profit for the year). The gross profit margin ratio is calculated as follows:

$$\text{Gross profit margin} = \frac{\text{Gross profit}}{\text{Sales revenue}} \times 100$$

For the year to 31 March 2004, the ratio for Alexis plc is:

$$\text{Gross profit margin} = \frac{495}{2,240} \times 100 = 22.1\%$$

ACTIVITY 7.5

Calculate the gross profit margin for Alexis plc for the year to 31 March 2005.

The gross profit margin for 2005 is:

$$\text{Gross profit margin} = \frac{409}{2,681} \times 100 = 15.3\%$$

The decline in this ratio means that gross profit was lower *relative* to sales revenue in 2005 than it had been in 2004. Bearing in mind that:

Gross profit = Sales revenue − Cost of sales (or cost of goods sold)

this means that cost of sales was higher *relative* to sales revenue in 2005, than in 2004. This could mean that sales prices were lower and/or that the purchase cost of goods sold had increased. It is possible that both sales prices and goods sold prices had reduced, but the former at a greater rate than the latter. Similarly they may both have increased, but with sales prices having increased at a lesser rate than costs of the goods sold.

Clearly, part of the decline in the net profit margin ratio is linked to the dramatic decline in the gross profit margin ratio. Whereas, after paying for the carpets sold, for each £1 of sales revenue 22.1p was left to cover other operating expenses and leave a profit in 2004, this was only 15.3p in 2005.

The profitability ratios for the business over the two years can be set out as follows:

	2004 %	2005 %
ROSF	33.0	2.0
ROCE	34.7	5.9
Net profit margin	10.8	1.8
Gross profit margin	22.1	15.3

ACTIVITY 7.6

What do you deduce from a comparison of the declines in the net profit and gross profit margin ratios?

It occurs to us that the decline in the net profit margin was 9% (that is, 10.8% to 1.8%), whereas that of the gross profit margin was only 6.8% (that is, from 22.1% to 15.3%). This can only mean that operating expenses were greater, compared with sales revenue in 2005, than they had been in 2004. Thus, the declines in both ROSF and ROCE were caused partly by the business incurring higher stock purchasing costs relative to sales revenue and partly through higher operating expenses to sales revenue. We should need to compare these ratios with the planned levels for them before we could usefully assess the business's success.

The analyst must now carry out some investigation to discover what caused the increases in both cost of sales and operating costs, relative to sales revenue, from 2004 to 2005. This will involve checking on what has happened with sales and stock prices over the two years. Similarly, it will involve looking at each of the individual expenses that make up operating costs to discover which ones were responsible for the increase, relative to sales revenue. Here further ratios, for example staff costs (wages and salaries) to sales revenue, could be calculated in an attempt to isolate the cause of the change from 2004 to 2005. In fact, as we discussed when we took an overview of the financial statements, the increase in staffing may well account for most of the increase in operating costs.

Real World 7.1 shows how one well-known international business is seeking to improve its ROCE.

REAL WORLD 7.1

Lazy assets raise the ROCE at Shell

During 2003 Shell, the oil business (The 'Shell' Transport and Trading Company plc) disposed of $4 billion of what it called 'lazy assets'. These are assets that the business felt were not earning their keep and were holding the ROCE below the target range of 13–15%. The business had also identified a further $3 billion of assets that could be 'improved', so that they could also boost the business's ROCE.

Source: Based on information in 'Shell disposals of $4 billion double initial estimate', Toby Shelley, FT.com, 22 December 2003.

Efficiency

Efficiency ratios examine the ways in which various resources of the business are managed. The following ratios consider some of the more important aspects of resource management:

● average stock (inventory) turnover period;
● average settlement period for debtors (receivable);
● average settlement period for creditors (payables);
● sales revenue to capital employed; and
● sales revenue per employee.

We shall now look at each of these in turn.

Average stock (inventory) turnover period

Stocks often represent a significant investment for a business. For some types of business (for example, manufacturers), stocks may account for a substantial proportion of the total assets held (see Real World 16.1, p. 562). The **average stock turnover period** measures the average period for which stocks are being held. The ratio is calculated as follows:

$$\text{Average stock turnover period} = \frac{\text{Average stock held}}{\text{Cost of sales}} \times 365$$

The average stock for the period can be calculated as a simple average of the opening and closing stock levels for the year. However, in the case of a highly seasonal business, where stock levels may vary considerably over the year, a monthly average may be more appropriate.

In the case of Alexis plc, the stock turnover period for the year ended 31 March 2004 is:

$$\text{Average stock turnover period} = \frac{(241 + 300)/2}{1{,}745} \times 365 = 56.6 \text{ days}$$

This means that, on average, the stock held is being 'turned over' every 56.6 days. So, a carpet bought by the business on a particular day would, on average, have been sold about eight weeks later. A business will normally prefer a short stock turnover period to a long one, as funds tied up in stocks cannot be used for other purposes. When judging the amount of stock to carry, the business must consider such things as the likely demand for the stock, the possibility of supply shortages, the likelihood of price rises, the amount of storage space available and the perishability of the stock. The management of stocks will be considered in more detail in Chapter 16.

This ratio is sometimes expressed in terms of months rather than days. Multiplying by 12 rather than 365 will achieve this.

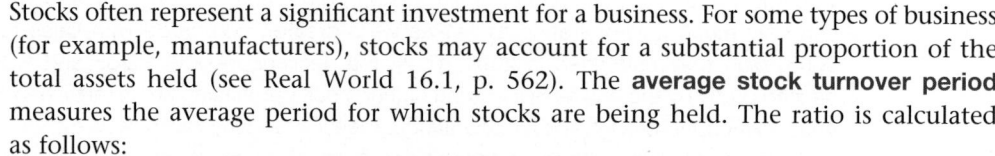

ACTIVITY 7.7

Calculate the average stock turnover period for Alexis plc for the year ended 31 March 2005.

The stock turnover period for 2005 is:

$$\text{Average stock turnover period} = \frac{(300 + 406)/2}{2{,}272} \times 365 = 56.7 \text{ days}$$

Thus the stock turnover period is virtually the same in both years.

Average settlement period for debtors

A business will usually be concerned with how long it takes for customers to pay the amounts owing. The speed of payment can have a significant effect on the business's cash flow. The **average settlement period for debtors** calculates how long, on average, credit customers take to pay the amounts that they owe to the business. The ratio is as follows:

$$\text{Average settlement period for debtors} = \frac{\text{Trade debtors}}{\text{Credit sales revenue}} \times 365$$

A business will normally prefer a shorter average settlement period to a longer one as, once again, funds are being tied up that may be used for more profitable purposes. Though this ratio can be useful, it is important to remember that it produces an *average* figure for the number of days for which debts are outstanding. This average may be badly distorted by, for example, a few large customers who are very slow or very fast payers.

Since all sales made by Alexis plc are on credit, the average settlement period for debtors for the year ended 31 March 2004 is:

$$\text{Average settlement period for debtors} = \frac{240}{2,240} \times 365 = 39.1 \text{ days}$$

As no figures for opening debtors are available, the year-end debtors figure only is used. This is common practice.

ACTIVITY 7.8

Calculate the average settlement period for Alexis plc's debtors for the year ended 31 March 2005. (In the interests of consistency, use the year-end debtors figure rather than an average figure.)

The average settlement period for 2005 is:

$$\text{Average settlement period for debtors} = \frac{273}{2,681} \times 365 = 37.2 \text{ days}$$

On the face of it, this reduction in the settlement period is welcome. It means that less cash was tied up in debtors for each £1 of sales revenue in 2005 than in 2004. Only if the reduction were achieved at the expense of customer goodwill or a high direct financial cost, might the desirability of the reduction be questioned. For example, the reduction may have been due to chasing customers too vigorously or as a result of incurring higher costs, such as discounts allowed to customers who pay quickly.

Average settlement period for creditors

The **average settlement period for creditors** measures how long, on average, the business takes to pay its trade creditors. The ratio is calculated as follows:

$$\text{Average settlement period for creditors} = \frac{\text{Trade creditors}}{\text{Credit purchases}} \times 365$$

This ratio provides an average figure, which, like the average settlement period for debtors ratio, can be distorted by the payment period for one or two large suppliers.

As trade creditors provide a free source of finance for the business, it is perhaps not surprising that some businesses attempt to increase their average settlement period for trade creditors. However, such a policy can be taken too far and result in a loss of good-will of suppliers. We shall return to the issues concerning the management of trade debtors and trade creditors in Chapter 16.

For the year ended 31 March 2004, Alexis plc's average settlement period for creditors is:

$$\text{Average settlement period for creditors} = \frac{221}{1,804} \times 365 = 44.7 \text{ days}$$

Once again, the year-end figure rather than an average figure for creditors has been used in the calculations.

ACTIVITY 7.9

Calculate the average settlement period for creditors for Alexis plc for the year ended 31 March 2005. (For the sake of consistency, use a year-end figure for creditors.)

The average settlement period for creditors is:

$$\text{Average settlement period for creditors} = \frac{314}{2,378} \times 365 = 48.2 \text{ days}$$

There was an increase, between 2004 and 2005, in the average length of time that elapsed between buying stock and paying for it. On the face of it, this is beneficial because the business is using free finance provided by suppliers. If, however, this is leading to a loss of supplier goodwill that could have adverse consequences for Alexis plc, it is not necessarily advantageous.

Sales revenue to capital employed

The **sales revenue to capital employed ratio** (or asset turnover ratio) examines how effectively the assets of the business are being used to generate sales revenue. It is calculated as follows:

$$\frac{\text{Sales revenue to}}{\text{capital employed ratio}} = \frac{\text{Sales revenue}}{\text{Share capital} + \text{Reserves} + \text{Non-current liabilities}}$$

Generally speaking, a higher asset turnover ratio is preferred to a lower one. A higher ratio will normally suggest that assets are being used more productively in the genera-tion of revenue. However, a very high ratio may suggest that the business is 'overtrad-ing on its assets', that is, it has insufficient assets to sustain the level of sales revenue achieved. (Overtrading will be discussed in more detail later in the chapter.) When comparing this ratio for different businesses, factors such as the age and condition of assets held, the valuation bases for assets and whether assets are rented or purchased outright can complicate interpretation.

A variation of this formula is to use the total assets less current liabilities (which is equivalent to long-term capital employed) in the denominator (lower part of the fraction) – the identical result is obtained.

For the year ended 31 March 2004 this ratio for Alexis plc is as follows:

$$\text{Sales revenue to capital employed} = \frac{2,240}{(638 + 763)/2} = 3.19 \text{ times}$$

ACTIVITY 7.10

Calculate the sales revenue to capital employed ratio for Alexis plc for the year ended 31 March 2005.

The sales revenue to capital employed ratio for the 2005 is:

$$\text{Sales revenue to capital employed} = \frac{2,681}{(763 + 834)/2} = 3.36 \text{ times}$$

This seems to be an improvement, since in 2005 more sales revenue was being generated for each £1 of capital employed (£3.36) than was the case in 2004 (£3.19). Provided that overtrading is not an issue, this is to be welcomed.

Sales revenue per employee

The **sales revenue per employee ratio** relates sales revenue generated to a particular business resource, that is, labour. It provides a measure of the productivity of the workforce. The ratio is:

$$\text{Sales revenue per employee} = \frac{\text{Sales revenue}}{\text{Number of employees}}$$

Generally, businesses would prefer to have a high value for this ratio, implying that they are using their staff efficiently.

For the year ended 31 March 2004, the ratio for Alexis plc is:

$$\text{Sales revenue per employee} = \frac{£2,240m}{13,995} = £160,057$$

ACTIVITY 7.11

Calculate the sales revenue per employee for Alexis plc for the year ended 31 March 2005.

The ratio for 2005 is:

$$\text{Sales revenue per employee} = \frac{£2,681m}{18,623} = £143,962$$

This represents a fairly significant decline and probably one that merits further investigation. As we discussed previously, the number of employees had increased quite notably (by about 33%) during 2005 and the analyst will probably try to discover why this had not generated sufficient additional sales revenue to maintain the ratio at its 2004 level. It could be that the additional employees were not appointed until late in the year ended 31 March 2005.

The efficiency, or activity, ratios may be summarised as follows:

	2004	*2005*
Average stock turnover period	56.6 days	56.7 days
Average settlement period for debtors	39.1 days	37.2 days
Average settlement period for creditors	44.7 days	48.2 days
Sales revenue to capital employed (asset turnover)	3.19 times	3.36 times
Sales revenue per employee	£160,057	£143,962

ACTIVITY 7.12

What do you deduce from a comparison of the efficiency ratios over the two years?

We feel that maintaining the stock turnover period at the 2004 level seems reasonable, though whether this represents a satisfactory period can probably only be assessed by looking at the business's planned stock period. The stock holding period for other businesses operating in carpet retailing, particularly those regarded as the market leaders, may have been helpful in formulating the plans. On the face of things, a shorter debtor collection period and a longer creditor payment period are both desirable. On the other hand, these may have been achieved at the cost of a loss of the goodwill of customers and suppliers, respectively. The increased asset turnover ratio seems beneficial, provided that the business can manage this increase. The decline in the sales revenue per employee ratio is undesirable but, as we have already seen, is probably related to the dramatic increase in the level of staffing. As with the stock turnover period, these other ratios need to be compared with the planned standard of efficiency.

The relationship between profitability and efficiency

In our earlier discussions concerning profitability ratios on page 214, we saw that return on capital employed (ROCE) is regarded as a key ratio by many businesses. The ratio is:

$$\text{ROCE} = \frac{\text{Net profit before interest and taxation}}{\text{Long-term capital employed}} \times 100$$

(where long-term capital comprises share capital plus reserves plus long-term loans). This ratio can be broken down into two elements, as shown in Figure 7.2. The first ratio is the net profit margin ratio, and the second is the sales revenue to capital employed (asset turnover) ratio, which we discussed earlier.

By breaking down the ROCE ratio in this manner, we highlight the fact that the overall return on funds employed within the business will be determined both by the profitability of sales and by efficiency in the use of capital.

Figure 7.2 **The main elements comprising the ROCE ratio**

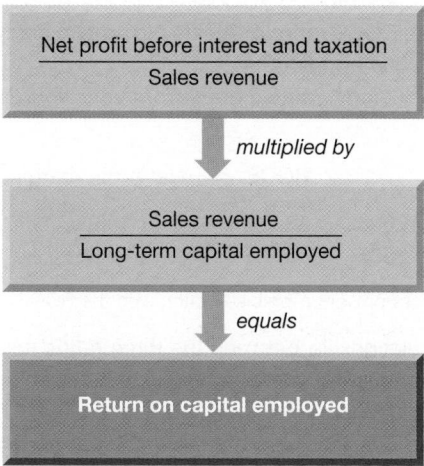

The ROCE ratio can be divided into two elements: net profit to sales revenue and sales revenue to capital employed. By analysing ROCE in this way, we can see the influence of both profitability and efficiency on this important ratio.

Example 7.2

Consider the following information concerning two different businesses operating in the same industry:

	Antler plc	*Baker plc*
Profit before interest and tax	£20m	£15m
Long-term capital employed	£100m	£75m
Sales revenue	£200m	£300m

The ROCE for each business is identical (20 per cent). However, the manner in which the return was achieved by each business was quite different. In the case of Antler plc, the net profit margin is 10% and the sales revenue to capital employed ratio is 2 times (so, ROCE = 10% × 2 = 20%). In the case of Baker plc, the net profit margin is 5% and the sales revenue to capital employed ratio is 4 times (and so, ROCE = 5% × 4 = 20%).

Example 7.2 demonstrates that a relatively low net profit margin can be compensated for by a relatively high sales revenue to capital employed ratio, and a relatively low sales revenue to capital employed ratio can be compensated for by a relatively high net profit margin. In many areas of retail and distribution (for example, supermarkets and delivery services) the net profit margins are quite low but the ROCE can be high, provided that the assets are used productively.

ACTIVITY 7.13

Show how the ROCE ratio for Alexis plc can be analysed into the two elements for each of the years 2004 and 2005.

What conclusions can we draw from your figures?

	ROCE	=	Net profit margin	×	Sales revenue to capital employed
2004	34.7%*		10.8%		3.19
2005	5.9%		1.8%		3.36

* Rounding errors prevent a precise match with the ROCE figures.

Thus the relationship between the three ratios holds for Alexis plc, for both years. The small apparent differences arise because the three ratios are stated above only to one or two decimal places.

Though the business was more effective at generating sales (sales revenue to capital employed ratio increased) from 2004 to 2005, it fell well below the level necessary to compensate for the sharp decline in the effectiveness of each sale (net profit margin). As a result, the 2005 ROCE was well below the 2004 value.

Liquidity

Liquidity ratios are concerned with the ability of the business to meet its short-term financial obligations. The following ratios are widely used:

- current ratio;
- acid test ratio; and
- operating cash flows to maturing obligations.

These three will now be considered.

Current ratio

The **current ratio** compares the 'liquid' assets (that is, cash and those assets held that will soon be turned into cash) of the business with the current liabilities. The ratio is calculated as follows:

$$\text{Current ratio} = \frac{\text{Current assets}}{\text{Current liabilities}}$$

Some people seem to suggest that there is an 'ideal' current ratio (usually 2 times or 2:1) for all businesses. However, this fails to take into account the fact that different types of business require different current ratios. For example, a manufacturing business will often have a relatively high current ratio because it is necessary to hold stocks of finished goods, raw materials and work in progress. It will also normally sell goods on credit, thereby incurring debtors. A supermarket chain, on the other hand, will have a relatively low ratio, as it will hold only fast-moving stocks of finished goods and will generate mostly cash sales revenue. (See **Real World 16.1** on p. 562.)

The higher the ratio, the more liquid the business is considered to be. As liquidity is vital to the survival of a business, a higher current ratio might be thought to be preferable to a lower one. If a business has a very high ratio, however, it may be that funds are tied up in cash or other liquid assets and are not, therefore, being used as productively as they might otherwise be.

As at 31 March 2004, the current ratio of Alexis plc is:

$$\text{Current ratio} = \frac{544}{291} = 1.9 \text{ times (or 1.9:1)}$$

ACTIVITY 7.14

Calculate the current ratio for Alexis plc as at 31 March 2005.

....

The current ratio as at 31 March 2005 is:

$$\text{Current ratio} = \frac{679}{432} = 1.6 \text{ times (or 1.6:1)}$$

Though this is a decline from 2004 to 2005, it is not necessarily a matter of concern. The next ratio may provide a clue as to whether there seems to be a problem.

Acid test ratio
....

The **acid test ratio** is very similar to the current ratio, but it represents a more stringent test of liquidity. It can be argued that, for many businesses, stock cannot be converted into cash quickly. (Note that, in the case of Alexis plc, the stock turnover period was about 57 days in both years (see p. 218).) As a result, it may be better to exclude this particular asset from any measure of liquidity. The acid test ratio is a variation of the current ratio, but excluding stock.

The minimum level for this ratio is often stated as 1.0 times (or 1:1 – that is, current assets (excluding stock) equals current liabilities). In many highly successful businesses that are regarded as having adequate liquidity, however, it is not unusual for the acid test ratio to be below 1.0 without causing particular liquidity problems. (See **Real World 16.1** on p. 562.)

The acid test ratio is calculated as follows:

$$\text{Acid test ratio} = \frac{\text{Current assets (excluding stock)}}{\text{Current liabilities}}$$

The acid test ratio for Alexis plc as at 31 March 2004 is:

$$\text{Acid test ratio} = \frac{544 - 300}{291} = 0.8 \text{ times (or 0.8:1)}$$

We can see that the 'liquid' current assets do not quite cover the current liabilities, so the business may be experiencing some liquidity problems.

ACTIVITY 7.15

Calculate the acid test ratio for Alexis plc as at 31 March 2005.

Acid test ratio as at 31 March 2005 $= \dfrac{679 - 406}{432} = 0.6$ times

The 2005 ratio is significantly below that for 2004. The 2005 level may well be a cause for concern. The rapid decline in this ratio should lead to steps being taken, at least, to stop further decline.

Cash generated from operations to maturing obligations

The **cash generated from operations to maturing obligations ratio** compares the cash generated from operations (taken from the cash flow statement) to the current liabilities of the business. It provides a further indication of the ability of the business to meet its maturing obligations. The ratio is expressed as:

$$\frac{\text{Cash generated from operations}}{\text{to maturing obligations}} = \frac{\text{Cash generated from operations}}{\text{Current liabilities}}$$

The higher this ratio, the better the liquidity of the business. This ratio has the advantage over the current ratio that the operating cash flows for a period usually provide a more reliable guide to the liquidity of a business than the current assets held at the balance sheet date. Alexis plc's ratio for the year ended 31 March 2004 is:

$$\text{Cash generated from operations to maturing obligations} = \frac{251}{291} = 0.9 \text{ times}$$

This ratio indicates that the operating cash flows for the period are just sufficient to cover the current liabilities at the end of the period.

ACTIVITY 7.16

Calculate the cash generated from operations to maturing obligations ratio for Alexis plc for the year ended 31 March 2005.

Cash generated from operations to maturing obligations ratio $= \dfrac{34}{432} = 0.1$ times

This ratio shows an alarming decline in the ability of the business to meet its maturing obligations from its operating cash flows. This confirms that liquidity is a real cause for concern for the business.

The liquidity ratios for the two-year period may be summarised as follows:

	2004	2005
Current ratio	1.9	1.6
Acid test ratio	0.8	0.6
Cash generated from operations to maturing obligations	0.9	0.1

ACTIVITY 7.17

What do you deduce from the liquidity ratios set out above?

Though it is probably not really possible to make a totally valid judgement without knowing the planned ratios, there appears to have been an alarming decline in liquidity. This is indicated by all three of these ratios. The most worrying is in the last ratio because it shows that the ability of the business to generate cash from trading operations has declined, relative to the short-term debts, from 2004 to 2005. The apparent liquidity problem may, however, be planned, short term and linked to the expansion in non-current assets and staffing. It may be that when the benefits of the expansion come on stream, liquidity will improve. On the other hand, short-term creditors may become anxious when they see signs of weak liquidity. This anxiety could lead to steps being taken to press for payment and this could cause problems for Alexis plc.

Gearing

Financial gearing occurs when a business is financed, at least in part, by borrowing, instead of by finance provided by the owners (the shareholders). A business's level of gearing (that is, the extent to which it is financed from sources that require a fixed return) is an important factor in assessing risk. Where a business borrows heavily, it takes on a commitment to pay interest charges and make capital repayments. This can be a significant financial burden; it can increase the risk of the business becoming insolvent. Nevertheless, most businesses are geared to some extent.

Given the risks involved, we may wonder why a business would want to take on gearing (that is, to borrow). One reason may be that the owners have insufficient funds, so the only way to finance the business adequately is to borrow from others. Another reason is that gearing can be used to increase the returns to owners. This is possible provided the returns generated from borrowed funds exceed the cost of paying interest. Example 7.3 illustrates this point.

Example 7.3

The long-term capital structures of two new businesses, Lee Ltd and Nova Ltd, are as follows:

	Lee Ltd £	Nova Ltd £
£1 ordinary shares	100,000	200,000
10% loan	200,000	100,000
	300,000	300,000

In their first year of operations, they each make a profit before interest and taxation of £50,000. The tax rate is 30 per cent of the net profit after interest.

Lee Ltd would probably be considered relatively highly geared, as it has a high proportion of borrowed funds in its long-term capital structure. Nova Ltd is much lower geared. The profit available to the shareholders of each business in the first year of operations will be:

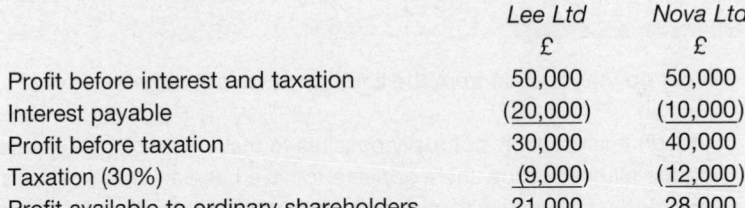

	Lee Ltd	Nova Ltd
	£	£
Profit before interest and taxation	50,000	50,000
Interest payable	(20,000)	(10,000)
Profit before taxation	30,000	40,000
Taxation (30%)	(9,000)	(12,000)
Profit available to ordinary shareholders	21,000	28,000

The return on ordinary shareholders' funds (ROSF) for each business will be:

Lee Ltd	Nova Ltd
$\dfrac{21,000}{100,000} \times 100 = 21\%$	$\dfrac{28,000}{200,000} \times 100 = 14\%$

We can see that Lee Ltd, the more highly geared business, has generated a better ROSF than Nova Ltd. This is despite the fact that the ROCE (return on capital employed) is identical for both businesses (that is (£50,000/£300,000) × 100 = 16.7%).

An effect of gearing is that returns to shareholders become more sensitive to changes in profits. For a highly geared business, a change in profits can lead to a proportionately greater change in the ROSF ratio.

ACTIVITY 7.18

Assume that the profit before interest and tax was 20 per cent higher for each business than stated above (that is, a profit of £60,000). What would be the effect of this on ROSF?

The revised profit available to the shareholders of each business in the first year of operations will be:

	Lee Ltd	Nova Ltd
	£	£
Profit before interest and taxation	60,000	60,000
Interest payable	(20,000)	(10,000)
Profit before taxation	40,000	50,000
Taxation (30%)	(12,000)	(15,000)
Profit available to ordinary shareholders	28,000	35,000

The ROSF for each business will now be:

Lee Ltd	Nova Ltd
$\dfrac{28,000}{100,000} \times 100 = 28\%$	$\dfrac{35,000}{200,000} \times 100 = 17.5\%$

We can see that for Lee Ltd, the higher-geared business, the returns to shareholders have increased by a third (from 21 per cent to 28 per cent), whereas for the lower-geared business, Nova Ltd, the benefits of gearing are less pronounced, increasing by

| Figure 7.3 | **The effect of financial gearing** |

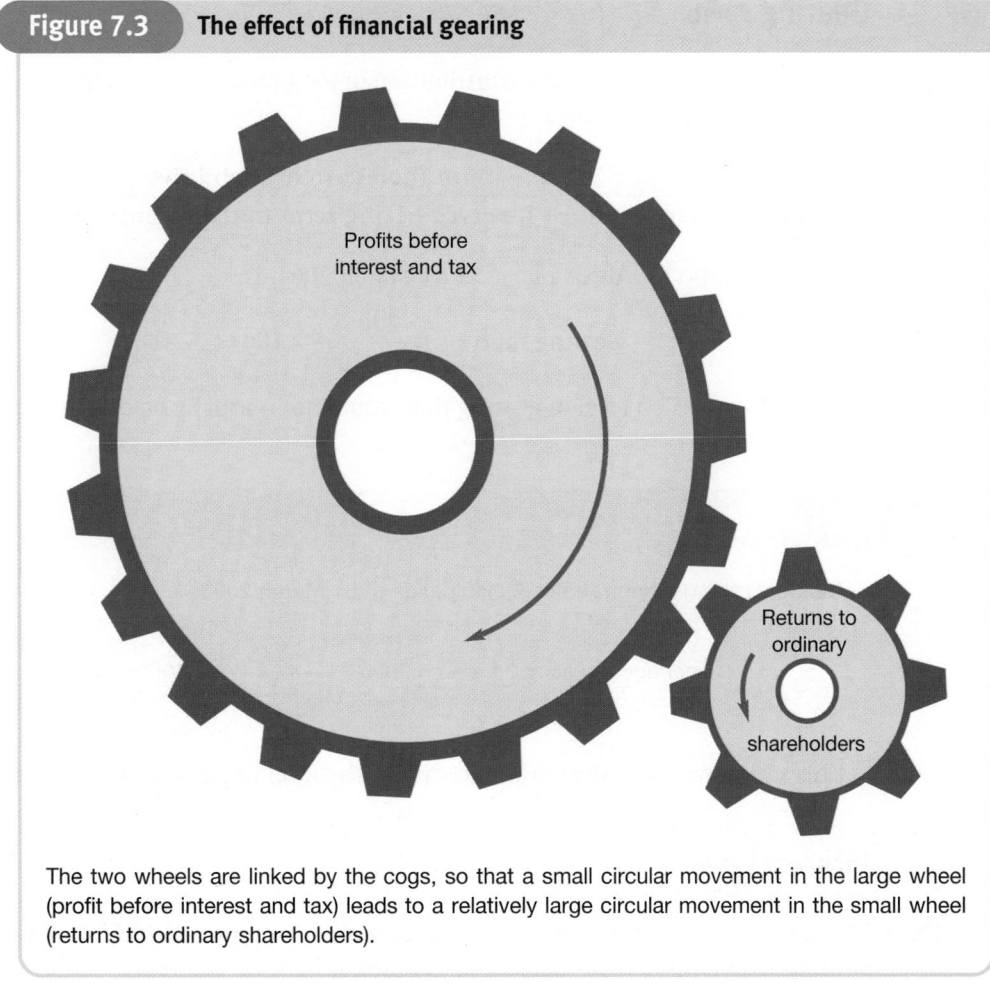

The two wheels are linked by the cogs, so that a small circular movement in the large wheel (profit before interest and tax) leads to a relatively large circular movement in the small wheel (returns to ordinary shareholders).

only a quarter (from 14 per cent to 17.5 per cent). The effect of gearing, of course, can work in both directions. Thus, for a highly geared business, a small decline in profits may bring about a much greater decline in the returns to shareholders.

The reason that gearing tends to be beneficial to shareholders is that loan interest rates are relatively low, compared with the returns that the typical business can earn. On top of this, interest costs are tax deductible, in the way shown in Example 7.3 and Activity 7.18, making the effective cost of borrowing quite cheap. It is debatable whether the apparent low interest rates really are beneficial to the shareholders. Some argue that since borrowing increases the risk to shareholders, there is a hidden cost of borrowing. What are not illusory, however, are the benefits to the shareholders of the tax deductibility of loan interest.

The effect of gearing is like that of two intermeshing cogwheels of unequal size (see Figure 7.3). The movement in the larger cog (profit before interest and tax) causes a more than proportionate movement in the smaller cog (returns to ordinary shareholders). The subject of gearing is discussed further in Chapter 15.

Real World 7.2, which appears later in this section on gearing ratios, provides an example of the effective use of gearing by a well-known business (Tesco plc).

Two ratios are widely used to assess gearing:

● gearing ratio;
● interest cover ratio.

Gearing ratio

➡ The **gearing ratio** measures the contribution of long-term lenders to the long-term capital structure of a business:

$$\text{Gearing ratio} = \frac{\text{Long-term (non-current) liabilities}}{\text{Share capital + Reserves + Long-term (non-current) liabilities}} \times 100$$

The gearing ratio for Alexis plc, as at 31 March 2004, is:

$$\text{Gearing ratio} = \frac{200}{(563 + 200)} \times 100 = 26.2\%$$

This ratio reveals a level of gearing that would not normally be considered to be very high.

ACTIVITY 7.19

Calculate the gearing ratio of Alexis plc as at 31 March 2005.

$$\text{Gearing ratio as at 31 March 2005} = \frac{300}{(534 + 300)} \times 100 = 36.0\%$$

This ratio reveals a substantial increase in the level of gearing over the year.

Interest cover ratio

➡ The **interest cover ratio** measures the amount of profit available to cover interest payable. The ratio may be calculated as follows:

$$\text{Interest cover ratio} = \frac{\text{Profit before interest and taxation}}{\text{Interest payable}}$$

The ratio for Alexis plc for the year ended 31 March 2004 is:

$$\text{Interest cover ratio} = \frac{243}{18} = 13.5 \text{ times}$$

This ratio shows that the level of profit is considerably higher than the level of interest payable. Thus a significant fall in profits could occur before profit levels failed to cover interest payable. The lower the level of profit coverage, the greater the risk to lenders that interest payments will not be met, and the greater the risk to the shareholders that the lenders will take action against the business to recover the interest due.

ACTIVITY 7.20

Calculate the interest cover ratio of Alexis plc for the year ended 31 March 2005.

$$\text{Interest cover ratio for 2005} = \frac{47}{32} = 1.5 \text{ times}$$

Real World 7.2 shows how Tesco plc, the UK and, increasingly, international super-market chain has been able to use increasing loan financing to boost ROSF in the early 2000s.

REAL WORLD 7.2

Tesco gears up for shareholders' returns

The following information relates to Tesco plc for its accounting years to the end of February 1999 to 2003:

	1999	2000	2001	2002	2003
ROCE (%)	17.2	16.1	16.6	16.1	15.3
Interest cover (times)	10.7	10.5	9.4	8.7	8.4
ROSF (%)	21.3	20.9	22.7	23.2	23.3

Over the five years, there was a decline in ROCE, but a steady increase in gearing (as measured by a decline in the interest cover ratio) had the effect of broadly increasing ROSF. The business must have been able to borrow at a lower rate of interest rate than its rate of ROCE. This boosted the returns to shareholders.

There is absolutely no suggestion here that Tesco's increased gearing was unwise. This is an extremely well-managed and successful business.

Source: Tesco plc Annual Report and Financial Statements 2003.

Alexis plc's gearing ratios are:

	2004	2005
Gearing ratio	26.2%	36.0%
Interest cover ratio	13.5 times	1.5 times

ACTIVITY 7.21

What do you deduce from a comparison of Alexis plc's gearing ratios over the two years?

....

The gearing ratio altered significantly. This is mainly due to the substantial increase in the long-term loan during 2005, which has had the effect of increasing the relative contribution of long-term lenders to the financing of the business.

The interest cover ratio has declined dramatically from a position where profit covered interest 13.5 times in 2004, to one where profit covered interest only 1.5 times in 2005. This was partly caused by the increase in borrowings in 2005, but mainly caused by the dramatic decline in profitability in that year. The later situation looks hazardous; only a small decline in future profitability in 2005 would leave the business with insufficient profit to cover the interest payments. The gearing ratio at 31 March 2005 would not necessarily be considered to be very high for a business that was trading successfully. It is the low profitability that is the problem.

Without knowing what the business planned these ratios to be, it is not possible to reach a totally valid conclusion on Alexis plc's gearing.

Real World 7.3 below provides some evidence concerning the gearing of listed businesses.

REAL WORLD 7.3

The gearing of listed businesses   FT

Larger listed businesses tend to have higher levels of gearing than smaller ones. A Bank of England report on the financing of small businesses found that the average level of gearing among smaller listed businesses was 27% compared with 37% for the top 350 listed businesses. Over recent years the level of borrowing by larger listed businesses has risen steadily [Tesco – see **Real World 7.2** – provides an example of this] whereas the level of borrowing for smaller listed businesses has remained fairly stable. This difference in gearing levels between larger and smaller businesses flies in the face of conventional wisdom.

Recent government investigations have found that smaller listed businesses often find it hard to attract the interest of investors. Many large institutional investors, who dominate the stock market, are not interested in the shares of smaller listed businesses because the amount of investment required is too small. As a result, shares in smaller businesses are less marketable. In such circumstances, it may be imagined that smaller businesses would become more reliant on loan financing and so would have higher levels of gearing than larger businesses. However, this is clearly not the case.

Although smaller businesses increase the level of shareholder funds by issuing relatively low dividends and retaining more profits, they tend to be less profitable than larger businesses. Thus, higher retained profits do not seem to explain satisfactorily this phenomenon.

The only obvious factors that could explain this difference between smaller and larger businesses are the level of tax relief on loan interest and borrowing capacity. Broadly, larger businesses pay tax at a higher rate than their smaller counterparts. This means that the tax benefits of borrowing tend to be greater per £ of interest paid for larger businesses than for smaller ones. It may well be that larger businesses can borrow at lower interest rates than smaller ones, if only because they tend to borrow larger sums and so the economies of scale may apply. Also larger businesses tend to be less likely to get into financial difficulties than smaller ones, so they may be able to borrow at lower interest rates.

Source: Adapted from 'Small companies surprise on lending', *Financial Times*, 25 April 2003.

Investment ratios

There are various ratios available that are designed to help investors assess the returns on their investment. The following are widely used:

- dividend payout ratio;
- dividend yield ratio;
- earnings per share;
- operating cash flow per share; and
- price/earnings ratio.

Dividend payout ratio
....

The **dividend payout ratio** measures the proportion of earnings that a business pays out to shareholders in the form of dividends. The ratio is calculated as follows:

$$\text{Dividend payout ratio} = \frac{\text{Dividends announced for the year}}{\text{Earnings for the year available for dividends}} \times 100$$

In the case of ordinary shares, the earnings available for dividend will normally be the net profit after taxation and after any preference dividends announced during the period. This ratio is normally expressed as a percentage.

The dividend payout ratio for Alexis plc for the year ended 31 March 2004 is:

$$\text{Dividend payout ratio} = \frac{40}{165} \times 100 = 24.2\%$$

The information provided by this ratio is often expressed slightly differently as the → **dividend cover ratio**. Here the calculation is:

$$\text{Dividend cover ratio} = \frac{\text{Earnings for the year available for dividend}}{\text{Dividend announced for the year}}$$

In the case of Alexis plc, (for 2004) it would be 165/40 = 4.1 times. That is to say, the earnings available for dividend cover the actual dividend by just over four times.

ACTIVITY 7.22

Calculate the dividend payout ratio of Alexis plc for the year ended 31 March 2005.

The ratio for 2005 is:

$$\text{Dividend payout ratio} = \frac{40}{11} \times 100 = 363.6\%$$

This would normally be considered to be a very alarming decline in the ratio over the two years. Paying a dividend of £40m in 2005 would probably be regarded as very imprudent.

Dividend yield ratio

→ The **dividend yield ratio** relates the cash return from a share to its current market value. This can help investors to assess the cash return on their investment in the business. The ratio, expressed as a percentage is:

$$\text{Dividend yield} = \frac{\text{Dividend per share}/(1 - t)}{\text{Market value per share}} \times 100$$

where t is the 'lower' rate of income tax. This requires some explanation. In the UK, investors who receive a dividend from a business also receive a tax credit. This tax credit is equal to the amount of tax that would be payable on the dividends received by a lower-rate taxpayer. As this tax credit can be offset against any tax liability arising from the dividends received, the dividends are effectively issued net of tax to lower-rate income taxpayers.

Investors may wish to compare the returns from shares with the returns from other forms of investment. As these other forms of investment are often quoted on a 'gross' (that is, pre-tax) basis it is useful to 'gross up' the dividend to make comparison easier. We can achieve this by dividing the **dividend per share** by $(1 - t)$, where t is the 'lower' rate of income tax.

Assuming a lower rate of income tax of 10 per cent, the dividend yield for Alexis plc for the year ended 31 March 2004 is:

$$\text{Dividend yield} = \frac{0.067^*/(1 - 0.10)}{2.50} \times 100 = 3.0\%$$

* Dividend proposed/number of shares = 40/(300 × 2) = £0.067 dividend per share (the 300 is multiplied by 2 because they are £0.50 shares).

ACTIVITY 7.23

Calculate the dividend yield for Alexis plc for the year ended 31 March 2005.

···

Your answer to this activity should be as follows:

$$\text{Dividend yield} = \frac{0.067^*/(1 - 0.10)}{1.50} \times 100 = 5.0\%$$

* 40/(300 × 2) = £0.067

Earnings per share
·························

The **earnings per share** (EPS) ratio relates the earnings generated by the business, and available to shareholders, during a period to the number of shares in issue. For equity (ordinary) shareholders, the amount available will be represented by the net profit after tax (less any preference dividend, where applicable). The ratio for equity shareholders is calculated as follows:

$$\text{Earnings per share} = \frac{\text{Earnings available to ordinary shareholders}}{\text{Number of ordinary shares in issue}}$$

In the case of Alexis plc, the earnings per share for the year ended 31 March 2004 is as follows:

$$\text{EPS} = \frac{£165}{600} = 27.5\text{p}$$

Many investment analysts regard the EPS ratio as a fundamental measure of share performance. The trend in earnings per share over time is used to help assess the investment potential of a business's shares. Though it is possible to make total profits rise through ordinary shareholders investing more in the business, this will not necessarily mean that the profitability *per share* will rise as a result.

It is not usually very helpful to compare the earnings per share of one business with those of another. Differences in capital structure (for example, in the nominal value of shares issued) can render any such comparison meaningless. However, it can be very useful to monitor the changes that occur in this ratio for a particular business over time.

ACTIVITY 7.24

Calculate the earnings per share of Alexis plc for the year ended 31 March 2005.

The earnings per share for 2005 is:

$$EPS = \frac{£11}{600} = 1.8p$$

Cash generated from operations per share

It can be argued that, in the short term at least, cash generated from operations (found in the cash flow statement) provides a better guide to the ability of a business to pay dividends and to undertake planned expenditures than the earnings per share figure. The **cash generated from operations (CGO) per ordinary share** is calculated as follows:

$$\text{Cash generated from operations per share} = \frac{\text{Cash generated from operations less preference dividend (if any)}}{\text{Number of ordinary shares in issue}}$$

The ratio for Alexis plc for the year ended 31 March 2004 is as follows:

$$\text{CGO per share} = \frac{£251}{600} = 41.8p$$

ACTIVITY 7.25

Calculate the CGO per ordinary share for Alexis plc for the year ended 31 March 2005.

The CGO per share for 2005 is:

$$\text{CGO per share} = \frac{£34}{600} = 5.7p$$

There has been a dramatic decrease in this ratio over the two-year period.

Note that, for both years, the CGO per share for Alexis plc is higher than the earnings per share. This is not unusual. The effect of adding back depreciation to derive the CGO figures will often ensure that a higher figure is derived.

Price/earnings (P/E) ratio

The **price/earnings ratio** relates the market value of a share to the earnings per share. This ratio can be calculated as follows:

$$\text{P/E ratio} = \frac{\text{Market value per share}}{\text{Earnings per share}}$$

The P/E ratio for Alexis plc as at 31 March 2004 is:

$$\text{P/E ratio} = \frac{£2.50}{27.5p^*} = 9.1 \text{ times}$$

* The EPS figure (27.5p) was calculated on p. 234.

This ratio reveals that the capital value of the share is 9.1 times higher than its current level of earnings. The ratio is a measure of market confidence in the future of a business. The higher the P/E ratio, the greater the confidence in the future earning power of the business and, consequently, the more investors are prepared to pay in relation to the earnings stream of the business.

P/E ratios provide a useful guide to market confidence concerning the future and they can, therefore, be helpful when comparing different businesses. However, differences in accounting policies between businesses can lead to different profit and earnings per share figures, and this can distort comparisons.

ACTIVITY 7.26

Calculate the P/E ratio of Alexis plc as at 31 March 2005.

Your answer to this activity should be as follows:

$$\text{P/E ratio} = \frac{£1.50}{1.8p} = 83.3 \text{ times}$$

The investment ratios for Alexis plc over the two-year period are as follows:

	2004	2005
Dividend payout ratio	24.2%	363.6%
Dividend yield ratio	3.0%	5.0%
Earnings per share	27.5p	1.8p
Cash generated from operations per share	41.8p	5.7p
P/E ratio	9.1 times	83.3 times

ACTIVITY 7.27

What do you deduce from the investment ratios set out above?
    Can you offer an explanation why the share price has not fallen as much as it might have done, bearing in mind the very poor (relative to 2004) trading performance in 2005?

We thought that, though:

● the EPS and the CGO per share figures have both fallen dramatically; and
● the dividend payment for 2005 seems very imprudent,

the share price seems to have held up remarkably well (fallen from £2.50 to £1.50, see p. 211). This means that dividend yield and P/E value for 2005 look better than those for 2004. This is an anomaly of these two ratios, which stems from using a forward-looking value (the share price) in conjunction with historic data (dividends and earnings). Share prices are based on investors' assessments of the business's future. It seems with Alexis plc that, at the end of 2005, the 'market' was not happy with the business, relative to 2004. This is evidenced by the fact that the share price had fallen by £1 a share. On the other hand, the share price has not fallen as much as profits. It appears that investors believe that the business will perform better in the future than it did in 2005. This may well be because they believe that the large expansion in assets and employee numbers that occurred in 2005 will yield benefits in the future; benefits that the business was not able to generate during 2005.

Real World 7.4 gives some information about the shares of several large, well-known UK businesses. This type of information is provided on a daily basis by several newspapers, notably the *Financial Times*.

REAL WORLD 7.4

Market statistics for some well-known businesses   FT

The following shares were extracted from the *Financial Times* on 3 January 2004, relating to the previous day's trading of the shares of some well-known businesses on the London Stock Exchange:

Share	Price	(+/−)	52 week		Y'ld	P/E	Volume
			High	Low	Gr's		000s
BP	$454^3/_4$	$+1^3/_4$	$459^1/_2$	$348^3/_4$	3.4	20.1	21,113
JD Wetherspoon	286	+6	290	158	1.2	16.8	784
Manchester United	264	$+6^1/_2$	275	103	0.9	43.3	153
Marks and Spencer	$289^1/_4$	$+^1/_4$	339	$258^1/_2$	3.8	13.6	7,243
Rolls-Royce	178	$+^3/_4$	194	$64^1/_4$	4.6	19.4	5,170
Vodafone	$139^1/_4$	$+1^1/_4$	$140^1/_2$	$100^3/_4$	1.3	28.5	81,870

The column headings are as follows:

Price   Mid-market price (that is, the price midway between buying and selling price) of the shares at the end of 2 January 2004.

(+/−)   Gain or loss (usually stated in pence) from the previous day's mid-market price.

High/Low   Highest and lowest prices reached by the share during the year (stated in pence).

Y'ld gr's   Gross dividend yield, based on the most recent year's dividend and the current share price.

P/E   Price/earnings ratio, based on the most recent year's after-tax profit and the current share price.

Volume   The number of shares (in thousands) that were bought and sold on 2 January 2004.

Real World 7.5 shows how investment ratios can vary between different industry sectors.

REAL WORLD 7.5

How investment ratios vary between industries

Investment ratios can vary significantly between businesses and between industries. To give some indication of the range of variations that occur, the average dividend yield ratios and average P/E ratios for listed businesses in 12 different industries are shown in Figures 7.4 and 7.5 respectively.

These ratios are calculated from the current market value of the shares and the most recent year's dividend paid (dividend yield) or earnings per share (P/E).

Some industries tend to pay out lower dividends than others, leading to lower dividend yield ratios. Pharmaceutical businesses tend to invest heavily in developing new drugs, hence their tendency to pay low dividends compared with their share prices. Electricity businesses probably tend to invest less heavily than pharmaceuticals, hence their rather higher level of dividend yields. Some of the inter-industry differences in the dividend yield ratio can be explained by the nature of the calculation of the ratio. The prices of shares at any given moment are based on expectations of their economic futures; dividends are actual past events. A business that had a good trading year recently may have paid a dividend that, in the light of investors' assessment on the business's economic future, may be high (a high dividend yield).

Businesses that have a high share price relative to their recent historic earnings have high P/E ratios. This may be because their future is regarded as economically bright, which may be the result of investing heavily in the future at the expense of current profits (earnings). On the other hand, high P/Es also arise where businesses have recent low earnings, but investors believe that their future is brighter.

Figure 7.4	Average dividend yield ratios for businesses in a range of industries

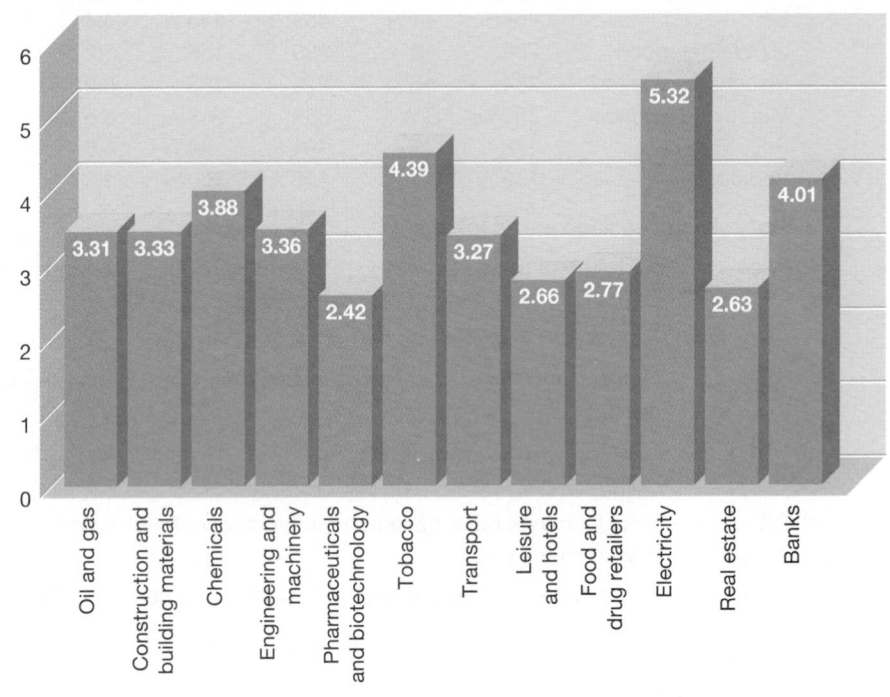

Average levels of dividend yield tend to vary from one industry to the next.

Source: Constructed from data appearing in *Financial Times*, 3 January 2004.

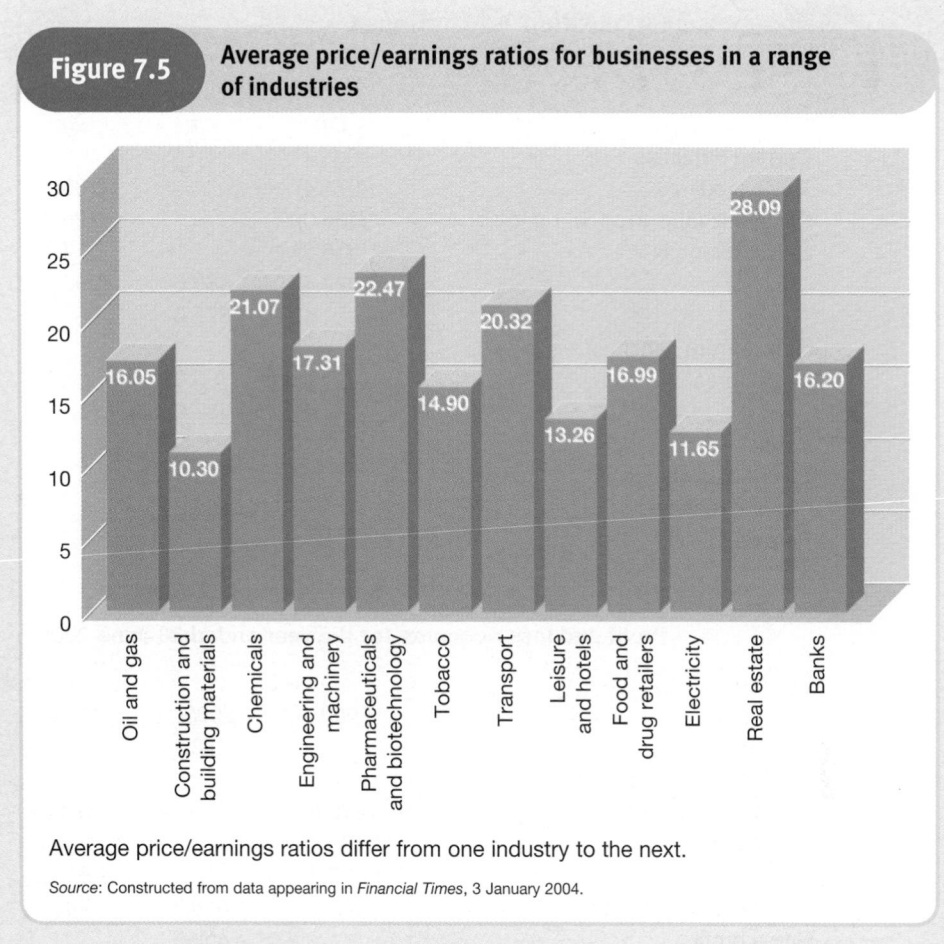

Figure 7.5   **Average price/earnings ratios for businesses in a range of industries**

Average price/earnings ratios differ from one industry to the next.

Source: Constructed from data appearing in *Financial Times*, 3 January 2004.

Both Ali plc and Bhaskar plc operate electrical stores throughout the UK. The financial statements of each business for the year ended 30 June 2005 are as follows:

Balance sheets as at 30 June 2005

	Ali plc		Bhaskar plc	
	£m	£m	£m	£m
Non-current assets				
Property, plant and equipment (cost less depreciation)				
Freehold land and buildings at cost		360.0		510.0
Fixtures and fittings at cost		87.0		91.2
		447.0		601.2
Current assets				
Stock at cost	592.0		403.0	
Debtors	176.4		321.9	
Cash at bank	84.6		91.6	
	853.0		816.5	

Self-assessment question 7.1 continued

	Ali plc		Bhaskar plc	
	£m	£m	£m	£m
Current liabilities				
Trade creditors	(271.4)		(180.7)	
Dividends (approved, but unpaid)	(135.0)		(95.0)	
Corporation tax	(16.0)		(17.4)	
	(422.4)	430.6	(293.1)	523.4
		877.6		1,124.6
Non-current liabilities				
Debentures		(190.0)		(250.0)
		687.6		874.6
Equity				
£1 ordinary shares		320.0		250.0
General reserves		355.9		289.4
Retained profit		11.7		335.2
		687.6		874.6

Profit and loss accounts for the year ended 30 June 2005

	Ali plc		Bhaskar plc	
	£000	£000	£000	£000
Revenue		1,478.1		1,790.4
Less Cost of sales				
Opening stock	480.8		372.6	
Purchases	1,129.5		1,245.3	
	1,610.3		1,617.9	
Less Closing stock	592.0	1,018.3	403.0	1,214.9
Gross profit		459.8		575.5
Less Operating expenses		308.5		408.6
Net profit before interest and tax		151.3		166.9
Less Interest payable		19.4		27.5
Net profit before tax		131.9		139.4
Less Corporation tax		32.0		34.8
Net profit after taxation		99.9		104.6
Add Retained profit brought forward		46.8		325.6
		146.7		430.2
Less Dividends approved, but unpaid		135.0		95.0
Retained profit carried forward		11.7		335.2

All purchases and sales were on credit. The dividends for both years had been approved by the shareholders before the respective year ends, but were paid after those times. The market values of a share in each business at the end of the year were £6.50 and £8.20 respectively.

Required:
For each business, calculate two ratios that are concerned with liquidity, gearing and investment (six ratios in total). What can you conclude from the ratios that you have calculated?

Financial ratios and the problem of overtrading

→ **Overtrading** occurs where a business is operating at a level of activity that cannot be supported by the amount of finance that has been committed. For example, the business has inadequate finance to fund the level of debtors and stocks necessary for the level of sales revenue that it is achieving. This situation usually reflects a poor level of financial control over the business. The reasons for overtrading are varied. It may occur:

● in young, expanding businesses that fail to prepare adequately for the rapid increase in demand for its goods or services;
● in businesses where the managers may have miscalculated the level of expected sales demand or have failed to control escalating project costs;
● as a result of a fall in the value of money (inflation), causing more finance to be committed to stock-in-trade and debtors, even where there is no expansion in the real volume of trade;
● where the owners are unable both to inject further funds into the business and to persuade others to invest in the business.

Whatever the reason, the problems that it brings must be dealt with if the business is to survive over the longer term.

Overtrading results in liquidity problems such as exceeding borrowing limits, or slow repayment of lenders and creditors. It can also result in suppliers withholding supplies, thereby making it difficult to meet customer needs. The managers of the business might be forced to direct all their efforts to dealing with immediate and pressing problems, such as finding cash to meet interest charges due or paying wages. Longer-term planning becomes difficult and managers may spend their time going from crisis to crisis. At the extreme, a business may fail because it cannot meet its maturing obligations.

ACTIVITY 7.28

If a business is overtrading, do you think the following ratios would be higher or lower than normally expected?

(a) Current ratio.
(b) Average stock turnover period.
(c) Average settlement period for debtors.
(d) Average settlement period for creditors.

Your answer should be as follows:

(a) The current ratio would be lower than normally expected. This is a measure of liquidity, and lack of liquidity is an important symptom of overtrading.
(b) The average stock turnover period would be lower than normally expected. Where a business is overtrading, the level of stocks held will be low because of the problems of financing stocks. In the short term, sales revenue may not be badly affected by the low stock levels and therefore stocks will be turned over more quickly.
(c) The average settlement period for debtors may be lower than normally expected. Where a business is suffering from liquidity problems it may chase debtors more vigorously so as to improve cash flows.
(d) The average settlement period for creditors may be higher than normally expected. The business may try to delay payments to creditors because of the liquidity problems arising.

To deal with the overtrading problem, a business must ensure that the finance available is commensurate with the level of operations. Thus, if a business that is overtrading is unable to raise new finance, it should cut back its level of operations in line with the finance available. Although this may mean lost sales and lost profits in the short term, it may be necessary to ensure survival over the longer term.

Trend analysis

It is often helpful to see whether ratios are indicating trends. Key ratios can be plotted on a graph to provide a simple visual display of changes occurring over time. The trends occurring within a business may, for example, be plotted against trends for the industry as a whole for comparison purposes. An example of trend analysis is shown in Figure 7.6. Here the current ratio of a particular business (XYZ Ltd) at various dates is plotted against the average current ratio for other businesses in the same industry as XYZ Ltd. This enables a comparison of the business and similar businesses to be tracked over time.

Many larger businesses publish certain key financial ratios as part of their annual reports to help users identify significant trends. These ratios typically cover several years' activities. **Real World 7.6** shows part of the table of 'key performance measures' of Marks and Spencer plc (M&S), the well-known UK high street store. After many years of profitable growth, M&S suffered a decline in its fortunes during the late 1990s. This was seen by the directors, and by many independent commentators, as arising from the business allowing itself to be drawn away from its traditional areas of strength into such activities as operating overseas businesses. Steps were taken to deal with the problem and the business now seems to have 'turned the corner'. M&S seems to have reached its low point in the year ended March 2001 when it incurred a significant overall loss, with a trading profit only about 40 per cent of that achieved in 1998. We

Figure 7.6	Graph plotting current ratio against time

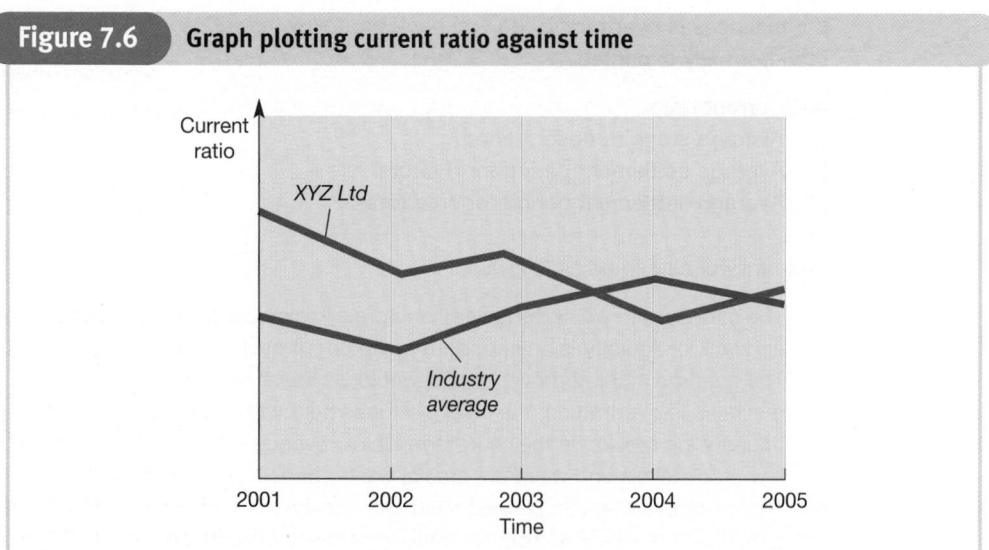

The current ratio for a particular business (XYZ Ltd) is plotted over time. On the same graph the same ratio for the average of businesses in the same industry is also plotted, enabling comparison to be made between the ratio for the particular business and the industry average.

can see from the table that the gross profit margin was not the cause of the problem. In fact, turnover was down in 2001 and expenses were up. The improvements in 2002 and 2003 are very clear. The return on equity (return on shareholders funds) in 2003 is significantly better than for any others of the five years. Also in 2003, both the gross (profit) and net (profit) margins are the best of the five years.

REAL WORLD 7.6

Key performance measures of Marks and Spencer plc

		2003 52 weeks	2002 52 weeks	2001 52 weeks	2000 53 weeks	1999 52 weeks
Gross margin	$\dfrac{\text{Gross profit}}{\text{Turnover}}$	36.4%	35.8%	34.3%	31.8%	31.1%
Net margin	$\dfrac{\text{Operating profit}}{\text{Turnover}}$	8.9%	8.3%	6.2%	6.6%	8.0%
Net margin excluding exceptional items		9.4%	8.3%	6.5%	7.5%	8.4%
Profitability	$\dfrac{\text{Profit before tax}}{\text{Turnover}}$	8.4%	9.0%	5.2%	6.3%	8.6%
Profitability excluding exceptional items		8.9%	8.5%	6.7%	7.3%	8.8%
Earnings per share	$\dfrac{\text{Standard earnings}}{\substack{\text{Weighted average ordinary} \\ \text{shares in issue}}}$	20.7p	5.4p	(0.2)p	9.6p	13.0p
Earnings per share adjusted for exceptional items		22.2p	16.3p	11.2p	13.8p	15.6p
Dividend per share		10.5p	9.5p	9.0p	9.0p	14.4p
Dividend cover	$\dfrac{\substack{\text{Profit attributable to} \\ \text{shareholders}}}{\text{Dividends}}$	2.0x	2.2x	n/a	1.1x	0.9x
Return on equity	$\dfrac{\substack{\text{Profit after tax and} \\ \text{minority interests}}}{\text{Average shareholders' funds}}$	16.5%	11.1%	(0.1)%	5.7%	7.8%

Source: Marks and Spencer plc Annual Report 2003. Reproduced by kind permission of Marks and Spencer plc.

Using ratios to predict financial failure

Financial ratios, based on current or past performance, are often used to help predict the future. However, both the choice of ratios and the interpretation of results are normally dependent on the judgement and opinion of the analyst. In recent years, however, attempts have been made to develop a more rigorous and systematic approach to the use of ratios for prediction purposes. In particular, researchers have shown an interest in the ability of ratios to predict the financial failure of a business.

By financial failure, we mean a business either going out of business or being severely adversely affected by its inability to meet its financial obligations. It is often referred to as 'going bust' or 'going bankrupt'. This, of course, is an area with which all those connected with the business are likely to be concerned.

Using single ratios

Many methods and models employing ratios have now been developed that claim to predict future financial failure. Early research focused on the examination of ratios on an individual basis to see whether they were good or bad predictors of financial failure. Here a particular ratio (for example the current ratio), for a business that had failed, was tracked over several years leading up to the date of the failure. This was to see whether it was possible to say that the ratio had showed a trend that could have been taken as a warning sign.

Beaver (see reference 1 at the end of the chapter) carried out the first research in this area. He calculated the average (mean) of various ratios for 79 businesses that had actually failed, over the ten-year period leading up to their failure. Beaver then compared these average ratios with similarly derived ratios for a sample of 79 businesses that did not fail over this period. (The research used a matched-pair design, where each failed business was matched with a non-failed business of similar size and industry type.) Beaver found that some ratios exhibited a marked difference between the failed and non-failed businesses for up to five years prior to failure. This is shown in Figure 7.7.

To explain Figure 7.7, let us take a closer look at graph (a). This plots the ratio, cash flow (presumably the operating cash flow figure, taken from the cash flow statement) divided by total debt. For the non-failed businesses this stayed fairly steady at about +0.45 over the period. For the failed businesses, however, this was already well below the non-failed businesses at about +0.15 even five years before those businesses eventually failed. It then declined steadily until, by one year before the failure, it was less than −0.15. Note that the scale of the horizontal axis shows the most recent year (Year 1) on the left and the earliest one (Year 5) on the right. The other graphs ((b) to (f)) show a similar picture for five other ratios. In each case there is a deteriorating average ratio for the failed businesses, as the time of failure approaches.

What is shown in Figure 7.7 implied that failure could be predicted by careful assessment of the trend shown by particular key ratios.

Research by Zmijewski (see reference 2 at the end of the chapter), using a sample of 72 failed and 3,573 non-failed businesses over a six-year period, found that failed businesses were characterised by lower rates of return, higher levels of gearing, lower levels of coverage for their fixed interest payments and more variable returns on shares. Whilst we may not find these results very surprising, it is interesting to note that Zmijewski, like a number of other researchers in this area, did not find liquidity ratios particularly useful in predicting financial failure. Intuition might have led us (wrongly it seems) to believe that the liquidity ratios would have been particularly helpful in this context.

 The approach adopted by Beaver and Zmijewski is referred to as **univariate analysis** because it looks at one ratio at a time. Though this approach can produce interesting results, there are practical problems associated with its use. Let us say, for example, that past research has identified two ratios as being good predictors of financial failure. When applied to a particular business, however, it may be found that one ratio predicts financial failure whereas the other does not. Given these conflicting signals, how should the decision maker interpret the results?

Using combinations of ratios

The weaknesses of univariate analysis have led researchers to develop models that combine ratios in such a way as to produce a single index that can be interpreted more

Figure 7.7   Average (mean) ratios of failed and non-failed businesses

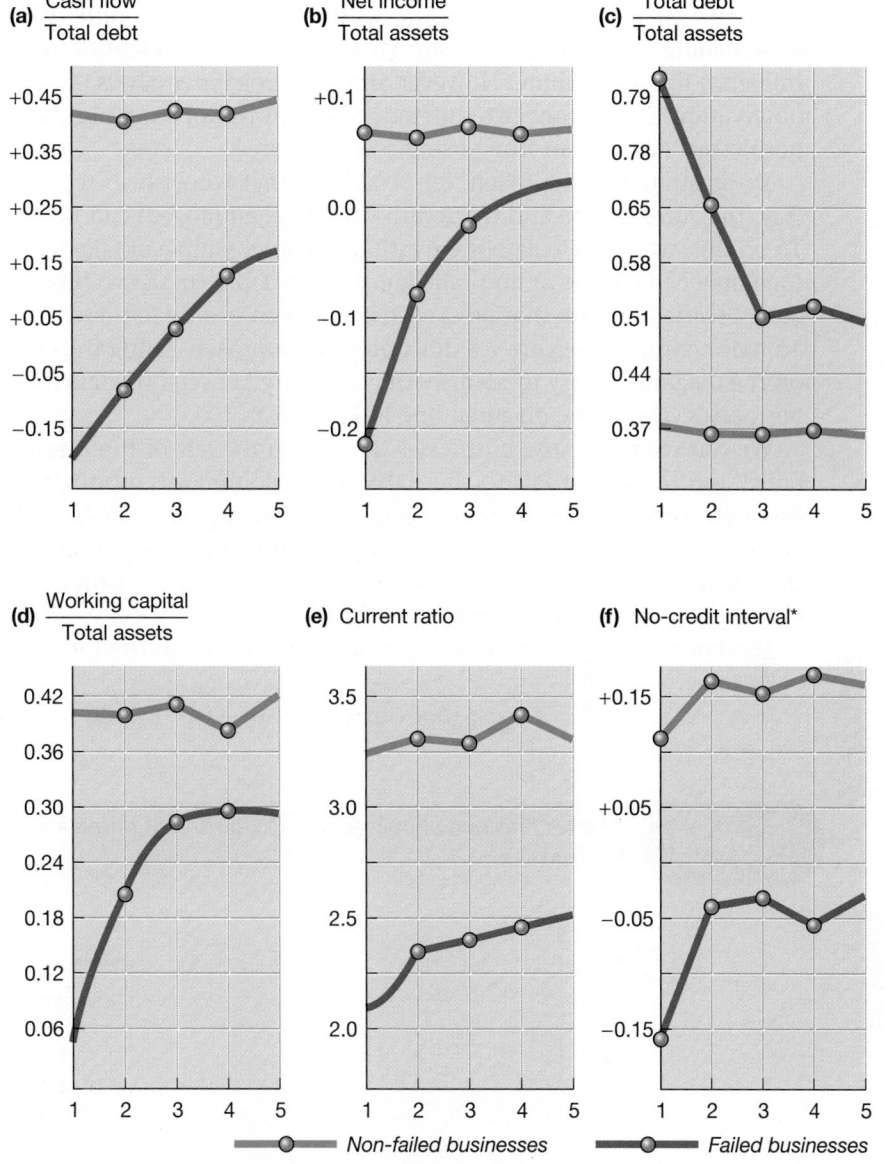

Each of the ratios (a) to (f) above indicates a marked difference in the average ratio between the sample of failed businesses and a matched sample of non-failed businesses. The vertical scale of each graph is the average value of the particular ratio for each group of businesses (failed and non-failed). The horizontal axis is the number of years before failure. Thus Year 1 is the most recent year and Year 5 the earliest of the years. For each of the six ratios, the difference between the average for the failed and the non-failed businesses can be detected five years prior to the failure of the former group. (From Beaver – see reference 1 at the end of the chapter.)

* The no-credit interval is the same as the cash generated from operations to maturing obligations ratio discussed earlier in the chapter.

Source: Beaver (see reference 1 at the end of the chapter).

clearly. One approach to model development, much favoured by researchers, applies **multiple discriminate analysis (MDA)**. This is, in essence, a statistical technique that is similar to regression analysis and which can be used to draw a boundary between those businesses that fail and those businesses that do not. This boundary is referred to as the **discriminate function**. In this context, MDA attempts to identify those factors likely to influence financial failure. However, unlike regression analysis, MDA assumes that the observations come from two different populations (for example, failed and non-failed businesses) rather than from a single population.

To illustrate this approach, let us assume that we wish to test whether two ratios (say, the current ratio and the return on capital employed) can help to predict failure. To do this, we can calculate these ratios, first for a sample of failed businesses and then for a matched sample of non-failed businesses. From these two sets of data we can produce a scatter diagram that plots each business according to these two ratios to produce a single coordinate. Figure 7.8 illustrates this approach. Using the observations plotted on the diagram, we try to identify the boundary between the failed and the non-failed businesses. This is the diagonal line in Figure 7.8.

We can see that those businesses that fall to the left of the line are predominantly failed and those that fall to the right are predominantly non-failed ones. Note that there is some overlap between the two populations. The boundary produced is unlikely, in practice, to eliminate all errors. Some businesses that fail may fall on the side of the boundary with non-failed businesses, and the other way round as well. However, it will *minimise* the misclassification errors.

The boundary shown in Figure 7.8 can be expressed in the form:

$$Z = a + (b \times \text{Current ratio}) + (c \times \text{ROCE})$$

Figure 7.8	**Scatter diagram showing the distribution of failed and non-failed businesses**

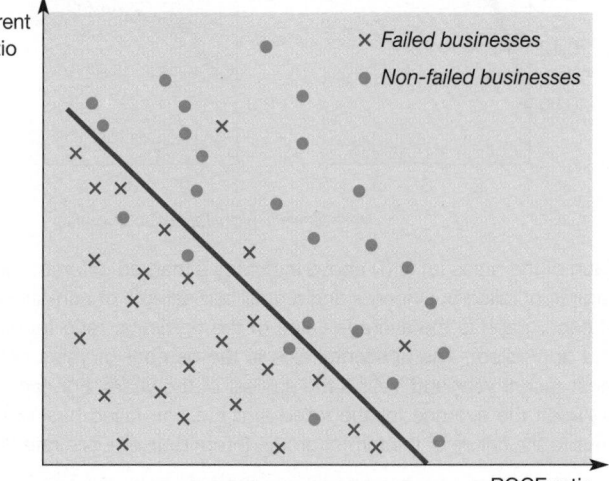

The distribution of failed and non-failed businesses is based on two ratios. The line represents a boundary between the samples of failed and non-failed businesses. Although there is some crossing of the boundary, the boundary represents the line that minimises the problem of misclassifying particular businesses.

where *a* is a constant and *b* and *c* are weights to be attached to each ratio. A weighted average or total score (*Z*) is then derived. The weights given to the two ratios will depend on the slope of the line and its absolute position.

Z score models

Altman (see reference 3 at the end of the chapter) was the first to develop a model using financial ratios that was able to predict financial failure. His model, the *Z* score model, is based on five financial ratios and is as follows:

$$Z = 1.2a + 1.4b + 3.3c + 0.6d + 1.0e$$

where *a* = Working capital/Total assets
 b = Accumulated retained profits/Total assets
 c = Profit before interest and taxation/Total assets
 d = Market value of ordinary and preference shares/Total liabilities at book value
 e = Sales revenue/Total assets

 In developing this model, Altman carried out experiments using a paired sample of failed businesses and non-failed businesses and collected relevant data for each business for five years prior to failure. He found that the model represented by the formula above was able to predict failure for up to two years before it occurred. However, the predictive accuracy of the model became weaker the further the period from failure.

 The ratios used in this model were identified by Altman through a process of trial and error, as there is no underlying theory of financial failure to help guide researchers in their selection of appropriate ratios. According to Altman, those businesses with a *Z* score of less than 1.81 tend to fail, and the lower the score the greater the probability of failure. Those with a *Z* score greater than 2.99 tended not to fail. Those businesses with a *Z* score between 1.81 and 2.99 occupied a 'zone of ignorance' and were difficult to classify. However, the model was able overall to classify 95 per cent of the businesses correctly. Altman based his model on US businesses.

 In recent years, this model has been updated and other models, using a similar approach, have been developed throughout the world. In the UK, Taffler (see reference 4 at the end of the chapter) has developed separate *Z* score models for different types of business.

 The prediction of financial failure is not the only area where research into the predictive ability of ratios has taken place. Researchers have also developed ratio-based models that claim to assess the vulnerability of a business to takeover by another. This is another area that is of vital importance to all those connected with the business.

Limitations of ratio analysis

Though ratios offer a quick and useful method of analysing the position and performance of a business, they are not without their problems and limitations. Some of the more important limitations are as follows:

● *Quality of financial statements*. It must always be remembered that ratios are based on financial statements, and the results of ratio analysis are dependent on the quality of these underlying statements. Ratios will inherit the limitations of the financial statements on which they are based. A significant example of this arises from the application of the prudence convention to internally generated intangible non-current assets (as compared with purchased ones). This convention tends to lead to assets of considerable value, like goodwill and brand names, being excluded from the balance sheet. This can mean that ratios, like ROSF, ROCE and the gearing ratio, fail to take account of these assets.

There is also the problem of deliberate attempts to make the financial statements misleading. We discussed this problem of *creative accounting* in Chapter 5.

● *Inflation*. A persistent, though recently less severe, problem, in most western countries is that the financial results of businesses can be distorted as a result of inflation. One effect of inflation is that the values of assets held for any length of time may bear little relation to current values. Generally speaking, the value of assets will be understated in current terms during a period of inflation as they are usually recorded at their original cost (less any amounts written off for depreciation). This means that comparisons, either between businesses or between periods, will be hindered. A difference in, say, return on capital employed may simply be owing to the fact that assets in one of the balance sheets being compared were acquired more recently (ignoring the effect of depreciation on the asset values). Another effect of inflation is to distort the measurement of profit. Sales revenue for a period is often matched against costs from an earlier period, because there is often a time lag between acquiring a particular resource and using it in the business. For example, stocks may be acquired in one period and sold in a later period. During a period of inflation, this will mean that the costs do not reflect current prices. The cost of goods sold figure is usually based on the historic cost of the stock concerned. As a result, costs will be understated in the current profit and loss account and this, in turn, means that profit will be overstated. One effect of this will be to distort the profitability ratios discussed earlier.

● *The restricted vision of ratios*. It is important not to rely exclusively on ratios, thereby losing sight of information contained in the underlying financial statements. As we saw earlier in the chapter, some items reported in these statements can be vital in assessing position and performance. For example, the total sales revenue, capital employed and profit figures may be useful in assessing changes in absolute size that occur over time, or differences in scale between businesses. Ratios do not provide such information. When comparing one figure with another, ratios measure *relative* performance and position, and therefore provide only part of the picture. Thus, when comparing two businesses, it will often be useful to assess the absolute size of profits, as well as the relative profitability of each business. For example, Business A may generate £1m profit and have a ROCE of 15 per cent, and Business B may generate £100,000 profit and have a ROCE of 20 per cent. Although Business B has a higher level of *profitability*, as measured by ROCE, it generates lower total profits.

● *The basis for comparison*. We saw earlier that for ratios to be useful they require a basis for comparison. Moreover, it is important that the analyst compares like with like. When comparing businesses, however, no two businesses will be identical, and the greater the differences between the businesses being compared, the greater the limitations of ratio analysis. Also, when comparing businesses, differences in such matters as accounting policies, financing methods (gearing levels) and financial year ends will add to the problems of evaluation.

● *Balance sheet ratios*. Because the balance sheet is only a 'snapshot' of the business at a particular moment in time, any ratios based on balance sheet figures, such as the liquidity ratios above, may not be representative of the financial position of the business for the year as a whole. For example, it is common for a seasonal business to have a financial year end that coincides with a low point in business activity.

Thus stocks and debtors may be low at the balance sheet date, and the liquidity ratios may also be low as a result. A more representative picture of liquidity can only really be gained by taking additional measurements at other points in the year.

Real World 7.7 points out another way in which ratios are limited.

REAL WORLD 7.7

Remember, it's people that really count . . .

Lord Weinstock (1924–2002) was an influential industrialist whose management style and philosophy helped to shape management practice in many UK businesses. During his long and successful reign at GEC plc, a major engineering business, Lord Weinstock relied heavily on financial ratios to assess performance and to exercise control. In particular, he relied on ratios relating to sales revenue, costs, debtors, profit margins and stock turnover. However, he was keenly aware of the limitations of ratios and recognised that, ultimately, people produce profits.

In a memo written to GEC managers he pointed out that ratios are an aid to good management, rather than a substitute for it. He wrote:

> The operating ratios are of great value as measures of efficiency but they are only the measures and not efficiency itself. Statistics will not design a product better, make it for a lower cost or increase sales. If ill-used, they may so guide action as to diminish resources for the sake of apparent but false signs of improvement.
>
> Management remains a matter of judgement, of knowledge of products and processes and of understanding and skill in dealing with people. The ratios will indicate how well all these things are being done and will show comparison with how they are done elsewhere. But they will tell us nothing about how to do them. That is what you are meant to do.

Source: Extract from *Arnold Weinstock and the Making of GEC*, by S. Aris (Aurum Press, 1998), published in *The Sunday Times*, 22 February 1998, p. 3.

SUMMARY

The main points of this chapter may be summarised as follows:

Ratio analysis

- Compares two related figures, usually both from the same set of financial statements.
- Is an aid to understanding what the financial statements say.
- Is an inexact science so results must be interpreted cautiously.
- Past periods – the performance of similar businesses and planned performance are often used to provide benchmark ratios.
- A brief overview of the financial statements can often provide insights that may not be revealed by ratios and/or may help in the interpretation of them.

Profitability ratios – concerned with effectiveness at generating profit

- Return on ordinary shareholders' funds (ROSF).
- Return on capital employed (ROCE).

- Net profit margin.
- Gross profit margin.

Efficiency ratios – concerned with efficiency of using assets/resources

- Average stock turnover period.
- Average settlement period for debtors.
- Average settlement period for creditors.
- Sales revenue to capital employed.
- Sales revenue per employee.

Liquidity ratios – concerned with the ability to meet short-term obligations

- Current ratio.
- Acid test ratio.
- Cash generated from operations to maturing obligations.

Gearing ratios – concerned with relationship between equity and debt financing

- Gearing ratio.
- Interest cover ratio.

Investment ratios – concerned with returns to shareholders

- Dividend payout ratio.
- Dividend yield ratio.
- Earnings per share.
- Cash generated from operations per share.
- Price/earnings ratio.

Overtrading = trading at a level of activity that the business is insufficiently funded to sustain

Individual ratios can be tracked (for example, plotted on a graph) to detect trends

Ratios can be used to predict financial failure

- Univariate analysis – looking at just one ratio over time in an attempt to predict financial failure.
- Multiple discriminate analysis – looking at several ratios, put together in a model, over time in an attempt to predict financial failure – Z scores.

Limitations of ratio analysis

- Ratios are only as reliable as the financial statements from which they derive.
- Inflation can distort the information.
- Ratios have restricted vision.
- It can be difficult to find a suitable benchmark (for example, another business) to compare with.
- Some ratios could mislead due to the 'snapshot' nature of the balance sheet.

 **Key terms**

return on ordinary shareholders' funds (ROSF) p. 213	**cash generated from operations to maturing obligations** p. 226
return on capital employed (ROCE) p. 214	**financial gearing** p. 227
	gearing ratio p. 230
net profit margin ratio p. 215	**interest cover ratio** p. 230
gross profit margin ratio p. 215	**dividend payout ratio** p. 232
average stock turnover period p. 218	**dividend cover ratio** p. 233
average settlement period for debtors p. 218	**dividend yield ratio** p. 233
	dividend per share p. 234
average settlement period for creditors p. 219	**earnings per share** p. 234
sales revenue to capital employed ratio p. 220	**cash generated from operations per ordinary share** p. 235
	price/earnings ratio p. 235
sales revenue per employee ratio p. 221	**overtrading** p. 241
	univariate analysis p. 244
current ratio p. 224	**multiple discriminate analysis** p. 246
acid test ratio p. 225	**discriminate function** p. 246

Further reading

If you would like to explore the topics covered in this chapter in more depth, we recommend the following books:

Financial Accounting and Reporting, *Elliott B. and Elliott J.*, 8th edn, Financial Times Prentice Hall, 2004, chapters 25 and 26.

International Financial Reporting and Analysis, *Alexander D., Britton A. and Jorissen A.*, Prentice Hall, 2003, chapters 26 and 27.

Financial Analysis, *Rees B.*, 2nd edn, Prentice Hall International, 1995, chapters 1–3.

The Analysis and Use of Financial Statements, *White G., Sondhi A. and Fried D.*, 3rd edn, Wiley, 2003, chapter 4.

References

1 'Financial ratios as predictors of failure', *Beaver W. H.*, in **Empirical Research in Accounting: Selected studies**, 1966, pp. 71–111.

2 'Predicting corporate bankruptcy: an empirical comparison of the extent of financial distress models', *Zmijewski M. E.*, Research Paper, State University of New York, 1983.

3 'Financial ratios, discriminant analysis and the prediction of corporate bankruptcy', *Altman E. I.*, in **Journal of Finance**, September 1968, pp. 589–609.

4 'The assessment of company solvency and performance using a statistical model: a comparative UK-based study', *Taffler R.*, in **Accounting and Business Research**, Autumn 1983, pp. 295–307.

REVIEW QUESTIONS

Answers to these questions can be found on the students' side of the Companion Website at **www.pearsoned.co.uk/atrillmclaney**.

7.1 Some businesses operate on a low net profit margin (for example, a supermarket chain). Does this mean that the return on capital employed from the business will also be low?

7.2 What potential problems arise for the external analyst from the use of balance sheet figures in the calculation of financial ratios?

7.3 Two businesses operate in the same industry. One has a stock turnover period that is higher than the industry average. The other has a stock turnover period that is lower than the industry average. Give three possible explanations for each business's stock turnover period ratio.

7.4 Identify and discuss three reasons why the P/E ratio of two businesses operating within the same industry may differ.

EXERCISES

Exercises 7.5 to 7.8 are more advanced than 7.1 to 7.4. Those with a coloured number have an answer at the back of the book.

7.1 Jiang Ltd has recently produced its financial statements for the current year. The directors are concerned that the return on capital employed (ROCE) had decreased from 14% last year to 12% for the current year.

The following reasons were suggested as to why this reduction in ROCE had occurred:

(i)   an increase in the gross profit margin;
(ii)   a reduction in sales revenue;
(iii) an increase in overhead expenses;
(iv)   an increase in amount of stock held;
(v)   the repayment of a loan at the year end; and
(vi)   an increase in the time taken for debtors to pay.

Required:
Taking each of these six suggested reasons in turn, state, with reasons, whether each of them could lead to a reduction in ROCE.

7.2 Amsterdam Ltd and Berlin Ltd are both engaged in retailing, but they seem to take a different approach to it according to the following information:

Ratio	Amsterdam Ltd	Berlin Ltd
Return on capital employed (ROCE)	20%	17%
Return on ordinary shareholders' funds (ROSF)	30%	18%
Average settlement period for debtors	63 days	21 days
Average settlement period for creditors	50 days	45 days
Gross profit margin	40%	15%
Net profit margin	10%	10%
Stock turnover period	52 days	25 days

Required:

Describe what this information indicates about the differences in approach between the two businesses. If one of them prides itself on personal service and one of them on competitive prices, which do you think is which and why?

7.3 Conday and Co. Ltd has been in operation for three years and produces antique reproduction furniture for the export market. The most recent set of financial statements for the business is set out as follows:

Balance sheet as at 30 November

	£000	£000	£000
Non-current assets			
Property, plant and equipment			
Freehold land and buildings at cost			228
Plant and machinery at cost		942	
Less Accumulated depreciation		180	762
			990
Current assets			
Stocks		600	
Trade debtors		820	
		1,420	
Less **Current liabilities**			
Trade creditors	665		
Taxation	48		
Bank overdraft	432	1,145	275
			1,265
Less **Non-current liabilities**			
9% debentures (Note 1)			200
			1,065
Equity			
Ordinary shares of £1 each			700
Retained profits			365
			1,065

Profit and loss account for the year ended 30 November

	£000	£000
Revenue		2,600
Less Cost of sales		1,620
Gross profit		980
Less Selling and distribution expenses (Note 2)	408	
Administration expenses	194	
Finance expenses	58	660
Net profit before taxation		320
Less Corporation tax		95
Net profit after taxation		225
Less Proposed dividend		160
Retained profit for the year		65

Notes

1 The debentures are secured on the freehold land and buildings.
2 Selling and distribution expenses include £170,000 in respect of bad debts.

The directors have invited an investor to take up a new issue of ordinary shares in the business at £6.40 each making a total investment of £200,000. The directors wish to use the funds to finance a programme of further expansion.

Required:

(a) Analyse the financial position and performance of the business and comment on any features that you consider to be significant.

(b) State, with reasons, whether or not the investor should invest in the business on the terms outlined.

7.4 The directors of Helena Beauty Products Ltd have been presented with the following abridged financial statements:

Helena Beauty Products Ltd
Profit and loss account for the year ended 30 September

	2004		2005	
	£000	£000	£000	£000
Revenue		3,600		3,840
Less Cost of sales				
Opening stock	320		400	
Purchases	2,240		2,350	
	2,560		2,750	
Less Closing stock	400	2,160	500	2,250
Gross profit		1,440		1,590
Less Expenses		1,360		1,500
Net profit		80		90

Balance sheet as at 30 September

	2004		2005	
	£000	£000	£000	£000
Non-current assets		1,900		1,860
Current assets				
Stock	400		500	
Debtors	750		960	
Bank	8		4	
	1,158		1,464	
Less Current liabilities	390	768	450	1,014
		2,668		2,874
Equity				
£1 ordinary shares		1,650		1,766
Reserves		1,018		1,108
		2,668		2,874

Required:

Using six ratios, comment on the profitability (three ratios) and efficiency (three ratios) of the business as revealed by the statements shown above.

7.5 Threads Limited manufactures nuts and bolts, which are sold to industrial users. The abbreviated financial statements for 2004 and 2005 are as follows:

Profit and loss account for the year ended 30 June

	2004 £000	2004 £000	2005 £000	2005 £000
Revenue		1,180		1,200
Cost of sales		(680)		(750)
Gross profit		500		450
Operating expenses	(200)		(208)	
Depreciation	(66)		(75)	
Interest	(–)		(8)	
		(266)		(291)
Profit before tax		234		159
Tax		(80)		(48)
Profit after tax		154		111
Dividend – paid		(70)		(72)
Retained profit for year		84		39

Balance sheet as at 30 June

	2004 £000	2004 £000	2005 £000	2005 £000
Non-current assets		702		687
Current assets				
Stocks	148		236	
Debtors	102		156	
Cash	3		4	
	253		396	
Current liabilities				
Trade creditors	(60)		(76)	
Other creditors and accruals	(18)		(16)	
Tax	(40)		(24)	
Bank overdraft	(81)		(122)	
	(199)		(238)	
Net current assets		54		158
Non-current liabilities				
Bank loan		–		(50)
		756		795
Equity				
Ordinary share capital of £1 (fully paid)		500		500
Retained profits		256		295
		756		795

Required:

(a) Calculate the following financial ratios for *both* 2004 and 2005 (using year-end figures for balance sheet items):

   (i)   return on capital employed;

   (ii)   net profit margin;

   (iii) gross profit margin;

   (iv) current ratio;

   (v)   acid test ratio;

   (vi) settlement period for debtors;

   (vii) settlement period for creditors; and

   (viii) stock turnover period.

(b) Comment on the performance of Threads Limited from the viewpoint of a business considering supplying a substantial amount of goods to Threads Limited on usual trade credit terms.

7.6   Bradbury Ltd is a family-owned clothes manufacturer based in the southwest of England. For a number of years the chairman and managing director was David Bradbury. During his period of office, sales revenue had grown steadily at a rate of 2 to 3 per cent each year. David Bradbury retired on 30 November 2004 and was succeeded by his son Simon. Soon after taking office, Simon decided to expand the business. Within weeks he had successfully negotiated a five-year contract with a large clothes retailer to make a range of sports and leisurewear items. The contract will result in an additional £2 million in sales revenue during each year of the contract. To fulfil the contract, Bradbury Ltd acquired new equipment and premises.

Financial information concerning the business is given below.

Profit and loss account for the year ended 30 November

	2004 £000	2005 £000
Turnover	9,482	11,365
Profit before interest and tax	914	1,042
Interest charges	22	81
Profit before tax	892	961
Taxation	358	386
Profit after tax	534	575
Dividend paid	120	120
Retained profit	414	455

Balance sheet as at 30 November

	2004 £000	2004 £000	2005 £000	2005 £000
Non-current assets				
Property, plant and equipment				
Freehold premises at cost		5,240		7,360
Plant and equipment (net)		2,375		4,057
		7,615		11,417
Current assets				
Stock	2,386		3,420	
Trade debtors	2,540		4,280	
	4,926		7,700	
Current liabilities				
Trade creditors	(1,157)		(2,245)	
Taxation	(179)		(193)	
Bank overdraft	(172)		(2,736)	
	(1,508)		(5,174)	
Net current assets		3,418		2,526
		11,033		13,943
Non-current liabilities				
Loans		(1,220)		(3,674)
Total net assets		9,813		10,269
Equity				
Share capital		2,000		2,000
Reserves		7,813		8,269
		9,813		10,269

Required:

(a) Calculate, for each year (using year-end figures for balance sheet items), the following ratios:
   (i) net profit margin;
   (ii) return on capital employed;

(iii) current ratio;
(iv) gearing ratio;
(v) days debtors (settlement period); and
(vi) sales revenue to capital employed.

(b) Using the above ratios, and any other ratios or information you consider relevant, comment on the results of the expansion programme.

7.7 The financial statements for Harridges Limited are given below for the two years ended 30 June 2004 and 2005. Harridges Limited operates a department store in the centre of a small town.

Harridges Limited
Profit and loss account for the years ended 30 June

	2004 £000	2004 £000	2005 £000	2005 £000
Revenue		2,600		3,500
Cost of sales		(1,560)		(2,350)
Gross profit		1,040		1,150
Expenses: Wages and salaries	(320)		(350)	
Overheads	(260)		(200)	
Depreciation	(150)		(250)	
		(730)		(800)
Operating profit		310		350
Interest payable		(50)		(50)
Profit before taxation		260		300
Taxation		(105)		(125)
Profit after taxation		155		175
Dividend (approved, but unpaid at the year end)		(65)		(75)
Profit retained for the year		90		100

Balance sheet as at 30 June

	2004 £000	2004 £000	2005 £000	2005 £000
Non-current assets		1,265		1,525
Current assets				
Stocks	250		400	
Debtors	105		145	
Cash at bank	380		115	
	735		660	
Current liabilities				
Trade creditors	(235)		(300)	
Dividend (approved, but unpaid)	(65)		(75)	
Other	(100)		(110)	
	(400)		(485)	
Net current assets		335		175
Total assets less current liabilities		1,600		1,700
Non-current liabilities				
10% loan stock		(500)		(500)
		1,100		1,200
Equity				
Share capital: £1 shares fully paid		490		490
Share premium		260		260
Profit and loss account		350		450
		1,100		1,200

Required:

(a) Choose and calculate eight ratios that would be helpful in assessing the performance of Harridges Limited. Use end-of-year values and calculate ratios for both 2004 and 2005.

(b) Using the ratios calculated in (a) and any others you consider helpful, comment on the business's performance from the viewpoint of a prospective purchaser of a majority of shares.

7.8 Genesis Ltd was incorporated in 2001 and has grown rapidly over the past three years. The rapid rate of growth has created problems for the business, which the directors have found difficult to deal with. Recently, a firm of management consultants has been asked to help the directors to overcome these problems.

In a preliminary report to the board of directors, the management consultants state: 'Most of the difficulties faced by the business are symptoms of an underlying problem of overtrading.'

The most recent financial statements of the business are set out below:

Balance sheet as at 31 October 2004

	£000	£000	£000
Non-current assets			
Property, plant and equipment			
Freehold land and buildings at cost		530	
Less Accumulated depreciation		88	442
Fixtures and fittings at cost		168	
Less Accumulated depreciation		52	116
Motor vans at cost		118	
Less Accumulated depreciation		54	64
			622
Current assets			
Stock-in-trade		128	
Trade debtors		104	
		232	
Less **Current liabilities**			
Trade creditors	184		
Taxation	8		
Bank overdraft	358	550	(318)
			304
Less **Non-current liabilities**			
10% debentures (secured)			(120)
			184
Equity			
Ordinary £0.50 shares			60
General reserve			50
Retained profit			74
			184

Profit and loss account for the year ended 31 October 2004

	£000	£000
Revenue		1,640
Less Cost of sales		
Opening stock	116	
Purchases	1,260	
	1,376	
Less Closing stock	128	(1,248)
Gross profit		392
Less Selling and distribution expenses	204	
Administration expenses	92	
Interest expenses	44	(340)
Net profit before taxation		52
Corporation tax		(16)
Net profit after taxation		36
Dividends paid		(4)
Retained profit for the year		32

All purchases and sales were on credit.

Required:
(a) Explain the term 'overtrading' and state how overtrading might arise for a business.
(b) Discuss the kinds of problem that overtrading can create for a business.
(c) Calculate and discuss *five* financial ratios that might be used to establish whether or not the business is overtrading.
(d) State the ways in which a business may overcome the problem of overtrading.

PART 2

Management accounting

Part 2 deals with the area of accounting usually known as 'management accounting' or 'managerial accounting'. This area is concerned with providing information to help managers to manage the business: it is intended to help them to plan, to ensure that plans are actually achieved and to make decisions.

Part 2 begins with a consideration of the basics of financial decision making. Chapter 8 deals with how we identify information that is relevant to a particular decision. In practice, we may be confronted with a large volume of financial information and we must be able to discriminate between that which is relevant to a particular decision and that which can be ignored. Unless we can do this, we run the risk of making poor decisions. Chapter 9 continues to examine the basics by considering the relationship between costs, volume of activity and profit. We shall see that an understanding of this relationship can be helpful in developing plans and in making a variety of decisions. This chapter incorporates an examination of break-even analysis, which is concerned with deducing the volume of activity at which the sales revenue generated exactly cover the costs incurred so that neither profit nor loss is made by the activity. Knowledge of the break-even figure can be useful in assessing the degree of risk associated with the operations.

In Chapter 10 we look at how businesses can determine the full cost of each unit of their output. By 'full cost' we mean that the figure takes account of all of the costs of producing a product or service. This includes not just those costs that are directly caused by the unit of output, but those, like rent and administrative costs, that are indirectly involved. This topic is continued in Chapter 11, where we consider some recent developments in determining the full cost of a product or service. In this chapter we also consider how a business can set prices for its output and how costs can be controlled.

Chapter 12 deals with the way in which businesses convert their general objectives and long-term plans into workable short-term plans or budgets. Budgets are an important feature of business life and we shall be looking at the budgeting process in some detail. We shall examine the purpose of budgets and the way in which budgets are prepared. In Chapter 13 we shall consider how, after the period of the budget, the actual performance can be compared with the budgeted performance. This is done to assess performance and to help identify the reasons for any failure to meet budget targets. By finding out what has gone wrong, managers may be able to put things right for the future. The chapter concludes with a discussion of the impact of budgets on the attitudes and behaviour of managers.

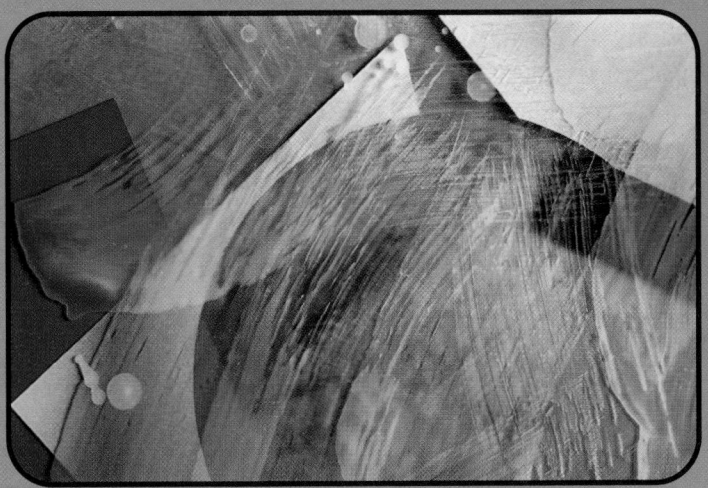

CHAPTER 8

Relevant costs for decision making

OBJECTIVES

When you have completed this chapter, you should be able to:

● Define and distinguish between relevant costs, outlay costs and opportunity costs.

● Identify and quantify the costs that are relevant to a particular decision.

● Use the relevant costs to make decisions.

● Set out the analysis in a logical form so that the conclusion may be communicated to managers.

INTRODUCTION

S o far in this book, we have mainly been considering reporting past events (for example through the profit and loss account (income statement)), but in this and the following chapters the focus will move to making decisions about the future. In this chapter we shall consider the identification and use of costs in making management decisions. We shall see that not all of the costs that appear to be linked to a particular business decision are relevant to it. It is important to distinguish carefully between costs (and revenue) that are relevant and those that are not. Failure to do this could well lead to bad decisions being made. The principles outlined here will provide the basis for much of the rest of the book.

What is meant by 'cost'?

Let us begin this chapter by asking 'what is meant by cost?' The answer to this question may seem, at first sight, very obvious. Many people might say that **cost** is how much was paid for an item of goods being supplied or a service being provided. However, the following activity illustrates that the definition of 'cost' is not always as obvious as might first be thought.

ACTIVITY 8.1

Let us assume that you own a motor car, for which you paid a purchase price of £5,000 – much below the list price – at a recent car auction. You have just been offered £6,000 for this car.

What is the cost to you of keeping the car for your own use? (*Note*: Ignore running costs and so on; just consider the 'capital' cost of the car.)

By retaining the car, you are forgoing an offer of £6,000. Thus, the real sacrifice, or cost, incurred by keeping the car for your own use is £6,000. Any decision that you make with respect to the car's future should logically take account of this figure. This cost is known as the 'opportunity cost' since it is the value of the opportunity forgone in order to pursue the other course of action. (In this case, the other course of action is to retain the car.)

We can see that the cost of retaining the car is not the same as the purchase price. In one sense, of course, the cost of the car in Activity 8.1 is £5,000 because that is how much was paid for it. However, this cost, which for obvious reasons is known as the **historic cost**, is only of academic interest. It cannot logically ever be used to make a decision on the car's future. If we disagree with this point, we should ask ourselves how we should assess an offer of £5,500, from another person, for the car. The answer is that we should compare the offer price of £5,500 with the **opportunity cost** of £6,000. This should lead us to reject the offer as it is less than the £6,000 opportunity cost. In these circumstances, it would not be logical to accept the offer of £5,500 on the basis that it was more than the £5,000 that we originally paid. (The only other figure that should concern us is the value to us, in terms of pleasure, usefulness and so on, of retaining the car. If we valued this more highly than the £6,000 opportunity cost, we should reject both offers.)

We may still feel, however, that the £5,000 is relevant here because it will help us in assessing the profitability of the decision. If we sold the car, we will make a profit of either £500 (£5,500 – £5,000) or £1,000 (£6,000 – £5,000) depending on which offer we accept. Since we should seek to make the higher profit, the right decision is to sell the car for £6,000. However, we do not need to know the historic cost of the car to make the right decision. What decision should we make if the car cost us £4,000 to buy? Clearly we should still sell the car for £6,000 rather than for £5,500 as the important comparison is between the offer price and the opportunity cost. We should reach the same conclusion whatever the historic cost of the car.

To emphasise the above point, let us assume that the car cost £10,000. Even in this case the historic cost would still be irrelevant. Had we just bought a car for £10,000 and found that shortly after it is only worth £6,000, we may well be fuming with rage at

 our mistake, but this does not make the £10,000 a **relevant cost**. The only relevant factors, in a decision on whether to sell the car or to keep it, are the £6,000 opportunity cost and the value of the benefits of keeping it. Thus, the historic cost can never be relevant to a future decision.

Historic cost is normally used in accounting statements, like the balance sheet and the profit and loss account (income statement). This is logical, however, since these statements are intended to be accounts of what has actually happened and are drawn up after the event. In the context of decision making, which is always related to the future, historic cost is always irrelevant.

Real World 8.1 gives an example of a decision made by Manchester United.

REAL WORLD 8.1

Transferring players: a game of two halves

In August 2003, Manchester United Football Club transferred one of its midfield players, Juan Sebastian Veron, to Chelsea Football Club for a reported £15 million. Manchester United had purchased the player's services two years earlier for a reported club transfer record of £28.1 million. As the transfer price to Chelsea Football Club was only a little more than half of the amount originally paid, Manchester United made a huge loss on the transaction. However, the offer of £15 million from Chelsea must have been greater than the sacrifice, or cost, of losing Veron's services for Manchester United to agree to the transfer. The original amount paid for the player's services should not have been an issue in arriving at the agreed transfer price.

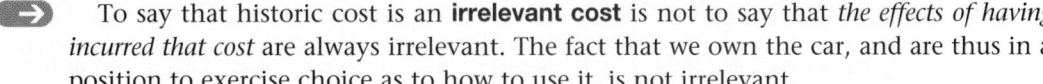 To say that historic cost is an **irrelevant cost** is not to say that *the effects of having incurred that cost* are always irrelevant. The fact that we own the car, and are thus in a position to exercise choice as to how to use it, is not irrelevant.

It might be useful to formalise what we have discussed so far.

A definition of cost

Cost may be defined as the amount of resources, usually measured in monetary terms, sacrificed to achieve a particular objective.

The objective might be to retain a car, to buy a particular house, to make a particular product or to render a particular service.

Relevant costs: opportunity and outlay costs

 We have just seen that, when we are making decisions concerning the future, **past costs** (that is, historic costs) are irrelevant. It is future opportunity costs and future **outlay costs** that are of concern. An opportunity cost can be defined as the value in monetary terms of being deprived of the next-best opportunity in order to pursue the particular objective. An outlay cost is an amount of money that will have to be spent to achieve that objective. We shall shortly meet plenty of examples of both of these types of cost.

To be relevant to a particular decision, a future outlay cost, or opportunity cost, must satisfy both of the following criteria:

- *It must relate to the objectives of the business.* Most businesses have some wealth-enhancement objective, that is, they are seeking to become richer (see Chapter 1). Thus, assuming a wealth-enhancement objective, to be relevant to a particular decision, a cost must have an effect on the wealth of the business.
- *It must differ from one possible decision outcome to the next.* Only costs (and revenue) that are different between outcomes can be used to distinguish between them. Thus the reason that the historic cost of the car that we discussed earlier, is irrelevant, is that it is the same whichever decision is taken about the future of the car. This means that all past costs are irrelevant because what has happened in the past must be the same for all possible future outcomes.

It is not only past costs that are the same from one decision outcome to the next; some future costs may also be the same. Take, for example, a road haulage business that has decided that it will buy a new lorry and the decision lies between two different models. The load capacity, the fuel and maintenance costs are different for each lorry. The potential costs and revenue associated with these are relevant items. The lorry will require a driver, so the business will need to employ one, but a suitably qualified driver could drive either lorry equally well, for the same wage. The cost of employing the driver is thus irrelevant to the decision as to which lorry to buy. This is despite the fact that this cost is a future one.

If, however, the decision did not concern a choice between two models of lorry but rather whether to operate an additional lorry or not, the cost of employing the additional driver would be relevant. This is because it would then be a cost that would vary with the decision made.

ACTIVITY 8.2

A garage has an old car that it bought several months ago for £3,000. The car needs a replacement engine before it can be sold. It is possible to buy a reconditioned engine for £300. This would take seven hours to fit by a mechanic who is paid £8 an hour. At present the garage is short of work, but the owners are reluctant to lay off any mechanics or even to cut down their basic working week because skilled labour is difficult to find and an upturn in repair work is expected soon.

Without the engine, the car could be sold for an estimated £3,500. What is the minimum price at which the garage should sell the car, with a reconditioned engine fitted?

The minimum price is the amount required to cover the relevant costs of the job. At this price, the business will make neither a profit nor a loss. Any price lower than this amount will mean that the wealth of the business is reduced. Thus, the minimum price is:

	£
Opportunity cost of the car	3,500
Cost of the reconditioned engine	300
Total	3,800

The original cost of the car is irrelevant for reasons that have already been discussed: it is the opportunity cost of the car that concerns us. The cost of the new engine is relevant because, if the work is done, the garage will have to pay £300 for the engine; but will pay nothing if the job is not done. The £300 is an example of a future outlay cost.

The labour cost is irrelevant because the same cost will be incurred whether the mechanic undertakes the work or not. This is because the mechanic is being paid to do nothing if this job is not undertaken; thus the additional labour cost arising from this job is zero.

It should be emphasised that the garage will not seek to sell the car with its reconditioned engine for £3,800; it will attempt to charge as much as possible for it. However, any price above the £3,800 will make the garage better off financially than not undertaking the engine replacement.

ACTIVITY 8.3

Assume exactly the same circumstances as in Activity 8.2, except that the garage is quite busy at the moment. If a mechanic is to be put on the engine replacement job, it will mean that other work that the mechanic could have done during the seven hours, all of which could be charged to a customer, will not be undertaken. The garage's labour charge is £20 an hour, though the mechanic is only paid £8 an hour.

What is the minimum price at which the garage should sell the car, with a reconditioned engine fitted, under these altered circumstances?

The minimum price is:

	£
Opportunity cost of the car	3,500
Cost of the reconditioned engine	300
Labour cost (7 × £20)	140
Total	3,940

We can see that the opportunity cost of the car and the cost of the engine is the same as in Activity 8.2 but now a charge for labour has been added to obtain the minimum price. The relevant labour cost here is that which the garage will have to sacrifice in making the time available to undertake the engine replacement job. While the mechanic is working on this job, the garage is losing the opportunity to do work for which a customer would pay £140. Note that the £8 an hour mechanic's wage is still not relevant. This is because the mechanic will be paid £8 an hour irrespective of whether it is the engine-replacement work or some other job that is undertaken.

ACTIVITY 8.4

A business is considering offering a tender to undertake a contract. Fulfilment of the contract will require the use of two types of raw material, both of which are held in stock by the business. All of the stock (inventory) of these two raw materials will need to be used on the contract. Information on the stock required is as follows:

Stock item	Quantity units	Historic cost £/unit	Sales value £/unit	Replacement cost £/unit
A1	500	5	3	6
B2	800	7	8	10

Stock item A1 is in frequent use in the business on a variety of work. The stock of item B2 was bought a year ago for a contract that was abandoned. It has recently become obvious that there is no likelihood of ever using this stock if the contract currently being considered does not proceed.

Management wishes to deduce the minimum price at which the business could undertake the contract without reducing its wealth as a result. This can be used as the baseline in deducing the tender price.

How much should be included in the minimum price in respect of the two stock items detailed above?

The relevant costs to be included in the minimum price are:

$$\text{Stock item:} \quad \text{A1} \quad £6 \times 500 = £3,000$$
$$\text{B2} \quad £8 \times 800 = £6,400$$

We are told that the stock of item A1 is in frequent use and so, if it is used on the contract, it will need to be replaced. Sooner or later, the business will have to buy 500 units (currently costing £6 a unit) additional to that which would have been required had the contract not been undertaken.

We are told that the stock of item B2 will never be used by the business unless the contract is undertaken. Thus, if the contract is not undertaken, the only reasonable thing for the business to do is to sell the stock. This means that if the contract is undertaken and the stock is used, it will have an opportunity cost equal to the potential proceeds from disposal, which is £8 a unit.

Note that the historic cost information about both materials is irrelevant and this will always be the case.

ACTIVITY 8.5

HLA Ltd is in the process of preparing a quotation for a special job for a customer. The job will have the following material requirements:

Material	Units required	Units currently held in stock			
		Quantity held	Historic cost £/unit	Sales value £/unit	Replacement cost £/unit
P	400	0	–	–	40
Q	230	100	62	50	64
R	350	200	48	23	59
S	170	140	33	12	49
T	120	120	40	0	68

Material Q is used consistently by the business on various jobs. Materials R, S and T are in stock as the result of previous overbuying. No other use can be found for R, but the 140 units of S could be used in another job as a substitute for 225 units of material V that are about to be purchased at a price of £10 a unit. Material T has no other use, it is difficult to store and the business has been informed that it will cost £160 to dispose of the material currently in stock.

What is the relevant cost of the materials for the job specified above?

The relevant cost is as follows:

	£
Material P	
This will have to be purchased at £40 a unit (400 × £40)	16,000
Material Q	
This will have to be replaced, therefore, the relevant price is (230 × £64)	14,720
Material R	
200 units of this are in stock and could be sold. The relevant price of these is the sales revenue forgone (200 × £23)	4,600
The remaining 150 units of R would have to be purchased (150 × £59)	8,850
Material S	
This could be sold or used as a substitute for material V.	
The existing stock (inventory) could be sold for £1,680 (140 × £12), however, the saving on material V is higher and therefore should be taken as the relevant amount (225 × £10)	2,250
The remaining units of material S must be purchased (30 × £49)	1,470
A saving on disposal will be made if material T is used	(160)
Total relevant cost	£47,730

Sunk costs and committed costs

When trying to identify relevant costs for a particular decision, we may come across the terms **sunk cost** and **committed cost**. In order to deal with such costs we need to understand what these terms mean. A sunk cost is simply another way of saying past cost and the two expressions can be used interchangeably. A committed cost is also, in effect, a past cost to the extent that an irrevocable decision has been made to incur the cost because, for example, the business has entered into a binding contract. As a result, it is more or less a past cost despite the fact that the cash may not be paid in respect of it until some point in the future. Since the business has no choice as to whether it incurs the cost or not, a committed cost can never be a relevant cost.

It is important to remember that, to be relevant, a cost must be capable of varying according to the decision made. If the business is already committed by a legally binding contract to a cost, that cost cannot vary with the decision.

ACTIVITY 8.6

Past costs are irrelevant costs. Does this mean that what happened in the past is irrelevant?

No, it does not mean this. The fact that the business has an asset that it can deploy in the future is highly relevant. What is not relevant is how much it cost to acquire that asset. This point was examined in the discussion that followed Activity 8.1.

Another reason why the past is not irrelevant is that it generally – though not always – provides us with our best guide to the future. Suppose that we need to estimate the cost of doing something in the future to help us to decide whether it is worth doing. In these circumstances our own experience, or that of others, on how much it has cost to do the thing in the past may provide us with a valuable guide to how much it is likely to cost in the future.

Figure 8.1 summarises the relationship between relevant, irrelevant, opportunity, outlay and past costs.

Qualitative factors of decisions

Though businesses must look closely at the obvious financial effects when making decisions, they must also consider factors that are not directly economic. These are likely to be factors that have a broader but less immediate impact on the business. Ultimately, however, these factors are likely to have economic effect – that is, to affect the wealth of the business.

Figure 8.1   **Summary of the relationship between relevant and irrelevant costs**

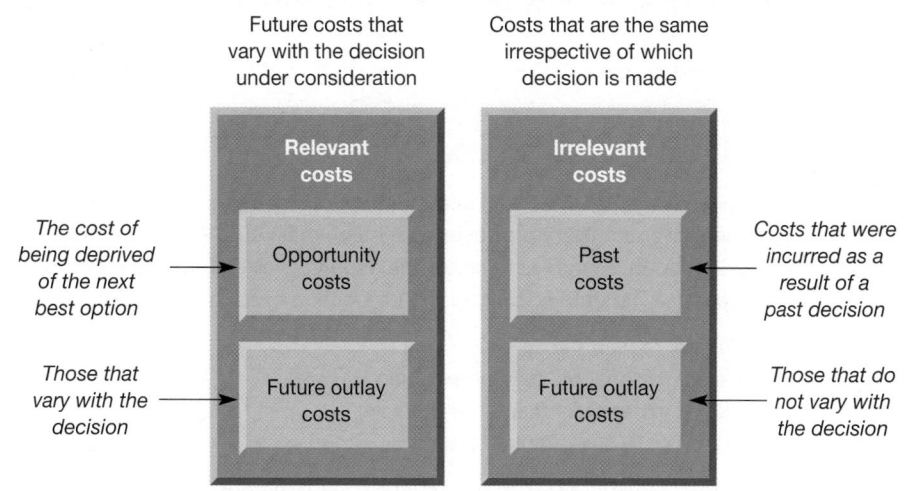

Note in particular that future outlay costs may be either relevant or irrelevant costs depending on whether they vary with the decision. Future opportunity costs and outlay costs, which vary with the decision, are relevant; future outlay costs, which do not vary with the decision and all past costs are irrelevant.

ACTIVITY 8.7

Activity 8.3 was concerned with the cost of putting a car into a marketable condition. Apart from whether the car could be sold for more than the relevant cost of doing this, are there any other factors that should be taken into account in making a decision as to whether or not to do the work?

We can think of three points:

● Turning away another job in order to do the engine replacement may lead to customer dissatisfaction.
● On the other hand, having the car available for sale may be useful commercially for the garage, beyond the profit that can be earned from that particular car sale. For example, having a good stock of second-hand cars may attract potential customers.
● There is also a more immediate economic point. It has been assumed that the only labour opportunity cost is the charge-out rate for the seven hours concerned. In practice, most car repairs involve the use of some materials and spare parts. These are usually charged to customers at a profit to the garage. Any such profit from a job turned away would be lost to the garage, and this lost profit would be an opportunity cost of the engine replacement and should, therefore, be included in the calculation of the minimum price to be charged for the sale of the car.

You may have thought of additional points.

It is important to consider 'qualitative' factors carefully. They can seem unimportant because they are virtually impossible to assess in terms of their ultimate economic effect. This effect can nevertheless be very significant.

SELF-ASSESSMENT QUESTION   8.1

JB Limited is a small specialist manufacturer of electronic components. Makers of aircraft, for both civil and military purposes, use much of its output. One of the aircraft makers has offered a contract to JB Limited for the supply, over the next 12 months, of 400 identical components. The data relating to the production of each component are as follows:

(i)   *Material requirements*:
   3 kg of material M1 (see note 1 below)
   2 kg of material P2 (see note 2 below)
   1 part no. 678 (see note 3 below)

   Note 1: Material M1 is in continuous use by the business; 1,000 kg are currently held in stock. Their original cost was £4.70/kg, but it is known that future purchases will cost £5.50/kg.

   Note 2: 1,200 kg of material P2 are held in stock. The original cost of this material was £4.30/kg. The material has not been required for the last two years. Its scrap value is £1.50/kg. The only foreseeable alternative use is as a substitute for material P4 (in constant use) but this would involve further processing costs of £1.60/kg. The current cost of material P4 is £3.60/kg.

   Note 3: It is estimated that part no. 678 could be bought in for £50 each.

(ii) *Labour requirements*:   Each component would require five hours of skilled labour and five hours of semi-skilled. A skilled employee is available and is currently paid £7/hour. A replacement would, however, have to be obtained at a rate of £6/hour for the work, which would otherwise be done by the skilled employee. The current rate for semi-skilled work is £5/hour and an additional employee could be appointed for this work.

(iii) *General manufacturing costs*:   It is JB Limited's policy to charge a share of the general costs (rent, heating and so on) to each contract undertaken at the rate of £20 for each machine-hour used on the contract. If the contract is undertaken, the general costs are expected to increase as a result of undertaking the contract by £3,200.

Spare machine capacity is available and each component would require four machine-hours. A price of £150 a component has been offered by the potential customer.

Required:
(a) Should the contract be accepted? Support your conclusion with appropriate figures to present to management.
(b) What other factors ought management to consider that might influence the decision?

SUMMARY

The main points in this chapter may be summarised as follows:

Cost = amount of resources, usually measured in monetary terms, sacrificed to achieve a particular objective

Relevant costs must

● Relate to the objective being pursued by the business.
● Differ from one possible decision output to the next.

Relevant costs therefore include

● Opportunity costs.
● Differential future outlay costs.

Irrelevant costs therefore include

● All past (or sunk) costs.
● All committed costs.
● Non-differential outlay costs.

Financial/economic decisions almost inevitably have qualitative aspects that financial analysis cannot really handle, despite their importance

 Key terms

cost p. 264	past cost p. 266
historic cost p. 264	outlay cost p. 266
opportunity cost p. 264	sunk cost p. 270
relevant cost p. 265	committed cost p. 270
irrelevant cost p. 265	

Further reading

If you would like to explore the topics covered in this chapter in more depth, we recommend the following books:

Accounting for Management Decisions, *Arnold J. and Turley S.*, 3rd edn, Prentice Hall International, 1996, chapter 9.

Management and Cost Accounting, *Drury C.*, 5th edn, Thomson Learning Business Press, 2000, chapter 9.

Cost Accounting: A managerial emphasis, *Horngren C., Foster G. and Datar S.*, 11th edn, Prentice Hall International, 2002, chapter 11.

Cost and Management Accounting, *Williamson D.*, Prentice Hall International, 1996, chapter 12.

REVIEW QUESTIONS

Answers to these questions can be found on the students' side of the Companion Website at www.pearsoned.co.uk/atrillmclaney.

8.1 To be relevant to a particular decision, a cost must have two attributes. What are they?

8.2 Distinguish between a sunk cost and an opportunity cost.

8.3 Define the word 'cost' in the context of management accounting.

8.4 What is meant by the expression 'committed cost'? How do committed costs arise?

EXERCISES

Exercises 8.7 and 8.8 are more advanced than 8.1 to 8.6. Those with coloured numbers have answers at the back of the book.

8.1 Lombard Ltd has been offered a contract for which there is available production capacity. The contract is for 20,000 identical items, manufactured by an intricate assembly operation, to be produced and delivered in the next financial year at a price of £80 each. The specification for one item is as follows:

Assembly labour	4 hours
Component X	4 units
Component Y	3 units

There would also be the need to hire equipment, for the duration of the contract, at an outlay cost of £200,000.

The assembly is a highly skilled operation and the workforce is currently underutilised. It is the business's policy to retain this workforce on full pay in anticipation of high demand in a few years' time, for a new product currently being developed. Skilled workers are paid £10 an hour.

Component X is used in a number of other subassemblies produced by the business. It is readily available. A stock of 50,000 units of component X is currently held. Component Y was a special purchase in anticipation of an order that did not in the end materialise. It is, therefore, surplus to requirements and 100,000 units that are in stock may have to be sold at a loss. An estimate of alternative values for components X and Y provided by the materials planning department is as follows:

	X £/unit	Y £/unit
Historic cost	4	10
Replacement cost	5	11
Net realisable value	3	8

It is estimated that any additional relevant costs associated with the contract (beyond the above) will amount to £8 an item.

Required:

Analyse the information in order to advise Lombard on the desirability of the contract.

8.2 The local authority of a small town maintains a theatre and arts centre for the use of a local repertory company, other visiting groups and exhibitions. Management decisions are taken by a committee that meets regularly to review the financial statements and to plan the use of the facilities.

The theatre employs a full-time staff and a number of artistes at costs of £4,800 and £17,600 a month, respectively. They mount a new production every month for 20 performances. Other monthly costs of the theatre are as follows:

	£
Costumes	2,800
Scenery	1,650
Heat and light	5,150
A share of the administration costs of local authority	8,000
Casual staff	1,760
Refreshments	1,180

On average the theatre is half full for the performances of the repertory company. The capacity and seat prices in the theatre are:

200 seats at £12 each
500 seats at £8 each
300 seats at £6 each

In addition, the theatre sells refreshments during the performances for £3,880 a month. Programme sales cover their costs but advertising in the programme generates £3,360 a month.

The management committee has been approached by a popular touring group, which would like to take over the theatre for one month (25 performances). The group is prepared to pay half of its ticket income for the booking. It expects to fill the theatre for 10 nights and achieve two-thirds capacity on the remaining 15 nights. The prices charged are £1 less than normally applies in the theatre.

The local authority will pay for heat and light costs and will still honour the contracts of all artistes and pay the full-time employees who will sell refreshments, programmes and so on. The committee does not expect any change in the level of refreshments or programme sales if they agree to this booking.

Note: The committee includes the share of the local authority administration costs when making profit calculations. It assumes occupancy applies equally across all seat prices.

Required:

(a) On financial grounds should the management committee agree to the approach from the touring group? Support your answer with appropriate workings.
(b) What other factors may have a bearing on the decision by the committee?

8.3 Andrews and Co. Ltd has been invited to tender for a contract. It is to produce 10,000 metres of a cable in which the business specialises. The estimating department of the business has produced the following information relating to the contract:

- *Materials.* The cable will require a steel core, which the business buys in. The steel core is to be coated with a special plastic, also bought in, using a special process. Plastic for the covering will be required at the rate of 0.10 kg/metre of completed cable.
- *Direct labour.* Skilled: 10 minutes/metre
  Unskilled: 5 minutes/metre

The business already has sufficient stock of each of the materials required, to complete the contract. Information on the cost of the stock is as follows:

	Steel core £/metre	Plastic £/kg
Historic cost	1.50	0.60
Current buying-in cost	2.10	0.70
Scrap value	1.40	0.10

The steel core is in constant use by the business for a variety of work that it regularly undertakes. The plastic is a surplus from a previous contract where a mistake was made and an excess quantity ordered. If the current contract does not go ahead, this plastic will be scrapped.

Unskilled labour, which is paid at the rate of £5 an hour, will need to be taken on specifically to undertake the contract. The business is fairly quiet at the moment which means that a pool of skilled labour exists that will still be employed at full pay of £7 an hour to do nothing if the contract does not proceed. The pool of skilled labour is sufficient to complete the contract.

Required:

Indicate the minimum price at which the contract could be undertaken, such that the business would neither be better or worse off as a result of doing it.

8.4 SJ Services Ltd has been asked to quote a price for a special contract to render a service that will take the business one week to complete. Information relating to labour for the contract is as follows:

Grade of labour	Hours required	Basic rate/hour
Skilled	27	£9
Semi-skilled	14	£7
Unskilled	20	£5

A shortage of skilled labour means that the necessary staff to undertake the contract would have to be moved from other work that is currently yielding an excess of sales revenue over labour and other costs of £8 an hour.

Semi-skilled labour is currently being paid at semi-skilled rates to undertake unskilled work. If the relevant members of staff are moved to work on the contract, unskilled labour will have to be employed for the week to replace them.

The unskilled labour actually needed to work on the contract will be specifically employed for the week of the contract.

All labour is charged to contracts at 50 per cent above the rate paid to the employees, so as to cover the contract's fair share of the business's overheads. It is estimated that these will increase by £50 as a result of undertaking the contract.

Undertaking the contract will require the use of a specialised machine for the week. The business owns such a machine, which it depreciates at the rate of £120 a week. This machine is currently being hired out to another business at a weekly rental of £175 on a week-by-week contract.

To derive the above estimates, the business has had to spend £300 on a specialised study. If the contract does not proceed, the results of the study can be sold for £250.

An estimate of the contract's fair share of the business's rent is £150 a week.

Required:

Deduce the minimum price at which SJ Services Ltd could undertake the contract such that it would be neither better nor worse off as a result of undertaking it.

8.5 A business in the food industry is currently holding 2,000 tonnes of material in bulk storage. This material deteriorates with time, and so in the near future it needs to be repackaged for sale or sold in its present form.

The stock (inventory) was acquired in two batches: 800 tonnes at a price of £40 a tonne and 1,200 tonnes at a price of £44 a tonne. The current market price of any additional purchases is

£48 a tonne. If the business were to dispose of the material, it could sell any quantity but only for £36 a tonne; it does not have the contacts or reputation to command a higher price.

Repackaging this bulk material may be undertaken to develop either Product A or Product X. No weight loss occurs with repackaging, that is, one tonne of material will make one tonne of A or X. For Product A, there is an additional cost of £60 a tonne, after which it will sell for £105 a tonne. The marketing department estimates that 500 tonnes could be sold in this way.

In the development of Product X, the business incurs additional costs of £80 a tonne for repackaging. A market price for X is not known and no minimum price has been agreed. The management is currently engaged in discussions over the minimum price that may be charged for Product X in the current circumstances.

Required:
Identify the relevant unit cost for pricing the increments of Product X, given sales volumes of X of:
(a) up to 1,500 tonnes
(b) over 1,500 tonnes, up to 2,000 tonnes
(c) over 2,000 tonnes.

Explain your answer.

8.6 A local education authority is faced with a predicted decline in the demand for school places in its area. It is believed that some schools will have to close in order to remove up to 800 places from current capacity levels. The schools that may face closure are referenced as A, B, C or D. Their details are as follows:

- *School A.* (capacity 200) was built 15 years ago at a cost of £1.2m. It is situated in a 'socially disadvantaged' community area. The authority has been offered £14m for the site by a property developer.
- *School B.* (capacity 500) was built 20 years ago and cost £1m. It was renovated only two years ago at a cost of £3m to improve its facilities. An offer of £8m has been made for the site by a business planning a shopping complex in this affluent part of the town.
- *School C.* (capacity 600) cost £5m to build five years ago. The land for this school is rented from a local business for an annual cost of £300,000.
- *School D.* (capacity 800) cost £7m to build eight years ago; last year £1.5m was spent on an extension. It offers considerable space, which is currently used for sporting events. This factor makes it popular with developers, who have recently offered £9m for the site.

In the accounting system, the local authority depreciates non-current assets based on 2 per cent a year on the original cost. It also differentiates between one-off, large items of capital expenditure or revenue, and annually recurring items.

The land rented for School C is based on a 100-year lease. If the school closes, the property reverts immediately to the owner. If School C is not closed, it will require a £3m investment to improve safety at the school.

If School D is closed, it will be necessary to pay £1.8m to adapt facilities at other schools to accommodate the change.

The local authority has a central staff, which includes administrators for each school costing £200,000 a year each, and a chief education officer costing £40,000 a year in total.

Required:
(a) Prepare a summary of the relevant cash flows (costs and revenue, relative to not making any closures) under the following options:
    (i) closure of D only,
    (ii) closure of A and B,
    (iii) closure of A and C.

Show separately the one-off effects and annually recurring items, rank the options open to the local authority, and briefly interpret your answer. *Note*: Various approaches are acceptable provided that they are logical.

(b) Identify and comment on any two different types of irrelevant cost contained in the information given.

(c) Discuss other factors that might have a bearing on the decision.

8.7 Rob Otics Ltd, a small business that specialises in building electronic-control equipment, has just received an order from a customer for eight identical robotic units. These will be completed using Rob Otic's own labour force and factory capacity. The product specification prepared by the estimating department shows the following:

- Material and labour requirements for each robotic unit:
  Component X   2 a unit
  Component Y   1 a unit
  Component Z   4 a unit.
- Other miscellaneous items:
  Assembly labour   25 hours a unit (but see below)
  Inspection labour   6 hours a unit.

As part of the costing exercise, the business has collected the following information:

- *Component X*. This is a stock item normally held by the business as it is in constant demand. The 10 units currently in stock were invoiced to Rob Otics at £150 a unit, but the sole supplier has announced a price rise of 20 per cent effective immediately. Rob Otics has not yet paid for the items in stock.
- *Component Y*. 25 units are in stock. This component is not normally used by Rob Otics but is in stock because of a cancelled order following the bankruptcy of a customer. The stock (inventory) originally cost the business £4,000 in total, although Rob Otics has recouped £1,500 from the liquidator. As Rob Otics can see no use for it, the finance director proposes to scrap the 25 units (zero proceeds).
- *Component Z*. This is in regular use by Rob Otics. There is none in stock but an order is about to be sent to a supplier for 75 units, irrespective of this new proposal. The supplier charges £25 a unit on small orders but will reduce the price by 20 per cent to £20 a unit for all units on any order over 100 units.
- *Other miscellaneous items*. These are expected to cost £250 in total.

Assembly labour is currently in short supply in the area and is paid at £10 an hour. If the order is accepted, all necessary labour will have to be transferred from existing work, and other orders will be lost. It is estimated that for each hour transferred to this contract £38 will be lost (calculated as lost sales revenue £60, less materials £12 and labour £10). The production director suggests that, owing to a learning process, the time taken to make each unit will reduce, from 25 hours to make the first one, by one hour a unit made.

Inspection labour can be provided by paying existing personnel overtime which is at a premium of 50 per cent over the standard rate of £12 an hour.

When the business is working out its contract prices, it normally adds an amount equal to £20 for each assembly hour to cover its general costs (such as, rent and electricity). To the resulting total, 40 per cent is normally added as a profit mark-up.

Required:

(a) Prepare an estimate of the minimum price that you would recommend Rob Otics to charge for the proposed contract, and provide explanations for any items included.

(b) Identify any other factors that you would consider before fixing the final price.

8.8 A business places substantial emphasis on customer satisfaction and, to this end, delivers its product in special protective containers. These containers have been made in a department within the business. Management has recently become concerned that this internal supply of containers is very expensive. As a result, outside suppliers have been invited to submit tenders for the provision of these containers. A quote of £250,000 a year has been received for a volume that compares with current internal supply.

An investigation into the internal costs of container manufacture has been undertaken and the following emerges:

(a) The annual cost of material is £120,000, according to the stores records maintained, at actual historic cost. Three-quarters (by cost) of this represents material that is regularly stocked and replenished. The remaining 25 per cent of the material cost is a special foaming chemical that is not used for any other purpose. There are 40 tonnes of this chemical currently held in stock. It was bought in bulk for £750 a tonne. Today's replacement price for this material is £1,050 a tonne but it is unlikely that the business could realise more than £600 a tonne if it had to be disposed of owing to the high handling costs and special transport facilities required.

(b) The annual labour cost is £80,000 for this department, however, most are casual employees or recent starters, and so, if an outside quote was accepted, little redundancy would be payable. There are, however, two long-serving employees who would each accept as a salary £15,000 a year until they reached retirement age in two years' time.

(c) The department manager has a salary of £30,000 a year. The closure of this department would release him to take over another department for which a vacancy is about to be advertised. The salary, status and prospects are similar.

(d) A rental charge of £9,750 a year, based on floor area, is allocated to the containers department. If the department was closed, the floor space released would be used for warehousing and, as a result, the business would give up the tenancy of an existing warehouse for which it is paying £15,750 a year.

(e) The plant cost £162,000 when it was bought five years ago. Its market value now is £28,000 and it could continue for another two years, at which time its market value would have fallen to zero. (The plant depreciates evenly over time.)

(f) Annual plant maintenance costs are £9,900 and allocated general administrative costs £33,750 for the coming year.

Required:
Calculate the annual cost of manufacturing containers for comparison with the quote using relevant figures for establishing the cost or benefit of accepting the quote. Indicate any assumptions or qualifications you wish to make.

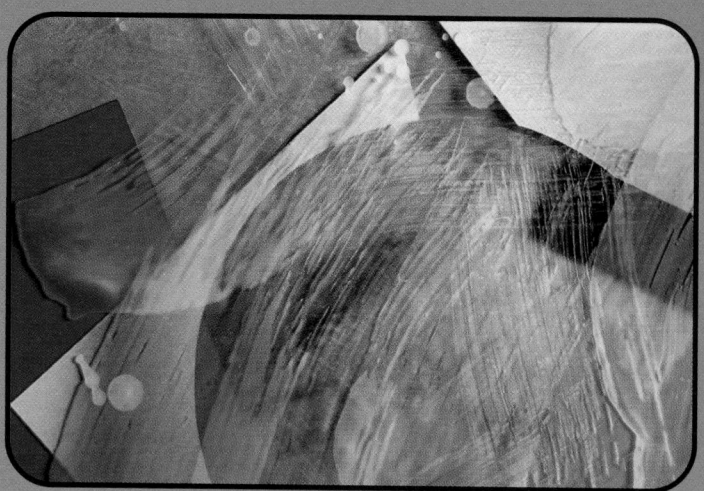

Cost–volume–profit analysis

INTRODUCTION

This chapter is concerned with the relationship between volume of activity, costs and profit. Broadly, costs can be analysed between those that are fixed, relative to the volume of activity, and those that vary with the volume of activity. We shall consider how we can use knowledge of this relationship to make decisions and to assess risk, particularly in the context of short-term decisions. This continues the theme of Chapter 8, but here we shall be looking at situations where a whole class of costs (fixed costs) can be treated as being irrelevant for decision-making purposes.

The behaviour of costs

We saw in the previous chapter that costs represent the resources that have to be sacrificed to achieve a business objective. The objective may be to make a particular product, to provide a particular service and so on. The costs incurred by a business may be classified in various ways and one important way is according to how they behave in relation to changes in the volume of activity. There are:

● those that are fixed (stay the same) when changes occur to the volume of activity;
● those that vary according to the volume of activity.

➡ These are known as **fixed costs** and **variable costs** respectively.

A restaurant manager's salary would normally provide an example of a fixed cost of operating the restaurant. The cost to the restaurant of buying the raw food would be a typical variable cost of operating the restaurant.

We shall see in this chapter that knowledge of how much of each type of cost is associated with some particular activity can be of great value to the decision maker.

Fixed costs

The way fixed costs behave can be shown by preparing a graph that plots the fixed costs of a business against the level of activity, as in Figure 9.1. The distance 0F represents the amount of fixed costs, and this stays the same irrespective of the volume of activity.

ACTIVITY 9.1

A business operates a small chain of hairdressing salons. Can you give some examples of costs that are likely to be fixed for this business?

We came up with the following:

● rent
● insurance
● cleaning costs
● staff salaries.

These costs seem likely to be the same irrespective of the number of customers having their hair cut or styled.

| Figure 9.1 | Graph of fixed cost(s) against the volume of activity |

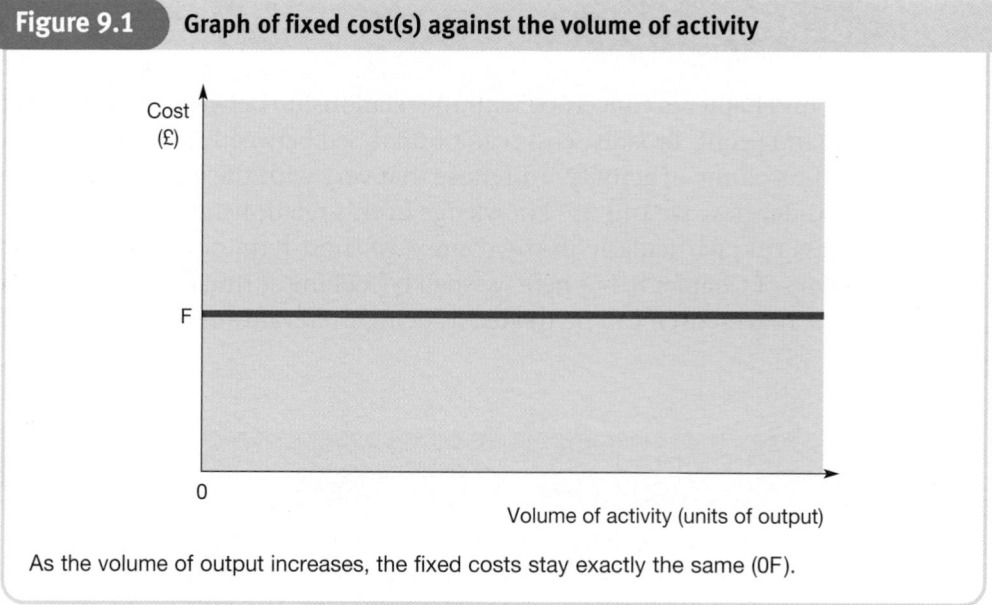

As the volume of output increases, the fixed costs stay exactly the same (0F).

Staff salaries and wages are sometimes automatically assumed always to be variable costs. In practice, they tend to be fixed. People are generally not paid according to the volume of output, and it is not normal to dismiss staff when there is a short-term downturn in activity. If there is a long-term downturn in activity, or at least if it looks that way to management, redundancies may occur, with fixed-cost savings. This, however, is true of all costs. If there is seen to be a likely reduction in demand, the business may decide to close some branches and make rental cost savings. Thus 'fixed' does not mean set in stone for all time; it usually means fixed over the short to medium term.

Nevertheless, in some circumstances, labour costs are variable (for example, where employees are paid according to how much output they produce), but this is unusual.

It is important to be clear that 'fixed', in this context, means only that the cost is not altered by changes in the volume of activity. Fixed costs are likely to be affected by inflation. If rent (a typical fixed cost) goes up because of inflation, a fixed cost will have increased, but not because of a change in the volume of activity.

The level of fixed costs does not stay the same, irrespective of the time period involved. Fixed costs are almost always *time-based*: that is, they vary with the length of time concerned. The rental charge for two months is normally twice that for one month. Thus fixed costs normally vary with time, but (of course) not with the volume of output. We should note that when we talk of fixed costs being, say, £1,000, we must add the period concerned, say, £1,000 a month.

ACTIVITY 9.2

Do fixed costs stay the same irrespective of the volume of output, even where there is a massive rise in that volume?
Think in terms of the rent cost for the hairdressing business.

In fact, the rent is only fixed over a particular range (known as the 'relevant' range). If the number of people wanting to have their hair cut by the business increased, and the business wished to meet this increased demand, it would eventually have to expand its physical size. This might be achieved by opening additional branches, or perhaps by moving existing branches to larger premises in the same vicinity. It may be possible to cope with relatively minor increases in activity by using existing space more efficiently, or by having longer opening hours. If activity continued to expand, increased rent charges would seem inevitable, however.

| Figure 9.2 | Graph of rent cost against the volume of activity |

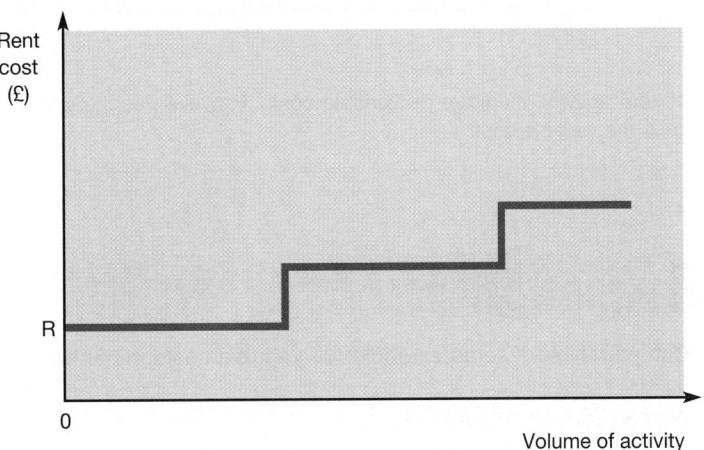

As the volume of activity increases from zero, the rent (a fixed cost) is unaffected. At a particular point, the volume of activity cannot increase further without additional space being rented. The cost of renting the additional space will cause a 'step' in the rent cost. The higher rent cost will continue unaffected if volume rises further until eventually another step point would be reached.

In practice, the situation described in Activity 9.2 would look something like Figure 9.2.

At lower volumes of activity, the rent cost shown in Figure 9.2 would be 0R. As the volume of activity expands, the accommodation becomes inadequate and further expansion requires an increase in premises and, therefore, cost. This higher level of accommodation provision will enable further expansion to take place. Eventually, further costs will need to be incurred if further expansion is to occur. Fixed costs that behave like this are often referred to as **stepped fixed costs**.

Variable costs

We saw earlier that variable costs are costs that vary with the volume of activity. In a manufacturing business, for example, this would include raw materials used.

Figure 9.3   **Graph of variable costs against the volume of activity**

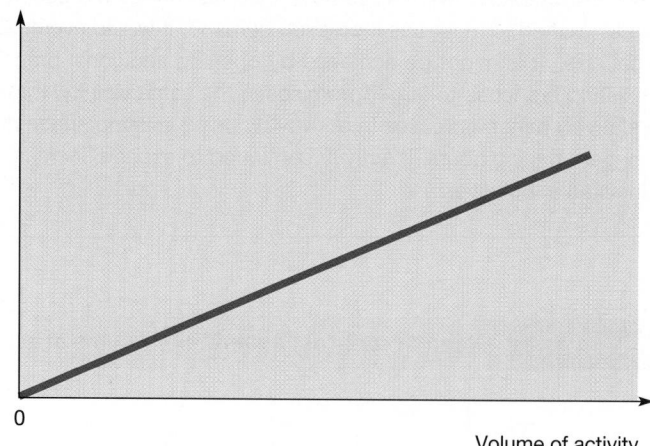

At zero activity, there are no variable costs. However, as the volume of activity increases, so does the variable cost.

As with many types of business activity, variable costs of hairdressers tend to be relatively light in comparison with fixed costs: that is, fixed costs tend to make up the bulk of total costs.

Variable costs can be represented graphically as in Figure 9.3. At zero volume of activity the variable cost is zero. The cost increases in a straight line as activity increases.

The straight line for variable cost on this graph implies that the variable cost will normally be the same per unit of activity, irrespective of the volume of activity concerned. We shall consider the practicality of this assumption a little later in this chapter.

Semi-fixed (semi-variable) costs

In some cases, costs have an element of both fixed and variable cost. These can be described as **semi-fixed (semi-variable) costs**. An example might be the electricity cost for the hairdressing business. Some of this will be for heating and lighting, and this part is probably fixed, at least until the volume of activity expands to a point where

REAL WORLD 9.1

BEP at BA, Ryanair and easyJet

Commercial airlines seem to pay a lot of attention to their BEPs and their 'load factors', that is, their actual level of activity. Figure 9.7 shows the BEP and load factor for three well-known airlines operating from the UK. British Airways (BA) is a traditional airline. Ryanair and easyJet are 'no frills' carriers, which means that passengers receive lower levels of service in return for lower fares. All three operate flights within the UK and from the UK to other European countries. Only BA operates flights beyond Europe. We can see that all three airlines are making operating profits as each has a load factor greater than its BEP.

Figure 9.7   Break-even and load factors in the airline industry

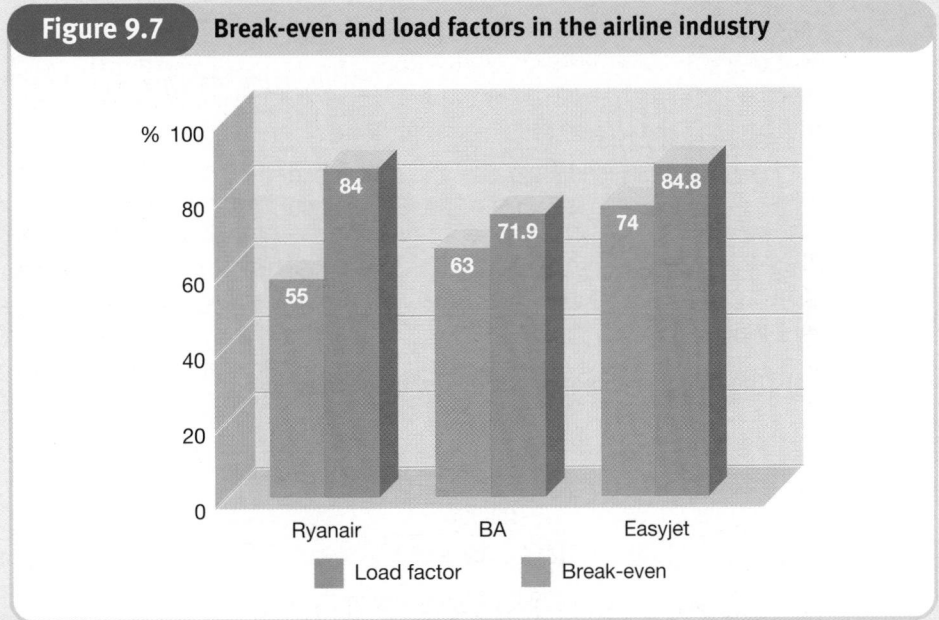

Source: Derived from information contained in the article 'Ryanair alert hits shares' by Jon Ashworth, *The Times*, 4 June 2003, p. 21. The data are based on the year ended 31 March 2003.

ACTIVITY 9.5

Can you think of reasons why the managers of a business might find it useful to know the BEP of some activity that they are planning to undertake?

The usefulness of being able to deduce the BEP is that it makes it possible to compare the planned or expected volume of activity with the BEP and so make a judgement about risk. Planning to operate only just above the volume of activity necessary in order to break even may indicate that it is a risky venture, since only a small fall from the planned volume of activity could lead to a loss. **Real World 9.1**, above, reveals that Ryanair's operations look rather less risky than those of the other two airlines in that the difference between its load factor and its BEP is largest.

ACTIVITY 9.6

Cottage Industries Ltd (see Example 9.1) expects to sell 500 baskets a month. The business has the opportunity to rent a basket-making machine. Doing so would increase the total fixed costs of operating the workshop for a month to £3,000. Using the machine would reduce the labour time to one hour per basket. The basket makers would still be paid £5 an hour.

(a) How much profit would the business make each month from selling baskets (i) assuming that the basket-making machine is not rented and (ii) assuming that it is rented?

(b) What is the BEP if the machine is rented?

(c) What do you notice about the figures that you calculate?

(a) Estimated monthly profit from basket making:

	Without the machine		With the machine	
	£	£	£	£
Sales (500 × £14)		7,000		7,000
Less Materials (500 × £2)	1,000		1,000	
Labour (500 × 2 × £5)	5,000			
(500 × 1 × £5)			2,500	
Fixed costs	500		3,000	
		6,500		6,500
Profit		500		500

(b) The BEP (in number of baskets) with the machine:

$$= \frac{\text{Fixed costs}}{\text{Sales revenue per unit} - \text{Variable costs per unit}}$$

$$= \frac{£3,000}{[£14 - (£2 + £5)]}$$

$$= 429 \text{ baskets a month}$$

The BEP without the machine is 250 baskets per month (see Example 9.1).

(c) There seems to be nothing to choose between the two manufacturing strategies regarding profit, at the estimated sales volume. There is, however, a distinct difference between the two strategies regarding the BEP. Without the machine, the actual volume of sales could fall by a half of that which is expected (from 500 to 250) before the business would fail to make a profit. With the machine, however, a 14 per cent fall (from 500 to 429) would be enough to cause the business to fail to make a profit. On the other hand, for each additional basket sold above the estimated 500, an additional profit of only £2 (that is, £14 – (£2 + £10)) would be made without the machine, whereas £7 (that is, £14 – (£2 + £5)) would be made with the machine. (Note that knowledge of the BEP and the planned volume of activity gives some basis for assessing the riskiness of the activity.)

We shall take a closer look at the relationship between fixed costs, variable costs and break-even together with any advice that we might give the management of Cottage Industries Ltd after we have briefly considered the notion of contribution.

Contribution

The bottom part of the break-even formula (sales revenue per unit less variable costs per unit) is known as the **contribution** per unit. Thus for the basket-making activity, without the machine the contribution per unit is £2, and with the machine it is £7. This can be quite a useful figure to know in a decision-making context. It is called 'contribution' because it contributes to meeting the fixed costs and, if there is any excess, it also contributes to profit.

We shall see, a little later in this chapter, how knowing the amount of the contribution generated by a particular activity can be valuable in making short-term decisions of various types, as well as being useful in the BEP calculation.

Margin of safety and operating gearing

The **margin of safety** is the extent to which the planned volume of output or sales lies above the BEP. Going back to Activity 9.6, we saw that the following situation exists:

	Without the machine (number of baskets)	With the machine (number of baskets)
Expected volume of sales	500	500
BEP	250	429
Difference (margin of safety):		
Number of baskets	250	71
Percentage of estimated volume of sales	50%	14%

ACTIVITY 9.7

What advice would you give Cottage Industries Ltd about renting the machine, on the basis of the values for margin of safety?

It is a matter of personal judgement, which in turn is related to individual attitudes to risk, as to which strategy to adopt. Most people, however, would prefer the strategy of not renting the machine, since the margin of safety between the expected volume of activity and the BEP is much greater. Thus, for the same level of return the risk will be lower without renting the machine.

The relative margins of safety are directly linked to the relationship between the selling price per basket, the variable costs per basket, and the fixed costs per month. Without the machine the contribution (selling price less variable costs) per basket is £2; with the machine it is £7. On the other hand, without the machine the fixed costs are £500 a month; with the machine they are £3,000. This means that, with the machine, the contributions have more fixed costs to 'overcome' before the activity becomes profitable. However, the rate at which the contributions can overcome fixed costs is higher with the machine, because variable costs are lower. This means that one more, or one less, basket sold has a greater impact on profit than it does if the machine is not rented. The contrast between the two scenarios is shown graphically in Figures 9.8(a) and 9.8(b).

The relationship between contribution and fixed costs is known as **operating gearing**. An activity with relatively high fixed costs compared with its variable costs is said to

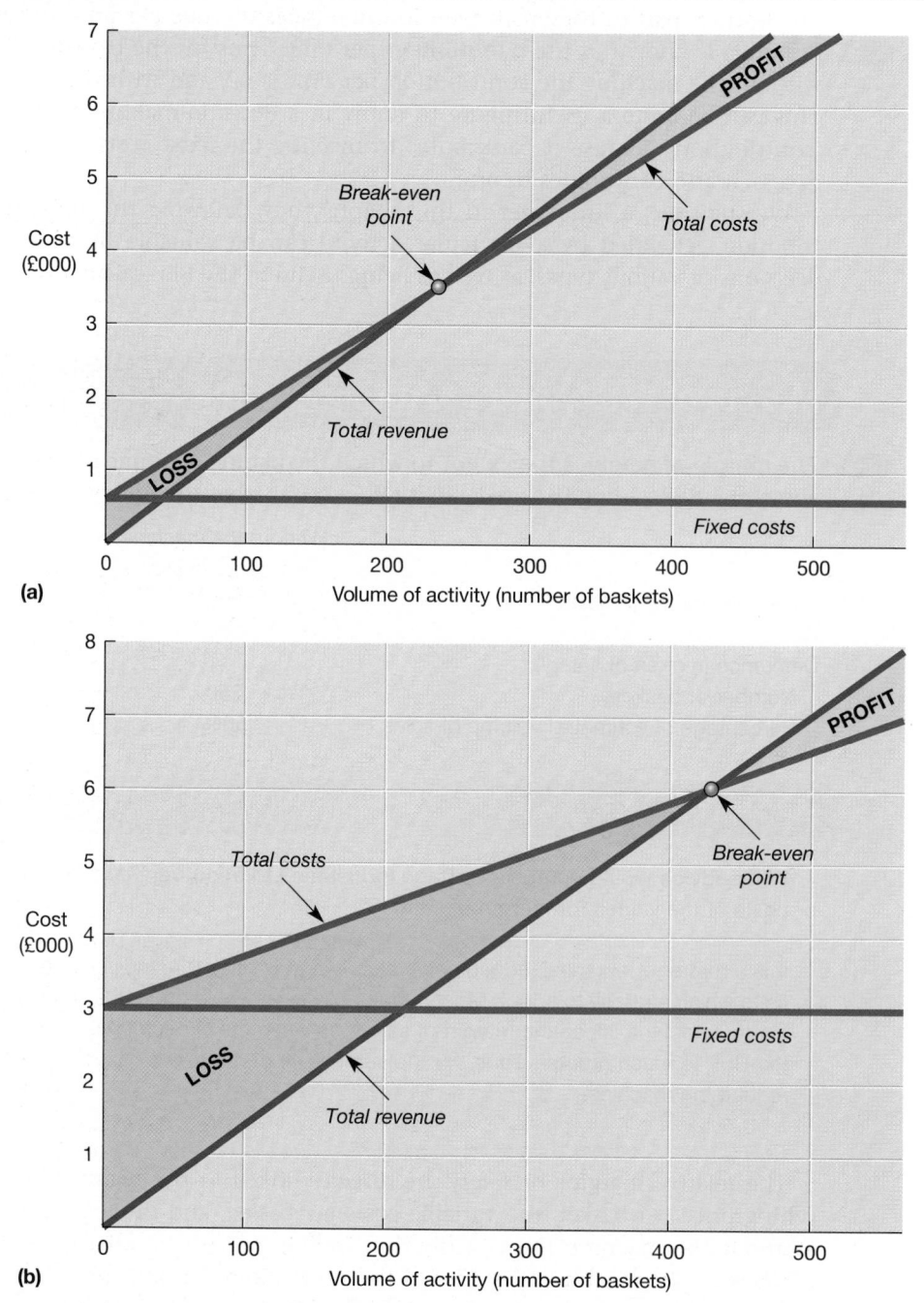

| Figure 9.8 | Break-even charts for Cottage Industries' basket-making activities (a) without the machine and (b) with the machine |

Without the machine the contribution is low. Thus, each additional basket sold does not make a dramatic difference to the profit or loss. With the machine, however, the opposite is true, and small increases or decreases in the sales volume will have a marked effect on the profit or loss.

| Figure 9.9 | The effect of operating gearing |

Where operating gearing is relatively high, as in the diagram, a small amount of circular motion in the volume wheel causes a relatively large amount of circular motion in the profit wheel. An increase in volume would cause a disproportionately greater increase in profit. The equivalent would also be true of a decrease in activity, however.

have high operating gearing. Thus, Cottage Industries Ltd is more highly operationally geared using the machine than not using it. Renting the machine increases the level of operating gearing quite dramatically because it causes an increase in fixed costs, but at the same time it leads to a reduction in variable costs per basket.

The reason why the word 'gearing' is used in this context is that, as with inter-meshing gear wheels of different circumferences, a movement in one of the factors (volume of output) causes a more-than-proportionate movement in the other (profit) as illustrated by Figure 9.9.

Increasing the level of operating gearing tends to make profits more sensitive to changes in the volume of activity. We can demonstrate operating gearing with Cottage Industries Ltd's basket-making activities as follows:

	Without the machine			*With the machine*		
Volume	500	1,000	1,500	500	1,000	1,500
	£	£	£	£	£	£
Contributions*	1,000	2,000	3,000	3,500	7,000	10,500
Less Fixed costs	500	500	500	3,000	3,000	3,000
Profit	500	1,500	2,500	500	4,000	7,500

* £2 per basket without the machine and £7 per basket with it.

Note that, without the machine (low operating gearing), a doubling of the output from 500 to 1,000 units brings a trebling of the profit. With the machine (high operating gearing), doubling output causes profit to rise by eight times. At the same time, reductions in the volume of output tend to have a more damaging effect on profit where the operating gearing is higher.

Operating gearing is quite similar in nature and effect to the financial gearing that we met in Chapter 7.

ACTIVITY 9.8

In general terms, what types of business activity tend to be most highly operationally geared? (*Hint*: Cottage Industries Ltd might give you some idea.)

In general, activities that are capital intensive tend to be more highly operationally geared. This is because renting or owning capital equipment gives rise to additional fixed costs, but it can also give rise to lower variable costs. **Real World 9.2** shows how a very well-known business has benefited from high operating gearing.

REAL WORLD 9.2

Sky-high operating gearing

British Sky Broadcasting Group plc (Sky), the satellite television broadcaster, is an obvious example of a business with high operating gearing. Nearly all of its costs are fixed in that they do not vary with the number of subscribers that it has or the value of its advertising revenue. This means that any increase in total revenue is likely to have a strong favourable effect on profit. The business acknowledged this in its 2003 annual report where it said, 'Sky continues to benefit from strong operational gearing', before going on to explain how a 15 per cent increase in revenue led to an increase of 94 per cent in operating profit.

Source: British Sky Broadcasting Group plc Annual Report 2003.

Profit–volume charts

A slight variant of the break-even chart is the **profit–volume (PV) chart**. A typical PV chart is shown in Figure 9.10.

The PV chart is obtained by plotting loss or profit against volume of activity. The slope of the graph is equal to the contribution per unit, since each additional unit sold decreases the loss, or increases the profit, by the sales revenue per unit less the variable cost per unit. At zero volume of activity there are no contributions, so there is a loss equal to the amount of the fixed costs. As the volume of activity increases, the amount of the loss gradually decreases until BEP is reached. Beyond BEP, profits increase as activity increases.

As we can see, the PV chart does not tell us anything not shown by the break-even chart. On the other hand, information is perhaps more easily absorbed from the PV chart. This is particularly true of the profit (loss) at any volume of activity. The break-even chart shows this as the vertical distance between the total cost and total

Figure 9.10   Profit–volume chart

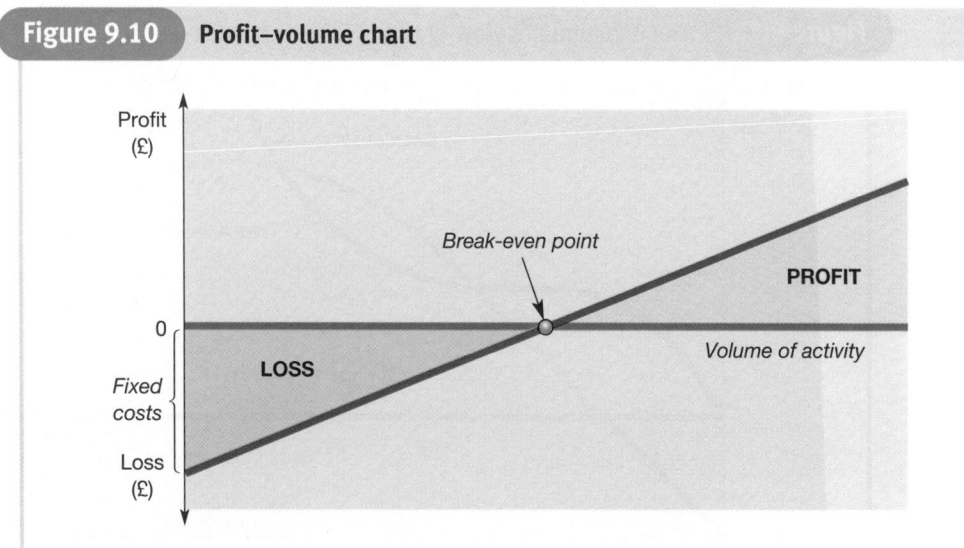

The sloping line is profit (loss) plotted against activity. As activity increases, so does total contribution (sales revenue less variable costs). At zero activity there are no contributions, so there will be a loss equal in amount to the total fixed costs.

sales revenue lines. The PV chart, in effect, combines the total sales revenue and total variable cost lines, which means that profit (or loss) is plotted directly.

The economist's view of the break-even chart

So far in this chapter we have treated all the relationships as linear – that is, all of the lines in the graphs have been straight. This is typically the approach taken in accounting, though it may not be strictly valid.

Consider, for example, the variable cost line in the break-even chart; accountants would normally treat this as being a straight line. Strictly, however, the line perhaps should not be straight because at high levels of output **economies of scale** may be available to an extent not available at lower levels. For example, a raw material (a typical variable cost) may be able to be used more efficiently with higher volumes of activity. Similarly, the relatively large quantities of material and services bought may enable the business to benefit from bulk discounts and general power in the marketplace to negotiate lower prices.

There is also a general tendency for sales revenue per unit to reduce as volume is expanded, since to sell more units of the product or service, it will probably be necessary to lower the selling price.

Economists tend to recognise that, in real life, the relationships portrayed in the break-even chart are usually non-linear. The typical economist's view of the chart is shown in Figure 9.11.

Note that, in Figure 9.11, the variable costs start to increase quite steeply with volume but that, around point A, economies of scale start to take effect. After this point, further increases in volume do not cause such a large increase, for each additional unit of output, in variable costs. These economies of scale continue to have a benign effect on costs until a point is reached where the business will be operating towards the end of its efficient range. Here the business may have problems with finding supplies

...ear relationships. The normal approach to break-even analysis assumes that the ...nships between sales revenue, variable costs and volume are strictly straight-...nes. In real life this is unlikely to be so. This is probably not a major problem, ...as we have just seen:

...ak-even analysis is normally conducted in advance of the activity actually ...ing place. Our ability to predict future costs, revenue and so on is somewhat ...ited: hence what are probably minor variations from strict linearity are ...likely to be significant, compared with other forecasting errors;

...st businesses operate within a narrow range of volume of activity. Over short ...ges, curved lines tend to be relatively straight.

...ed fixed costs. Most fixed costs are not fixed over all volumes of activity. They ...to be 'stepped' in the way depicted in Figure 9.2. This means that, in practice, ...care must be taken in making assumptions about fixed costs. The problem is ...cularly heightened because most activities will probably involve fixed costs of ...us types (rent, supervisory salaries, administration costs), all of which are likely ...ave steps at different points.

...i-product businesses. Most businesses do not offer just one product or service. ...is a problem for break-even analysis since it raises the question of the effect ...dditional sales of one product or service on sales of another of the business's ...lucts or services. There is also the problem of identifying the fixed costs of ...particular activity. Fixed costs tend to relate to more than one activity – for ...mple, two activities may be carried out in the same rented premises. There are ...s of dividing fixed costs between activities, but these tend to be arbitrary, which ...s into question the value of the break-even analysis.

...pite some problems, the notion of break-even analysis and BEP seem to be widely ...The media frequently refer to the BEP for businesses and activities. For example, ...was much discussion at the turn of this century about the BEP, in terms of the ...er of visitors, for the London Millennium Dome. Eurotunnel's BEP, and whether ...l be reached, also seems to be a much-reported topic. Similarly, the number of ...e regularly needed to pay to watch a football team so that the club breaks even ...seems to be referred to. **Real World 9.3** provides an insight to the extent of break-...analysis by managers in practice.

REAL WORLD 9.3

...reak-even analysis in practice

...survey of management accounting practice in the US was conducted in 2003. Nearly ...000 businesses replied to the survey. These tended to be larger businesses, of which ...bout 40 per cent were manufacturers and about 16 per cent financial services; the ...emainder were across a range of other industries.

The survey revealed that 62 per cent use break-even analysis extensively, with a further ...2 per cent considering using the technique in the future.

Though the survey relates to the US, in the absence of UK evidence it provides some ...nsight to what is likely also to be practice in the UK and elsewhere in the developed world.

...ource: Taken from the 2003 Survey of Management Accounting, Ernst and Young, 2003.

Marginal analysis

If we cast our minds back to Chapter 8, where we discussed relevant costs for decision making, we should recall that when we are trying to decide between two or more possible courses of action, *only costs that vary with the decision should be included in the decision analysis.*

For many decisions that involve:

● relatively small variations from existing practice, and/or
● relatively limited periods of time,

fixed costs are not relevant to the decision, because they will be the same irrespective of the decision made. This is because:

● fixed costs tend to be impossible to alter in the short term, or
● managers are reluctant to alter them in the short term.

ACTIVITY   9.9

Ali plc occupies premises that it owns in order to provide a service. There is a downturn in demand for the service, and it would be possible for Ali plc to carry on the business from smaller, cheaper premises.

Can you think of any reasons why the business might not immediately move to smaller, cheaper premises?

....

We thought of broadly three reasons:

1 It is not usually possible to find a buyer for premises at very short notice.
2 It may be difficult to move premises quickly where there is, say, delicate equipment to be moved.
3 Management may feel that the downturn might not be permanent, and would thus be reluctant to take such a dramatic step and deny itself the opportunity to benefit from a possible revival of trade.

The business's premises in Activity 9.9 may provide an example of one of the more inflexible types of cost, but most fixed costs tend to be broadly similar in this context.

We shall now consider some types of decisions where fixed costs can be regarded as irrelevant. These decisions are short-term in nature, which means that the objective of wealth enhancement will be promoted by trying to generate as much net cash inflow as possible.

In **marginal analysis** we concern ourselves just with costs and revenue that vary with the decision and so this usually means that fixed costs are ignored. Marginal analysis tends to assume that the variable cost per unit will be equal to the **marginal cost**, which is the additional cost of producing one more unit of output. Although this is normally the case, there may be times when producing one more will involve a step in the fixed costs. If this occurs, the marginal cost is not just the variable cost, it will include the increment, or step, in the fixed costs as well.

VOLUME–PROFIT ANALYSIS

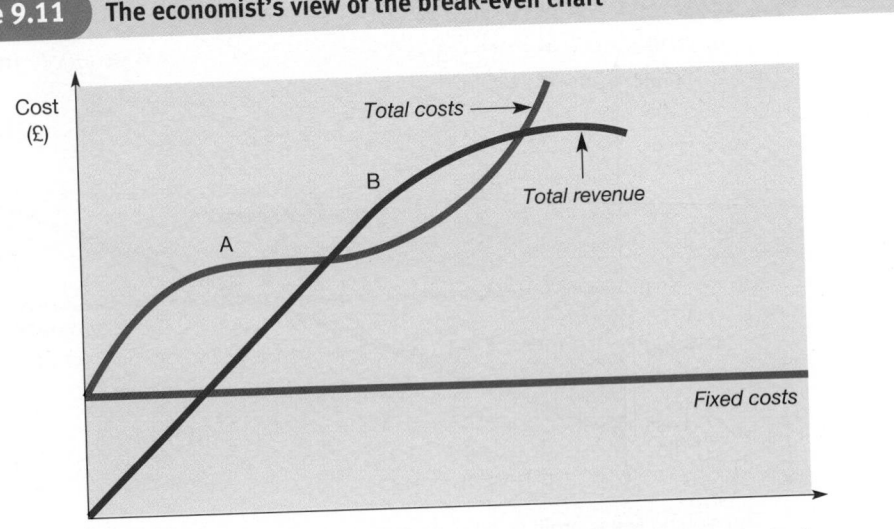

re 9.11   The economist's view of the break-even chart

...s volume increases, economies of scale have a favourable effect on variable costs, but this ...ffect is reversed at still higher levels of output. At the same time, sales revenue per unit will ...end to decrease at higher levels to encourage additional buyers.

...the variable-cost elements, which will normally adversely affect their price. Also, ... business may find it more difficult to produce, there may be machine breakdowns, ...d so on.

...At low levels of output, sales may be made at a relatively high price per unit. To ...rease sales output beyond point B it may be necessary to lower the average sales ...ce per unit.

...Note how this 'curvilinear' representation of the break-even chart can easily lead to ...e existence of two break-even points.

...Accountants justify their approach to this topic by the fact that, though the lines ...ay not in practice be perfectly straight, this defect is probably not worth taking ...to account in most cases. This is partly because all of the information used in the ...alysis is based on estimates of the future. As this will inevitably be flawed, it seems ...ointless to be pedantic about minor approximations, such as treating the total cost ...d revenue lines as straight ones when strictly this is invalid. Only where signifi-...nt economies or diseconomies of scale are involved should the non-linearity of the ...ariable costs be taken into account. Also, for most businesses, the range of possible ...olumes of activity at which they are capable of operating (the **relevant range**) is pretty ...arrow. Over very short distances, it is perfectly reasonable to treat a curved line as ...eing straight.

Weaknesses of break-even analysis

...s we have seen, break-even analysis can provide some useful insights to the import-...nt relationship between fixed costs, variable costs and the volume of activity. It does, ...owever, have its weaknesses. There are three general problems:

Marginal analysis may be used in four key areas of decision making:

- accepting/rejecting special contracts;
- determining the most efficient use of scarce resources;
- make-or-buy decisions;
- closing or continuation decisions.

We shall now consider each of these areas in turn.

Accepting/rejecting special contracts

To understand how marginal analysis may be used in decisions as to whether to accept or reject special contracts, let us consider the following activity.

ACTIVITY 9.10

Cottage Industries Ltd (see Example 9.1) has spare capacity in that its basket makers have some spare time. An overseas retail chain has offered the business an order for 300 baskets at a price of £13 each.

Without considering any wider issues, should the business accept the order? (Assume that the business does not rent the machine.)

··

Since the fixed costs will be incurred in any case, they are not relevant to this decision. All we need to do is see whether the price offered will yield a contribution. If it will, the business will be better off by accepting the contract than by refusing it.

	£
Additional revenue per unit	13
Less Additional cost per unit	12
Additional contribution per unit	1

For 300 units, the additional contribution will be £300 (that is, 300 × £1). Since no fixed cost increase is involved, irrespective of what else is happening to the business, it will be £300 better off by taking this contract than by refusing it.

As ever with decision making, there are other factors that are either difficult or impossible to quantify. These should be taken into account before reaching a final decision. In the case of Cottage Industries Ltd's decision on the overseas customer, these could include the following:

- The possibility that spare capacity will have been 'sold off' cheaply when there might be another potential customer who will offer a higher price, but, by which time, the capacity will be fully committed. It is a matter of commercial judgement as to how likely this will be.
- Selling the same product, but at different prices, could lead to a loss of customer goodwill. The fact that a different price will be set for customers in different countries (that is, in different markets) may be sufficient to avoid this potential problem.

- If the business is going to suffer continually from being unable to sell its full production potential at the 'regular' price, it might be better, in the long run, to reduce capacity and make fixed cost savings. Using the spare capacity to produce marginal benefits may lead to the business failing to address this issue.
- On a more positive note, the business may see this as a way of breaking into the overseas market. This is something that might be impossible to achieve if the business charges its regular price.

The most efficient use of scarce resources

We tend to think in terms of the size of the market being the brake on output. This is to say that the ability of a business to sell will limit production, rather than the ability to produce will limit sales. In some cases, however, it is a limit on what can be produced that limits sales. Limited production might stem from a shortage of any factor of production – labour, raw materials, space, machinery and so on. Such scarce factors are often known as *key* or *limiting* factors.

The most profitable combination of products will occur where the *contribution per unit of the scarce factor* is maximised. Example 9.2 should illustrate this point.

Example 9.2

A business provides three different services, the details of which are as follows:

Service (code name)	AX107	AX109	AX220
	£	£	£
Selling price per unit	50	40	65
Variable cost per unit	(25)	(20)	(35)
Contribution per unit	25	20	30
Labour time per unit	5 hours	3 hours	6 hours

Within reason, the market will take as many units of each service as can be provided, but the ability to provide the service is limited by the availability of labour, all of which needs to be skilled. Fixed costs are not affected by the choice of service provided because all three services use the same facilities.

The most profitable service is AX109 because it generates a contribution of £6.67 (£20/3) an hour. The other two generate only £5.00 each an hour (£25/5 and £30/6). So, to maximise profit, priority should be given to the production that maximises the contribution per unit of limiting factor.

Our first reaction may have been that the business should provide only service AX220, because this is the one that yields the highest contribution per unit sold. If so, we should have been making the mistake of thinking that it is the ability to sell that is the limiting factor. If the above analysis is not convincing, we can take an imaginary number of available labour-hours and ask ourselves what is the maximum contribution (and, therefore, profit) that could be made by providing each service exclusively. Bear in mind that there is no shortage of anything else, including market demand, just a shortage of labour.

ACTIVITY 9.11

A business makes three different products, the details of which are as follows:

Product (code name)	B14	B17	B22
Selling price per unit (£)	25	20	23
Variable cost per unit (£)	10	8	12
Weekly demand (units)	25	20	30
Machine time per unit (hours)	4	3	4

Fixed costs are not affected by the choice of product because all three products use the same machine. Machine time is limited to 148 hours a week.

Which combination of products should be manufactured if the business is to produce the highest profit?

Product (code name)	B14	B17	B22
	£	£	£
Selling price per unit	25	20	23
Variable cost per unit	(10)	(8)	(12)
Contribution per unit	15	12	11
Machine time per unit (hours)	4	3	4
Contribution per machine-hour	£3.75	£4.00	£2.75
Order of priority	2nd	1st	3rd

Therefore:

Produce	20 units of product B17 using	60 hours
	22 units of product B14 using	88 hours
		148 hours

This leaves unsatisfied the market demand for a further 3 units of product B14 and 30 units of product B22.

ACTIVITY 9.12

What steps could be contemplated that could lead to a higher level of contribution for the business in Activity 9.11?

The possibilities for improving matters that occurred to us are as follows:

- Consider obtaining additional machine time. This could mean obtaining a new machine, subcontracting the machining to another business, or perhaps squeezing a few more hours a week out of the business's own machine. Perhaps a combination of two or more of these is a possibility.
- Redesign the products in a way that requires less time per unit on the machine.
- Increase the price per unit of the three products. This might well have the effect of dampening demand, but the existing demand cannot be met at present, and it may be more profitable in the long run to make a greater contribution on each unit sold than to take one of the other courses of action to overcome the problem.

ACTIVITY 9.13

Going back to Activity 9.11, what is the maximum price that the business concerned would logically be prepared to pay to have the remaining B14s machined by a subcontractor, assuming that no fixed or variable costs would be saved as a result of not doing the machining in-house?

Would there be a different maximum if we were considering the B22s?

If the remaining three B14s were subcontracted at no cost, the business would be able to earn a contribution of £15 a unit, which it would not otherwise be able to gain. Therefore, any price up to £15 a unit would be worth paying to a subcontractor to undertake the machining. Naturally, the business would prefer to pay as little as possible, but anything up to £15 would still make it worthwhile subcontracting the machining.

This would not be true of the B22s because they have a different contribution per unit; £11 would be the relevant figure in their case.

Make-or-buy decisions

Businesses are frequently confronted by the need to decide whether to produce the product or service that they sell themselves, or to buy it in from some other business. Thus, a producer of electrical appliances might decide to subcontract the manufacture of one of its products to another business, perhaps because there is a shortage of production capacity in the producer's own factory, or because it believes it to be cheaper to subcontract than to make the appliance itself.

It might just be part of a product or service that is subcontracted. For example, the producer may have a component for the appliance made by another manufacturer. In principle, there is hardly any limit to the scope of make-or-buy decisions. Virtually any part, component or service that is required in production of the main product or service, or the main product or service itself, could be the subject of a make-or-buy decision. So, for example, the personnel function of a business, which is normally performed in-house, could be subcontracted. At the same time, electrical power, which is typically provided by an outside electrical utility business, could be generated in-house.

 Obtaining services or products from a subcontractor is often called **outsourcing**.

Real World 9.4 provides an example of outsourcing by a well-known UK business.

REAL WORLD 9.4

Outsourcing at Boots

During 2002, Boots Company plc, the UK health-care manufacturer and retailer, decided to subcontract or 'outsource' its IT activities. Now, instead of employing its own IT staff, it has a contract for another business to run Boots' IT facility. Boots estimates that this will save it £100 million over a ten-year period. Outsourcing this type of activity is becoming very common in the UK and elsewhere.

Source: Boots Company plc Annual Report 2003.

Example 9.3

Shah Ltd needs a component for one of its products. It can subcontract production of the component to a subcontractor who will provide the components for £20 each. The business can produce the components internally for total variable costs of £15 per component. Shah Ltd has spare capacity.

Should the component be subcontracted or produced internally?

The answer is that Shah Ltd should produce the component internally, since the variable cost of subcontracting is greater by £5 than the variable cost of internal manufacture.

ACTIVITY 9.14

Now assume that Shah Ltd (Example 9.3) has no spare capacity, so it can only produce the component internally by reducing its output of another of its products. While it is making each component, it will lose contributions of £12 from the other product.

Should the component be subcontracted or produced internally?

The answer is to subcontract.

The relevant cost of internal production of each component is:

	£
Variable cost of production of the component	15
Opportunity cost of lost production of the other product	12
	27

This is obviously more costly than the £20 per component that will have to be paid to the subcontractor.

ACTIVITY 9.15

What factors, other than the immediately financially quantifiable, would you consider when making a make-or-buy decision?

We feel that there are two major factors:

1 The general problems of subcontracting:
   (a) loss of control of quality;
   (b) potential unreliability of supply.
2 Expertise and specialisation. It is possible for most businesses, with sufficient determination, to do virtually everything in-house. This may, however, require a level of skill and facilities that most businesses neither have nor feel inclined to acquire. For example, though it is true that most businesses could generate their own electricity, their managements tend to take the view that this is better done by a specialist generator business. Specialists can often do things more cheaply, with less risk of things going wrong.

Closing or continuation decisions

It is quite common for businesses to produce separate financial statements for each department or section, to try to assess the relative effectiveness of each one.

Example 9.4

Goodsports Ltd is a retail shop that operates through three departments, all in the same premises. The three departments occupy roughly equal-sized areas of the premises. The trading results for the year just finished showed the following:

	Total	Sports equipment	Sports clothes	General clothes
	£000	£000	£000	£000
Sales	534	254	183	97
Costs	(482)	(213)	(163)	(106)
Profit/(loss)	52	41	20	(9)

It would appear that if the general clothes department were to close, the business would be more profitable, by £9,000 a year, assuming last year's performance to be a reasonable indication of future performance.

When the costs are analysed between those that are variable and those that are fixed, however, the contribution of each department can be deduced and the following results obtained:

	Total	Sports equipment	Sports clothes	General clothes
	£000	£000	£000	£000
Sales	534	254	183	97
Variable costs	(344)	(167)	(117)	(60)
Contribution	190	87	66	37
Fixed costs (rent and so on)	(138)	(46)	(46)	(46)
Profit/(loss)	52	41	20	(9)

Now it is obvious that closing the general clothes department, without any other developments, would make the business worse off by £37,000 (the department's contribution). The department should not be closed, because it makes a positive contribution. The fixed costs would continue whether the department were closed or not. As can be seen from the above analysis, distinguishing between variable and fixed costs, and deducing the contribution, can make the picture a great deal clearer.

ACTIVITY 9.16

In considering Goodsports Ltd (in Example 9.4), we saw that the general clothes department should not be closed 'without any other developments'.

What 'other developments' could affect this decision, making continuation either more attractive or less attractive?

....

The things that we could think of are as follows:

● Expansion of the other departments or replacing the general clothes department with a completely new activity. This would make sense only if the space currently occupied by the general clothes department could generate contributions totalling at least £37,000 a year.
● Subletting the space occupied by the general clothes department. Once again, this would need to generate a net rent greater than £37,000 a year to make it more financially beneficial than keeping the department open.
● Keeping the department open, even if it generated no contribution whatsoever (assuming that there is no other use for the space), may still be beneficial. If customers are attracted into the shop because it has general clothing, they may then buy something from one of the other departments. In the same way, the activity of a sub-tenant might attract customers into the shop. (On the other hand, it might drive them away!)

SELF-ASSESSMENT QUESTION 9.1

Khan Ltd can render three different types of service (Alpha, Beta and Gamma) using the same staff. Various estimates for next year have been made as follows:

Service	Alpha £/unit	Beta £/unit	Gamma £/unit
Selling price	30	39	20
Variable material cost	15	18	10
Other variable costs	6	10	5
Share of fixed costs	8	12	4
Staff time required (hours)	2	3	1

Fixed costs for next year are expected to total £40,000.

Required:
(a) If the business were to render only service Alpha next year, how many units of the service would it need to provide in order to break even? (Assume for this part of the question that there is no effective limit to market size and staffing level.)
(b) If the business has a maximum of 10,000 staff-hours next year, in which order of preference would the three services come?
(c) If the maximum market for next year for the three services is as follows:

Alpha	3,000 units
Beta	2,000 units
Gamma	5,000 units

what quantities of which service should the business provide next year and how much profit would this be expected to yield?

SUMMARY

The main points in this chapter may be summarised as follows:

Behaviour of costs

- Fixed costs are those that are independent of the level of activity (for example, rent).
- Variable costs are those that vary with the level of activity (for example, raw materials).
- Semi-fixed (semi-variable) costs are a mixture of the two (for example, electricity).

Break-even analysis

- The break-even point (BEP) is the level of activity (in units of output or sales revenue) at which total costs (fixed + variable) = total sales revenue.
- Calculation of BEP is as follows:

$$\text{BEP (in units of output)} = \frac{\text{Fixed costs for the period}}{\text{Contribution per unit}}$$

- Use of knowledge of BEP for a particular activity – risk assessment.
- Contribution per unit = sales revenue per unit less variable cost per unit.
- Margin of safety = excess of planned volume of activity over BEP.
- Operating gearing = the extent to which the total costs of some activity are fixed rather than variable.
- Profit–volume (PV) chart is an alternative approach to BE chart.
- Economists tend to take a different approach to BE, taking account of economies (and diseconomies) of scale and of the fact that, generally, in order to sell large volumes, price per unit may need to fall.

Weaknesses of BE analysis

- Non-linear relationships.
- Stepped fixed costs.
- Multi-product businesses.

Marginal analysis (ignores fixed costs where these are not affected by the decision)

- Accepting/rejecting special contracts – consider only the effect on contributions.
- Using scarce resources – the limiting factor is most effectively used by maximising its contribution per unit.
- Make-or-buy decisions – take the action that leads to the highest total contributions.
- Closing/continuing an activity – should be assessed by net effect on total contributions.

→ Key terms

fixed costs p. 281	margin of safety p. 291
variable costs p. 281	operating gearing p. 291
stepped fixed costs p. 283	profit–volume (PV) chart p. 294
semi-fixed (semi-variable)	economies of scale p. 295
costs p. 284	relevant range p. 296
break-even analysis p. 286	marginal analysis p. 298
break-even chart p. 287	marginal cost p. 298
break-even point p. 287	outsourcing p. 302
contribution p. 291	

Further reading

If you would like to explore the topics covered in this chapter in more depth, we recommend the following books:

Management Accounting, *Atkinson A., Banker R., Kaplan R. and Young S.M.*, 3rd edn, Prentice Hall, 2001, chapter 3.

Management and Cost Accounting, *Drury C.*, 5th edn, Thomson Learning, 2000, chapter 8.

Cost Accounting: A managerial emphasis, *Horngren C., Foster G.* and *Datar S.*, 11th edn, Prentice Hall International, 2002, chapter 3.

Cost and Management Accounting, *Williamson D.*, Prentice Hall International, 1996, chapters 3 and 11.

REVIEW QUESTIONS

Answers to these questions can be found on the students' side of the Companion Website at **www.pearsoned.co.uk/atrillmclaney**.

9.1 Define the terms *fixed cost* and *variable cost.* Explain how an understanding of the distinction between fixed costs and variable costs can be useful to managers.

9.2 What is meant by the *BEP* for an activity? How is the BEP calculated? Why is it useful to know the BEP?

9.3 When we say that some business activity has *high operating gearing*, what do we mean? What are the implications for the business of high operating gearing?

9.4 If there is a scarce resource that is restricting sales, how will the business maximise its profit? Explain the logic of the approach that you have identified for maximising profit.

EXERCISES

Exercises 9.4 to 9.8 are more advanced than 9.1 to 9.3. Those with a coloured number have answers at the back of the book.

9.1 The management of a business is concerned at its inability to obtain enough fully trained labour to enable it to meet its present budget projection.

Service:	Alpha £000	Beta £000	Gamma £000	Total £000
Variable costs				
Materials	6	4	5	15
Labour	9	6	12	27
Expenses	3	2	2	7
Allocated fixed costs	13	8	12	33
Total cost	31	20	31	82
Profit	8	9	2	19
Sales revenue	39	29	33	101

The amount of labour likely to be available amounts to £20,000. All of the variable labour is paid at the same hourly rate. You have been asked to prepare a statement of plans ensuring that at least 50 per cent of the budget sales are achieved for each service, and the balance of labour is used to produce the greatest profit.

Required:

(a) Prepare a statement, with explanations, showing the greatest profit available from the limited amount of skilled labour available, within the constraint stated. *Hint*: Remember that all labour is paid at the same rate.

(b) What steps could the business take in an attempt to improve profitability, in the light of the labour shortage?

9.2 Lannion and Co. is engaged in providing and marketing a standard advice service. Summarised results for the past two months reveal the following:

	October	November
Sales (units of the service)	200	300
Sales revenue (£)	5,000	7,500
Operating profit (£)	1,000	2,200

There were no price changes of any description during these two months.

Required:
(a) Deduce the BEP (in units of the service) for Lannion.
(b) State why the business might find it useful to know its BEP.

9.3 A hotel group prepares financial statements on a quarterly basis. The senior management is reviewing the performance of one hotel and making plans for next year.

They have in front of them the results for this year (based on some actual results and some forecasts to the end of this year):

Quarter	Sales	Profit/(loss)
	£000	£000
1	400	(280)
2	1,200	360
3	1,600	680
4	800	40
Total	4,000	800

The total estimated number of visitors (guest nights) for this year is 50,000. The results follow a regular pattern; there are no unexpected cost fluctuations beyond the seasonal trading pattern shown above. The management intends to incorporate into its plans for next year an anticipated increase in unit variable costs of 10 per cent and a profit target for the hotel of £1m.

Required:
(a) Calculate the total variable and total fixed costs of the hotel for this year. Show the provisional annual results for this year in total, showing variable and fixed costs separately. Show also the revenue and costs per visitor.
(b) (i) If there is no increase in visitors for next year, what will be the required revenue rate per hotel visitor to meet the profit target?
(ii) If the required revenue rate per visitor is not raised above this year's level, how many visitors will be required to meet the profit target?
(c) Outline and briefly discuss the assumptions that are made in typical PV or break-even analysis, and assess whether they limit its usefulness.

9.4 Motormusic Ltd makes a standard model of car radio, which it sells to car manufacturers for £60 each. Next year the business plans to make and sell 20,000 radios. The business's costs are as follows:

Manufacturing	
Variable materials	£20 per radio
Variable labour	£14 per radio
Other variable costs	£12 per radio
Fixed costs	£80,000 per year
Administration and selling	
Variable	£3 per radio
Fixed	£60,000 per year

Required:
(a) Calculate the break-even point for next year, expressed both in quantity of radios and sales value.

(b) Calculate the margin of safety for next year, expressed both in quantity of radios and sales value.

9.5 A business makes three products, A, B and C. All three products require the use of two types of machine: cutting machines and assembling machines. Estimates for next year include the following:

Product	A	B	C
Selling price (£ per unit)	25	30	18
Sales demand (units)	2,500	3,400	5,100
Material cost (£ per unit)	12	13	10
Variable production cost (£ per unit)	7	4	3
Time required per unit on cutting machines (hours)	1.0	1.0	0.5
Time required per unit on assembling machines (hours)	0.5	1.0	0.5

Fixed costs for next year are expected to total £42,000. It is the business's policy for each unit of production to absorb these in proportion to its total variable costs. The business has cutting machine capacity of 5,000 hours a year and assembling machine capacity of 8,000 hours a year.

Required:
(a) State, with supporting workings, which products in which quantities the business should plan to make next year on the basis of the above information. *Hint*: First determine which machines will be a limiting factor (scarce resource).
(b) State the maximum price per product that it would be worth the business paying a sub-contractor to carry out that part of the work that could not be done internally.

9.6 Darmor Ltd has three products, which require the same production facilities. Information about the production costs for one unit of its products is as follows:

Product	X	Y	Z
	£	£	£
Labour: Skilled	6	9	3
Unskilled	2	4	10
Materials	12	25	14
Other variable costs	3	7	7
Fixed costs	5	10	10

All labour and materials are variable costs. Skilled labour is paid £6 an hour, and unskilled labour is paid £5 an hour. All references to labour costs above, are based on basic rates of pay. Skilled labour is scarce, which means that the business could sell more than the maximum that it is able to make of any of the three products.

Product X is sold in a regulated market, and the regulators have set a price of £30 per unit for it.

Required:
(a) State, with supporting workings, the price that must be charged for Products Y and Z, such that the business would find it equally profitable to make and sell any of the three products.
(b) State, with supporting workings, the maximum rate of overtime premium that the business would logically be prepared to pay its skilled workers to work beyond the basic time.

9.7 Intermediate Products Ltd produces four types of water pump. Two of these (A and B) are sold by the business. The other two (C and D) are incorporated, as components, into other of the business's products. Neither C nor D is incorporated into A or B. Costings (per unit) for the products are as follows:

	A £	B £	C £	D £
Variable materials	15	20	16	17
Variable labour	25	10	10	15
Other variable costs	5	3	2	2
Other fixed costs	20	8	8	12
	£65	£41	£36	£46
Selling price (per unit)	£70	£45		

There is an outside supplier who is prepared to supply unlimited quantities of products C and D to the business, charging £40 per unit for product C and £55 per unit for product D.

Next year's estimated demand for the products, from the market (in the case of A and B) and from other production requirements (in the case of C and D) is as follows:

	Units
A	5,000
B	6,000
C	4,000
D	3,000

For strategic reasons, the business wishes to supply a minimum of 50 per cent of the above demand for products A and B.

Manufacture of all four products requires the use of a special machine. The products require time on this machine as follows:

	Hours per unit
A	0.5
B	0.4
C	0.5
D	0.3

Next year there are expected to be a maximum of 6,000 special-machine-hours available. There will be no shortage of any other factor of production.

Required:

(a) State, with supporting workings and assumptions, which products the business should plan to make next year.

(b) Explain the maximum amount that it would be worth the business paying per hour to rent a second special machine.

(c) Suggest ways, other than renting an additional special machine, that could solve the problem of the shortage of special machine time.

9.8 Gandhi Ltd renders a promotional service to small retailing businesses. There are three levels of service: the 'basic', the 'standard' and the 'comprehensive'. On the basis of past experience, the business plans next year to work at absolute full capacity as follows:

Service	Number of units of the service	Selling price £	Variable cost per unit £
Basic	11,000	50	25
Standard	6,000	80	65
Comprehensive	16,000	120	90

The business's fixed costs total £660,000 a year. Each service takes about the same length of time, irrespective of the level.

One of the accounts staff has just produced a report that seems to show that the standard service is unprofitable. The relevant extract from the report is as follows:

Standard service cost analysis

	£	
Selling price per unit	80	
Variable cost per unit	(65)	
Fixed cost per unit	(20)	(£660,000/(11,000 + 6,000 + 16,000))
Net loss	(5)	

The producer of the report suggests that the business should not offer the standard service next year.

Required:

(a) Should the standard service be offered next year, assuming that the quantity of the other services could not be expanded to use the spare capacity?

(b) Should the standard service be offered next year, assuming that the released capacity could be used to render a new service, the 'nova', for which customers would be charged £75, and which would have variable costs of £50 and take twice as long as the other three services?

(c) What is the minimum price that could be accepted for the basic service, assuming that the necessary capacity to expand it will come only from not offering the standard service?

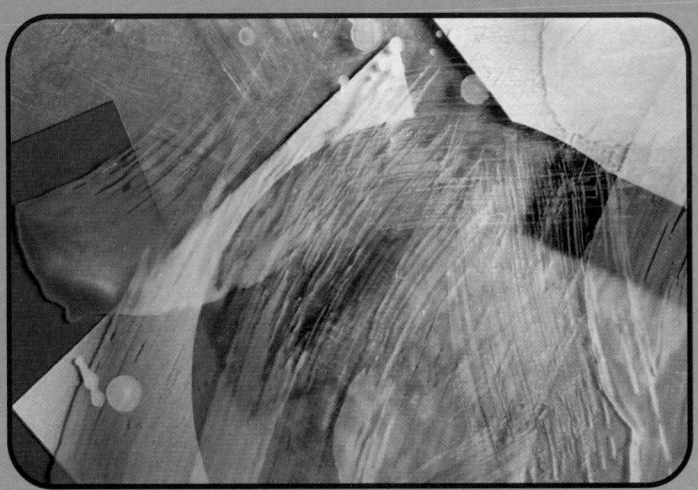

Full costing

INTRODUCTION

This chapter continues our examination of management accounting by looking at an approach to deducing the cost of a unit of output that takes account of all of the costs of producing it. This full-costing approach, as it is called, is very widely used in practice. Many businesses set their selling prices based on full cost information. Unless the prices charged for the products or services exceed all the costs incurred, no profit will be made.

We saw in Chapter 3 that, when measuring profit, we need to know the cost of the goods or services sold. Full cost information is normally used for this purpose and so it can help us assess the profitability of the business. It can also be used to assess the profitability of particular products or services provided by a business.

This chapter looks at the traditional, but widely used, form of full costing. Chapter 11 goes on to consider activity-based costing, which represents an alternative form of full costing.

The nature of full costing

→ With **full costing** we are concerned with all costs involved with achieving some objective, such as providing a particular service. The logic of full costing is that all of the costs of running a particular facility, say an office, are part of the cost of the output of that office. For example, the rent may be a cost that will not alter merely because we provide one more unit of the service, but if the office were not rented there would be nowhere from which to provide the service, so rent is an important element of the cost of each unit of output.

→ **Full cost** is the total amount of resources, usually measured in monetary terms, sacrificed to achieve a particular objective. It takes account of all resources sacrificed to achieve the objective. Thus, if the objective were to supply a customer with a product or service, all costs relating to the production of the product or provision of the service would be included as part of the full cost. To derive the full cost figure, we must accumulate the costs incurred and then assign them to the particular product or service. In the sections that follow we shall first see how this is done for a single product operation and then see how it is done for a multi-product operation.

Deriving full costs in a single-product operation

The simplest case for which to deduce the full cost per unit is where the business has only one product line, that is, each unit of its product is identical. Here it is simply a question of adding up all the costs of production incurred in the period (materials, labour, rent, fuel and power and so on) and dividing this total by the total number of units of output for the period.

ACTIVITY 10.1

Fruitjuice Ltd has just one product, a sparkling orange drink that is marketed as 'Orange Fizz'. During last month the business produced 7,300 litres of the drink. The costs incurred were as follows:

	£
Ingredients (oranges and so on)	390
Fuel	85
Rent of premises	350
Depreciation of equipment	75
Labour	880

What is the full cost per litre of producing 'Orange Fizz'?

This figure is found by simply adding together all of the costs incurred and then dividing by the number of litres produced:

$$£(390 + 85 + 350 + 75 + 880)/7,300 = £0.24 \text{ per litre}$$

In practice, there can be problems in deciding exactly how much cost was incurred. In the case of Fruitjuice Ltd, for example, how is the cost of depreciation deduced? It is certainly an estimate, and so its reliability is open to question. The cost of raw materials may also be a problem. Should we use the 'relevant' cost of the raw materials (almost certainly the replacement cost), or the actual price paid for the stock (inventory) used? If it is worth calculating the cost per litre, it must be because this information will be used for some decision-making purpose, so the replacement cost is probably more logical. In practice, however, it seems that historic costs are more often used to deduce full costs.

There can also be problems in deciding precisely how many units of output there were. If making Orange Fizz is not a very fast process, some of the drink will be in the process of being made at any given moment. This, in turn, means that some of the costs incurred last month were for some Orange Fizz that was work in progress at the end of the month, so is not included in the output quantity of 7,300 litres. Similarly, part of the 7,300 litres was started and incurred costs in the previous month, yet all of those litres were included in the 7,300 litres that we used in our calculation of the cost per litre. Work in progress is not a serious problem, but some adjustment for opening and closing work in progress for a period needs to be made if reliable full cost information is to be obtained.

The approach to full costing described above, which can be taken with identical, or near identical units of output, is often referred to as **process costing**.

Deriving full costs in multi-product operations

Most businesses produce more than one type of product or service. In this situation, the units of output of the product, or service, will not be identical and so the approach that we used with litres of 'Orange Fizz' in Activity 10.1 cannot be used. Although it is reasonable to assign an identical cost to units of output that are identical; it is not reasonable to do this where the units of output are obviously different. It would not be reasonable, for example, to assign the same costs to each car repair carried out by a garage, irrespective of the complexity and size of the repair.

Direct and indirect costs

To provide full cost information, we need to have a systematic approach to accumulating costs and then assigning these costs to particular units of product or service on some reasonable basis. Where units of output are not identical, the starting point is to separate costs into two categories: direct costs and indirect costs.

 ● **Direct costs**. These are costs that can be identified with specific cost units. That is to say, the effect of the cost can be measured in respect of each particular unit of output. The main examples of these are direct materials and direct labour. Thus, in costing a motor car repair by a garage, both the cost of spare parts used in the repair and the cost of the mechanic's time would be direct costs. Collecting direct costs is a simple matter of having a cost-recording system that is capable of capturing the cost of direct materials used on each job and the cost, based on the hours worked and the rate of pay, of direct workers.

● **Indirect costs** (or **overheads**). These are all other costs, that is, those that cannot be directly measured in respect of each particular unit of output. Thus the rent of the garage premises would be an indirect cost of a motor car repair.

We shall use the terms 'indirect costs' and 'overheads' interchangeably for the remainder of this book. Overheads are sometimes known as **common costs** because they are common to all production of the production unit (for example, factory or department) for the period.

Real World 10.1 provides some insight to the direct/indirect cost balance in practice.

REAL WORLD 10.1

Direct and indirect costs in practice

A survey of 176 fairly large UK businesses, conducted during 1999, revealed that, on average, total costs of businesses are in the following proportions:

Direct costs	70%
Indirect costs	30%

Perhaps surprisingly, these proportions did not vary greatly between manufacturers, retailers and service businesses. The only significant variation from the 70/30 proportions was with financial and commercial businesses, which had an average 52/48 split.

Source: Based on information taken from Drury and Tayles (see reference 1 at the end of the chapter).

An extensive (nearly 2,000 responses) and more recent (2003) survey of management accounting practice in the US showed similar results. Like the 1999 UK survey, this tended to relate to larger businesses. About 40 per cent were manufacturers and about 16 per cent financial services; the remainder were from a range of other industries.

This survey revealed that, of total costs, indirect costs accounted for between:

34%	for retailers (lowest)
42%	for manufacturers (highest)

with other industries' proportion of indirect costs falling within the 34–42 per cent range. Financial and commercial businesses showed an indirect cost percentage of 38 per cent.

Source: Ernst and Young (see reference 2 at the end of the chapter).

The differences between the UK and the US could be accounted for by a higher level of capital intensity in US industry, which would tend to increase indirect costs relative to direct ones.

Job costing

The term **job costing** is used to describe the way in which we identify the full cost per unit of output (job) where the units of output differ. To cost (that is, deduce the full cost of) a particular unit of output (job), we first identify the direct costs of the job, which, by the definition of direct costs, is capable of being done. We then seek to 'charge' each unit of output with a fair share of indirect costs. This is shown graphically in Figure 10.1.

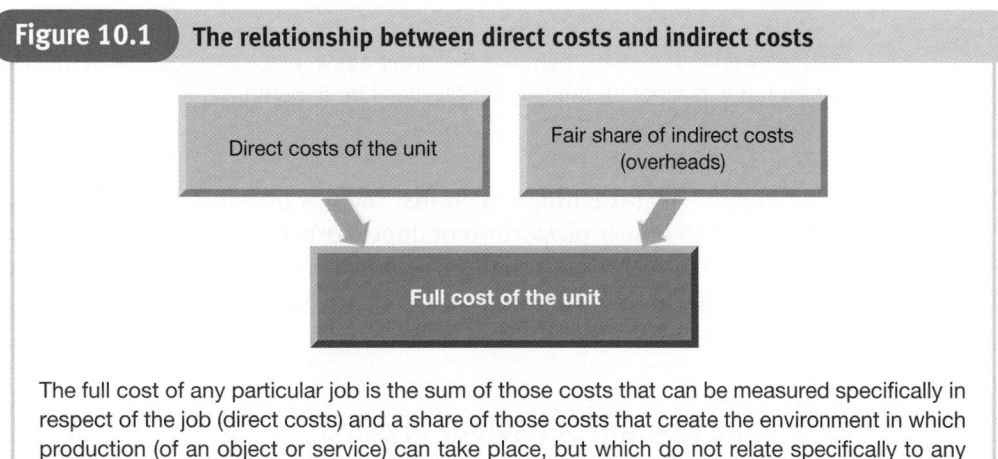

Figure 10.1   The relationship between direct costs and indirect costs

| Direct costs of the unit | Fair share of indirect costs (overheads) |

Full cost of the unit

The full cost of any particular job is the sum of those costs that can be measured specifically in respect of the job (direct costs) and a share of those costs that create the environment in which production (of an object or service) can take place, but which do not relate specifically to any particular job (overheads).

ACTIVITY 10.2

Sparky Ltd is a business that employs a number of electricians. The business undertakes a range of work for its customers, from replacing fuses to installing complete wiring systems in new houses.

In respect of a particular job done by Sparky Ltd, into which category (direct or indirect) would each of the following costs fall?

- the wages of the electrician who did the job;
- depreciation (wear and tear) of the tools used by the electrician;
- the salary of Sparky Ltd's accountant;
- the cost of cable and other materials used on the job;
- rent of the premises where Sparky Ltd stores its stock (inventory) of cable and other materials.

Only the electrician's wages earned while working on the particular job and the cost of the materials used on the job are direct costs. This is because it is possible to measure how much time was spent on (and therefore the labour cost of) the particular job and the amount of materials used in the job.

All of the other costs are general costs of running the business and, as such, must form part of the full cost of doing the job, but they cannot be directly measured in respect of the particular job.

It is important to note that whether a cost is direct or indirect depends on the item being costed – the cost objective. People tend to refer to overheads without stating what the cost objective is; this is incorrect.

Into which category, direct or indirect, would each of the costs listed in Activity 10.2 fall if we were seeking to find the cost of operating the entire business of Sparky Ltd for a month?

....

The answer is that all of them will be direct costs, since they can all be related to, and measured in respect of, running the business for a month.

Naturally, broader-reaching cost units, such as operating Sparky Ltd for a month, tend to include a higher proportion of direct costs than do more limited ones, such as a particular job done by Sparky Ltd. As we shall see shortly, this makes costing broader cost units rather more straightforward than costing narrower ones, since direct costs are easier to deal with than indirect ones.

Full costing and the behaviour of costs

We saw in Chapter 9 that the full cost of doing something (or total cost, as it is usually known in the context of marginal analysis) can be analysed between the fixed and the variable elements. This is illustrated in Figure 10.2.

The similarity of what is shown in Figure 10.2 to that depicted in Figure 10.1 seems to lead some people to believe, mistakenly, that variable costs and direct costs are the same and that fixed costs and overheads are the same. This is incorrect.

The notions of fixed and variable are concerned entirely with **cost behaviour** in the face of changes to the volume of activity. Directness of costs, on the other hand, is entirely concerned with collecting together the elements that make up full cost, that is, with the extent to which costs can be measured directly in respect of particular units

Figure 10.2 **The relationship between fixed costs, variable costs and total costs**

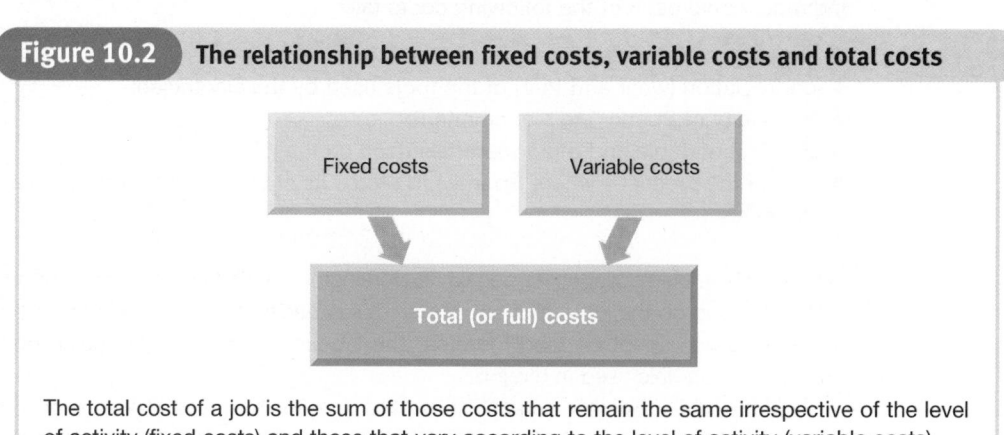

The total cost of a job is the sum of those costs that remain the same irrespective of the level of activity (fixed costs) and those that vary according to the level of activity (variable costs).

of output or jobs. These are two entirely different concepts. Though it may be true that there is a tendency for fixed costs to be indirect costs (overheads) and for variable costs to be direct costs, there is no link, and there are many exceptions to this tendency. For example, most activities have variable overheads. Labour is a major element of direct cost in most types of business activity but is usually a fixed cost, at least over the short term.

The relationship between the reaction of costs to volume changes (cost behaviour), on the one hand, and how costs need to be gathered to deduce the full cost (cost collection), on the other, in respect of a particular job is shown in Figure 10.3.

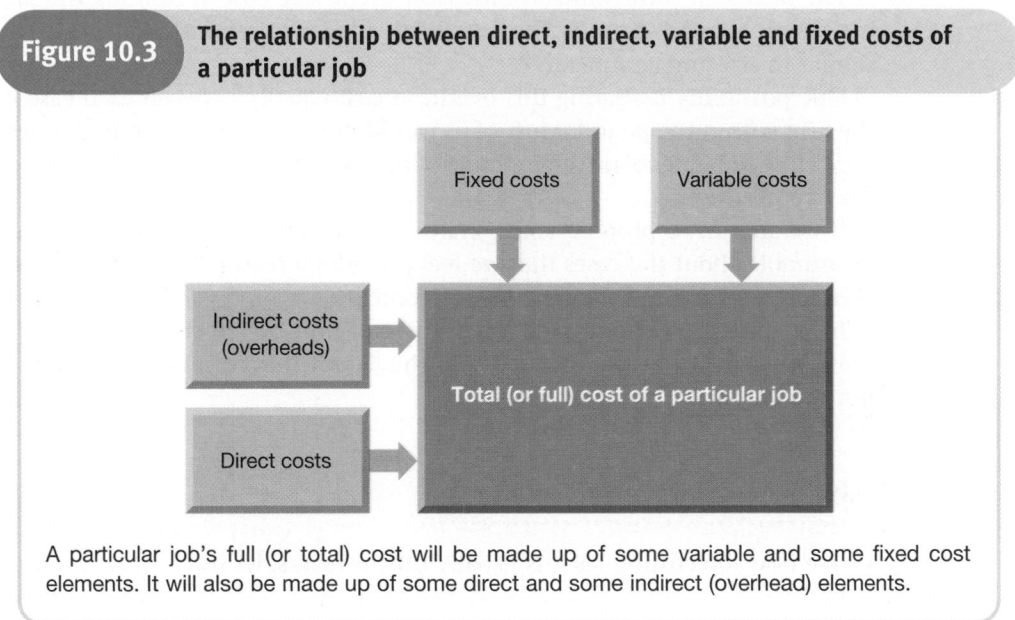

| Figure 10.3 | The relationship between direct, indirect, variable and fixed costs of a particular job |

A particular job's full (or total) cost will be made up of some variable and some fixed cost elements. It will also be made up of some direct and some indirect (overhead) elements.

Total cost is the sum of direct and indirect costs. It is also the sum of fixed and variable costs. These two facts are independent of one another. Thus a particular cost may, for example, be fixed relative to the level of output on the one hand, and be either direct or indirect on the other.

The problem of indirect costs

Distinguishing between direct and indirect costs is related only to deducing full cost in a job-costing environment, that is, where units of output differ. When we were considering costing a litre of 'Orange Fizz' drink in Activity 10.1, whether particular elements of cost were direct or indirect was of absolutely no consequence, because all costs were shared equally between the litres of 'Orange Fizz'. However, where we have units of output that are not identical, we have to look more closely at the make-up of the costs to achieve a fair measure of the full cost of a particular job.

Indirect costs of any activity must form part of the cost of each unit of output. By definition, however, they cannot be directly related to individual **cost units**. This raises a major practical issue: how are indirect costs to be apportioned to individual cost units?

Overheads as service renderers

It is reasonable to view the overheads as rendering a service to the cost units. A legal case undertaken by a firm of solicitors can be seen as being rendered a service by the office in which the work is done. In this sense, it is reasonable to charge each case (cost unit) with a share of the costs of running the office (rent, lighting, heating, cleaning, building maintenance, and so on). It also seems reasonable to relate the charge for the 'use' of the office to the level of service that the particular case has received from the office.

The next step is the difficult one. How might the cost of running the office, which is a cost of all work done by the firm, be divided between individual cases that are not similar in size and complexity?

One possibility is sharing this overhead cost equally between each case handled by the firm within the period. Most of us would not propose this method unless the cases were close to being identical, in terms of the extent to which they had 'benefited' from the overheads.

If we are not to propose equal shares, we must identify something observable and measurable about the cases that we feel provides a reasonable basis for distinguishing between one case and the next in this context.

In practice, time spent working on the cost unit by direct labour is the basis that is most popular. It must be stressed that this is not the 'correct' way, and it certainly is not the only way.

Job costing: a worked example

To see how job costing (as it is usually called) works, let us consider Example 10.1.

Example 10.1

Johnson Ltd, a business that provides a television repair service to its customers, has overheads of £10,000 each month. Each month 1,000 direct-labour-hours are worked and charged to units of output (repairs carried out by the business). A particular repair undertaken by the business used direct materials costing £15. Direct labour worked on the repair was 3 hours and the wage rate is £8 an hour. Overheads are charged to jobs on a direct labour hour basis. What is the full cost of the repair?

 First, let us establish the **overhead absorption (recovery) rate**, that is, the rate at which individual repairs will be charged with overheads. This is £10 (that is, £10,000/1,000) per direct labour hour.

Thus, the full cost of the repair is:

	£
Direct materials	15
Direct labour (3 × £8)	24
	39
Overheads (3 × £10)	30
Full cost of the job	69

Note, in Example 10.1, that the number of labour-hours (3 hours) appears twice in deducing the full cost: once to deduce the direct labour cost and a second time to deduce the overheads to be charged to the repair. These are really two separate issues, though they are both based on the same number of labour-hours.

Note also that if all of the repair jobs that are undertaken during the month are assigned overheads in a similar manner, all £10,000 of overheads will be charged to the jobs between them. Jobs that involve a lot of direct labour will be assigned a large share of overheads, and those that involve little direct labour will be assigned a small share of overheads.

ACTIVITY 10.4

Can you think of reasons why direct-labour-hours is regarded as the most logical basis for sharing overheads between cost units?

The reasons that occurred to us are as follows:

● Large jobs should logically attract large amounts of overheads because they are likely to have been rendered more 'service' by the overheads than small ones. The length of time that they are worked on by direct labour may be seen as a rough and ready way of measuring relative size, though other means of doing this may be found – for example, relative physical size, where the cost unit is a physical object, like a manufactured product.

● Most overheads are related to time. Rent, heating, lighting, non-current asset depreciation, supervisors' and managers' salaries and loan interest, which are all typical overheads, are all more or less time based. That is to say that the overhead cost for one week tends to be about half of that for a similar two-week period. Thus, a basis of apportioning overheads to jobs that takes account of the length of time that the units of output benefited from the 'service' rendered by the overheads seems logical.

● Direct labour hours are capable of being measured in respect of each job. They will normally be measured to deduce the direct labour element of cost in any case. Thus, a direct-labour-hour basis of dealing with overheads is practical to apply in the real world.

It cannot be emphasised enough that there is no 'correct' way to apportion overheads to jobs. Overheads (indirect costs), by definition, do not naturally relate to individual jobs. If, nevertheless, we wish to take account of the fact that overheads are part of the cost of all jobs, we must find some acceptable way of including a share of the total overheads in each job. If a particular means of doing this is accepted by those who use the full cost deduced, then the method is as good as any other method. Accounting is concerned only with providing useful information to decision makers. In practice, the method that seems to be regarded as being the most useful is the direct-labour-hour method. **Real World 10.2**, which we shall consider later in the chapter, provides some evidence of this.

ACTIVITY 10.5

Marine Suppliers Ltd undertakes a range of work, including making sails for small sailing boats on a made-to-measure basis.

The business expects to incur the following costs during the next month:

Activity 10.5 continued

Direct labour costs	£60,000
Direct labour time	6,000 hours
Indirect labour cost	£9,000
Depreciation of machinery	£3,000
Rent and rates	£5,000
Heating, lighting and power	£2,000
Machine time	2,000 hours
Indirect materials	£500
Other miscellaneous indirect costs	£200
Direct materials cost	£3,000

The business has received an enquiry about a sail, and it is estimated that the sail will take 12 direct-labour-hours to make and will require 20 square metres of sailcloth, which costs £2 per square metre.

The business normally uses a direct-labour-hour basis of charging overheads to individual jobs.

What is the full cost of making the sail?

The direct costs of making the sail can be identified as follows:

	£
Direct materials (20 × £2)	40.00
Direct labour (12 × (£60,000/6,000))	<u>120.00</u>
	<u>160.00</u>

To deduce the indirect cost element that must be added to derive the full cost of the sail, we first need to total these costs as follows:

	£
Indirect labour	9,000
Depreciation	3,000
Rent and rates	5,000
Heating, lighting and power	2,000
Indirect materials	500
Other miscellaneous indirect costs	<u>200</u>
Total indirect costs	<u>19,700</u>

Since the business uses a direct-labour-hour basis of charging overheads to jobs, we need to deduce the indirect cost, or overhead recovery rate, per direct-labour-hour. This is simply:

$$£19,700/6,000 = £3.28 \text{ per direct-labour-hour}$$

Thus, the full cost of the sail would be expected to be:

	£
Direct materials (20 × £2)	40.00
Direct labour (12 × (£60,000/6,000))	120.00
Indirect costs (12 × £3.28)	<u>39.36</u>
Full cost	<u>199.36</u>

ACTIVITY 10.6

Suppose that Marine Suppliers Ltd (Activity 10.5) used a machine-hour basis of charging overheads to jobs. What would be the cost of the job detailed if it was expected to take 5 machine-hours (as well as 12 direct-labour-hours)?

The total overheads of the business will of course be the same irrespective of the method of charging them to jobs. Thus, the overhead recovery rate, on a machine-hour basis, will be:

$$£19,700/2,000 = £9.85 \text{ per machine-hour}$$

Thus, the full cost of the sail would be expected to be:

	£
Direct materials (20 × £2)	40.00
Direct labour (12 × (£60,000/6,000))	120.00
Indirect costs (5 × £9.85)	49.25
Full cost	209.25

Selecting a basis for charging overheads

A question now presents itself as to which of the two costs for this sail is the correct one, or simply the better one. The answer is that neither is the correct one, as was pointed out earlier. Which is the better one is a matter of judgement. This judgement is concerned entirely with usefulness of information, which in this context is probably concerned with the attitudes of those who will be affected by the figure used. Thus, reasonableness, as those people perceive it, is likely to be the important issue.

Most people would probably feel that the nature of the overheads should influence the choice of the basis of charging the overheads to jobs. Where the operation is capital-intensive and overheads are primarily machine-based (such as depreciation, machine maintenance, power and so on), machine-hours might be favoured. Otherwise direct-labour-hours might be preferred.

It could appear that one of these bases might be preferred to the other one simply because it apportions either a higher or a lower amount of overheads to a particular job. This would probably be irrational, however. Since the total overheads are the same irrespective of the method of dividing that total between individual jobs, a method that gives a higher share of overheads to one particular job must give a lower share to the remaining jobs. There is one cake of fixed size. If one person is to be given a relatively large slice, the other people, between them, must receive relatively small slices. To illustrate further this issue of apportioning overheads, consider Example 10.2.

Example 10.2

A business that provides a service expects to incur overheads totalling £20,000 next month. The total direct labour time worked is expected to be 1,600 hours and machines are expected to operate for a total of 1,000 hours.

During the next month, the business expects to do just two large jobs. Information concerning each job is as follows:

	Job 1	Job 2
Direct-labour-hours	800	800
Machine-hours	700	300

How much of the total overheads will be charged to each job if overheads are to be charged on:

→

(a) a direct-labour-hour basis; and
(b) a machine-hour basis?

What do you notice about the two sets of figures that you calculate?

(a) Direct-labour-hour basis

Overhead recovery rate = £20,000/1,600 = £12.50 per direct-labour-hour.

Job 1   £12.50 × 800 = £10,000
Job 2   £12.50 × 800 = £10,000

(b) Machine-hour basis

Overhead recovery rate = £20,000/1,000 = £20.00 per machine-hour.

Job 1   £20.00 × 700 = £14,000
Job 2   £20.00 × 300 = £ 6,000

It is clear from these calculations that the total of the overheads charged to jobs is the same (that is, £20,000) whichever method is used. So, whereas the machine-hour basis gives Job 1 a higher share than does the direct-labour-hour method, the opposite is true for Job 2.

It is not practical to charge overheads on one basis to one job and on the other basis to the other job. This is because either total overheads will not be fully charged to the jobs, or the jobs will be overcharged with overheads. For example, using the direct-labour-hour method for Job 1 (£10,000) and the machine hour basis for Job 2 (£6,000) will mean that only £16,000 of a total £20,000 of overheads will be charged to jobs. As a result, the objective of full costing, which is to charge all overheads to jobs done, will not be achieved. In this particular case, if selling prices are based on full costs, the business may not charge prices high enough to cover all of its costs.

ACTIVITY 10.7

The point was made above that it would normally be irrational to prefer one basis of charging overheads to jobs simply because it apportions either a higher or a lower amount of overheads to a particular job. The total overheads are the same irrespective of the method of charging the total to individual jobs. Can you think of any circumstances where it would not necessarily be so irrational?

This might apply where a customer has agreed to pay (for a particular job) a price based on full cost plus an agreed fixed percentage for profit. Here it would be beneficial to the producer for the total cost of the job to be as high as possible. This would be relatively unusual, but sometimes public-sector organisations, particularly central and local government departments, have entered into contracts to have work done, with the price to be deduced, after the work has been completed, on a cost-plus basis. Such contracts are pretty rare these days, probably because they are open to abuse in the way described. Usually, contract prices are agreed in advance, typically in conjunction with competitive tendering.

Real World 10.2 provides some insight to the basis of overhead recovery in the practice.

REAL WORLD 10.2

Overhead recovery rates in practice

A survey of 303 UK manufacturing businesses, published in 1993, showed that the direct-labour-hour basis of charging overheads to cost units was overwhelmingly the most popular, used by 73 per cent of the respondents to the survey. Where the work has a strong labour element this seems reasonable, but the survey also showed that 68 per cent of businesses used this basis for automated activities. It is surprising that direct-labour-hours should have been used as the basis of charging overheads in an environment dominated by machines and machine-related costs.

Though this survey is not very recent and applied only to manufacturing businesses, in the absence of other information, it provides some impression of what happens in practice. There is no reason to believe that current practice is very different from that which applied at the beginning of the 1990s.

Source: Based on information taken from Drury *et al*. (see reference 3 at the end of the chapter).

Segmenting the overheads

As we have just seen, charging the same overheads to different jobs on different bases is not possible. It is possible, however, to charge one segment of the total overheads on one basis and another segment, or other segments, on another basis.

ACTIVITY 10.8

Taking the same business as in Example 10.2, on closer analysis we find that of the overheads totalling £20,000 next month, £8,000 relate to machines (depreciation, maintenance, rent of the space occupied by the machines and so on) and the remaining £12,000 to more general overheads. The other information about the business is exactly as it was before.

How much of the total overheads will be charged to each job if the machine-related overheads are to be charged on a machine-hour basis and the remaining overheads are charged on a direct-labour-hour basis?

Direct-labour-hour basis

Overhead recovery rate = £12,000/1,600 = £7.50 per direct labour hour

Machine-hour basis

Overhead recovery rate = £8,000/1,000 = £8.00 per machine hour

→

Activity 10.8 continued

Overheads charged to jobs

	Job 1 £	Job 2 £
Direct-labour-hour basis		
£7.50 × 800	6,000	
£7.50 × 800		6,000
Machine-hour basis		
£8.00 × 700	5,600	
£8.00 × 300		2,400
Total	11,600	8,400

We can see from this that the expected overheads of £20,000 are charged in total.

Segmenting the overheads in this way may well be seen as providing a better basis of charging overheads to jobs. This is quite often found in practice, usually by dividing a business into separate 'areas' for costing purposes, charging overheads differently from one area to the next.

Remember that there is no correct basis of charging overheads to jobs, so our frequent reference to the direct-labour- and machine-hour bases should not be taken to imply that these are the correct methods. However, it should be said that these two methods do have something to commend them and are popular in practice. As we have already discussed, a sensible method does need to identify something about each job that can be measured and which distinguishes it from other jobs. There is also a lot to be said for methods that are concerned with time because most overheads are time related.

Dealing with overheads on a departmental basis

In general, all but the smallest businesses are divided into departments. Normally, each department deals with a separate activity.

The reasons for dividing a business into departments include the following:

- Many businesses are too large and complex to be managed as a single unit. It is usually more practical to operate each business as a series of relatively independent units (departments) with each one having its own manager.
- Each department normally has its own area of specialism and is managed by a specialist.
- Each department can have its own accounting records that enable its performance to be assessed. This can lead to greater management control and motivation among the staff.

Very many businesses deal with charging overheads to cost units on a department-by-department basis. They do this in the expectation that it will give rise to a more useful way of charging overheads. It is probably often the case that it does not lead to any great improvement in the usefulness of the resulting full costs. Though it may not be of enormous benefit in many cases, it is probably not an expensive exercise to apply overheads on a departmental basis. Since costs are collected department by department for other purposes (particularly control), to apply overheads on a department-by-department basis is a relatively simple matter.

We shall now take a look at how the departmental approach to deriving full costs works, in a service-industry context, through Example 10.3.

Example 10.3

Autosparkle Ltd offers a motor vehicle paint-respray service. The jobs that it undertakes range from painting a small part of a saloon car, usually following a minor accident, to a complete respray of a double-decker bus.

Each job starts life in the Preparation Department, where it is prepared for the Paintshop. In the Preparation Department the job is worked on by direct workers, in most cases taking some direct materials from the stores with which to treat the old paintwork to render the vehicle ready for respraying. Thus the job will be charged with direct materials, direct labour and with a share of the Preparation Department's overheads. The job then passes into the Paintshop Department, already valued at the costs that it picked up in the Preparation Department.

In the Paintshop, the staff draws direct materials from the stores and direct workers spend time respraying the job, using a sophisticated spraying apparatus as well as working by hand. So, in the Paintshop, the job is charged with direct materials, direct labour plus a share of that department's overheads. The job now passes into the Finishing Department, valued at the cost of the materials, labour and overheads that it accumulated in the first two departments.

In the Finishing Department, jobs are cleaned and polished ready to go back to the customers. Further direct labour and, in some cases, materials are added. All jobs also pick up a share of that department's overheads. The job, now complete, passes back to the customer.

Figure 10.4 shows graphically how this works for a particular job.

Figure 10.4 — A cost unit (Job A) passing through Autosparkle Ltd's process

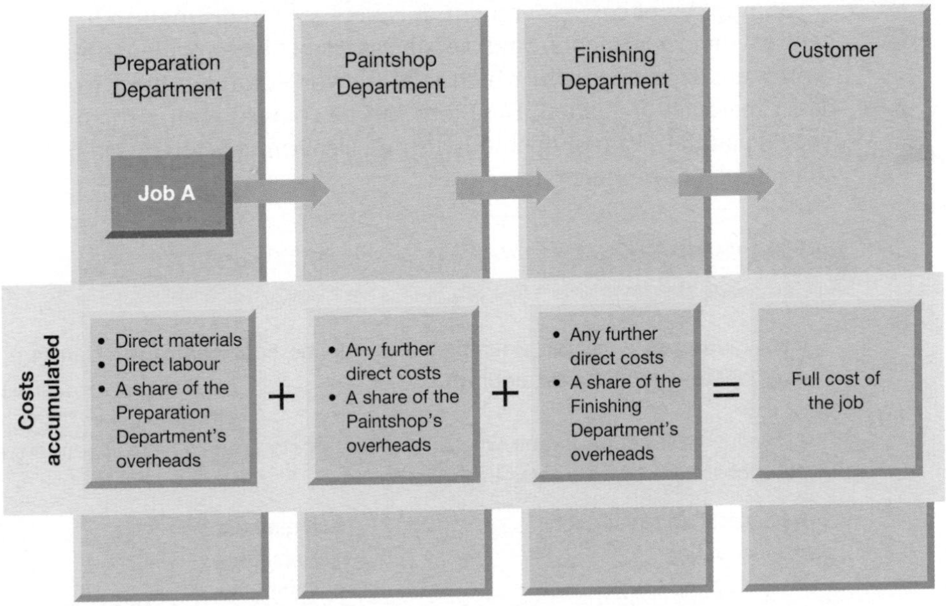

As the particular paint job passes through the three departments, where work is carried out on it, the job 'gathers' costs of various types.

→ The basis of charging overheads to jobs (for example direct labour hours) might be the same for all three departments, or it might be different from one department to another. It is possible that spraying apparatus costs dominate the Paintshop costs, so overheads might well be charged to jobs on a machine-hour basis. The other two departments are probably labour intensive, so that direct-labour-hours may be seen as being appropriate there.

The passage of the job through the departments can be compared to a snowball being rolled across snow: as it rolls, it picks up more and more snow.

→ Where costs are dealt with departmentally, each department is known as a **cost centre**. A cost centre can be defined as some physical area or some activity or function for which costs are separately identified. Charging direct costs to jobs, in a departmental system, is exactly the same as where the whole business is one single cost centre. It is simply a matter of keeping a record of:

- the number of hours of direct labour worked on the particular job and the grade of labour, assuming that there are different grades with different rates of pay;
- the cost of the direct materials taken from stores and applied to the job; and
- any other direct costs, for example some subcontracted work, associated with the job.

This record-keeping will normally be done departmentally in a departmental system.

It is obviously necessary to break down the production overheads of the entire business on a departmental basis. This means that the total overheads of the business must be divided between the departments, such that the sum of the departmental overheads equals the overheads for the entire business. By charging all of their overheads to jobs, the departments will, between them, charge all of the overheads of the business to jobs.

Real World 10.3 provides an indication of the number of different cost centres that businesses tend to use, in practice.

→
→ For purposes of cost assignment, it is necessary to distinguish between **product cost centres** (or departments) and **service cost centres** (or departments). Product cost centres are departments in which jobs are worked on by direct workers and/or where direct materials are added. Here jobs can be charged with a share of their overheads. The Preparation, Paintshop and Finishing Departments, discussed in Example 10.3, are all examples of product cost centres.

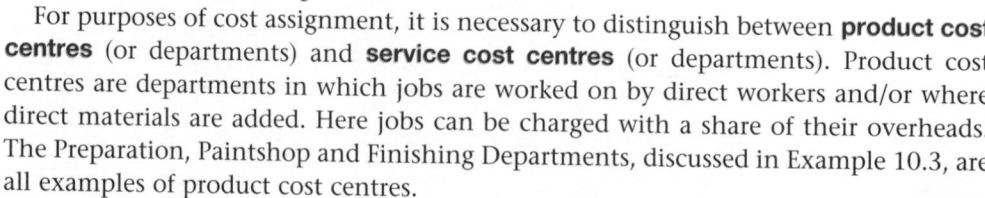

ACTIVITY 10.9

Can you guess what the definition of a service cost centre is? Can you think of an example of a service cost centre?

A service cost centre is one where no direct costs are involved. It renders a service to other cost centres. Examples include:

- General administration
- Accounting
- Stores
- Maintenance
- Personnel
- Catering.

All of these render services to product cost centres and, possibly, to other service cost centres.

REAL WORLD 10.3

Cost centres in practice

It is not unusual for a large business to have several cost centres. The survey of large UK businesses by Drury and Tayles referred to earlier (see **Real World 10.1**), revealed that 86 per cent of businesses surveyed had 6 or more cost centres and that 36 per cent of businesses had more than 20 cost centres (see Figure 10.5). Though not shown on the diagram, 3 per cent of businesses surveyed had a single cost centre (that is, there was business-wide or overall overhead rate only used).

Source: Based on information taken from Drury and Tayles (see reference 1 at the end of the chapter).

Figure 10.5   **Analysis of the number of cost centres within a business**

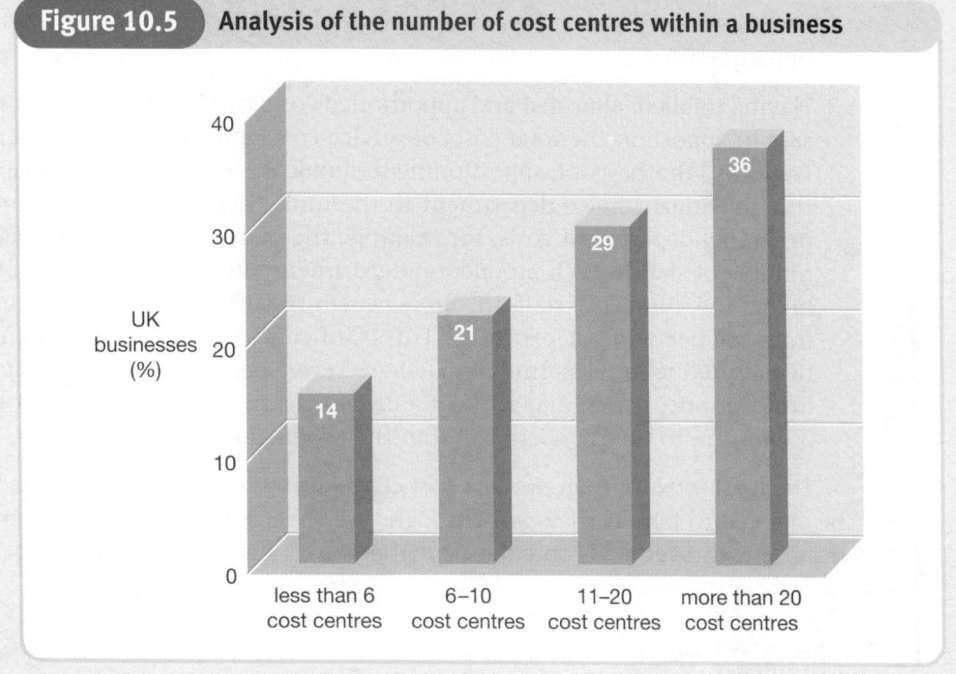

Service cost centre costs must be charged to product cost centres, and become part of the product cost centres' overheads, so that those overheads can be recharged to jobs. This must be done so that all of the overheads of the business find their way into the cost of the jobs. If this is not done, the 'full' cost derived will not really be the full cost of the jobs.

Logically, the costs of a service cost centre should be charged to product cost centres on the basis of the level of service provided to the product cost centre concerned. For example, a production department that has a lot of machine maintenance carried out relative to other production departments should be charged with a larger share of the maintenance department's costs than should those other product cost centres.

The process of dividing overheads between departments is as follows:

➡ 1 **Cost allocation**. Allocate costs that are specific to the departments. These are costs that relate to, and are measurable in respect of, individual departments, that is, they are direct costs of running the department. Examples include:

   (a) salaries of indirect workers whose activities are wholly within the department, for example the salary of the departmental manager;

(b) rent, where the department is housed in its own premises for which rent can be separately identified;

(c) electricity, where it is separately metered for each department.

→ 2 **Cost apportionment.** Apportion the more general overheads to the departments. These are overheads that relate to more than one department, perhaps to them all. These would include:

(a) rent, where more than one department is housed in the same premises;

(b) electricity, where it is not separately metered;

(c) salaries of cleaning staff who work in a variety of departments.

These costs would be apportioned to departments on some fair basis, such as by square metres of floor area, in the case of rent, or by level of mechanisation, for electricity used to power machinery. As with charging overheads to individual jobs, usefulness is the issue; there is no correct basis of apportioning general overheads to departments.

3 Having totalled, allocated and apportioned costs to all departments, it is now necessary to apportion the total costs of service cost centres to production departments. Logically, the basis of apportionment should be the level of service rendered by the individual service department to the individual production department. With personnel department costs, for example, the basis of apportionment might be the number of staff in each production department, because it could be argued that the higher the number of staff, the more benefit the production department has derived from the personnel department. This is, of course, rather a crude approach. A particular production department may have severe personnel problems and a high staff turnover rate, which may make it a user of the personnel service that is way out of proportion to the number of staff in the production department.

The final total for each product cost centre is that cost centre's overheads. These can be charged to jobs as they pass through. We shall now go on to consider an example dealing with overheads on a departmental basis (see Example 10.4).

Example 10.4

A business consists of four departments: 1 Preparation department; 2 Machining department; 3 Finishing department; 4 General administration (GA) department. The first three are product cost centres and the last renders a service to the other three. The level of service rendered is thought to be roughly in proportion to the number of employees in each production department.

Overhead costs, and other data, for next month are expected to be as follows:

	£
Rent	10,000
Electricity to power machines, etc.	3,000
Electricity for heating and lighting	800
Insurance of premises	200
Cleaning	600
Depreciation of machines	2,000

Salaries of each of the indirect workers are as follows:

	£
Preparation department	2,000
Machining department	2,400
Finishing department	1,800
General administration department	1,800

The general administration department has a staff consisting of only indirect workers (including managers). The other departments have both indirect workers (including managers) and direct workers. There are 100 indirect workers within each of the four departments and none do any 'direct' work.

Each direct worker is expected to work 160 hours next month. The number of direct workers in each department is:

Preparation department	600
Machining department	900
Finishing department	500

Machining department direct workers are paid £12 an hour; other direct workers are paid £10 an hour.

All of the machinery is in the machining department. Machines are expected to operate for 120,000 hours next month.

The floorspace (in square metres) occupied by the departments is as follows:

	Sq m
Preparation department	16,000
Machining department	20,000
Finishing department	10,000
General administration department	2,000

Deducing the overheads department by department can be done, using a schedule, as follows:

	Total £000	Prep'n £000	Mach'g £000	Fin'g £000	GA £000
Allocated costs:					
Machine power	3,000		3,000		
Machine depreciation	2,000		2,000		
Indirect salaries	8,000	2,000	2,400	1,800	1,800
Apportioned costs					
Rent	10,000				
Heating and lighting	800				
Insurance of premises	200				
Cleaning	600				
Apportioned by floor area	11,600	3,867	4,833	2,417	483
Departmental overheads	24,600	5,867	12,233	4,217	2,283
Reapportion GA costs by number of staff (including the indirect workers)		695	993	595	(2,283)
	24,600	6,562	13,226	4,812	–

ACTIVITY 10.10

Assume that the machining department overheads (in Example 10.4) are to be charged to jobs on a machine-hour basis, but that the direct-labour-hour basis is to be used for the other two departments. What will be the full cost of a job with the following characteristics?

	Preparation	Machining	Finishing
Direct-labour-hours	10	7	5
Machine-hours	–	6	–
Direct materials (£)	85	13	6

(*Hint*: This should be tackled as if each department were a separate business, then departmental costs are added together for the job so as to arrive at the total full cost.)

....

Firstly, we need to deduce the overhead recovery rates for each department:
Preparation department (direct-labour-hour based):

$$\frac{£6,562,000}{600 \times 160} = £68.35$$

Machining department (machine-hour based):

$$\frac{£13,226,000}{120,000} = £110.22$$

Finishing department (direct-labour-hour based):

$$\frac{£4,812,000}{500 \times 160} = £60.15$$

The cost of the job is as follows:

	£	£
Direct labour:		
Preparation department (10 × £10)	100.00	
Machining department (7 × £12)	84.00	
Finishing department (5 × £10)	50.00	
		234.00
Direct materials:		
Preparation department	85.00	
Machining department	13.00	
Finishing department	6.00	
		104.00
Overheads:		
Preparation department (10 × £68.35)	683.50	
Machining department (6 × £110.22)	661.32	
Finishing department (5 × £60.15)	300.75	
		1,645.57
Full cost of the job		1,983.57

ACTIVITY 10.11

The manufacturing costs for Buccaneers Ltd for next year are expected to be as follows:

	£000
Direct materials:	
Forming department	450
Machining department	100
Finishing department	50
Direct labour:	
Forming department	180
Machining department	120
Finishing department	75
Indirect materials:	
Forming department	40
Machining department	30
Finishing department	10
Administration department	10
Indirect labour:	
Forming department	80
Machining department	70
Finishing department	60
Administration department	60
Maintenance costs	50
Rent and rates	100
Heating and lighting	20
Building insurance	10
Machinery insurance	10
Depreciation of machinery	120
Total manufacturing costs	1,645

The following additional information is available:

(i)   All direct labour is paid £6 an hour for all hours worked.
(ii) The administration department renders personnel and general services to the production departments.
(iii) The area of the premises in which the business manufactures amounts to 50,000 square metres, divided as follows:

	Sq m
Forming department	20,000
Machining department	15,000
Finishing department	10,000
Administration department	5,000

(iv) The maintenance employees are expected to divide their time between the production departments as follows:

	%
Forming department	15
Machining department	75
Finishing department	10

Activity 10.11 continued

(v) Machine-hours are expected to be as follows:

	Hours
Forming department	5,000
Machining department	15,000
Finishing department	5,000

On the basis of this information:

(a) Allocate and apportion overheads to the three production departments.
(b) Deduce overhead recovery rates for each department using two different bases for each department's overheads.
(c) Calculate the full cost of a job with the following characteristics:

Direct labour hours:	
Forming department	4 hours
Machining department	4 hours
Finishing department	1 hour
Machine hours:	
Forming department	1 hour
Machining department	2 hours
Finishing department	1 hour
Direct materials:	
Forming department	£40
Machining department	£9
Finishing department	£4

Use whichever of the two bases of overhead recovery, deduced in (b), that you consider more appropriate.
(d) Explain why you consider the basis used in (c) to be the more appropriate.

(a) Overheads can be allocated and apportioned as follows:

Cost	Basis of apport't	Total £000	Forming £000	Machining £000	Finishing £000	Admin. £000
Indirect materials	Specifically allocated	90	40	30	10	10
Indirect labour	Specifically allocated	270	80	70	60	60
Maintenance	Staff time	50	7.5	37.5	5	–
Rent/rates	100					
Heat/light	20					
Buildings insurance	10					
	Area	130	52	39	26	13
Machine insurance	10					
Machine depreciation	120					
	Machine-hours	130	26	78	26	–
		670	205.5	254.5	127	83
Admin.	Direct labour		39.84	26.56	16.6	(83)
		670	245.34	281.06	143.6	–

Note that direct costs are not included in the above because they are allocated *directly* to jobs.

(b) Overhead recovery rates are as follows:

Basis 1: direct-labour-hours

$$\text{Forming} = \frac{£245,340}{180,000/6} = £8.18 \text{ per direct-labour-hour}$$

$$\text{Machining} = \frac{£281,060}{120,000/6} = £14.05 \text{ per direct-labour-hour}$$

$$\text{Finishing} = \frac{£143,600}{75,000/6} = £11.49 \text{ per direct-labour-hour}$$

Basis 2: machine-hours

$$\text{Forming} = \frac{£245,340}{5,000} = £49.07 \text{ per machine-hour}$$

$$\text{Machining} = \frac{£281,060}{15,000} = £18.74 \text{ per machine-hour}$$

$$\text{Finishing} = \frac{£143,600}{5,000} = £28.72 \text{ per machine-hour}$$

(c) Full cost of job – on direct-labour-hour basis of overhead recovery

	£	£
Direct labour cost (9 × £6)		54.00
Direct materials (£40 + £9 + £4)		53.00
Overheads:		
Forming (4 × £8.18)	32.72	
Machining (4 × £14.05)	56.20	
Finishing (1 × £11.49)	11.49	100.41
Full cost		£207.41

(d) The reason for using the direct-labour-hour basis rather than the machine-hour basis was that labour is more important, in terms of the number of hours applied to output, than is machine time. Strong arguments could have been made for the use of the alternative basis; certainly, a machine-hour basis could have been justified for the machining department.

It would be possible, and it may be reasonable, to use one basis in respect of one department's overheads and a different one for those of another department. For example, machine hours could have been used for the machining department and a direct-labour-hours basis for the other two.

Batch costing

The production of many types of goods and services (particularly goods) involves producing in a batch of identical, or nearly identical, units of output, but where each batch is distinctly different from other batches. For example, a theatre may put on a production whose nature (and therefore costs) is very different from that of other productions. On the other hand, ignoring differences in the desirability of the various types of seating, all of the individual units of output (tickets to see the production) are identical.

In these circumstances, we should normally deduce the cost per ticket by using a job costing approach (taking account of direct and indirect costs and so on) to find the cost of mounting the production and then we should simply divide this by the expected number of tickets to be sold to find the cost per ticket. This is known as **batch costing**.

Full cost as the break-even price

We should recognise that if all goes according to plan (so that direct costs, overheads and the basis of charging overheads, for example direct-labour-hours, prove to be as expected), then selling the output for its full cost should cause the business to break even exactly. Therefore, whatever profit (in total) is loaded onto full cost to set actual selling prices will result in that level of profit being earned for the period.

The forward-looking nature of full costing

Though deducing full costs can be done after the work has been completed, it is often done in advance. In other words, costs are frequently predicted. Where, for example, full costs are needed as a basis on which to set selling prices, it is usually the case that prices need to be set before the customer will accept the job being done. Even where no particular customer has been identified, some idea of the ultimate price will need to be known before the business will be able to make a judgement as to whether potential customers will buy the product, and in what quantities. There is a risk, of course, that the actual outcome will differ from that which was predicted. If this occurs, corrections are subsequently made to the full costs originally calculated.

SELF-ASSESSMENT QUESTION 10.1

Hector and Co. Ltd has been invited to tender for a contract to produce 1,000 clothes hangers. The following information relates to the contract.

- *Materials*: The clothes hangers are made of metal wire covered with a padded fabric. Each hanger requires 2 metres of wire and 0.5 square metres of fabric.
- *Direct labour*:
  - Skilled 10 minutes per hanger
  - Unskilled 5 minutes per hanger.

The business already has sufficient stock of each of the materials required to complete the contract. Information on the cost of the stock is as follows:

	Metal wire £/m	Fabric £/m²
Historic cost	2.20	1.00
Current buying-in cost	2.50	1.10
Scrap value	1.70	0.40

The metal wire is in constant use by the business for a range of its products. The fabric has no other use for the business and is scheduled to be scrapped.

Unskilled labour, which is paid at the rate of £5.00 an hour, will need to be taken on specifically to undertake the contract. The business is fairly quiet at the moment, which means that a pool of skilled labour exists that will still be employed at full pay of £7.50 an hour to do nothing if the contract does not proceed. The pool of skilled labour is sufficient to complete the contract.

The business charges jobs with overheads on a direct-labour-hour basis. The production overheads of the entire business for the month in which the contract will be undertaken are estimated at £50,000. The estimated total direct-labour-hours that will be worked are 12,500. The business tends not to alter the established overhead recovery rate to reflect increases or reductions to estimated total hours arising from new contracts. The total overhead cost is not expected to increase as a result of undertaking the contract.

The business normally adds 12.5 per cent profit loading to the job cost to arrive at a first estimate of the tender price.

Required:

(a) Price this job on a traditional job-costing basis.
(b) Indicate the minimum price at which the contract could be undertaken such that the business would be neither better nor worse off as a result of doing it.

Uses of full-cost information

Why do we need to deduce full-cost information? There are probably two main reasons:

- *For pricing purposes.*   In some industries and circumstances, full costs are used as the basis of pricing. Here, the full cost is deduced and a percentage is added for profit. This is known as **cost-plus pricing**. Garages, carrying out vehicle repairs, typically operate in this way. Solicitors and accountants doing work for clients often use this approach as well.

  In many circumstances, suppliers are not in a position to deduce prices on a cost-plus basis, however. Where there is a competitive market, a supplier will usually have to accept the price that the market offers: that is, most suppliers are *price takers* not *price makers*. We shall take a closer look at pricing, and the place of full costs in it, in Chapter 11.

- *For income measurement purposes.*   As we saw in Chapter 3, to provide a valid means of measuring a business's income it is necessary to match expenses with the revenue realised in the same accounting period. Where a service is partially rendered in one accounting period but the revenue is realised in the next, or where manufactured stock (inventory) is made or partially made in one period but sold in the next, the full cost (including an appropriate share of overheads) must be carried from the first accounting period to the second one. Unless we are able to identify the full cost of work done in one period that is the subject of a sale in the next, the profit figures of the periods concerned will become meaningless. This will mean that users of accounting information will not have a reliable means of assessing the effectiveness of the business as a whole, or the effectiveness of individual parts of it. This second reason for needing full cost information can be illustrated by Example 10.5.

Example 10.5

During the accounting year that ended on 31 December last year, Engineers Ltd made a special machine for a customer. At the beginning of this year, after having a series of tests successfully completed by a subcontractor, the machine was delivered to the customer. The business's normal practice (typical of most businesses and following the realisation convention) is to take account of sales revenue when the product passes to the customer. The sale price of the machine was £25,000.

During last year, materials costing £3,500 were used on making the machine and 1,200 hours of direct labour, costing £9,300, were worked on the machine. The business uses a direct-labour-hour basis of charging overheads to jobs, which is believed to be fair because most of its work is labour intensive. The total manufacturing overheads for the business for last year were £77,000, and the total direct-labour-hours worked were 22,000. Testing the machine cost £1,000.

How much profit or loss did the business make on the machine during last year? How much profit or loss did the business make on the machine during this year? At what value should the business have included the machine on its balance sheet at the end of last year so that the correct profit will be recorded for each of the two years?

No profit or loss was made during last year, following the business's (and the generally accepted) approach to recognising revenue (sales). If the sale were not to be recognised until this year it would be illogical (and in contravention of the matching convention) to treat the costs of making the machine as expenses until that time.

During this year, the sale would be recognised and all of the costs, including a reasonable share of overheads, would be set against it in this year's profit and loss account (income statement) as follows:

	£	£
Sales price		25,000
Costs:		
Direct labour	(9,300)	
Direct materials	(3,500)	
Overheads (1,200 × (£77,000/22,000))	(4,200)	
Total incurred last year	(17,000)	
Testing cost	(1,000)	
Total cost		(18,000)
This year's profit from the machine		7,000

The machine needs to be shown as an asset of the business (valued at £17,000) in the balance sheet as at 31 December last year.

Unless all production costs are charged in the same accounting period as that in which the sale is recognised in the profit and loss account (income statement), distortions will occur that will render the profit and loss account much less useful. Thus it is necessary to deduce the full cost of any production undertaken completely or partially in one accounting period, but sold in a subsequent one.

Criticisms of full costing

Full costing has been criticised because, in practice, it tends to use past costs and to restrict its consideration of future costs to outlay costs. It can be argued that past costs are irrelevant, irrespective of the purpose for which the information is to be used. This is basically because it is not possible to make decisions about the past, only about the future. Advocates of full costing would argue that it provides an informative long-run average cost.

Despite the criticisms that are made of full costing, it is, according to research evidence, very widely practised.

The main points in this chapter may be summarised as follows:

Full cost = the total amount of resources sacrificed to achieve a particular objective

Single-product operations

- Where all the units of output are identical, the full cost can be calculated as follows:

$$\text{Cost per unit} = \frac{\text{Total cost of output}}{\text{Number of units produced}}$$

Multi-product operations – job costing

- Where units of output are not identical, it is necessary to divide the costs into two categories: direct costs and indirect costs.
- Direct costs = costs that can be identified with specific cost units (for example, labour of a garage mechanic).
- Indirect costs (overheads) = costs that cannot be directly measured in respect of particular cost units (for example, the rent of a garage).
- Full cost = direct cost + indirect cost.
- Direct/indirect is not linked to variable/fixed.
- Indirect costs are difficult to relate to individual cost units – arbitrary bases used and there is no single correct method.
- Traditionally, indirect costs are seen as the costs of providing a 'service' to cost units.
- Direct-labour-hour basis of applying indirect costs to cost units is the most popular in practice.

Dealing with overheads on a departmental basis

- Indirect costs can be segmented – usually on departmental basis – each department has its own overhead recovery rate.
- Each department is a separate cost centre – that is an area, activity or function for which costs are separately collected.
- Overheads must be allocated or apportioned to cost centres.
- Service cost centre costs must then be apportioned to product cost centres and product cost centre overheads absorbed by cost units (jobs).

Batch costing

- A variation of job costing where each job consists of a number of identical (or near identical) cost units:

$$\text{Cost per unit} = \frac{\text{Cost of the batch (direct + indirect)}}{\text{Number of units in the batch}}$$

If the full cost is charged as the sales price and things go according to plan, the business will break even

Uses of full cost information

1 Pricing (full cost) on a cost-plus basis.
2 Income measurement.

Full cost information is seen by some as not very useful because it can be backward looking: it includes information irrelevant to decision making, but excludes some relevant information

Key terms

full costing p. 314	overhead absorption (recovery)
full cost p. 314	rate p. 320
process costing p. 315	cost centre p. 328
direct costs p. 316	product cost centre p. 328
indirect costs p. 316	service cost centre p. 328
overheads p. 316	cost allocation p. 329
common costs p. 316	cost apportionment p. 330
job costing p. 317	batch costing p. 336
cost behaviour p. 318	cost-plus pricing p. 337
cost unit p. 319	

Further reading

If you would like to explore the topics covered in this chapter in more depth, we recommend the following books:

Management Accounting, *Atkinson A., Barker R., Kaplan R. and Young S.M.*, 3rd edn, Prentice Hall, 2001, chapter 4.

Management and Cost Accounting, *Drury C.*, 5th edn, Thomson Learning, 2000, chapters 3, 4 and 5.

Cost Accounting: A managerial emphasis, *Horngren C., Foster G. and Datar S.*, 11th edn, Prentice Hall International, 2002, chapter 4.

Cost and Management Accounting, *Williamson D.*, Prentice Hall International, 1996, chapters 6, 8 and 10.

References

1 **Cost Systems Design and Profitability Analysis in UK Manufacturing Companies**, *Drury C. and Tayles M.*, CIMA Publishing, 2000.

2 **2003 Survey of Management Accounting**, *Ernst and Young*, Ernst and Young, 2003.

3 **A Survey of Management Accounting Practices in UK Manufacturing Companies**, *Drury C., Braund S., Osborne P. and Tayles M.*, Chartered Association of Certified Accountants, 1993.

REVIEW QUESTIONS

Answers to these questions can be found on the students' side of the Companion Website at **www.pearsoned.co.uk/atrillmclaney**.

10.1 What problem does the existence of work in progress cause in process costing?

10.2 What is the point of distinguishing direct costs from indirect ones? Why is this not necessary in process costing environments?

10.3 Are direct costs and variable costs the same thing? Explain your answer.

10.4 It is sometimes claimed that the full cost of pursuing some objective represents the long-run break-even selling price. Why is this said, and what does it mean?

EXERCISES

Exercises 10.4 to 10.8 are more advanced than exercises 10.1 to 10.3. Those with a coloured number have answers at the back of the book.

10.1 Bodgers Ltd, a business that provides a market research service, operates a job costing system. Towards the end of each financial year, the overhead recovery rate (the rate at which overheads will be charged to jobs) is established for the forthcoming year.

(a) Why does the business bother to predetermine the recovery rate in the way outlined?
(b) What steps will be involved in predetermining the rate?
(c) What problems might arise with using a predetermined rate?

10.2 Athena Ltd is an engineering business doing work for its customers to their particular requirements and specifications. It determines the full cost of each job taking a 'job costing' approach, accounting for overheads on a departmental basis. It bases its prices to customers on this full cost figure. The business has two departments: a Machining Department, where each job starts, and a Fitting Department, which completes all of the jobs. Machining Department overheads are charged to jobs on a machine hour basis and those of the Fitting Department on a direct labour hour basis. The budgeted information for next year is as follows:

Heating and lighting	£25,000	(allocated equally between the two departments)
Machine power	£10,000	(all allocated to the Machining Department)
Direct labour	£200,000	(£150,000 allocated to the Fitting Department and £50,000 to the Machining Department. All direct workers are paid £5 an hour)
Indirect labour	£50,000	(apportioned to the departments in proportion to the direct labour cost)
Direct materials	£120,000	(all applied to jobs in the Machining Department)
Depreciation	£30,000	(all relates to the Machining Department)
Machine time	200,000 hours	(all worked in the Machining Department)

Required:

(a) Prepare a statement showing the budgeted overheads for next year, analysed between the two departments. This should be in the form of three columns: one for the total figure for each type of overhead and one column each for the two departments, where each type of overhead is analysed between the two departments. Each column should also show the total of overheads for the year.

(b) Derive the appropriate rate for charging the overheads of each department to jobs (that is, a separate rate for each department).

(c) Athena Ltd has been asked by a customer to specify the price that it will charge for a particular job that will, if the job goes ahead, be undertaken early next year. The job is expected to use direct materials costing Athena Ltd £1,200, to need 50 hours of machining time, 10 hours of Machine Department direct labour and 40 hours of Fitting Department direct labour. Athena Ltd charges a profit loading of 20% to the full cost of jobs to determine the selling price.

Show workings to derive the proposed selling price for this job.

10.3 Pieman Products Ltd makes road trailers to the precise specifications of individual customers. The following are predicted to occur during the forthcoming year, which is about to start:

Direct materials cost	£50,000
Direct labour costs	£80,000
Direct labour time	16,000 hours
Indirect labour cost	£25,000
Depreciation of machine	£8,000
Rent and rates	£10,000
Heating, lighting and power	£5,000
Indirect materials	£2,000
Other indirect costs	£1,000
Machine time	3,000 hours

All direct labour is paid at the same hourly rate.

A customer has asked the business to build a trailer for transporting a racing motorcycle to races. It is estimated that this will require materials and components that will cost £1,150. It will take 250 direct-labour-hours to do the job, of which 50 will involve the use of machinery.

Required:
Deduce a logical cost for the job, and explain the basis of dealing with overheads that you propose.

10.4 Promptprint Ltd, a printing business, has received an enquiry from a potential customer for the quotation of a price for a job. The pricing policy of the business is based on the plans for the next financial year shown below.

	£
Sales revenue (billings to customers)	196,000
Materials (direct)	(38,000)
Labour (direct)	(32,000)
Variable overheads	(2,400)
Advertising (for business)	(3,000)
Depreciation	(27,600)
Administration	(36,000)
Interest	(8,000)
Profit (before tax)	49,000

A first estimate of the direct costs for the job are:

	£
Direct materials	4,000
Direct labour	3,600

Required:

(a) Prepare a recommended price for the job based on the plans, commenting on your method, ignoring the information given in the Appendix (below).

(b) Comment on the validity of using financial plans in pricing, and recommend any improvements you would consider desirable for the pricing policy used in (a).

(c) Incorporate the effects of the information shown in the Appendix (below) into your estimates of direct material costs, explaining any changes you consider it necessary to make to the above direct materials cost of £4,000.

Appendix to Exercise 10.4

Direct material costs were computed as follows based on historic costs:

	£
Paper grade 1	1,200
Paper grade 2	2,000
Card (zenith grade)	500
Inks and other miscellaneous items	300
	4,000

Paper grade 1 is in stock and in regular use. Because it is imported, it is estimated that if it is used for this job, a new stock order will have to be placed shortly. Sterling has depreciated against the foreign currency by 25% since the last purchase.

Paper grade 2 is purchased from the same source as grade 1. However, current stock (inventory) was bought in for a special order. This order was cancelled, although the defaulting customer was required to pay £500 towards the cost of the paper. The accountant has offset this against the original cost to arrive at the figure of £2,000 shown above. This paper is rarely used, and due to its special chemical coating will be unusable if it is not used on the job in question.

The card is another specialist item currently in stock. There is no use foreseen, and it would cost £750 to replace if required. However, the stock (inventory) controller had planned to spend £130 on overprinting to use the card as a substitute for other materials costing £640.

Inks and other items are in regular use in the print shop.

10.5 Bookdon plc manufactures three products, X, Y and Z, in two production departments: a machine shop and a fitting section; it also has two service departments: a canteen and a machine maintenance section. Shown below are next year's planned production data and manufacturing costs for the business.

	X	Y	Z
Production	4,200 units	6,900 units	1,700 units
Direct materials	£11/unit	£14/unit	£17/unit
Direct labour			
Machine shop	£6/unit	£4/unit	£2/unit
Fitting section	£12/unit	£3/unit	£21/unit
Machine hours	6 hr/unit	3 hr/unit	4 hr/unit

(continued over)

Planned overheads are as follows:

	Machine shop	Fitting section	Canteen	Machine maintenance section	Total
Allocated overheads	£27,660	£19,470	£16,600	£26,650	£90,380
Rent, rates, heat and light					£17,000
Depreciation and insurance of equipment					£25,000
Additional data:					
Gross book value of equipment	£150,000	£75,000	£30,000	£45,000	
Number of employees	18	14	4	4	
Floorspace occupied	3,600 m²	1,400 m²	1,000 m²	800 m²	

All machining is carried out in the machine shop. It has been estimated that approximately 70% of the machine maintenance section's costs are incurred servicing the machine shop and the remainder servicing the fitting section.

Required:

(a) Calculate the following planned overhead absorption rates:
   (i) A machine-hour rate for the machine shop.
   (ii) A rate expressed as a percentage of direct wages for the fitting section.
(b) Calculate the planned full cost per unit of product X.

10.6   Shown below is an extract from next year's plans for a business manufacturing three products, A, B and C, in three production departments.

	A	B	C
Production	4,000 units	3,000 units	6,000 units
Direct material cost	£7 per unit	£4 per unit	£9 per unit
Direct labour requirements:			
Cutting department:			
Skilled operatives	3 hr/unit	5 hr/unit	2 hr/unit
Unskilled operatives	6 hr/unit	1 hr/unit	3 hr/unit
Machining department	½ hr/unit	¼ hr/unit	⅓ hr/unit
Pressing department	2 hr/unit	3 hr/unit	4 hr/unit
Machine requirements:			
Machining department	2 hr/unit	1½ hr/unit	2½ hr/unit

The skilled operatives employed in the cutting department are paid £8 per hour and the unskilled operatives are paid £5 per hour. All the operatives in the machining and pressing departments are paid £6 per hour.

	Production departments			Service departments	
	Cutting	Machining	Pressing	Engineering	Personnel
Planned total overheads	£154,482	£64,316	£58,452	£56,000	£34,000
Service department costs incurred for the benefit of other departments, as follows:					
Engineering services	20%	45%	35%	–	–
Personnel services	55%	10%	20%	15%	–

The business operates a full absorption costing system.

Required:

Calculate, as equitably as possible, the total planned cost of:

(a) One completed unit of product A.

(b) One incomplete unit of product B, which has been processed by the cutting and machining departments but which has not yet been passed into the pressing department.

10.7 'In a job costing system, it is necessary to divide up the business into departments. Fixed costs (or overheads) will be collected for each department. Where a particular fixed cost relates to the business as a whole, it must be divided between the departments. Usually this is done on the basis of area of floorspace occupied by each department relative to the entire business. When the total fixed costs for each department have been identified, this will be divided by the number of hours that were worked in each department to deduce an overhead recovery rate. Each job that was worked on in a department will have a share of fixed costs allotted to it according to how long it was worked on. The total cost for each job will therefore be the sum of the variable costs of the job and its share of the fixed costs. It is essential that this approach is taken in order to deduce a selling price for the business's output.'

You are required to prepare a table of two columns. In the first column you should show any phrases or sentences in the above statement with which you do not agree, and in the second column you should show your reason for disagreeing with each one.

10.8 Many businesses charge overheads to jobs on a departmental basis.

Required:

(a) What is the advantage that is claimed for charging overheads to jobs on a departmental basis, and why is it claimed?

(b) What circumstances need to exist to make a difference to a particular job whether overheads are charged on a business-wide basis or on a departmental basis. (Note that the answer to this part of the question is not specifically covered in the chapter. You should, nevertheless, be able to deduce the reason from what you know.)

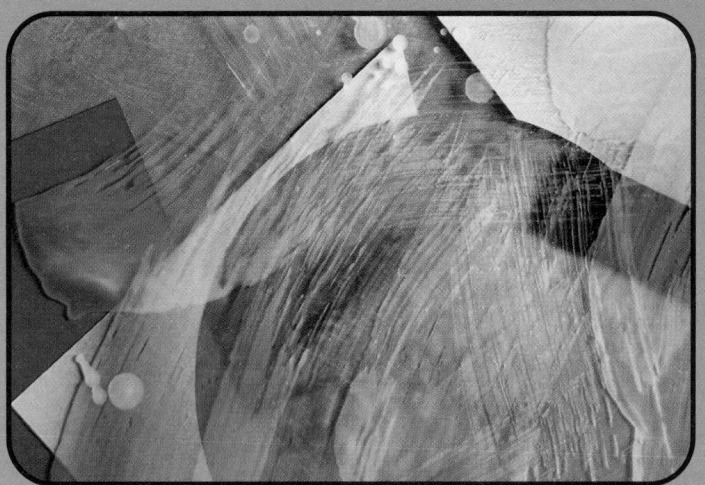

Managing in a competitive environment

When you have completed this chapter, you should be able to:

● Discuss the nature and practicalities of activity-based costing.

● Explain the theoretical underpinning of pricing and discuss the issues involved in reaching a pricing decision in real-world situations.

● Explain how new developments such as total life-cycle costing and target costing can be used to control costs.

● Discuss the importance of non-financial measures of performance in managing a business and the way in which the Balanced Scorecard attempts to integrate financial and non-financial measures.

● Explain the term 'shareholder value' and describe the role of EVA® in measuring and delivering shareholder value.

INTRODUCTION

Recent years have witnessed major changes in the business world, such as deregulation, privatisation, the growing expectations of shareholders and the impact of new technology. These have led to a much more fast-changing and competitive environment that has radically changed the way in which businesses need to be managed. This chapter considers some of the financial techniques that are being used to manage in this new era.

We begin by considering the impact of this new, highly competitive environment on the full-costing approach that we considered in Chapter 10. We shall see that activity-based costing, which is a development of the traditional full-costing approach, takes a much more enquiring, much less accepting attitude towards overheads. We shall see how, in theory and in practice, a business can use costing information to aid pricing decisions. This will pick up some of the points on relevant cost and cost–volume–profit relationships that we considered in Chapters 8 and 9. Some recent approaches to costing that can lower costs and, therefore, increase the ability of a business to compete on price are also examined.

Management accounting embraces both financial and non-financial measures and, in this chapter, we shall consider the increasing importance of non-financial measures in managing a business. These include the Balanced Scorecard approach, which seeks to integrate financial and non-financial measures into a framework for the achievement of business objectives.

Finally, the idea of shareholder value is considered. This has been a 'hot' issue among managers in recent years. Many leading businesses now claim that the quest for shareholder value is the driving force behind strategic and operational decisions. In this chapter, we consider what the term 'shareholder value' means and look at one of the main methods of measuring shareholder value.

Costing and the changed business environment

The background to traditional costing and pricing

The traditional, but still widely used, approach to costing and pricing productive output first developed when the notion of trying to determine the cost of industrial production originally emerged. This was around the time of the Industrial Revolution when industry showed the following features:

● *Direct-labour-intensive and direct-labour-paced production*. Labour was at the heart of production. To the extent that machinery was used, it was to support the efforts of direct labour, and the speed of production was dictated by direct labour.
● *A low level of overheads relative to direct costs*. Little was spent on power, personnel services, machinery (leading to low depreciation charges) and other areas typical of the overheads of modern businesses.

- *A relatively uncompetitive market.* Transport difficulties, limited industrial production worldwide and a lack of knowledge by customers of competitors' prices meant that businesses could prosper without being too scientific in costing and pricing their output.

Since overheads then represented a pretty small element of total costs, it was acceptable and practical to deal with them in a fairly arbitrary manner. Not too much effort was devoted to trying to control the cost of overheads because the rewards of better control were relatively small, certainly when compared with the rewards from controlling direct labour and material costs. It was also reasonable to charge overheads to individual jobs on a direct-labour-hour basis. Most of the overheads were incurred directly in support of direct labour: providing direct workers with a place to work, heating and lighting that workplace, employing people to supervise the direct workers and so on. Direct workers, perhaps aided by machinery, carried out all production.

At that time service industries were a relatively unimportant part of the economy and would have largely consisted of self-employed individuals. These individuals would probably have been too unsophisticated to try to do more than work out a rough hourly/daily rate for their time and to try to base prices on this.

The current full costing and pricing environment

In more recent years, the world of much industrial production had fundamentally altered. Most of it is now characterised by:

- *Capital-intensive and machine-paced production.* Machines are at the heart of much production, including service provision. Most labour supports the efforts of machines, for example, technically maintaining them, and the pace of production is often dictated by machines.
- *A higher level of overheads relative to direct costs.* Modern businesses tend to have very high depreciation, servicing and power costs. There are also high costs of a nature scarcely envisaged in the early days of industrial production, such as personnel and staff welfare costs. At the same time, there are very low (sometimes no) direct labour costs. Although direct materials cost often remains an important element of total cost, more efficient production methods lead to less waste and, therefore, less material total cost, again tending to make overheads more dominant.
- *A highly competitive international market.* Production, much of it highly sophisticated, is carried out worldwide. Transport, including fast airfreight, is relatively cheap. Fax, telephone and the Internet ensure that potential customers can quickly and cheaply find the prices of a range of suppliers. So the market is likely to be highly competitive. This means that businesses need to know their costs with a greater degree of accuracy than historically has been the case. Businesses also need to take a considered and informed approach to pricing their output.

In the UK, service industries now dominate the economy, employing the great majority of the workforce and producing most of the value of productive output. Though there are many self-employed individuals supplying services, many service providers are vast businesses like banks, insurance businesses and cinema operators. For most of these larger service providers, the activities very closely resemble modern manufacturing activity. They too are characterised by high capital intensity, overheads dominating direct costs and a competitive international market.

Activity-based costing

Chapter 10 considered the traditional approach to job costing (deriving the full cost of output where one unit of output differs from another). This approach is to collect those costs for each job, which can be unequivocally linked to and measured in respect of the particular job (direct costs). All other costs (overheads) are thrown into a pool of costs and charged to individual jobs according to some formula. As we saw in Chapter 10, survey evidence indicates that this formula has usually been on the basis of the number of direct-labour-hours worked on each particular job.

In the past, overhead recovery rates (that is, rates at which overheads are absorbed by jobs) were typically much less for each direct-labour-hour than the actual rate paid to direct workers. It is now, however, becoming increasingly common for overhead recovery rates to be between five and ten times the hourly rate of pay, because overheads are now much more significant. When production is dominated by direct labour paid, say, £8 an hour, it might be reasonable to have an overhead recovery rate of, say, £1 an hour. When, however, direct labour plays a relatively small part in production, to have overhead recovery rates of, say, £50 for each direct-labour-hour is likely to lead to very arbitrary costing. Even a small change in the amount of direct labour worked on a job could massively affect the total cost deduced. This is not because the direct worker is very highly paid, but because of the effect of the direct labour change on the overhead loading. Overheads are charged on a direct-labour-hour basis even though they may not be particularly related to direct labour.

An alternative approach to full costing

As a result of changes in the business environment, the whole question of overheads, what causes them and how they are charged to jobs, has been receiving much closer attention. Historically, businesses have been content to accept that overheads exist and, therefore, for costing purposes they must be dealt with in as practical a way as possible. In recent years, however, there has been an increasing realisation that overheads do not just happen; they must be caused by something. To illustrate this point, let us consider Example 11.1.

Example 11.1

Modern Producers Ltd has, like virtually all manufacturers, a storage area that is set aside for finished goods. The costs of running the stores include a share of the factory rent and other establishment costs, such as heating and lighting. They also include the salaries of staff employed to look after the stock (inventory), and the cost of financing the stock held in the stores.

The business has two product lines: A and B. Product A tends to be made in small batches, and low levels of finished stock are held. The business prides itself on its ability to supply Product B in relatively large quantities instantly. As a consequence, much of the finished goods store is filled with finished Product Bs ready to be despatched immediately an order is received.

Traditionally, the whole cost of operating the stores would have been treated as a general overhead and included in the total of overheads charged to jobs on a

→

direct-labour-hour basis. This means that when assessing the cost of products A and B, the cost of operating the stores has fallen on them according to the number of direct-labour-hours worked on each one. In fact, most of the stores cost should be charged to Product B, since this product causes (and benefits from) the stores cost much more than is true of Product A. Failure to account more precisely for the cost of running the stores is masking the fact that Product B is not as profitable as it seems to be. It may even be leading to losses as a result of the relatively high stores-operating cost that it causes. So far much of this cost has been charged to Product A, without regard to the fact that Product A causes little of it. The products absorb the stores cost in proportion to the direct-labour-hour content, a factor that has nothing to do with storage.

Cost drivers

Realisation that overheads do not just occur, but that they are caused by activities – like holding products in stores – that 'drive' the costs, is at the heart of **activity-based** **costing (ABC)**. The traditional approach is that direct-labour-hours are the **cost driver**, which probably used to be true. ABC recognises that this is often not the case.

There is a basic philosophical difference between the traditional and the ABC approaches. Traditionally we tend to think of overheads as *rendering a service to cost units*, the cost of which must be charged to those units. ABC sees overheads as being *caused by cost units*, and those cost units must be charged with the costs that they cause.

ACTIVITY 11.1

Can you think of any other purpose that identification of the cost drivers serves, apart from deriving more accurate costs?

Identification of the activities that cause costs puts management in a position where it may well be able to control them.

The opaque nature of overheads has traditionally made them more difficult to control than direct labour and material costs. If, however, an analysis of overheads can identify the cost drivers, questions can be asked about whether the activity driving certain costs is necessary at all, and whether the cost justifies the benefit. In Example 11.1, it may be a good marketing policy that Product B can be supplied immediately from stock, but this causes a cost that should be recognised and assessed against the benefit.

Adopting ABC requires that most overheads can be analysed and the cost drivers identified. This means that it might be possible to gain much clearer insights to the overhead costs that are caused, activity by activity, so that fairer and more accurate product costs can be identified, and costs can be controlled more effectively.

Cost pools

Under ABC, an overhead **cost pool** is established for each cost driver in which all of the costs caused by that driver are placed. So, the business in Example 11.1 would create a cost pool for operating the stores. All costs associated with this activity would be allocated to that cost pool. The total costs in that pool would then be allocated to output (goods or services) according to the extent to which each unit of output 'drove' those costs, using the cost driver identified.

Example 11.2

The accountant at Modern Producers Ltd (see Example 11.1) has estimated that the costs of running the finished goods stores for next year will be £90,000. This will be the amount allocated to the 'finished goods stores cost pool'.

It is estimated that each Product A will spend an average of one week in the stores before being sold. With Product B, the equivalent period is four weeks. Both products are of roughly similar size and have very similar storage needs. It is felt, therefore, that the quantity of each product and the period spent in the stores are the cost drivers.

It is estimated that, next year, 50,000 Product As and 25,000 Product Bs will pass though the stores. So the total number of 'product weeks' in store will be:

$$
\begin{array}{llll}
\text{Product A} & 50,000 \times 1 \text{ week} & = & 50,000 \\
\text{B} & 25,000 \times 4 \text{ weeks} & = & \underline{100,000} \\
& & & \underline{150,000}
\end{array}
$$

The stores cost for each 'product week' is given by

$$£90,000/150,000 = £0.60$$

Therefore each Product A will be charged with £0.60 for finished stores costs, and each Product B with £2.40 (that is, £0.60 × 4).

Allocating overhead costs to cost pools, as is necessary with ABC, contrasts with the traditional approach, where the overheads are allocated to production departments. In both cases, however, the overheads are then charged to cost units (goods or services). The two different approaches are illustrated in Figure 11.1.

With the traditional approach, overheads are apportioned to product departments. Each department would then derive an overhead recovery rate, typically overheads per direct labour hour. Overheads would then be applied to units of output according to how many direct-labour-hours were worked on them.

With ABC, the overheads are analysed into cost pools, with one cost pool for each cost driver. The overheads are then charged to units of output, through activity cost driver rates. These rates are an attempt to represent the extent to which each particular cost unit is believed to cause the particular part of the overheads.

ABC and service industries

Much of our discussion of ABC has concentrated on manufacturing industry, perhaps because early users of ABC were manufacturing businesses. In fact, ABC is possibly even more relevant to service industries because, in the absence of a direct materials element, a service business's total costs are likely to be largely made up of overheads. There is certainly evidence that ABC has been adopted more readily by businesses that sell services rather than goods, as we shall see later.

Figure 11.1   Traditional versus activity-based costing

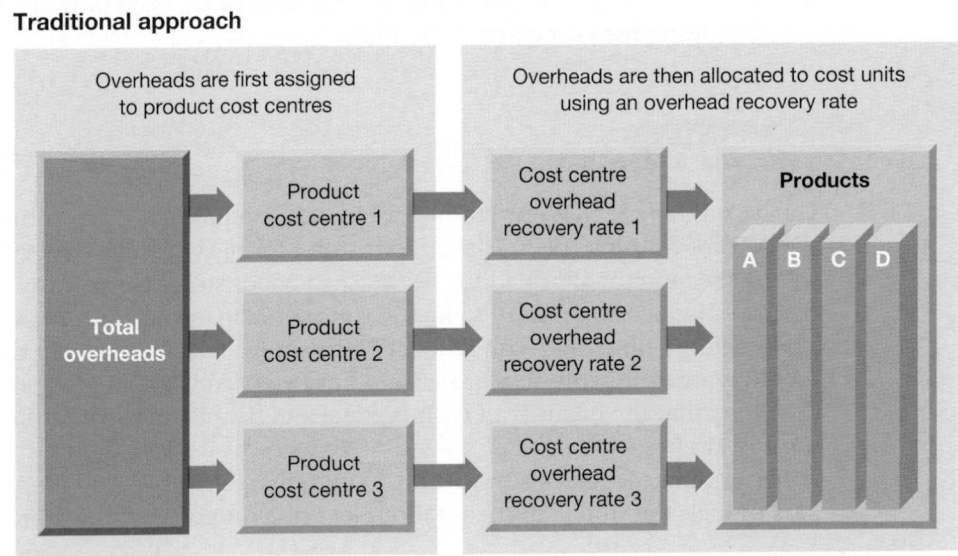

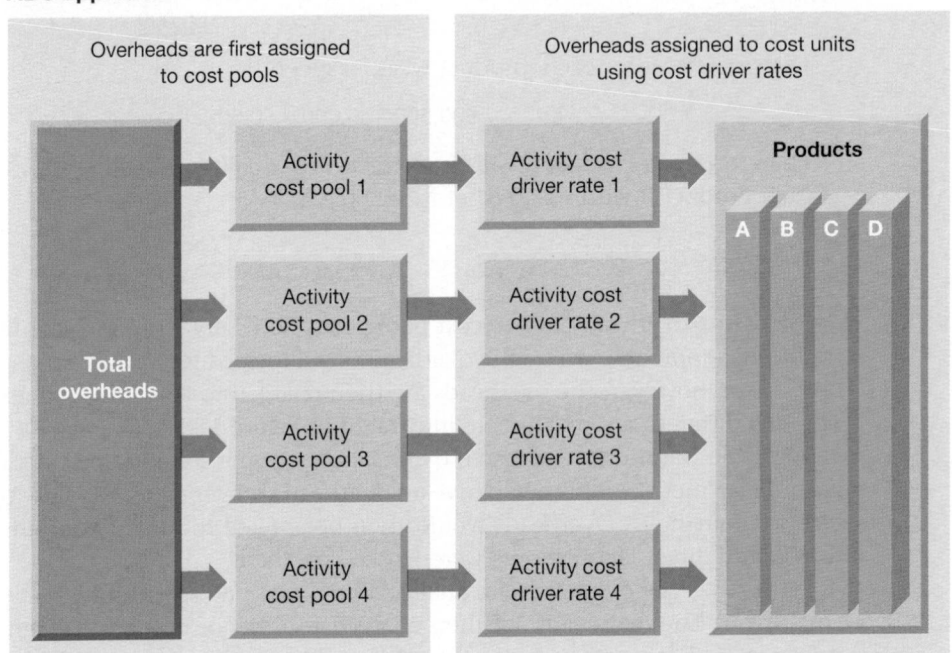

With the traditional approach, overheads are first assigned to product cost centres. Then, overheads are absorbed by cost units on the basis of an overhead recovery rate (using direct-labour-hours worked on the cost units or some other approach) for each cost centre. With activity-based costing, overheads are assigned to cost pools and then cost units are charged with overheads to the extent that each individual cost unit drives the costs in the various pools.

Source: Adapted from Innes and Mitchell (see reference 1 at the end of the chapter).

ACTIVITY 11.2

What is the difference in the way in which direct costs are accounted for when using ABC, relative to their treatment taking a traditional approach to full costing?

The answer is no difference at all. ABC is concerned only with the way in which overheads are charged to jobs to derive the full cost.

Criticisms of ABC

Critics of ABC argue that analysis of overheads in order to identify cost drivers is time-consuming and costly, and that the benefit of doing so, in terms of more accurate costing and the potential for cost control, does not justify the cost of carrying out the analysis.

ABC is also criticised for the same reason that full costing generally is criticised: because it does not provide very relevant information for decision making. The point was made in Chapter 10 that full costing tends to use past costs and to ignore opportunity costs. Since past costs are always irrelevant in decision making and opportunity costs can be significant, full costing information is an expensive irrelevance. In contrast, advocates of full costing claim that it *is* relevant, in that it provides a long-run average cost, whereas 'relevant costing', which we considered in Chapter 8, relates only to the specific circumstances of the short term.

Despite the criticisms that are made of full costing (whether 'traditional' or ABC), it is, according to survey evidence, very widely practised.

Real World 11.1 provides some indication of the extent to which ABC is used in practice.

REAL WORLD 11.1

ABC in practice

A survey of large UK businesses in 1999 revealed that, on average, 15 per cent of businesses fully use an ABC approach to dealing with full costing. A further 8 per cent use it partially. The remaining 77 per cent do not use ABC at all. Even so, there was a surprising range in the level of usage of ABC from industry to industry (see Figure 11.2). It is particularly surprising that so few manufacturing businesses use ABC. The survey showed that it tends to be larger businesses that adopt ABC.

There is some evidence of a decrease in the use of ABC over recent years. A different survey of large UK businesses (conducted by Innes, Mitchell and Sinclair) in 1999, replicated a 1994 survey conducted by the same researchers. They found the following:

	1994 %	1999 %
Currently using ABC	21.0	17.5
Currently considering using ABC	29.6	20.3
Rejected using ABC after assessing it	13.3	15.3

Thus, it seems that both as to current and potential usage of ABC, it was less popular in 1999 than it had been five years previously.

Source: Innes *et al*. (see reference 3 at the end of the chapter).

Real World 11.1 continued

Figure 11.2

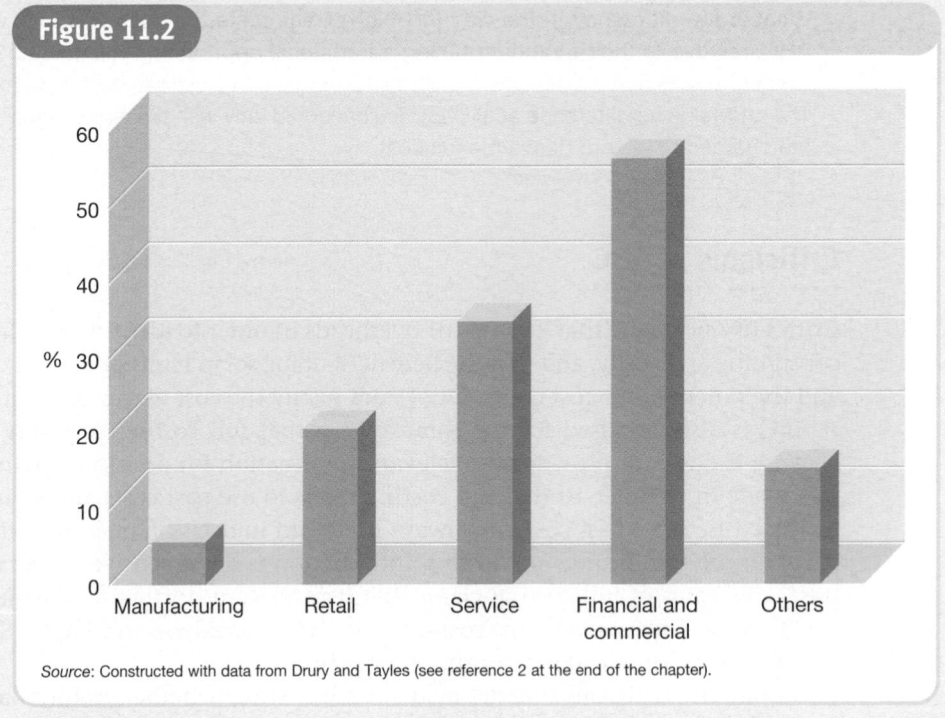

Source: Constructed with data from Drury and Tayles (see reference 2 at the end of the chapter).

SELF-ASSESSMENT QUESTION 11.1

Psilis Ltd makes a product in two qualities, called 'Basic' and 'Super'. The business is able to sell these products at a price that gives a standard profit mark-up of 25 per cent of full cost. Management is concerned by the lack of profit.

Full cost for one unit is calculated by charging overheads to each type of product on the basis of direct labour hours. The costs are as follows:

	Basic £	Super £
Direct labour (all £5/hour)	20	30
Direct material	15	20

Total overheads are £1,000,000. Based on experience over recent years, in the forthcoming year the business expects to make and sell 40,000 Basics and 10,000 Supers.

Recently, the business's management accountant has undertaken an exercise to try to identify cost drivers in an attempt to be able to deal with the overheads on a more precise basis than had been possible before. This exercise has revealed the following analysis of the annual overheads:

Activity (and cost driver)	Cost £000	Annual number of activities		
		Total	Basic	Super
Number of machine set-ups	280	100	20	80
Number of quality-control inspections	220	2,000	500	1,500
Number of sales orders processed	240	5,000	1,500	3,500
General production (machine-hours)	260	500,000	350,000	150,000
Total	1,000			

The management accountant explained the analysis of the £1,000,000 overheads as follows:

● The two products are made in relatively small batches, so that storage of finished stock (inventory) is negligible. The Supers are made in very small batches because their demand is relatively low. Each time a new batch is produced, the machines have to be reset by skilled staff. Resetting for Basic production occurs about 20 times a year and for Supers about 80 times: about 100 times in total. The cost of employing the machine-setting staff is about £280,000 a year. It is clear that the more set-ups that occur, the higher the total set-up costs; in other words, the number of set-ups is the factor that drives set-up costs.

● All production has to be inspected for quality and this costs about £220,000 a year. The higher specifications of the Supers mean that there is more chance that there will be quality problems. Thus the Supers are inspected in total 1,500 times annually, whereas the Basics only need about 500 inspections. The number of inspections is the factor that drives these costs.

● Sales order processing (dealing with customers' orders, from receiving the original order to despatching the products) costs about £240,000 a year. Despite the larger amount of Basic production, there are only 1,500 sales orders each year because the Basics are sold to wholesalers in relatively large-sized orders. The Supers are sold mainly direct to the public by mail order, usually in very small-sized orders. It is believed that the number of orders drives the costs of processing orders.

● The remaining general production overheads, totalling £260,000 a year, are thought to be driven by the number of hours for which the machines operate. The machine time for one unit of the product is somewhat higher for Supers than for Basics.

Required:
(a) Deduce the full cost of each of the two products on the basis used at present and, from these, deduce the current selling price.
(b) Deduce the full cost of each product on an ABC basis, taking account of the management accountant's recent investigations.
(c) What conclusions do you draw? What advice would you offer the management of the business?

Pricing

As we have just seen, full costing can be used as a basis for setting prices for the business's output. We have also seen that it can be criticised in that role. In this section we are going to take a closer look at pricing. We shall begin by considering some theoretical aspects of the subject before going on to look at some more practical issues, particularly the role of management accounting information in pricing decisions.

Economic theory

In most market conditions found in practice, the price charged by a business will determine the number of units sold. This is shown graphically in Figure 11.3.

Figure 11.3 shows the number of units of output that the market would demand at various prices. As price increases, the less willing are people to buy the commodity (call it commodity A). At a relatively low price a unit (P_1), the quantity of units demanded by the market (Q_1) is fairly high. When the price is increased to P_2, the demand decreases to Q_2. The graph shows a linear (straight-line) relationship between the price and demand. In practice, the relationship, though broadly similar, may not be quite so straightforward.

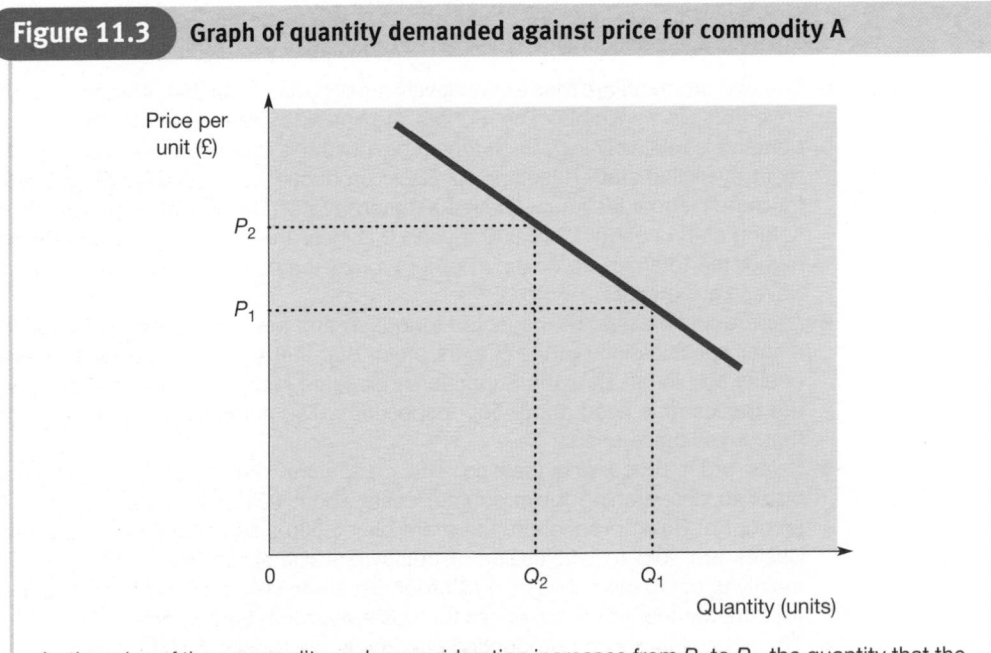

Figure 11.3   Graph of quantity demanded against price for commodity A

As the price of the commodity under consideration increases from P_1 to P_2, the quantity that the market will buy falls from Q_1 to Q_2.

Not all commodities show exactly the same slope of line. Figure 11.4 shows the demand/price relationship for commodity B, a different commodity from the one depicted in Figure 11.3.

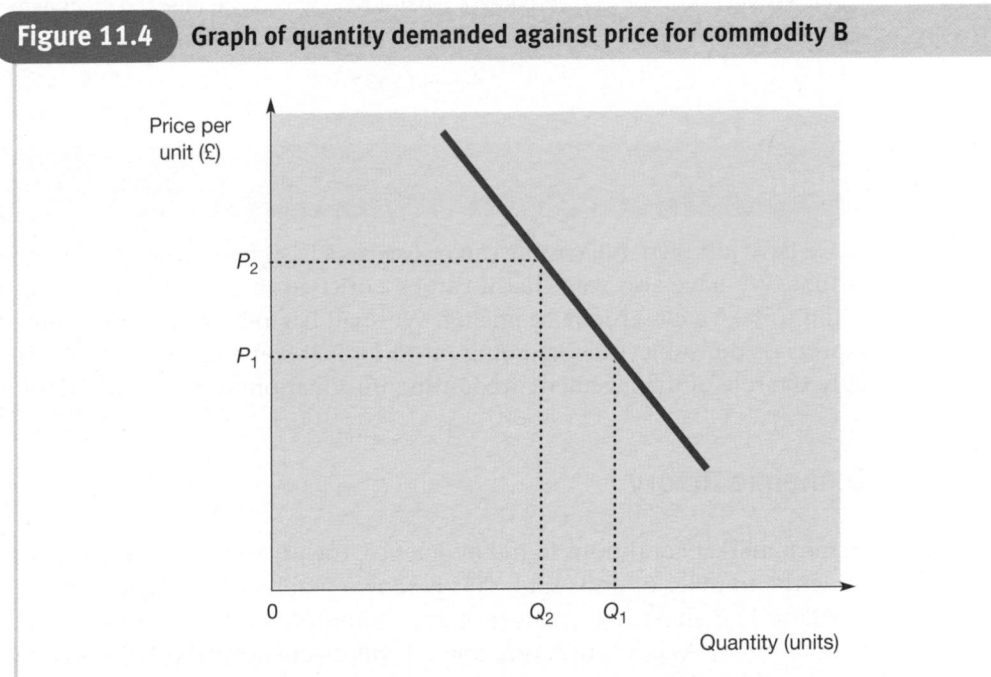

Figure 11.4   Graph of quantity demanded against price for commodity B

As the price of the commodity increases from P_1 to P_2, the quantity that the market will buy falls from Q_1 to Q_2. This fall in demand is less than was the case for commodity A, which has the greater elasticity of demand.

Though a rise in price of commodity B, from P_1 to P_2, causes a fall in demand, the fall in demand is much smaller than is the case for commodity A with a similar rise in price. As a result, we say that commodity A has a higher **elasticity of demand** than commodity B. Demand for A reacts much more dramatically (stretches more) to price changes than demand does for B. Elastic demand tends to be associated with commodities that are not essential, perhaps because there is a ready substitute.

ACTIVITY 11.3

Which would be the more elastic of the following commodities?

● A particular brand of chocolate bar
● Mains electricity supply.

A branded chocolate bar seems likely to have a fairly *elastic* demand. This is for several reasons, including the following:

● Few buyers of the bar would feel that chocolate bars are essentials.
● Other chocolate bars, probably quite similar to the one in question, will be easily available.

Mains electricity probably has a relatively *inelastic* demand. This is because:

● Many users of electricity would find it very difficult to manage without fuel of some description.
● For neither household nor business users of electricity is there an immediate, practical substitute. For some uses of electricity – for example, powering machinery – there is probably no substitute. Even for a purpose such as heating, where there are substitutes such as gas and oil, it may be impractical to switch to the substitute because gas and oil heating appliances are not immediately available and are costly to acquire.

It is very helpful for those involved with pricing decisions to have some feel for the elasticity of demand of the commodity that will be the subject of a decision. The sensitivity of the demand to the pricing decision is obviously much greater (and the pricing decision more crucial) with commodities whose demand is elastic than with commodities whose demand is relatively inelastic.

Real World 11.2 provides an example of pricing some well-known elastic-demand products.

REAL WORLD 11.2

Sony and Microsoft in European console price war   **FT**

The battle for control of the European games console market intensified on Wednesday as Sony and Microsoft went head to head with price cuts for their respective Playstation 2 and Xbox consoles.

Sony sought to solidify its leading position in the market by aggressively cutting the price of the Playstation 2 console by 15 per cent in the UK to £169.99 ($260.30) and by up to 17 per cent in continental Europe to between €249 and €259 ($244.10–$253.90).

An hour later, Microsoft responded by slashing the European retail price of the Xbox to €249.99.

Real World 11.2 continued

In the run up to the lucrative Christmas period, console makers have intensified sales and marketing initiatives, racing to carve out a share of a market estimated to be worth £27bn.

'The games market has a lot of price elasticity – the lower the price, the more people tend to buy consoles. Sony, Microsoft and Nintendo are looking to get their user-base as large as possible, by putting the hardware out at almost cost price. They can then make their money from selling software,' said Peter Reed, analyst at Beeson Gregory.

Making a push on hardware sales now, he noted, will allow them to prepare for games sales in the pre-Christmas period, which can account for more than one-third of total yearly sales.

Source: 'Sony and Microsoft in European console price war', FT.com, 28 August 2002.

As we saw in Chapter 1, the objective of most businesses is to enhance the wealth of their owners. Broadly speaking, this will be best achieved by seeking to maximise profits – that is, having the largest possible difference between total costs and total revenue. Thus, prices should be set in a way that is likely to have this effect. To be able to do this, the price decision maker needs to have some insight to the way in which costs and prices relate to volume of output.

Figure 11.5 shows the relationship between cost and volume of output, which we have already met in Chapter 9. The figure shows that the total cost of providing a particular commodity (service X) increases as the quantity of output increases. It is shown here as a straight line. In practice it may be curved, either curving upwards (tending to become closer to the vertical) or flattening out (tending to become closer to the horizontal). The figure assumes that the marginal cost of each unit is constant over the range shown.

Figure 11.5   **Graph of total cost against quantity (volume) of output of service X**

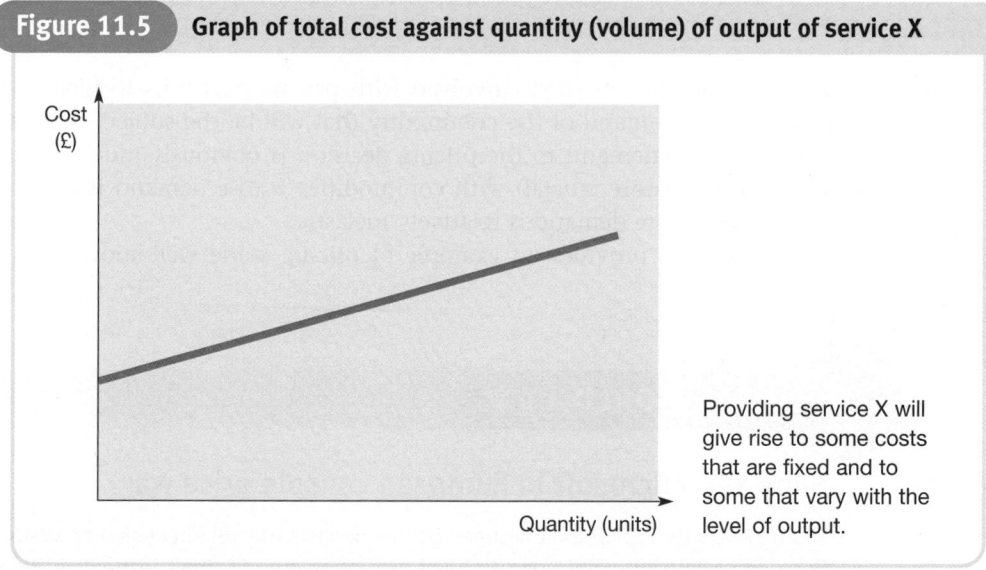

Providing service X will give rise to some costs that are fixed and to some that vary with the level of output.

ACTIVITY   11.4

What general effect would tend to cause the total cost line in Figure 11.5 to (a) curve towards the vertical, and (b) curve towards the horizontal? (You may recall that we considered this issue in Chapter 9.)

(a) Curving towards the vertical would mean that the marginal cost (additional cost of making one more) of each successive unit of output would become greater. This would probably imply that increased activity would be causing a shortage of supply of some factor of production, which had the effect of increasing cost prices. This might be caused by a shortage of labour, meaning that overtime payments would need to be made to encourage people to work the hours necessary for increased production. It might also/alternatively be caused by a shortage of raw materials. Perhaps normal supplies were exhausted at lower levels of output and more expensive sources had to be used to expand output.

(b) Curving towards the horizontal might be caused by the business being able to exploit the economies of scale at higher levels of output, making the marginal cost of each successive unit of output cheaper. Perhaps higher volumes of output enable division of labour or more mechanisation. Possibly, suppliers of raw materials offer better deals for larger orders.

Figure 11.6 shows the total sales revenue against quantity of service X sold. The total sales revenue increases as the quantity of output increases, but only up to a certain point.

Figure 11.6   Graph of total sales revenue against quantity (volume) sold of service X

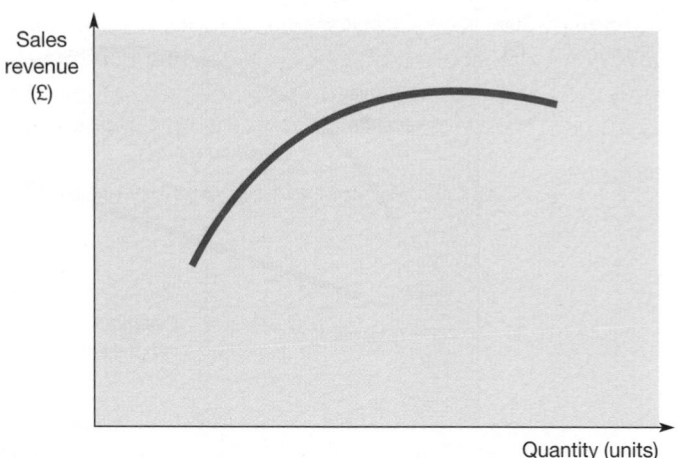

As more units of service X are sold, the total sales revenue initially increases, but at a declining rate. This is because, to persuade people to buy increasing quantities, the price must be reduced. Eventually the price will have to be reduced so much, to encourage additional sales, that the total sales revenue will fall as the number of units sold increases.

ACTIVITY 11.5

What assumption does Figure 11.6 make about the price for a unit of service X at which output can be sold as the number of units sold increases?

The graph suggests that, to sell more units, the price must be lowered, meaning that the average price for each unit of output reduces as volume sold increases. As we discussed earlier in this section, this is true of most markets found in practice.

Figure 11.6 implies that there will come a point where, to make increased sales, prices will have to be reduced so much that total sales revenue will not increase; it may even reduce.

In Chapter 9, when we considered break-even analysis, we assumed a steady price per unit over the range that we were considering. Now we are saying that, in practice, it does not work like this. How can these two positions be reconciled? The answer is that, when we dealt with break-even analysis, we were only considering a relatively small range of output, namely from zero sales up to the break-even point. It may well be that over a small range, particularly at low levels of output, a constant sales price a unit is a reasonable assumption. That is to say that, to the left of the curve in Figure 11.6, there may be a straight line from zero up to the start of the curve.

There is nothing in break-even analysis that demands that the assumption about steady selling prices is made, but making it does mean that the analysis is very straightforward.

Figure 11.7 combines information about total sales revenue and total cost for service X over a range of output levels.

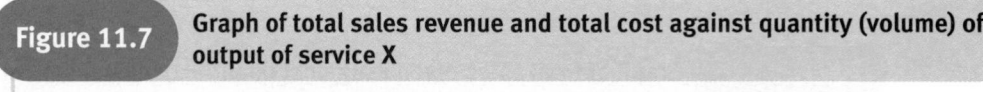

Figure 11.7   **Graph of total sales revenue and total cost against quantity (volume) of output of service X**

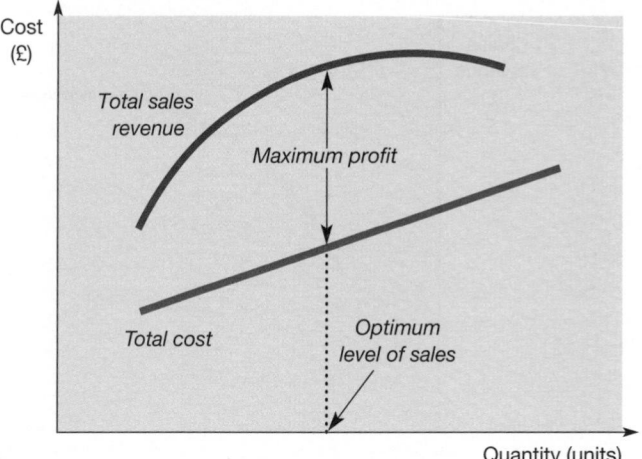

Profit is the vertical distance between the total-cost and total-sales-revenue lines. For a wealth-maximising business, the optimum level of sales will occur when this is at a maximum.

The total sales revenue increases, but at a decreasing rate, and the total cost of production increases as the quantity of output increases. The maximum profit is made where the total sales revenue and total cost lines are vertically furthest apart. At the left-hand end of the graph, we are clearly above break-even point because the total-sales-revenue line has already gone above the total-cost line. At the lower levels of volume of sales and output, the total-sales-revenue line is climbing faster than the total cost line. The business will wish to keep expanding output as long as this continues to be the case, because profit is the vertical distance between the two lines. A point will be reached where the total sales revenue line flattens towards the horizontal to such an extent that further expansion will reduce profit.

The point at which profit is maximised is where the two lines stop diverging, that is, the point at which the two lines are climbing at exactly the same rate. Thus we can say that profit is maximised at the point where:

Marginal sales revenue = Marginal cost of production

that is,

$$\begin{bmatrix}\text{Increase in total sales}\\ \text{revenue from selling}\\ \text{one more unit}\end{bmatrix} = \begin{bmatrix}\text{Increase in total costs}\\ \text{that will result from}\\ \text{selling one more unit}\end{bmatrix}$$

To see how this approach can be applied, consider Example 11.3.

Example 11.3

A schedule of predicted total sales revenue and total costs at various levels of provision for service Y are shown in columns (a) and (c) of the table.

Quantity of output	Total sales revenue £ (a)	Marginal sales revenue £ (b)	Total cost £ (c)	Marginal cost £ (d)	Profit (loss) £ (e)
0	0		0		0
1	1,000	1,000	2,300	2,300	(1,300)
2	1,900	900	2,600	300	(700)
3	2,700	800	2,900	300	(200)
4	3,400	700	3,200	300	200
5	4,000	600	3,500	300	500
6	4,500	500	3,800	300	700
7	4,900	400	4,100	300	800
8	5,200	300	4,400	300	800
9	5,400	200	4,700	300	700
10	5,500	100	5,000	300	500

Column (b) is deduced by taking the total sales revenue for one less unit sold from the total sales revenue at the sales level under consideration (column (a)). For example, the marginal sales revenue of the fifth unit of the service sold (£600) is deduced by taking the total sales revenue for four units sold (£3,400) away from the total sales revenue for five units sold (£4,000).

Column (d) is deduced similarly, but using total cost figures from column (c). Column (e) is found by deducting column (c) from column (a).

It can be seen by looking at the profit (loss) column that the maximum profit occurs with an output of seven or eight units (£800). Thus the maximum output should be eight units of the service. This is the point where marginal cost and marginal revenue are equal (at £300).

ACTIVITY 11.6

Specialist Ltd makes a very specialised machine that is sold to manufacturing businesses. The business is about to commence production of a new model of machine for which facilities exist to produce a maximum of 10 machines each week. To assist management in a decision on the price to charge for the new machine, two pieces of information have been collected:

- *Market demand*. The business's marketing staff believes that, at a price of £3,000 a machine, the demand would be zero. Each £100 reduction in unit price below £3,000 would generate one additional sale a week. Thus, for example, at a price of £2,800 each, two machines could be sold each week.
- *Manufacturing costs*. Fixed costs associated with manufacture of the machine are estimated at £3,000 a week. Since the work is highly labour-intensive and labour is in short supply, unit variable costs are expected to be progressive. The manufacture of one machine each week is expected to have a variable cost of £1,100, but each additional machine produced will increase the variable cost for the entire output by £100 a machine. For example, if the output were three machines a week, the variable cost for each machine (for all three machines) would be £1,300.

It is the policy of the business always to charge the same price for its entire output of a particular model. What is the most profitable level of output of the new machine?

Output	Unit sales revenue £	Total sales revenue £	Marginal sales revenue £	Unit variable cost £	Total variable cost £	Total cost £	Marginal cost £	Profit (loss) £
0	0	0	0	0	0	3,000	3,000	(3,000)
1	2,900	2,900	2,900	1,100	1,100	4,100	1,100	(1,200)
2	2,800	5,600	2,700	1,200	2,400	5,400	1,300	200
3	2,700	8,100	2,500	1,300	3,900	6,900	1,500	1,200
4	2,600	10,400	2,300	1,400	5,600	8,600	1,700	1,800
5	2,500	12,500	2,100	1,500	7,500	10,500	1,900	2,000
6	2,400	14,400	1,900	1,600	9,600	12,600	2,100	1,800
7	2,300	16,100	1,700	1,700	11,900	14,900	2,300	1,200
8	2,200	17,600	1,500	1,800	14,400	17,400	2,500	200
9	2,100	18,900	1,300	1,900	17,100	20,100	2,700	(1,200)
10	2,000	20,000	1,100	2,000	20,000	23,000	2,900	(3,000)

An output of five machines each week will maximise profit at £2,000 a week.

The additional cost of producing the fifth machine compared with the cost of producing the first four (£1,900) is just below the marginal revenue (the amount by which the total revenue from five machines exceeds that from selling four (£2,100)).

The additional cost of producing the sixth machine compared with the cost of producing the first five (£2,100) is just above the marginal revenue (the amount by which the total revenue from six machines exceeds that from selling five (£1,900)).

Some practical considerations

Despite the analysis in Activity 11.6, in practice the answer of five machines a week may prove not to be the best answer. This might be for one or more of several reasons:

- Demand is notoriously difficult to predict, even assuming no changes in the environment.
- The effect of sales of the new machine on the other of the business's products may mean that the machine cannot be considered in isolation. Five machines a week may be the optimum level of output if sales were being taken from a rival business or a new market were being created, but possibly not in other circumstances.
- Costs are difficult to estimate.
- Since labour is in short supply, the relevant labour cost should probably include an element for opportunity cost.
- The level of sales is calculated on the assumption that short-run profit maximisation is the goal of the business. Unless this is consistent with wealth enhancement in the longer term, it may not be in the business's best interests.

These points highlight some of the weaknesses of the theoretical approaches to pricing, particularly the fact that costs and demands are difficult to predict. It would be wrong, however, to dismiss the theory. The fact that the theory does not work perfectly in practice does not mean that it cannot offer helpful insights to the nature of markets, how profit relates to volume, and the notion of an optimum level of output.

Full cost (cost-plus) pricing

Now that we have considered pricing theory, let us return to the subject of using full cost as the basis for setting prices. We saw in Chapter 10 that one of the reasons why some businesses deduce full costs is to base selling prices on them. There is a lot of logic in this. If a business charges the full cost of its output as a selling price, the business will, in theory, break even, because the sales revenue will exactly cover all of the costs. Charging something above full cost will yield a profit.

    If a **full cost (cost-plus) pricing** approach is to be taken, the issue that must be addressed is the level of profit that is required from each unit sold. This must logically be based on the total profit that is required for the period. Normally, businesses seek to enhance their wealth through trading. The extent to which they expect to do this is normally related to the amount of wealth that is invested to promote wealth enhancement. Businesses tend to seek to produce a particular percentage increase in wealth. In other words, businesses seek to generate a target return on capital employed. It seems logical, therefore, that the profit loading on full cost should reflect the business's target profit and that the target should itself be based on a target return on capital employed.

ACTIVITY 11.7

A business has just completed a service job whose full cost has been calculated at £112. For the current period, the total costs (direct and indirect) are estimated at £250,000. The profit target for the period is £100,000.

Suggest a selling price for the job.

Activity 11.7 continued

If the profit is to be earned by jobs in proportion to their full cost, then the profit for each pound of full cost must be £0.40 (that is, £100,000/250,000). Thus, the profit on the job must be:

$$£0.40 \times 112 = £44.80$$

This means that the price for the job must be:

$$£112 + £44.80 = £156.80$$

Other ways could be found for apportioning a share of profit to jobs – for example, direct-labour- or machine-hours. Such bases may be preferred where it is believed that these factors are better representatives of effort and, therefore, profitworthiness. It is clearly a matter of judgement as to how profit is apportioned to units of output.

An obvious problem with cost-plus pricing is that the market may not agree with the price. Put another way, cost-plus pricing takes no account of the market demand function (the relationship between price and quantity demanded, which we considered above). A business may fairly deduce the full cost of some product and then add what might be regarded as a reasonable level of profit, only to find that a rival producer is offering a similar product for a much lower price, or that the market simply will not buy at the cost-plus price.

Most suppliers are not strong enough in the market to dictate pricing. Most are 'price takers' not 'price makers'. They must accept the price offered by the market or they do not sell any of their products. Cost-plus pricing may be appropriate for price makers, but it has less relevance for price takers.

Real World 11.3 illustrates how adopting a cost-plus approach to pricing may lead to a situation where falling demand leads to price rises, which, in turn lead to falling demand.

REAL WORLD 11.3

A vicious circle in the library

Librarians have long complained about the price rises of academic journals and Derek Haan chairman and chief executive of Elsevier Science, which publishes more than 1,600 journals, admits that journal price inflation has been a problem for the industry. He says the problem is due to falling subscription numbers as more readers make photocopies or use interlibrary lending. With fewer subscribers to share the cost of each publication, publishers have to increase prices. To stay within budgets, libraries start cancelling titles, which creates a vicious circle of dwindling subscriber numbers, soaring prices and reduced collections.

Source: Based on information from 'Case Study: Elsevier', FT.com, 19 June 2002.

The cost-plus price is not entirely useless to price takers, however. When contemplating entering a market, knowing the cost-plus price will give useful information. It will tell the price taker whether it can profitably enter the market or not. As has been said already in this chapter, the full cost can be seen as a long-run break-even selling price. If entering a market means that this break-even price, plus an acceptable profit, cannot be achieved, then the business should probably stay out. Having a breakdown of the full cost may put the business in a position to examine where costs might be capable of being cut in order to bring the full cost, plus profit within a figure acceptable to the market.

Being a price maker does not always imply that the business dominates a particular market. Many small businesses are, to some extent, price makers. This tends to be where buyers find it difficult to make clear distinctions between the prices offered by various suppliers. An example of this might be a car repair. Though it may be possible to obtain a series of binding estimates for the work from various garages, most people would not normally do so. As a result, garages normally charge cost-plus prices for car repairs.

Real World 11.4 considers the extent to which cost-plus pricing seems to be used in practice.

REAL WORLD 11.4

Cost-plus pricing in practice

The 1999 survey of fairly large UK businesses by Drury and Tayles (see reference 2 at the end of the chapter) revealed that cost-plus pricing is used by 60 per cent of businesses. Of that 60 per cent, not all use it to set the price of all of the business's sales, however. The 60 per cent breaks down as follows:

% of sales accounted for by cost-plus pricing	% of businesses
1 to 20	26
21 to 50	11
51 to 100	<u>23</u>
	<u>60</u>

Thus, for example, 26 per cent of all businesses responding to the survey used a cost-plus approach to pricing for between 1 per cent and 20 per cent of their total sales.

It is difficult to interpret these data to reach a general conclusion, but it is fair to say that cost-plus is an important approach to pricing in the UK.

The 1993 survey by Drury *et al*. (see reference 4) indicated that 39 per cent of respondents used the cost-plus approach to most of their pricing decisions. This might indicate that the cost-plus approach was more popular in 1993 than in 1999, when only 23 per cent of respondents used it for more than 50 per cent of their output.

Relevant/marginal cost pricing

The relevant/marginal-cost approach deduces the minimum price for which the business can offer the product for sale. This minimum price will leave the business better off as a result of making the sale than it would have been by pursuing the next best opportunity instead. We considered the more general approach to relevant-cost pricing in Chapter 8. In Chapter 9, we looked at the more restricted case of relevant cost pricing: **marginal cost pricing**. Here it is assumed that fixed costs will not be affected by the decision to produce and, therefore, only the variable-cost element need be considered.

It would normally be the case that a relevant/marginal cost approach would only be used where there is not the opportunity to sell at a price that will cover the full cost. The business can sell at any price above the marginal cost and still be better off, simply because it happens to find itself in the position that certain costs will be incurred in any case.

ACTIVITY 11.8

A commercial aircraft is due to take off in one hour's time with 20 seats unsold. What is the minimum price at which these seats could be sold such that the airline would be no worse off as a result?

The answer is that any price above the additional cost of one more passenger, caused by people occupying the previously unsold seats, would represent an acceptable minimum. If there are no such costs, the minimum price is zero.

This is not to say that the airline will seek to charge the minimum price; it will presumably seek to charge the highest price that the market will bear. The fact that the market will not bear the full cost, plus a profit margin, should not, in principle, be sufficient for the airline to refuse to sell seats.

Relevant/marginal pricing must be regarded as a short-term approach that can be adopted because a business finds itself in a particular position, for example, having spare aircraft seats. Ultimately, if the business is to be profitable, all costs must be covered by sales revenue.

ACTIVITY 11.9

When we considered marginal costing in Chapter 9, we identified three problems with its use. Can you remember what these problems are?

The three problems are as follows:

● The possibility that spare capacity will be 'sold off' cheaply when there is another potential customer who will offer a higher price, but by which time the capacity will be fully committed. It is a matter of commercial judgement as to how likely this will be. With reference to Activity 11.8, would an hour before take-off be sufficiently close to be fairly confident that no 'normal' passenger will come forward to buy a seat?
● The problem that selling the same product but at different prices could lead to a loss of customer goodwill. Would a 'normal' passenger be happy to be told by another passenger that the latter had bought his or her ticket very cheaply, compared with the normal price?
● If the business is going to suffer continually from being unable to sell its full production potential at the 'regular' price, it might be better, in the long run, to reduce capacity and make fixed-cost savings. Using the spare capacity to produce marginal benefits may lead to the business failing to address this issue. Would it be better for the airline to operate smaller aircraft or to have fewer flights, either of these leading to fixed-cost savings, than to sell off surplus seats at marginal prices?

Real World 11.5 provides an unusual example where humanitarian issues are the driving force for adopting marginal pricing.

REAL WORLD 11.5

Drug prices in developing countries

In recent years, large pharmaceutical businesses based in the West have been under con-siderable pressure to provide cheap drugs to developing countries. It has been suggested that life-saving therapeutic drugs should be sold to these countries at a price that is close to their marginal cost. However, two obstacles to such a pricing policy have been identified:

● Firstly, it may lead to customer revolts in the West (the 'loss of customer goodwill' referred to above).

● Secondly, there is a concern that the drugs may not reach their intended patients and could be re-exported to western countries. A major cost of producing a new drug is the research and development costs incurred and marginal costs of production are usually very low. Thus, a selling price based on marginal cost is likely to be considerably lower than the (full-cost) selling price in the West. This, it is feared, may lead to the cheap drugs provided leaking back into the West. Acquiring drugs at a price near to their marginal cost and reselling them at a figure close to the selling price in the West offers unscrupulous individuals an opportunity to make huge profits.

The above problems are not insurmountable and are not the only problems surrounding this issue, but they do appear to have slowed progress towards a speedier response to a humanitarian crisis.

Source: Based on information from 'Patent nonsense', *Financial Times*, 24 August 2001.

Pricing strategies

Costs and the market-demand function are not the only determinants of price. Businesses often employ pricing strategies that, in the short term, may not maximise profit. They do this in the expectation that they will gain in the long term. An example of such a strategy is **penetration pricing**. Here, the product is sold relatively cheaply in order to sell in quantity and to gain a large share of the market. This would tend to have the effect of dissuading competitors from entering the market. Subsequently, once the business has established itself as the market leader, prices would be raised to more profitable levels. By its nature, penetration pricing would tend to apply to new products.

Price skimming is almost the opposite of penetration pricing. It seeks to exploit the notion that the market can be stratified according to resistance to price. Here a new product is initially priced highly and sold only to those buyers in the stratum that is fairly unconcerned by high prices. Once this stratum of the market is saturated, the price is lowered to attract the next stratum. The price is gradually lowered as each stratum is saturated. This strategy tends only to be able to be employed where there is some significant barrier to entry for other potential suppliers, such as patent protection. Mobile telephones are an example of a price-skimming strategy.

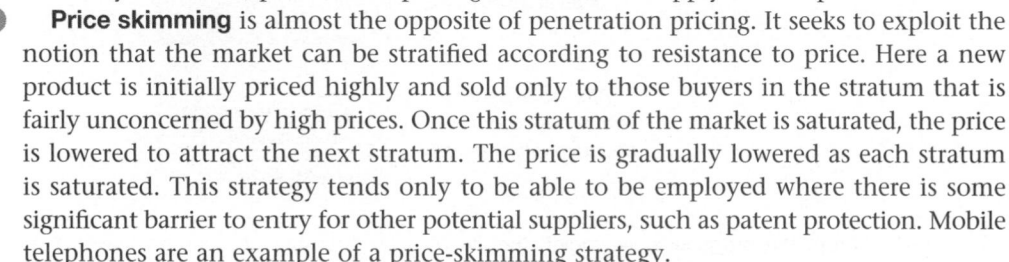

Recent developments in pricing and cost management

The increasingly competitive environment in which modern businesses operate is leading to increased effort being applied in trying to manage costs. Businesses need to keep costs to a minimum so that they can supply goods and services at a price that customers will be prepared to pay and, at the same time, generate a level of profit necessary to meet the businesses' objectives of enhancing shareholder wealth. We shall now outline some techniques that have recently emerged in an attempt to meet these goals of competitiveness and profitability.

Firstly, we need to appreciate that the total life-cycle of a product or service has three phases. These are:

1 The *pre-production phase*. This is the period that precedes production of the product or service for sale. During this phase, research and development – both of the product or service and of the market – is conducted. The product or service is invented/ designed and so is the means of production. The phase culminates with acquiring and setting up the necessary production facilities and with advertising and promotion.

2 The *production phase* comes next, being the one in which the product is made and sold or the service is rendered to customers.

3 The *post-production phase* comes last. During this phase, any costs necessary to correct faults that arose with products or services that have been sold (after-sales service) are incurred. There would also be the costs of closing production at the end of the product's or service's life-cycle, such as the cost of decommissioning production facilities. Since after-sales service will tend to arise from as early as the first product or service being sold and, therefore, well before the last one is sold, this phase would typically overlap the manufacturing/service-rendering phase.

The total life cycle is shown in Figure 11.8.

Figure 11.8 **The total life-cycle of a product or service**

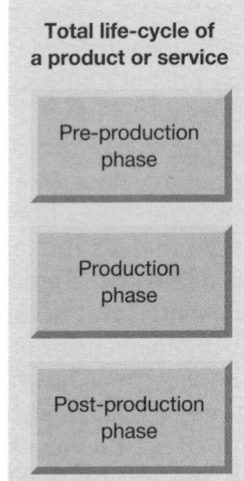

Total life-cycle of a product or service

Research and development, production set-up, pre-production marketing costs → Pre-production phase

Manufacturing and marketing costs → Production phase

After-sales service and production facility decommissioning costs → Post-production phase

From the producer's viewpoint, the life of a product can be seen as having three distinct phases. During the first the product is developed and everything is prepared so that production and marketing can start. Next comes production and sales. Lastly, dealing with post-production activities is undertaken.

Total life-cycle costing

In some types of business, particularly those engaged in an advanced manufacturing environment, it is estimated that a very high proportion (as much as 80 per cent) of the total costs that will be incurred over the total life of a particular product are either incurred or committed at the pre-production phase. For example, a motor car manufacturer, when designing, developing and setting up production of a new model, incurs a high proportion of the total costs that will be incurred on that model during the whole of its life. Not only are pre-production costs specifically incurred during this phase but the need to incur particular costs during the production phase is also established. This is because the design will incorporate features that will lead to particular manufacturing costs. Once the design of the car has been finalised and the manufacturing plant set up, it may be too late to 'design out' a costly feature without incurring another large cost.

ACTIVITY 11.10

A decision taken at the design stage could well commit the business to costs after the manufacture of the product has taken place. Can you suggest a potential cost that could be built in at the design stage that will show itself after the manufacture of the product?

After-sales service costs could be incurred as a result of some design fault. Once the manufacturing facilities have been established, it may not be economic to revise the design but merely to deal with the problem through after-sales service procedures.

Total life-cycle costing seeks to focus management's attention on the fact that it is not just during the production phase that attention needs to be paid to cost management. By the start of the production phase it is too late to try to manage a large element of the product's or service's total life-cycle cost. Efforts need to be made to assess the costs of alternative designs.

There needs to be a review of the product or service over its entire life-cycle, which could be a period of twenty years or more. Traditional management accounting, however, tends to be concerned with assessing performance over periods of just one year or less.

Real World 11.6 provides some idea of the extent to which total life-cycle costing is used in practice.

REAL WORLD 11.6

Total life-cycle costing in practice

A survey of management accounting practice in the US was conducted in 2003. Nearly 2,000 businesses replied to the survey. These tended to be larger businesses, of which about 40 per cent were manufacturers and about 16 per cent financial services; the remainder were across a range of other industries.

The survey revealed that 22 per cent extensively use a total life-cycle approach to cost control, with a further 37 per cent considering using the technique in the future.

Though the survey relates to the US, in the absence of UK evidence, it provides some insight to what is likely also to be practised in the UK and elsewhere in the developed world.

Source: Ernst and Young (see reference 5 at the end of the chapter).

Target costing

With traditional cost-plus pricing, costs are totalled for a product or service and a percentage is added for profit to give a selling price. This, for reasons raised earlier in this chapter, is not a very practical basis on which to price output for many businesses – certainly not those operating in a price-competitive market. The cost-plus price may well be totally unacceptable to the market.

    Target costing approaches the problem from the other direction. First, with the help of market research or other means, a unit selling price and sales volume are established. From the unit selling price is taken an amount for profit. This unit profit figure must be such as to be acceptable to meet the business's profit objective. The resulting figure is the target cost. Efforts are then made to establish a way of providing the service or producing the product that will enable the target cost to be met. This may involve revising the design, finding more efficient means of production or requiring suppliers of goods and services to supply more cheaply.

Target costing is seen as a part of a total life-cycle costing approach, in that cost savings are sought at a very early stage in the life cycle, during the pre-production phase.

Real World 11.7 indicates the level of usage of target costing. This shows quite a low level of usage in both the UK and US. In contrast, survey evidence shows that target costing is very widely used by Japanese manufacturing businesses.

REAL WORLD 11.7

Target costing in practice on both sides of the Atlantic

The ACCA survey suggests that target costing is not much used by UK businesses: 22 per cent of respondents never use this approach and only 26 per cent use it often or always.

Source: Drury *et al*. (see reference 4 at the end of the chapter).

The Ernst and Young survey of management accounting practice in the US, conducted in 2003, revealed that 27 per cent extensively use target costing, with a further 41 per cent considering using the technique in the future.

Source: Ernst and Young (see reference 5 at the end of the chapter).

ACTIVITY 11.11

Though target costing seems effective and has its enthusiasts, some people feel it has its problems. Can you suggest what these problems might be?

There seem to be three main problem areas:

1 It can lead to various conflicts – for example, between the business, its suppliers and its own staff.
2 It can cause a great deal of stress for employees who are trying to meet target costs that are sometimes extremely difficult to meet.
3 Although, in the end, ways may be found to meet a target cost (through product or service redesign, negotiating lower prices with suppliers and so on), the whole process can be very expensive.

Kaizen costing
·······················

 ***Kaizen* costing** is linked to total life-cycle costing and focuses on cost saving during the production phase. Since that is at a relatively late stage in the life-cycle (from a cost control point of view), in the production phase only relatively small cost savings can be made. Also, the major production-phase cost savings should already have been made through target costing. The Japanese word *kaizen* implies 'small changes'.

With *kaizen* costing, efforts are made to reduce the unit manufacturing or service provision cost of the particular product or service under review, if possible taking it below the unit cost in the previous period. Target percentage reductions can be set. Usually, production workers are encouraged to identify ways of reducing costs. This is something that the 'hands on' experience of those workers may enable them to do. Even though the scope to reduce costs is limited at the production stage, valuable savings can still be made.

Value chain analysis
·······························

Another approach that seeks cost control and recognises the total life-cycle concept is **value chain analysis**. The value chain is the linking sequence of activities, through the three phases of the product life-cycle (see Figure 11.8) from research and development to after-sales activities. In a wealth-seeking business, the objective for the product is that it should create value for the business and its owners. Each link in the value chain represents a particular activity. All of the activities will lead to a cost. Ideally, each link should add value to the product, making the product more valuable to the customer. Any links in the chain that fail to add value should be examined very critically. The objective of this examination is to assess whether the particular link could be eliminated completely or, at least, have its cost reduced.

An example of a typical non-value-added activity is inspection of the completed product or service by a quality controller. This activity does not add value to the product or service, yet it adds cost. This inspection cost might well be capable of being reduced, or even completely eliminated. The introduction of a 'quality' culture in the business could lead to all output being reliable and not needing to be inspected. This is a development that many modern businesses have achieved.

An example of a value-added activity would be the rendering of a service to a customer, for which the customer is prepared to pay more than it cost.

Real World 11.8 gives some indication of the extent that value chain analysis is used in practice.

REAL WORLD 11.8

Value chain analysis in practice

The Ernst and Young survey of management accounting practice in the US, conducted in 2003, revealed that 27 per cent extensively use value chain analysis, with a further 47 per cent considering using the technique in the future.

Source: Ernst and Young (see reference 5 at the end of the chapter).

Real World 11.9 reveals how the elimination of non-value-creating activities may lead to a transformation in the nature of the business.

REAL WORLD 11.9

Driving in a different direction

In the US, the big three car makers, General Motor, Ford and Chrysler, have suffered from intense competition for market share. They have responded by re-examining all aspects of their business in order to save costs and to eliminate non-value-creating activities. They have standardised components across vehicle platforms and brands and have streamlined their purchasing systems so that they deal with fewer suppliers. In the future, they are expected to collaborate strongly with key suppliers over the engineering aspects of cars to explore whether further costs may be saved. It is predicted that this will lead to greater pressure for suppliers to assume responsibility for engineering. This part of the car makers' task will be passed down the 'value chain' so that, ultimately, car makers may simply market and design cars.

Source: Based on information from 'Parts companies feel knock-on effect', FT.com, 4 March 2003.

Benchmarking

→ **Benchmarking** is an activity – usually a continuing one – where a business, or one of its divisions, seeks to emulate a successful business or division and so achieve a similar level of success. The successful business or division provides a benchmark against which the business can measure its own performance, as well as examples of approaches that can lead to success. Sometimes the benchmark business will help with the activity, but even where no co-operation is given, outside observers can still learn quite a lot about what makes that business successful.

Real Worlds **11.10** and **11.11** outline the use of benchmarking in practice in the UK.

REAL WORLD 11.10

Benchmarking in local government

The Audit Commission is a public body that has a statutory right to investigate public-sector organisations and report on the extent to which those organisations provide value for money to the public.

In the context of local government, the Commission sees benchmarking as one way of assessing value for money. It has been doing this since the 1980s, and so while benchmarking may be seen as a recent innovation in the private sector, it has a fairly long history in the public sector.

Since the Commission has legal powers, it has been able to insist that the various local government authorities provide information to enable a comprehensive benchmarking operation to take place. Contrast this with the private sector where benchmarking between businesses is difficult because there is no compulsion. Businesses are reluctant to divulge commercially sensitive information to other businesses with which they may be in competition. Often, the best that can be achieved in the private sector is for businesses to benchmark internally, with one division or department comparing itself with another part of the same business.

REAL WORLD 11.11

A new look at benchmarking

New Look plc is a large womenswear retail chain, with branches in the UK and in Europe. The annual report for 2002/3 describes how the business was able to reduce its cost of sales to sales ratio from 43 per cent to 41 per cent (gross profit margin of 59 per cent). This was achieved by benchmarking against, what the business regards as, the standard of the better businesses in the industry. This 'world class standard', the business believes, is a 38 per cent ratio.

Source: New Look Group plc, Annual Report 2003, p. 6.

Real World 11.12 gives an indication of the extent to which benchmarking is used in practice.

REAL WORLD 11.12

Benchmarking in practice

The Ernst and Young survey of management accounting practice in the US, conducted in 2003, revealed that 53 per cent benchmark extensively, with a further 36 per cent considering using the technique in the future.

Source: Ernst and Young (see reference 5 at the end of the chapter).

Non-financial measures of performance

Financial measures have long been regarded as the most important measures for a business. They provide us with a valuable means of summarising and evaluating business achievement, and there is no serious doubt about the continued importance of financial measures in this role. However, in recent years there has been increasing recognition that financial measures alone will not provide managers with the information that they require to manage a business effectively. Non-financial measures should also be used to help gain a deeper understanding of the business and to achieve business objectives.

Financial measures portray various aspects of business achievement (for example, sales, profits, return on capital employed and so on) that can help managers determine whether the business is increasing the wealth of its owners. This is vital in an increasingly competitive environment, but managers also need to understand what particular things drive the creation of wealth. These **value drivers**, as they are often called, may be such things as employee satisfaction, customer loyalty and the level of product innovation. Often, they do not lend themselves to financial measurement. Non-financial measures may be used to arrive at some indirect means of assessment, however.

ACTIVITY 11.12

How might we measure the following?

(a) Employee satisfaction.
(b) Customer loyalty.
(c) The level of product innovation.

....

(a) *Employee satisfaction* may be measured through the use of an employee survey. This could examine attitudes towards various aspects of the job, the degree of autonomy that is permitted, the level of recognition and reward received, the level of participation in decision making, the degree of support received in carrying out tasks and so on. Less direct measures of satisfaction may include employee turnover rates and employee productivity; however, other factors may have a significant influence on these measures.

(b) *Customer loyalty* may be measured through the proportion of total sales generated from existing customers, the number of repeat sales made to customers, the percentage of customers renewing subscriptions or other contracts, and so on.

(c) *The level of product innovation* may be measured through the number of innovations during a period compared with those of competitors, the percentage of sales attributable to recent product innovations, the number of innovations that are brought successfully to market and so on.

Real World 11.13 gives an example of a very well known international business that focuses a lot of attention on non-financial measures.

REAL WORLD 11.13

Non-financial measures at Pepsi

Pepsi Cola attaches considerable importance to non-financial measures when assessing the success of the business. This is reflected in the fact that managers' bonuses are linked to meeting targets based on non-financial measures, as well as more conventional financial measures. The non-financial measures include:

● market-oriented measures, based on quality, customer attitudes and market share (known as marketplace profit and loss account); and

● employee motivation, based on regular surveys.

Source: Based on information from 'The marketing route to value', *Financial Times*, 14 October 2002.

It has been argued that financial measures are normally 'lag' indicators, in that they tell us about outcomes. In other words, they measure the consequences arising from management decisions that were made earlier. Non-financial measures can also be used as lag indicators of course. They can, however, also be used as 'lead' indicators by focusing on those things that drive the creation of wealth. It is argued that if we measure changes in these value drivers, we may be able to predict changes in future financial performance. For example, we may find from experience that if, during a particular period, there is a 10 per cent fall in the level of product innovation, this will lead to a 20 per cent fall in sales over the following three periods. In this case, the levels of product innovation can be regarded as a lead indicator that can alert managers to a future decline in sales unless corrective action is taken.

The Balanced Scorecard

One of the most impressive, and widely used, attempts to integrate the use of financial and non-financial measures has been the **Balanced Scorecard**, which was developed by Robert Kaplan and David Norton. The Balanced Scorecard is really a framework that translates the aims and objectives of a business into a series of key performance measures and targets. This framework should make the strategy of the business clearer and more easily communicated to employees. It should also help managers to assess the extent to which the objectives of the business are being fulfilled.

The Balanced Scorecard involves setting objectives and developing appropriate measures and targets in four main areas:

1 *Financial*. This area will specify the financial returns required by shareholders and may involve the use of financial measures such as return on capital employed, net profit margin, percentage sales growth and so on.
2 *Customer*. This area will specify the kind of customer and/or markets the business wishes to service and will establish appropriate measures such as customer satisfaction, new customer growth levels and so on.
3 *Internal business process*. This area will specify those business processes (for example, innovation, types of operation and after-sales service) that are important to the success of the business. It will also establish appropriate measures such as percentage of sales from new products, time to market for new products, product cycle times and speed of response to customer complaints.
4 *Learning and growth*. This area will specify the kind of people, the systems and the procedures that are necessary to deliver long-term business growth. This area is often the most difficult for the development of appropriate measures, however, examples of measures may include employee motivation, employee skills profiles, information systems capabilities and so on.

These four areas are shown in Figure 11.9.

The Balanced Scorecard approach does not prescribe the particular objectives, measures or targets that a business should adopt. This is a matter for the individual business to determine. It simply sets out the framework for developing a coherent set of objectives for the business and ensuring that they are then pursued in a systematic manner.

According to Kaplan and Norton (see reference 6 at the end of the chapter), this framework is referred to as a *Balanced* Scorecard because it aims to strike a balance between external measures relating to customers and shareholders, and internal measures relating to internal business process and learning and growth. It also aims to strike a balance between the measures that portray outcomes (lag indicators) and measures that help predict future performance (lead indicators). Finally, the framework aims to strike a balance between 'hard' financial measures and 'soft' non-financial measures.

Real World 11.14 shows how the Balanced Scorecard is used by one very well-known UK business.

Figure 11.9	The Balanced Scorecard, for translating a strategy into operational processes

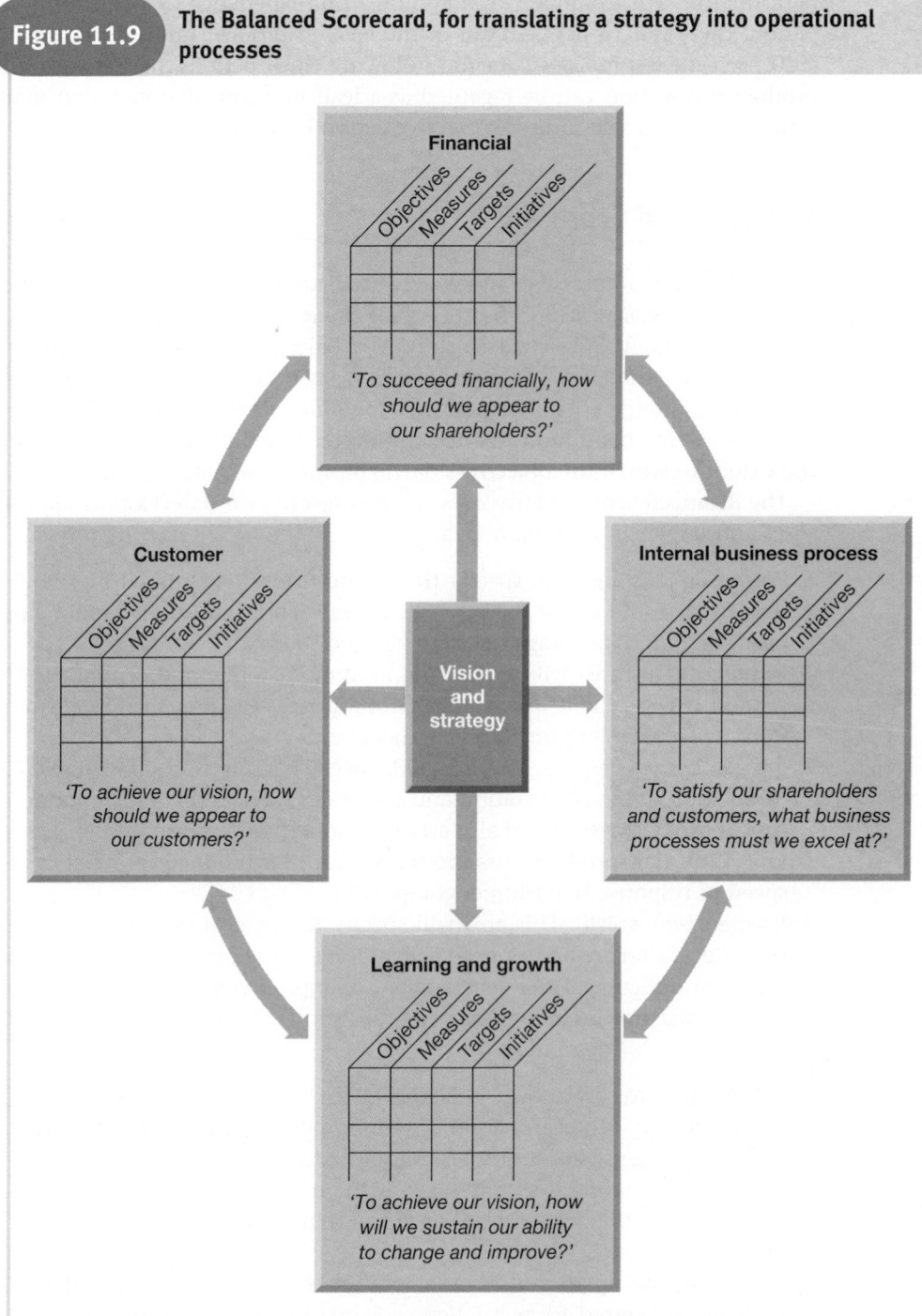

There are four main areas covered by the Balanced Scorecard. Note that, for each area, a fundamental question must be addressed. By answering this question, managers should be able to develop the key objectives of the business. Once this has been done, suitable measures and targets can be developed that are relevant to those objectives. Finally, appropriate management initiatives will be developed to achieve the targets set.

Source: Kaplan and Norton (see reference 6 at the end of the chapter).

REAL WORLD 11.14

The Balanced Scorecard at Tesco

Tesco plc, the major supermarket chain, said in its 2003 annual report:

> The Steering Wheel is the term used to describe our balanced scorecard approach, which we believe is the best way to achieve results for our shareholders. It sets out a broad range of targets under quadrant headings of customers, operations, people and finance. This allows the business to be operated and monitored on a balanced basis with due regard for all stakeholders. The Board undertakes a formal review of progress on a quarterly basis and any resulting actions considered appropriate are communicated throughout the business.

Source: Tesco plc, Annual Report 2003, p. 8.

Real World 11.15 provides an indication of the extent that the Balanced Scorecard is applied in practice.

REAL WORLD 11.15

The Balanced Scorecard in practice

The Ernst and Young survey of management accounting practice in the US, conducted in 2003, revealed that 43 per cent employ a balanced scorecard approach, with a further 40 per cent considering using the technique in the future.

Source: Ernst and Young (see reference 5 at the end of the chapter).

As a footnote to our consideration of the Balanced Scorecard, **Real World 11.16** provides an interesting analogy with aeroplane pilots limiting themselves to just one control device.

(UN)REAL WORLD 11.16

Flying blind

Kaplan and Norton invite us to imagine the following conversation with the pilot of a jet aeroplane on entering the cockpit:

Q: I'm surprised to see you operating the plane with only a single instrument. What does it measure?

A: Airspeed. I'm really working on airspeed this flight.

Q: That's good. Airspeed certainly seems important. But what about altitude, wouldn't an altimeter be helpful?

A: I worked on altitude for the last few flights and I've gotten pretty good at it. Now I have to concentrate on proper airspeed.

Q: But I notice you don't even have a fuel gauge. Wouldn't that be useful?

A: You're right; fuel is significant, but I can't concentrate on doing too many things well at the same time. So on this flight I'm focusing on airspeed. Once I get to be excellent at airspeed, as well as altitude, I intend to concentrate on fuel consumption on the next set of flights.

Source: Kaplan and Norton (see reference 6 at the end of the chapter).

The point they are trying to make (apart from warning us against flying with a pilot like this!) is that, to fly a complex machine like an aeroplane, a wide range of instruments is required. A business, however, can be even more complex to navigate than an aeroplane, so a wide range of measures, both financial and non-financial, is necessary.

The quest for shareholder value

Many leading businesses now claim that the quest for shareholder value is the driving force behind their strategic and operational decisions. In simple terms, this means that they are committed to putting the needs of shareholders at the heart of management decisions. It is argued that shareholders invest in a business with a view to maximising their financial returns in relation to the risks that they are prepared to take. As managers are appointed by the shareholders to act on their behalf, management decisions and actions should therefore reflect a concern for maximising shareholder returns. Though the business may have other 'stakeholder' groups, such as employees, customers and suppliers, the shareholders should be seen as the most important group.

This, of course, is not a new idea. As we discussed in Chapter 1, maximising shareholder returns is assumed to be the key objective of a business. However, not everyone accepts this idea. Some believe that a balance must be struck between the competing claims of the various stakeholders. What we can say, however, is that changes in the economic environment over recent years have often forced managers to focus their attention on the needs of shareholders.

In the past, shareholders have been accused of being too passive and of accepting too readily the profits and dividends that managers have delivered. However, this has changed. Now, shareholders are much more assertive, and, as owners of the business, are in a position to insist that their needs are given priority. Since the 1980s we have witnessed the deregulation and globalisation of business, as well as enormous changes in technology. The effect has been to create a much more competitive world. This has meant not only competition for products and services but also competition for funds. Businesses must now compete more strongly for shareholder funds and so must offer competitive rates of return.

Thus, self-interest may be the most powerful reason for managers to commit themselves to maximising shareholder returns. If they do not do this, there is a real risk that shareholders will either replace them with managers who will do so, or shareholders may allow the business to be taken over by another business, which has managers who are dedicated to maximising shareholder returns. In either case, the situation of the business's managers will be threatened.

Creating shareholder value

Creating shareholder value involves a four-stage process:

1 Set objectives for the business that recognise the central importance of maximising shareholder returns. This will set a clear direction for the business.
2 Establish an appropriate means of measuring the returns, or value, that have been generated for shareholders. For reasons that we shall discuss later, the traditional methods of measuring returns to shareholders are inadequate for this purpose.

3 Manage the business in such a manner as to ensure that shareholder returns are maximised. This means:
   (a) setting demanding targets and then achieving them through the best possible use of resources;
   (b) the use of incentive systems; and
   (c) embedding the shareholder value culture throughout the business.
4 Measure the shareholder returns over a period of time to see whether the objectives have actually been achieved.

Figure 11.10 shows the shareholder value creation process.

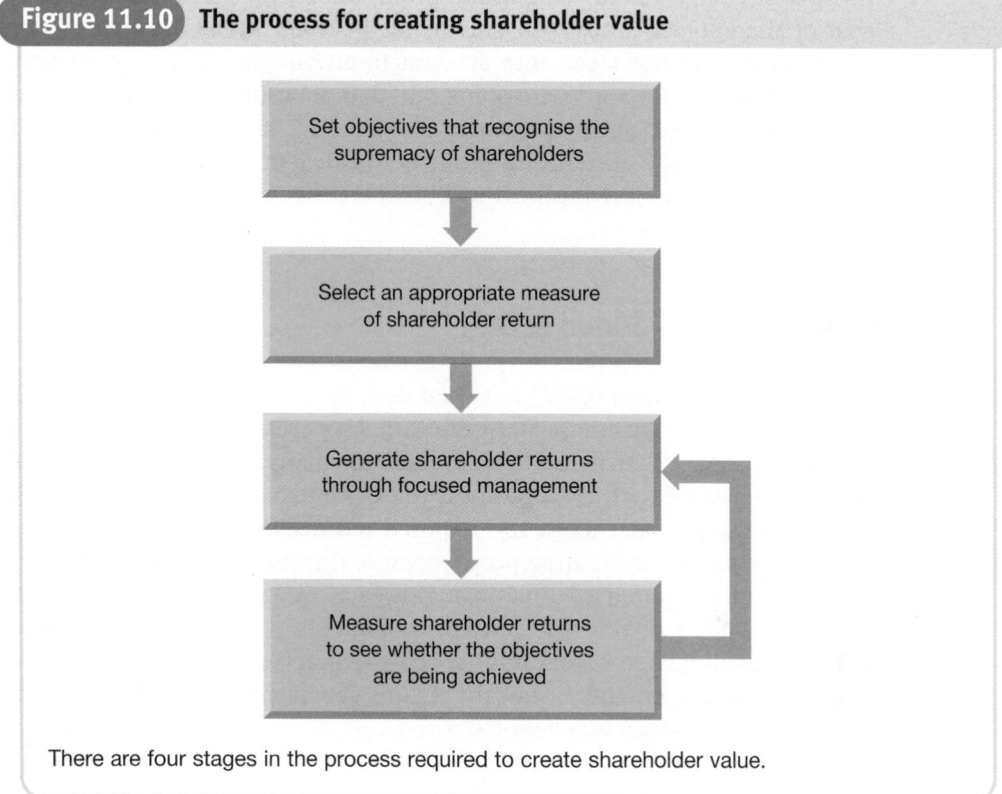

Figure 11.10 The process for creating shareholder value

There are four stages in the process required to create shareholder value.

The need for new forms of measurement

Given a commitment to maximise shareholder returns, we must select an appropriate measure that will help us assess the returns to shareholders over time. It is argued that the traditional methods for measuring shareholder returns are seriously flawed and so should not be used for this purpose.

ACTIVITY 11.13

What are the traditional methods of measuring shareholder returns?

The traditional approach is to use accounting profit or some ratio that is based on accounting profit, such as return on shareholders' funds or earnings per share.

One problem which arises with conventional methods of measuring shareholder returns is that risk is ignored. A fundamental principle in finance is that there is a clear relationship between the level of returns achieved and the level of risk that must be taken to achieve those returns. The higher the level of returns required, the higher the level of risk that must be taken to achieve the returns. A management strategy which produces an increase in profits can reduce shareholder value if the increase in profits is achieved by taking on high-risk activities. Profit alone is not enough.

A second problem with the use of profit, or a ratio based on profit, is that it does not take account of all of the costs of the capital invested by the business. The conventional approach to measuring profit takes account of the cost of loan capital (that is, interest charges) in arriving at net profit, but there is no similar deduction for the cost of shareholder funds. (Any dividends payable, which are part of the return to shareholders, are not taken into account in arriving at the net profit figure.) Critics of the conventional approach point out that a business will not make a profit, in an economic sense, unless it covers the cost of all capital invested, including shareholder funds. If the accounting profit is insufficient to cover the cost of using the shareholders' funds, the business will be operating at a loss and so shareholder value will be reduced.

Economic value added (EVA®)

Economic value added (EVA®) has been developed and trademarked by a US management consultancy business, Stern Stewart. However, EVA® is based on the idea of 'economic profit', which has been around for many years. The measure reflects the point made above that, for a business to be profitable in an economic sense, it must generate returns that exceed the required returns from investors. It is not enough simply to make an accounting profit, because this measure does not take full account of the returns required by investors. However, by taking account of these required returns, the level of risk associated with business operations is considered, because higher risk will lead to higher returns being required by shareholders.

EVA® indicates whether or not the returns generated exceed the required returns by investors. The formula is as follows:

$$\text{EVA}^{\circledR} = \text{NOPAT} - (R \times C)$$

where:
NOPAT = Net operating profit after tax
     R = Required returns of investors
     C = Capital invested (that is, the net assets of the business)

Only when EVA® is positive can we say that the business is increasing shareholder wealth. To maximise shareholder wealth, managers must increase EVA® by as much as possible.

ACTIVITY 11.14

Can you suggest how managers might be able to increase EVA®?
(*Hint*: Use the formula shown above as your starting point.)

The formula suggests that in order to increase EVA® managers may try to:

● Increase NOPAT. This may be done by either reducing expenses or increasing sales.
● Use capital invested more efficiently. This means selling off any assets that are not generating adequate returns and investing in assets that are generating a satisfactory NOPAT.
● Reduce the required rates of return for investors. This may be achieved by changing the capital structure by increasing the proportion of loan capital (which tends to be cheaper to service than share capital). However, this strategy can create problems.

EVA® relies on conventional financial statements (the profit and loss account (income statement) and balance sheet) to measure the wealth created for shareholders. However, the NOPAT and capital figures shown on these statements are used only as a starting point. They have to be adjusted because of the problems and limitations of conventional measures. According to Stern Stewart, the major problem is that profit and capital tend to be understated. This is caused by the conservative bias in accounting measurement. Profit is understated as a result of judgemental 'expenses' such as goodwill written off, research and development expenditure written off and as a result of excessive provisions being created (such as a provision for doubtful debts). Capital is understated because assets are reported at their original cost (less amounts written off for depreciation), which can produce figures considerably below current market values. In addition, certain assets, such as internally generated goodwill and brand names, are omitted from the financial statements because no external transactions have occurred.

Stern Stewart has identified more than 100 adjustments that could be made to the conventional financial statements to eliminate the conservative bias. However, it is believed that, in practice, only a handful of adjustments will usually have to be made to the accounting figures of any particular business. Unless an adjustment is going to have a significant effect on the calculation of EVA®, it is really not worth making. The adjustments made should reflect the nature of the particular business. Each business is unique and so must customise the calculation of EVA® to its particular circumstances. (This aspect of EVA® can be seen as either indicating flexibility or as being open to manipulation depending on whether or not we support the use of this measure!)

EVA® has now taken root throughout the world, particularly in the US and in Europe. A number of large businesses including Coca-Cola, Monsanto, Tate and Lyle, the Burton Group and Pirelli now adopt this measure to assess performance. **Real World 11.17** gives some examples of recent values added by some well-known businesses.

REAL WORLD 11.17

Measuring EVA®

Each year, Stern Stewart measures the economic value added (or destroyed) by large US businesses and publishes this information on its website. Below are the EVA® measures for some well-known businesses for 2002:

	EVA® $m
Microsoft Corporation	2,201
Wal-Mart Stores	2,928
IBM	(8,032)
Exxon Mobil	(2,175)
Coca-Cola Co.	2,496
Dell Computer Corporation	360

→

Real World 11.17 continued

We can see that, in two cases, there is a significant loss of shareholder value for the year. It is interesting to note that, for both of these businesses, the net operating profit after tax expressed as a percentage of average capital employed for the year is positive (3.7 per cent for IBM and 6.6 per cent for Exxon Mobil). Based on this information alone, it may therefore appear that these two businesses created value for their shareholders. However, when EVA® is used, a large loss of economic value is revealed. This apparent anomaly can be explained by the fact that EVA® also takes account of the required rates of return from investors, and, therefore risk.

Source: www.eva.com, Stern Stewart and Co.

Real World 11.18 provides an example of the use of EVA® by a well-known German business in an attempt to generate shareholder value.

 **REAL WORLD 11.18**

VW changes gear

Following a change in top management, the German car maker VW has begun to focus more attention on controlling its capital spending. In particular, research and development expenditure is seen as a key area to be contained. The size of the problem is partly illustrated by the fact that the first-half-year results for 2003 showed that the cash flow from auto operations was €1bn less than needed to cover the €3.9bn of investment and research and development expenditure. In the drive to contain capital spending, performance measures such as return on sales are being abandoned in favour of performance measures that focus on the profitable use of capital. One effect of this change is that bonuses of managers are to be linked to EVA® to encourage them to reduce their capital requirements.

Source: Based on 'VW signals passing of the age of engineers', FT.com, 7 September 2003.

Real World 11.19 gives some indication of the extent of the usage of value-based management (of which EVA® is an example) in the US.

 **REAL WORLD 11.19**

The extent of the use of value-based management in practice

The Ernst and Young survey of management accounting practice in the US, conducted in 2003, revealed that 52 per cent use value-based management, with a further 40 per cent considering using this approach in the future.

Source: Ernst and Young (see reference 5 at the end of the chapter).

The main points of this chapter may be summarised as follows:

Activity based costing = an approach to dealing with overheads (in full costing) that treats all costs as being caused or 'driven' by activities. Advocates argue that it is more relevant to the modern commercial environment than is the traditional approach

- Identification of the cost drivers can lead to more relevant indirect cost treatment in full costing.
- Critics argue that ABC is time consuming and expensive to apply – not justified by the possible improvement in the quality of information.

Pricing output

- In theory, profit is maximised where the price is such that:

  Marginal sales revenue = Marginal cost of production

- Elasticity of demand indicates the sensitivity of demand to price changes.
- Full cost (cost-plus) pricing, takes the full cost and adds a mark up for profit.
  - Popular.
  - The market may not accept the price (most businesses are 'price takers').
  - Can provide a useful benchmark.
- Relevant/marginal cost pricing, takes the marginal/relevant cost and adds a mark-up for profit.
  - Can be useful in the short term, but in the longer term it may be better to charge a full cost plus price.
- Various pricing strategies can be used, including:
  - penetration pricing;
  - price skimming;

Total life-cycle costing = taking account of all of the costs incurred over a product's entire life

- The life cycle of a product can be broken down into three phases: pre-production, production and post-production.
  - A high proportion of costs incurred and/or committed during the pre-production phase.
- Target costing = attempting to reduce costs so that the market price covers the cost plus an acceptable profit.
- Kaizen costing = attempting to reduce costs at the production stage, but since most costs will have been saved at the pre-production phase and through target costing, only small cost savings are likely to be possible.
- Value chain analysis = analysing the various activities in the product life-cycle. By distinguishing between activities that add value and those that do not, it may be possible to save costs by eliminating or reducing the cost of the non-value-added ones.
- Benchmarking = attempting to emulate a successful aspect of, for example, another business or division.

Balanced Scorecard = a management tool that attempts to integrate financial and non-financial measures to give a balanced approach to the pursuit of key performance indicators

● Four areas: financial, customer, internal business process and learning and growth:
  – Encourages a balanced approach to managing the business.
  – Seems to be used effectively in practice.

Economic value added = a means of measuring whether the returns generated by the business exceed the required returns from investors

● EVA® = NOPAT – ($R \times C$)
where:
NOPAT = Net operating profit after tax
R = Required returns from investors
C = Capital invested (that is, the net assets of the business)

 Key terms

activity-based costing (ABC) p. 350	total life-cycle costing p. 369
cost driver p. 350	target costing p. 370
cost pool p. 350	*kaizen* costing p. 371
elasticity of demand p. 357	value chain analysis p. 371
full cost (cost-plus) pricing p. 363	benchmarking p. 372
marginal cost pricing p. 365	value driver p. 373
penetration pricing p. 367	Balanced Scorecard p. 375
price skimming p. 367	economic value added (EVA®) p. 380

Further reading

If you would like to explore the topics covered in this chapter in more depth, we recommend the following books:

Management and Cost Accounting, Drury C., 5th edn, Thomson Learning Business Press, 2000, chapters 10, 11 and 23.

Cost Accounting: A managerial emphasis, Horngren C., Foster G. and Datar S., 11th edn, Prentice Hall International, 2002, chapters 5, 12 and 13.

Cost and Management Accounting, Williamson D., Prentice Hall International, 1996, chapters 7, 13 and 20.

Management Accounting, Atkinson A., Banker R., Kaplan R. and Young S.M., 3rd edn, Prentice Hall, 2001, chapters 5, 7 and 9.

The EVA Challenge, Stern J. and Shelly J., John Wiley, 2001.

References

1 **Activity Based Costing – A review with case studies**, *Innes J. and Mitchell F.*, CIMA Publishing, 1990.

2 **Cost Systems Design and Profitability Analysis in UK Companies**, *Drury C. and Tayles M.*, CIMA Publishing, 2000.

3 'Activity-based costing in the UK's largest companies', *Innes J., Mitchell F. and Sinclair D.*, in **Management Accounting Research**, Vol. 11, No. 3, 2000.

4 **A Survey of Management Accounting Practices in UK Manufacturing Companies**, *Drury C., Braund S., Osborne P. and Tayles M.*, Chartered Association of Certified Accountants, 1993.

5 **2003 Survey of Management Accounting**, *Ernst and Young*, Ernst and Young, 2003.

6 **The Balanced Scorecard**, *Kaplan R. and Norton D.*, Harvard Business School Press, 1996.

REVIEW QUESTIONS

Answers to these questions can be found on the students' side of the Companion Website at www.pearsoned.co.uk/atrillmclaney.

11.1 How does activity-based costing differ from the traditional approach? What is the underlying difference in the philosophy of each of them?

11.2 The use of activity-based costing in helping to deduce full costs has been criticised. What has tended to be the basis of this criticism?

11.3 What is meant by elasticity of demand? How does knowledge of the elasticity of demand affect pricing decisions?

11.4 According to economic theory, at what point is profit maximised? Why is it at this point?

EXERCISES

Exercises 11.6 to 11.8 are more advanced than 11.1 to 11.5. Those with coloured numbers have answers at the back of the book.

11.1 Woodner Ltd provides a standard service. It is able to provide a maximum of 100 units of this service each week. Experience shows that at a price of £100, no unit of the service would be sold. For every £5 below this price, the business is able to sell 10 more units. For example, at a price of £95, 10 units would be sold, at £90, 20 units would be sold, and so on. The business's fixed costs total £2,500 a week. Variable costs are £20 a unit over the entire range of possible output. The market is such that it is not feasible to charge different prices to different customers.

Required:
What is the most profitable level of output of the service?

11.2 It appears from research evidence that a cost-plus approach influences pricing decisions in practice. What is meant by cost-plus pricing and what are the problems of using this approach?

11.3 Kaplan plc makes a range of suitcases of various sizes and shapes. There are 10 different models of suitcase produced by the business. In order to keep stocks (inventories) of finished suitcases to a minimum, each model is made in a small batch. Each batch is costed as a separate job and the cost for each suitcase deduced by dividing the batch cost by the number of suitcases in the batch.

At present, the business derives the cost of each batch using a traditional job-costing approach. Recently, however, a new management accountant was appointed, who is advocating the use of activity-based costing (ABC) to deduce the cost of the batches. The management accountant claims that ABC leads to much more reliable and relevant costs and that it has other benefits.

Required:
(a) Explain how the business deduces the cost of each suitcase at present.
(b) Discuss the purposes to which the knowledge of the cost for each suitcase, deduced on a traditional basis, can be put and how valid the cost is for the purpose concerned.

(c) Explain how ABC could be applied to costing the suitcases, highlighting the differences between ABC and the traditional approach.

(d) Explain what advantages the new management accountant probably believes ABC to have over the traditional approach.

11.4 Comment critically on the following statements that you have overheard:

(a) 'To maximise profit you need to sell your output at the highest price.'

(b) 'Elasticity of demand deals with the extent to which costs increase as demand increases.'

(c) 'Provided that the price is large enough to cover the marginal cost of production, the sale should be made.'

(d) 'According to economic theory, profit is maximised where total cost equals total revenue.'

(e) 'Price skimming is charging low prices for the output until you have a good share of the market, and then putting up your prices.'

Explain clearly all technical terms.

11.5 Comment critically on the following statements that you have overheard:

(a) 'Direct-labour-hours are the most appropriate basis to use to charge overheads to jobs in the modern manufacturing environment where people are so important.'

(b) 'Activity-based costing is a means of more accurately accounting for direct labour cost.'

(c) 'Activity-based costing cannot really be applied to the service sector because the "activities" that it seeks to analyse tend to be related to manufacturing.'

(d) '*Kaizen* costing is an approach where great efforts are made to reduce the costs of developing a new product and setting up its production processes.'

(e) 'Benchmarking is an approach to job costing where each direct worker keeps a record of the time spent on each job on his or her workbench before it is passed on to the next direct worker or into finished stock stores.'

11.6 The GB Company manufactures a variety of electric motors. The business is currently operating at about 70% of capacity and is earning a satisfactory return on investment.

The management of GB has been approached by International Industries (II) with an offer to buy 120,000 units of an electric motor. II manufactures a motor that is almost identical to GB's motor, but a fire at the II plant has shut down its manufacturing operations. II needs the 120,000 motors over the next four months to meet commitments to its regular customers; II is prepared to pay £19 each for the motors, which it will collect from the GB plant.

GB's product cost, based on current planned cost for the motor is:

	£
Direct materials	5.00
Direct labour (variable)	6.00
Manufacturing overhead	9.00
Total	20.00

Manufacturing overhead is applied to production at the rate of £18.00 a direct-labour-hour. This overhead rate is made up of the following components:

	£
Variable factory overhead	6.00
Fixed factory overhead – direct	8.00
– allocated	4.00
Applied manufacturing overhead rate	18.00

Additional costs usually incurred in connection with sales of electric motors include sales commissions of 5% and freight expense of £1.00 a unit.

In determining selling prices, GB adds a 40% mark-up to product costs. This provides a suggested selling price of £28 for the motor. The marketing department, however, has set the current selling price at £27.00 to maintain market share. The order would, however, require additional fixed factory overhead of £15,000 a month in the form of supervision and clerical costs. If management accepts the order, 30,000 motors will be manufactured and delivered to II each month for the next four months.

Required:

(a) Prepare a financial evaluation showing the impact of accepting the Industrial Industries order. What is the minimum unit price that the business's management could accept without reducing its operating profit?

(b) State clearly any assumptions contained in the analysis of (a) above and discuss any other organisational or strategic factors that GB should consider.

11.7 Sillycon Ltd is a business engaged in the development of new products in the electronics industry. Subtotals on the spreadsheet of planned overheads reveal:

	Electronics department	Testing department	Service department
Overheads – variable (£000)	1,200	600	700
– fixed (£000)	2,000	500	800
Planned activity: Direct-labour-hours ('000)	800	600	–

For the purposes of reallocation of service department's overheads, it is agreed that variable overheads vary with the direct-labour-hours worked in each department. Fixed overheads of the service department are to be reallocated on the basis of maximum practical capacity of the two departments, which is the same for each.

The business has a long-standing practice of marking up full manufacturing costs by between 25% and 35% to establish selling prices.

One new product, which is in a final development stage, is hoped to offer some improvement over competitors' products, which are currently marketed at between £110 and £130 each. Product development engineers have determined that the direct material content is £7 a unit. The product will take 4 labour-hours in the electronics department and 3 hours in testing. Hourly labour rates are £10 and £6, respectively.

Management estimates that the fixed costs that would be specifically incurred in relation to the product are: supervision £13,000, depreciation of a recently acquired machine £100,000 and advertising £37,000 a year. These fixed costs are included in the table given above.

Market research indicates that the business could expect to obtain and hold about 25% of the market or, optimistically, 30%. The total market is estimated at 20,000 units.

Note: It may be assumed that the existing plan has been prepared to cater for a range of products and no single product decision will cause the business to amend it.

Required:

(a) Prepare a summary of information that would help with the pricing decision. Such information should include marginal cost and full cost implications after allocation of service department overheads.

(b) Explain and elaborate on the information prepared.

11.8 A business manufactures refrigerators for domestic use. There are three models: Lo, Mid and Hi. The models, their quality and their price are aimed at different markets.

Product costs are computed on a blanket overhead-rate basis using a labour-hour method. Prices as a general rule are set based on cost plus 20 per cent. The following information is provided about next year:

	Lo	Mid	Hi
Material cost (£/unit)	25	62.5	105
Direct-labour-hours (per unit)	$1/2$	1	1
Planned production/sales (units)	20,000	1,000	10,000

The planned overheads for the business for next year amount to £4,410,000. Direct labour is costed at £8 an hour.

The business is currently facing increasing competition, especially from imported goods. As a result, the selling price of Lo has been reduced to a level that produces very little profit margin. To address this problem, an activity-based costing approach has been suggested. The overheads are examined and these are grouped round main business activities of machining (£2,780,000), logistics (£590,000) and establishment (£1,040,000) costs. It is maintained that these costs could be allocated based respectively on cost drivers of machine-hours, material orders and space, to reflect the use of resources in each of these areas. After analysis, the following proportionate statistics are available related to the total volume of products:

	Lo %	Mid %	Hi %
Machine-hours	40	15	45
Material orders	47	6	47
Space	42	18	40

Required:
(a) Calculate for each product the full cost and selling price determined by:
   (i) The original costing method.
   (ii) The activity-based costing method.
(b) What are the implications of the two systems of costing in the situation given?
(c) What business/strategic options exist for the business in the light of the new information?

CHAPTER 12

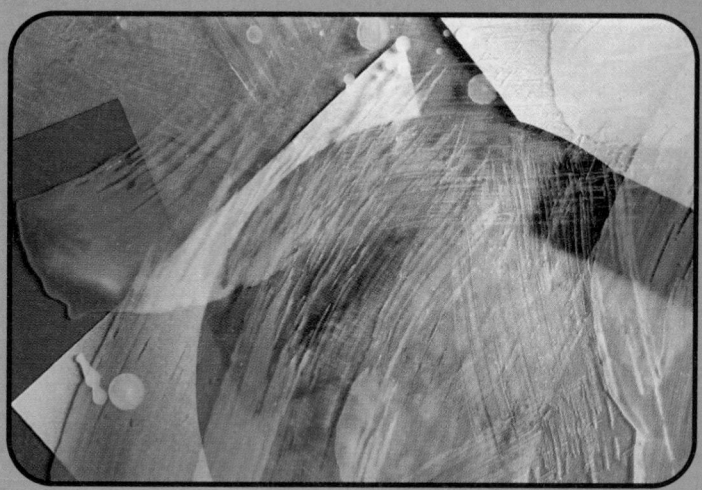

Budgeting

OBJECTIVES

When you have completed this chapter, you should be able to:

- Define a budget and show how budgets, corporate objectives and long-term plans are related.

- Explain the budgeting process and the interlinking of the various budgets within the business.

- Indicate the uses of budgeting and construct various budgets, including the cash budget, from relevant data.

- Discuss the criticisms that are made of budgeting.

INTRODUCTION

Budgets are an important tool for management planning and control. This chapter considers the role and nature of budgets, and shows how budgets are prepared. Preparing budgets relies on an understanding of the financial statements (balance sheet and profit and loss account (income statement)) considered in Chapters 2 and 3. It also picks up on many of the issues relating to the behaviour of costs and full costing, topics explored in Chapters 9 and 10 respectively. So, if you are unsure about these topics, you may wish to revise them before reading this chapter.

Budgets do not exist in a vacuum; they are an integral part of a planning framework that is adopted by well-run businesses. To understand fully the nature of budgets we must, therefore, understand the planning framework within which they are set. The chapter begins with a discussion of this framework and then goes on to consider detailed aspects of the budgeting process.

Budgets, long-term plans and corporate objectives

It is vital that businesses develop plans for the future. Whatever a business is trying to achieve, it is unlikely to be successful unless its managers are clear what the future direction of the business is going to be.

The development of plans involves five key steps:

1 Setting the aims and objectives of the business.
2 Identifying the options available.
3 Evaluating the options and making a selection.
4 Setting detailed short-term plans or budgets.
5 Collecting information on performance and exercising control.

Step 1: Setting the aims and objectives of the business

The aims and objectives set out what the business is basically trying to achieve. It is sometimes useful to make a distinction between aims and objectives. The aims of the business are often couched in broad terms and may be set out in the form of a **mission statement**. This statement is usually brief and will often identify high standards or ideals for the business. **Real World 12.1** provides an example of a mission statement.

REAL WORLD 12.1

BT's mission

BT, the multinational telecommunications business, states its mission as follows:

> BT's strategy is to create value for shareholders through being the best provider of communications services and solutions for everybody in the UK, and for corporate customers in Europe, achieving global reach through partnership.

Source: BT Group plc Annual Report 2003.

The objectives of a business are more specific than its aims. They will set out more precisely what has to be achieved. The objectives will vary between businesses but may include the following aspects of operations and performance:

● the kind of market the business seeks to serve;
● the share of that market it wishes to achieve;
● the level of operating efficiency (for example, striving to be the lowest-cost producer);
● the kinds of product and/or service that should be offered;
● the levels of profit and returns to shareholders (for example, a particular return on capital employed or dividends) that are required;
● the levels of growth required (for example, increases in assets or sales revenue);
● technological leadership (for example, the degree of innovation).

Objectives should be quantifiable and should be consistent with the aims of the business as set out in its mission statement.

Step 2: Identifying the options available

A number of possible options (strategies) may be available to the business to help it to achieve its objectives. A creative search for the various strategic options should be undertaken. This will involve collecting information – an activity that can be extremely time-consuming, particularly when the business is considering entering new markets or investing in new technology.

The type of information collected should include an external analysis of the competitive environment and will relate to such matters as:

● market size and growth prospects;
● level of competition within the industry;
● bargaining power of suppliers and customers;
● threat of new entrants to the market;
● threat of substitute products;
● relative power of trade unions, community interest groups and so on.

Information should also be collected that provides an *internal* analysis of the resources and expertise of the business that are available to pursue each option. Information concerning the capabilities of the business in each of the following areas may be collected:

● marketing and distribution;
● manufacturing and production operations;
● finance and administration;
● research and development;
● information systems;
● human resources.

Any deficiencies or gaps in these areas that could affect the ability of the business to pursue a particular option must be identified.

Step 3: Evaluating the options and making a selection

When deciding on the most appropriate option(s) to choose, the managers must thoroughly examine the information relating to each option. This is to see whether the option fits with the objectives that have been set. It is also to assess whether the resources to pursue the option are available. For each identified option, the managers must also consider the effect of pursuing it on the financial performance and position of the business.

Humans have a restricted ability to process information. Too much information can be as bad as too little, as it can overload individuals and create confusion. This, in turn, can lead to poor evaluations and poor decisions. The information provided to managers is best restricted to what is relevant to a particular decision and that which is capable of being absorbed. This may mean that, in practice, information is produced in summary form. It may also mean that only a restricted range of options will be considered.

The option selected will form the basis of the long-term plan for the business. This plan will usually cover a period of five years or more and will specify such things as:

- the market that the business will seek to serve;
- the products or services to be offered;
- amounts and sources of finance to be raised by the business;
- capital investments to be made;
- amounts and sources of bought-in goods and services required;
- personnel requirements.

Step 4: Setting detailed short-term plans or budgets

A **budget** is a business plan for the short term – typically one year. It is likely to be expressed mainly in financial terms. Its role is to convert the long-term plans into actionable blueprints for the immediate future. Budgets will define precise targets concerning:

- cash receipts and payments;
- sales, broken down into amounts and prices for each of the products or services provided by the business;
- detailed stock (inventory) requirements;
- detailed labour requirements;
- specific production requirements.

Clearly, the relationship between objectives, long-term plans and budgets is that the objectives, once set, are likely to last for quite a long time – perhaps throughout the life of the business. A series of long-term plans identifies how each objective is to be pursued, and budgets identify how the long-term plan is to be fulfilled.

An analogy might be found in terms of a student enrolling on a course of study. His or her objective might be to embark on a career that will be rewarding in various ways. He or she might have identified the particular study course as the most effective way to work towards this objective. In working towards this, passing a particular stage of the course might be identified as the target for the forthcoming year. Here the intention to complete the entire course is analogous to a long-term plan, and passing each stage is analogous to the budget. Having achieved the 'budget' for the first year, the 'budget' for the second year becomes passing the second stage.

Step 5: Collecting information on performance and exercising control

However well planned the activities of a business might be, they will come to nothing unless steps are taken to try to achieve them in practice. The process of making planned events actually occur is known as *control*.

Control can be defined as compelling events to conform to plan. This definition is valid in any context. For example, when we talk about controlling a motor car, we mean making the car do what we plan that it should do. In a business context, accounting is very useful in the control process. This is because it is possible to state plans in accounting terms (as budgets) and it is also possible to state *actual* outcomes in the same terms, thus making comparison between actual and planned outcomes a relatively easy matter. Where actual outcomes are at variance with budgets, this variance should be highlighted by accounting information. Managers can then take steps to get the business back on track towards the achievement of the budgets.

Figure 12.1 shows the planning and control process in diagrammatic form.

It should be emphasised that planning (including budgeting) is the responsibility of managers rather than accountants. Though accountants can play a role in the planning process, by supplying relevant information to managers and by contributing to decision making as part of the management team, they should not dominate the process. In practice, it seems that the budgeting aspect of planning is in danger of being dominated by accountants, perhaps because most budgets are expressed in financial terms. However, managers are avoiding their responsibilities if they allow this to happen.

Time horizon of plans and budgets

The setting of plans is typically performed as a major exercise every five years, and budgets are usually set annually. It need not necessarily be the case that long-term plans are set for five years and that budgets are set for one year: it is up to the management of the business concerned. Businesses involved in certain industries – say, information technology – may feel that five years is too long a planning period since new developments can, and do, occur virtually overnight. Such businesses may feel that a planning horizon of two or three years is more feasible. Similarly, a budget need not be set for one year, although this appears to be a widely used time horizon.

Figure 12.1 **The planning and control process**

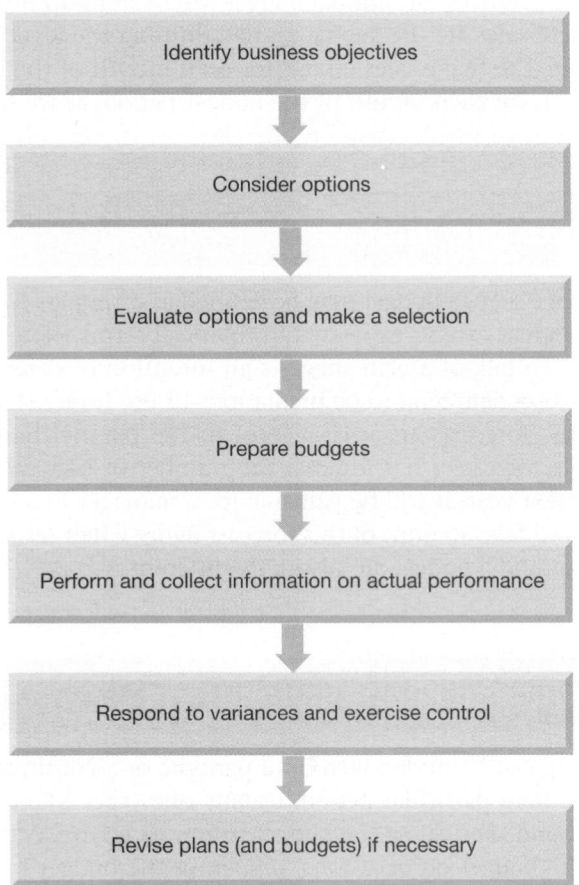

Once the objectives of the business have been determined, the various options that can fulfil these objectives must be considered and evaluated in order to derive a strategic plan. The budget is a short-term financial plan for the business that is prepared within the framework of the strategic plan. Control can be exercised through the comparison of budgeted and actual performance. Where a significant divergence emerges, some form of corrective action should be taken. If the budget figures prove to be based on incorrect assumptions about the future, it might be necessary to revise the budget.

ACTIVITY 12.2

Can you think of any reason why most businesses prepare detailed budgets for the forthcoming year, rather than for a shorter or longer period?

The reason is probably that a year represents a long enough time for the budget preparation exercise to be worthwhile, yet short enough into the future for detailed plans to be capable of being made. As we shall see later in this chapter, the process of formulating budgets can be a time-consuming exercise, but there are economies of scale – for example, preparing the budget for the next twelve months would not normally take twice as much time and effort as preparing the budget for the next six months.

An annual budget sets targets for the forthcoming year for all aspects of the business. It is usually broken down into monthly budgets, which define monthly targets. Indeed, in many instances, the annual budget will be built up from monthly figures. For example, where sales are the key factor determining the level of activity, the sales staff will be required to make sales targets for each month of the budget period. Other budgets will be set, for each month of the budget period, as we shall explain below.

Budgets and forecasts

As we have seen, a budget may be defined as a *business plan* for the short-term. Budgets are, to a great extent, expressed in financial terms. Note that a budget is a *plan*, not a forecast. To talk of a plan suggests an intention or determination to achieve planned targets; **forecasts** tend to be predictions of the future state of the environment.

Clearly, forecasts are very helpful to the planner/budget-setter. If, for example, a reputable forecaster has forecast the number of new cars to be purchased in the UK during next year, it will be valuable for a manager in a car manufacturing business to obtain and take account of this forecast figure when setting its sales budgets. However, a forecast and a budget are distinctly different.

Periodic and continual budgets

Budgeting can be undertaken on a periodic or a continual basis. A **periodic budget** is prepared for a particular period (usually one year). Managers will agree the budget for the year and then allow the budget to run its course. Although it may be necessary to revise the budget on occasions, preparing the budget is in essence a one-off exercise during a financial year. A **continual budget**, as the name suggests, is continually updated. We have seen that an annual budget will normally be broken down into smaller time intervals (usually monthly periods) to help control the activities of a business. A continual budget will add a new month to replace the month that has just passed, thereby ensuring that, at all times, there will be a budget for a full planning period. Continual budgets are also referred to as **rolling budgets**.

ACTIVITY 12.3

What do you think are the advantages and disadvantages of each form of budgeting?

Periodic budgeting will usually take less time and effort to prepare and will therefore be less costly. However, as time passes, the budget period shortens and towards the end of the financial year managers will be working to a very short planning period indeed. Continual budgeting, on the other hand, will ensure that managers always have a full year's budget to help them make decisions. It is claimed that continual budgeting ensures that managers plan throughout the year rather than just once each year. In this way it encourages a forward-looking attitude. However, there is a danger that budgeting will become a mechanical exercise as managers may not have time to step back from their other tasks each month and consider the future carefully. It may be unreasonable to expect managers continually to take this future-oriented perspective.

The interrelationship of various budgets

For a particular business for a particular period, there is more than one budget. Each one will relate to a specific aspect of the business. It is generally considered that the ideal situation is that there should be a separate budget for each person who is in a managerial position, no matter how junior. The contents of all of the individual budgets will be summarised in **master budgets** consisting usually of a budgeted profit and loss account (income statement) and balance sheet. The cash flow statement (in summarised form) is considered by some to be a third master budget.

Figure 12.2 illustrates the interrelationship and interlinking of individual budgets, in this particular case using a manufacturing business as an example.

Figure 12.2   **The interrelationship of various budgets**

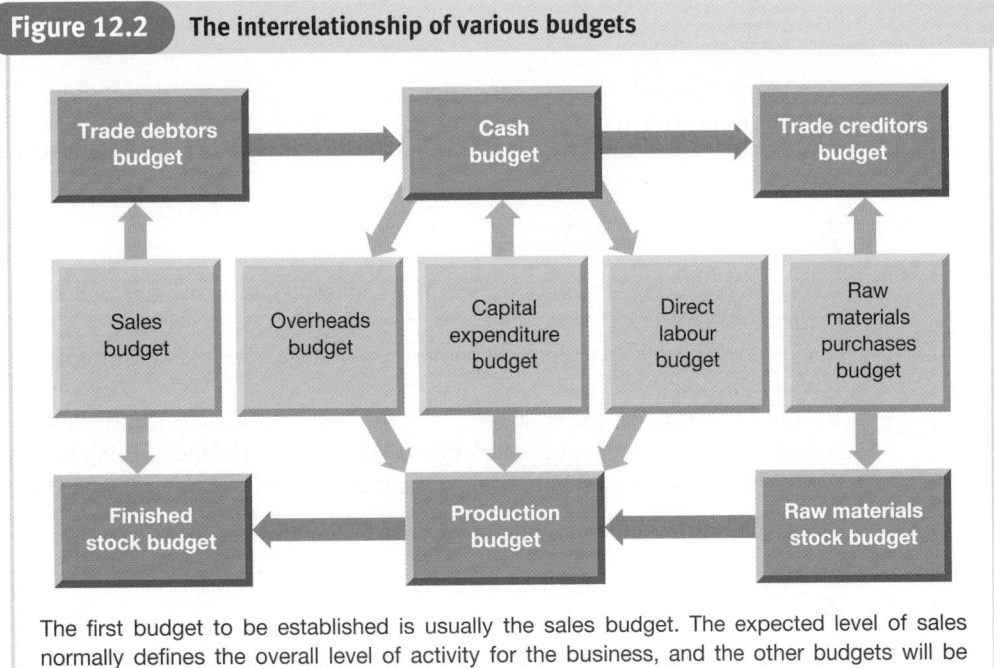

The first budget to be established is usually the sales budget. The expected level of sales normally defines the overall level of activity for the business, and the other budgets will be drawn up in accordance with this. Thus, the sales budget will largely define the finished stock requirements, and from this we can define the production requirements and so on.

The figure shows the interrelationship of budgets for a manufacturing business.

Starting at the top of Figure 12.2, the sales budget is usually the first budget to be prepared, as this tends to determine the overall level of activity for the forthcoming period. Sales demand is probably the most common factor that limits activity. The level of sales would tend to dictate the finished stock (inventory) requirement, though it would also be dictated by the policy of the business on finished stockholding. The requirement for finished stock would define the required production levels, which would, in turn, dictate the requirements of the individual production departments or sections. The demands of manufacturing, in conjunction with the business's policy on raw materials stock, define the raw materials stock budget. The purchases budget will be dictated by the materials stock budget which will, in conjunction with the policy of the business on creditor payment, dictate the trade creditors (payables) budget. One of the determinants of the cash budget will be the trade creditors budget; another will be the trade debtors (receivables) budget, which itself derives, through the debtor policy of the business, from the sales budget. Cash will also be affected by overheads and direct labour costs (themselves linked to production) and by capital expenditure. The factors that affect policies on matters such as stockholding and debtor collection and creditor payment periods will be discussed in some detail in Chapter 16.

It may actually prove to be the case that it is not sales demand that limits activities. Assuming that the budgeting process takes the order just described, it might be found in practice that there is some constraint other than sales. For example, the production capacity of the business may be incapable of meeting the necessary levels of output to match the sales budget for one or more months. In this case, it might be reasonable to look at the ways of overcoming the problem. As a last resort, it might be necessary to revise the sales budget to a lower level to enable production to meet the target.

ACTIVITY 12.4

Can you think of any ways in which a short-term shortage of production facilities might be overcome?

We thought of the following:

- Higher production in previous months and stockpiling to meet period(s) of higher demand.
- Increasing production capacity, perhaps by working overtime and/or acquiring (buying or leasing) additional plant.
- Subcontracting some production.
- Encouraging potential customers to change the timing of their buying by offering discounts or other special terms during the months that have been identified as quiet.

You might well have thought of other approaches.

There will be the horizontal relationships between budgets, which we have just looked at, but there will usually be vertical ones as well. For example, the sales budget may be broken down into a number of subsidiary budgets, perhaps one for each regional sales manager. The overall sales budget will be a summary of the subsidiary ones. The same may be true of virtually all of the other budgets, most particularly the production budget.

Figure 12.2, which was considered earlier, gives a very simplified outline of the budgetary framework of a typical manufacturing business. We have looked at the interlinking of budgets in the context of a manufacturing business. This is not because such businesses are particularly significant, but purely because they have all of the types of budget that we tend to find in practice. A service supplier, for example, would have a similar set of budgets, but without some or all of those relating to stocks. All of the issues relating to budgets apply equally well to all types of business.

All of the operating budgets that we have just reviewed have to be consistent with the overall short-term plans laid out in the master budget: that is, the budgeted profit and loss account and balance sheet.

The uses of budgets

Budgets are generally regarded as having five areas of usefulness. These are:

1 *Budgets tend to promote forward thinking and the possible identification of short-term problems.* We saw (above) that a shortage of production capacity might be identified during the budgeting process. Making this discovery in good time could leave a number of means of overcoming the problem open to exploration. If the potential production problem is picked up early enough, all of the suggestions in the answer to Activity 12.4 and, possibly, other ways of overcoming the problem can be explored. Early identification of the potential problem gives managers time for calm and rational consideration of the best way of overcoming it. The best solution to the potential problem may only be feasible if action can be taken well in advance. This would be true of all of the suggestions made in the answer to Activity 12.4.

2 *Budgets can be used to help co-ordination between the various sections of the business.* It is crucial that the activities of the various departments and sections of the business are linked so that the activities of one are complementary to those of another. For example, the activities of the purchasing/procurement department of a manufacturing business should dovetail with the raw materials needs of the production departments. If this is not the case, production could run out of stock, leading to expensive production stoppages. Possibly, just as undesirably, excessive stocks (inventories) could be bought, leading to large and unnecessary stockholding costs. We shall see how this co-ordination tends to work in practice later in this chapter.

3 *Budgets can motivate managers to better performance.* Having a stated task can motivate managers and staff in their performance. It is a well-established view that to tell a manager to do his or her best is not very motivating, but to define a required level of achievement is likely to be. It is felt that managers will be better motivated by being able to relate their particular role in the business to the overall objectives of the business. Since budgets are directly derived from corporate objectives, budgeting makes this possible. It is clearly not possible to allow managers to operate in an unconstrained environment. Having to operate in a way that matches the goals of the business is a price of working in an effective business. We shall consider the role of budgets as motivators in Chapter 13.

4 *Budgets can provide a basis for a system of control.* As mentioned earlier in the chapter, control is concerned with ensuring that events conform to plans. If senior management wishes to control and to monitor the performance of more junior staff, it needs some yardstick against which the performance can be measured and assessed. It is possible to compare current performance with past performance or perhaps with what happens in another business. However, the most logical yardstick is usually planned performance. If there is information available concerning the actual performance for a period, and this can be compared with the planned performance, then a basis for control will have been established. Such a basis will enable the use of **management by exception**, a technique where senior managers can spend most of their time dealing with those staff or activities that have failed to achieve the budget (the exceptions). This means that the senior managers do not have to spend too much time on those that are performing well. It also allows junior managers to exercise self-control. By knowing what is expected of them and what they have actually achieved, they can assess how well they are performing and take steps to correct matters where they are failing to achieve. We shall consider the effect of making plans and being held accountable for their achievement in Chapter 13.

Figure 12.3 **Benefits of budgeting**

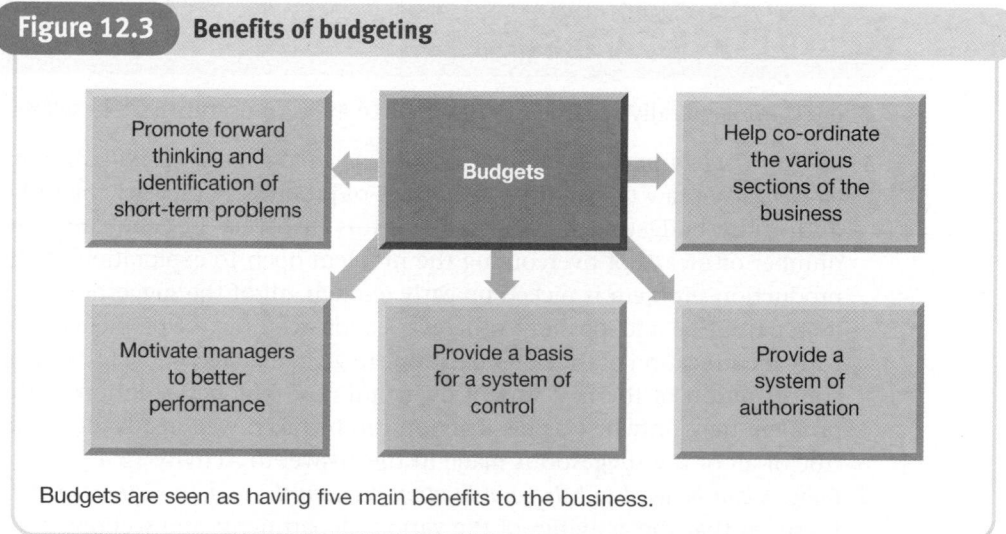

Budgets are seen as having five main benefits to the business.

5 *Budgets can provide a system of authorisation* for managers to spend up to a particular limit. A good example of this is where there are certain activities (for example, staff development and research expenditure) that are allocated a fixed amount of funds at the discretion of senior management.

Figure 12.3 shows the benefits of budgets in diagrammatic form.

The following three activities pick up on some issues that relate to some of the uses of budgets.

ACTIVITY 12.5

The third on the above list of the uses of budgets (motivation), implies that managers are set stated tasks. Do you think there is a danger that requiring managers to work towards such predetermined targets will stifle their skill, flair and enthusiasm?

If the budgets are set in such a way as to offer challenging yet achievable targets, the manager is still required to show skill, flair and enthusiasm. There is the danger, however, that if targets are badly set (either unreasonably demanding or too easy to achieve), they could be a demotivating force. This could well stifle managers' skill, flair and enthusiasm.

ACTIVITY 12.6

The fourth on the above list of the uses of budgets (control), implies that current management performance is compared with some yardstick. What is wrong with comparing actual performance with past performance, or the performance of others, in an effort to exercise control?

There is no automatic reason to believe that what happened in the past, or is happening elsewhere, represents a sensible target for this year in this business. Considering what happened last year, and in other businesses, may help in the formulation of plans, but past events and the performance of others should not automatically be seen as the target.

Could the five identified uses of budgets conflict with one another on occasions? For example, can you think of a possible conflict:

(a) between the budget as a motivational device and the budget as a means of control?

(b) between the budget as a means of control and the budget as a system of authorisation?

It is quite possible for the uses identified to be in conflict with one another.

(a) Where the budget is being used as a motivational device, some businesses set the budget targets at a more difficult level than the managers are expected to achieve. This is in attempt to motivate managers to strive to reach their targets. For control purposes, however, the budget becomes less meaningful as a benchmark against which to compare actual performance.

(b) Where a budget is being used as a system of authorisation, managers may be motivated to spend to the limit of their budget, even though this may be wasteful. This may occur where the managers are not allowed to carry over unused funds to the next budget period or if they believe that the budget for the next period will be reduced because not all the funds for the current period were spent. The wasting of resources in this way conflicts with the role of budgets as a means of exercising control.

Conflict between the different uses will mean that managers must decide which particular uses for budgets should be given priority; managers must be prepared, if necessary, to trade off the benefits resulting from one particular use for the benefits of another.

The budget-setting process

Budgeting is such an important area for businesses, and other organisations, that it tends to be approached in a fairly methodical and formal way. This usually involves a number of steps, described below and shown in diagrammatic form in Figure 12.4.

Step 1: Establish who will take responsibility

It is usually seen as crucial that those responsible for the budget-setting process have real authority within the organisation.

Why is it crucial that those responsible for the budget-setting process have real authority in the organisation?

→

Activity 12.8 continued

One of the crucial aspects of the process is establishing co-ordination between budgets so that the plans of one department match and are complementary to those of other departments. This usually requires compromise where adjustment of initial budgets must be undertaken. This in turn means that someone on the board of directors (or its equivalent) has to be closely involved; only people of this rank are likely to have the necessary moral and, if needed, formal managerial authority to force departmental managers to compromise.

Quite commonly, a **budget committee** is formed to supervise and take responsibility for the budget-setting process. This committee usually comprises a senior representative of most of the functional areas of the business – marketing, production, personnel and so on. Often, a **budget officer** is appointed to carry out, or to take immediate responsibility for others carrying out, the tasks of the committee. Not surprisingly, given their technical expertise in the activity, accountants are often required to take budget officer roles.

Figure 12.4   Steps in the budget-setting process

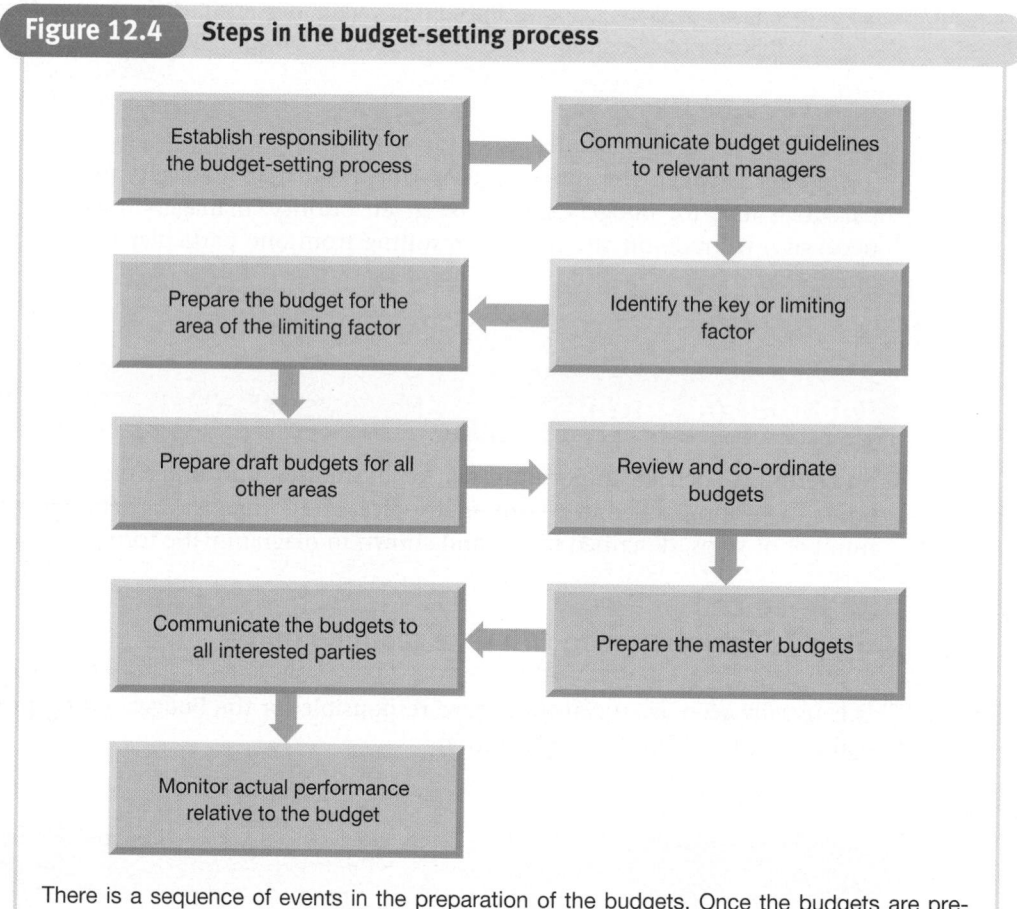

There is a sequence of events in the preparation of the budgets. Once the budgets are prepared, they are communicated to all interested parties and, over time, actual performance is monitored in relation to the targets set out in the budgets.

Step 2: Communicate budget guidelines to relevant managers

Budgets are intended to be the short-term plans that seek to work towards the achievement of long-term plans and to the overall objectives of the business. It is therefore important that, in drawing up budgets, managers are well aware of what the long-term plans are and how the forthcoming budget period is intended to work towards them. Managers also need to be made well aware of the commercial/economic environment in which they will be operating. It is the responsibility of the budget committee to see that managers have all the necessary information.

Step 3: Identify the key, or limiting, factor

There will always be some aspect of the business that will stop it achieving its objectives to the maximum extent. This is often a limited ability of the business to sell its products; sometimes, it is some production shortage (such as labour, materials or plant) that is the **limiting factor**, or, linked to these, a shortage of funds. Often, production shortages can be overcome by an increase in funds – for example, more plant can be bought or leased. This is not always a practical solution, because no amount of money will buy certain labour skills or increase the world supply of some raw material.

As has been pointed out earlier in this chapter, it is sometimes possible to ease an initial limiting factor: for example, subcontracting can eliminate a plant capacity problem. This means that some other factor, perhaps sales, will replace the production problem, though at a higher level of output. Ultimately, however, the business will hit a ceiling; some limiting factor will prove impossible to ease.

For entirely practical reasons, it is important that the limiting factor is identified. Ultimately, most, if not all, budgets will be affected by the limiting factor, and so if it can be identified at the outset, all managers can be informed of the restriction early in the process.

Step 4: Prepare the budget for the area of the limiting factor

The limiting factor will determine the overall level of activity for the business. The limiting-factor budget will quite often be the sales budget since the ability to sell is frequently the limiting factor that simply cannot be eased. (When discussing the interrelationship of budgets earlier in the chapter, we started with the sales budget for this reason.) As we have seen, sales is not always the limiting factor.

Real World 12.2 looks at the methods favoured by businesses of different sizes to determine their sales budgets.

REAL WORLD 12.2

Sources of the sales budget in practice

Determining the future level of sales can be a difficult problem. In practice, a business may rely on the judgements of sales staff, statistical techniques or market surveys (or some combination of these) to arrive at a sales budget. A 1993 survey of UK manufacturing businesses provides the following insights concerning the use of such techniques and methods.

Real World 12.2 continued

	All respondents	Small businesses	Large businesses
Number of respondents	281	47	46
	%	%	%
Technique			
Statistical forecasting	31	19	29
Market research	36	13	54
Subjective estimates based on sales staff experience	85	97	80

We can see that the most popular approach by far is the opinion of sales staff. We can also see that there are differences between large and small businesses, particularly concerning the use of market surveys. This evidence is now pretty old, but in the absence of more up-to-date research, it provides some idea of how businesses determine their sales targets.

Source: Drury *et al*. (see reference 1 at the end of the chapter).

Step 5: Prepare draft budgets for all other areas

The other budgets are prepared, complementing the budget for the area of the limiting factor. In all budget preparation, the computer has become an almost indispensable tool. Much of the work of preparing budgets is repetitive and tedious, yet the resultant budget has to be a reliable representation of the actual plans made. Computers are ideally suited to such tasks and human beings are not. It is often the case that budgets have to be redrafted several times because of some minor alteration, and, again, computers do this without complaint.

There are two broad approaches to setting individual budgets. The *top-down approach* is where the senior management of each budget area originates the budget targets, perhaps discussing them with lower levels of management and, as a result, refining them before the final version is produced. With the *bottom-up approach*, the targets are fed upwards from the lowest level. For example, junior sales managers will be asked to set their own sales targets, which then become incorporated into the budgets of higher levels of management until the overall sales budget emerges.

Where the bottom-up approach is adopted, it is usually necessary to haggle and negotiate at different levels of authority to achieve agreement. This may be because the plans of some departments do not fit in with those of others or because the targets set by junior managers are not acceptable to their superiors. This approach seems rarely to be found in practice.

ACTIVITY 12.9

What are the advantages and disadvantages of each type of budgeting approach?

The bottom-up approach allows greater involvement among managers in the budgeting process and this, in turn, may increase the level of commitment to the targets set. It also allows the business to draw more fully on the local knowledge and expertise of its managers. However, this approach can be time-consuming and may result in some managers setting undemanding targets for themselves in order to have an easy life.

> The top-down approach enables senior management to communicate plans to employees and to co-ordinate the activities of the business more easily. It may also help in establishing more demanding targets for managers. However, the level of commitment to the budget may be lower as many of those responsible for achieving the budgets will have been excluded from the budget-setting process.

There will be a brief discussion of the benefits of participation in target setting in Chapter 13.

Step 6: Review and co-ordinate budgets

A business's budget committee must at this stage review the various budgets and satisfy itself that the budgets complement one another. Where there is a lack of co-ordination, steps must be taken to ensure that the budgets mesh. Since this will require that at least one budget must be revised, this activity normally benefits from a diplomatic approach. Ultimately, however, the committee may be forced to assert its authority and insist that alterations are made.

Step 7: Prepare the master budgets

The master budgets are the budgeted profit and loss account (income statement) and budgeted balance sheet (and perhaps a summarised, budgeted cash flow statement). All of the information required to prepare these statements should be available from the individual budgets that have already been prepared. The budget committee usually undertakes the task of preparing the master budgets.

Step 8: Communicate the budgets to all interested parties

The formally agreed budgets are now passed to the individual managers who will be responsible for their implementation. This is, in effect, senior management formally communicating to the other managers the targets that they are expected to achieve.

Step 9: Monitor performance relative to the budget

Much of the budget-setting activity will have been pointless unless each manager's actual performance is compared with planned performance, which is embodied in the budget. This issue is examined in detail in Chapter 13.

Incremental and zero-base budgeting

Traditionally, much budget setting has tended to be on the basis of what happened last year, with some adjustment for any changes in factors that are expected to affect the forthcoming budget period (for example, inflation). This approach is sometimes known as **incremental budgeting**; it is often used for 'discretionary' budgets, such as research and development and staff training, where the **budget holder** (the manager responsible for the budget) is allocated a sum of money to be spent in the area of activity concerned. They are referred to as **discretionary budgets** because the sum allocated is normally at the discretion of senior management. These budgets are very common in local and central government (and in other public bodies), but are also used in commercial businesses to cover certain types of activity.

A feature of the types of activity for which discretionary budgets exist is the lack of a clear relationship between inputs (resources applied) and outputs (benefits). Compare this with, say, a raw materials usage budget in a manufacturing business, where the amount of material used and, therefore, the amount of funds taken by it is clearly related to the level of production and, ultimately, to sales. It is easy for discretionary budgets to eat up funds with no clear benefit being derived. It is often only proposed increases in these budgets that are closely scrutinised.

Zero-base budgeting (ZBB) rests on the philosophy that all spending needs to be justified. Thus, when establishing, say, the training budget each year, it is not automatically accepted that training courses should be financed in the future simply because they were undertaken this year. The training budget will start from a zero base and will only be increased above zero if a good case can be made for the scarce resources of the business to be allocated to this form of activity. Top management will need to be convinced that the proposed activities represent 'value for money'.

ZBB encourages managers to adopt a more questioning approach to their areas of responsibility. To justify the allocation of resources, they are often forced to think carefully about the particular activities and the ways in which they are undertaken. This questioning approach should result in a more efficient use of business resources. With an increasing portion of the total costs of most businesses being in areas where the link between outputs and inputs is not always clear, and where commitment of resources is discretionary rather than demonstrably essential to production, ZBB is increasingly relevant.

ACTIVITY 12.10

Can you think of any disadvantages of using ZBB? How might any disadvantages be partially overcome?

The principal problems with ZBB are:

● It is time-consuming and therefore expensive to undertake.
● Managers, whose sphere of responsibility is subjected to ZBB, can feel threatened by it.

The benefits of a ZBB approach can be gained to some extent – perhaps at not too great a cost – by using the approach on a selective basis. For example, a particular budget area could be subjected to ZBB-type scrutiny only every third or fourth year. In any case, if ZBB is used more frequently, there is the danger that managers will use the same arguments each year to justify their activities. The process will simply become a mechanical exercise and the benefits will be lost. For a typical business, some areas are likely to benefit from ZBB more than others. ZBB could, in these circumstances, be applied only to those areas that will benefit from it, and not to the others. The areas that are most likely to benefit from ZBB are discretionary spending ones, such as training, advertising, and research and development.

If senior management is aware of the potentially threatening nature of this form of budgeting, care can be taken to apply ZBB with sensitivity. However, in the quest for value for money, the application of ZBB can result in some tough decisions being made.

The extent to which budgets are utilised

There is recent survey evidence that reveals the extent to which budgeting is used by larger US businesses. It shows that most of them prepare and use budgets (see **Real World 12.3**).

REAL WORLD 12.3

Budgeting in practice

A survey of management accounting practice in the US was conducted in 2003. Nearly 2,000 businesses replied to the survey. These tended to be larger businesses, of which about 40 per cent were manufacturers and about 16 per cent financial services; the remainder were across a range of other industries.

The survey revealed that 75 per cent extensively use operational budgeting, with a further 16 per cent considering using the technique in the future.

Though the survey relates to the US, in the absence of UK evidence, it provides some insight to what is likely also to be practice in the UK and elsewhere in the developed world.

Source: Ernst and Young (see reference 4 at the end of the chapter).

A fairly recent survey of budgeting practice in small and medium-sized enterprises (SMEs) (see **Real World 12.4**) revealed that not all such businesses fully use budgeting.

REAL WORLD 12.4

Preparation of budgets in SMEs

A study of budgeting practice in small and medium-sized enterprises revealed that the most frequently prepared budget is the sales budget, followed by the budgeted profit and loss account (income statement) and the overheads budget (see Figure 12.5).

Figure 12.5

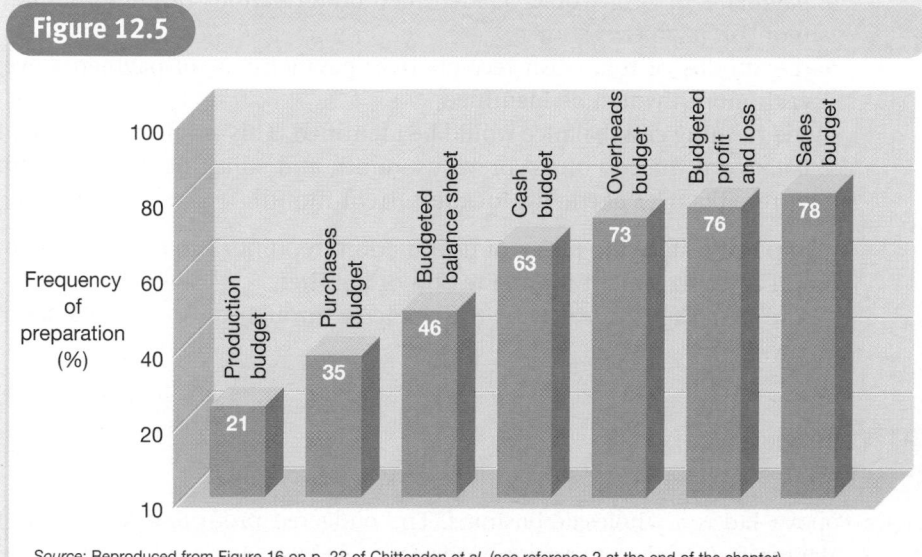

Source: Reproduced from Figure 16 on p. 22 of Chittenden *et al.* (see reference 2 at the end of the chapter).

It seems that some smaller businesses prepare budgets only for what they see as key areas. The budget that is most frequently prepared by such businesses is the sales budget, followed by the budgeted profit and loss account (income statement) and the overheads budget. Perhaps surprisingly, the cash budget is prepared by less than two-thirds of the small businesses surveyed.

Preparing the cash budget

We shall now look in some detail at how the various budgets used by the typical business are prepared, starting with the cash budget and then looking at the others. It might be helpful for us to start with the cash budget because:

● it is a key budget; most economic aspects of a business are reflected in cash sooner or later, so that for a typical business the cash budget reflects the whole business more than any other single budget;
● very small, unsophisticated businesses (for example, a corner shop) may feel that full-scale budgeting is not appropriate to their needs, but almost certainly they should prepare a cash budget as a minimum (despite the survey evidence mentioned above!).

We shall consider other budgets later in the chapter.

Since budgets are documents that are to be used only internally by a business, their style and format is a question of management choice and will therefore vary from one business to the next. However, since managers, irrespective of the business, are likely to be using budgets for similar purposes, there is a tendency for some consistency of approach to exist. We can probably say that, in most businesses, the cash budget would possess the following features:

1 the budget period would be broken down into sub-periods, typically months;
2 the budget would be in columnar form, with one column for each month;
3 receipts of cash would be identified under various headings and a total for each month's receipts shown;
4 payments of cash would be identified under various headings and a total for each month's payments shown;
5 the surplus of total cash receipts over payments or of payments over receipts for each month would be identified;
6 the running cash balance would be identified. This would be achieved by taking the balance at the end of the previous month and adjusting it for the surplus or deficit of receipts over payments for the current month.

Typically, all of the pieces of information in points 3 to 6 in the above list would be useful to management for one reason or another.

The best way to deal with this topic is through an example – see Example 12.1 below.

Example 12.1

Vierra Popova Ltd is a wholesale business. The budgeted profit and loss accounts (income statements) for each of the next six months are as follows:

	Jan £000	Feb £000	Mar £000	Apr £000	May £000	June £000
Sales revenue	52	55	55	60	55	53
Cost of goods sold	30	31	31	35	31	32
Salaries and wages	10	10	10	10	10	10
Electricity	5	5	4	3	3	3
Depreciation	3	3	3	3	3	3
Other overheads	2	2	2	2	2	2
Total expenses	50	51	50	53	49	50
Net profit	2	4	5	7	6	3

The business allows all of its customers one month's credit (this means, for example, that cash from January sales will be received in February). Sales revenue during December totalled £60,000.

The business plans to maintain stocks (inventories) at their existing level until some time in March, when they are to be reduced by £5,000. Stocks will remain at this lower level indefinitely. Stock purchases are made on one month's credit. December purchases totalled £30,000. Salaries, wages and 'other overheads' are paid in the month concerned. Electricity is paid quarterly in arrears in March and June. The business plans to buy and pay for a new delivery van in March. This will cost a total of £15,000, but an existing van will be traded in for £4,000 as part of the deal.

The business expects to have £12,000 in cash at the beginning of January.

The cash budget for the six months ending in June will look as follows:

	Jan £000	Feb £000	Mar £000	Apr £000	May £000	June £000
Receipts						
Debtors (note 1)	60	52	55	55	60	55
Payments						
Creditors (note 2)	30	30	31	26	35	31
Salaries and wages	10	10	10	10	10	10
Electricity			14			9
Other overheads	2	2	2	2	2	2
Van purchase	–	–	11	–	–	–
Total payments	42	42	68	38	47	52
Cash surplus	18	10	(13)	17	13	3
Opening balance (note 3)	12	30	40	27	44	57
Closing balance	30	40	27	44	57	60

Notes

1 The cash receipts from trade debtors (receivables) lag a month behind sales because customers are given a month in which to pay for their purchases. So, December sales will be paid for in January and so on.

2 In most months, the purchases of stock will equal the cost of goods sold. This is because the business maintains a constant level of stock. For stock to remain constant at the end of each month, the business must replace exactly the amount that has been used. During March, however, the business plans to reduce its stock by £5,000. This means that stock purchases will be lower than stock usage in that month. The payments for stock purchases lag a month behind purchases because the business expects to be allowed a month to pay for what it buys.

3 Each month's cash balance is the previous month's figure plus the cash surplus (or minus the cash deficit) for the current month. The balance at the start of January is £12,000 according to the information provided earlier.

4 Depreciation does not give rise to a cash payment. In the context of profit measurement (in the profit and loss account), depreciation is a very important aspect. Here, however, we are only interested in cash.

ACTIVITY 12.11

Looking at the cash budget of Vierra Popova Ltd (see Example 12.1), what conclusions do you draw and what possible course of action do you recommend regarding the cash balance over the period concerned?

There appears to be a fairly large cash balance, given the size of the business, and it seems to be increasing. Management might give consideration to putting some of the cash into an income-yielding deposit. Alternatively, it could be used to expand the trading activities of the business by, for example, increasing the investment in non-current assets.

ACTIVITY 12.12

Vierra Popova Ltd (see Example 12.1) now wishes to prepare its cash budget for the second six months of the year. The budgeted profit and loss accounts (income statements) for each of the second six months are as follows:

	July £000	Aug £000	Sept £000	Oct £000	Nov £000	Dec £000
Sales revenue	57	59	62	57	53	51
Cost of goods sold	32	33	35	32	30	29
Salaries and wages	10	10	10	10	10	10
Electricity	3	3	4	5	6	6
Depreciation	3	3	3	3	3	3
Other overheads	2	2	2	2	2	2
Total expenses	50	51	54	52	51	50
Net profit	7	8	8	5	2	1

The business will continue to allow all of its customers one month's credit.

It plans to increase stocks (inventories) from the 30 June level by £1,000 each month until, and including, September. During the following three months, stock levels will be decreased by £1,000 each month.

Stock purchases, which had been made on one month's credit until the June payment, will, starting with the purchases made in June, be made on two months' credit.

Salaries, wages and 'other overheads' will continue to be paid in the month concerned. Electricity is paid quarterly in arrears in September and December.

At the end of December the business intends to pay off part of a loan. This payment is to be such that it will leave the business with a cash balance of £5,000 with which to start next year.

Required:
Prepare the cash budget for the six months ending in December. (Remember that any information you need that relates to the first six months of the year, including the cash balance that is expected to be brought forward on 1 July, is given in Example 12.1.)

The cash budget for the six months ended 31 December is:

	July £000	Aug £000	Sept £000	Oct £000	Nov £000	Dec £000
Receipts						
Debtors	53	57	59	62	57	53
Payments						
Creditors (note 1)	–	32	33	34	36	31
Salaries and wages	10	10	10	10	10	10
Electricity			10			17
Other overheads	2	2	2	2	2	2
Loan repayment (note 2)	–	–	–	–	–	131
Total payments	12	44	55	46	48	191
Cash surplus	41	13	4	16	9	(138)
Opening balance	60	101	114	118	134	143
Closing balance	101	114	118	134	143	5

Notes:

1 There will be no payment to creditors in July because the June purchases will be made on two months' credit and will therefore be paid in August. The July purchases, which will equal the July cost of sales revenue figure plus the increase in stock made in July, will be paid for in September, and so on.

2 The repayment is simply the amount that will cause the balance at 31 December to be £5,000.

Preparing other budgets

Though each one will have its own particular features, other budgets will tend to follow the same sort of pattern as the cash budget, that is, they will show inflows and outflows during each month and the opening and closing balances in each month.

Example 12.2

To illustrate some of the other budgets, we shall continue to use the example of Vierra Popova Ltd that we considered in Example 12.1, on p. 408. To the information given there, we need to add the fact that the stock balance at 1 January was £30,000.

Show the debtors (receivables), creditors (payables) and stock (inventory) budgets for the six months.

Solution

Debtors (receivables) budget

This would normally show the planned amount owing from credit sales to the business at the beginning and at the end of each month, the planned total sales

→

revenue for each month, and the planned total cash receipts from debtors. The layout would be something like the following:

	Jan £000	Feb £000	Mar £000	Apr £000	May £000	June £000
Opening balance	60	52	55	55	60	55
Add Sales revenue	52	55	55	60	55	53
	112	107	110	115	115	108
Less Cash receipts	60	52	55	55	60	55
Closing balance	52	55	55	60	55	53

The opening and closing balances represent the amount that the business plans to be owed (in total) by debtors at the beginning and end of the month, respectively.

Creditors (payables) budget

Typically this shows the planned amount owed to suppliers by the business at the beginning and at the end of each month, the planned purchases for each month, and the planned total cash payments to creditors. The layout would be something like the following:

	Jan £000	Feb £000	Mar £000	Apr £000	May £000	June £000
Opening balance	30	30	31	26	35	31
Add Purchases	30	31	26	35	31	32
	60	61	57	61	66	63
Less Cash payment	30	30	31	26	35	31
Closing balance	30	31	26	35	31	32

The opening and closing balances represent the amount planned to be owed (in total) by the business to creditors, at the beginning and end of the month respectively.

Stock (inventory) budget

This would normally show the planned amount of stock to be held by the business at the beginning and at the end of each month, the planned total stock purchases for each month, and the planned total monthly stock usage. The layout would be something like the following:

	Jan £000	Feb £000	Mar £000	Apr £000	May £000	June £000
Opening balance	30	30	30	25	25	25
Add Purchases	30	31	26	35	31	32
	60	61	56	60	56	57
Less Stock used	30	31	31	35	31	32
Closing balance	30	30	25	25	25	25

The opening and closing balances represent the amount of stock, at cost, planned to be held by the business at the beginning and end of the month respectively.

A *raw materials stock budget*, for a manufacturing business, would follow a similar pattern, with the 'stock usage' being the cost of the stock put into production. A *finished stock budget* for a manufacturer would also be similar to the above, except that 'stock manufactured' would replace 'purchases'. A manufacturing business would normally prepare both a raw materials stock budget and a finished stock budget.

The stock budget will normally be expressed in financial terms, but may also be expressed in physical terms (for example, kg or metres) for individual stock items.

Note how the debtors, creditors and stock budgets in Example 12.2 link to one another, and to the cash budget for the same business in Example 12.1. Note particularly that:

● the rows of purchases figures in both the creditors budget and the stock budget are identical;
● the rows of cash payments figures in both the creditors budget and the cash budget are identical; and
● the rows of cash receipts figures in both the debtors budget and the cash budget are identical to the cash budget: the cash receipts row of figures is the same in both. The debtors budget would link to the sales budget in a similar way.

This is how the linking (co-ordination), which was discussed earlier in this chapter, is achieved.

ACTIVITY 12.13

Have a go at preparing the debtors budget for Vierra Popova Ltd for the six months, July to December (see Activity 12.12).

The debtors budget for the six months ended 31 December is:

	July £000	Aug £000	Sept £000	Oct £000	Nov £000	Dec £000
Opening balance (note 1)	53	57	59	62	57	53
Add Sales revenue (note 2)	57	59	62	57	53	51
	110	116	121	119	110	104
Less Cash receipts (note 3)	53	57	59	62	57	53
Closing balance (note 4)	57	59	62	57	53	51

Notes:
1 The opening debtors figure is the previous month's sales revenue figure (sales are on one month's credit).
2 The sales revenue is the current month's figure.
3 The cash received each month is equal to the previous month's sales revenue figure.
4 The closing balance is equal to the current month's sales revenue figure.

Note that if we knew three of the four figures each month, we could deduce the fourth.

This budget could, of course, be set out in any manner that would have given the sort of information that management would require in respect of planned levels of debtors and associated transactions.

ACTIVITY 12.14

Have a go at preparing the creditors budget for Vierra Popova Ltd for the six months of July to December (see Activity 12.12). (*Hint*: Remember that the creditors' payment period alters from the June purchases onwards.)

The creditors budget for the six months ended 31 December is:

	July £000	Aug £000	Sept £000	Oct £000	Nov £000	Dec £000
Opening balance	32	65	67	70	67	60
Add Purchases	33	34	36	31	29	28
	65	99	103	101	96	88
Less Cash payments	–	32	33	34	36	31
Closing balance	65	67	70	67	60	57

This, again, could be set out in any manner that would have given the sort of information that management would require in respect of planned levels of creditors and associated transactions.

SELF-ASSESSMENT QUESTION 12.1

Antonio Ltd has planned production and sales for the next nine months as follows:

	Production (units)	Sales (units)
May	350	350
June	400	400
July	500	400
August	600	500
September	600	600
October	700	650
November	750	700
December	750	800
January	750	750

During the period, the business plans to advertise heavily to generate these increases in sales. Payments for advertising of £1,000 and £1,500 will be made in July and October respectively.

The selling price a unit will be £20 throughout the period. Forty per cent of sales revenue is normally made on two months' credit. The other 60 per cent is settled within the month of the sale.

Raw materials will be held in stock for one month before they are taken into production. Purchases of raw materials will be on one month's credit (buy one month, pay the next). The cost of raw materials is £8 a unit of production.

Other direct production expenses, including labour, are £6 a unit of production. These will be paid in the month concerned.

Various production overheads, which during the period to 30 June had run at £1,800 a month, are expected to rise to £2,000 each month from 1 July to 31 October. These are expected to rise again from 1 November to £2,400 a month and to remain at that level for the foreseeable future. These overheads include a steady £400 each month for depreciation. Overheads are planned to be paid 80 per cent in the month of production and 20 per cent in the following month.

To help to meet the planned increased production, a new item of plant will be bought and will be delivered in August. The cost of this item is £6,600; the contract with the supplier will specify that this will be paid in three equal amounts in September, October and November.

Raw materials stock (inventory) is planned to be 500 units on 1 July. The balance at the bank the same day is planned to be £7,500.

Required:
(a) Draw up the following for the six months ending 31 December:
   (i)   a raw materials budget, showing both physical quantities and financial values;
   (ii) a creditors budget;
   (iii) a cash budget.
(b) The cash budget reveals a potential cash deficiency during October and November. Can you suggest any ways in which a modification of plans could overcome this problem?

Activity-based budgeting

Activity-based budgeting (ABB) applies the philosophy of activity-based costing (ABC), which we discussed in Chapter 11, to planning and control through budgets. We should recall that ABC recognises that it is activities that cause or 'drive' costs. If the cost-driving activities can be identified, ascertaining the cost of the output of a business can be achieved with greater accuracy. Not only this, but costs become easier to control simply because their cause is known.

It is a central feature of budgeting that those who are responsible for meeting a particular budget (budget holders) should have control over the events that affect performance in their area. Ensuring that this is always the case can be problematical. For example, a decision is made at a senior level to increase the volume of activity for the business. This leads to an increase in the costs of a particular junior manager, that takes those costs above the budgeted level. The junior manager might be held responsible for the cost increase, yet the volume change was beyond that manager's control. In other words, the costs are driven by activities not controlled by the manager who is being held accountable for those costs.

ABB seeks to generate budgets in such a way that the manager who has control over the cost drivers is accountable for the costs that are caused.

Non-financial measures in budgeting

The efficiency of internal operations and customer satisfaction have become of critical importance to businesses striving to survive in an increasingly competitive environment. Non-financial measures have an important role to play in assessing performance in such key areas as customer/supplier delivery times, set-up times, defect levels and customer satisfaction levels. These non-financial measures are of much the same type as are used in the Balanced Scorecard that we considered in Chapter 11. The Balanced Scorecard uses a mix of financial and non-financial measures.

There is no reason why budgeting need be confined to just financial targets and measures. Non-financial measures can also be used as the basis for targets and can be incorporated into the budgeting process and reported alongside the financial targets for the business. **Real World 12.5** gives some idea of the extent of the use of non-financial measures in practice in the UK.

REAL WORLD 12.5

Non-financial measures used in practice

A 1993 survey of UK manufacturing businesses revealed that non-financial measures are widely used by businesses. The following table is taken from this study.

| | Extent to which performance is measured | | | | | |
| | Never/rarely | | Sometimes | | Often/always | |
	Smaller businesses %	Larger businesses %	Smaller businesses %	Larger businesses %	Smaller businesses %	Larger businesses %
Customer satisfaction/ product quality	22	2	11	7	67	91
Customer delivery efficiency	16	2	22	7	62	91
Supplier quality/delivery	16	4	32	15	52	81
Throughput times	33	6	24	20	43	74
Set-up times	59	32	19	22	22	46
	businesses	businesses	businesses	businesses	businesses	businesses

We can see that customer-based measures are the most widely used form of non-financial performance measures. There are also clear differences between the smaller businesses and larger businesses in the extent to which non-financial measures are used. Though this evidence is now quite old, in the absence of more up-to-date research, it provides some insight to what happens in practice.

Source: Drury *et al*. (see reference 1 at the end of the chapter).

Budgets and management behaviour

All accounting statements and reports are intended to affect the behaviour of one or another group of people. Budgets are intended to affect the behaviour of managers, for example, to encourage them to work towards the business's objectives and to do this in a co-ordinated manner.

Whether budgets seem to be effective and how they can be made more effective are crucial issues for managers. We shall examine this topic in detail in the next chapter, after we have seen how budgets can be used to help managers to exercise control.

Who needs budgets?

Until recently it would have been a heresy to suggest that budgeting was not of central importance to any business. The benefits of budgeting, mentioned earlier in this chapter, have been widely recognised and the vast majority of businesses prepare annual budgets. However, there is increasing concern that, in today's highly dynamic and competitive environment, budgets may actually be harmful to the achievement of business objectives. This has led a small but growing number of businesses to abandon budgets as a tool of planning and control.

Various charges have been levelled against the conventional budgeting process. It is claimed that budgets:

● cannot deal with a fast-changing environment and that budgets are often out of date before the start of the budget period;

● focus too much management attention on the achievement of short-term financial targets. Instead, managers should focus on the things that create value for the business (for example, innovation, building brand loyalty, responding quickly to competitive threats and so on);

● reinforce a 'command and control' structure that prevents junior managers from exercising autonomy. This may be particularly true where a top-down approach, that allocates budgets to managers, is being used. Where managers feel constrained, attempts to retain and recruit able managers can be difficult;

● take up an enormous amount of management time that could be better used. In practice, budgeting can be a lengthy process that may involve much negotiation, reworking and updating. However, this may add little to the achievement of business objectives;

● are based around business functions (sales, marketing, production and so on). However, to achieve the business's objectives, the focus should be on business processes that cut across functional boundaries and reflect the needs of the customer;

● encourage incremental thinking by employing a 'last year plus *x* per cent' approach to planning. This can inhibit the development of 'break out' strategies that may be necessary in a fast-changing environment;

● can protect costs rather than lower costs. In some cases, a fixed budget for an activity, such as research and development, is allocated to a manager. If the amount is not spent, the budget may be taken away and, in future periods, the budget for this activity may be either reduced or eliminated. Such a response to unused budget allocations can encourage managers to spend the whole of the budget, irrespective of need, in order to protect the allocations they receive;

● promote 'sharp' practice among managers. In order to meet budget targets, managers may try to negotiate lower sales targets or higher cost allocations than they feel is really necessary. This helps them to build some 'slack' into the budgets and so meeting the budget becomes easier (see reference 5 at the end of the chapter).

Although, some believe that many of the problems identified can be solved by better budgeting systems such as activity-based budgeting and zero-base budgeting, others believe that a more radical solution is required.

Beyond conventional budgeting

In recent years, some businesses have abandoned budgeting, although they still recognise the need for forward planning. No one seriously doubts that there must be appropriate systems in place to steer a business towards its objectives. It is claimed, however, that the systems adopted should reflect a broader, more integrated approach to planning. The new systems that have been implemented are often based around a 'leaner' financial planning process that is more closely linked to other measurement and reward systems. Emphasis is placed on the use of rolling forecasts, key performance indicators (such as market share, customer satisfaction and innovations) and/or 'scorecards' (like the Balanced Scorecard, which we met in Chapter 11) that identify both monetary and non-monetary targets to be achieved over the long term and short term. These are often very demanding ('stretch') targets, based on benchmarks that have been set by world-class businesses.

The new 'beyond budgeting' model promotes a more decentralised, participative approach to managing the business. It is claimed that the traditional hierarchical management structure, where decision making is concentrated at the higher levels of the hierarchy, encourages a culture of dependency where meeting the budget targets set by senior managers is the key to managerial success. This traditional structure is replaced by a network structure where decision making is devolved to 'front-line' managers. In the new structure a more open, questioning attitude among employees is encouraged. There is a sharing of knowledge and best practice and protective behaviour by managers is discouraged. In addition, rewards are linked to targets based on improvement in relative performance rather than to meeting the budget. It is claimed that this new approach allows greater adaptability to changing conditions, increases performance and increases motivation among staff.

Figure 12.6 sets out the main differences between the traditional and 'beyond budgeting' planning models.

Real World 12.6 below reveals the experience of one business that decided to abandon conventional budgets.

It is too early to predict whether or not the trickle of businesses that are now seeking an alternative to budgets will turn into a flood. However, it is clear that in today's highly competitive environment a business must be flexible and responsive to changing conditions. Management systems that in any way hinder these attributes will not survive.

Despite the criticisms made of budgeting, it remains a very widely used technique. Real Worlds 12.3 and 12.4 provide evidence for this. In the next chapter we shall look in some detail at how budgets can be adapted for use as devices for exercising management control.

Figure 12.6   Traditional versus 'beyond budgeting' planning model

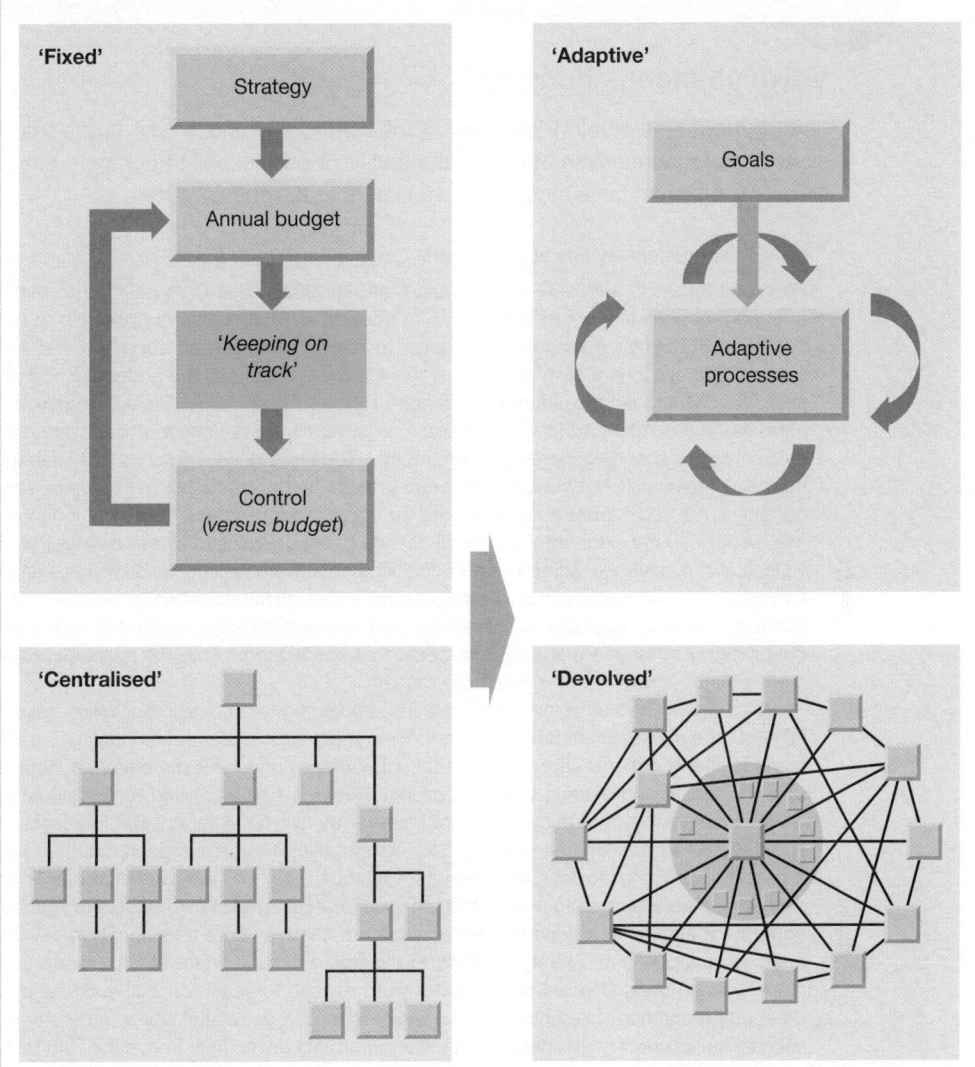

The traditional model is based on the use of fixed targets, which determine the future actions of managers. The 'beyond budgeting' model, on the other hand, is based on the use of stretch targets that can be adapted. The traditional hierarchical management structure is replaced by a network structure.

Source: www.bbrt.org

REAL WORLD 12.6

Volvo abandons budgets

Jeremy Hope and Robin Fraser are at the forefront of those who argue that budgeting systems have an adverse effect on the ability of businesses to compete effectively. The following is a short case study of Volvo Cars that they have written.

New steering mechanisms at Volvo Cars

Following losses in 1990–92 and a small profit in 1993, Volvo Cars decided to make a number of important changes, one of which was to adopt a radically different approach to managing the business. But senior managers were quick to realise that such an approach was unlikely to be successful in the longer term unless they tackled the problems of the budgeting and planning process that encouraged the old mindset of compliance and control. As Ole Johannesson, VP finance, explains, 'the budget and long-range planning systems are no longer efficient when the business environment is changing more and more rapidly. Today we need a process that enables us to react not only immediately but even beforehand'. In 1994 there was no budget requested by the Group company, AB Volvo, from operating units for the forthcoming year, 1995. As Johannesson notes, 'we recognised the extent of the cultural change needed. We wanted less and less of order giving, victims of circumstance, administration, checking, reactive positions, functional ties and hierarchical thinking, and more and more of creating opportunities, communication, development, confidence-building, proactive positions, network ties, and process thinking'. Since that time Volvo Cars has built a highly advanced management model that has helped it face the intense competitive pressures that are endemic to the world car market.

Volvo reckoned that its previous planning, budgeting and control processes absorbed around 20% of total management time. By abandoning these processes and managing in a different way, managers have not only saved significant costs but they now have more time to focus on strategy, action planning and beating the competition. This is a battle not tied to an annual cycle, but is waged continuously month by month and quarter by quarter. Strategy and forecasts are reviewed and updated several times a year with four distinct cycles apparent. Each month a 'flash' forecast is prepared covering the next three months; each quarter a two-year rolling forecast is updated; and each year sees a revised four-year and ten-year strategic plan. While targets are broad-brush and comprise a number of key performance indicators, there is more time spent on developing action plans to support them. Monthly reports to the board include financial information (actual month, actual year-to-date, forecast remainder of year, revised forecast for total years, and last year-to-date) and a number of key performance indicators such as market share, order intake, customer satisfaction, product costs, dealer profitability, warranty costs, fault frequency, and total ownership cost (all where possible compared with the competition). Four years after dismantling the budgeting process there is now a strong 'responsibility' and 'no blame' culture at Volvo Cars.

According to Ole Johannesson, 'managers now know that they mustn't come to meetings with problems, but with explanations about what they've done to solve them'. The management accountants now spend more time collecting a whole range of measurement data but, more importantly, they see their role as one of analysing and interpreting the data so that operating managers can take the appropriate action. Indeed the whole emphasis is on 'actions' rather than 'problems'. Volvo has transformed itself into an action-orientated company in which decisions are made by people at the appropriate level to meet changing conditions. This has contributed to Volvo's remarkable turnaround. It now ranks as the sixteenth largest motor vehicle manufacturer in the world, but in terms of profitability it is second only to Ford on profits on sales and assets.

Source: Hope and Fraser (see reference 3 at the end of the chapter), p. 17.

Note: Since this case study was written, Volvo has become part of the Ford Motor Company. It is possible that the success of the business led Ford to acquire Volvo.

SUMMARY

The main points of this chapter may be summarised as follows:

Budget = a short-term financial plan

- Budgets are the short-term means of working towards the business's objectives.
- They are usually prepared for a one-year period with sub-periods of a month.
- There is usually a separate budget for each key area.

Uses of budgets

They:

- promote forward thinking;
- help co-ordinate the various aspects of the business;
- motivate performance;
- provide the basis of a system of control.
- provide a system of authorisation.

The budget setting process

- Establish who will take responsibility.
- Communicate guidelines.
- Identify key factors.
- Prepare budget for key factor area.
- Prepare draft budgets for all other areas.
- Review and co-ordinate.
- Prepare master budgets (profit and loss account (income statement) and balance sheet).
- Communicate the budgets to interested parties.
- Monitor performance relative to budget.

Preparing budgets

- There is no standard style – practicality and usefulness are the key issues.
- They are usually prepared in columnar form, with a column for each month (or similarly short period).
- Each budget must link (co-ordinate) with others.

Criticisms of budgets

- Cannot deal with rapid change.
- Focus on short-term financial targets, rather than value creation.
- Encourage a 'top-down' management style.
- Time-consuming.
- Based around traditional business functions and do not cross boundaries.
- Encourage incremental thinking (last year's figure plus x per cent).
- Protect rather than lower costs.
- Promote 'sharp' practice among managers.
- Budgeting is very widely practised despite the criticisms.

→ Key terms

mission statement   p. 391
budget   p. 393
forecast   p. 396
periodic budget   p. 396
continual (rolling) budget   p. 396
master budget   p. 397
management by exception   p. 399
budget committee   p. 402

budget officer   p. 402
limiting factor   p. 403
incremental budgeting   p. 406
budget holder   p. 406
discretionary budget   p. 406
zero-base budgeting (ZBB)   p. 406
activity-based budgeting
   (ABB)   p. 415

Further reading

If you would like to explore the topics covered in this chapter in more depth, we recommend the following books:

Management Accounting, *Atkinson A., Banker R., Kaplan R. and Young, S.M.*, 3rd edn, Prentice Hall International, 2001, chapter 11.

Management and Cost Accounting, *Drury C.*, 5th edn, Thomson Learning Business Press, 2000, chapter 15.

Cost Accounting: A managerial emphasis, *Horngren C., Foster G. and Datar S.*, 11th edn, Prentice Hall International, 2002, chapter 6.

References

1 **A Survey of Management Accounting Practices in UK Manufacturing Companies**, *Drury C., Braund S., Osborne P. and Tayles M.*, Chartered Association of Certified Accountants, 1993.

2 **Financial Management and Working Capital Practices in UK SMEs**, *Chittenden F., Poutziouris P. and Michaelis N.*, Manchester Business School, 1998.

3 'Beyond budgeting', *Hope J. and Fraser R.*, in **Management Accounting**, January 1999.

4 **2003 Survey of Management Accounting**, *Ernst and Young*, Ernst and Young, 2003.

5 **Beyond Budgeting**, www.beyondbudgeting.plus.com

REVIEW QUESTIONS

Answers to these questions can be found on the students' side of the Companion Website at **www.pearsoned.co.uk/atrillmclaney**.

12.1 Define a budget. How is a budget different from a forecast?

12.2 What were the five uses of budgets that were identified in the chapter?

12.3 What do budgets have to do with control?

12.4 What is a budget committee? What purpose does it serve?

EXERCISES

Exercises 12.5 to 12.8 are more advanced than 12.1 to 12.4. Those with coloured numbers have answers at the back of the book.

12.1 Daniel Chu Ltd, a new business, will start production on 1 April, but sales will not commence until 1 May. Planned sales for the next nine months are as follows:

	Sales units
May	500
June	600
July	700
August	800
September	900
October	900
November	900
December	800
January	700

The selling price a unit will be a consistent £100, and all sales will be made on one month's credit. It is planned that sufficient finished goods stock for each month's sales should be available at the end of the previous month.

Raw materials purchases will be such that there will be sufficient raw materials stock available at the end of each month precisely to meet the following month's planned production. This planned policy will operate from the end of April. Purchases of raw materials will be on one month's credit. The cost of raw material is £40 a unit of finished product.

The direct labour cost, which is variable with the level of production, is planned to be £20 a unit of finished production. Production overheads are planned to be £20,000 each month, including £3,000 for depreciation. Non-production overheads are planned to be £11,000 a month, of which £1,000 will be depreciation.

Various non-current assets costing £250,000 will be bought and paid for during April.

Except where specified, assume that all payments take place in the same month as the cost is incurred.

The business will raise £300,000 in cash from a share issue in April.

CHAPTER 12 BUDGETING

Required:

Draw up the following for the six months ending 30 September:

(a) A finished stock budget, showing just physical quantities.
(b) A raw materials stock budget showing both physical quantities and financial values.
(c) A trade creditors budget.
(d) A trade debtors budget.
(e) A cash budget.

12.2 You have overheard the following statements:

(a) 'A budget is a forecast of what is expected to happen in a business during the next year.'
(b) 'Monthly budgets must be prepared with a column for each month so that you can see the whole year at a glance, month by month.'
(c) 'Budgets are OK but they stifle all initiative. No manager worth employing would work for a business that seeks to control through budgets.'
(d) 'Activity-based budgeting is an approach that takes account of the planned volume of activity in order to deduce the figures to go into the budget.'
(e) 'Any sensible person would start with the sales budget and build up the other budgets from there.'

Required:

Critically discuss these statements, explaining any technical terms.

12.3 A nursing home, which is linked to a large hospital, has been examining its budgetary control procedures, with particular reference to overhead costs.

The level of activity in the facility is measured by the number of patients treated in the budget period. For the current year, the budget stands at 6,000 patients and this is expected to be met.

For months 1 to 6 of this year (assume 12 months of equal length), 2,700 patients were treated. The actual variable overhead costs incurred during this six-month period are as follows:

Expense	£
Staffing	59,400
Power	27,000
Supplies	54,000
Other	8,100
Total	148,500

The hospital accountant believes that the variable overhead costs will be incurred at the same rate during months 7 to 12 of the year.

Fixed overhead costs are budgeted for the whole year as follows:

Expense	£
Supervision	120,000
Depreciation/financing	187,200
Other	64,800
Total	372,000

Required:

(a) Present an overheads budget for months 7 to 12 of the year. You should show each expense, but should not separate individual months. What is the total overhead cost for each patient that would be incorporated into any statistics?
(b) The home actually treated 3,800 patients during months 7 to 12, the actual variable overheads were £203,300, and the fixed overheads were £190,000. In summary form, examine how well the home exercised control over its overheads.
(c) Interpret your analysis and point out any limitations or assumptions.

12.4 Linpet Ltd is to be incorporated on 1 June. The opening balance sheet of the business will then be as follows:

Assets	£
Cash at bank	60,000
Share capital	
£1 ordinary shares	60,000

During June, the business intends to make payments of £40,000 for a leasehold property, £10,000 for equipment and £6,000 for a motor vehicle. The business will also purchase initial trading stock costing £22,000 on credit.

The business has produced the following estimates:

(i)   Sales revenue for June will be £8,000 and will increase at the rate of £3,000 a month until September. In October, sales revenue will rise to £22,000 and in subsequent months will be maintained at this figure.

(ii) The gross profit percentage on goods sold will be 25%.

(iii) There is a risk that supplies of trading stock will be interrupted towards the end of the accounting year. The business therefore intends to build up its initial level of stock (£22,000) by purchasing £1,000 of stock each month in addition to the monthly purchases necessary to satisfy monthly sales. All purchases of stock (including the initial stock) will be on one month's credit.

(iv) Sales revenue will be divided equally between cash and credit sales. Credit customers are expected to pay two months after the sale is agreed.

(v)   Wages and salaries will be £900 a month. Other overheads will be £500 a month for the first four months and £650 thereafter. Both types of expense will be payable when incurred.

(vi) 80% of sales revenue will be generated by salespeople, who will receive 5 per cent commission on sales revenue. The commission is payable one month after the sale is agreed.

(vii) The business intends to purchase further equipment in November for £7,000 cash.

(viii) Depreciation is to be provided at the rate of 5% a year on freehold property and 20% a year on equipment. (Depreciation has not been included in the overheads mentioned in (v) above.)

Required:

(a) State why a cash budget is required for a business.

(b) Prepare a cash budget for Linpet Ltd for the six-month period to 30 November.

12.5 Lewisham Ltd manufactures one product line – the Zenith. Sales of Zeniths over the next few months are planned to be as follows:

1 *Demand*

	Units
July	180,000
August	240,000
September	200,000
October	180,000

Each Zenith sells for £3.

2 *Debtor receipts*. Debtors are expected to pay as follows:

– 70% during the month of sale
– 28% during the following month.

The remaining debtors are expected to go bad (that is, to be uncollectable). Debtors who pay in the month of sale are entitled to deduct a 2% discount from the invoice price.

3 *Finished goods stocks*. Stocks of finished goods are expected to be 40,000 units at 1 July. The business's policy is that, in future, the stock at the end of each month should equal 20% of the following month's planned sales requirements.

4 *Raw materials stock*. Stocks of raw materials are expected to be 40,000 kg on 1 July. The business's policy is that, in future, the stock at the end of each month should equal 50% of the following month's planned production requirements. Each Zenith requires 0.5 kg of the raw material, which costs £1.50/kg. Raw materials purchases are paid in the month after purchase.

5 *Labour and overheads*. The direct labour cost of each Zenith is £0.50. The variable overhead element of each Zenith is £0.30. Fixed overheads, including depreciation of £25,000, total £47,000 a month. All labour and overheads are paid during the month in which they arise.

6 *Cash in hand*. At 1 August the business plans to have a bank balance (in funds) of £20,000.

Required:

Prepare the following budgets:

(a) Finished stock budget (expressed in units of Zenith) for each of the three months July, August and September.

(b) Raw materials budget (expressed in kilograms of the raw material) for the two months July and August.

(c) Cash budget for August and September.

12.6 Newtake Records Ltd owns a chain of 14 shops selling cassette tapes and compact discs. At the beginning of June the business had an overdraft of £35,000 and the bank had asked for this to be eliminated by the end of November. As a result, the directors have recently decided to review their plans for the next six months.

The following plans were prepared for the business some months earlier:

	May £000	June £000	July £000	August £000	Sept £000	Oct £000	Nov £000
Sales revenue	180	230	320	250	140	120	110
Purchases	135	180	142	94	75	66	57
Administration expenses	52	55	56	53	48	46	45
Selling expenses	22	24	28	26	21	19	18
Taxation payment				22			
Finance payments	5	5	5	5	5	5	5
Shop refurbishment	–	–	14	18	6	–	–

Notes:

(i) Stock held at 1 June was £112,000. The business believes it is preferable to maintain a minimum stock level of £40,000 of goods over the period to 30 November.

(ii) Suppliers allow one month's credit. The first three months' purchases are subject to a contractual agreement, which must be honoured.

(iii) The gross profit margin is 40%.

(iv) All sales revenue is received in the month of sale. However, 50 per cent of customers pay with a credit card. The charge made by the credit card business to Newtake Records Ltd is 3% of the sales value. These charges are in addition to the selling expenses identified above. The credit card business pays Newtake Records Ltd in the month of sale.

(v) The business has a bank loan, which it is paying off in monthly instalments of £5,000. The interest element represents 20% of each instalment.

(vi) Administration expenses are paid when incurred. This item includes a charge of £15,000 each month in respect of depreciation.

(vii) Selling expenses are payable in the following month.

Required (working to the nearest £1,000):

(a) Prepare a cash budget for the six months ending 30 November which shows the cash balance at the end of each month.

(b) Compute the stock levels at the end of each month for the six months to 30 November.

(c) Prepare a budgeted profit and loss account for the six months period ending 30 November. (A monthly breakdown of profit is *not* required.)

(d) What problems is Newtake Records Ltd likely to face in the next six months? Can you suggest how the business might deal with these problems?

12.7 Prolog Ltd is a small wholesaler of personal computers. It has in recent months been selling 50 machines a month at a price of £2,000 each. These machines cost £1,600 each. A new model has just been launched and this is expected to offer greatly enhanced performance. Its selling price and cost will be the same as for the old model. From the beginning of January, sales are planned to increase at a rate of 20 machines each month until the end of June, when sales will amount to 170 units a month. They are planned to continue at that level thereafter. Operating costs including depreciation of £2,000 a month, are planned as follows:

	January	February	March	April	May	June
Operating costs (£000)	6	8	10	12	12	12

Prolog expects to receive no credit for operating costs. Additional shelving for storage will be bought, installed and paid for in April, costing £12,000. Corporation tax of £25,000 is due at the end of March. Prolog anticipates that debtors will amount to two months' sales revenue. To give its customers a good level of service, Prolog plans to hold enough stock at the end of each month to fulfil anticipated demand from customers in the following month. The computer manufacturer, however, grants one month's credit to Prolog. Prolog Ltd's balance sheet appears below.

Balance sheet at 31 December

	£000	£000
Non-current assets		80
Current assets		
Stock	112	
Debtors	200	
Cash	–	
	312	
Current liabilities		
Trade creditors	112	
Taxation	25	
Overdraft	68	
	205	
Net current assets		107
Total assets less current liabilities		187
Equity		
Share capital (25p ordinary shares)		10
Profit and loss account		177
		187

Required:

(a) Prepare a cash budget for Prolog Ltd showing the cash balance or required overdraft for the six months ending 30 June.

(b) State briefly what further information a banker would require from Prolog before granting additional overdraft facilities for the anticipated expansion of sales.

12.8   Brown and Jeffreys, a West Midlands business, makes one standard product for use in the motor trade. The product, known as the Fuel Miser, for which the business holds the patent, when fitted to the fuel system of production model cars has the effect of reducing petrol consumption.

Part of the production is sold direct to a local car manufacturer, which fits the Fuel Miser as an optional extra to several of its models and the rest of the production is sold through various retail outlets, garages and so on.

Brown and Jeffreys assemble the Fuel Miser, but all three components are manufactured by local engineering businesses. The three components are codenamed A, B and C. One Fuel Miser consists of one of each component.

The planned sales for the first seven months of the forthcoming accounting period, by channels of distribution and in terms of Fuel Miser units, are as follows:

	Jan	Feb	Mar	Apr	May	June	July
Manufacturers	4,000	4,000	4,500	4,500	4,500	4,500	4,500
Retail, and so on	2,000	2,700	3,200	3,000	2,700	2,500	2,400
	6,000	6,700	7,700	7,500	7,200	7,000	6,900

The following further information is available:

(i)   There will be a stock of finished units at 1 January of 7,000 Fuel Misers.

(ii)   The stocks of raw materials at 1 January will be:
    A   10,000 units
    B   16,500 units
    C   7,200 units

(iii)   The selling price of Fuel Misers is to be £10 each to the motor manufacturer and £12 each to retail outlets.

(iv)   The maximum production capacity of the business is 7,000 units a month. There is no possibility of increasing this output.

(v)   Assembly of each Fuel Miser will take 10 minutes of direct labour. Direct labour is paid at the rate of £7.20 an hour during the month of production.

(vi)   The components are each expected to cost the following:
    A   £2.50
    B   £1.30
    C   £0.80

(vii)   Indirect costs are to be paid at a regular rate of £32,000 each month.

(viii)   The cash at the bank at 1 January will be £2,620.

The business plans to pursue the following policies for as many months as possible and in a manner consistent with the planned sales:

● Finished stocks at the end of each month are to equal the following month's total sales to retail outlets, and half the total of the following month's sales to the motor manufacturer.

● Raw materials at the end of each month are to be sufficient to cover production requirements for the following month. The production for July will be 6,800 units.

● Creditors for raw materials are to be paid during the month following purchase. The creditors payment for January will be £21,250.

● Debtors will pay in the month of sale, in the case of sales to the motor manufacturer, and the month after sale, in the case of retail sales. Retail sales during December were 2,000 units at £12 each.

Required:
Prepare the following budgets in monthly columnar form, both in terms of money and units (where relevant), for the six months of January to June inclusive:

(a) Sales budget.*
(b) Finished stock budget (valued at direct cost).†
(c) Raw materials stock budget.†
(d) Production budget (direct costs only).*
(e) Debtors' budget.†
(f) Creditors' budget.†
(g) Cash budget.†

* The sales and production budgets should merely state each month's sales or production in units and in money terms.
† The other budgets should all seek to reconcile the opening balance of stocks, debtors, creditors or cash with the closing balance through movements of the relevant factors over the month.

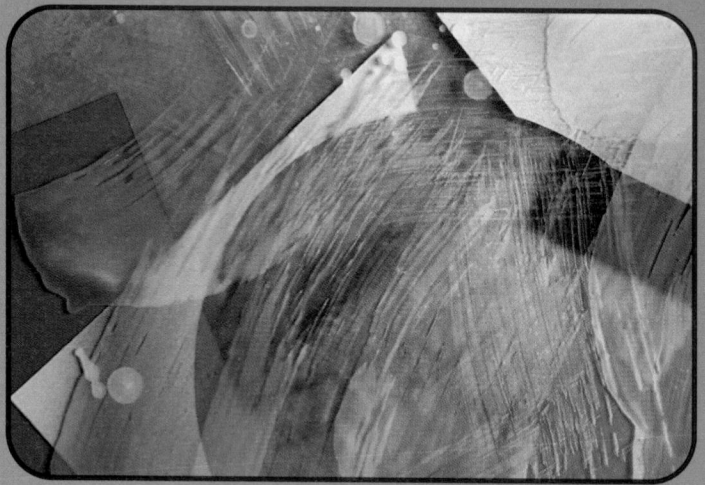

Accounting for control

INTRODUCTION

This chapter deals with the role of budgets in management control. It, therefore, continues some of the themes that we discussed in Chapter 12, and considers how a budget can be used in helping to control a business. By collecting information on actual performance and comparing it with the revised budget, it is possible to identify fairly precisely which activities are in control and which seem to be out of control. The chapter picks up some of the issues relating to the behaviour of costs with changing volumes of activity; a topic that we considered in Chapter 8.

Using budgets for control – flexible budgets

In Chapter 12, we saw that budgets can provide a useful basis for exercising control over the business. This is because control is usually seen as making events conform to a plan. Since the budget represents the plan, making events conform to it is the obvious way to try to control the business. Using budgets in this way is popular in practice.

As we saw in Chapter 12, for most businesses the routine is as shown in Figure 13.1.

These steps in the control process are fairly easy to understand. The point is that, if plans are drawn up sensibly, we have a basis for exercising control over the business. It also requires us to have the means of measuring actual performance, in the same terms as those in which the budget is stated. If they are not in the same terms, comparison will not usually be possible.

Taking steps to exercise control means finding out where and why things did not go according to plan and seeking ways to put things right for the future. One of the reasons why things may have gone wrong is that the plans may, in reality, prove to be

Figure 13.1   The budgetary control process

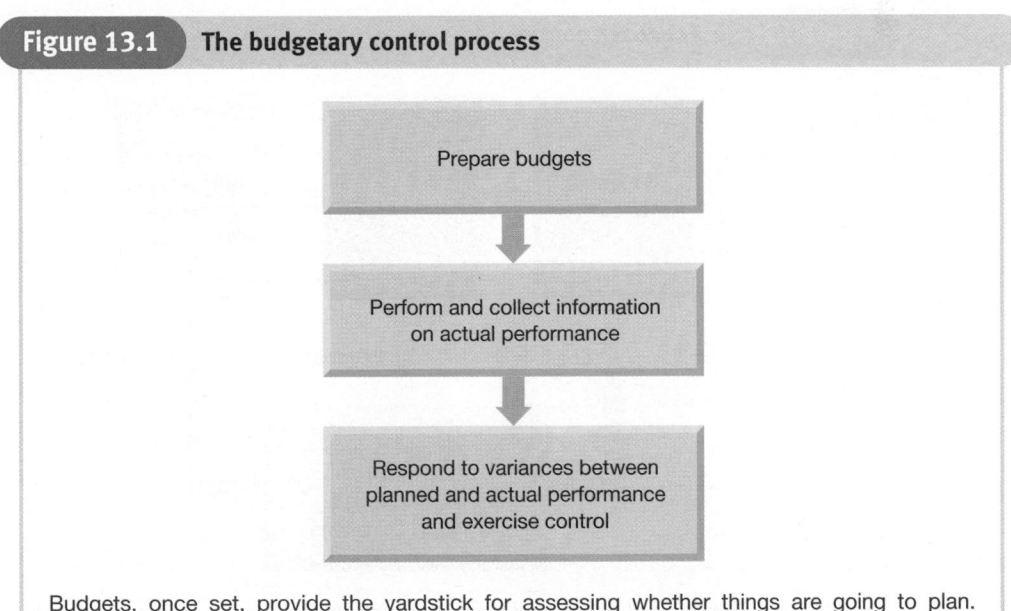

Budgets, once set, provide the yardstick for assessing whether things are going to plan. Variances between budgeted and actual performance can be identified and reacted to.

unachievable. In this case, if budgets are to be a useful basis for exercising control in the future, it may be necessary to revise the budgets for future periods to bring targets into the realms of achievability.

This last point should not be taken to mean that budget targets can simply be ignored if the going gets tough; rather that they should be adaptable. However, budgets may prove to be totally unrealistic. This could be for a variety of reasons, including unexpected changes in the commercial environment (for example, an unexpected collapse in demand for services of the type that the business provides). In this case, nothing whatsoever will be achieved by pretending that the targets can be met.

By having a system of budgetary control, a position can be established where decision making and responsibility can be delegated to junior management, yet senior management can still retain control. This is because senior managers can use the budgetary control system to ascertain which junior managers are meeting targets and, therefore, working towards the objectives of the business. (We should remember that budgets are the short-term plans for achieving the business's objectives.) This enables a management-by-exception environment to be created. Here senior management concentrates its energy on areas where things are not going according to plan (the exceptions – it is to be hoped). Junior managers who are performing to budget can be left to get on with their jobs.

Feedback and feedforward controls

The control process that we have just outlined is known as **feedback control**. Its main feature is that steps are taken to get operations back on track as soon as there is a signal that they have gone wrong. This is similar to the thermostatic control that is a feature of most central heating systems. The thermostat senses when the temperature has fallen below a preset level (analogous to the budget), and takes action to correct matters by activating the heating device that restores the required minimum temperature. Figure 13.2 depicts the stages in a feedback control system using budgets.

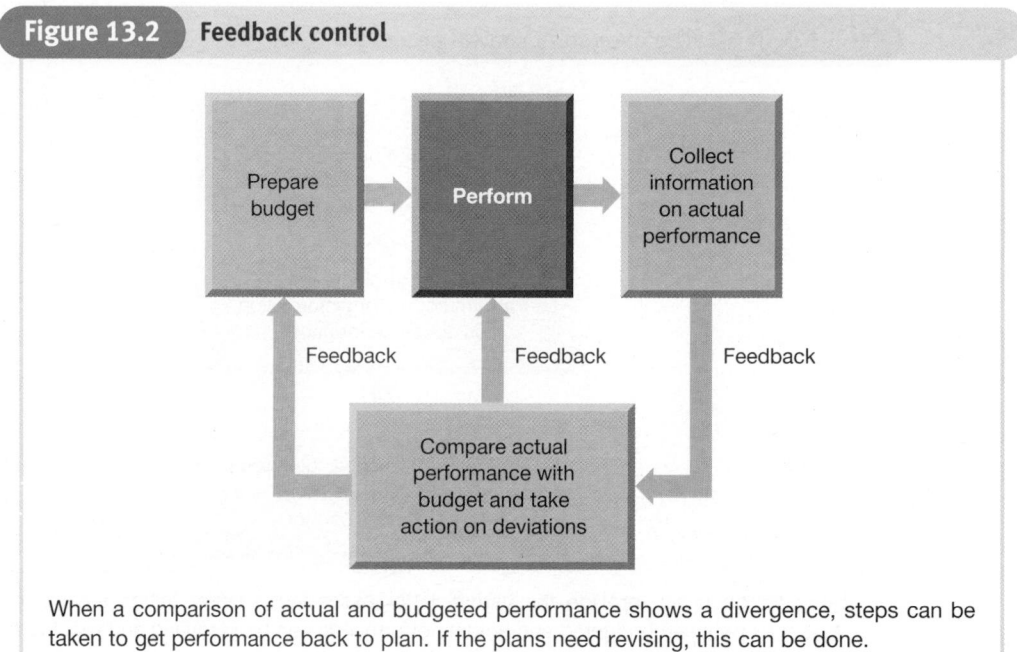

Figure 13.2 **Feedback control**

When a comparison of actual and budgeted performance shows a divergence, steps can be taken to get performance back to plan. If the plans need revising, this can be done.

→ There is an alternative type of control, known as **feedforward control**. Here predictions are made as to what can go wrong and steps taken to avoid any undesirable outcome. The preparation of budgets, which we discussed in Chapter 12, provides an example of this type of control. Preparing a particular budget may reveal a problem that will arise unless the business changes its plans. For example, preparing the cash budget may reveal that if the original plans are followed there will be a negative cash balance for some part of the budget period. By recognising this, the plans may be able to be revised to eliminate the problem.

We have just seen that budgeting embraces both forms of control. Comparing the budget with actual results is a form of feedback control whereas preparing a budget is a form of feedforward control. Generally speaking, the latter form of control is better. Things should not go wrong in the first place when steps are taken to ensure that they do not go wrong. Feedforward controls try to anticipate future problems, whereas feedback controls simply react to problems that have already occurred. In many situations, however, it is not possible to install feedforward controls.

Comparing the actual performance with the budget

The principal objective of most private-sector businesses is to enhance their shareholders' wealth. Since profit is the net increase in wealth as a result of trading, the most important budget target to meet is the profit target. In view of this, we shall begin with that aspect in our consideration of making the comparison between the budget and the actual results. Example 13.1 shows the budgeted and actual profit and loss account (income statement) for Baxter Ltd for the month of May.

Example 13.1

The following are the budgeted and actual profit and loss accounts (income statements) for Baxter Ltd for the month of May:

	Budget	Actual
Output (production and sales)	1,000 units	900 units
	£	£
Sales revenue	100,000	92,000
Raw materials	(40,000) (40,000 metres)	(36,900) (37,000 metres)
Labour	(20,000) (2,500 hours)	(17,500) (2,150 hours)
Fixed overheads	(20,000)	(20,700)
Operating profit	20,000	16,900

From these figures, it is clear that the budgeted profit was not achieved. As far as May is concerned, this is a matter of history. However, the business (or at least one aspect of it) is out of control. Senior management must discover where things went wrong during May and try to ensure that these mistakes are not repeated in later months. It is not enough to know that, overall, things went wrong. We need to know where and why. The approach taken is to compare the budgeted and actual figures for the various items (sales revenue, raw materials and so on) in the above statement.

ACTIVITY 13.1

Can you see any problems in comparing the various items (sales revenue, raw materials and so on) for the budget and the actual performance of Baxter Ltd in order to draw conclusions as to which aspects were out of control?

The problem is that the actual level of output was not as budgeted. The actual level of output was 10 per cent less than budget. This means that we cannot, for example, say that there was a labour cost saving of £2,500 (that is, £20,000 – £17,500) and conclude that all is well in that area.

Flexing the budget

One practical way to overcome our difficulty is to 'flex' the budget to what it would have been had the planned level of output been 900 units rather than 1,000 units. **Flexing the budget** simply means revising it, assuming a different volume of output.

In the context of control, the budget is usually flexed to reflect the volume that actually occurred, where this is higher or lower than the originally planned volume. To be able to do this we need to know which items are fixed and which are variable, relative to the volume of output. Once we have this knowledge, flexing is a simple operation. We shall assume that sales revenue, material cost and labour cost vary strictly with volume. Fixed overheads, by definition, will not. Whether, in real life, labour cost does vary with the volume of output is not so certain, but it will serve well enough as an assumption for our purposes.

On the basis of our assumptions regarding the behaviour of revenue and costs, the flexed budget would be as follows:

	Flexed budget
Output	900 units
(production and sales)	
	£
Sales revenue	90,000
Raw materials	(36,000) (36,000 metres)
Labour	(18,000) (2,250 hours)
Fixed overheads	(20,000)
Operating profit	16,000

This is simply the original budget, with the sales, raw materials and labour figures scaled down by 10 per cent (the same factor as the actual output fell short of the budgeted one).

Putting the original budget, the flexed budget and the actual for May together, we obtain the following:

	Original budget	Flexed budget	Actual
Output	1,000 units	900 units	900 units
(production and sales)			
	£	£	£
Sales revenue	100,000	90,000	92,000
Raw materials	(40,000)	(36,000) (36,000 m)	(36,900) (37,000 m)
Labour	(20,000)	(18,000) (2,250 hr)	(17,500) (2,150 hr)
Fixed overheads	(20,000)	(20,000)	(20,700)
Operating profit	20,000	16,000	16,900

Flexible budgets enable us make a more valid comparison between budget (using the flexed figures) and actual. We can now see that there was a genuine labour cost saving, even after allowing for the output shortfall.

Sales volume variance

It may seem as if we are saying that it does not matter if there are volume shortfalls, because we just revise the budget and carry on as if nothing had happened. However, this is not the case, because losing sales means losing profit. The first point we must pick up, therefore, is the loss of profit arising from the loss of sales of 100 units of the product.

ACTIVITY 13.2

What will be the loss of profit arising from the sales shortfall, assuming that everything except sales volume was as planned?

The answer is simply the difference between the original and flexed budget profit figures. The only difference between these two profit figures is the volume of sales; everything else was the same. Thus the figure is £4,000 (that is, £20,000 – £16,000).

As we saw in Chapter 9, when we considered the relationship between cost, volume and profit, selling one unit less will result in one less contribution to profit. The contribution is sales revenue for one unit less variable cost. We can see from the original budget that the unit sales revenue is £100 (that is, £100,000/1,000), raw material cost is £40 a unit (that is, £40,000/1,000) and labour cost is £20 a unit (that is, £20,000/1,000). Thus the contribution is £40 a unit (that is, £100 – (£40 + £20)).

If, therefore, 100 units of sales are lost, £4,000 (that is, 100 × £40) of contributions, and therefore profit, are foregone. This would be an alternative means of finding the sales volume variance, instead of taking the difference between the original and flexed budget profit figures; nevertheless once we have produced the flexed budget, it is generally easier simply to compare the two profit figures.

The difference between the original and flexed budget profit figures is called the *sales volume variance*. It is an **adverse variance** because, taken alone, it has the effect of making the actual profit lower than that which was budgeted. A variance that has the effect of increasing profit above that which is budgeted is known as a **favourable variance**. We can therefore say that a **variance** is the effect of that factor (taken alone) on the budgeted profit. When looking at some particular aspect, such as sales volume, we assume that all other factors went according to plan. This is shown in Figure 13.3.

> **Sales volume variance**
> The difference between the profit as shown in the original budget and the profit as shown in the flexed budget for the period.

ACTIVITY 13.3

What else does the senior management of Baxter Ltd need to know about the May sales volume variance?

It needs to know why the volume of sales fell below the budgeted figure. Only by discovering this information will management be in a position to try to see that it does not occur again.

Figure 13.3	Relationship between the budgeted and actual profit

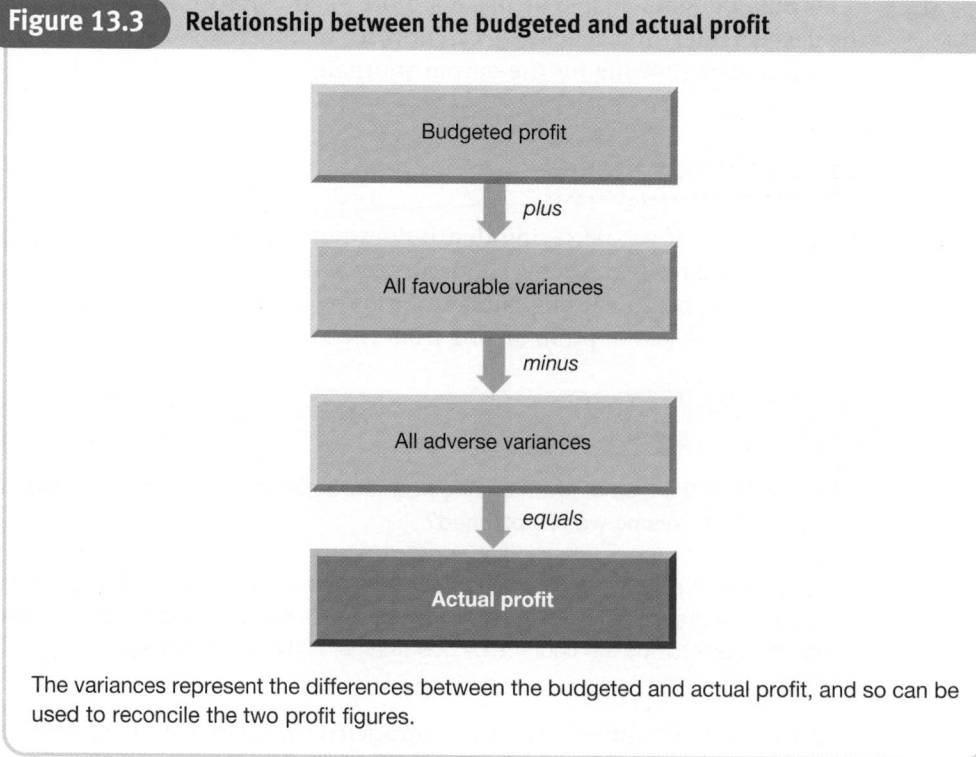

The variances represent the differences between the budgeted and actual profit, and so can be used to reconcile the two profit figures.

Who should be asked about this sales volume variance? The answer would probably be the sales manager. This person should know precisely why the departure from budget has occurred. This is not the same as saying that it was the sales manager's fault. The reason for the problem could easily have been that production was at fault in not having produced the budgeted quantities, meaning that there were not sufficient items to sell. What is not in doubt is that, in the first instance, it is the sales manager who should know the reason for the problem.

The budget and actual figures for Baxter Ltd for June are given in Activity 13.4. They will be used as the basis for a series of activities which you should work through as we look at variance analysis. Note that the business had budgeted for a higher level of output for June than it did for May.

ACTIVITY 13.4

	Budget for June	Actual for June
Output	1,100 units	1,150 units
(production and sales)		
	£	£
Sales revenue	110,000	113,500
Raw materials	(44,000) (44,000 metres)	(46,300) (46,300 metres)
Labour	(22,000) (2,750 hours)	(23,200) (2,960 hours)
Fixed overheads	(20,000)	(19,300)
Operating profit	24,000	24,700

Try flexing the June budget, comparing it with the original June budget, and so find the sales volume variance.

	Flexed budget
Output (production and sales)	1,150 units
	£
Sales revenue	115,000
Raw materials	(46,000) (46,000 metres)
Labour	(23,000) (2,875 hours)
Fixed overheads	(20,000)
Operating profit	26,000

The sales volume variance is £2,000 (favourable) (that is, £26,000 – £24,000). It is favourable since the original budget profit was lower than the flexed budget profit. This is because more sales were actually made than were budgeted.

Having dealt with the sales volume variance, we have picked up the profit difference caused by any variation between the budgeted and the actual volumes of sales. This means that, for the remainder of the analysis of the difference between the actual and budgeted profits, we can ignore the original budget. We can concentrate exclusively on the differences between the figures in the flexed budget and the actual figures.

Sales price variance

Sales price variance
The difference between the actual sales revenue figure for the period and the sales revenue figure as shown in the flexed budget.

Starting with the sales revenue figure, we can see that there is a difference of £2,000 (favourable) between the flexed budget and the actual figures. This can only arise from higher prices being charged than were envisaged in the original budget, because any variance arising from the volume difference has already been 'stripped out' in the flexing process. This price difference is known as the *sales price variance*. Higher sales prices will, all other things being equal, mean more profit. So there is a favourable variance.

ACTIVITY 13.5

Using the figures in Activity 13.4, what is the sales price variance for June?

The sales price variance for June is £1,500 (adverse) (that is, £115,000 – £113,500). Actual sales prices, on average, must have been lower than those budgeted. The actual price averaged £98.70 (that is, £113,500/1,150) whereas the budgeted price was £100. Selling output at a lower price than the budgeted one must tend to reduce profit, hence an adverse variance.

We shall now move on to look at the expenses.

Materials variances

Total direct materials variance
The difference between the actual direct materials cost and the direct materials cost according to the flexed budget (budgeted usage for the actual output).

In May, there was an overall or *total direct materials variance* of £900 (adverse) (that is, £36,900 – £36,000). It is adverse because the actual materials cost was higher than budgeted, which has an adverse effect on profit. Who should be held accountable for this variance? The answer depends on whether the difference arises from excess usage of the raw material, in which case it is the production manager, or whether it is a higher-than-budgeted price per metre being paid, in which case it is the responsibility of the buying manager.

Direct materials usage variance
The difference between the actual quantity of direct materials used and the quantity of direct materials according to the flexed budget (budgeted usage for actual output). This quantity is multiplied by the budgeted direct materials cost for one unit of the direct materials.

Fortunately, we have the means available to go beyond this total variance. We can see from the figures that there was a 1,000 metre excess usage of the raw material (that is, 37,000 metres – 36,000 metres). All other things being equal, this alone would have led to a profit shortfall of £1,000, since clearly the budgeted price per metre is £1. The £1,000 (adverse) variance is known as the *direct materials usage variance*. Normally, this variance would be the responsibility of the production manager.

ACTIVITY 13.6

Using the figures in Activity 13.4, what was the direct materials usage variance for June?

The direct materials usage variance for June was £300 (adverse) (that is, (46,300 – 46,000) × £1). It is adverse because more material was used than was budgeted for an output of 1,150 units. Excess usage of material will tend to reduce profit.

Direct materials price variance
The difference between the actual cost of the direct materials used and the direct materials cost allowed (actual quantity of materials used at the budgeted direct materials cost).

The other aspect of direct materials is the *direct materials price variance*. Here we simply take the actual cost of materials used and compare it with the cost that was allowed, given the quantity used. In May the actual cost of direct materials used was £36,900, whereas the allowed cost of the 37,000 metres was £37,000. Thus we have a favourable variance of £100. Paying less than the budgeted price will tend to increase profit, hence a favourable variance.

ACTIVITY 13.7

Using the figures in Activity 13.4, what was the direct materials price variance for June?

The direct materials price variance for June was zero (that is, (46,300 – 46,300) × £1).

As we have just seen, the total direct materials variance is the sum of the usage variance and the price variance. This is illustrated in Figure 13.4.

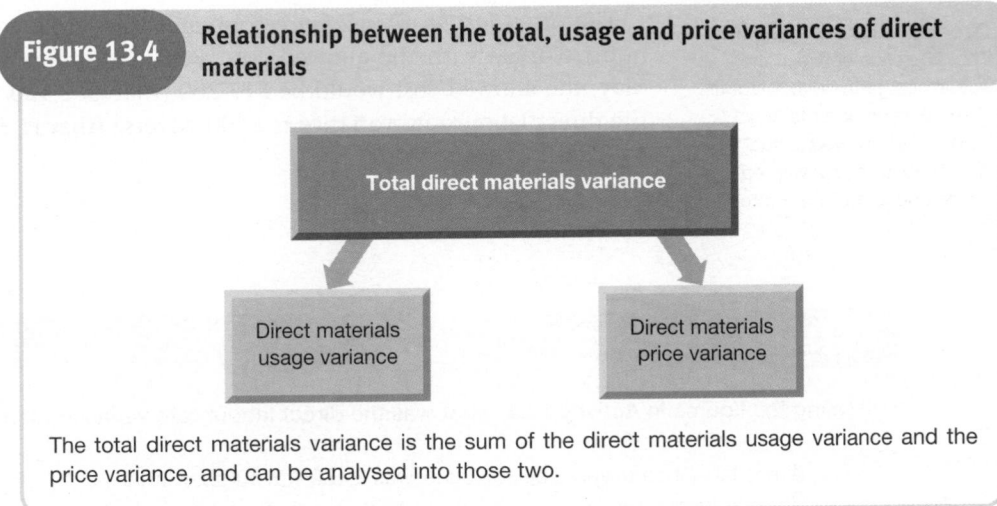

Figure 13.4 Relationship between the total, usage and price variances of direct materials

The total direct materials variance is the sum of the direct materials usage variance and the price variance, and can be analysed into those two.

Labour variances

Total direct labour variance
The difference between the actual direct labour cost and the direct labour cost according to the flexed budget (budgeted direct-labour-hours for the actual output).

Direct labour efficiency variance
The difference between the actual direct-labour-hours worked and the number of direct-labour-hours according to the flexed budget (budgeted direct-labour-hours for the actual output). This figure is multiplied by the budgeted direct-labour rate for one hour.

Direct labour variances are similar in form to those for raw materials. The *total direct labour variance* for May was £500 (favourable) (that is, £18,000 – £17,500). It is favourable because £500 less was spent on labour than was budgeted for the actual level of output achieved. Again, this information is not particularly helpful, and needs to be analysed further, since the responsibility for the rate of pay lies primarily with the personnel manager, whereas the number of hours taken to complete a particular quantity of output is the responsibility of the production manager.

The *direct labour efficiency variance* compares the number of hours that would be allowed for the achieved level of production with the actual number of hours. It then costs this difference at the allowed hourly rate. Thus, for May, it was (2,250 – 2,150) × £8 = £800 (favourable). We know that the budgeted hourly rate is £8 because the original budget shows that 2,500 hours were budgeted to cost £20,000. The variance is favourable because fewer hours were used than would have been allowed for the actual level of output. Working more quickly would tend to lead to higher profit.

ACTIVITY 13.8

Using the figures in Activity 13.4, what was the direct labour efficiency variance for June?

The direct labour efficiency variance for June was £680 (adverse) (that is, (2,960 – 2,875) × £8). It is adverse because the work took longer than the budget allowed. This would tend to lead to less profit.

Direct labour rate variance
The difference between the actual cost of the direct-labour-hours worked and the direct labour cost allowed (actual direct-labour-hours worked at the budgeted labour rate).

The *direct labour rate variance* compares the actual cost of the hours worked with the allowed cost. For 2,150 hours worked in May, the allowed cost would be £17,200 (that is, 2,150 × £8). So, the direct labour rate variance is £300 adverse (that is, £17,500 – £17,200).

ACTIVITY 13.9

Using the figures in Activity 13.4, what was the direct labour rate variance for June?

The direct labour rate variance for June was £480 (favourable) (that is, (2,960 × £8) – 23,200). It is favourable because a lower rate was paid than the budgeted one. Paying a lower wage rate will tend to increase profit.

Fixed overhead variance

The remaining area is that of overheads. In our example, we have assumed that all of the overheads are fixed. Variable overheads certainly exist in practice, but they have been omitted here simply to restrict the amount of detailed coverage. Variances involving variable overheads are similar in style to labour and materials variances.

Fixed overhead spending variance
The difference between the actual fixed overhead cost and the fixed overhead cost according to the flexed (and the original) budget.

The *fixed overhead spending variance* is simply the difference between the flexed (or original – they will be the same) budget and the actual figures. For May, this was £700 (adverse) (that is, £20,700 – £20,000). It is adverse because more overheads cost was actually incurred than was budgeted. This would tend to lead to less profit. In theory, this is the responsibility of whoever controls overheads expenditure. In practice, this tends to be a very slippery area, and one that is notoriously difficult to control.

ACTIVITY 13.10

Using the figures in Activity 13.4, what was the fixed overhead spending variance for June?

The fixed overhead spending variance for June was £700 (favourable) (that is, £20,000 – £19,300). It was favourable because less was spent on overheads than was budgeted, tending to increase profit.

We are now in a position to reconcile the original May budget profit with the actual profit, as follows:

	£	£
Budgeted profit		20,000
Add **Favourable variances**		
Sales price variance	2,000	
Direct materials price	100	
Direct labour efficiency	800	2,900
		22,900
Less **Adverse variances**		
Sales volume	4,000	
Direct materials usage	1,000	
Direct labour rate	300	
Fixed overhead spending	700	6,000
Actual profit		16,900

ACTIVITY 13.11

Using the figures in Activity 13.4, try reconciling the original profit figure for June with the actual June figure.

	£	£
Budgeted profit		24,000
Add **Favourable variances**		
Sales volume	2,000	
Direct labour rate	480	
Fixed overhead spending	700	
		3,180
		27,180
Less **Adverse variances**		
Sales price	1,500	
Direct materials usage	300	
Direct labour efficiency	680	
		2,480
Actual profit		24,700

ACTIVITY 13.12

The following are the budgeted and actual profit and loss accounts (income statements) for Baxter Ltd for the month of July:

	Budget	Actual
Output (production and sales)	1,000 units	1,050 units
	£	£
Sales revenue	100,000	104,300
Raw materials	(40,000) (40,000 metres)	(41,200) (40,500 metres)
Labour	(20,000) (2,500 hours)	(21,300) (2,600 hours)
Fixed overheads	(20,000)	(19,400)
Operating profit	20,000	22,400

Produce a reconciliation of the budgeted and actual operating profit, going into as much detail as possible with the variance analysis.

Activity 13.12 continued

The original budget, the flexed budget and the actual are as follows:

	Original budget 1,000 units	Flexed budget 1,050 units	Actual 1,050 units
Output (production and sales)			
	£	£	£
Sales revenue	100,000	105,000	104,300
Raw materials	(40,000)	(42,000)	(41,200)
Labour	(20,000)	(21,000)	(21,300)
Fixed overheads	(20,000)	(20,000)	(19,400)
Operating profit	20,000	22,000	22,400

Reconciliation of the budgeted and actual operating profits for July

	£	£
Budgeted profit		20,000
Add Favourable variances:		
Sales volume (22,000 – 20,000)	2,000	
Direct materials usage {[(1,050 × 40) – 40,500] × £1}	1,500	
Direct labour efficiency {[(1,050 × 2.50) – 2,600] × £8}	200	
Fixed overhead spending (20,000 – 19,400)	600	4,300
		24,300
Less Adverse variances:		
Sales price variance (105,000 – 104,300)	700	
Direct materials price [(40,500 × £1) – 41,200]	700	
Direct labour rate [(2,600 × £8) – 21,300]	500	1,900
Actual profit		22,400

Real World 13.1 gives some indication of the extent of use of **variance analysis** in practice.

REAL WORLD 13.1

Accounting for control in practice

A 1993 survey of UK manufacturing businesses showed variance analysis to be very widely used: 76 per cent of all the survey respondents used it, with 83 per cent of larger businesses using it. Interestingly, 11 per cent of businesses had abandoned using variance analysis during the 10 years preceding the date of the survey. Does this imply that there is a significant shift away from its use?

The variances that are widely used, and regarded as important, are those that we have looked at in some detail in this chapter.

Though this survey was conducted some time ago, it represents the most recent such survey and is worth noting.

Source: Taken from information appearing in Drury *et al*. (see reference 1 at the end of the chapter).

Standard quantities and costs

We have already seen that a budget is a business plan for the short term – typically one year – and it is likely to be expressed mainly in financial terms. It is built up from standards. **Standard quantities and costs** (or revenue) are those planned for individual units of input or output. Thus standards are the building blocks of the budget.

We can say about Baxter Ltd's operations that:

- the standard selling price is £100 for one unit of output;
- the standard raw materials cost is £40 for one unit of output;
- the standard raw materials usage is 40 metres for one unit of output;
- the standard raw materials price is £1 a metre (that is, for one unit of input);
- the standard labour cost is £20 for one unit of output;
- the standard labour time is 2.50 hours for one unit of output;
- the standard labour rate is £8 an hour (that is, for one unit of input).

The standards, like the budgets to which they are linked, represent targets and, therefore, yardsticks by which actual performance is measured. They are derived from experience and judgements of what is a reasonable quantity of input (for labour time and materials usage) and from assessments of the market for the product (standard selling price) and the market for the inputs (labour rate and material price). These should be subject to frequent review and, where necessary, revision. It is vital, if they are to be used as part of the control process, that they represent realistic targets.

Calculation of most variances is, in effect, based on standards. For example, the material usage variance is the difference between the standard materials usage for the level of output and the actual usage, costed at the standard materials price.

Standards can have uses other than in the context of budgetary control. Standards provide the business with a database of costs, usages, selling prices and so on, that are known to be broadly realistic. This provides managers with a ready set of information for their decision making and income measurement purposes.

Real World 13.2 provides some information on the use of standard costs in practice.

REAL WORLD 13.2

Standard costing in practice

The Drury, Braund, Osborne and Tayles survey from 1993 showed that the respondent businesses found standard costs important to them for the following purposes:

	Percentage of respondents
Cost control and performance evaluation	72
Valuing stock (inventory) and work in progress	80
Deducing costs for decision-making purposes	62
To help in constructing budgets	69

Thus, standards are seen as very important in the context of the subject of this chapter (cost control and performance evaluation), but they also seem to be widely used for other financial and management accounting purposes.

The conventional wisdom on the level of standards is that they should be demanding but achievable. Thus, if the standard direct labour time for some activity is five minutes,

Real World 13.2 continued

this should be capable of being achieved yet require staff to be working efficiently to achieve it. The survey showed that 44 per cent of respondents deliberately set standards of this type; 46 per cent, however, set standards based on past performance. Perhaps this was because the businesses' managements felt that past performance represents an achievable (obviously) yet demanding level of achievement. Only 5 per cent of respondents set standards at a level that could be achieved if everything went perfectly all of the time. Many people believe that such standards are not helpful because they do not represent a realistic target in a world where things *do* go wrong from time to time.

Standards are formally reviewed annually or more frequently by 91 per cent of the respondent businesses. This would amount to considering whether the existing standards are set at an appropriate level and amending them where necessary.

Source: Drury *et al*. (see reference 1 at the end of the chapter).

Labour cost standards and the learning-curve effect

Where a particular activity undertaken by direct workers has been unchanged in nature for some time, and the workers are experienced at performing it, normally an established standard labour time will be unchanged over time. Where a new activity is introduced, or new people are involved with performing an existing task, a **learning-curve** effect will normally occur. This is shown in Figure 13.5.

The first unit of output takes a long time to produce. As experience is gained, the person takes less time to produce each unit of output. The rate of reduction in the time taken will, however, decrease as experience is gained. Thus, for example, the reduction in time taken between the first and second unit produced will be much bigger than the reduction between, say, the ninth and the tenth. Eventually, the rate of reduction in time taken will reduce to zero so that each unit will take as long as the preceding one. At this point, the point where the curve in Figure 13.5 becomes horizontal (the bottom

Figure 13.5 **The learning-curve effect**

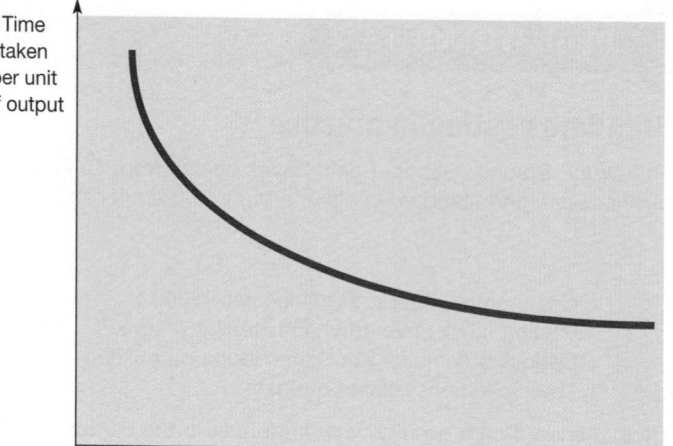

Each time a particular task is performed, people become quicker at it. This learning-curve effect becomes less and less significant until, after performing the task a number of times, no further learning occurs.

right of the graph), the learning-curve effect will have been eliminated and a steady, long-term standard time for the activity will have been established.

The learning-curve effect seems to have little to do with whether workers are skilled or unskilled; if they are unfamiliar with the task, the learning-curve effect will arise. Practical experience shows that learning curves show remarkable regularity and, therefore, predictability from one activity to the next.

Clearly, the learning-curve effect must be taken into account when setting standards, and when interpreting any adverse labour efficiency variances, where a new process and/or new personnel are involved.

Reasons for adverse variances

A constant possible reason why variances occur is that the standards against which performance is being measured are not reasonable targets. This is certainly not to say that the immediate reaction to an adverse variance should be that the standard is unreasonably harsh. On the other hand, standards that are not achievable are useless.

ACTIVITY 13.13

The variances that we have considered are:

- sales volume
- sales price
- direct materials usage
- direct materials price
- direct labour efficiency
- direct labour rate
- fixed overhead spending.

Ignoring the possibility that standards may be unreasonable, jot down any ideas that occur to you as possible practical reasons for adverse variances in each case.

The reasons that we thought of included the following:

Sales volume
- Poor performance by sales personnel.
- Deterioration in market conditions between the setting of the budget and the actual event.
- Lack of stock (inventory) or services to sell as a result of some production problem.

Sales price
- Poor performance by sales personnel.
- Deterioration in market conditions between the setting of the budget and the actual event.

Direct materials usage
- Poor performance by production department staff, leading to high rates of scrap.
- Substandard materials, leading to high rates of scrap.
- Faulty machinery, causing high rates of scrap.

Direct materials price
- Poor performance by buying department staff.
- Change in market conditions between setting the standard and the actual event.

Activity 13.13 continued

Labour efficiency
- Poor supervision.
- A low skill grade of worker taking longer to do the work than was envisaged for the correct skill grade.
- Low-grade materials, leading to high levels of scrap and wasted labour time.
- Problems with a customer for whom a service is being rendered.
- Problems with machinery, leading to labour time being wasted.
- Dislocation of materials supply, leading to workers being unable to proceed with production.

Labour rate
- Poor performance by the personnel function.
- Using a higher grade of worker than was planned.
- Change in labour market conditions between setting the standard and the actual event.

Fixed overheads
- Poor supervision of overheads.
- General increase in costs of overheads not taken into account in the budget.

Though we have tended to use the example of a manufacturing business to explain variance analysis, this should not be taken to imply that variance analysis is not equally applicable and useful in service-sector businesses. It is simply that manufacturing businesses tend to have all of the variances found in practice. Service businesses, for example, may not have materials variances.

Non-operating profit variances

There are many areas of business that have a budget but where a failure to meet the budget does not have a direct effect on profit. Frequently, however, it has an indirect effect on profit, and sometimes a profound effect. For example, the cash budget sets out the planned receipts, payments and resultant cash balance for the period. If the person responsible for the cash budget gets things wrong, or is forced to make unplanned expenditures, this could lead to unplanned cash shortages and accompanying costs. These costs might be limited to lost interest on possible investments, which could otherwise have been made, or to the need to pay overdraft interest. If the cash shortage cannot be covered by some form of borrowing, the consequences could be more profound, such as the loss of profits on business that was not able to be undertaken because of the lack of funds.

It is clearly necessary that control be exercised over areas such as cash management as well as over those like production and sales in an attempt to avoid adverse ➔ **non-operating profit variances**.

Investigating variances

It is unreasonable to expect budget targets to be met precisely each month and so variances will usually occur. Whatever the reason for a variance, finding that reason will take time, and time is costly. Small variances are almost inevitable, yet investigating variances can be expensive. Management needs, therefore, to establish a policy concerning which variances to investigate and which to accept. For example, for Baxter Ltd (Example 13.1 on p. 433) the budgeted usage of materials during May was 40,000 metres at a cost of £1 a metre. Suppose that production had been the same as the budgeted quantity of output, but that 40,005 metres of material, costing £1 a metre, had actually been used. Would this adverse variance of £5 be investigated? Probably not. What, though, if the variance were £50 or £500 or £5,000?

ACTIVITY 13.14

What broad approach do you feel should be taken as to whether to spend money investigating a particular variance?

The general approach to this policy must be concerned with cost and benefit. The benefit likely to be gained from knowing why a variance arose needs to be balanced against the cost of obtaining that knowledge. The issue of balancing the benefit of having information with the cost of having it was discussed in Chapter 1.

Unfortunately, as is often the case in practice, both the cost of investigation and the value of the benefit are difficult to assess in advance of the investigation.

Knowing the reason for a variance can have a value only when it might provide management with the means to bring things back under control, enabling future targets to be met. It should be borne in mind here that variances will normally be either zero, or very close to zero. This is to say that achieving targets, give or take small variances, should be normal.

Broadly, we suggest that the following approach seems sensible:

1 Significant *adverse* variances should be investigated because the continuation of the fault that they represent could be very costly. Management must decide what 'significant' means. A certain amount of science, in the form of statistical models, can be brought to bear in making this decision. Ultimately, however, it must be a matter of managerial judgement as to what is significant. Perhaps a variance of 5 per cent from the budgeted figure would be deemed to be significant.

2 Significant *favourable* variances should probably be investigated as well as those that are unfavourable. Though such variances would not cause such immediate management concern as adverse ones, they still represent things not going according to plan. If actual performance is significantly better than target, it may well mean that the target is unrealistically low.

3 Insignificant variances, though not triggering immediate investigation, should be kept under review. For each aspect of operations, the cumulative sum of variances, over a series of control periods, should be zero, with small adverse variances in some periods being compensated for by small favourable ones in others. This should be the case with variances that are caused by chance factors, which will not necessarily repeat themselves.

Where a variance is caused by a more systematic factor, which will repeat itself, the cumulative sum of the periodic variances will not be zero but an increasing figure. Where the increasing figure represents a set of adverse variances it may well be worth investigating the situation, even though the individual variances may be insignificant. Even where the direction of the cumulative total points to favourable variances, investigation may still be considered to be valuable.

To illustrate this last point, let us consider Example 13.2.

Example 13.2

Indisurers Ltd finds that the variances for direct labour efficiency for processing motor insurance claims, since the beginning of the year, are as follows:

	£			£
January	25 (adverse)		July	20 (adverse)
February	15 (favourable)		August	15 (favourable)
March	5 (favourable)		September	23 (adverse)
April	20 (adverse)		October	15 (favourable)
May	22 (adverse)		November	5 (favourable)
June	8 (favourable)		December	26 (adverse)

The average total cost of labour performing this task is about £1,200 a month. Management believes that none of these variances, taken alone, is significant given the labour cost each month. The question is, are they significant when taken together? If we add them together, taking account of the signs, we find that we have a net adverse variance for the year of £73. Of itself this, too, is probably not significant, but we should expect the cumulative total to be close to zero, were the variances random. We might feel that a pattern is developing and, given long enough, a net adverse variance of significant size might build up.

Investigating the labour efficiency might be worth doing. (We should note that 12 periods are probably not enough to reach a statistically sound conclusion on whether the variances are random or not, but it provides an illustration of the point.)

Plotting the cumulative variances, from month to month, as in Figure 13.6, makes it clear what is happening at Indisurers Ltd as time proceeds.

Real World 13.3 is taken from the research of Drury, Braund, Osborne and Tayles. The table shows the methods used by respondents to the survey to make the decision on whether to investigate a particular variance.

REAL WORLD 13.3

Methods used to make decisions on investigation of variances

	% 'Often' or 'Always'
Decisions based on managerial judgement	75
Variance exceeds a specific monetary amount	41
Variance exceeds a given percentage of standard	36
Statistical models	3

Source: Reproduced from Table 5.7 on p. 39 of Drury *et al*. (see reference 1 at the end of the chapter).

It is interesting to note the large extent, revealed by this survey, to which decisions on whether to investigate variances are made on the basis of some, presumably subjective, judgement. We might have expected businesses to adopt a more systematic

Figure 13.6	The cumulative variances for labour efficiency in motor insurance claim handling at Indisurers Ltd

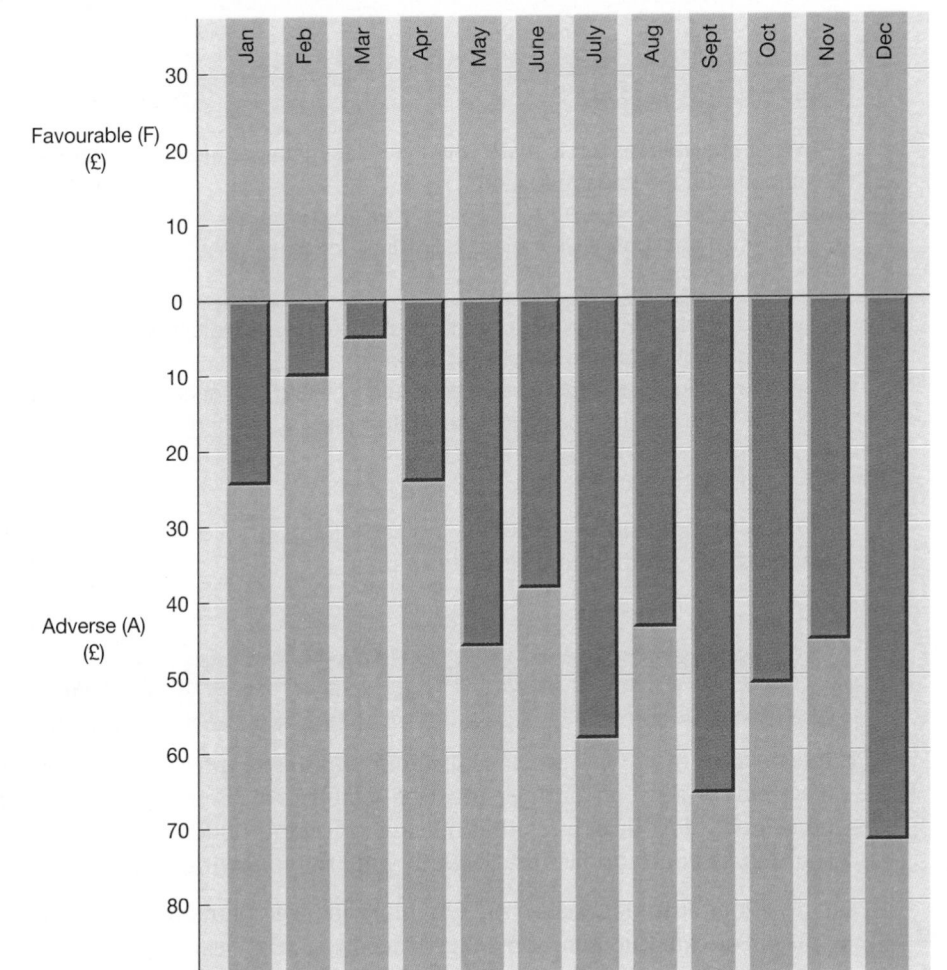

Starting at zero at the beginning of January, each month the cumulative variance (that is, the sum (taking account of the plus and minus signs)) is plotted. The January figure is £25 (A). The February one is £10 (A) (that is £25 (A) plus £15 (F)) and so on. The graph seems to show an overall trend of adverse variances, but with several favourable variances involved.

approach. The survey is not very recent, but it probably provides some helpful insights to current practice.

Compensating variances

There is superficial appeal in the idea of **compensating variances**. This is, trading off linked favourable and adverse variances against each other, without further consideration. For example, a sales manager believes that she could sell more of a particular service if prices were lowered, and that this would feed through to increased net operating profit. This would lead to a favourable sales volume variance, but also to an adverse sales price variance. On the face of it, provided that the former is greater than the latter, all would be well.

ACTIVITY 13.15

What possible reason is there why the sales manager mentioned above should not go ahead with the price reduction?

The change in policy will have ramifications for other areas of the business, including the following:

● The need for more provision of the service to be available to sell. Staff and other factors might not be able to supply this increase.
● Increased sales would involve an increased need for finance to pay for increased activity, for example to pay additional staff costs.

Thus 'trading off' variances is not automatically acceptable, without a more far-reaching consultation and revision of plans.

Making budgetary control effective

It is obvious from what we have seen of **budgetary control** that, if it is to be successful, a system, or a set of routines, must be established to enable the potential benefits to be gained. Most businesses that operate successful budgetary control systems tend to share some common factors. These include the following:

1 A serious attitude taken to the system by all levels of management, right from the very top. For example, senior managers need to make clear to junior managers that they take notice of the monthly variance reports and base some of their actions on them.
2 Clear demarcation between areas of managerial responsibility so that accountability can more easily be ascribed for any area that seems to be going out of control. It needs to be clear which manager is responsible for each aspect of the business.
3 Budget targets being reasonable, so that they represent a rigorous yet achievable target. This may be promoted by managers being involved in setting their own targets. It is argued that this can increase the managers' commitment and motivation. We shall consider this in more detail shortly.
4 Established data collection, analysis and dissemination routines, which take the actual results and the budget figures, and calculate and report the variances. This should be part of the business's regular accounting information system, so that the required reports are automatically produced each month.
5 Reports aimed at individual managers, rather than general-purpose documents. This avoids managers having to wade through reams of reports to find the part that is relevant to them.
6 Fairly short reporting periods, typically a month, so that things cannot go too far wrong before they are picked up.
7 Variance reports being produced and disseminated shortly after the end of the relevant reporting period. If it is not until the end of June that a manager is informed

that the performance in May was below the budgeted level, it is quite likely that the performance for June will be below target as well. Reports on the performance in May ideally need to emerge in early June.

8 Action being taken to get operations back under control if they are shown to be out of control. The report will not change things by itself. Managers need to take action to try to ensure that the reporting of significant adverse variances leads to action to put things right for the future.

Limitations of the traditional approach to control through variances and standards

Budgetary control of the type that we have reviewed in this chapter has obvious appeal and, judging by the wide extent of its use in practice, it has value as well. It is somewhat limited at times, however. Some of its limitations are as follows:

1 Vast areas of most business and commercial activities simply do not have the same direct relationship between inputs and outputs as is the case with, say, level of output and the number of direct-labour-hours worked. Many of the expenses of a modern business are in areas such as training and advertising, where the expense is discretionary and not linked to the level of output in a direct way.

2 Standards can quickly become out of date as a result of both technological change and price changes. This does not pose insuperable problems, but it does require that the potential problem be systematically addressed. Standards that are unrealistic are, at best, useless. At worst, they could have adverse effects on performance. A personnel manager who knows that it is impossible to meet targets on rates of pay for labour, because of general labour cost rises, may have a reduced incentive to minimise costs.

3 Sometimes factors that are outside the control of the manager concerned can affect the calculation of the variance for which that manager is held accountable. This may have an adverse effect on the assessment of the manager's performance. The situation can often be overcome by a more considered approach to the calculation of the variance, resulting in those factors controllable by the manager being separated from those that are not.

4 In practice, creating clear lines of demarcation between the areas of responsibility of various managers may be difficult. Thus, one of the prerequisites of good budgetary control is lost.

Behavioural aspects of budgetary control

Budgets, perhaps more than any other accounting statement, are prepared with the objective of affecting the attitudes and behaviour of managers. The point was made in Chapter 12 that budgets are intended to motivate managers, and research evidence generally shows this to be true. More specifically, the research shows:

● The existence of budgets generally tends to improve performance.
● Demanding, yet achievable, budget targets tend to motivate better than less demanding targets. It seems that setting the most demanding targets that will be accepted by managers is a very effective way to motivate them.

- Unrealistically demanding targets tend to have an adverse effect on managers' performance.
- The participation of managers in setting their targets tends to improve motivation and performance. This is probably because those managers feel a sense of commitment to the targets and a moral obligation to achieve them.

It has been suggested that allowing managers to set their own targets will lead to slack (that is, easily achievable targets) being introduced. This would make achievement of the target that much easier. On the other hand, in an effort to impress, a manager may select a target that is not really achievable. These points imply that care must be taken in the extent to which managers have unfettered choice of their own targets.

The impact of management style

There has been a great deal of literature published on the way in which managers use information generated by the budgeting system and the impact of its use on the attitudes and behaviour of subordinates. A pioneering study by Hopwood (see reference 2 at the end of the chapter) examined the way in which managers working within a manufacturing environment used budget information to evaluate the performance of subordinates. He argued that three distinct styles of management could be observed. These are:

- *Budget-constrained style.* This management style focuses rigidly on the ability of subordinates to meet the budget. Other factors relating to the performance of subordinates are not given serious consideration, even though they might include improving the long-term effectiveness of the area for which the subordinate has responsibility,
- *Profit-conscious style.* This management style uses budget information in a more flexible way and often in conjunction with other data. The main focus is on the ability of each subordinate to improve long-term effectiveness.
- *Non-accounting style.* In this case, budget information plays no significant role in the evaluation of a subordinate's performance.

ACTIVITY 13.16

How might a manager respond to budget information that indicates a subordinate has not met the budget targets for the period, assuming the manager adopts:

(a) a budget-constrained style?
(b) a profit-conscious style?
(c) a non-accounting style?

(a) A manager adopting a budget-constrained style is likely to take the budget information very seriously. This may result in criticism of the subordinate and, perhaps, some form of punishment.
(b) A manager adopting a profit-conscious style is likely to take a broader view when examining the budget information and so will take other factors into consideration (for example, factors that could not have been anticipated at the time of preparing the budgets), before deciding whether criticism or punishment is justified.
(c) A manager adopting a non-accounting style will regard the failure to meet the budget as being relatively unimportant and so no action may be taken.

Hopwood found that subordinates working for a manager who adopts a budget-constrained style had unfortunate experiences. They suffered higher levels of job-related stress and had poorer working relationships, with both their colleagues and their manager, than those subordinates whose manager adopted one of the other two styles. Hopwood also found that the subordinates of a budget-constrained style of manager were more likely to manipulate the budget figures, or to take other undesirable actions, to ensure the budgets were met.

Reservations about the Hopwood study

Though Hopwood's findings are interesting, subsequent studies have cast doubt on their universal applicability. Later studies confirm that human attitudes and behaviour are complex and can vary according to the particular situation. For example, it has been found that the impact of different management styles on such factors as job-related stress and the manipulation of budget figures seems to vary. The impact is likely to depend on such factors as the level of independence enjoyed by the subordinates and the level of uncertainty associated with the tasks to be undertaken.

It seems that where there is a high level of interdependence between business divisions, subordinate managers are more likely to feel that they have less control over their performance, because the performance of staff in other divisions could be an important influence on the final outcome. In such a situation, rigid application of the budget could be viewed as being unfair and may lead to undesirable behaviour. However, where managers have a high degree of independence, the application of budgets as a measure of performance is likely to be more acceptable. In this case, the managers are likely to feel that the final outcome is much less dependent on the performance of others.

Later studies have also shown that where a subordinate is undertaking a task that has a high degree of uncertainty concerning the outcome (for example, developing a new product for the market), budget targets are unlikely to be an adequate measure of performance. In such a situation, other factors and measures should be taken into account in order to derive a more complete assessment of performance. However, where a task has a low degree of uncertainty concerning the outcome (for example, producing a standard product using standard equipment and an experienced workforce), budget measures may be regarded as more reliable indicators of performance. It appears that a budget-constrained style is more likely to work where subordinates enjoy a fair amount of independence and where the tasks set have a low level of uncertainty concerning their outcomes.

Failing to meet the budget

The existence of budgets gives senior managers a ready means to assess the performance of their subordinates. Where a manager fails to meet a budget, the failure must be dealt with carefully by his/her senior manager. A harsh, critical approach may demotivate the manager. Adverse variances may imply that the manager needs some help.

Real World 13.4 gives some indication of the effects of the **behavioural aspects of budgetary control** in practice.

REAL WORLD 13.4

Behavioural aspects of budgetary control in practice

The 1993 survey by Drury, Braund, Osborne and Tayles indicates that there is a large degree of participation in setting budgets by those who will be expected to perform to the budget standard (the budget holders). It also indicates that senior management has greater influence in setting the targets than the budget holders.

Where there is a conflict between the cost estimates submitted by the budget holders and their managers, in 40 per cent of respondent businesses the senior manager's view would prevail without negotiation, but in nearly 60 per cent of cases there would be reduction, but it would be negotiated between the budget holder and the senior manager. The general philosophy of the respondent businesses, regarding budget holders influencing the setting of their own budgets, is:

- 23 per cent of respondents believe that budget holders should not have too much influence since they will seek to obtain easy budgets (build in slack) if they do;
- the opposite view was taken by 69 per cent of respondents.

The general view on how senior managers should judge their subordinates is:

- 46 per cent of respondent businesses think that senior managers should judge junior managers mainly on their ability to achieve the budget;
- 40 per cent think otherwise.

Though this research is not very recent, in the absence of more recent evidence it provides some feel for budget setting in practice.

Source: Drury *et al.* (see reference 1 at the end of the chapter).

SELF-ASSESSMENT QUESTION 13.1

Toscanini Ltd makes a standard product, which is budgeted to sell at £4.00 a unit, in a competitive market. It is made by taking a budgeted 0.4 kg of material, budgeted to cost £2.40/kg, and working on it by hand by an employee, paid a budgeted £8.00/hour, for a budgeted 6 minutes. Monthly fixed overheads are budgeted at £4,800. The output for May was budgeted at 4,000 units.

The actual results for May were as follows:

	£
Sales revenue (3,500 units)	13,820
Materials (1,425 kg)	(3,420)
Labour (345 hours)	(2,690)
Fixed overheads	(4,900)
Actual operating profit	2,810

No stocks of any description existed at the beginning and end of the month.

Required:
(a) Deduce the budgeted profit for May, and reconcile it with the actual profit in as much detail as the information provided will allow.
(b) State which manager should be held accountable, in the first instance, for each variance calculated.
(c) Assuming that the standards were all well set in terms of labour times and rates and material usage and price, suggest at least one feasible reason for each of the variances that you identified in (a), given what you know about the business's performance for May.
(d) If it were discovered that the actual total world market demand for the business's product was 10 per cent lower than estimated when the May budget was set, explain how and why the variances that you identified in (a) could be revised to provide information that would be potentially more useful.

SUMMARY

The main points of this chapter may be summarised as follows:

Controlling through budgets

- Budgets act as a system of both feedback and feedforward control.
- Budgets can be flexed to match actual volume of output.
- Variance = increase (favourable) or decrease (adverse) in profit, relative to the budgeted profit, as a result of some aspect of the business's activities taken alone.
- Budgeted profit plus all favourable variances less all adverse variances equals actual profit.
- Commonly calculated variances:
  - Sales volume variance = difference between budgeted and actual volume (in units) multiplied by the standard contribution (for one unit).
  - Sales price variance = difference between actual sales revenue and actual volume at the standard sales price.
  - Direct materials usage variance = difference between actual usage and budgeted usage, for the actual volume of output, multiplied by the standard materials cost.
  - Direct materials price variance = difference between the actual materials cost and the actual usage multiplied by the standard materials cost.
  - Direct labour efficiency variance = difference between actual labour time and budgeted time, for the actual volume of output, multiplied by the standard labour rate.
  - Direct labour rate variance = difference between the actual labour cost and the actual labour time multiplied by the standard labour rate.
  - Fixed overhead spending variance = difference between the actual and budgeted spending on fixed overheads.
- Standards = budgeted physical quantities and financial values for one unit of inputs and outputs.
- Standards are useful in providing data for decision making and income measurement.
- There tends to be a learning-curve effect: routine tasks are performed more quickly with experience.
- Significant and/or persistent variances need to be investigated to establish their cause.
- Good budgetary control requires establishing systems and routines to ensure such things as a clear distinction between individual managers' areas of responsibility; prompt, frequent and relevant variance reporting; and senior management commitment.
- Not all activities can usefully be controlled through traditional variance analysis.
- There is a behavioural aspect of control and this should be taken into account by senior managers.

 **Key terms**

feedback control p. 432	standard quantities and costs p. 443
feedforward control p. 433	learning curve p. 444
flexing the budget p. 434	non-operating profit variances p. 446
flexible budget p. 435	compensating variances p. 449
adverse variance p. 435	budgetary control p. 450
favourable variance p. 435	behavioural aspects of budgetary
variance p. 435	control p. 453
variance analysis p. 442	

Further reading

If you would like to explore the topics covered in this chapter in more depth, we recommend the following books:

Management Accounting, *Atkinson A., Banker R., Kaplan R. and Young S.M.*, 3rd edn, Prentice Hall, 2001, chapter 12.

Management and Cost Accounting, *Drury C.*, 5th edn, Thomson Learning Business Press, 2000, chapters 16, 18 and 19.

Cost Accounting: A managerial emphasis, *Horngren C., Foster G. and Datar S.*, 11th edn, Prentice Hall International, 2002, chapters 7 and 8.

Cost and Management Accounting, *Williamson D.*, Prentice Hall International, 1996, chapter 15.

References

1 **A Survey of Managment Accounting Practices in UK Manufacturing Companies**, *Drury, C., Braund, S., Osborne, P. and Tayles, M.*, Chartered Association of Certified Accountants, 1993.

2 'An empirical study of the role of accounting data in performance evaluation', *Hopwood, A. G.*, in **Empirical Research in Accounting**, a supplement to the **Journal of Accounting Research**, 1972, pp. 156–82.

REVIEW QUESTIONS

Answers to these questions can be found on the students' side of the Companion Website.
at **www.pearsoned.co.uk/atrillmclaney**.

13.1 Explain what is meant by feedforward control and distinguish it from feedback control.

13.2 What is meant by a variance? What is the point in analysing variances?

13.3 What is the point in flexing the budget in the context of variance analysis? Does flexing imply that differences between budget and actual in the volume of output are ignored in variance analysis?

13.4 Should all variances be investigated to find their cause? Explain your answer.

EXERCISES

Exercises 13.4 to 13.8 are more advanced than 13.1 to 13.3. Those with coloured numbers have answers at the back of the book.

13.1 You have recently overheard the following remarks:

(a) 'A favourable direct labour rate variance can only be caused by staff working more efficiently than budgeted.'

(b) 'Selling more units than budgeted, because the units were sold at less than standard price, automatically leads to a favourable sales volume variance.'

(c) 'Using below-standard materials will tend to lead to adverse materials usage variances but cannot affect labour variances.'

(d) 'Higher-than-budgeted sales could not possibly affect the labour rate variance.'

(e) 'An adverse sales price variance can only arise from selling a product at less than standard price.'

Required:
Critically assess these remarks, explaining any technical terms.

13.2 Pilot Ltd makes a standard product, which is budgeted to sell at £5.00 a unit. It is made by taking a budgeted 0.5 kg of material, budgeted to cost £3.00 a kilogram, and working on it by hand by an employee, paid a budgeted £5.00 an hour, for a budgeted 15 minutes. Monthly fixed overheads are budgeted at £6,000. The output for March was budgeted at 5,000 units.

The actual results for March were as follows:

	£
Sales revenue (5,400 units)	26,460
Materials (2,830 kg)	(8,770)
Labour (1,300 hours)	(6,885)
Fixed overheads	(6,350)
Actual operating profit	4,455

No stocks existed at the start or end of March.

Required:
(a) Deduce the budgeted profit for March and reconcile it with the actual profit in as much detail as the information provided will allow.

(b) State which manager should be held accountable, in the first instance, for each variance calculated.

13.3 Antonio plc makes product X, the standard costs of which are:

	£
Sales revenue	31
Direct labour (2 hours)	(11)
Direct materials (1 kg)	(10)
Fixed overheads	(3)
Standard profit	7

The budgeted output for March was 1,000 units of product X; the actual output was 1,100 units, which was sold for £34,950. There were no stocks at the start or end of March.

The actual production costs were:

	£
Direct labour (2,150 hours)	12,210
Direct materials (1,170 kg)	11,630
Fixed overheads	3,200

Required:

Calculate the variances for March as fully as you are able from the available information, and use them to reconcile the budgeted and actual profit figures.

13.4 You have recently overheard the following remarks:

(a) 'When calculating variances, we in effect ignore differences of volume of output, between original budget and actual, by flexing the budget. If there were a volume difference, it is water under the bridge by the time that the variances come to be calculated.'
(b) 'It is very valuable to calculate variances because they will tell you what went wrong.'
(c) 'All variances should be investigated to find their cause.'
(d) 'Research evidence shows that the more demanding the target, the more motivated the manager.'
(e) 'Most businesses do not have feedforward controls of any type, just feedback controls through budgets.'

Required:

Critically assess these remarks, explaining any technical terms.

13.5 Bradley-Allen Ltd makes one standard product. Its budgeted operating statement for May is as follows:

		£	£
Sales revenue:	800 units		64,000
Direct materials:	Type A	12,000	
	Type B	16,000	
Direct labour:	Skilled	4,000	
	Unskilled	10,000	
Overheads:	(All Fixed)	12,000	
			54,000
Budgeted operating profit			10,000

The standard costs were as follows:

Direct materials:	Type A	£50/kg
	Type B	£20/m
Direct labour:	Skilled	£10/hour
	Unskilled	£8/hour

During May, the following occurred:

(i)   950 units were sold for a total of £73,000.
(ii) 310 kilos (costing £15,200) of type A material were used in production.
(iii) 920 metres (costing £18,900) of type B material were used in production.
(iv) Skilled workers were paid £4,628 for 445 hours.
(v)   Unskilled workers were paid £11,275 for 1,375 hours.
(vi) Fixed overheads cost £11,960.

There was no stock of finished production or of work in progress at either end of May.

Required:

(a) Prepare a statement that reconciles the budgeted to the actual profit of the business for May. Your statement should analyse the difference between the two profit figures in as much detail as you are able.

(b) Explain how the statement in (a) might be helpful to managers.

13.6 Mowbray Ltd makes and sells one product, the standard costs of which are as follows:

	£
Direct materials (3 kg at £2.50/kg)	7.50
Direct labour (15 minutes at £9.00/hr)	2.25
Fixed overheads	3.60
	13.35
Selling price	20.00
Standard profit margin	6.65

The monthly production and sales are planned to be 1,200 units.

The actual results for May were as follows:

	£	
Sales revenue	18,000	
Less Direct materials	(7,400)	(2,800 kg)
Direct labour	(2,300)	(255 hr)
Fixed overheads	(4,100)	
Operating profit	4,200	

There were no stocks at the start or end of May. As a result of poor sales demand during May, the business reduced the price of all sales by 10%.

Required:

Calculate the budgeted profit for May and reconcile it to the actual profit through variances, going into as much detail as is possible from the information available.

13.7 Varne Chemprocessors is a business that specialises in plastics. It uses a standard costing system to monitor and report its purchases and usage of materials. During the most recent month, accounting period six, the purchase and usage of chemical UK194 were as follows:

Purchases/usage:	28,100 litres
Total price:	£51,704

Because of fire risk and the danger to health, no stocks are held by the business. UK194 is used solely in the manufacture of a product called Varnelyne. The standard cost specification shows that, for the production of 5,000 litres of Varnelyne, 200 litres of UK194 is needed at a total standard cost of £392. During period six, 637,500 litres of Varnelyne were produced.

Required:

(a) Calculate the price and usage variances for UK194 for period six.

(b) The following comment was made by the production manager:

'I knew at the beginning of period six that UK194 would be cheaper than the standard cost specification, so I used rather more of it than normal; this saved £4,900 on other chemicals.'

What changes do you need to make in your analysis for (a) as a result of this comment?

(c) Calculate, for each material below, the cumulative variances and comment briefly on the results.

Variances: periods one to six

Period	UK500		UK800	
	£		£	
1	301	F	298	F
2	251	A	203	F
3	102	F	52	A
4	202	A	98	A
5	153	F	150	A
6	103	A	201	A

where F = cost saving and A = cost overrun.

13.8 Brive plc has the following standards for its only product:

Selling price:	£110/unit
Direct labour:	2 hours at £5.25/hour
Direct material:	3 kg at £14.00/kg
Fixed overheads:	£27.00, based on a budgeted output of 800 units/month

During May, there was an actual output of 850 units and the operating statement for the month was as follows:

	£
Sales revenue	92,930
Direct labour (1,780 hours)	(9,665)
Direct materials (2,410 kg)	(33,258)
Fixed overheads	(21,365)
Operating profit	28,642

There was no stock of any description at the beginning and end of May.

Required:

Prepare the original budget and a budget flexed to the actual volume. Use these to compare the budgeted and actual profits of the business for the month, going into as much detail with your analysis as the information given will allow.

Financial management

Part 3 is concerned with the area of accounting and finance usually known as 'business finance' or 'financial management'. Broadly, we shall be looking at decisions concerning the raising and investment of finance. Businesses can be seen, from a purely economic perspective, as organisations that raise money from investors and others (for example, shareholders and lenders) and use those funds to make investments (typically in plant and other assets) that will make the business and its owners wealthier. Clearly, these are important decision-making areas typically involving large amounts of money and relatively long-term commitments.

Chapter 14 considers how businesses make decisions about what represents a worthwhile investment. We shall be looking particularly at investments in such things as factories, offices and plant, which might enable businesses to provide some product or service for which a profitable market is seen. The decision-making techniques that we shall consider could equally well be applied to making investments in the shares of a business, or any other type of 'financial' investment, which individuals might make using their own money.

Chapter 15 deals with the other side of the investment: where the investment finance comes from. Here we shall be reviewing the various types of funding used by businesses of various sizes, including raising funds

→

from the owners of the business (the shareholders in the case of limited companies).

Chapter 16 looks at a particular area of fundraising and investment: the management of working capital. Working capital consists of the short-term assets and claims of the business: stock, trade debtors, cash and trade creditors. These items typically involve large amounts of finance and need to be managed carefully. The chapter considers how working capital can be managed effectively.

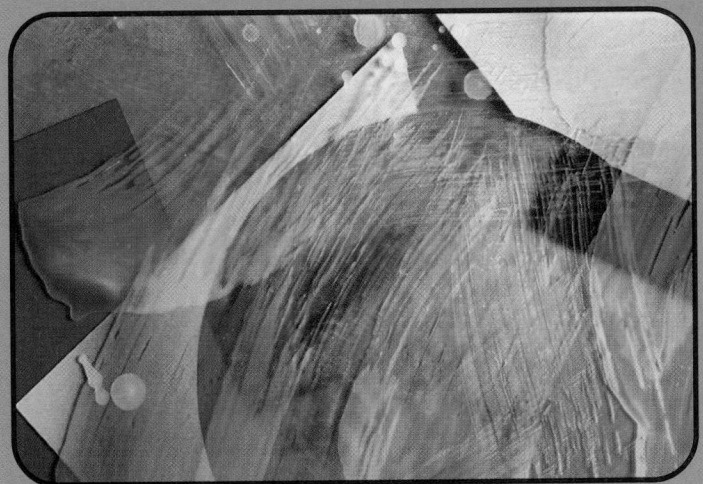

CHAPTER 14

Making capital investment decisions

When you have completed this chapter, you should be able to:

- Explain the nature and importance of investment decision making.

- Identify, use and discuss the qualities of the four main investment appraisal methods used in practice.

- Discuss the strengths and weaknesses of various techniques for dealing with risk in investment appraisal.

- Explain the methods used to review and control capital expenditure projects.

INTRODUCTION

This chapter looks at how businesses can make decisions involving investments in new plant, machinery, buildings and similar long-term assets. The general principles that apply to assessing investments in these types of assets can also be applied equally well to investments in the shares of businesses, irrespective of whether the investment is being considered by a business or by a private individual.

Investment decisions require the application of the same principles concerning the identification of relevant costs that were met in Chapters 8 and 9. Failure to identify relevant costs and benefits relating to an investment proposal could lead to poor decisions being made.

The research evidence relating to the use of the various appraisal techniques in practice is considered, as well as the problem of risk, which is a major aspect of all decision making. There are various ways in which risk can be incorporated into capital investment appraisal and we shall examine some of the more important of these.

Once a decision has been made to implement a particular capital investment proposal, proper review and control procedures must be in place, so the ways in which managers can oversee capital investment projects and how control may be exercised throughout the life of the project are discussed.

The nature of investment decisions

The essential feature of investment decisions is time. Investment involves making an outlay of something of economic value, usually cash, at one point in time, which is expected to yield economic benefits to the investor at some other point in time. Typically, the outlay precedes the benefits. Also, the outlay is typically one large amount and the benefits arrive as a series of smaller amounts over a fairly protracted period.

Investment decisions tend to be crucial to the business because:

● *Large amounts of resources are often involved.* Many investments made by businesses involve laying out a significant proportion of their total resources (see Real World 14.2 below). If mistakes are made with the decision, the effects on the businesses could be significant, if not catastrophic.

● *It is often difficult and/or expensive to 'bail out' of an investment once it has been undertaken.* It is often the case that investments made by a business are specific to its needs. For example, a hotel business may invest in a new, purposely designed hotel complex. The specialist nature of this complex will probably lead to it having a rather limited second-hand value to another potential user with different needs. If the business found, after having made the investment, that room occupancy rates were not as buoyant as planned, the only possible course of action might be to close down and sell the complex. This would probably mean that much less could be recouped from the investment than it had originally cost, particularly if the costs of design are included as part of the cost, as they logically should be.

Real World 14.1 gives an illustration of a major investment by a well-known business operating in the UK.

REAL WORLD 14.1

Brittany Ferries launches an investment

In the spring of 2004, Brittany Ferries, the cross-channel ferry operator, launched a new ship. The ship had cost the business about £100m. Though Brittany Ferries is a substantial business, this level of expenditure is significant. Clearly, the business believes that acquisition of the new ship will be profitable for it, but how would it have reached this conclusion? Presumably the anticipated future cash flows from passengers and freight operators will have been major inputs to the decision. The ship was specifically designed for Brittany Ferries, so it would be difficult for the business to recoup a large proportion of its £100m, should these projected cash flows not materialise.

Source: Publicity material published by Brittany Ferries.

The issues raised by the Brittany Ferries investment will be the main subject of this chapter.

Real World 14.2 indicates the level of annual investment for a number of randomly selected, well-known UK businesses. It can be seen that the scale of investment varies from one business to another. (It also tends to vary from one year to the next for a particular business.) In nearly all of these businesses the scale of investment is very significant. Real World 14.2 is limited to considering the non-current asset investment, but most such investment also requires a level of current asset investment to support it (additional stock-in-trade (inventory), for example), meaning that the real scale of investment is even greater than indicated below.

REAL WORLD 14.2

The scale of investment by UK businesses

Business	Expenditure on additional non-current assets as a percentage of:	
	Annual sales	*Start of year non-current assets*
Associated British Foods plc	10.1	28.6
The Boots Company plc	3.2	7.6
British Airways plc	9.3	7.0
British Sky Broadcasting Group plc	5.0	5.8
BT plc	19.9	17.0
J D Wetherspoon plc	25.1	24.1
Manchester United plc	27.5	20.5
Stagecoach Group plc	6.0	5.4
Tesco plc	8.5	20.1
Vodafone Group plc	79.4	11.8

Source: Annual reports of the businesses concerned for the accounting year ending in 2002

ACTIVITY 14.1

When managers are making decisions involving capital investments, what should the decision seek to achieve?

....

The answer to this question must be that any decision must be made in the context of the objectives of the business concerned. For a private-sector business, this is likely to include increasing the wealth of the shareholders of the business through long-term profitability.

Methods of investment appraisal

Given the importance of investment decisions to the viability of the business, it is essential that investment proposals are all properly screened. Ensuring that the business uses appropriate methods of evaluation is an important part of this screening process.

Research shows that there are basically four methods used in practice by businesses throughout the world to evaluate investment opportunities. They are:

- accounting rate of return (ARR)
- payback period (PP)
- net present value (NPV)
- internal rate of return (IRR).

It is possible to find businesses that use variants of these four methods. It is also possible to find businesses, particularly smaller ones, which do not use any formal appraisal method, but rely more on the 'gut feeling' of their managers. Most businesses, however, seem to use one of the four methods listed above that we shall now review.

We are going to assess the effectiveness of each of these methods and we shall see that only one of them (NPV) is not flawed to some extent. We shall also see how popular these four methods seem to be in practice.

To help us to examine each of the methods, it might be useful to consider how each of them would cope with a particular investment opportunity. Let us consider the following example.

Example 14.1

Billingsgate Battery Company has carried out some research that shows that the business could provide a standard service that it has recently developed.

Provision of the service would require investment in a machine that would cost £100,000, payable immediately. Sales of the service would take place throughout the next five years. At the end of that time, it is estimated that the machine could be sold for £20,000.

Sales of the service would be expected to occur as follows:

	Number of units
Next year	5,000
Second year	10,000
Third year	15,000
Fourth year	15,000
Fifth year	5,000

It is estimated that the new service can be sold for £12 a unit, and that the relevant (variable) costs will total £8 a unit.

To simplify matters, we shall assume that the cash from sales and for the costs of providing the service are paid and received, respectively, at the end of each year. (This is clearly unlikely to be true in real life. Money will have to be paid to employees (for salaries and wages) on a weekly or a monthly basis. Customers will pay within a month or two of buying the service. On the other hand, making the assumption probably does not lead to a serious distortion. It is a simplifying assumption that is often made in real life, and it will make things more straightforward for us now. We should be clear, however, that there is nothing about any of the four approaches that *demands* this assumption to be made.)

Bearing in mind that each unit of the service sold will give rise to a net cash inflow of £4 (that is £12 – £8), the total net cash flows (receipts less payments) for each year will be as follows:

Time		£000
Immediately	Cost of machine	(100)
1 year's time	Net profit before depreciation (£4 × 5,000)	20
2 years' time	Net profit before depreciation (£4 × 10,000)	40
3 years' time	Net profit before depreciation (£4 × 15,000)	60
4 years' time	Net profit before depreciation (£4 × 15,000)	60
5 years' time	Net profit before depreciation (£4 × 5,000)	20
5 years' time	Disposal proceeds from the machine	20

Note that, broadly speaking, the net profit before deducting depreciation (that is, before non-cash items) equals the net amount of cash flowing into the business. Apart from depreciation, all of this business's expenses cause cash to flow out of the business. Sales revenue leads to cash flowing in.

Having set up the example, we shall go on to look at the techniques used to assess investment opportunities and see how they deal with this particular decision.

Accounting rate of return (ARR)

The **accounting rate of return** method takes the average accounting profit that the investment will generate and expresses it as a percentage of the average investment in the project, as measured in accounting terms.

Thus:

$$ARR = \frac{\text{Average annual profit}}{\text{Average investment to earn that profit}} \times 100\%$$

We can see that to calculate the ARR, we need to deduce two pieces of information:

- the annual average profit
- the average investment for the particular project.

In our example, the average profit before depreciation over the five years is £40,000 (that is, £(20 + 40 + 60 + 60 + 20)/5). Assuming straight-line depreciation (that is, equal annual amounts), the annual depreciation charge will be £16,000 (that is, £(100,000 − 20,000)/5). Thus the average annual profit is £24,000 (that is, £40,000 − £16,000).

The average investment over the five years can be calculated as follows:

$$\text{Average investment} = \frac{\text{Cost of machine} + \text{disposal value}}{2}$$

$$= \frac{£100,000 + £20,000}{2}$$

$$= £60,000$$

Thus, the ARR of the investment is:

$$ARR = \frac{£24,000}{£60,000} \times 100\%$$

$$= 40\%$$

To decide whether the 40 per cent return is acceptable, we need to compare this percentage with the minimum required by the business.

ACTIVITY 14.2

Chaotic Industries is considering an investment in a fleet of ten delivery vans to take its products to customers. The vans will cost £15,000 each to buy, payable immediately. The annual running costs are expected to total £20,000 for each van (including the driver's salary). The vans are expected to operate successfully for six years, at the end of which period they will all have to be sold, with disposal proceeds expected to be about £3,000 a van. At present, the business uses a commercial carrier for all of its deliveries. It is expected that this carrier will charge a total of £230,000 each year for the next five years to undertake the deliveries.

What is the ARR of buying the vans? (Note that cost savings are as relevant a benefit from an investment as are net cash inflows.)

The vans will save the business £30,000 a year (that is, £230,000 – (£20,000 × 10)), before depreciation, in total.

Thus, the inflows and outflows will be:

Time		£000
Immediately	Cost of vans	(150)
1 year's time	Net saving before depreciation	30
2 years' time	Net saving before depreciation	30
3 years' time	Net saving before depreciation	30
4 years' time	Net saving before depreciation	30
5 years' time	Net saving before depreciation	30
6 years' time	Net saving before depreciation	30
6 years' time	Disposal proceeds from the vans (10 × 3)	30

The total annual depreciation expense (assuming a straight-line approach) will be £20,000 (that is, (£150,000 – £30,000)/6). Thus, the average annual saving, after depreciation, is £10,000 (that is, £30,000 – £20,000).

The average investment will be:

$$\text{Average investment} = \frac{£150,000 + £30,000}{2} = £90,000$$

Thus, the ARR of the investment is:

$$\text{ARR} = \frac{£10,000}{£90,000} \times 100\% = 11.1\%$$

ARR and ROCE

We should note that ARR and the return on capital employed (ROCE) ratio take the same approach to performance measurement, in that they both relate accounting profit to the cost of the assets invested to generate that profit. We may recall from Chapter 7 that ROCE is a popular means of assessing the performance of a business, as a whole, *after* it has performed. ARR is an approach that assesses the potential performance of a particular investment, taking the same approach as ROCE, *before* it has performed.

Since private-sector businesses are normally seeking to increase the wealth of their owners, ARR may seem to be a sound method of appraising investment opportunities. Profit can be seen as a net increase in wealth over a period, and relating it to the size of investment made to achieve it seems a logical approach.

A user of ARR would require that any investment undertaken by the business would be able to achieve a minimum target ARR. Perhaps the minimum target would be based on the rate that previous investments had actually achieved (as measured by ROCE). Perhaps it would be the industry-average ROCE.

Where there are competing projects that all seem capable of exceeding this minimum rate, the one with the higher or highest ARR would normally be selected.

ARR is said to have a number of advantages as a method of investment appraisal. It was mentioned earlier that ROCE seems a widely used measure of business performance. Shareholders seem to use this ratio to evaluate management performance, and sometimes the financial objective of a business will be expressed in terms of a target ROCE. It therefore seems sensible to use a method of investment appraisal that is consistent with this overall approach to measuring business performance. It also gives the result expressed as a percentage as some managers feel comfortable with using measures expressed in percentage terms.

Problems with ARR

ACTIVITY 14.3

ARR suffers from a very major defect as a means of assessing investment opportunities. Can you reason out what this is? Consider the three competing projects whose cash flows are shown below. All three of these involve investment in a machine that is expected to have no residual value at the end of the five years. Note that all of the projects have the same total net profits over the five years.

Project		A	B	C
Time		£000	£000	£000
Immediately	Cost of machine	(320)	(320)	(320)
1 year's time	Net profit after depreciation	20	10	160
2 years' time	Net profit after depreciation	40	10	10
3 years' time	Net profit after depreciation	60	10	10
4 years' time	Net profit after depreciation	60	10	10
5 years' time	Net profit after depreciation	20	160	10

(*Hint*: The defect is not concerned with the ability of the decision maker to forecast future events, though this too can be a problem. Try to remember what was the essential feature of investment decisions that we identified at the beginning of this chapter.)

The problem with ARR is that it almost completely ignores the time factor. In this example, exactly the same ARR would have been computed for each of the three projects.

Since the same total profit over the five years arises in all three of these projects (that is, £200,000) and the average investment in each project is £160,000 (that is, £320,000/2), this means that each case will give rise to the same ARR of 25% (that is, £40,000/£160,000).

Given a financial objective of increasing the wealth of the business, any rational decision maker faced with a choice between the three projects, set out in Activity 14.3, would strongly prefer Project C. This is because most of the benefits from the investment come in within 12 months of investing the £320,000 to establish the project. Project A would rank second, and Project B would come a poor third in the rankings. Any appraisal technique that is not capable of distinguishing between these three situations is seriously flawed.

Clearly the use of ARR can easily cause poor decisions to be made. We shall look in more detail at the reason for timing being so important later in the chapter.

There are other defects associated with the ARR method. For investment appraisal purposes, it is cash flows rather than accounting profits that are important. Cash is the ultimate measure of the economic wealth generated, because cash is used to acquire resources and for distribution to shareholders. Accounting profit is more appropriate for reporting achievement over the short term. It is a useful measure of productive effort for a relatively short period, such as a year, rather than for a long period.

The ARR method can also create problems when considering competing investments of different size.

ACTIVITY 14.4

Sinclair Wholesalers plc is currently considering opening a new sales outlet in Coventry. Two possible sites have been identified for the new outlet. Site A has a capacity of 30,000 sq m. It will require an average investment of £6m, and will produce an average profit of £600,000 a year. Site B has a capacity of 20,000 sq m. It will require an average investment of £4m, and will produce an average profit of £500,000 a year.

What is the ARR of each investment opportunity? Which site would you select, and why?

The ARR of Site A is £600,000/£6m = 10%. The ARR of Site B is £500,000/£4m = 12.5%. Thus, Site B has the higher ARR. However, in terms of the absolute profit generated, Site A is the more attractive. If the ultimate objective is to maximise the wealth of the shareholders of Sinclair Wholesalers plc, it might be better to choose Site A even though the percentage return is lower. It is the absolute size of the return rather than the relative (percentage) size that is important. This is a general problem of using comparative measures, like percentages, when the objective is measured in absolute ones. If businesses were seeking through their investments to generate a percentage rate of return on investment, ARR would be more helpful. The problem is that most businesses seek to achieve increases in their absolute wealth (measured in pounds, euros, dollars and so on), through their investment decisions.

Real World 14.3 illustrates how using percentage measures can lead to confusion.

REAL WORLD 14.3

Increasing road capacity by sleight of hand

During the 1970s, the Mexican government wanted to increase the capacity of a major four-lane road. It came up with the idea of repainting the lane markings so that there were six narrower lanes occupying the same space as four wider ones had previously done. This increased the capacity of the road by 50% (that is (6 − 4)/4 x 100). A tragic outcome of the narrower lanes was an increase in deaths from road accidents. A year later the Mexican government had the six narrower lanes changed back to the original four wider ones. This reduced the capacity of the road by 33% (that is, (4 − 6)/6 x 100). The Mexican government reported that it had increased the capacity of the road by 17% (that is 50% − 33%), despite the fact that its real capacity was identical to that which it had been originally. The confusion arose because each of the two percentages (50% and 33%) is based on different bases (four and six).

Source: Gigerenzer (see reference 1 at the end of the chapter).

Payback period (PP)

The **payback period** method seems to go some way to overcoming the timing problem of ARR, or at least at first glance it does.

It might be useful to consider PP in the context of the Billingsgate Battery example. We should recall that essentially the project's costs and benefits can be summarised as:

Time		£000
Immediately	Cost of machine	(100)
1 year's time	Net profit before depreciation	20
2 years' time	Net profit before depreciation	40
3 years' time	Net profit before depreciation	60
4 years' time	Net profit before depreciation	60
5 years' time	Net profit before depreciation	20
5 years' time	Disposal proceeds	20

Note that all of these figures are amounts of cash to be paid or received (we saw earlier that net profit before depreciation is a rough measure of the cash flows from the project).

The payback period is the length of time it takes for the initial investment to be repaid out of the net cash inflows from the project. In this case, it will be three years before the £100,000 outlay is covered by the inflows, still assuming that the cash flows occur at year ends. The payback period can be derived by calculating the cumulative cash flows as follows:

Time		Net cash flows £000	Cumulative cash flows £000	
Immediately	Cost of machine	(100)	(100)	
1 year's time	Net profit before depreciation	20	(80)	(−100 + 20)
2 years' time	Net profit before depreciation	40	(40)	(−80 + 40)
3 years' time	Net profit before depreciation	60	20	(−40 + 60)
4 years' time	Net profit before depreciation	60	80	(20 + 60)
5 years' time	Net profit before depreciation	20	100	(80 + 20)
5 years' time	Disposal proceeds	20	120	(100 + 20)

We can see that the cumulative cash flows become positive at the end of the third year. Had we assumed that the cash flows arise evenly over the year, the precise payback period would be:

$$2 \text{ years} + (40/60) = 2^2/_3 \text{ years}$$

(where 40 represents the cash flow still required at the beginning of the third year to repay the initial outlay, and 60 is the projected cash flow during the third year). Again we must ask how to decide whether $2^2/_3$ years is acceptable. A manager using PP would need to have a minimum payback period in mind. For example, if Billingsgate Battery had a minimum payback period of three years it would accept the project, but it would not go ahead if its minimum payback period were two years. If there were two competing projects that both met the minimum payback period requirement, the decision maker should select the project with the shorter payback period.

ACTIVITY 14.5

What is the payback period of the Chaotic Industries project from Activity 14.2?

The inflows and outflows are expected to be:

		Net cash flows £000	Cumulative net cash flows £000	
Time				
Immediately	Cost of vans	(150)	(150)	
1 year's time	Net saving before depreciation	30	(120)	(−150 + 30)
2 years' time	Net saving before depreciation	30	(90)	(−120 + 30)
3 years' time	Net saving before depreciation	30	(60)	(−90 + 30)
4 years' time	Net saving before depreciation	30	(30)	(−60 + 30)
5 years' time	Net saving before depreciation	30	0	(−30 + 30)
6 years' time	Net saving before depreciation	30	30	(0 + 30)
6 years' time	Disposal proceeds from the vans	30	60	(30 + 30)

The payback period here is five years; that is, it is not until the end of the fifth year that the vans will pay for themselves out of the savings that they are expected to generate.

The PP approach has certain advantages. It is quick and easy to calculate, and can be easily understood by managers. The logic of using PP is that projects that can recoup their cost quickly are economically more attractive than those with longer payback periods, that is, it emphasises liquidity. PP is probably an improvement on ARR in respect of the timing of the cash flows. PP is not, however, the whole answer to the problem.

Problems with PP

ACTIVITY 14.6

In what respect, in your opinion, is PP not the whole answer as a means of assessing investment opportunities? Consider the cash flows arising from three competing projects:

		Project 1 £000	Project 2 £000	Project 3 £000
Time				
Immediately	Cost of machine	(200)	(200)	(200)
1 year's time	Net profit before depreciation	40	10	80
2 years' time	Net profit before depreciation	80	20	100
3 years' time	Net profit before depreciation	80	170	20
4 years' time	Net profit before depreciation	60	20	200
5 years' time	Net profit before depreciation	40	10	500
5 years' time	Disposal proceeds	40	10	20

(*Hint*: Again, the defect is not concerned with the ability of the manager to forecast future events. This is a problem, but it is a problem whatever approach we take.)

Any rational manager would prefer Project 3 to either of the other two projects, yet PP sees all three of them as being equally attractive in that they all have a three-year payback

Activity 14.6 continued

period. The method cannot distinguish between those projects that pay back a significant amount early in the three-year payback period and those that do not. Project 3 is by far the best bet because the cash flows come in earlier (most of the cost of the machine has been repaid by the end of the second year) and they are greater in total, yet PP could not identify it as the best.

Figure 14.1   The cumulative cash flows of each project in Activity 14.6

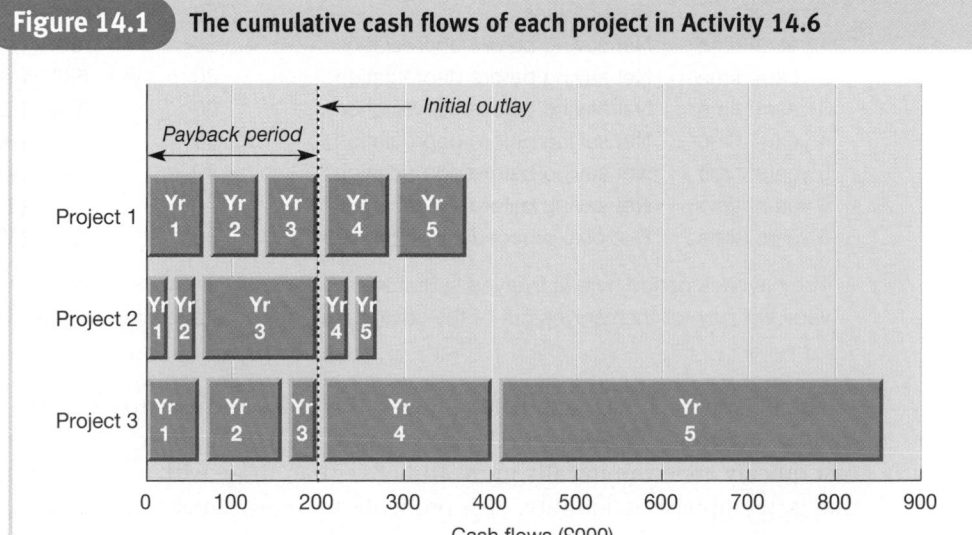

The payback method of investment appraisal would view Projects 1, 2 and 3 as being equally attractive. In doing so, the method completely ignores the fact that Project 3 provides the payback cash earlier in the three-year period and goes on to generate large benefits in later years.

The cumulative cash flows of each project in Activity 14.6 are set out in Figure 14.1.

Within the payback period, PP ignores the timing of the cash flows. Beyond the payback period, the method totally ignores both the size and the timing of the cash flows. While ignoring cash flows beyond the payback period neatly avoids the practical problems of forecasting cash flows over a long period, it means that crucial information may be ignored.

The PP approach is often seen as a means of dealing with the problem of risk by favouring projects with a short payback period. However, this is a fairly crude approach to the problem. Also it only looks at the risk that the project will end earlier than expected. This is only one of many risk areas. What, for example, about the risk that the demand for the product may be less than expected? There are more systematic approaches to dealing with risk that can be used and we shall look at these later in the chapter.

It seems that PP has the advantage of taking some note of the timing of the costs and benefits from the project. Its key deficiency, however, is that it is not linked to promoting increases in the wealth of the business. PP will tend to recommend undertaking projects that pay for themselves quickly. As we saw earlier, ARR ignores timing to a great extent, but it does take account of all benefits and costs. What we really need to help us to make sensible decisions is a method of appraisal that takes account of all of the costs and benefits of each investment opportunity, but which also makes a logical allowance for the timing of those costs and benefits.

Net present value (NPV)

To make sensible investment decisions, we need a method of appraisal that:

● considers *all* of the costs and benefits of each investment opportunity; and
● makes a logical allowance for the *timing* of those costs and benefits.

The **net present value** method provides us with this.

Consider the Billingsgate Battery example, which we should recall can be summarised as follows:

Time		£000
Immediately	Cost of machine	(100)
1 year's time	Net profit before depreciation	20
2 years' time	Net profit before depreciation	40
3 years' time	Net profit before depreciation	60
4 years' time	Net profit before depreciation	60
5 years' time	Net profit before depreciation	20
5 years' time	Disposal proceeds	20

Given that the principal financial objective of the business is to increase wealth, it would be very easy to assess this investment if all of the cash flows were to occur now (all at the same time). All that we should need to do would be to add up the benefits (total £220,000) and compare them with the cost (£100,000). This would lead us to the conclusion that the project should go ahead, because the business would be better off by £120,000. Of course, it is not as easy as this, because time is involved. The cash outflow (payment) will occur immediately if the project is undertaken. The inflows (receipts) will arise at a range of later times.

The time factor arises because normally people do not see £100 paid out now as equivalent in value to £100 receivable in a year's time. If we were to be offered £100 in 12 months' time, provided that we paid £100 now, we should not be prepared to do so, unless we wished to do someone (perhaps a friend or relation) a favour.

ACTIVITY 14.7

Why would you see £100 to be received in a year's time as unequal in value to £100 to be paid immediately? (There are basically three reasons.)

The reasons are:

● interest lost
● risk
● effects of inflation.

We shall now take a closer look at these three reasons in turn.

Interest lost

If we are to be deprived for a year of the opportunity to spend our money, we could equally well be deprived of its use by placing it on deposit in a bank or building society.

In this case, at the end of the year we could have our money back and have interest as well. Thus, unless the opportunity to invest will offer similar returns, we shall be incurring an *opportunity cost*. An opportunity cost occurs where one course of action, for example making an investment in a computer, deprives us of the opportunity to derive some benefit from an alternative action, for example putting the money in the bank.

From this we can see that any investment opportunity must, if it is to make us wealthiest, do better than the returns that are available from the next best opportunity. Thus, if Billingsgate Battery Company sees putting the money in the bank on deposit as the alternative to investment in the machine, the return from investing in the machine must be better than that from investing in the bank. If the bank offered a better return, the business would become wealthier by putting the money on deposit.

Risk
······

Buying a machine to manufacture a product, or to provide a service, to be sold in the market, on the strength of various estimates made in advance of buying the machine, exposes the business to **risk**. Things may not turn out as expected.

ACTIVITY 14.8

Can you suggest some areas where things could go other than according to plan in the Billingsgate Battery Company example?

We have come up with the following:

- The machine might not work as well as expected; it might break down, leading to loss of the service.
- Sales of the product or service may not be as buoyant as expected.
- Labour costs may prove to be higher than was expected.
- The sale proceeds of the machine could prove to be less than was estimated.

It is important to remember that the decision as to whether or not to invest in the machine must be taken *before* any of these things are known. It is only after the machine has been purchased that we could discover that the level of sales, which had been estimated before the event, is not going to be achieved. It is not possible to wait until we know for certain whether the market is behaving as we expected before we buy the machine. We can study reports and analyses of the market. We can commission sophisticated market surveys, and these may give us more confidence in the likely outcome. We can advertise strongly and try to expand sales. Ultimately, however, we have to decide whether or not to jump off into the dark and accept the risk if we want the opportunity to make profitable investments.

Normally, people expect to receive greater returns where they perceive risk to be a factor. Examples of this in real life are not difficult to find. One such example is that banks tend to charge higher rates of interest to borrowers whom the bank perceives as more risky. Those who can offer good security for a loan and who can point to a regular source of income tend to be charged fairly low rates of interest.

Going back to Billingsgate Battery Company's investment opportunity, it is not enough to say that we should not advise making the investment unless the returns from it are higher than those from investing in a bank deposit. Clearly we should want returns above the level of bank deposit interest rates, because the logical equivalent to investing in the machine is not putting the money on deposit but making an alternative investment that is risky.

In practice, we tend to expect a higher rate of return from investment projects where the risk is perceived as being higher. How risky a particular project is, and therefore how large this **risk premium** should be, are matters that are difficult to handle. In practice, it is necessary to make some judgement on these questions.

Inflation

If we are to be deprived of £100 for a year, when we come to spend that money it will not buy as many goods and services as it would have done a year earlier. Generally, we shall not be able to buy as many tins of baked beans or loaves of bread or bus tickets as we could have done a year earlier. This is because of the loss in the purchasing power of money, or **inflation**, that occurs over time. Clearly, the investor needs this loss of purchasing power to be compensated for if the investment is to be made. This is on top of a return that takes account of what could have been gained from an alternative investment of similar risk.

In practice, interest rates observable in the market tend to take inflation into account. Rates that are offered to potential building society and bank depositors include an allowance for the rate of inflation that is expected in the future.

Actions of a logical investor

To summarise these factors, we can say that the logical investor, who is seeking to increase his or her wealth, will only be prepared to make investments that will compensate for the loss of interest and purchasing power of the money invested and for the fact that the returns expected may not materialise (risk). This is usually assessed by seeing whether the proposed investment will yield a return that is greater than the basic rate of interest (which would include an allowance for inflation) plus a risk premium.

These three factors (interest lost, risk and inflation) are set out in Figure 14.2.

Naturally, investors need at least the minimum returns before they are prepared to invest. However, it is in terms of the effect on their wealth that they should logically assess an investment project. Usually it is the investment with the highest percentage return

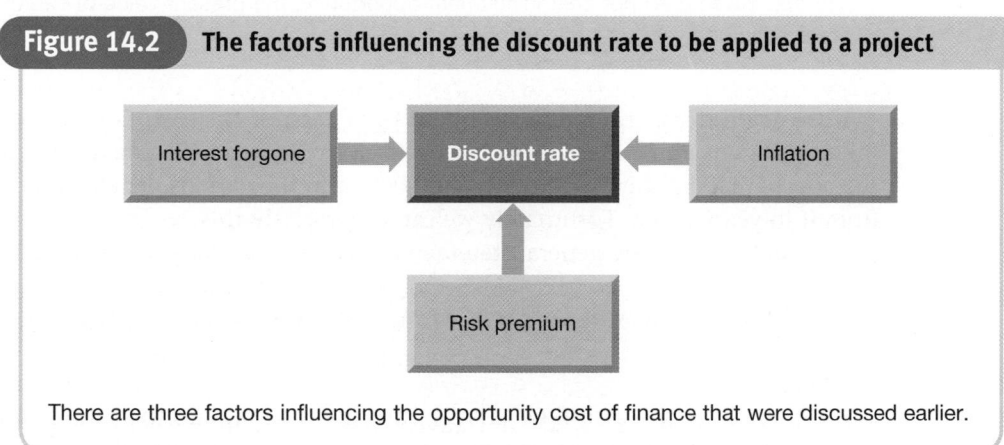

Figure 14.2   **The factors influencing the discount rate to be applied to a project**

There are three factors influencing the opportunity cost of finance that were discussed earlier.

that will make the investor most wealthy, but we shall see later in this chapter that this is not always the case. For the time being, therefore, we shall concentrate on wealth.

Let us now return to the Billingsgate Battery Company example and assume that instead of making this investment the business could make an alternative investment with similar risk and obtain a return of 20 per cent a year.

We should recall that we have seen that it is not sufficient just to compare the basic cash flow figures for the investment. It would therefore be useful if we could express each of these cash flows in similar terms, so that we could make a direct comparison between the sum of the inflows over time and the immediate £100,000 investment. Fortunately, we can do this.

ACTIVITY 14.9

We know that Billingsgate Battery Company could alternatively invest its money at a rate of 20 per cent a year. How much do you judge the present (immediate) value of the expected first year receipt of £20,000 to be? In other words, if instead of having to wait a year for the £20,000, and being deprived of the opportunity to invest it at 20 per cent, you could have some money now, what sum to be received now would you regard as exactly equivalent to getting £20,000, but having to wait a year for it?

We should obviously be happy to accept a lower amount if we could get it immediately than if we had to wait a year. This is because we could invest it at 20 per cent (in the alternative project). Logically, we should be prepared to accept the amount that, with a year's income, will grow to £20,000. If we call this amount PV (for present value) we can say:

$$PV + (PV \times 20\%) = £20,000$$

that is, the amount plus income from investing the amount for the year equals the £20,000.
If we rearrange this equation we find:

$$PV \times (1 + 0.2) = £20,000$$

Note that 0.2 is the same as 20 per cent, but expressed as a decimal.
Further rearranging gives:

$$PV = £20,000/(1 + 0.2)$$
$$PV = £16,667$$

Thus, rational investors who have the opportunity to invest at 20 per cent a year would not mind whether they have £16,667 now or £20,000 in a year's time. In this sense we can say that, given a 20 per cent investment opportunity, the present value of £20,000 to be received in one year's time is £16,667.

If we could derive the present value (PV) of each of the cash flows associated with Billingsgate's machine investment, we could easily make the direct comparison between the cost of making the investment (£100,000) and the various benefits that will derive from it in years 1 to 5. Fortunately we can do precisely this.

We can make a more general statement about the PV of a particular cash flow. It is:

PV of the cash flow of year n = Actual cash flow of year n divided by $(1 + r)^n$

where:
n is the year of the cash flow (that is, how many years into the future), and
r is the opportunity investing rate expressed as a decimal (instead of as a percentage).

We have already seen how this works for the £20,000 inflow for year 1. For year 2 the calculation would be:

$$\text{PV of year 2 cash flow (that is, £40,000)} = £40,000/(1 + 0.2)^2$$

$$PV = £40,000/(1.2)^2 = £40,000/1.44 = £27,778$$

Thus the present value of the £40,000 to be received in two years' time is £27,778.

ACTIVITY 14.10

See if you can show that an investor would be indifferent to £27,778 receivable now, or £40,000 receivable in two years' time, assuming that there is a 20 per cent investment opportunity.

....

The reasoning goes like this:

	£
Amount available for immediate investment	27,778
Add Interest for year 1 (20% × 27,778)	5,556
	33,334
Add Interest for year 2 (20% × 33,334)	6,667
	40,001

(The extra £1 is only a rounding error.)

Thus, because the investor can turn £27,778 into £40,000 in two years, these amounts are equivalent. We can say that £27,778 is the present value of £40,000 receivable after two years (given a 20 per cent rate of return).

Now let us deduce the present values of all of the cash flows associated with the Billingsgate machine project and hence the *net present value* of the project as a whole. The relevant cash flows and calculations are as follows:

Time	Cash flow	Calculation of PV	PV
	£000		£000
Immediately (time 0)	(100)	$(100)/(1 + 0.2)^0$	(100.00)
1 year's time	20	$20/(1 + 0.2)^1$	16.67
2 years' time	40	$40/(1 + 0.2)^2$	27.78
3 years' time	60	$60/(1 + 0.2)^3$	34.72
4 years' time	60	$60/(1 + 0.2)^4$	28.94
5 years' time	20	$20/(1 + 0.2)^5$	8.04
5 years' time	20	$20/(1 + 0.2)^5$	8.04
			24.19

(Note that $(1 + 0.2)^0 = 1$)

Once again, we must ask how we can decide whether the machine project is acceptable to the business. In fact, the decision rule is simple. If the NPV is positive we accept the project; if it is negative we reject the project. In this case, the NPV is positive, so we accept the project and buy the machine.

Investing in the machine will make the business £24,190 better off. What the above is saying is that the benefits from investing in this machine are worth a total of £124,190 today. Since the business can 'buy' these benefits for just £100,000 the investment should be made. If, however, the benefits were below £100,000 they would be less than the cost of 'buying' them.

ACTIVITY 14.11

What is the *maximum* the Billingsgate Battery Company would be prepared to pay for the machine, given the potential benefits of owning it?

The business would be prepared to pay up to £124,190 since the wealth of the owners of the business would be increased up to this price – though the business would prefer to pay as little as possible.

Using discount tables

Deducing the present values of the various cash flows is a little laborious using the approach that we have just taken. To deduce each PV we took the relevant cash flow and multiplied it by $1/(1 + r)^n$. Fortunately, there is a quicker way. Tables exist that show values of this **discount factor** for a range of values of r and n. Such a table appears at the end of this book in Appendix E. Take a look at it.

Look at the column for 20 per cent and the row for one year. We find that the factor is 0.833. Thus the PV of a cash flow of £1 receivable in one year is £0.833. So a cash flow of £20,000 receivable in one year's time is £16,660 (that is, 0.833 × £20,000), the same result as we found doing it in longhand.

ACTIVITY 14.12

What is the NPV of the Chaotic Industries project from Activity 14.2, assuming a 15 per cent opportunity cost of finance (discount rate)? You should use the discount table in Appendix E.

Remember that the inflows and outflow are expected to be:

Time		£000
Immediately	Cost of vans	(150)
1 year's time	Net saving before depreciation	30
2 years' time	Net saving before depreciation	30
3 years' time	Net saving before depreciation	30
4 years' time	Net saving before depreciation	30
5 years' time	Net saving before depreciation	30
6 years' time	Net saving before depreciation	30
6 years' time	Disposal proceeds from the vans	30

The calculation of the NPV of the project is as follows:

Time	Cash flows	Discount factor (15% – from the table)	Present value
	£000		£000
Immediately	(150)	1.000	(150.00)
1 year's time	30	0.870	26.10
2 years' time	30	0.756	22.68
3 years' time	30	0.658	19.74
4 years' time	30	0.572	17.16
5 years' time	30	0.497	14.91
6 years' time	30	0.432	12.96
6 years' time	30	0.432	12.96
		Net present value	(23.49)

ACTIVITY 14.13

How would you interpret the result in Activity 14.12?

The fact that the project has a negative NPV means that the present values of the benefits from the investment are worth less than the cost of entering into it. Any cost up to £126,510 (the present value of the benefits) would be worth paying, but not £150,000.

The discount tables reveal how the value of £1 diminishes as its receipt goes further into the future. Assuming an opportunity cost of finance of 20 per cent a year, £1 to be received immediately, obviously, has a present value of £1. However, as the time before it is to be received extends, the present value diminishes significantly, as is shown in Figure 14.3.

Figure 14.3	**Present value of £1 receivable at various times in the future, assuming an annual financing cost of 20 per cent**

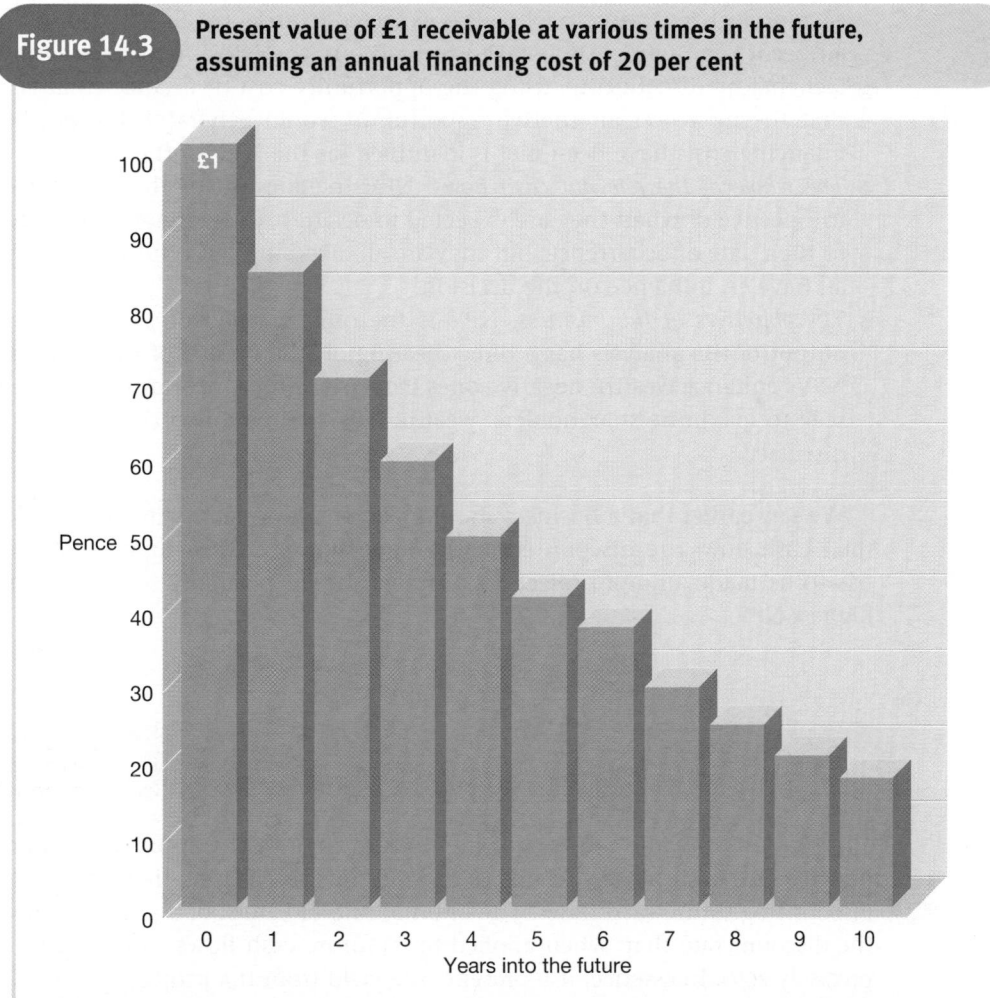

The present value of a future receipt (or payment) of £1 depends on how far in the future it will occur. Those that will occur in the near future will have a larger present value than those whose occurrence is more distant in time.

The discount rate and the cost of capital

We have seen that the appropriate discount rate to use in NPV assessments is the opportunity cost of finance. This is, in effect, the cost to the business of the finance that it will use to finance the investment, should it go ahead. This will normally be the cost of the mixture of funds (shareholders' funds and borrowings) used by the business. This is usually known as the cost of capital.

Why NPV is superior to ARR and PP

From what we have seen, NPV seems to be a better method of appraising investment opportunities than either ARR or PP. This is because it fully takes account of each of the following:

- *The timing of the cash flows.* By discounting the various cash flows associated with each project according to when it is expected to arise, the fact that cash flows do not all occur simultaneously is taken into account by NPV. Associated with this is the fact that by discounting, using the opportunity cost of finance (that is, the return that the next best alternative opportunity would generate), the net benefit after financing costs have been met is identified (as the NPV of the project).
- *The whole of the relevant cash flows.* NPV includes all of the relevant cash flows, irrespective of when they are expected to occur. It treats them differently according to their date of occurrence, but they are all taken into account in the NPV, and they all have an influence on the decision.
- *The objectives of the business.* NPV is the only method of appraisal in which the output of the analysis has a direct bearing on the wealth of the business. (Positive NPVs enhance wealth; negative ones reduce it.) Since most private-sector businesses seek to maximise shareholders' wealth, NPV is superior to the methods previously discussed.

We saw earlier that a business should take on all projects with positive NPVs, when their cash flows are discounted at the opportunity cost of finance. Where a choice has to be made among projects, a business should normally select the one with the highest NPV.

Internal rate of return (IRR)

This is the last of the four major methods of investment appraisal that are found in practice. It is quite closely related to the NPV method in that, like NPV, it also involves discounting future cash flows. The **internal rate of return** of a particular investment is the discount rate that, when applied to its future cash flows, will produce an NPV of precisely zero. In essence, it represents the yield from the project.

We should recall that when we discounted the cash flows of the Billingsgate Battery Company machine investment opportunity at 20 per cent, we found that the NPV was a positive figure of £24,190 (see p. 479).

What does the NPV of the machine project (that is, £24,190 (positive)) tell us about the rate of return that the investment will yield for the business?

....

The fact that the NPV is positive when discounting at 20 per cent implies that the rate of return that the project generates is more than 20 per cent. The fact that the NPV is a pretty large figure implies that the actual rate of return is quite a lot above 20 per cent. We should expect increasing the size of the discount rate to reduce NPV, because a higher discount rate gives a lower discounted figure.

It is somewhat laborious to deduce the IRR by hand, since it cannot usually be calculated directly. Thus iteration (trial and error) is the only approach. Fortunately, computer spreadsheet packages can deduce the IRR with ease. The package will also use a trial and error approach, but at high speed.

Let us try a higher rate and see what happens, say, 30 per cent:

Time	Cash flow £000	Discount factor 30%	PV £000
Immediately (time 0)	(100)	1.000	(100.00)
1 year's time	20	0.769	15.38
2 years' time	40	0.592	23.68
3 years' time	60	0.455	27.30
4 years' time	60	0.350	21.00
5 years' time	20	0.269	5.38
5 years' time	20	0.269	5.38
			(1.88)

In increasing the discount rate from 20 per cent to 30 per cent, we have reduced the NPV from £24,190 (positive) to £1,880 (negative). Since the IRR is the discount rate that will give us an NPV of exactly zero, we can conclude that the IRR of Billingsgate Battery Company's machine project is very slightly below 30 per cent. Further trials could lead us to the exact rate, but there is probably not much point, given the likely inaccuracy of the cash flow estimates. It is probably good enough, for practical purposes, to say that the IRR is about 30 per cent.

The relationship between the NPV method discussed earlier and the IRR is shown graphically in Figure 14.4 using the information relating to the Billingsgate Battery Company.

We can see that, where the discount rate is zero, the NPV will be the sum of the net cash flows. In other words, no account is taken of the time value of money. However, as the discount rate increases there is a corresponding decrease in the NPV of the project. When the NPV line crosses the horizontal axis there will be a zero NPV, and that represents the IRR.

Users of the IRR approach should apply the following decision rules:

● For any project to be acceptable, it must meet a minimum IRR requirement. Logically, this minimum should be the opportunity cost of finance.
● Where there are competing projects (for example, the business can choose one of the projects only) the one with the higher or highest IRR would be selected.

IRR has certain attributes in common with NPV. All cash flows are taken into account, and their timing is logically handled.

Figure 14.4   **The relationship between the NPV and IRR methods**

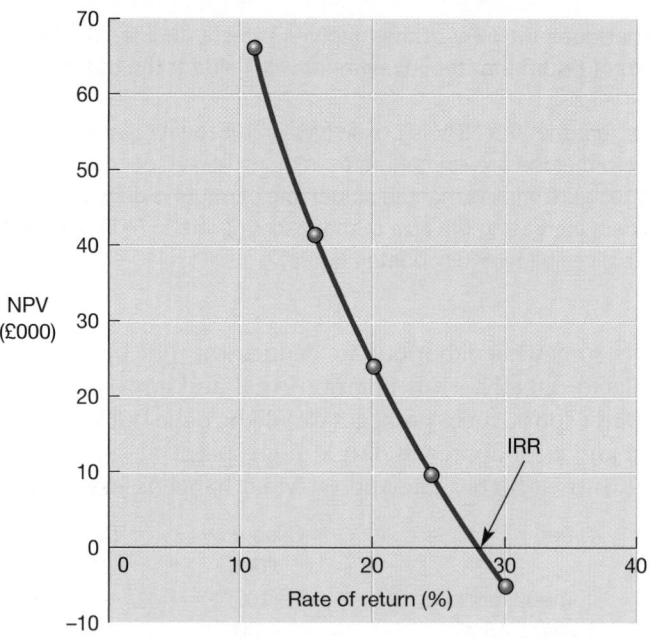

If the discount rate were zero, the NPV would be the sum of the net cash flows. In other words, no account would be taken of the time value of money. However, if we assume increasing discount rates, there is a corresponding decrease in the NPV of the project. When the NPV line crosses the horizontal axis there will be a zero NPV, and the point where it crosses is the IRR.

ACTIVITY 14.15

What is the internal rate of return of the Chaotic Industries project from Activity 14.2? You should use the discount table at the end of the book. (*Hint*: Remember that you already know the NPV of this project at 15 per cent.)

- -

Since we know (from Activity 14.12) that, at a 15 per cent discount rate, the NPV is a relatively large negative figure, our next trial is using a lower discount rate, say 10 per cent:

Time	Cash flows £000	Discount factor (10% – from the table)	Present value £000
Immediately	(150)	1.000	(150.00)
1 year's time	30	0.909	27.27
2 years' time	30	0.826	24.78
3 years' time	30	0.751	22.53
4 years' time	30	0.683	20.49
5 years' time	30	0.621	18.63
6 years' time	30	0.565	16.95
6 years' time	30	0.565	16.95
		Net present value	(2.40)

We can see that NPV increased by about £21,000 (£23,490 – £2,400) for a 5% drop in the discount rate: that is, about £4,200 for each 1%. We need to know the discount rate for a zero NPV: that is, a fall in the negative NPV of a further £2,400. This logically would be roughly 0.6% (that is, 2,400/4,200). Thus the IRR is close to 9.4%. However, to say that the IRR is about 9% is near enough for most purposes.

Problems with IRR

The main disadvantage of IRR is the fact that it does not correctly address the question of wealth generation. It could therefore lead to the wrong decision being made. This is because IRR would, for example, always see an IRR of 25 per cent being preferable to a 20 per cent IRR, assuming an opportunity cost of finance of, say, 15 per cent. Though this may well lead to the project being taken that could most effectively increase wealth, this may not always be the case, because IRR completely ignores the *scale of investment*. With a 15 per cent cost of finance, £15 million invested at 20 per cent (that is, $15 \times (20 - 15) = 0.75$) would make us richer than £5 million invested at 25 per cent (that is, $5 \times (25 - 15) = 0.50$). IRR does not recognise this. This problem with percentages is another example illustrated by the Mexican road discussed in **Real World 14.3**. It should be acknowledged that it is not usual for projects to be competing where there is such a large difference in scale. Even though the problem may be rare and so, typically, IRR will give the same signal as NPV, a method (NPV) that is always reliable must be better to use than IRR.

A further problem with the IRR method is that it has difficulty handling projects with unconventional cash flows. In the examples studied so far, each project has a negative cash flow arising at the start of its life and then positive cash flows thereafter. However, in some cases, a project may have both positive and negative cash flows at future points in its life. Such a pattern of cash flows can result in there being more than one IRR, or even no IRR at all.

Some practical points

When undertaking an investment appraisal, there are several practical points that we should bear in mind:

- *Relevant costs.* As with all decision making, we should only take account of cash flows that vary according to the decision in our analysis. Thus, cash flows that will be the same, irrespective of the decision under review, should be ignored. For example, overheads that will be incurred in equal amount whether or not the investment is made should be ignored, despite the fact that the investment could not be made without the infrastructure that the overhead costs create. Similarly, past costs should be ignored as they are not affected by, and do not vary with, the decision.
- *Opportunity costs.* Opportunity costs arising from benefits forgone must be taken into account. Thus, for example, when considering a decision concerning whether or not to continue to use a machine already owned by the business, the realisable value of the machine might be an important opportunity cost.
- *Taxation.* Tax will usually be affected by an investment decision. The profits will be taxed, the capital investment may attract tax relief, and so on. Tax is levied on these at significant rates. This means that, in real life, unless tax is formally taken into account, the wrong decision could easily be made.
- *Cash flows not profit flows.* We have seen that for the NPV, IRR and PP methods, it is cash flows rather than profit flows that are relevant to the evaluation of investment projects. In a problem requiring the application of any of these methods we may be given details of the profits for the investment period, and shall be required to adjust these in order to derive the cash flows. Remember, the net profit before depreciation is an approximation to the cash flows for the period, and so we should work back to this figure.

When the data are expressed in profit rather than cash flow terms, an adjustment in respect of working capital may also be necessary. Some adjustment should be made to take account of changes to working capital. For example, launching a new product may give rise to an increase in the net cash investment made in trade debtors (receivables), stock (inventories) and trade creditors (payables), requiring an immediate outlay of cash. This outlay for additional working capital should be shown in the NPV calculations as part of the initial cost. However, at the end of the life of the project, the additional working capital will be released. The resulting inflow of cash at the end of the life of the project should also be taken into account.

● *Interest payments*. When using discounted cash flow techniques, interest payments should not be taken into account in deriving the cash flows for the period. The discount factor already takes account of the costs of financing, so to take account of interest charges in deriving cash flows for the period would be double counting.

● *Other factors*. Investment decision making must not be viewed as simply a mechanical exercise. The results derived from a particular investment appraisal method will be only one input to the decision-making process. There may be broader issues connected to the decision that have to be taken into account, but which may be difficult or impossible to quantify. The reliability of the forecasts and the validity of the assumptions used in the evaluation will also have a bearing on the final decision.

ACTIVITY 14.16

The directors of Manuff (Steel) Ltd are considering closing one of the business's factories. There has been a reduction in the demand for the products made at the factory in recent years, and the directors are not optimistic about the long-term prospects for these products. The factory is situated, in an area where unemployment is high.

The factory is leased, and there are still four years of the lease remaining. The directors are uncertain as to whether the factory should be closed immediately or at the end of the period of the lease. Another business has offered to sublease the premises from Manuff at a rental of £40,000 a year for the remainder of the lease period.

The machinery and equipment at the factory cost £1,500,000, and have a balance sheet value of £400,000. In the event of immediate closure, the machinery and equipment could be sold for £220,000. The working capital at the factory is £420,000, and could be liquidated for that amount immediately, if required. Alternatively, the working capital can be liquidated in full at the end of the lease period. Immediate closure would result in redundancy payments to employees of £180,000.

If the factory continues in operation until the end of the lease period, the following operating profits (losses) are expected:

	Year 1 £000	Year 2 £000	Year 3 £000	Year 4 £000
Operating profit (loss)	160	(40)	30	20

The above figures include a charge of £90,000 a year for depreciation of machinery and equipment. The residual value of the machinery and equipment at the end of the lease period is estimated at £40,000.

Redundancy payments are expected to be £150,000 at the end of the lease period if the factory continues in operation. The business has an annual cost of capital of 12 per cent. Ignore taxation.

Required:

(a) Determine the relevant cash flows arising from a decision to continue operations until the end of the lease period rather than to close immediately.

(b) Calculate the net present value of continuing operations until the end of the lease period, rather than closing immediately.

(c) What other factors might the directors take into account before making a final decision on the timing of the factory closure?

(d) State, with reasons, whether or not the business should continue to operate the factory until the end of the lease period.

....

Your answer to this activity should be as follows:

(a) Relevant cash flows

	Years				
	0	1	2	3	4
	£000	£000	£000	£000	£000
Operating cash flow (Note 1)		250	50	120	110
Sale of machinery (Note 2)	(220)				40
Redundancy costs (Note 3)	180				(150)
Sublease rentals (Note 4)		(40)	(40)	(40)	(40)
Working capital invested (Note 5)	(420)				420
	(460)	210	10	80	380

Notes:

1 Each year's operating cash flow is calculated by adding back the depreciation charge for the year to the operating profit for the year. In the case of the operating loss, the depreciation charge is deducted.

2 In the event of closure, machinery could be sold immediately. Thus an opportunity cost of £220,000 is incurred if operations continue.

3 By continuing operations, there will be a saving in immediate redundancy costs of £180,000. However, redundancy costs of £150,000 will be paid in four years' time.

4 By continuing operations, the opportunity to sublease the factory will be forgone.

5 Immediate closure would mean that working capital could be liquidated. By continuing operations this opportunity is forgone. However, working capital can be liquidated in four years' time.

(b) Discount rate 12%	1.000	0.893	0.797	0.712	0.636
Present value	(460)	187.5	8.0	57.0	241.7
Net present value	34.2				

(c) Other factors that may influence the decision include:

- *The overall strategy of the business.* The business may need to set the decision within a broader context. It may be necessary to manufacture the products made at the factory because they are an integral part of the business's product range. The business may wish to avoid redundancies in an area of high unemployment for as long as possible.
- *Flexibility.* A decision to close the factory is probably irreversible. If the factory continues, however, there may be a chance that the prospects for the factory will brighten in the future.
- *Creditworthiness of sublessee.* The business should investigate the creditworthiness of the sublessee. Failure to receive the expected sublease payments would make the closure option far less attractive.

→

● *Accuracy of forecasts.* The forecasts made by the business should be examined carefully. Inaccuracies in the forecasts or any underlying assumptions may change the expected outcomes.

(d) The NPV of the decision to continue operations rather than close immediately is positive. Hence, shareholders would be better off if the directors took this course of action. The factory should therefore continue in operation rather than close down. This decision is likely to be welcomed by employees and would allow the business to maintain its flexibility.

SELF-ASSESSMENT QUESTION 14.1

Beacon Chemicals plc is considering buying some equipment to produce a chemical named X14. The new equipment's capital cost is estimated at £100,000. If its purchase is approved now, the equipment can be bought and production can commence by the end of this year. £50,000 has already been spent on research and development work. Estimates of revenues and costs arising from the operation of the new equipment appear below:

	Year 1	Year 2	Year 3	Year 4	Year 5
Sales price (£ per litre)	100	120	120	100	80
Sales volume (litres)	800	1,000	1,200	1,000	800
Variable costs (£ per litre)	50	50	40	30	40
Fixed costs (£000)	30	30	30	30	30

If the equipment is bought, sales of some existing products will be lost, and this will result in a loss of contribution of £15,000 a year over its life.

The accountant has informed you that the fixed costs include depreciation of £20,000 a year on the new equipment. They also include an allocation of £10,000 for fixed overheads. A separate study has indicated that if the new equipment were bought, additional overheads, excluding depreciation, arising from producing the chemical would be £8,000 a year. Production would require additional working capital of £30,000.

For the purposes of your initial calculations ignore taxation.

Required:
(a) Deduce the relevant annual cash flows associated with buying the equipment.
(b) Deduce the payback period.
(c) Calculate the net present value using a discount rate of 8 per cent.

(*Hint*: You should deal with the investment in working capital by treating it as a cash outflow at the start of the project and an inflow at the end.)

Investment appraisal in practice

Many surveys have been conducted in the UK into the methods of investment appraisal used in practice. They have tended to show the following features:

● businesses using more than one method to assess each investment decision, increasingly so over time;

- an increased use of the discounting methods (NPV and IRR) over time, with these two becoming the most popular in recent years;
- continued popularity of ARR and PP, despite their theoretical shortcomings and the rise in popularity of the discounting methods;
- a tendency for larger businesses to use the discounting methods and to use more than one method in respect of each decision.

Real World 14.4 shows the results of the most recent (1997) survey conducted of UK businesses regarding their use of investment appraisal methods.

REAL WORLD 14.4

A survey of UK business practice

Method	Percentage of businesses using the method
Net present value	80
Internal rate of return	81
Payback period	70
Accounting rate of return	56
	287

Source: Arnold and Hatzopoulos (see reference 2 at the end of the chapter). Reproduced by kind permission of Blackwell Publishing Ltd.

ACTIVITY 14.17

How do you explain the popularity of the PP method, given the theoretical limitations discussed earlier in this chapter?

A number of possible reasons may explain this finding:

- PP is easy to understand and use.
- It can avoid the problems of forecasting far into the future.
- It gives emphasis to the early cash flows when there is greater certainty concerning the accuracy of their predicted value.
- It emphasises the importance of liquidity. Where a business has liquidity problems, a short payback period for a project is likely to appear attractive.

PP can provide a convenient, though rough and ready, assessment of the profitability of a project, in the way that it is used in **Real World 14.5**, p. 490.

The popularity of PP may suggest a lack of sophistication among managers concerning investment appraisal. This criticism is most often made against managers of smaller businesses. In fact, the Arnold and Hatzopoulos and other surveys found that smaller businesses were much less likely to use discounted cash flow methods (NPV and IRR) than larger businesses.

IRR may be as popular as NPV, despite IRR's theoretical weaknesses, because it expresses outcomes in percentage terms rather than in absolute terms. This form of expression appears to be more acceptable to managers. This may be because managers are used to using percentage figures as targets (for example, return on capital employed).

REAL WORLD 14.5

Space to earn

SES Global is the world's largest commercial satellite operator. This means that it rents satellite capacity to broadcasters, governments, telecommunications groups and Internet service providers. It is a risky venture that few are prepared to undertake. As a result, a handful of businesses dominate the market.

Launching a satellite requires a huge initial outlay of capital, but relatively small cash outflows following the launch. Revenues only start to flow once the satellite is in orbit. A satellite launch costs around €250m. The main elements of this cost are the satellite (€120m), the launch vehicle (€80m), insurance (€40m) and ground equipment (€10m).

According to Romain Bausch, president and chief executive of SES Global, it takes three years to build and launch a satellite. However, the average lifetime of a satellite is fifteen years during which time it is generating revenues. The revenues generated are such that the payback period is around four to five years.

Source: 'Satellites need space to earn', Tim Burt, FT.com, 14 July 2003.

The sum of percentage usage for each appraisal method is 287 per cent (see Real World 14.4), which indicates that many businesses use more than one method to appraise investments. Real World 14.4 suggests that most businesses use one of the two discounted cash flow methods.

Generally survey evidence has shown a strong increase in the rate of usage of both NPV and IRR, in the UK, over the years.

Real World 14.6 shows extracts from the 2002 annual report of a well-known business: Rolls-Royce plc, the builder of engines for aircraft and other purposes.

REAL WORLD 14.6

The use of NPV at Rolls-Royce

In its 2002 annual report, Rolls-Royce said:

> The Group continues to subject all investments to rigorous examination of risks and future cash flows to ensure that they create shareholder value. All major investments require Board approval.
>
> The Group has a portfolio of projects at different stages of their life cycles. Discounted cash flow analysis of the remaining life of projects is performed on a regular basis.

Source: Rolls-Royce plc, Annual Report 2002.

Rolls-Royce makes clear that it uses NPV (the report refers to creating shareholder value and to discounted cash flow, which strongly implies NPV). It is interesting to note that Rolls-Royce not only assesses new projects, but also reassesses existing ones. This must be a sensible commercial approach. Businesses should not continue with existing projects unless those projects have a positive NPV based on future cash flows. Just because a project seemed to have a positive NPV before it started does not mean that this will persist, in the light of changing circumstances. Activity 14.16 (page 486) considered a decision to close down a project.

Dealing with risk in investment appraisal

We have already considered the fact that risk – the likelihood that what is projected to occur will not actually happen – is an important aspect of financial decision making. It is a particularly important issue in the context of investment decisions, because of:

- the relatively long timescales involved. There is more time for things to go wrong between the decision being made and the end of the project; and
- the size of the investment. If things go wrong, the impact can be both significant and lasting.

Various approaches to dealing with risk have been proposed. These fall into two categories: assessing the level of risk and reacting to the level of risk. We now consider formal methods of dealing with risk that fall within each category.

Assessing the level of risk

Sensitivity analysis

One popular way of attempting to assess the level of risk is to carry out a **sensitivity analysis** on the proposed project. This involves an examination of the key input values affecting the project to see how changes in each input might influence the viability of the project.

Firstly, the investment is appraised, using the best estimates for each of the input factors (for example, labour cost, material cost, discount rate and so on). Assuming that the NPV is positive, each input value is then examined to see how far the estimated figure could be changed before the project becomes unviable for that reason alone. Let us suppose that the NPV for an investment in a machine, to provide a particular service, is a positive value of £50,000. If we were to carry out a sensitivity analysis on this project, we should consider in turn each of the key input factors – cost of the machine, sales volume and price, relevant labour costs, length of the project and the discount rate. We should seek to find the value that each of them could have before the NPV figure would become negative (that is, the value for the factor at which NPV would be zero). The difference between the value for that factor at which the NPV would equal zero and the estimated value represents the margin of safety for that particular input. The process is set out in Figure 14.5.

A computer spreadsheet model of the project can be extremely valuable for this exercise because it then becomes a very simple matter to try various values for the input data and see the effect of each. As a result of carrying out a sensitivity analysis, the decision maker is able to get a 'feel' for the project, which otherwise might not be possible. The following activity can be undertaken without recourse to a spreadsheet, however.

ACTIVITY 14.18

S. Saluja (Property Developers) Ltd intends to bid at an auction, to be held today, for a manor house that has fallen into disrepair. The auctioneer believes that the house will be sold for about £450,000. The business wishes to renovate the property and to divide it into luxury flats, to be sold for £150,000 each. The renovation will be in two stages

Figure 14.5   **Factors affecting the sensitivity of NPV calculations**

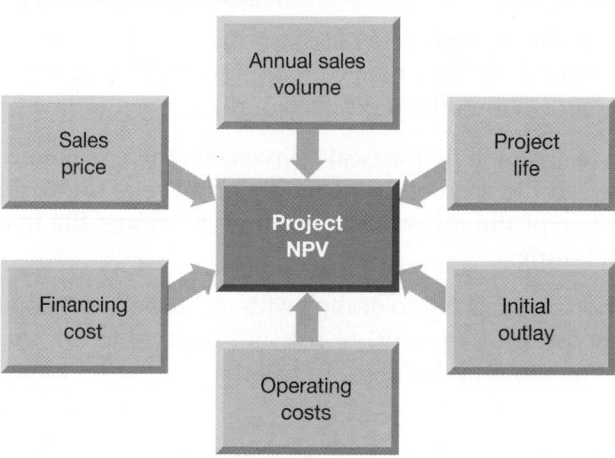

Sensitivity analysis involves identifying the key factors that affect the project. In the figure, six factors have been identified for the particular project. (In practice, the key factors are likely to vary between projects.) Once identified, each factor will be examined in turn to find the value it should have for the project to have a zero NPV.

Activity 14.18 continued

and will cover a two-year period. Stage 1 will cover the first year of the project. It will cost £500,000 and the six flats completed during this stage are expected to be sold for a total of £900,000 at the end of the first year. Stage 2 will cover the second year of the project. It will cost £300,000 and the three remaining flats are expected to be sold at the end of the second year for a total of £450,000. The cost of renovation is subject to an agreed figure with local builders; however, there is some uncertainty over the remaining input values. The business estimates its cost of capital at 12 per cent a year.

(a) What is the NPV of the proposed project?
(b) Assuming none of the other inputs deviates from the best estimates provided:
   (i)   What auction price would have to be paid for the manor house to cause the project to have a zero NPV?
   (ii) What cost of capital would cause the project to have a zero NPV?
   (iii) What is the sale price of each of the flats that would cause the project to have a zero NPV? (Each flat will be sold for the same price: £150,000.)
(c) Is the level of risk associated with the project high or low? Discuss your findings.

(a) The NPV of the proposed project is as follows:

	Cash flows £	Discount factor 12%	Present value £
Year 1 (£900,000 – £500,000)	400,000	0.893	357,200
Year 2 (£450,000 – £300,000)	150,000	0.797	119,550
Less Initial outlay			(450,000)
Net present value			26,750

(b) (i) To obtain a zero NPV, the auction price would have to be £26,750 higher than the current estimate – that is, a total price of £476,750. This is about 6% above the current estimated price.

(ii) As there is a positive NPV, the cost of capital that would cause the project to have a zero NPV must be higher than 12%. Let us try 20%.

	Cash flows £	Discount factor 20%	Present value £
Year 1 (£900,000 – £500,000)	400,000	0.833	333,200
Year 2 (£450,000 – £300,000)	150,000	0.694	104,100
Less Initial outlay			(450,000)
Net present value			(12,700)

The 'break-even' cost of capital lies somewhere between 12 and 20%. Increasing the discount rate by 8 percentage points (from 12 to 20%) causes the NPV to reduce by £39,450 (from £26,750 (positive) to £12,700 (negative)). This means £4,931 (that is £39,450/8) for each percentage point shift in the discount rate. At 12%, the NPV is £26,750 (above zero), so a discount rate of 12% + [(26,750/4,931) × 1%] = 17.4% applies.

This approach is, of course, the same as that used when calculating the IRR of the project. In other words, 17.4% is the IRR of the project.

(iii) To obtain a zero NPV, the sale price of each flat must be reduced so that the NPV is reduced by £26,750. In year 1, six flats are sold (and in year 2, three flats are sold). The discount factor at the 12% rate for year 1 is 0.893 and for year 2, 0.797. We can derive the fall in value per flat (Y) to give a zero NPV by using the equation:

$$(6Y \times 0.893) + (3Y \times 0.797) = £26,750$$
$$Y = £3,452$$

The sale price of each flat necessary to obtain a zero NPV is therefore:

$$£150,000 – £3,452 = £146,548$$

This represents a fall in the estimated price of 2.3%.

(c) These calculations indicate that the auction price would have to be about 6% above the estimated price before a zero NPV is obtained. The margin of safety is, therefore, not very high for this factor. The calculations also reveal that the price of the flats would only have to fall by 2.3% from the estimated price before the NPV is reduced to zero. Hence, the margin of safety for this factor is even smaller. However, the cost of capital is less sensitive to changes and there would have to be an increase from 12 to 17.4% before the project produced a zero NPV. It seems from the calculations that the sale price of the flats is the most sensitive factor to consider. A careful re-examination of the market value of the flats seems appropriate before a final decision is made.

There are two major drawbacks with the use of sensitivity analysis:

● It does not give managers clear decision rules concerning acceptance or rejection of the project and so they must rely on their own judgement.

● It is a static form of analysis. Only one input is considered at a time, while the rest are held constant. In practice, however, it is likely that more than one input value will differ from the best estimates provided. Even so it would be possible to deal with changes in various inputs simultaneously, were the project data put onto a spreadsheet model. This approach, where more than one variable is altered at a time, is known as **scenario building**.

Real World 14.7 below shows that it is not only the business that may carry out sensitivity analysis, or scenario building, in order to assess risk. A supplier or a lender may also use these tools to see whether the business is a credit risk.

REAL WORLD 14.7

No fear of flying

Ryanair is a low-cost airline that has enjoyed considerable success over recent years. As part of its expansion programme, the business has ordered 153 Boeing 737–800 aircraft, with an option to purchase a further 125 aircraft, over a period up to 2009. It has been reported that these aircraft cost Ryanair around $32m each. This represents a huge order for the Boeing Corporation and, of course, a huge risk if the aircraft were built for Ryanair and the business was then unable to pay for them. Around the time of the sale agreement, therefore, Boeing decided to evaluate the future profitability of Ryanair.

Boeing prepared a computer model to test whether changes in key variables such as a fall in passenger demand, changes in currency exchange rates and a rise in aviation fuel prices would damage the profitability of the low-cost airline. Ryanair passed the tests with flying colours: the worst scenario generated was that Ryanair would break even. According to Boeing's sales director for the UK and Ireland, the Ryanair model was probably the most robust that Boeing had encountered.

Source: 'How low can you go?', *Financial Times Magazine*, 21 June 2003, and 'Ryanair: feeding time at the zoo', 11 February 2003, Research report, Goodbody Stockbrokers.

Expected net present value

Another means of assessing risk is through the use of statistical probabilities. It may be possible to identify a range of feasible values for each of the items of input data and to assign a probability of occurrence to each of these values. Using this information, we can derive an **expected net present value (ENPV)**, that is, in effect, a weighted average of the possible outcomes where the probabilities are used as weights. To illustrate this method, let us consider Example 14.2.

Example 14.2

C. Piperis (Properties) Ltd has the opportunity to acquire a lease on a block of flats that has only two years remaining before it expires. The cost of the lease would be £100,000. The occupancy rate of the block of flats is currently around 70 per cent and the flats are let almost exclusively to naval personnel. There is a large naval base located nearby, and there is little other demand for the flats. The occupancy rate of the flats will change in the remaining two years of the lease, depending on the outcome of a defence review. The navy is currently considering three options for the naval base. These are:

● *Option 1.* Increase the size of the base by closing down a base in another region and transferring the personnel to the one located near the flats.

- *Option 2*. Close down the naval base near to the flats and leave only a skeleton staff there for maintenance purposes. The personnel would be moved to a base in another region.
- *Option 3*. Leave the base open but reduce staffing levels by 20 per cent.

The directors of Piperis have estimated the following net cash flows for each of the two years under each option and the probability of their occurrence:

	£	Probability
Option 1	80,000	0.6
Option 2	12,000	0.1
Option 3	40,000	0.3
		1.0

Note that the sum of the probabilities is 1.0 (in other words it is certain that one of the possible options will arise). The business has a cost of capital of 10 per cent.

Should the business purchase the lease on the block of flats?

Solution

To calculate the expected NPV of the proposed investment, we must first calculate the weighted average of the expected outcomes for each year where the probabilities are used as weights, by multiplying each cash flow by its probability of occurrence. Thus, the expected annual net cash flows will be:

	Cash flows	Probability	Expected cash flows
	£	£	
	(a)	(b)	(a × b)
Option 1	80,000	0.6	48,000
Option 2	12,000	0.1	1,200
Option 3	40,000	0.3	12,000
Expected cash flows in each year			61,200

Having derived the expected annual cash flows, we can now discount these using a rate of 10 per cent to reflect the cost of capital:

Year	Expected cash flows	Discount rate	Expected present value
	£	10%	£
1	61,200	0.909	55,631
2	61,200	0.826	50,551
			106,182
Less Initial investment			100,000
Expected NPV			6,182

We can see that the expected NPV is positive. Hence, the wealth of shareholders is expected to increase by purchasing the lease.

The expected NPV approach has the advantage of producing a single numerical outcome and of having a clear decision rule to apply. If the expected NPV is positive, we should invest; if it is negative, we should not.

However, the approach produces an average figure that may not be capable of occurring. This point was illustrated in Example 14.2 where the expected NPV does not correspond to any of the stated options.

Perhaps more importantly, using an average figure can obscure the underlying risk associated with the project. Simply deriving the ENPV, as in Example 14.2, can be misleading. Without some idea of the individual possible outcomes and their probability of occurring, the decision maker is in the dark. In Example 14.2, were either of Options 2 and 3 to occur, the investment would be adverse (wealth destroying). It is 40 per cent probable that one of these two options will occur, so this is a significant risk. Only should Option 1 arise (60 per cent probable) would investing in the flats represent a good decision. Of course, in advance of making the investment, which option will actually occur is not known. None of this should be taken to mean that the investment in the flats should not be made, simply that the decision maker is better placed to make a judgement where information on the possible outcomes is available. This point is further illustrated by Activity 14.19.

ACTIVITY 14.19

Qingdao Manufacturing Ltd is considering two competing projects. Details are as follows:

● Project A has a 0.9 probability of producing a negative NPV of £200,000 and a 0.1 probability of producing a positive NPV of £3.8 million.
● Project B has a 0.6 probability of producing a positive NPV of £100,000 and a 0.4 probability of producing a positive NPV of £350,000.

What is the expected net present value of each project?

The expected NPV of Project A is:

$$[(0.1 \times £3.8m) - (0.9 \times £200,000)] = £200,000$$

The expected NPV of Project B is:

$$[(0.6 \times £100,000) + (0.4 \times £350,000)] = £200,000$$

Although the expected NPV of each project in Activity 14.19 is identical, this does not mean that the business will be indifferent about which project to undertake. We can see from the information provided that Project A has a high probability of making a loss whereas Project B is not expected to make a loss under either possible outcome. If we assume that the shareholders dislike risk – which is usually the case – they will prefer the directors to take on Project B as this provides the same level of expected return as Project A but has a lower level of risk.

It can be argued that the problem identified above may not be significant where the business is engaged in several similar projects, as it will be lost in the averaging process. However, in practice, investment projects may be unique events and this argument will not then apply. Also, where the project is large in relation to other projects undertaken, the argument loses its force. There is also the problem that a factor that might cause one project to have an adverse outcome could also have adverse effects on other projects.

Where the expected NPV approach is being used, it is probably a good idea to make known to managers the different possible outcomes and the probability attached to each outcome. By so doing, the managers will be able to gain an insight to the *downside risk* attached to the project. The information relating to each outcome can be presented in the form of a diagram if required. The construction of such a diagram is illustrated in Example 14.3.

Example 14.3

Zeta Computing Services Ltd has recently produced some software for a client organisation. The software has a life of two years and will then become obsolete. The cost of producing the software was £10,000. The client has agreed to pay a licence fee of £8,000 a year for the software if it is used in only one of its two divisions, and £12,000 a year if it is used in both of its divisions. The client may use the software for either one or two years in either division but will definitely use it in at least one division in each of the two years.

Zeta Computing Services believes there is a 0.6 chance that the licence fee received in any one year will be £8,000 and a 0.4 chance that it will be £12,000. There are four possible outcomes attached to this project (where p denotes probability):

- *Outcome 1.* Year 1 cash flow £8,000 ($p = 0.6$) and Year 2 cash flow £8,000 ($p = 0.6$). The probability of both years having cash flows of £8,000 will be:

$$0.6 \times 0.6 = 0.36$$

- *Outcome 2.* Year 1 cash flow £12,000 ($p = 0.4$) and Year 2 cash flow £12,000 ($p = 0.4$). The probability of both years having cash flows of £12,000 will be:

$$0.4 \times 0.4 = 0.16$$

- *Outcome 3.* Year 1 cash flow £12,000 ($p = 0.4$) and Year 2 cash flow £8,000 ($p = 0.6$). The probability of this sequence of cash flows occurring will be:

$$0.4 \times 0.6 = 0.24$$

- *Outcome 4.* Year 1 cash flow £8,000 ($p = 0.6$) and Year 2 cash flow £12,000 ($p = 0.4$). The probability of this sequence of cash flows occurring will be:

$$0.6 \times 0.4 = 0.24$$

The information in Example 14.3 can be displayed in the form of a diagram (Figure 14.6).

The source of probabilities

As we might expect, assigning probabilities to possible outcomes can often be a problem. There may be many possible outcomes arising from a particular investment project, and to identify each outcome and then assign a probability to it may prove to be an impossible task. When assigning probabilities to possible outcomes, either an objective or a subjective approach may be used. **Objective probabilities** are based on information gathered from past experience. Thus, for example, the transport manager of a business operating a fleet of motor vans may be able to provide information concerning the possible life of a new motor van purchased based on the record of similar vans acquired in the past. From the information available, probabilities may be developed for different

Figure 14.6	The different possible project outcomes for Example 14.3

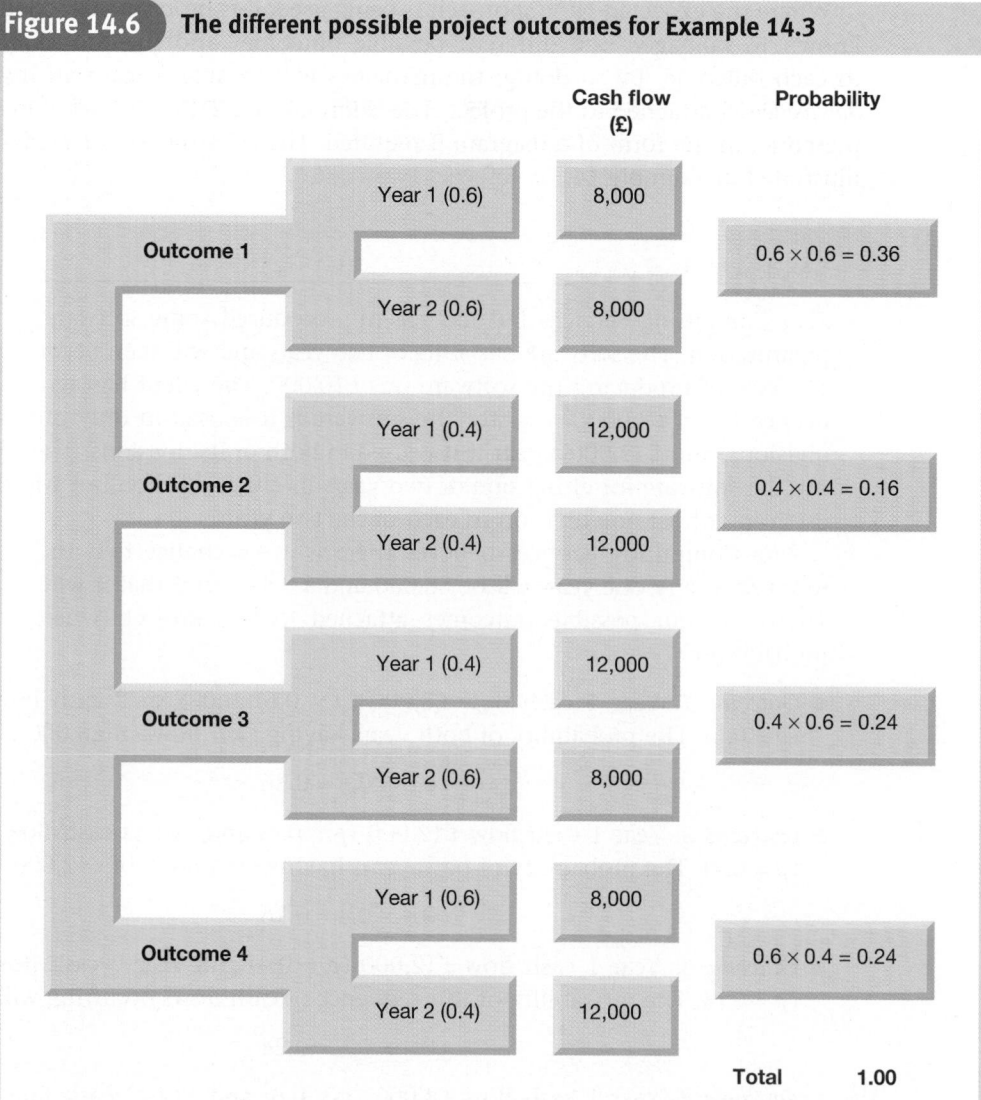

This sets out the different possible outcomes associated with a particular project and the probability of each outcome. The sum of the probabilities attached to each outcome must equal 1.00, in other words it is certain that one of the possible outcomes will occur. For example, outcome 1 would occur where only one division uses the software in each year.

possible lifespans. However, the past may not always be a reliable guide to the future, particularly during a period of rapid change. In the case of the motor vans, for example, changes in design and technology or changes in the purpose for which the vans are being used may undermine the validity of past data.

Subjective probabilities are based on opinion and will be used where past data are either inappropriate or unavailable. The opinions of independent experts may provide a useful basis for developing subjective probabilities, though even these may contain bias, which will affect the reliability of the judgements made.

Despite these problems, we should not be dismissive of the use of probabilities. Assigning probabilities can help to make explicit some of the risks associated with a project and should help decision makers to appreciate the uncertainties that have to be faced.

ACTIVITY 14.20

Devonia (Laboratories) Ltd has recently carried out successful clinical trials on a new type of skin cream that has been developed to reduce the effects of ageing. Research and development costs incurred by the business in relation to the new product amount to £160,000. In order to gauge the market potential of the new product, independent market research consultants were hired at a cost of £15,000. The market research report submitted by the consultants indicates that the skin cream is likely to have a product life of four years and could be sold to retail chemists and large department stores at a price of £20 per 100 ml container. For each of the four years of the new product's life, sales demand has been estimated as follows:

Number of 100 ml containers sold	Probability of occurrence
11,000	0.3
14,000	0.6
16,000	0.1

If the business decides to launch the new product, it is possible for production to begin at once. The equipment necessary to produce the skin cream is already owned by the business and originally cost £150,000. At the end of the new product's life, it is estimated that the equipment could be sold for £35,000. If the business decides against launching the new product, the equipment will be sold immediately for £85,000, as it will be of no further use.

The new skin cream will require one hour's labour for each 100 ml container produced. The cost of labour for the new product is £8.00 an hour. Additional workers will have to be recruited to produce the new product. At the end of the product's life, the workers are unlikely to be offered further work with the business and redundancy costs of £10,000 are expected. The cost of the ingredients for each 100 ml container is £6.00. Additional overheads arising from production of the new product are expected to be £15,000 a year.

The new skin cream has attracted the interest of the business's competitors. If the business decides not to produce and sell the skin cream, it can sell the patent rights to a major competitor immediately for £125,000.

Devonia has a cost of capital of 12 per cent. Ignore taxation.

(a) Calculate the expected net present value (ENPV) of the new product.
(b) State, with reasons, whether or not Devonia should launch the new product.

Your answer should be as follows:

(a) Expected sales volume per year = $(11,000 \times 0.3) + (14,000 \times 0.6) + (16,000 \times 0.1)$
    = 13,300 units
    Expected annual sales revenue = $13,300 \times £20$
    = £266,000
    Annual labour = $13,300 \times £8$
    = £106,400
    Annual ingredient costs = $13,300 \times £6$
    = £79,800

→

Activity 14.20 continued

Incremental cash flows:

	0 £000	1 £000	2 £000	3 £000	4 £000
			Years		
Sale of patent rights	(125.0)				
Sale of equipment	(85.0)				35.0
Sales revenue		266.0	266.0	266.0	266.0
Cost of ingredients		(79.8)	(79.8)	(79.8)	(79.8)
Labour costs		(106.4)	(106.4)	(106.4)	(106.4)
Redundancy					(10.0)
Additional overheads		(15.0)	(15.0)	(15.0)	(15.0)
	(210.0)	64.8	64.8	64.8	89.8
Discount factor (12%)	1.0	0.893	0.797	0.712	0.636
	(210.0)	57.9	51.6	46.1	57.1
ENPV	2.7				

(b) As the ENPV of the project is positive, the wealth of shareholders would be increased by accepting the project. However, the ENPV is very low in relation to the size of the project and careful checking of the key estimates and assumptions would be advisable. A relatively small downward revision of sales revenue or upward revision of costs could make the project ENPV negative.

It would be helpful to derive the NPV for each of the three possible outcomes regarding sales levels. This would enable the decision maker to have a clearer view of the risk involved with the investment.

Reacting to the level of risk

The logical reaction to a risky project is to demand a higher rate of return. Both theory and observable evidence show that there is a relationship between risk and the return required by investors. It was mentioned earlier, for example, that a bank would normally ask for a higher rate of interest on a loan where it perceives the lender to be less likely to be able to repay the amount borrowed.

When evaluating investment projects, it is normal to increase the NPV discount rate in the face of increased risk – that is, to demand a risk premium. The higher the level of risk, therefore, the higher the risk premium that will be demanded. The risk premium is usually added to a 'risk-free' rate of return to derive the total return required. The risk-free rate is normally taken to be equivalent to the rate of return from government loan stock. In practice, a business may divide projects into low-, medium- and high-risk categories and then assign a risk premium to each category. The cash flows from a particular project will then be discounted using a rate based on the risk-free rate plus the appropriate risk premium. This relationship between risk and return is illustrated in Figure 14.7.

Figure 14.7 **Relationship between risk and return**

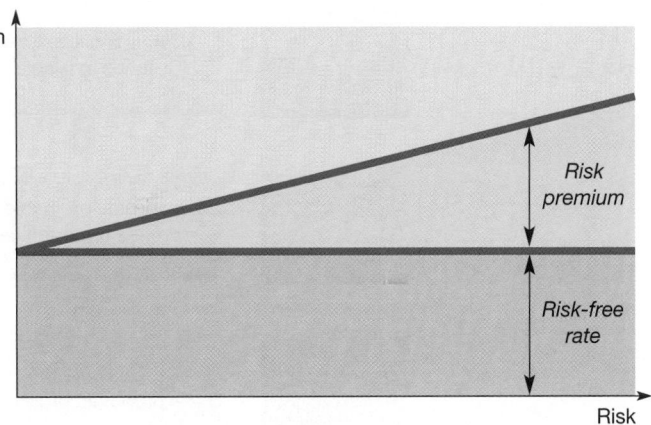

It is logical to take account of the riskiness of projects by changing the discount rate. A risk premium is added to the risk-free rate to derive the appropriate discount rate. A higher return will normally be expected from projects where the risks are higher. Thus, the riskier the project, the higher the risk premium.

The use of a **risk-adjusted discount rate** provides managers with a single value, which can be used when making a decision either to accept or to reject a project. Moreover, managers are likely to have an intuitive grasp of the relationship between risk and return and may well feel comfortable with this technique. However, there are practical difficulties with implementing this approach.

ACTIVITY 14.21

Can you think of any practical problems with the use of risk-adjusted discount rates?

Subjective judgement is required when assigning an investment project to a particular risk category and then in assigning a risk premium to each category. The choices made will reflect the personal views of the managers responsible and this may differ from the views of the shareholders they represent. The choices made can, nevertheless, make the difference between accepting and rejecting a particular project.

Managing investment projects

So far, we have been concerned with the process of carrying out the necessary calculations that enable managers to select among already identified investment opportunities. This topic is given a great deal of emphasis in the literature on investment appraisal. Though the evaluation of projects is undoubtedly important, we must bear in mind that it is only *part* of the process of investment decision making. There are other important aspects that managers must also consider.

It is possible to see the investment process as a sequence of five stages, each of which managers must consider. The five stages are set out in Figure 14.8 and described below.

| Figure 14.8 | Managing the investment decision |

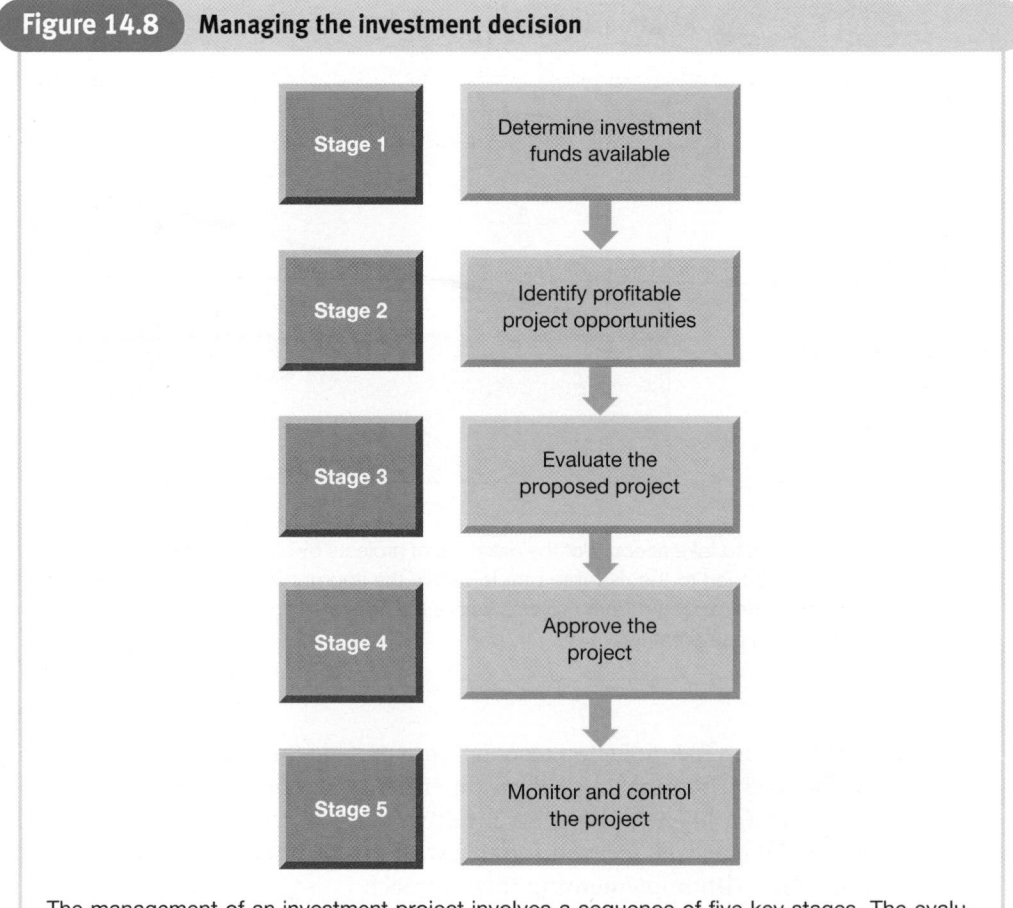

The management of an investment project involves a sequence of five key stages. The evaluation of projects using the appraisal techniques discussed earlier represents only one of these stages.

Stage 1: Determine investment funds available

The amount of funds available for investment may be determined by the external market for funds or by internal management. In practice, it is often the latter that has the greater influence on the amount available. In either case, it may be that the funds will not be sufficient to finance the profitable investment opportunities available. When this occurs, some form of **capital rationing** has to be undertaken. This means that managers are faced with the task of deciding on the most profitable use of the investment funds available.

Stage 2: Identify profitable project opportunities

A vital part of the investment process is the search for profitable investment opportunities. A business should carry out methodical routines for identifying feasible projects. This may be done through a research and development department or by some other means. Failure to do so will inevitably lead to the business losing its competitive position with respect to product development, production methods or market penetration. To help identify good investment opportunities, some businesses provide financial incentives to staff that have good ideas. The search process will, however, usually involve looking outside the business to identify changes in technology, customer demand, market conditions and so on. Information will need to be gathered and this may take some time, particularly for unusual or non-routine investment opportunities.

Stage 3: Evaluate the proposed project

If management is to agree to the investment of funds in a project, there must be a proper screening of each proposal. For projects of any size, this will involve providing answers to a number of questions, including:

● What is the nature and purpose of the project?
● Does the project align with the overall objectives of the business?
● How much finance is required?
● What other resources (such as expertise, factory space and so on) are required for successful completion of the project?
● How long will the project last and what are its key stages?
● What is the expected pattern of cash flows?
● What are the major problems associated with the project and how can they be overcome?
● What is the NPV/IRR of the project? How does this compare with other opportunities available?
● Have risk and inflation been taken into account in the appraisal process and, if so, what are the results?

It is important to appreciate that the ability and commitment of those responsible for proposing and managing the project will be vital to its success. Hence, when evaluating a new project, those proposing it will be judged by its success. In some cases, senior managers may decide not to support a project that appears profitable on paper if they lack confidence in the ability of key managers to see it through to completion.

Stage 4: Approve the project

Once the managers responsible for investment decision making are satisfied that the project should be undertaken, formal approval can be given. However, a decision on a project may be postponed if senior managers need more information from those proposing the project, or if revisions are required to the proposal. In some cases, the project proposal may be rejected if it is considered unprofitable or likely to fail. Before rejecting a proposal, however, the implications of not pursuing the project for such areas as market share, staff morale and existing business operations must be carefully considered.

Stage 5: Monitor and control the project

Making a decision to invest in, say, the plant needed to provide a new service does not automatically cause the investment to be made and provision of the service to go smoothly ahead. Managers will need to manage the project actively through to completion. This, in turn, will require further information-gathering exercises.

Management should receive progress reports at regular intervals concerning the project. These reports should provide information relating to the actual cash flows for each stage of the project, which can then be compared against the forecast figures provided when the proposal was submitted for approval. The reasons for significant variations should be ascertained and corrective action taken where possible. Any changes in the expected completion date of the project or any expected variations in future cash flows from budget should be reported immediately; in extreme cases, managers may even abandon the project if circumstances appear to have changed dramatically for the worse. We saw in Real World 14.6 that Rolls-Royce undertakes this kind of reassessment of existing projects. No doubt most other well-managed businesses do this too.

Project management techniques (for example, critical path analysis) should be employed wherever possible and their effectiveness reported to senior management.

 An important part of the control process is a **post-completion audit** of the project. This is, in essence, a review of the project performance in order to see whether it lived up to expectations and whether any lessons can be learned from the way that the investment process was carried out. In addition to an evaluation of financial costs and benefits, non-financial measures of performance such as the ability to meet deadlines and levels of quality achieved should also be reported. (See Chapter 11 for a discussion of total life-cycle costing, which is based on similar principles.)

The fact that a post-completion audit is an integral part of the management of the project should also encourage those who submit projects to use realistic estimates. Where over-optimistic estimates are used in an attempt to secure project approval, the managers responsible will find themselves accountable at the post-completion audit stage. Such audits, however, can be difficult and time-consuming to carry out, and so the likely benefits must be weighed against the costs involved. Senior management may feel, therefore, that only projects above a certain size should be subject to a post-completion audit.

Real World 14.8 reveals that Tesco and Premier Oil both use post-completion audit approaches to evaluating past investment projects. No doubt most well-managed businesses do the same.

REAL WORLD 14.8

Approaches to investment decisions

In its 2003 annual report, Tesco, the supermarket chain said:

> The capital investment programme is subject to formalised review procedures requiring key criteria to be met. All major initiatives require business cases to be prepared, normally covering a minimum of five years. Post investment appraisals are also carried out.

In its 2002 annual report, Premier Oil, the oil and gas exploration and production business, said:

> The group has clearly defined procedures for capital expenditure. These include authority levels, commitment records and reporting, annual budget and detailed appraisal and review procedures.

SUMMARY

The main points of this chapter may be summarised as follows:

Accounting rate of return (ARR) = the average accounting profit from the project expressed as a percentage of the average investment

- Decision rule – projects with an ARR above a defined minimum are acceptable; the greater the ARR, the more attractive the project becomes.
- Conclusions on ARR:
  - It does not relate directly to shareholders' wealth – can lead to illogical conclusions.
  - Takes almost no account of the timing of cash flows.
  - Ignores some relevant information and may take account of some irrelevant.
  - Relatively simple to use.
  - Much inferior to NPV.

Payback period (PP) = the length of time that it takes for the cash outflow for the initial investment to be repaid out of resulting cash inflows

- Decision rule – projects with a PP up to defined maximum period are acceptable; the shorter the PP, the more desirable.
- Conclusions on PP:
  - Does not relate to shareholders' wealth; ignores inflows after the payback date.
  - Takes little account of the timing of cash flows.
  - Ignores much relevant information.
  - Does not always provide clear signals and can be impractical to use.
  - Much inferior to NPV, but it is easy to understand and can offer a liquidity insight, which might be the reason for its widespread use.

Net present value (NPV) = the sum of the discounted values of the cash flows from the investment

- Money has a time value.
- Decision rule – all positive NPV investments enhance shareholders' wealth; the greater the NPV, the greater the enhancement and the more desirable.
- PV of a cash flow = cash flow $\times 1/(1 + r)^n$, assuming a constant discount rate.
- The act of discounting brings cash flows at different points in time to a common valuation basis (their present value), which enables them to be directly compared.
- Conclusions on NPV:
  - Relates directly to shareholders' wealth objective.
  - Takes account of the timing of cash flows.
  - Takes all relevant information into account.
  - Provides clear signals and practical to use.

Internal rate of return (IRR) = the discount rate that causes a project to have a zero NPV

- Represents the average percentage return on the investment, taking account of the fact that cash may be flowing into and out of the project at various points in its life.
- Decision rule – projects that have an IRR greater than the cost of capital are acceptable; the greater the IRR, the more attractive the project.

- Usually cannot be calculated directly; a trial and error approach is usually necessary.
- Conclusions on IRR:
  - Does not relate directly to shareholders' wealth. Usually gives the same signals as NPV – can mislead where there are competing projects of different scales.
  - Takes account of the timing of cash flows.
  - Takes all relevant information into account.
  - With unconventional cash flows, problems of multiple or no IRR.
  - Inferior to NPV.

Use of appraisal methods in practice

- All four methods are widely used.
- The discounting methods (NPV and IRR) show a strong increase in usage over time.
- Many businesses use more than one method.
- Larger businesses seem to be more sophisticated than smaller ones.

Risk in investment appraisal

- Sensitivity analysis (SA) = an assessment, taking each input factor in turn, of how much each one can vary from estimate before a project is not viable:
  - Provides useful insights to projects.
  - Does not give a clear decision rule, but provides an impression.
  - It can be rather static, but Scenario building solves this problem.
- Expected net present value (ENPV) = the weighted average of the possible outcomes for a project, based on probabilities for each of the inputs:
  - Provides a single value and a clear decision rule.
  - The single ENPV figure can hide the real risk.
  - Useful for the ENPV figure to be supported by information on the range and dispersion of possible outcomes.
  - Probabilities may be subjective (based on opinion) or objective (based on evidence).
- Reacting to the level of risk
  - Logically, high risk should lead to high returns.
  - Using a risk-adjusted discount rate, where a risk premium is added to the risk-free rate, is a logical response to risk.

Management of the investment project has five stages

1 Determine investment funds available – dealing, if necessary, with capital rationing problems.
2 Identify profitable project opportunities.
3 Evaluate the proposed project.
4 Approve the project.
5 Monitor and control the project – using a post-completion audit approach.

→ **Key terms**

accounting rate of return (ARR) p. 467	sensitivity analysis p. 491
payback period (PP) p. 472	scenario building p. 493
net present value (NPV) p. 475	expected net present value (ENPV) p. 494
risk p. 476	objective probabilities p. 497
risk premium p. 477	subjective probabilities p. 498
inflation p. 477	risk-adjusted discount rate p. 501
discount factor p. 480	capital rationing p. 502
internal rate of return (IRR) p. 482	post-completion audit p. 504

Further reading

If you would like to explore the topics covered in this chapter in more depth, we recommend the following books:

Corporate Financial Management, *Arnold G.*, 2nd edn, Financial Times Prentice Hall, 2002, chapters 2, 3 and 4.

Investment Appraisal and Financial Decisions, *Lumby S. and Jones C.*, 7th edn, International Thomson Business Press, 2003, chapters 3, 5 and 6.

Business Finance: Theory and practice, *McLaney E.*, 6th edn, Financial Times Prentice Hall, 2003, chapters 4–6.

Corporate Finance and Investment, *Pike R. and Neale B.*, 4th edn, Prentice Hall International, 2002, chapters 5, 6 and 7.

References

1 **Reckoning with Risk**, *Gigerenzer, G.*, Penguin, 2002.
2 'The theory–practice gap in capital budgeting: evidence from the United Kingdom', *Arnold G. C. and Hatzopoulos P. D.*, in **Journal of Business Finance and Accounting**, June/July 2000.

REVIEW QUESTIONS

Answers to these questions can be found on the students' side of the Companion Website at www.pearsoned.co.uk/atrillmclaney.

14.1 Why is the net present value method of investment appraisal considered to be theoretically superior to other methods that are found in practice?

14.2 The payback method has been criticised for not taking the time value of money into account. Could this limitation be overcome? If so, would this method then be preferable to the NPV method?

14.3 Research indicates that the IRR method is a more popular method of investment appraisal than the NPV method. Why might this be?

14.4 Why are cash flows rather than profit flows used in the IRR, NPV and PP methods of investment appraisal?

EXERCISES

Exercises 14.5 to 14.8 are more advanced than 14.1 to 14.4. Those with a coloured number have answers at the back of the book.

14.1 The directors of Mylo Ltd are currently considering two mutually exclusive investment projects. Both projects are concerned with the purchase of new plant. The following data are available for each project:

	Project 1 £	Project 2 £
Cost (immediate outlay)	100,000	60,000
Expected annual net profit (loss):		
Year 1	29,000	18,000
2	(1,000)	(2,000)
3	2,000	4,000
Estimated residual value of the plant	7,000	6,000

The business has an estimated cost of capital of 10%, and uses the straight-line method of depreciation for all non-current assets when calculating net profit. Neither project would increase the working capital of the business. The business has sufficient funds to meet all capital expenditure requirements.

Required:
(a) Calculate for each project:
   (i) The net present value.
   (ii) The approximate internal rate of return.
   (iii) The payback period.
(b) State which, if any, of the two investment projects the directors of Mylo Ltd should accept, and why.
(c) State, in general terms, which method of investment appraisal you consider to be most appropriate for evaluating investment projects, and why.

14.2 C. George (Controls) Ltd manufactures a thermostat that can be used in a range of kitchen appliances. The manufacturing process is, at present, semi-automated. The equipment used costs £540,000, and has a written-down (balance sheet) value of £300,000. Demand for the product has been fairly stable, and output has been maintained at 50,000 units a year in recent years.

The following data, based on the current level of output, have been prepared in respect of the product:

| | Per unit | |
	£	£
Selling price		12.40
Less		
Labour	3.30	
Materials	3.65	
Overheads: Variable	1.58	
Fixed	1.60	
		10.13
Profit		2.27

Although the existing equipment is expected to last for a further four years before it is sold for an estimated £40,000, the business has recently been considering purchasing new equipment that would completely automate much of the production process. The new equipment would cost £670,000 and would have an expected life of four years, at the end of which it would be sold for an estimated £70,000. If the new equipment is purchased, the old equipment could be sold for £150,000 immediately.

The assistant to the business's accountant has prepared a report to help assess the viability of the proposed change, which includes the following data:

| | Per unit | |
	£	£
Selling price		12.40
Less		
Labour	1.20	
Materials	3.20	
Overheads: Variable	1.40	
Fixed	3.30	
		9.10
Profit		3.30

Depreciation charges will increase by £85,000 a year as a result of purchasing the new machinery; however, other fixed costs are not expected to change.

In the report the assistant wrote:

> The figures shown above that relate to the proposed change are based on the current level of output and take account of a depreciation charge of £150,000 a year in respect of the new equipment. The effect of purchasing the new equipment will be to increase the net profit to sales revenue ratio from 18.3% to 26.6%. In addition, the purchase of the new equipment will enable us to reduce our stock level immediately by £130,000.
>
> In view of these facts, I recommend purchase of the new equipment.

The business has a cost of capital of 12%. Ignore taxation.

Required:

(a) Prepare a statement of the incremental cash flows arising from the purchase of the new equipment.

(b) Calculate the net present value of the proposed purchase of new equipment.

(c) State, with reasons, whether the business should purchase the new equipment.

(d) Explain why cash flow forecasts are used rather than profit forecasts to assess the viability of proposed capital expenditure projects.

14.3 The accountant of your business has recently been taken ill through overwork. In his absence his assistant has prepared some calculations of the profitability of a project, which are to be discussed soon at the board meeting of your business. His workings, which are set out below, include some errors of principle. You can assume that the statement below includes no arithmetical errors.

	Year 1 £000	Year 2 £000	Year 3 £000	Year 4 £000	Year 5 £000	Year 6 £000
Sales revenue		450	470	470	470	470
Less Costs						
Materials		126	132	132	132	132
Labour		90	94	94	94	94
Overheads		45	47	47	47	47
Depreciation		120	120	120	120	120
Working capital	180					
Interest on working capital		27	27	27	27	27
Write-off of development costs		30	30	30		
Total costs	180	438	450	450	420	420
Profit/(loss)	(180)	12	20	20	50	50

$$\frac{\text{Total profit (loss)}}{\text{Cost of equipment}} = \frac{(£28,000)}{£600,000} = \text{Return on investment (4.7\%)}$$

You ascertain the following additional information:

● The cost of equipment contains £100,000, being the book value of an old machine. If it were not used for this project it would be scrapped with a zero net realisable value. New equipment costing £500,000 will be purchased on 31 December Year 0. You should assume that all other cash flows occur at the end of the year to which they relate.
● The development costs of £90,000 have already been spent.
● Overheads have been costed at 50% of direct labour, which is the business's normal practice. An independent assessment has suggested that incremental overheads are likely to amount to £30,000 a year.
● The business's cost of capital is 12%.

Ignore taxation in your answer.

Required:

(a) Prepare a corrected statement of the incremental cash flows arising from the project. Where you have altered the assistant's figures you should attach a brief note explaining your alterations.
(b) Calculate:
  (i) The project's payback period.
  (ii) The project's net present value as at 31 December Year 0.
(c) Write a memo to the board advising on the acceptance or rejection of the project.

14.4 Arkwright Mills plc is considering expanding its production of a new yarn, code name X15. The plant is expected to cost £1m and have a life of five years and a nil residual value. It will be bought, paid for and ready for operation on 31 December, Year 0. £500,000 has already been spent on development costs of the product, and this has been charged in the profit and loss account (income statement) in the year it was incurred.

The following results are projected for the new yarn are:

	Year 1 £m	Year 2 £m	Year 3 £m	Year 4 £m	Year 5 £m
Sales revenue	1.2	1.4	1.4	1.4	1.4
Costs, including depreciation	1.0	1.1	1.1	1.1	1.1
Profit before tax	0.2	0.3	0.3	0.3	0.3

Tax is charged at 50% on annual profits (before tax and after depreciation) and paid one year in arrears. Depreciation of the plant has been calculated on a straight-line basis. Additional working capital of £0.6m will be required at the beginning of the project and released at the end of Year 5. You should assume that all cash flows occur at the end of the year in which they arise.

Required:
(a) Prepare a statement showing the incremental cash flows of the project relevant to a decision concerning whether or not to proceed with the construction of the new plant.
(b) Compute the net present value of the project using a 10% discount rate.
(c) Compute the payback period to the nearest year. Explain the meaning of this term.

14.5 Newton Electronics Ltd has incurred expenditure of £5m over the past three years researching and developing a miniature hearing aid. The hearing aid is now fully developed, and the directors are considering which of three mutually exclusive options should be taken to exploit the potential of the new product. The options are as follows:

1 The business could manufacture the hearing aid itself. This would be a new departure, since the business has so far concentrated on research and development projects. However, the business has manufacturing space available that it currently rents to another business for £100,000 a year. The business would have to purchase plant and equipment costing £9m and invest £3m in working capital immediately for production to begin.

A market research report, for which the business paid £50,000, indicates that the new product has an expected life of five years. Sales of the product during this period are predicted as follows:

	Predicted sales for the year ended 30 November				
	Year 1	Year 2	Year 3	Year 4	Year 5
Number of units ('000)	800	1,400	1,800	1,200	500

The selling price per unit will be £30 in the first year but will fall to £22 in the following three years. In the final year of the product's life, the selling price will fall to £20. Variable production costs are predicted to be £14 a unit, and fixed production costs (including depreciation) will be £2.4m a year. Marketing costs will be £2m a year.

The business intends to depreciate the plant and equipment using the straight-line method and based on an estimated residual value at the end of the five years of £1m. The business has a cost of capital of 10% per year.

2 Newton Electronics Ltd could agree to another business manufacturing and marketing the product under licence. A multinational business, Faraday Electricals plc, has offered to undertake the manufacture and marketing of the product, and in return will make a royalty payment to Newton Electronics Ltd of £5 per unit. It has been estimated that the annual number of sales of the hearing aid will be 10% higher if the multinational business, rather than if Newton Electronics Ltd, manufactures and markets the product.

3 Newton Electronics Ltd could sell the patent rights to Faraday Electricals plc for £24m, payable in two equal instalments. The first instalment would be payable immediately and the second at the end of two years. This option would give Faraday Electricals the exclusive right to manufacture and market the new product.

Ignore taxation. Assume it is now 30 November Year 0.

Required:

(a) Calculate the net present value of each of the options available to Newton Electronics Ltd.
(b) Identify and discuss any other factors that Newton Electronics Ltd should consider before arriving at a decision.
(c) State what you consider to be the most suitable option, and why.

14.6 Chesterfield Wanderers is a professional football club that has enjoyed considerable success in both national and European competitions in recent years. As a result, the club has accumulated £10m to spend on its further development. The board of directors is currently considering two mutually exclusive options for spending the funds available.

The first option is to acquire another player. The team manager has expressed a keen interest in acquiring Basil ('Bazza') Ramsey, a central defender, who currently plays for a rival club. The rival club has agreed to release the player immediately for £10m if required. A decision to acquire 'Bazza' Ramsey would mean that the existing central defender, Vinnie Smith, could be sold to another club. Chesterfield Wanderers has recently received an offer of £2.2m for this player. This offer is still open but will only be accepted if 'Bazza' Ramsey joins Chesterfield Wanderers. If this does not happen, Vinnie Smith will be expected to stay on with the club until the end of his playing career in five years' time. During this period, Vinnie will receive an annual salary of £400,000 and a loyalty bonus of £200,000 at the end of his five-year period with the club.

Assuming 'Bazza' Ramsey is acquired, the team manager estimates that gate receipts will increase by £2.5m in the first year and £1.3m in each of the following four years. There will also be an increase in advertising and sponsorship revenues of £1.2m for each of the next five years if the player is acquired. At the end of five years, the player can be sold to a club in a lower division and Chesterfield Wanderers will expect to receive £1m as a transfer fee. During his period at the club, 'Bazza' will receive an annual salary of £800,000 and a loyalty bonus of £400,000 after five years.

The second option is for the club to improve its ground facilities. The west stand could be extended and executive boxes could be built for businesses wishing to offer corporate hospitality to clients. These improvements would also cost £10m and would take one year to complete. During this period, the west stand would be closed, resulting in a reduction of gate receipts of £1.8m. However, gate receipts for each of the following four years would be £4.4m higher than current receipts. In five years' time, the club has plans to sell the existing grounds and to move to a new stadium nearby. Improving the ground facilities is not expected to affect the ground's value when it comes to be sold. Payment for the improvements will be made when the work has been completed at the end of the first year.

Whichever option is chosen, the board of directors has decided to take on additional ground staff. The additional wages bill is expected to be £350,000 a year over the next five years.

The club has a cost of capital of 10%. Ignore taxation.

Required:

(a) Calculate the incremental cash flows arising from each of the options available to the club.
(b) Calculate the net present value of each of the options.
(c) On the basis of the calculations made in (b) above, which of the two options would you choose and why?
(d) Discuss the validity of using the net present value method in making investment decisions for a professional football club.

14.7 Simtex Ltd has invested £120,000 to date in developing a new type of shaving foam. The shaving foam is now ready for production and it has been estimated that the new product will sell 160,000 cans a year over the next four years. At the end of four years, the product will be discontinued and replaced by a new product.

The shaving foam is expected to sell at £6 a can and variable costs are estimated at £4 per can. Fixed costs (excluding depreciation) are expected to be £300,000 a year. (This figure includes £130,000 in fixed costs incurred by the existing business that will be apportioned to this new product.)

To manufacture and package the new product, equipment costing £480,000 must be acquired immediately. The estimated value of this equipment in four years' time is £100,000. The business calculates depreciation using the straight-line method, and has an estimated cost of capital of 12%.

Required:

(a) Deduce the net present value of the new product.

(b) Calculate by how much each of the following must change before the new product is no longer profitable:
   (i)   the discount rate;
   (ii) the initial outlay on new equipment;
   (iii) the net operating cash flows;
   (iv) the residual value of the equipment.

(c) Should the business produce the new product?

14.8 Kernow Cleaning Services Ltd provides street-cleaning services for local councils in the far south west of England. The work is currently labour intensive and few machines are employed. However, the business has recently been considering the purchase of a fleet of street-cleaning vehicles at a total cost of £540,000. The vehicles have a life of four years and are likely to result in a considerable saving of labour costs. Estimates of the likely labour savings and their probability of occurrence are set out below:

	Estimated savings £	Probability of occurrence
Year 1	80,000	0.3
	160,000	0.5
	200,000	0.2
Year 2	140,000	0.4
	220,000	0.4
	250,000	0.2
Year 3	140,000	0.4
	200,000	0.3
	230,000	0.3
Year 4	100,000	0.3
	170,000	0.6
	200,000	0.1

Estimates for each year are independent of other years. The business has a cost of capital of 10%.

Required:

(a) Calculate the expected net present value (ENPV) of the street-cleaning machines.

(b) Calculate the net present value (NPV) of the worst possible outcome and the probability of its occurrence.

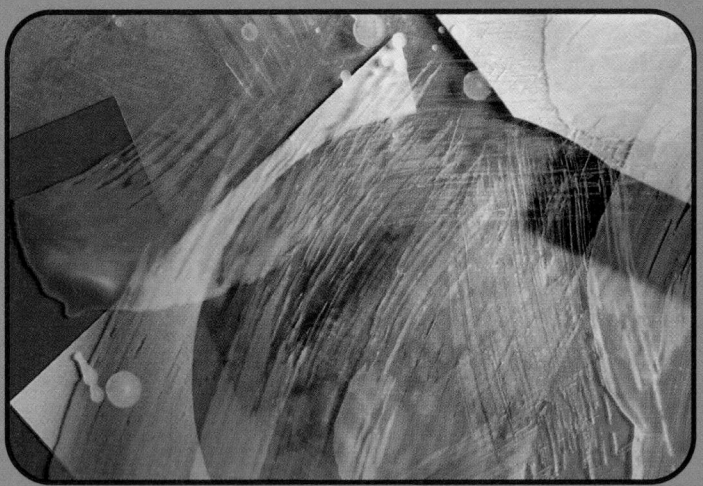

Financing a business

When you have completed this chapter, you should be able to:

● Identify the main sources of finance available to a business and explain the advantages and disadvantages of each source.

● Outline the ways in which share capital may be issued.

● Explain the role and nature of the Stock Exchange.

● Discuss the ways in which smaller businesses may seek to raise finance.

INTRODUCTION

This chapter examines various aspects of financing a business. It begins by considering the main sources of finance available to a business. Some of these sources have already been touched upon when financing of limited companies was discussed in Chapters 4 and 7. This chapter, discusses these sources in more detail as well as discussing other sources of finance that have not yet been mentioned. The factors to be taken into account when choosing an appropriate source of finance are considered.

Following a consideration of the main sources of finance, the chapter goes on to examine various aspects of the capital markets including the role of the Stock Exchange, the financing of smaller businesses, and the ways in which share capital may be issued.

Sources of finance

When considering the various sources of finance for a business, it is useful to distinguish between *internal* and *external* sources of finance. By internal sources we mean sources that do not require the agreement of anyone beyond the directors and managers of the business. Thus, retained profit is considered an internal source because the directors of the business have power to retain profits without the agreement of the shareholders, whose profits they are. Finance from an issue of new shares, on the other hand, is an external source because it requires the compliance of potential shareholders.

Within each of the two categories just described, we can further distinguish between *long-term* and *short-term* sources of finance. There is no agreed definition concerning each of these terms but, for the purpose of this chapter, long-term sources of finance are defined as sources of finance that are not due for repayment within one year. Short-term sources are those due for repayment within one year.

In the sections that immediately follow, we consider the various sources of internal finance. We shall then go on to consider the various sources of external finance available. This is probably an appropriate order to deal with these since, in practice, businesses tend to look first to internal sources before going outside for new funds.

Internal sources of financing

Internal sources of finance usually have the advantage that they are flexible. They may also be obtained quickly – particularly from working capital sources – and need not require the compliance of other parties. The main sources of internal funds are described below, and are summarised in Figure 15.1.

Figure 15.1	Major internal sources of finance

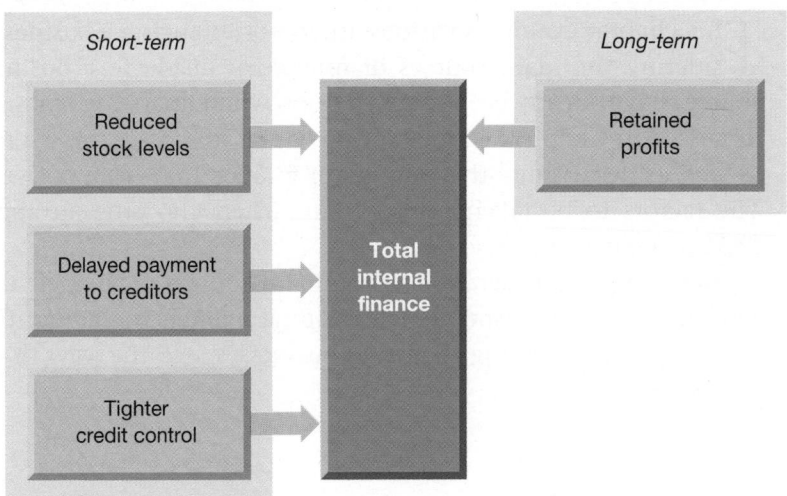

The major long-term source of internal finance is the profits that are retained rather than distributed to shareholders. The major short-term sources of internal finance involve reducing the level of debtors (receivables) and stocks (inventories) and increasing the level of creditors (payables).

Long-term sources of internal finance

Retained profits

Retained profits are the major source of finance for most businesses. By retaining profits within the business rather than distributing them to shareholders in the form of dividends, the funds of the business are increased.

ACTIVITY 15.1

Are retained profits a free source of finance to the business?

It is tempting to think that retained profits are a 'cost-free' source of funds for a business. However, this is not the case. If profits are reinvested rather than distributed to shareholders, those shareholders cannot invest the profits made in other forms of investment. They will therefore expect a rate of return from the profits reinvested that is equivalent to what they would have received had the funds been invested in another opportunity with the same level of risk.

The reinvestment of profits rather than the issue of new shares can be a useful way of raising capital from ordinary share investors. There are no issue costs associated with retaining profits, and the amount raised is certain, once the profit has been made. When issuing new shares, the issue costs may be substantial, and there may be uncertainty over the success of the issue. Retaining profits will have no effect on the control of the business by existing shareholders, whereas new shares may be issued to outside investors leading to some dilution of control.

The retention of profits is something that is determined by the directors. They may find it easier simply to retain profits rather than ask investors to subscribe to a new share issue. Retained profits are already held by the business, and so it does not have to wait to receive the funds. Moreover, there is often less scrutiny when profits are being retained for reinvestment purposes than when new shares are being issued. Investors and their advisers will closely examine the reasons for any new share issue. A problem with the use of profits as a source of finance, however, is that the timing and level of future profits cannot always be reliably determined.

Some shareholders may prefer profits to be retained by the business, rather than be distributed in the form of dividends. By ploughing back profits, it may be expected that the business will expand, and that share values will increase as a result. In the UK, not all capital gains are liable for taxation. (For the tax year 2004/5, an individual with capital gains totalling less than £8,200 would not be taxed on those gains.) A further advantage of capital gains over dividends is that the shareholder has a choice as to when the gain is realised. Research indicates that investors may be attracted to particular businesses according to the dividend/retention policies that they adopt.

Retained profit is much the most important source of new finance for UK businesses, on average, in terms of funds raised.

Short-term sources of internal finance

Tighter credit control
....

By exerting tighter control over trade debtors (receivables) it may be possible for a business to reduce the proportion of assets held in this form and so release funds for other purposes. Having funds tied up in trade debts represents an opportunity cost in that those funds could be used for profit generating activities. It is important, however, to weigh the benefits of tighter credit control against the likely costs in the form of lost customer goodwill and lost sales. To remain competitive, a business must take account of the needs of its customers and the credit policies adopted by rival businesses within the industry. We shall consider this further in Chapter 16.

ACTIVITY 15.2

H. Rusli Ltd provides a car valet service for car-hire businesses when their cars are returned from hire. Details of the service costs are as follows:

	Per car	
	£	£
Car valet charge		20
Less Variable costs	14	
Fixed costs	4	18
Net profit		2

Sales revenue is £10 million a year and is all on credit. The average credit period taken by the car-hire businesses is 45 days, although the terms of credit require payment within 30 days. Bad debts are currently £100,000 a year. Debtors are financed by a bank overdraft costing 15 per cent a year.

→

Activity 15.2 continued

The credit control department of H. Rusli Ltd believes it can eliminate bad debts and can reduce the average credit period to 30 days if new credit control procedures are implemented. These will cost £50,000 a year, and are likely to result in a reduction in sales revenue of 5 per cent a year.

Should the business implement the new credit control procedures? (*Hint*: To answer this activity it is useful to compare the current cost of trade credit with the costs under the proposed approach.)

The current annual cost of trade credit is:

	£
Bad debts	100,000
Overdraft interest [(£10m × 45/365) × 15%]	184,931
	284,931

The annual cost of trade credit under the new policy will be:

	£
Overdraft interest [((95% × 10m) × (30/365)) × 15%]	117,123
Cost of control procedures	50,000
Net cost of lost sales [((£10m/£20) × 5%) × (20 − 14*)]	150,000
	317,123

* The loss will be the contribution per unit (that is, the difference between the selling price and the variable costs).

The above figures reveal that the business will be worse off if the new policies are adopted.

Reducing stock (inventory) levels

This is an internal source of funds that may prove attractive to a business. If it has a proportion of its assets in the form of stock there is an opportunity cost, as the funds tied up cannot be used for other opportunities. By holding less stock, funds become available for those purposes. However, a business must try to ensure that there are sufficient stocks available to meet likely future sales demand. Failure to do so will result in lost customer goodwill and lost sales revenue.

The nature and condition of the stock held will determine whether it is possible to exploit this form of finance. A business may be overstocked as a result of poor buying decisions in the past. This may mean that a significant proportion of stocks held are slow moving or obsolete and cannot, therefore, be reduced easily. These issues will be picked up again in Chapter 16.

Delaying payment to trade creditors (payables)

By providing a period of credit, suppliers are effectively offering a business an interest-free loan. If the business delays payment, the period of the 'loan' is extended and funds can be retained within the business. This can be a cheap form of finance for a business, although this is not always the case. If a business fails to pay within the agreed credit period, there may be significant costs. For example, the business may find it difficult to buy on credit when it has a reputation as a slow payer.

Sources of external finance

Figure 15.2 summarises the main sources of long-term and short-term external finance.

| **Figure 15.2** | **The major sources of external finance** |

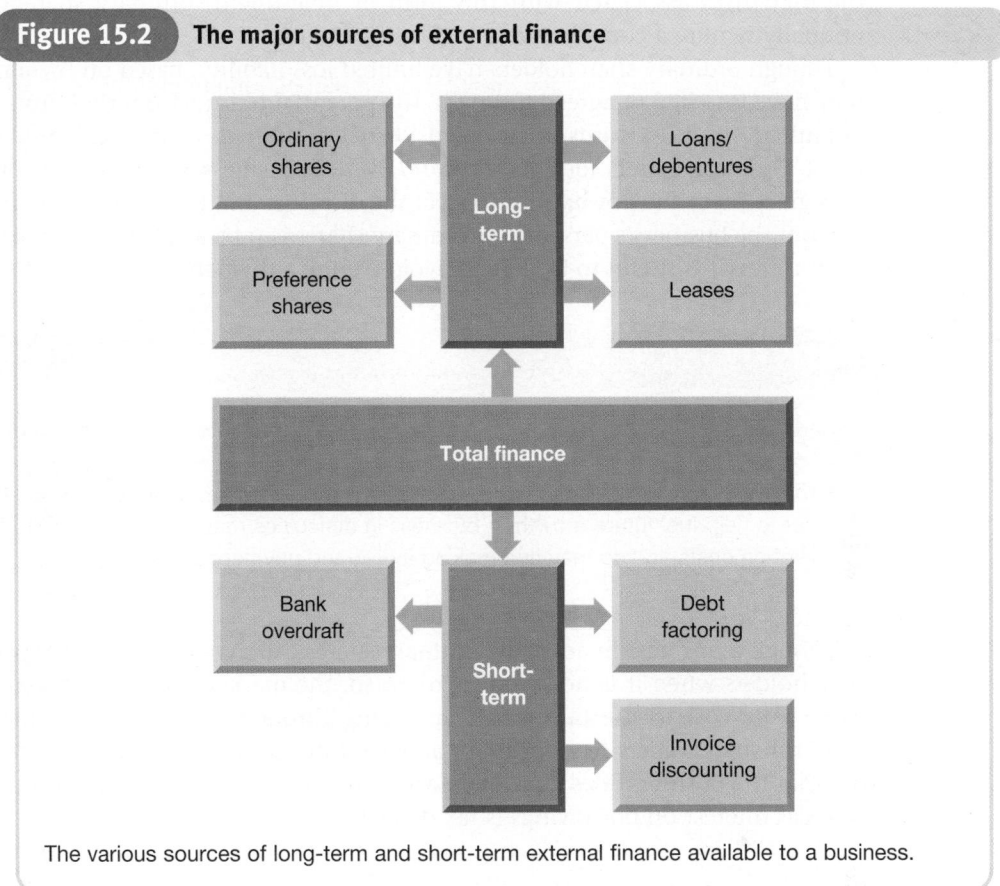

The various sources of long-term and short-term external finance available to a business.

Long-term sources of external finance

As Figure 15.2 reveals, the major forms of long-term external finance are:

● ordinary shares
● preference shares
● loans
● leases, that is, finance leases, including sale and leaseback arrangements.

   We shall now discuss each of the sources identified.

Ordinary shares
. . . .

Ordinary shares form the backbone of the financial structure of a business. Ordinary share capital represents the business's risk capital. There is no fixed rate of dividend, and ordinary shareholders will receive a dividend only if profits available for distribution still remain after other investors (preference shareholders and lenders) have received their dividend or interest payments. If the business is wound up, the ordinary shareholders will receive any proceeds from asset disposals only after lenders and creditors and, often, after preference shareholders have received their entitlements. Because of the high risks associated with this form of investment, ordinary shareholders will normally require a comparatively high rate of return.

Though ordinary shareholders have limited loss liability, based on the amount that they have invested or agreed to invest, the potential returns from their investment are unlimited. In other words, their downside risk is limited, while their upside potential is not. Ordinary shareholders have control over the business, through their voting rights. This gives them the power both to elect the directors and to remove them from office.

From the business's perspective, ordinary shares can be a valuable form of financing as, at times, it is useful to be able to avoid paying a dividend.

ACTIVITY 15.3

Under what circumstances might a business find it useful to avoid paying a dividend?

Two circumstances spring to mind. An expanding business may prefer to retain funds in order to help fuel future growth. A business in difficulties may need the funds to meet its operating costs and so may find making a dividend payment a real burden.

Though a business financed by ordinary shares can avoid making cash payments to shareholders when it is not prudent to do so, the market value of the shares may go down. The cost to the business of financing through ordinary shares may become higher if shareholders feel uncertain about future dividends. It is also worth pointing out that the business does not obtain any tax relief on dividends paid to shareholders, whereas interest on borrowings is tax deductible.

Preference shares

Preference shares offer investors a lower level of risk than ordinary shares. Provided there are sufficient profits available, preference shares will normally be given a fixed rate of dividend each year, and preference dividends will be paid before ordinary dividends are paid. Should the business be wound up, preference shareholders may be given priority over the claims of ordinary shareholders. (The business's particular documents of incorporation will state the precise rights of preference shareholders in this respect.)

ACTIVITY 15.4

Would you expect the returns to preference shares to be higher or lower than those of ordinary shares?

Because of the lower level of risk associated with this form of investment (preference shareholders have priority over ordinary shareholders regarding dividends), investors will be offered a lower level of return than that normally expected by ordinary shareholders.

Preference shares are no longer an important source of new finance. A major reason for this is that dividends paid to preference shareholders are not allowable against taxable profits, whereas interest on loan capital is an allowable expense. From the business's point of view, preference shares and loans are quite similar, so the tax deductibility of loan interest is an important issue.

ACTIVITY 15.5

Would you expect the market price of ordinary shares or preference shares to be the more volatile? Why?

The dividends of preference shares tend to be fairly stable over time, and there is usually an upper limit on the returns that can be received. As a result, the share price, which reflects the expected future returns from the share, will normally be less volatile than for ordinary shares.

Both preference shares and ordinary shares are, in effect, *redeemable*. The business is allowed to buy back the shares from shareholders at any time.

Loans and debentures

Most businesses rely on loans as well as share capital to finance operations. Lenders enter into a contract with the business in which the rate of interest, dates of interest payments, capital repayments and security for the loan are clearly stated. In the event that the interest payments or capital repayments are not made on the due dates, the lender will usually have the right, under the terms of the contract, to seize the assets on which the loan is secured and sell them in order to repay the amount outstanding. Security for a loan may take the form of a fixed charge on particular assets of the business (freehold land and premises are often favoured by lenders) or a floating charge on the whole of its assets. A floating charge will 'float' over the assets and will only fix on particular assets in the event that the business defaults on its loan obligations.

ACTIVITY 15.6

What do you think is the advantage for the business of having a floating charge rather than a fixed charge on its assets?

A floating charge on assets allows the managers greater flexibility in their day-to-day operations than a fixed charge. Assets can be traded without reference to the lenders.

Term loans

One form of long-term loan is the **term loan**. This type of loan is offered by banks and other financial institutions, and is usually tailored to the needs of the client business. The amount of the loan, the time period, the repayment terms and the interest payable are all open to negotiation and agreement, which can be very useful. For example, where all of the funds to be borrowed are not required immediately, a business may agree with the lender that funds are drawn only as and when required. This means that interest will be paid only on amounts drawn and the business will not have to pay interest on amounts borrowed that are temporarily surplus to requirements. Term loans tend to be cheap to set up (from the borrower business's perspective) and can be quite flexible as to conditions.

Debentures

→ Another form of long-term loan finance is the **debenture**. This is simply a loan that is evidenced by a trust deed. The debenture loan is frequently divided into units (rather like share capital), and investors are invited to purchase the number of units they require. The debenture loan may be redeemable or irredeemable. Debentures of public limited companies are often traded on the Stock Exchange, and their listed value will fluctuate according to the fortunes of the business, movements in interest rates and so on.

Eurobonds

→ **Eurobonds** are unsecured loan stocks denominated in a currency other than the home currency of the business that issued them. Eurobonds are issued by businesses (and other large organisations) in various countries, and the finance is raised on an international basis. They are often issued in US dollars, but many are issued in other major currencies. Interest is normally paid on an annual basis. Eurobonds are part of an emerging international capital market, and they are not subject to regulations imposed by authorities in particular countries. Numerous financial institutions throughout the world have created a market for eurobonds, where holders of eurobonds are able to sell them to would-be holders. Eurobonds are usually issued by the issuing business making them available to large banks and other financial institutions, which may either retain them as an investment or sell them to their clients.

The extent of borrowing, by UK businesses, in currencies other than sterling has expanded massively in recent years. Businesses are often attracted to issue eurobonds because of the size of the international capital market. Access to a large number of international investors is likely to increase the chances of a successful issue. In addition, the lack of regulation in the eurobond market means that national restrictions regarding loan issues may be overcome.

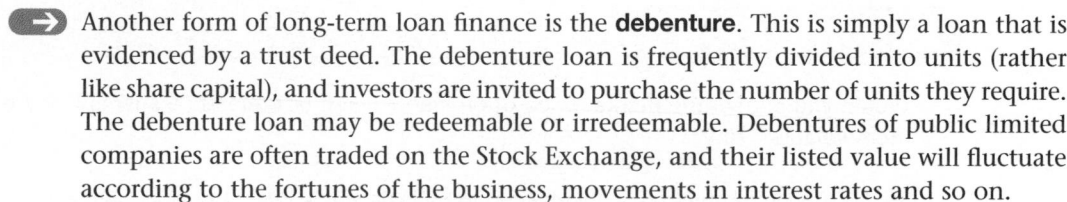

ACTIVITY 15.7

Would you expect the returns to loan capital to be higher or lower than those of preference shares?

....

Investors will normally view loans as being less risky than preference shares. Lenders have priority over any claims from preference shareholders, and will usually have security for their loans. As a result of the lower level of risk associated with this form of investment, investors are usually prepared to accept a lower rate of return.

The risk return characteristics of loan, preference share and ordinary share finance are shown graphically in Figure 15.3.

Interest rates and deep discount bonds

Interest rates on loan finance may be either floating or fixed. A floating rate means that the required rate of return from lenders will rise and fall with market rates of interest.

| Figure 15.3 | The risk/return characteristics of long-term capital |

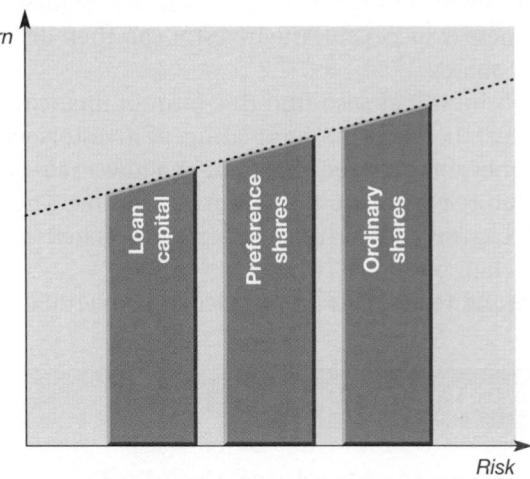

The higher the level of risk associated with a particular form of long-term capital, the higher will be the expected returns from investors. Ordinary shares are the most risky and have the highest expected return and, as a general rule, loan capital is the least risky and has the lowest expected return.

However, the market value of the lender's investment in the business is likely to remain fairly stable over time. The converse will normally be true for fixed-interest loans and debentures. The interest payments will remain unchanged with rises and falls in market rates of interest, but the value of the loan investment will fall when interest rates rise and will rise when interest rates fall.

A business may issue redeemable loan capital that offers a rate of interest below the market rate. In some cases, the loan capital may have a zero rate of interest. Such loans are issued at a discount to their redeemable value and are referred to as **deep discount bonds**. Thus loan capital may be issued at, say, £80 for every £100 of nominal value. Although lenders will receive little or no interest during the period of the loan, they will receive a gain when the loan is finally redeemed at the full £100. The redemption yield, as it is referred to, is often quite high and, when calculated on an annual basis, may compare favourably with returns from other forms of loan capital with the same level of risk. Deep discount bonds may have particular appeal to businesses with short-term cash flow problems. Such businesses receive an immediate injection of cash, and there are no significant cash outflows associated with the loan until the maturity date. Deep discount bonds are likely to appeal to investors who do not have short-term cash flow needs, since they must wait for the loan to mature before receiving a cash return.

Convertible loan stocks

Convertible loan stocks (or convertible debentures) give investors the right to convert a loan into ordinary shares at a given future date and at a specified price. The investor remains a lender to the business, and will receive interest on the amount of the loan until such time as the conversion takes place. The investor is not obliged to convert to ordinary shares. This will be done only if the market price of the shares at the conversion date exceeds the agreed conversion price.

An investor may find this form of investment a useful hedge against risk. This may be particularly useful when investment in a new business is being considered. Initially the investment is in the form of a loan, and regular interest payments will be made. If the business is successful, the investor can then decide to convert the investment into ordinary shares.

The business may also find this form of financing useful. If the business is successful, the loan becomes self-liquidating, as investors will exercise their option to convert. The business may also be able to offer a lower rate of interest to investors because they expect future benefits to arise from conversion. There will be, however, some dilution of both control and earnings for existing shareholders if holders of convertible loans exercise their option to convert.

Real World 15.1 details one particular convertible loan issue.

REAL WORLD 15.1

The answer is blowin' in the wind

In June 2003, Scottish Power plc issued convertible bonds to help finance research into new methods of creating energy, including the development of wind farms. The business initially intended to raise £343m from the issue, but the popularity of the bonds among investors allowed the business to raise $700m (£420m). The bonds were sold to specialist investors, mostly financial institutions. The investors can convert the bonds into 90 million ordinary shares in the future, which represent 5 per cent of Scottish Power's total share capital. Thus, there will not be a significant dilution of control for existing shareholders if the bonds are converted. The share price at which the bonds may be converted is 460 pence and, at the time of the issue, the market price of Scottish Power's shares was 372 pence.

Source: 'Generating cash from bonds', *Accountancy Age*, 17 July 2003, p. 7.

Public issues of ordinary shares, preference shares and loan stocks

Real World 15.2 provides an impression of the relative importance of the three principal types of public issue.

REAL WORLD 15.2

New issues by listed businesses

Figure 15.4 plots the issues of capital made by UK listed businesses (excluding financial businesses such as banks) in recent years. The chart reveals that loan capital and ordinary shares are the major sources of long-term external finance. Preference shares are a much less important source of new finance.

Warrants

 Holders of **warrants** have the right, but not the obligation, to acquire ordinary shares in a particular business at a given price (the 'exercise' price). In the case of both convertible

Figure 15.4 Capital issues of UK Stock Exchange listed businesses (excluding financial businesses), 1992–2001

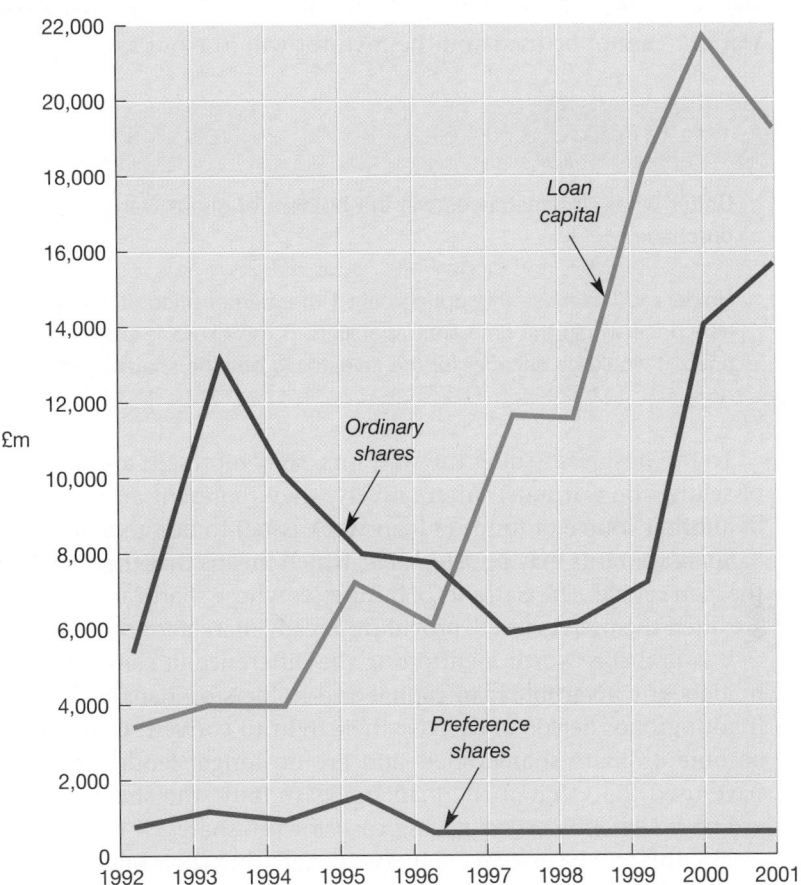

At times, the popularity of ordinary shares and that of loan capital seem to move counter to one another. When ordinary shares are popular loan capital is unpopular, and vice versa. This tends to reflect the level of interest rates and business confidence. However, in recent years, ordinary share issues and loan capital issues have both moved in the same direction. Preference shares have dwindled to virtually nothing, in terms of new issues. The chart, of course, is not the whole story. Most finance from ordinary shareholders comes from profit retentions rather than share issues. In addition, bank loans are not included.

Source: Based on information from Financial statistics, Office for National Statistics, December 2003, HMSO.

loan capital and warrants, the price at which shares may be acquired is usually higher than the market price of those ordinary shares at the time of issue. The warrant will usually state the number of shares that the holder may purchase and the time limit within which the option to buy shares can be exercised. Occasionally, perpetual warrants are issued that have no set time limits. Warrants do not confer voting rights or entitle the holders to make any claims on the assets of the business. Warrants are themselves neither shares nor loan stocks.

Share warrants are often provided as a 'sweetener' to accompany the issue of loan capital, that is, an incentive to potential lenders. The issue of warrants in this way may enable the business to offer lower rates of interest on the loan or to negotiate less restrictive loan conditions. Sometimes businesses sell share warrants without there being a link to a loan stock issue. Warrants enable investors to benefit from any future increases in the business's ordinary share price, without having to buy the shares themselves. On the other hand, if the share price remains below the exercise price, the warrant cannot be used and the investor will lose out as a result.

ACTIVITY 15.8

Under what circumstances will the holders of share warrants exercise their option to purchase?

Holders will exercise this option only if the market price of the shares exceeds the exercise price within the time limit specified. If the exercise price is higher than the market price, it would be cheaper for the investor to buy the shares in the market.

To the business issuing the warrants, they represent a source of funds (the proceeds of selling the warrants). Alternatively, they represent an encouragement for the issue of another source of funds (a loan stock issue) to be successful.

Share warrants may be *detachable*, which means that they can be sold separately from the loan capital. The warrants of businesses whose shares are listed on the Stock Exchange are often themselves listed, providing a ready market for buying and selling the warrants.

It is probably worth mentioning the difference in status within a business between holders of convertible loan capital and holders of loans with share warrants attached if both groups decide to exercise their right to convert. Convertible loan stock holders become ordinary shareholders and are no longer lenders to the business. They will have used the value of the loan stocks to 'buy' the shares. Warrant holders become ordinary shareholders by paying cash for the shares. If the warrant holders held loan stocks, this will be unaffected by their exercising their right to buy the shares bestowed by the warrant.

Both convertibles and warrants are examples of **financial derivatives**. These are any form of financial instrument, based on share or loan capital, that can be used by investors to increase their returns or reduce risk.

Mortgages

A **mortgage** is a form of loan that is secured on an asset, typically freehold property. Financial institutions such as banks, insurance businesses and pension funds are often prepared to lend to businesses on this basis. The mortgage may be over a long period (20 years or more).

Loan covenants

Lenders often impose certain obligations and restrictions on borrowers in order to protect themselves. **Loan covenants** (as they are called) often form part of a loan agreement, and may deal with such matters as:

● *Financial statements.* The lender may require access to the financial statements of the borrowing business on a regular basis.

- *Other loans.* The lender may require the business to ask the lender's permission before taking on further loans from other sources.
- *Dividend payments.* The lender may require dividend payments to be limited during the period of the loan.
- *Liquidity.* The lender may require the business to maintain a certain level of liquidity during the period of the loan. This would typically be a requirement that the borrower business's current ratio is maintained at, or above, a specified level.

Any breach of these restrictive covenants can have serious consequences for the business. The lender may require immediate repayment of the loan in the event of a material breach.

ACTIVITY 15.9

Both preference shares and loan capital are forms of finance that require the business to provide a particular rate of return to investors. What are the factors that may be taken into account by a business when deciding between these two sources of finance?

The main factors are as follows:

- Preference shares have a higher rate of return than loan capital. From the investor's point of view, preference shares are more risky. The amount invested cannot be secured, and the return is paid after the returns paid to lenders.
- A business has a legal obligation to pay interest and make capital repayments on loans at the agreed dates. It will usually make every effort to meet its obligations because failure to do so can have serious consequences. (These consequences have been mentioned earlier.) Failure to pay a preference dividend, on the other hand, is less important. There is no legal obligation to pay if profits are not available for distribution. Failure to pay a preference dividend may prove an embarrassment for the business, however. It may make it difficult to persuade investors to take up future preference share issues.
- It was mentioned above that the taxation system in the UK permits interest on loans to be allowable against profits for taxation, whereas preference dividends are not. As a result, the cost of servicing loan capital is usually much less for a business than the cost of servicing preference shares.
- The issue of loan capital may result in the management of a business having to accept some restrictions on its freedom of action. We saw earlier that loan agreements often contain covenants that can be onerous. However, preference shareholders can impose no such restrictions.

A further point is that preference shares issued form part of the permanent capital base of the business. If they are redeemed, the law requires that they be replaced, either by a new issue of shares or by a transfer from revenue reserves, so that the business's capital base stays intact. Loan capital, however, is not viewed in law as part of the business's permanent capital base, and therefore there is no legal requirement to replace any loan capital that has been redeemed.

Finance leases and sale and leaseback arrangements

When a business needs a particular asset (for example an item of plant), instead of buying it direct from a supplier, the business may decide to arrange for another business (typically a bank) to buy it and then lease it to the first business. The business that owns the asset and leases it out is known as a 'lessor'.

 A **finance lease**, as such an arrangement is known, is, in essence, a form of lending. This is because, had the lessee borrowed the funds and then used them to buy the asset itself, the effect would be much the same. The lessee would have use of the asset, but have a financial obligation to the lender – much the same position as the leasing arrangement would lead to.

Though, with finance leasing, legal ownership of the asset rests with the financial institution (the lessor), a finance lease agreement transfers to the user (the lessee) virtually all the rewards and risks that are associated with the item being leased. The finance lease agreement covers a significant part of the life of the item being leased, and often cannot be cancelled.

Real World 15.3 gives an example of the use of finance leasing in a leading airline business.

REAL WORLD 15.3

Finance leasing at BA
FT

Many airline businesses use finance leasing as a means of acquiring new aeroplanes. The financial statements for British Airways plc (BA) for the year ended 31 March 2003 reveal that approximately 28 per cent (totalling £2,220m) of the net book value of its fleet of aircraft had been acquired through this method.

Source: British Airways plc, Annual Report and Accounts, year ended 31 March 2003.

 A finance lease can be contrasted with an **operating lease**, where the rewards and risks of ownership stay with the owner and where the lease is short term. An example of an operating lease is where a builder hires some earthmoving equipment for a week to carry out a particular job.

In recent years, some important benefits associated with finance leasing have disappeared. Changes in UK tax law no longer make it such a tax-efficient form of financing, and changes in accounting disclosure requirements no longer make it possible to conceal this form of 'borrowing' from investors. Nevertheless, the popularity of finance leases has continued. Other reasons must therefore exist for businesses to adopt this form of financing. These reasons are said to include the following:

● *Ease of borrowing.* Leasing may be obtained more easily than other forms of long-term finance. Lenders normally require some form of security and a profitable track record before making advances to a business. However, a lessor may be prepared to lease assets to a new business without a track record, and to use the leased assets as security for the amounts owing.

● *Cost.* Leasing agreements may be offered at reasonable cost. As the asset leased is used as security, standard lease arrangements can be applied and detailed credit checking of lessees may be unnecessary. This can reduce administrative costs for the lessor and, thereby, help in providing competitive lease rentals.

● *Flexibility.* Leasing can help provide flexibility where there are rapid changes in technology. If an option to cancel can be incorporated into the lease, the business may be able to exercise this option and invest in new technology as it becomes available. This will help the business to avoid the risk of obsolescence.

● *Cash flows.*   Leasing, rather than purchasing an asset outright, means that large cash outflows can be avoided. The leasing option allows cash outflows to be smoothed out over the asset's life. In some cases, it is possible to arrange for low lease payments to be made in the early years of the asset's life, when cash inflows may be low, and for these to increase over time as the asset generates positive cash flows.

Real World 15.4 provides some impression of the importance of finance leasing over recent years.

REAL WORLD 15.4

The importance of finance leasing in the UK

| Figure 15.5 | Finance leases 1998–2002 |

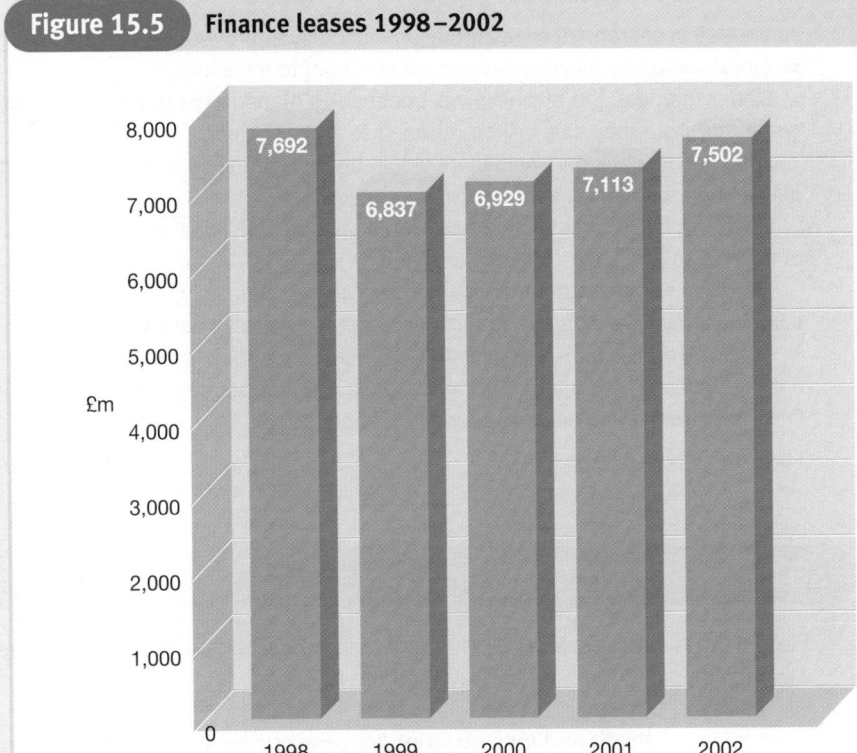

There was a decline in the amount of finance leasing in 1999. However, since then there has been a steady increase and, in 2002, the amount of finance leasing was near to its 1998 level.

Source: Compiled from information provided by the Finance and Leasing Association (www.fla.org.uk). Copyright © 2003 Finance and Leasing Association.

     A **sale and leaseback** arrangement involves a business raising finance by selling an asset to a financial institution. The sale is accompanied by an agreement to lease the asset back to the business to allow it to continue to use the asset. The lease payment is allowable against profits for taxation purposes. There are usually reviews at regular intervals throughout the period of the lease, and the amounts payable in future years may be difficult to predict. At the end of the lease agreement, the business must either try to renew the lease or find an alternative asset. Although the sale of the asset will result in an immediate injection of cash for the business, it will lose benefits from any future capital appreciation on the asset. Where a capital gain arises on the sale of the asset to the financial institution, a liability for taxation may also arise. Freehold property is often the asset that is the subject of such an arrangement.

A sale and leaseback agreement can be used to help a business focus on its core areas of competence. **Real World 15.5**, which is an extract from an article in the *Financial Times*, shows how a leading leisure hotels group used a sale and leaseback agreement to do this and, at the same time, return some cash to shareholders.

REAL WORLD 15.5

Approval for Jarvis sale and leaseback

FT

Jarvis Hotels shareholders yesterday unanimously approved the sale of nine of the group's properties in a £150m deal that will return £85m to investors.

Under the deal, the business will continue to manage the hotels but some of the cash generated from their sale will be returned to shareholders.

John Jarvis, chairman, said there would be 'opportunities for further sale and leaseback deals when the market becomes more suitable'.

However, it is thought such deals would concern individual properties rather than a sale of several as a block.

'We are evolving into a management services business,' said Mr Jarvis. 'But if you are a business that wants a strong balance sheet, you always have to retain a core of assets.'

Peter Joseph, leisure analyst with KBC Peel Hunt, said: 'Jarvis is doing the right things. If it continues on this route it will end up as a hotel operator, not a hotel owner, which is fine – provided it has security over all of its contracts.'

Source: Financial Times, 8 November 2002, p. 28.

SELF-ASSESSMENT QUESTION 15.1

Helsim Ltd is a wholesaler and distributor of electrical components. The most recent financial statements of the business revealed the following:

Profit and loss account (income statement) for the year

	£m	£m
Sales revenue		14.2
Opening stock	3.2	
Purchases	8.4	
	11.6)	
Closing stock	(3.8)	(7.8)
Gross profit		6.4
Administration expenses	(3.0)	
Selling and distribution expenses	(2.1)	
Finance charges	(0.8)	(5.9)
Net profit before taxation		0.5
Corporation tax		(0.2)
Net profit after taxation		0.3

Balance sheet as at the end of the year

	£m	£m	£m
Non-current assets			
Land and buildings			3.8
Equipment			0.9
Motor vehicles			0.5
			5.2
Current assets			
Stock		3.8	
Trade debtors		3.6	
Cash at bank		0.1	
		7.5	
Less: **Current liabilities**			
Trade creditors	1.8		
Bank overdraft	3.6	5.4	2.1
			7.3
Less: **Non-current liabilities**			
Debentures (secured on freehold land)			3.5
			3.8
Equity			
Ordinary £1 shares			2.0
Profit and loss account			1.8
			3.8

Notes

1 Land and buildings are shown at their current market value. Equipment and motor vehicles are shown at their written-down values.
2 No dividends have been paid to ordinary shareholders for the past three years.

In recent months, trade creditors have been pressing for payment. The managing director has therefore decided to reduce the level of trade creditors to an average of 40 days outstanding. To achieve this, he has decided to approach the bank with a view to increasing the overdraft. The business is currently paying 12% a year interest on the overdraft.

Required:

(a) Comment on the liquidity position of the business.
(b) Calculate the amount of finance required to reduce trade creditors, from the level shown on the balance sheet, to an average of 40 days outstanding.
(c) State, with reasons, how you consider the bank would react to the proposal to grant an additional overdraft facility.
(d) Identify four sources of finance (internal or external, but excluding a bank overdraft) that may be suitable to finance the reduction in trade creditors, and state, with reasons, which of these you consider the most appropriate.

Gearing and the long-term financing decision

In Chapter 7 we saw that financial gearing occurs when a business is financed, at least in part, by contributions from fixed-charge capital (preference shares and loans). We also saw that the level of gearing associated with a business is often an important factor in assessing the risk and returns to ordinary shareholders. In the example that follows, we consider the implications of making a choice between a geared and an ungeared approach to raising long-term finance.

Example 15.1

The following are the summarised financial statements of Woodhall Engineers plc:

Woodhall Engineers plc
Profit and loss account year ended 31 December

	Year 1 £m	Year 2 £m
Turnover	47	50
Operating costs	(41)	(47)
Operating profit	6	3
Interest payable	(2)	(2)
Profit on ordinary activities before tax	4	1
Taxation on profit on ordinary activities	–	–
Profit on ordinary activities after tax	4	1
Dividends	(1)	(1)
Profit retained for the financial year	3	–

Balance sheet at 31 December

	Year 1 £m	Year 2 £m
Non-current assets (less depreciation)	21	20
Current assets		
Stocks	10	18
Debtors	16	17
Cash at bank	3	1
	29	36
Current liabilities		
Short-term loans	(5)	(11)
Trade creditors	(10)	(10)
	(15)	(21)
Total assets less current liabilities	35	35
Less Non-current liabilities		
Long-term loans (secured)	15	15
	20	20
Equity		
Called-up share capital 25p ordinary shares	16	16
Profit and loss account	4	4
	20	20

The business is making plans to expand its premises. New plant will cost £8m, and an expansion in output will increase working capital by £4m. Over the 15 years' life of the project, incremental profits arising from the expansion will be £2m a year before interest and tax. In addition, Year 3's profits before interest and tax from its existing activities are expected to return to Year 1 levels.

Two possible methods of financing the expansion have been discussed by Woodhall's directors. The first is the issue of £12m 15% loan capital repayable in Year 18. The second is a rights issue of 40m 25p ordinary shares, which will give the business 30p per share after expenses.

The business has substantial tax losses, which can be offset against future profits, so taxation can be ignored in the calculations. The Year 3 dividend per share is expected to be the same as that for Year 2.

Prepare a forecast of Woodhall's projected profit and loss account (excluding turnover and operating costs) for the year ended 31 December Year 3, and of its capital and reserves, long-term loans and number of shares outstanding at that date assuming that the business issues:

● loan capital
● ordinary shares.

The first part of the example requires the preparation of a forecast profit and loss account (income statement) under each financing option. These will be as follows:

Projected profit and loss account for the year ended 31 December Year 3

	Loan issue	Share issue
	£m	£m
Profit before interest and taxation (6.0 + 2.0)	8.0	8.0
Loan interest	(3.8)	(2.0)
Profit before tax	4.2	6.0
Taxation	–	–
Profit after tax	4.2	6.0
Dividends	(1.0)	(1.6)
Retained profit for the year	3.2	4.4

The capital structure of the business under each option as at the end of Year 3 will be as follows:

	Loan issue	Share issue
	£m	£m
Equity		
Share capital 25p ordinary shares	16.0	26.0
Share premium account*	–	2.0
Profit and loss account	7.2	8.4
	23.2	36.4
Number of shares in issue (25p shares)	64 million	104 million

* This represents the amount received from the issue of shares that is above the nominal value of the shares. The amount is calculated as follows:

40m shares × (30p − 25p) = £2m

ACTIVITY 15.10

Compute Woodhall's interest cover and earnings per share for the year ended 31 December Year 3 and its gearing on that date, assuming that the business issues:

- loan capital
- ordinary shares.

Your answer should be as follows:

	Loan issue	*Share issue*
Interest cover ratio		
$\dfrac{\text{Profit before interest and tax}}{\text{Interest payable}} = $	$\dfrac{8.0}{3.8}$	$\dfrac{8.0}{2.0}$
	= 2.1 times	4.0 times
Earning per share		
$\dfrac{\text{Earning available to equity}}{\text{Number of ordinary shares}} = $	$\dfrac{£4.2m}{64m}$	$\dfrac{£6.0m}{104m}$
	= 6.6p	5.8p
Gearing ratio		
$\dfrac{\text{Long-term liabilities}}{\text{Share capital + Reserves + Long-term liabilities}} = $	$\dfrac{£27m}{£23.2m + £27m}$	$\dfrac{£15m}{£36.4m + £15m}$
	= 53.8%	29.2%

ACTIVITY 15.11

What would your views of the proposed schemes be in each of the following circumstances?

(a) If you were a banker and you were approached for a loan.
(b) If you were an ordinary share investor in Woodhall and you were asked to subscribe to a rights issue.

(a) A banker may be unenthusiastic about lending money to the business. The gearing ratio of 53.8 per cent is rather high, and would leave the bank in an exposed position. The existing loan is already secured on the business's assets, and it is not clear whether the business is in a position to offer an attractive form of security for the new loan. The interest cover ratio of 2:1 is also rather low. If the business is unable to achieve the expected returns from the new project, or if it is unable to restore profits from the remainder of its operations to Year 1 levels, this ratio would be even lower.

(b) Ordinary share investors may need some convincing that it would be worthwhile to make further investments in the business. The return on ordinary shareholders' funds in Year 1 was 20 per cent (£4m/£20m). The incremental profit from the new project is £2m and the investment required is £12m, which represents a return of 16.7 per cent. Thus, the returns from the project are expected to be lower than for existing operations. In making their decision, investors should discover whether the new investment is of a similar level of risk to their existing investment and how the returns from the investment compare with those available from other opportunities with similar levels of risk.

Share issues

A business may issue shares in a number of ways. These may involve direct appeals to investors, or the use of financial intermediaries. The most common methods of share issues for cash are:

- rights issues
- offers for sale and public issue
- private placing.

These are discussed below.

Rights issues

 Rights issues are made when businesses that have been established for some time seek to raise additional share capital for expansion, or even to solve a liquidity problem (cash shortage) by issuing additional shares for cash. Company law gives existing shareholders the first right of refusal on these new shares, so the new shares would be offered to shareholders in proportion to their existing holding. Thus existing shareholders are each given the right to buy some new shares. Only where the existing shareholders agree to waive their right would the shares be offered to the investing public generally. Rights issues are now the most common form of share issue. The business (in effect, the existing shareholders) would typically prefer that the shares are bought by existing shareholders, irrespective of the legal position. This is for two reasons:

- The ownership (and, therefore, control) of the business remains in the same hands.
- The costs of making the issue (advertising, complying with various company law requirements) tend to be less if the shares are to be offered to existing shareholders.

To encourage existing shareholders to take up their 'rights' to buy some new shares, those shares are always offered at a price below the current market price of the existing ones.

ACTIVITY 15.12

In Chapter 4 (Example 4.2, p. 118) the point was illustrated that issuing new shares at below their current worth was to the advantage of the new shareholders at the expense of the old ones. In view of this, does it matter that rights issues are always made at below the current value of the shares?

The answer is that it does not matter *in these particular circumstances*, because, in a rights issue, the existing shareholders and the new shareholders are exactly the same people. Moreover, the new shares will be held by the shareholders in the same proportion as they currently hold the existing shares. Thus, shareholders will gain on the new shares exactly as much as they lose on the existing ones: in the end, no one is better or worse off as a result of the rights issue being made at a discount.

Rights issues are frequently made to raise cash for expansion, but **Real World 15.6** gives an example of where a rights issue was made for exactly the opposite reason.

Laura Ashley to close 35 European stores   **FT**

Laura Ashley has taken the unusual step of launching a rights issue, not to fund expansion but to assist it in the closure of 35 of its loss-making European stores, including all its remaining shops in Germany.

The UK clothing and home furnishing retailer, which earlier this month warned that full-year results would be below market expectations, is hoping to raise £9m ($14.6m) through the issue priced at about 8p a share.

It will go some way to pay for the estimated £7.7m cost of closing the stores, which have dragged down results at the group that is known for its floral offerings, both in clothing and furniture.

In its Christmas trading statement Laura Ashley blamed the fall in profits, that knocked almost 20% off its already battered shares, on the heavy discounting in its European stores.

KC Ng, chief executive, said the rights issue and closures would place the company on a 'firmer footing' for further development.

Laura Ashley said that it remained committed to its remaining 18 European stores, despite the closure of 35 stores. The group is looking for franchise partners to keep the profitable stores going . . .

Source: 'Laura Ashley to close 35 European stores', Lisa Urquhart, *Financial Times*, 23 January 2003, FT.com.

Calculating the value of the rights offer received by shareholders is quite straight-forward, as shown in Example 15.2.

Example 15.2

Shaw Holdings plc has 20 million ordinary shares of 50p in issue. These shares are currently valued on the Stock Exchange at £1.60 a share. The directors have decided to make a one-for-four issue (that is, one new share for every four shares held) at £1.30 a share.

The first step in the valuation process is to calculate the price of a share following the rights issue. This is known as the *ex-rights price*, and is simply a weighted average of the price of shares before the issue of rights and the price of the rights shares. In the above example, we have a one-for-four rights issue. The theoretical ex-rights price is therefore calculated as follows:

	£
Price of four shares before the rights issue (4 × £1.60)	6.40
Price of taking up one rights share	1.30
	7.70

$$\text{Theoretical ex-rights price} = \frac{7.70}{5} \qquad = \underline{\underline{£1.54}}$$

As the price of each share, in theory, should be £1.54 following the rights issue and the price of a rights share is £1.30, the value of the rights offer will be the difference between the two:

$$£1.54 - £1.30 = £0.24 \text{ per share}$$

Market forces will usually ensure that the actual and theoretical price of rights will be fairly close.

ACTIVITY 15.13

An investor with 2,000 shares in Shaw Holdings plc (see Example 15.2) has contacted you for investment advice. She is undecided whether to take up the rights issue, sell the rights, or allow the rights offer to lapse.

Calculate the effect on the net wealth of the investor of each of the options being considered.

	£
Before the rights issue the investor had shares worth (2,000 x £1.60)	3,200

If she takes up the rights issue, she will be in the following position:

	£
Value of holding after rights issue ((2000 + 500) × £1.54)	3,850
Less Cost of buying the rights shares (500 × £1.30)	650
	3,200

If the investor sells the rights, she will be in the following position:

	£
Value of holding after rights issue (2,000 × £1.54)	3,080
Sale of rights (500 × £0.24)	120
	3,200

If the investor lets the rights offer lapse, she will be in the following position:

	£
Value of holding after rights issue (2,000 × £1.54)	3,080

As we can see, the first two options should leave her in the same position concerning net wealth as she was before the rights issue. Before the rights issue she had 2,000 shares worth £1.60 each or £3,200. However, she will be worse off if she allows the rights offer to lapse than under the other two options. In practice, however, the business may sell the rights, on behalf of the investor, and pass on the proceeds in order to ensure that she is not worse off as a result of the issue.

When considering a rights issue, the directors must first consider the amount of funds that needs to be raised. This will depend on the future plans and commitments of the business. The directors must then decide on the issue price of the rights shares. Normally, this decision is not critical. In Example 15.2 above, the business made a one-for-four issue with the price of the rights shares set at £1.30. However, it could have raised the same amount by making a one-for-two issue and setting the rights price at £0.65, a one-for-one issue and setting the price at £0.325, and so on. The issue price that is finally decided upon will not affect the value of the underlying assets of the business or the proportion of the underlying assets and earnings to which the shareholder is entitled. The directors must, however, ensure that the issue price is not above the current market price of the shares, or the issue will be unsuccessful.

Offer for sale and public issue

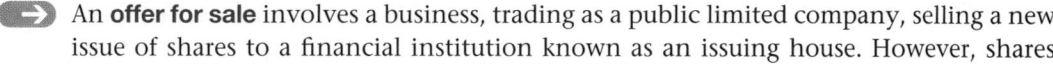 An **offer for sale** involves a business, trading as a public limited company, selling a new issue of shares to a financial institution known as an issuing house. However, shares

that are already in issue may also be sold to an issuing house. In this case, existing shareholders agree to sell their shares to the issuing house. The issuing house will, in turn, sell the shares, purchased from either the business or its shareholders, to the public. The issuing house will publish a prospectus that sets out details of the business and the type of shares to be sold and investors will be invited to apply for shares. The advantage of this type of issue, from the business's viewpoint, is that the sale proceeds of the shares are certain.

→ A **public issue** involves the business making a direct invitation to the public to purchase its shares. Typically, this is done through a newspaper advertisement. The shares may, once again, be a new issue or those already in issue. An offer for sale and a public issue will both result in a widening of share ownership in the business.

In practical terms, the net effect on the business is much the same whether there is an offer for sale or a public issue.

Issues by tender

When making an issue of shares, the business or the issuing house will usually set a price for the shares. Establishing this, however, may not be an easy task, particularly where the market is volatile or where the business has unique characteristics. One way → of dealing with this issue-price problem is to make a **tender issue** of shares. This involves the investors determining the price at which the shares are issued. Though the business (or issuing house) may publish a reserve price to help guide investors, it will be up to the individual investor to determine the number of shares to be purchased and the price the investor wishes to pay. Once the offers from investors have been received, a price at which all the shares can be sold will be established (known as the *striking price*). Investors who have made offers at, or above, the striking price will be issued shares at the striking price; offers received below the striking price will be rejected. Note that all of the shares will be issued at the same price, irrespective of the prices actually offered by individual investors. Though this form of issue is adopted occasionally, it is not popular with investors, and is therefore not in widespread use.

Private placings

→ A **private placing** does not involve an invitation to the public to subscribe to shares. Instead the shares are 'placed' with selected investors, such as large financial institutions. This can be a quick and relatively cheap form of raising funds, because savings can be made in advertising and legal costs. However, it can result in the ownership of the business being concentrated in a few hands. Usually, unlisted businesses seeking relatively small amounts of cash will make this form of issue.

Bonus issues

We should recall from Chapter 4 that bonus issues are not means of raising finance. They are simply converting one part of the owners' claim (reserves) into another (ordinary shares). No cash changes hands; this benefits neither the business nor the shareholders.

The role of the Stock Exchange

Earlier we considered the various forms of long-term capital that are available to a business. In this section, we examine the role that the **Stock Exchange** plays in the provision of finance for businesses. The Stock Exchange acts as an important *primary* and *secondary* market in capital for businesses. As a primary market, its function is to enable businesses to raise new capital. As a secondary market, its function is to enable investors to sell their securities (including shares and loan capital) with ease. Thus, it provides a 'second-hand' market where shares and loan capital already in issue may be bought and sold.

In order to issue shares or loan capital through the Stock Exchange, a business must be 'listed'. This means that the business must meet fairly stringent requirements concerning size, profit history, information disclosure and so on. Some share issues on the Stock Exchange arise from the initial listing of the business, often known as an *initial public offering (IPO)*. Other share issues are undertaken by businesses that are already listed and that are seeking additional finance from investors.

Real World 15.7 explains how new issues are not always good investments for those who take up the shares concerned.

REAL WORLD 15.7

New issues but old problems   **FT**

It seems that we should be cautious when invited to subscribe to a new issue of shares arising from an initial listing on the Stock Exchange. The following extract from the *Financial Times* tells us why investing in new business flotations may be bad for our wealth.

> Back in 1940 Benjamin Graham and David Dodd, the fathers of security analysis wrote: 'the odds are so strongly against the man who buys into these new flotations that he might as well throw three-quarters of the money out the window and keep the rest in the bank.'
>
> Now confirmation of the poor record of recent new issues comes from an Ernst and Young survey. The accountancy group looked at the records of 200 companies that floated on the UK market between 1998 and 2002. It found that only 39% of the sample had increased profits since flotation (although 82% had seen their sales grow).
>
> This should not come as too much of a surprise. Companies are most likely to float on the market when their recent trading record is impressive. But periods of rapid growth can be very dangerous for a company – costs and management ambitions can get out of hand. Furthermore, no business can grow rapidly forever, and there is a risk that the flotation occurs just at the moment when the decline is beginning.
>
> And, as Ernst and Young points out, the very act of flotation incurs significant costs and can divert management focus from the business. The money raised can also burn a hole in the management's pockets, leading to a flurry of spending that would disgrace a football manager.
>
> All this is slightly discouraging, given that the primary role of the stock market is to allow growing businesses to raise capital. But perhaps a certain amount of investor greed (and gullibility) is necessary if industry is to gain access to finance. New issue investors have been fooled before; they will be fooled again.

Source: Financial Times, 8 August 2003, p. 22.

Advantages of a listing

The secondary market role of the Stock Exchange means that shares and other financial claims are easily transferable. Furthermore, the prices of shares and other financial claims are constantly under scrutiny by investors and skilled analysts. This helps to ensure that the prices quoted for a particular share reflect its true worth. These factors can bring real benefits to a business.

ACTIVITY 15.14

What kind of benefits might a business gain from its shares being listed?

If investors know that their shares can easily be sold for prices that reflect the true worth of the shares, they will have more confidence to invest. The business may benefit from this greater investor confidence by finding it easier to raise long-term finance and by obtaining this finance at a lower cost, as investors will view their investment as being less risky.

It is worth pointing out that investors are not obliged to use the Stock Exchange as the means of transferring shares in a listed business. However, it is usually the most convenient way of buying or selling shares.

The Stock Exchange can be a useful vehicle for a successful entrepreneur wishing to realise the value of the business that has been built up. By floating (listing) the shares on the Stock Exchange, and thereby making the shares available to the public, the entrepreneur will usually benefit from a gain in the value of the shares held and will be able to realise that gain easily, if required, by selling some shares. **Real Worlds 15.8** and **15.9** give examples of businesses 'floating' on the Stock Exchange and making their owners a lot of money.

REAL WORLD 15.8

Privatised stationer 'to float'

Ray Peck is an entrepreneur who runs a business that was the government's former stationery division. Newspaper reports revealed that he wished to float the business on the Stock Exchange and that stock market investors were likely to value the business at around £80m to £100m. Mr Peck, his senior managers and a financial institution bought the whole business for about £10m two years before the intention to float the business was reported. At the time, Ray Peck owned 20% of the shares of the business, which means that his stake in the business would be valued somewhere between £16m and £20m, assuming that predictions concerning the value of the business were accurate.

Source: Sunday Times, Business Section, 30 June 2002, p. 3.

Disadvantages of a listing

A Stock Exchange listing can have certain disadvantages for a business. These include:

1 Strict rules are imposed on listed businesses, including requiring additional levels of financial disclosure to that already imposed by law (for example, the listing rules require that half-yearly financial reports are published).

REAL WORLD 15.9

Cashing in

Mark Mills, a 33 year-old entrepreneur, made himself a fortune in the form of the value of shares worth £4.6m, when his business (Cardpoint) was floated. The business owns 1,900 cash dispensing machines installed in garages and other locations. Everyone using the machines is charged £1.50 to withdraw cash. The business also owns 3,600 mobile phone top-up terminals.

Cardpoint was not Mark Mills' first business venture. He started young, selling bags of broken biscuits to his friends at age 6. At 18 he was in business as a party organiser. He then moved on to selling payphone systems to publicans, then to selling advertising to go on the outside of post boxes. These businesses had mixed success, but he really hit the jackpot with Cardpoint.

Source: Based on information in *Sunday Times*, Business Section, 11 January 2004, p. 11.

2 Financial analysts, financial journalists and others closely monitor the activities of listed businesses. Such scrutiny may not be welcome, particularly if the business is dealing with sensitive issues or is experiencing operational problems.
3 It is often suggested that listed businesses are under pressure to perform well over the short term. This pressure may detract from undertaking projects that will only yield benefits in the longer term. If the market becomes disenchanted with the business, and the price of its shares falls, this may make it vulnerable to a takeover bid from another business.
4 The costs of obtaining a listing are vast and this may be a real deterrent for some businesses.

Real World 15.10 explains how the larger businesses tend to dominate investment on the London Stock Exchange.

REAL WORLD 15.10

Big is beautiful

There are more than 2,000 listed businesses on the London Stock Exchange. However, the 100 largest businesses account for more than 80 per cent of the value of the market and it is these large companies that provide the main focus of interest for investors. Smaller businesses often claim that they are overlooked, particularly by large institutional investors. These investors are normally only interested in large businesses because of the size of the investments that they make in each business. It has been suggested that businesses valued at less £100m are unlikely to be of interest. This makes it hard for smaller businesses to raise new capital, unless, perhaps, they can convince investors that they are fast growing. Thus, for some small businesses the advantages of listing are outweighed by the disadvantages.

Source: Based on information in 'Climbing aboard the flight from flotation', Philip Coggan, *Financial Times*, 6 September 2003.

Short-term sources of external finance

Short-term, in this context, is usually taken to mean up to one year. Figure 15.2 revealed that the major sources of short-term external finance were:

● bank overdrafts
● debt factoring
● invoice discounting.

These are discussed below.

Bank overdrafts

A **bank overdraft** enables a business to maintain a negative balance on its bank account. It represents a very flexible form of borrowing as the size of the overdraft can (subject to bank approval) be increased or decreased according to the financing requirements of the business. It is relatively inexpensive to arrange, and interest rates are often very competitive, though often higher than those for a term loan. As with all loans, the rate of interest charged on an overdraft will vary, however, according to how creditworthy the customer is perceived to be by the bank. It is also fairly easy to arrange – sometimes an overdraft can be agreed by a telephone call to the bank. In view of these advantages, it is not surprising that this is an extremely popular form of short-term finance.

Banks prefer to grant overdrafts that are self-liquidating: that is, the funds applied will result in cash inflows that will extinguish the overdraft balance. The banks may ask for a cash budget (projected cash flow statement) from the business to see when the overdraft will be repaid and how much finance is required. The bank may also require some form of security on amounts advanced. One potential drawback with this form of finance is that it is repayable on demand. This may pose problems for a business that is illiquid. However, many businesses operate for many years using an overdraft. This form of borrowing, though in theory regarded as short term, can often become a long-term source of finance.

Debt factoring

Debt factoring is a service offered by a financial institution (known as a 'factor'). Many of the large factors are subsidiaries of commercial banks. Debt factoring involves the factor taking over the business's debt collection. In addition to operating normal credit control procedures, a factor may offer to undertake credit investigations and to provide protection for approved credit sales. The factor is usually prepared to make an advance to the business of a maximum of 80 per cent of approved trade debtors. The charge made for the factoring service is based on total turnover, and is often 2 to 3 per cent of turnover. Any advances made to the business by the factor will attract a rate of interest similar to the rate charged on bank overdrafts.

Debt factoring is, in effect, outsourcing the trade debtors control to a specialist subcontractor. Many businesses find a factoring arrangement very convenient. It can result in savings in credit management and create more certain cash flows. It can also release the time of key personnel for more profitable activities. This may be extremely important for smaller businesses that rely on the talent and skills of a few key individuals. However, there is a possibility that some will see a factoring arrangement as

| Figure 15.6 | **The factoring process** |

There are three main parties to the factoring agreement. The client business will sell goods on credit and the factor will take responsibility for invoicing the customer and collecting the amount owing. The factor will then pay the client business the invoice amount, less fees and interest, in two stages. The first stage represents 80 per cent of the invoice value and will be paid immediately after the goods have been delivered to the customer. The second stage will represent the balance outstanding and will usually be paid when the customer has paid the factor the amount owing.

an indication that the business is experiencing financial difficulties. This may have an adverse effect on confidence. For this reason, some businesses try to conceal the factoring arrangement by collecting debts on behalf of the factor. When considering a factoring agreement, the costs and likely benefits arising must be identified and carefully weighed.

Figure 15.6 above shows the factoring process diagrammatically.

Invoice discounting

Invoice discounting involves a factor or other financial institution providing a loan based on a proportion of the face value of a business's credit sales outstanding. The amount advanced is usually 75 to 80 per cent of the value of the approved sales invoices outstanding. The business must agree to repay the advance within a relatively short period – perhaps 60 or 90 days. The responsibility for collecting the trade debts outstanding remains with the business, and repayment of the advance is not dependent on the trade debts being collected. Invoice discounting will not result in such a close relationship developing between the business and the financial institution as factoring. It may be a short-term arrangement whereas debt factoring usually involves a longer-term relationship.

Invoice discounting is a much more important source of funds than factoring (see Figure 15.7). There are three main reasons for this:

1 It is a confidential form of financing that the business's customers will know nothing about.

2 The service charge for invoice discounting is generally only 0.2 to 0.3 per cent of turnover, compared with 2.0 to 3.0 per cent for factoring.

3 Many businesses are unwilling to relinquish control of their customers' records. Customers are an important resource of the business, and many wish to retain control over all aspects of their relationship with their customers.

Real World 15.11 shows the relative importance of invoice discounting and factoring.

REAL WORLD 15.11

The popularity of invoice discounting and factoring

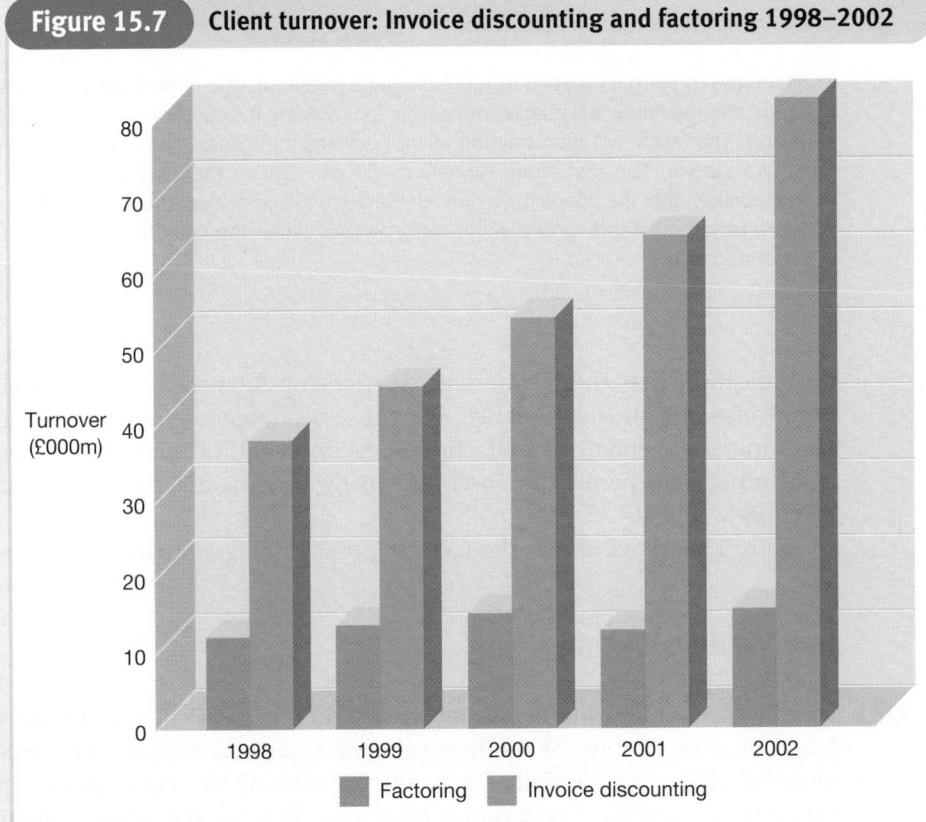

| Figure 15.7 | Client turnover: Invoice discounting and factoring 1998–2002 |

In recent years, client turnover for invoice discounting has risen much more sharply than client turnover from factoring. The turnover for invoice discounting for the year 2002 is more than four times the turnover for factoring.

Source: Compiled from information published by Factors & Discounters Association (www.factors.org.uk).

→ Factoring and invoice discounting are forms of **asset-based finance** as the assets of debtors are in effect used as security for the cash advances received by the business.

Long-term versus short-term borrowing

Having decided that some form of borrowing is required to finance the business, managers must then decide whether it should be long-term or short-term in form. There are many issues that should be taken into account when making this decision. These include the following:

● *Matching.* The business may attempt to match the type of borrowing with the nature of the assets held. Thus, long-term borrowing might finance assets that form part of the permanent operating base of the business, including non-current assets and a certain level of current assets. This leaves assets held for a short period, such as current assets held to meet seasonal increases in demand, to be financed by short-term borrowing, because short-term borrowing tends to be more flexible in that funds can be raised and repaid at short notice. Figure 15.8 shows this funding division graphically.

    A business may wish to match the asset life exactly with the period of the related loan; however, this may not be possible because of the difficulty of predicting the life of many assets.

● *Flexibility.* Short-term borrowing may be a useful means of postponing a commitment to taking on a long-term loan. This may be seen as desirable if interest rates are high and it is forecast that they will fall in the future. Short-term borrowing does not usually incur penalties if there is early repayment of the amount outstanding, whereas some form of financial penalty may arise if long-term debt is repaid early.

● *Refunding risk.* Short-term borrowing has to be renewed more frequently than long-term borrowing. This may create problems for the business if it is already in financial difficulties, or if there is a shortage of funds available for lending.

● *Interest rates.* Interest payable on long-term debt is often higher than for short-term debt, as lenders require a higher return where their funds are locked up for a long period. This fact may make short-term borrowing a more attractive source of

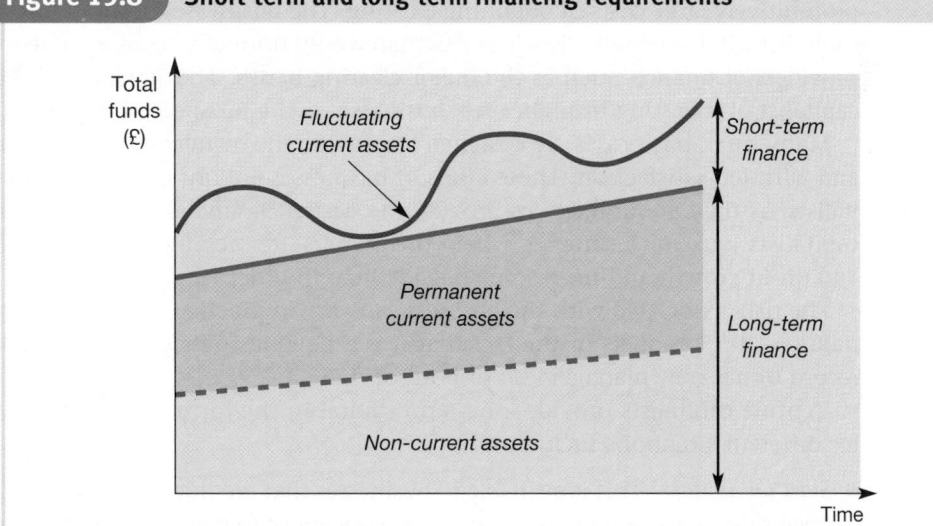

Figure 15.8   Short-term and long-term financing requirements

The broad consensus on financing seems to be that all of the permanent financial needs of the business should come from long-term sources. Only that part of current assets that fluctuates on a short-term, probably a seasonal, basis should be financed from short-term sources.

finance for a business. However, there may be other costs associated with borrowing (arrangement fees, for example) to be taken into account. The more frequently borrowings must be renewed, the higher these costs will be.

ACTIVITY 15.15

Some businesses may take up a less cautious financing position than that shown in Figure 15.8, and others may take up a more cautious one. How would the diagram differ under each of these options?

A less cautious position would mean relying on short-term finance to help fund part of the permanent capital base. A more cautious position would mean relying on long-term finance to help finance the fluctuating assets of the business.

Providing long-term finance for the small business

Though the Stock Exchange provides an important source of long-term finance for large businesses, it is not really suitable for small businesses. The aggregate market value of shares that are to be listed on the Stock Exchange must be at least £700,000 and, in practice, the amounts are much higher because of the high costs of listing. Thus, small businesses must look elsewhere for help in raising long-term finance. Some of the more important sources of finance that are available are considered below.

Venture capital and other long-term financing

Venture capital is long-term capital provided to small and medium-sized businesses wishing to grow but which do not have ready access to stock markets because of the prohibitively large costs of obtaining a listing. The businesses of interest to the venture capitalist will have higher levels of risk than would normally be acceptable to traditional providers of finance, such as the major clearing banks. The attraction for the venture capitalist of investing in higher-risk businesses is the prospect of higher returns.

Many small businesses are designed to provide the owners with a particular lifestyle and with job satisfaction. These kinds of businesses are not of interest to venture capitalists, as they are unlikely to provide the desired financial returns. Instead, venture capitalists look for businesses where the owners are seeking significant sales revenue and profit growth and need some outside help in order to achieve this.

The risks associated with the business can vary in practice. They are often due to the nature of the products or the fact that it is a new business that either lacks a trading record or has new management or both of these.

Venture capitalists provide long-term capital in the form of share and loan finance for different situations including:

● *Start-up capital.* This is available to businesses that are not fully developed. They may need finance to help refine the business concept or to engage in product development or initial marketing. They have not yet reached the stage where they are trading.
● *Early stage capital.* This is available for businesses that are ready to commence trading.
● *Expansion capital.* This is aimed at providing additional funding for existing, growing businesses.

- *Buy-out or buy-in capital.*   This is used to fund the acquisition of a business either by the existing management team ('buy-out') or by a new management team ('buy-in'). Management buy-outs (MBOs) and buy-ins (MBIs) often occur where a large business wishes to divest itself of one of its operating units or where a family business wishes to sell out because of succession problems.

Real World 15.12 provides some information on the use of venture capital by UK businesses.

REAL WORLD 15.12

Nothing ventured, nothing gained

The average level of investment by venture capitalists in each of the above categories during 2002 is shown in Figure 15.9. We can see that management buy-outs attract the highest average level of investment.

The total UK investment by venture capitalists in each of the above categories during 2002 is shown in Figure 15.10 below. We can see that management buy-outs account for approximately 60 per cent of the total investment.

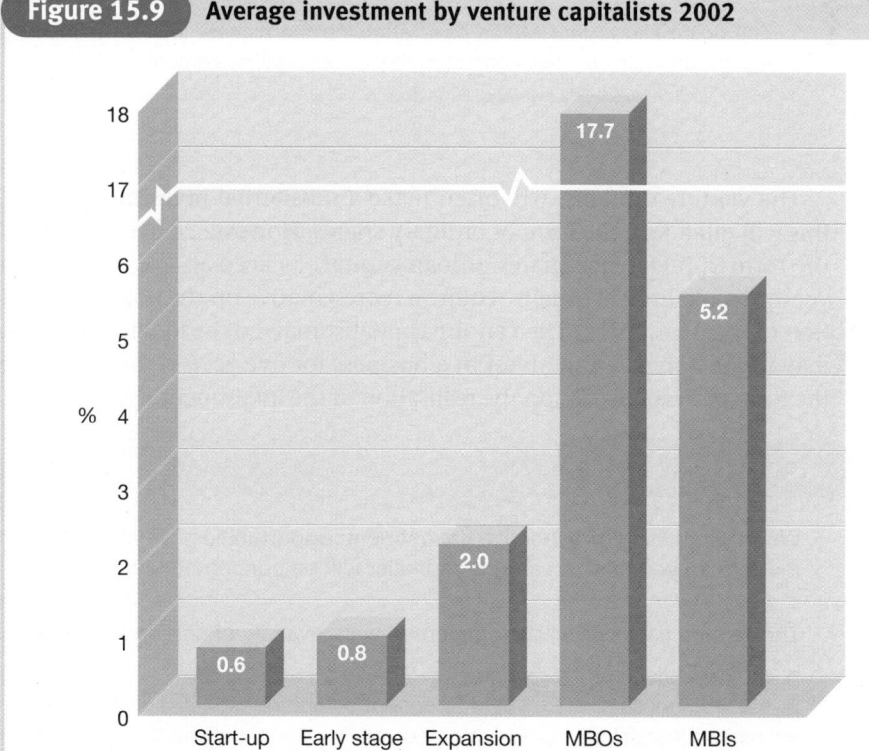

Figure 15.9   Average investment by venture capitalists 2002

MBOs have attracted the highest average investment, and start-up capital the lowest average investment. Start-ups often need relatively small amounts of funding and so this finding is, perhaps, to be expected.

Source: British Venture Capital Association BVCA report on investment activity, 2002.

Real World 15.12 continued

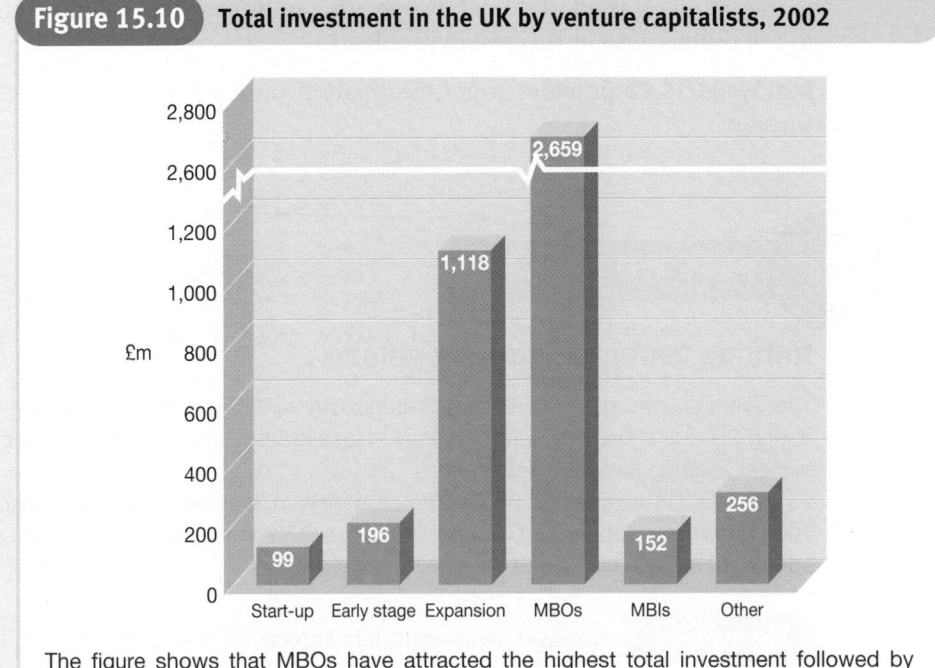

Figure 15.10 Total investment in the UK by venture capitalists, 2002

The figure shows that MBOs have attracted the highest total investment followed by expansion. Start-ups have attracted the lowest total investment.

Source: British Venture Capital Association BVCA report on investment activity, 2002.

The venture capitalist will often make a substantial investment in the business, and this will often take the form of ordinary shares. However, some of the funding may be in the form of preference shares or loan capital. To keep an eye on the sum invested, the venture capitalist will usually require a representative on the board of directors as a condition of the investment. The venture capitalist may not be looking for a quick return, and may well be prepared to invest in a business for five years or more. The return may take the form of a capital gain on the realisation of the investment (typically selling the shares).

ACTIVITY 15.16

When examining prospective investment opportunities, what kind of non-financial matters do you think a venture capitalist will be concerned with?

The venture capitalist will be concerned with a variety of non-financial matters, including:

- the aspirations of the owners;
- the willingness of the owners to accept a venture capitalist as a partner;
- the commercial advantage or unique selling point that the business provides;
- the growth potential of the market;
- the plans made to exploit business opportunities;
- the quality of management;
- the personal stake or commitment made by the owners to the business;
- the quality and nature of the product; and
- the possible ways in which the investment can be realised at the end of the investment period.

Though venture capital is extremely important for some small businesses, the vast majority of small businesses obtain their finance from other sources. **Real World 15.13** below shows the main sources of finance for small businesses in the UK.

REAL WORLD 15.13

Small business funding

Bank finance, such as overdrafts and loans, is the main source of external finance as the pie chart in Figure 15.11 shows.

Figure 15.11   **Financing small businesses 1997–1999**

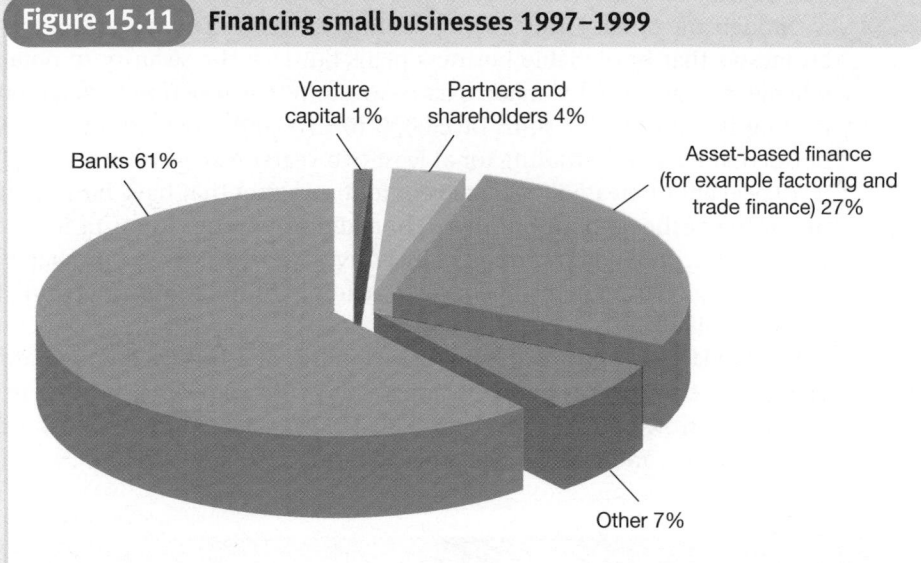

Venture capital, though very important to some small businesses, represents a very small part of the total finance raised. Bank finance remains the most important source of external finance, followed by trade finance, such as trade creditors, and asset-based finance, such as invoice discounting and factoring.

Source: ESRC reprinted in Accountany Age, 19 June 2003.

Business angels

Business angels are often wealthy individuals who have been successful in business. They are usually willing to invest, through a shareholding, somewhere between £10,000 and £100,000 in a start-up business or in a business that is at an early stage of development. They will often invest for a period of between three and five years, and sometimes even longer. They normally have a minority stake in the business and do not become involved in its day-to-day management. Business angels fill an important gap in the market as the size and the nature of the investment that they find appealing will not often appeal to venture capitalists.

Business angels may be attractive to small businesses for a number of reasons, including:

● They may be able to make investment decisions quickly, particularly if they are familiar with the industry in which the new business operates.
● They may also be able to offer a wealth of business experience to budding tycoons.

● Some may be prepared to accept lower financial returns than those required from venture capitalists in order to have the opportunity to become involved in a new and interesting project (see reference 1 at the end of the chapter).

Business angels offer an informal source of share finance and it is not always easy for owners of small businesses to identify a suitable angel. However, numerous business angel networks have now developed to help owners of small businesses find their 'perfect partner'.

Government assistance

One of the most effective ways in which the UK government assists small businesses is through the Small Firms Loan Guarantee Scheme. This scheme aims to help small businesses that have viable business plans but lack the security to obtain a loan. The scheme guarantees loans made over a two- to ten-year period to small businesses from lending institutions for sums of £5,000 to £100,000 (increased to £250,000 for businesses that have been trading for at least two years). The government will guarantee up to 70 per cent (increased to 85 per cent for businesses that have been trading for at least two years) of the amount borrowed. In addition to other forms of financial assistance, such as government grants and tax incentives for investors to buy shares in small businesses, the government also helps by providing information concerning the sources of finance available.

Real World 15.14 records the financing phases of a very well known dotcom retailer. The business started (as many businesses do) with the owner putting in personal savings and borrowings, to start it up. This led in stages to major Stock Exchange listed issues of shares and bonds (loan stocks) during 1997 and 1998.

 **REAL WORLD 15.14**

The financing of Amazon.com

Amazon.com is an online retailer that has enjoyed considerable growth in recent years. The following table shows the key financing stages in the early years of the business.

Financing of Amazon.com (1994–1999)

Dates	Share price	Source of funds
1994: July to Nov	$0.0010	*Founder*: Jeff Bezos starts Amazon.com with $10,000; borrows $44,000
1995: Feb to July	$0.1717	*Family*: founder's father and mother invest $245,000
1995: Aug to Dec	$0.1287–0.3333	*Business angels*: two angels invest $54,408
1995/96: Dec to May	$0.3333	*Business angels*: 20 angels invest $937,000
1996: May	$0.3333	*Family*: founder's siblings invest $20,000
1996: June	$2.3417	*Venture capitalists*: two venture capital funds invest $8m
1997: May	$18.00	*IPO**: 3m shares issued raising $49.1m
1997/98: Dec to May	$52.11	*Bond issue*: $326m bond issue

* Initial public offering of shares

Source: Van Osnabrugge and Robinson 2000. Reprinted in *Financial Times*, 6 November 2000.

SUMMARY

The main points in this chapter may be summarised as follows:

Sources of finance

- Internal sources of finance do not require the agreement of anyone beyond the directors and managers of the business, whereas external sources of finance do require the compliance of 'outsiders'.

- Long-term sources of finance are not due for repayment within one year whereas short-term sources are due for repayment within one year.

- The higher the level of risk associated with investing in a particular form of finance, the higher the level of return that will be expected by investors.

Internal sources of finance

- The major internal source of long-term finance is retained profits.

- The main short-term sources of internal finance are tighter credit control of debtors (receivables), reducing stock (inventory) levels and delaying payments to trade creditors (payables).

External sources of finance

- The main external, *long-term* sources of finance are ordinary shares, preference shares, loans and leases.

- Ordinary shares are normally considered to be the most risky form of investment and, therefore, provide the highest expected returns. Loan capital is normally the least risky and provides the lowest expected returns to investors.

- The level of gearing associated with a business is often an important factor in assessing the level of risk and returns to ordinary shareholders.

- The main sources of external *short-term* finance are bank overdrafts, debt factoring and invoice discounting.

- When considering the choice between long-term and short-term sources of borrowing, factors such as matching the type of borrowing with the nature of the assets held, the need for flexibility, refunding risk and interest rates should be taken into account.

Share issues

- Share issues that involve the payment of cash by investors can take the form of a rights issue, public issue, offer for sale or a private placing.

- A rights issue is made to existing shareholders. Most share issues are of this type as the law requires that shares that are to be issued for cash must first be offered to existing shareholders.

- A public issue involves a direct issue to the public and an offer for sale involves an indirect issue to the public.

- A private placing is an issue of shares to selected investors.

The Stock Exchange

- The Stock Exchange is an important primary and secondary market in capital for large businesses. However, obtaining a Stock Exchange listing can have certain drawbacks for a business.

Small businesses

● Venture capital is long-term capital for small or medium-sized businesses that are not listed on the Stock Exchange. These businesses often have higher levels of risk but provide the venture capitalist with the prospect of higher levels of return.

● Business angels are wealthy individuals who are willing to invest in businesses at an early stage of development.

● The government assists small businesses through guaranteeing loans and by providing grants and tax incentives.

→ **Key terms**

term loan p. 521	rights issues p. 535
debenture p. 522	offer for sale p. 537
eurobond p. 522	public issue p. 538
deep discount bond p. 523	tender issue p. 538
convertible loan stocks p. 523	private placing p. 538
warrants p. 524	Stock Exchange p. 539
financial derivatives p. 526	bank overdraft p. 542
mortgage p. 526	debt factoring p. 542
loan covenants p. 526	invoice discounting p. 543
finance lease p. 528	asset-based financing p. 544
operating lease p. 528	venture capital p. 546
sale and leaseback p. 529	business angel p. 549

Further reading

If you would like to explore the topics covered in this chapter in more depth, we recommend the following books:

Corporate Financial Management, *Arnold G.*, 2nd edn, Financial Times Prentice Hall, 1998, chapters 11 and 12.

Business Finance: Theory and practice, *McLaney E.*, 6th edn, Financial Times Prentice Hall, 2003, chapter 8.

Corporate Finance and Investment, *Pike R. and Neale B.*, 4th edn, Prentice Hall International, 2003, chapters 16 and 18.

Financial Management: An introduction, *McMenamin J.*, Routledge, 1999, chapters 4 and 19.

Reference

1 **Sources of Business Angel Capital 1998/99**, Business Venture Capital Association.

REVIEW QUESTIONS

Answers to these questions can be found on the students' side of the Companion Website at www.pearsoned.co.uk/atrillmclaney.

15.1 What are the benefits to a business of issuing share warrants?

15.2 Why might a business that has a Stock Exchange listing revert to being unlisted?

15.3 Distinguish between an offer for sale and a public issue of shares.

15.4 Distinguish between invoice discounting and factoring.

EXERCISES

Exercises 15.4 to 15.8 are more advanced than 15.1 to 15.3. Those with a coloured number have an answer at the back of the book.

15.1 H. Brown (Portsmouth) Ltd produces a range of central heating systems for sale to builders' merchants. As a result of increasing demand for the business's products, the directors have decided to expand production. The cost of acquiring new plant and machinery and the increase in working capital requirements are planned to be financed by a mixture of long-term and short-term borrowing.

Required:
(a) Discuss the major factors that should be taken into account when deciding on the appropriate mix of long-term and short-term borrowing necessary to finance the expansion programme.
(b) Discuss the major factors that a lender should take into account when deciding whether to grant a long-term loan to the business.
(c) Identify three conditions that might be included in a long-term loan agreement, and state the purpose of each.

15.2 Devonian plc has the following equity as at 30 November Year 4:

	£m
Ordinary shares 25p fully paid	50.0
General reserve	22.5
Retained profit	25.5
	98.0

The business has no long-term loans.

In the year to 30 November Year 4, the operating profit (net profit before interest and taxation) was £40m and it is expected that this will increase by 25% during the forthcoming year. The business is listed on the London Stock Exchange and the share price as at 30 November Year 4 was £2.10.

The business wishes to raise £72m in order to re-equip one of its factories and is considering two possible financing options. The first option is to make a one-for-five rights issue at a discount price of £1.80 per share. The second option is to take out a long-term loan at an interest rate of 10% a year. If the first option is taken, it is expected that the price earnings (P/E) ratio will remain the same for the forthcoming year. If the second option is taken, it is estimated that the P/E ratio will fall by 10% by the end of the forthcoming year.

Assume a corporation tax rate of 30%.

Required:

(a) Assuming a rights issue of shares is made, calculate
   (i)   the theoretical ex-rights price of an ordinary share in Devonian plc; and
   (ii) the value of the rights for each original ordinary share.

(b) Calculate the price of an ordinary share in Devonian plc in one year's time assuming:
   (i)   a rights issue is made; and
   (ii) a loan issue is made.
   and comment on your findings.

(c) Explain why rights issues are usually made at a discount.

(d) From the business's viewpoint, how critical is the pricing of a rights issue likely to be?

15.3   Brocmar plc has 10m ordinary £0.50 shares in issue. The market price of the shares is £1.80. The board of the business wishes to finance a major project at a cost of £2.88m. Forecasts suggest that the implementation of the project will add £0.4m to after-tax earnings available to ordinary shareholders in the coming year. After-tax earnings for the year just completed were £2m, but this figure is expected to decline to £1.8m in the coming year if the project proposed is not undertaken. A rights issue at a 20% discount on the existing market price is proposed. Issue expenses can be ignored.

Required:

(a) To assist the board in coming to a final decision, you are required to present information in the following format:
   ● Project not undertaken
      (i)   earnings per share for the coming year.
   ● Project undertaken and financed by a rights issue
      (ii)   rights issue price per share
      (iii) number of shares to be issued
      (iv)   earnings per share for the coming year
      (v)   the theoretical ex-rights price per share.
   All workings should be shown separately.

(b) What information, other than that provided in the question, is needed before the board can make the investment decision?

15.4   Raphael Ltd is a small engineering business that has annual credit sales revenue of £2.4m. In recent years, the business has experienced credit-control problems. The average collection period for sales has risen to 50 days even though the stated policy of the business is for payment to be made within 30 days. In addition, 1.5% of sales are written off as bad debts each year.

The business has recently been in talks with a factor who is prepared to make an advance to the business equivalent to 80% of debtors, based on the assumption that customers will, in future, adhere to a 30-day payment period. The interest rate for the advance will be 11% a year. The trade debtors are currently financed through a bank overdraft, which has an interest rate of 12% a year. The factor will take over the credit-control procedures of the business and this will result in a saving to the business of £18,000 a year; however, the factor will make a charge of 2% of sales revenue for this service. The use of the factoring service is expected to eliminate the bad debts incurred by the business.

Required:

Calculate the net cost of the factor agreement to the business and state whether or not the business should take advantage of the opportunity to factor its trade debts.

15.5 Russell Ltd installs and services heating and ventilation systems for commercial premises. The business's most recent balance sheet and profit and loss account is set out below:

Balance sheet as at 31 May Year 4

	£000	£000	£000
Non-current assets			
Property, plant and equipment			
Machinery and equipment at cost		883.6	
Less Accumulated depreciation		328.4	555.2
Motor vehicles at cost		268.8	
Less Accumulated depreciation		82.2	186.6
			741.8
Current assets			
Stock at cost	293.2		
Trade debtors	510.3	803.5	
Current liabilities			
Trade creditors	(199.7)		
Corporation tax due	(128.0)		
Bank overdraft	(135.2)	(462.9)	340.6
			1,082.4
Non-current liabilities			
12% debentures (repayable Year 10/11)			(250.0)
			832.4
Equity			
£1 ordinary shares			400.0
General reserve			50.2
Retained profit			380.2
			832.4

Profit and loss account for the year ended 31 May Year 4

	£000
Sales revenue	5,207.8
Net profit before interest and taxation	542.0
Interest payable	(30.0)
Net profit before taxation	512.0
Corporation tax (25%)	(128.0)
Net profit after taxation	384.0
Dividend paid	(153.6)
Retained profit for the year	230.4

The business wishes to invest in more machinery and equipment in order to cope with an upsurge in demand for its services. An additional profit before interest and taxation of £120,000 a year is expected if an investment of £600,000 is made in plant and machinery.

The directors are considering an offer from venture capitalists to finance the expansion programme. The finance will be made available immediately through either:

(i)   an issue of £1 ordinary shares at a premium on par of £3 a share; or
(ii) an issue of £600,000 10% debentures at par.

The directors wish to maintain the same dividend payout ratio in future years as in past years whichever method of finance is chosen.

Required:
(a) For each of the financing schemes:
    (i)   prepare a projected profit and loss account for the year ended 31 May Year 5;
    (ii) calculate the projected earnings per share for the year ended 31 May Year 5;
    (iii) calculate the projected level of gearing as at 31 May Year 5.
(b) Briefly assess both of the financing schemes under consideration from the viewpoint of the existing shareholders.

15.6 Carpets Direct plc wishes to increase the number of its retail outlets in the south of England. The board of directors has decided to finance this expansion programme by raising the funds from existing shareholders through a one-for-four rights issue. The most recent profit and loss account of the business is as follows:

Profit and loss account for the year ended 30 April

	£m
Sales revenue	164.5
Profit before interest and taxation	12.6
Interest	(6.2)
Profit before taxation	6.4
Corporation tax	(1.9)
Profit after taxation	4.5
Ordinary dividends paid	(2.0)
Retained profit for the year	2.5

The share capital consists of 120m ordinary shares with a par value of £0.50 a share. These are currently being traded on the Stock Exchange at a price earnings ratio of 22 times and the board of directors has decided to issue the new shares at a discount of 20% on the current market value.

Required:
(a) Calculate the theoretical ex-rights price of an ordinary share in Carpets Direct plc.
(b) Calculate the price at which the rights in Carpet Direct plc are likely to be traded.
(c) Identify and evaluate, at the time of the rights issue, each of the options arising from the rights issue to an investor who holds 4,000 ordinary shares before the rights announcement.

15.7 Gainsborough Fashions Ltd operates a small chain of fashion shops in North Wales. In recent months the business has been under pressure from its trade creditors to reduce the average credit period taken from three months to one month. As a result, the directors have approached the bank to ask for an increase in the existing overdraft for one year to be able to comply with the creditors' demands. The most recent financial statements of the business are as follows:

Balance sheet as at 31 May

	£	£	£
Non-current assets			
Property, plant and equipment			
Fixtures and fittings at cost		90,000	
Less Accumulated depreciation		23,000	67,000
Motor vehicles at cost		34,000	
Less Accumulated depreciation		27,000	7,000
			74,000
Current assets			
Stock at cost		198,000	
Trade debtors		3,000	
		201,000	
Current liabilities			
Trade creditors	(162,000)		
Accrued expenses	(10,000)		
Bank overdraft	(17,000)		
Taxation	(5,000)		
	(194,000)		7,000
			81,000
Non-current liabilities			
Debentures repayable in just over one year's time			(40,000)
			41,000
Equity			
£1 ordinary shares			20,000
General reserve			4,000
Retained profit			17,000
			41,000

Abbreviated profit and loss account for the year ended 31 May

	£
Sales revenue	740,000
Net profit before interest and taxation	38,000
Interest charges	(5,000)
Net profit before taxation	33,000
Taxation	(10,000)
Net profit after taxation	23,000
Dividend paid	(10,000)
Retained profit for the year	13,000

Notes
1 The debentures are secured by personal guarantees from the directors.
2 The current overdraft bears an interest rate of 12 per cent a year.

Required:
(a) Identify and discuss the major factors that a bank would take into account before deciding whether or not to grant an increase in the overdraft of a business.
(b) State whether, in your opinion, the bank should grant the required increase in the overdraft for Gainsborough Fashions Ltd. You should provide reasoned arguments and supporting calculations where necessary.

15.8 Telford Engineers plc, a medium-sized Midlands manufacturer of automobile components, has decided to modernise its factory by introducing a number of robots. These will cost £20m and will reduce operating costs by £6m a year for their estimated useful life of 10 years starting next year (Year 10). To finance this scheme, the business can raise £20 million either:

1 by the issue of 20 million ordinary shares at 100p; or
2 by loan capital at 14% interest a year, capital repayments of £3m a year commencing at the end of Year 11.

Extracts from Telford Engineers' financial statements appear below:

Summary of balance sheet at 31 December

	Year 6 £m	Year 7 £m	Year 8 £m	Year 9 £m
Non-current assets	48	51	65	64
Current assets	55	67	57	55
Current liabilities				
Trade creditors	(20)	(27)	(25)	(18)
Bank overdraft	(5)	–	(6)	(8)
	78	91	91	93
Equity	48	61	61	63
Non-current liabilities	30	30	30	30
	78	91	91	93
Number of issued 25p shares	80 million	80 million	80 million	80 million
Share price	150p	200p	100p	145p

Summary of profit and loss accounts for years ended 31 December

	Year 6 £m	Year 7 £m	Year 8 £m	Year 9 £m
Sales revenue	152	170	110	145
Profit before interest and taxation	28	40	7	15
Interest payable	(4)	(3)	(4)	(5)
Profit before taxation	24	37	3	10
Taxation	(12)	(16)	(0)	(4)
Profit after taxation	12	21	3	6
Dividends	(6)	(8)	(3)	(4)
Retained profit	6	13	0	2

For your answer you should assume that the corporate tax rate for Year 10 is 40%, that sales revenue and operating profit will be unchanged except for the £6 million cost saving arising from the introduction of the robots, and that Telford Engineers will pay the same dividend per share in Year 10 as in Year 9.

Required:

(a) Prepare, for each financing arrangement, Telford Engineers' projected profit and loss account for the year ending 31 December Year 10 and a statement of its share capital, reserves and loans on that date.

(b) Calculate Telford's projected earnings per share for Year 10 for both schemes.

(c) Which scheme would you advise the business to adopt? You should give your reasons and state what additional information you would require.

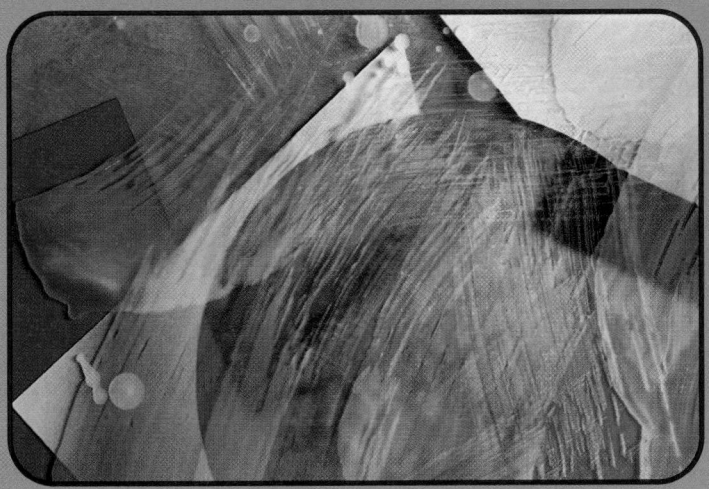

CHAPTER 16

Managing working capital

OBJECTIVES

When you have completed this chapter, you should be able to:

● Identify the main elements of working capital.

● Discuss the purpose of working capital and the nature of the working capital cycle.

● Explain the importance of establishing policies for the control of working capital.

● Explain the factors that have to be taken into account when managing each element of working capital.

INTRODUCTION

T his chapter considers the factors that must be taken into account when managing the working capital of a business. Each element of working capital will be
identified, and the major issues surrounding them will be discussed. Working capital
represents a significant investment for many businesses and so its proper management and control can be vital. We saw in Chapter 14 that it may be an important
aspect of new investment proposals. Some useful tools in the management of working capital are accounting ratios, which were explored in Chapter 7, and budgets,
which were considered in Chapter 12.

The nature and purpose of working capital

Working capital is usually defined as current assets less current liabilities.
The major elements of current assets are:

- stocks (inventories)
- trade debtors (receivables)
- cash (in hand and at bank).

The major elements of current liabilities are:

- trade creditors (payables)
- bank overdrafts.

The size and composition of working capital can vary between industries. For some
types of business, the investment in working capital can be substantial. For example, a
manufacturing business will typically invest heavily in raw material, work in progress
and finished goods, and will often sell its goods on credit, thereby generating trade
debtors. A retailer, on the other hand, will hold only one form of stock (finished
goods), and will usually sell goods for cash. Many service businesses hold no stocks.
Most businesses buy goods and/or services on credit, giving rise to trade creditors. Few,
if any, businesses operate without a cash balance, though in some cases it is a negative
one (bank overdraft).

Working capital represents a net investment in short-term assets. These assets are
continually flowing into and out of the business, and are essential for day-to-day
operations. The various elements of working capital are interrelated, and can be seen
as part of a short-term cycle. For a manufacturing business, the working capital cycle
can be depicted as shown in Figure 16.1.

For a retailer the situation would be as in Figure 16.1, except that there would be
no work in progress and the raw materials and the finished stock would be the same.
For a purely service business, the working capital cycle would also be similar to that
depicted in Figure 16.1, except that there would be no stock of raw materials and
finished goods. There may well be work in progress, however, since many services, for
example a case handled by a firm of solicitors, will take some time to complete and
costs will build up before the client is billed for them.

Figure 16.1	The working capital cycle

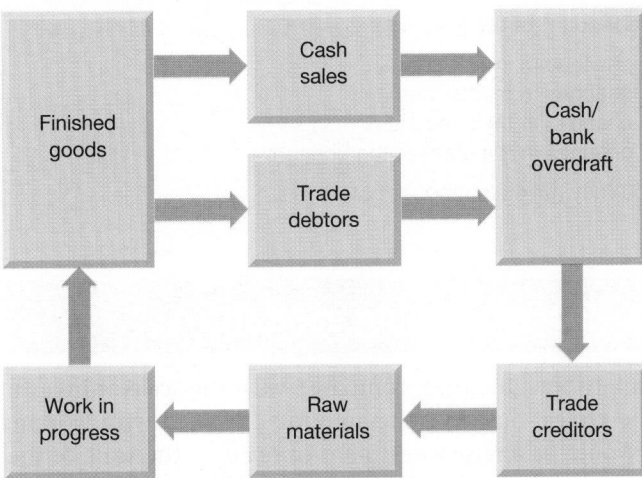

Cash is used to pay trade creditors for raw materials, or raw materials are bought for immediate cash settlement; cash is spent on labour and other aspects that turn raw materials into work in progress and, finally, into finished goods. The finished goods are sold to customers either for cash or on credit. In the case of credit customers, there will be a delay before the cash is received from the sales. Receipt of cash completes the cycle.

Managing working capital

The management of working capital is an essential part of the business's short-term planning process. It is necessary for management to decide how much of each element should be held. As we shall see later in this chapter, there are costs associated with holding either too much or too little of each element. Management must be aware of these costs, which include opportunity costs, in order to manage effectively. Hence, the potential benefits must be weighed against the likely costs in an attempt to achieve the optimum investment.

The working capital needs of a particular business are likely to change over time as a result of changes in the business environment. This means that working capital decisions are constantly being made. Managers must try to identify changes in an attempt to ensure that the level of investment in working capital is appropriate (see Activity 16.1, below).

In addition to changes in the external environment, changes arising within the business could alter the required level of investment in working capital. Examples of such internal changes include using different production methods (resulting, perhaps, in a need to hold less stock) and changes in the level of risk that managers are prepared to take.

ACTIVITY 16.1

What kind of changes in the commercial environment might lead to a decision to change the level of investment in working capital? Try to identify four possible changes that could affect the working capital needs of a business.

Activity 16.1 continued

We thought of the following:

- changes in interest rates
- changes in market demand
- changes in the seasons
- changes in the state of the economy.

You may have also thought of others.

The scale of working capital

We might imagine that, compared with the scale of investment in non-current assets by the typical business, the amounts involved with working capital are pretty trivial. This would be a false assessment of reality – the scale of the working capital elements for most businesses is vast.

Real World 16.1 gives some impression of the working capital involvement for five UK businesses that are either very well known by name, or whose products are everyday

 **REAL WORLD 16.1**

A summary of the balance sheets of five UK businesses

Business	The Boots Company plc	Go-Ahead Group plc	Rolls-Royce plc	Tesco plc	United Utilities plc
Balance sheet date	31.3.03	28.6.03	31.12.02	22.2.03	31.3.03
	%	%	%	%	%
Non-current assets	74	126	70	126	104
Current assets					
Stock	25	2	27	10	–
Trade debtors	13	23	23	–	3
Other debtors	12	29	33	6	4
Cash and near cash	19	16	17	6	10
	69	70	100	22	17
Current liabilities					
Trade creditors	14	25	11	20	1
Tax and dividends	12	15	9	6	5
Other short-term liabilities	12	55	44	10	12
Overdrafts and short-term loans	5	1	6	12	3
	43	96	70	48	21
Working capital	26	(26)	30	(26)	(4)
Total long-term investment	100	100	100	100	100

The non-current assets, current assets and current liabilities are expressed as a percentage of the total net investment (equity plus non-current liabilities) of the business concerned. The businesses were randomly selected, except that they were deliberately taken from different industries. Boots is a major UK health-care manufacturer that operates a chain of high-street retail stores. Go-Ahead is a major passenger transport provider, principally through buses and trains. It runs much of the Central London bus service and owns South Central and Thames Trains. Rolls-Royce builds engines for aircraft and for other purposes. Tesco is one of the major UK supermarkets. United Utilities is a major distributor of electricity and water, particularly in the north west of England.

Source: The table was constructed from information which appeared in the annual reports of the five businesses concerned.

commodities for most of us. These businesses were randomly selected, except that each one is high profile and from a different industry. For each business the major balance sheet items are expressed as a percentage of the total investment by the providers of long-term finance.

The totals for current assets are pretty large when compared with the total long-term investment. This is particularly true of Boots, Go-Ahead and Rolls-Royce. The amounts vary considerably from one type of business to the next. Rolls-Royce is the only one of the five businesses that is solely a manufacturer. Boots and Tesco are both retailers, though Boots is also a manufacturer. These three are the only ones that hold significant amounts of stock. The other two are service providers. Tesco does not sell on credit and little of United Utilities sales are on credit, so they have little or nothing invested in trade debtors. It is interesting to note that Tesco's trade creditors are much higher than its stock. Since most of these creditors will be suppliers of stock, it means that the business is able, on average, to have the cash from a particular sale in the bank before it needs to pay for the goods concerned.

These types of variation in the amounts and types of working capital elements are typical of other businesses. In the sections that follow, we shall consider each element of working capital separately and how they might be properly managed.

Managing stocks (inventories)

A business may hold stocks for various reasons, the most common of which is to meet the immediate day-to-day requirements of customers and production. However, a business may hold more than is necessary for this purpose if it is believed that future supplies may be interrupted or scarce. Similarly, if the business believes that the cost of stocks will rise in the future, it may decide to stockpile.

For some types of business the stock held may represent a substantial proportion of the total assets held. For example, a car dealership that rents its premises may have nearly all of its total assets in the form of stock. As we have seen, manufacturing businesses' stock levels tend to be higher than in many other types of business. For some types of business, the level of stock held may vary substantially over the year owing to the seasonal nature of the industry. An example of such a business is a greetings card manufacturer. For other businesses, stock levels may remain fairly stable throughout the year.

Where a business holds stock simply to meet the day-to-day requirements of its customers and for production, it will normally seek to minimise the amount of stock held, because there are significant costs associated with holding stocks. These include storage and handling costs, financing costs, the risks of pilferage and obsolescence, and the opportunities forgone in tying up funds in this form of asset. However, a business must also recognise that, if the level of stocks held is too low, there will also be associated costs.

ACTIVITY 16.2

What costs might a business incur as a result of holding too low a level of stocks? Try to jot down at least three types of cost.

In answering this activity you may have thought of the following costs:

- loss of sales, from being unable to provide the goods required immediately;
- loss of goodwill from customers, for being unable to satisfy customer demand;

Activity 16.2 continued

- high transport costs incurred to ensure that stocks are replenished quickly;
- lost production due to shortage of raw materials;
- inefficient production scheduling due to shortages of raw materials;
- purchasing stocks at a higher price than might otherwise have been possible in order to replenish stocks quickly.

Before we go on to deal with the various approaches that can be taken to managing stock, **Real World 16.2** provides an example of how badly things can go wrong if stock is not adequately controlled.

REAL WORLD 16.2

Pallets lost at Brambles

Brambles Industries plc (BI) is an Anglo-Australian industrial services business, formed in 2001 when the industrial services subsidiary of GKN plc, the UK engineering business, was merged with the Australian business Brambles Ltd.

BI uses 'pallets' on which it delivers its products to customers. These are returnable by customers so BI holds a stock or 'pool' of pallets. Each pallet costs the business about £10. Unfortunately, BI lost 14m pallets during the year ended in June 2002 as a result of poor stock control and this led to a significant decline in the business's profits and share price.

At BI's annual general meeting in Sydney, Australia, one of the shareholders was quoted as saying: 'Running a pallet pool is not rocket science. I can teach one of my employees about pallets in 20 minutes.'

Source: Information taken from an article appearing in the *Financial Times*, 27 November 2002.

To try to ensure that the stocks are properly managed, a number of procedures and techniques may be used. These are reviewed below.

Budgeting future demand

One of the best means of a business trying to ensure that there will be stock (inventory) available to meet future production requirements and sales is to make appropriate plans.

REAL WORLD 16.3

Dreaming of a bright Christmas

Wal-Mart is the world's largest retailer and has extremely sophisticated stock planning and control systems. Nevertheless, things can still go wrong. During 2002, there was a rise in sales revenue of 12 per cent and a rise in stock levels of 10 per cent. The large rise in stock in relation to the rise in sales revenue was unplanned and was largely due to sales revenue over the Christmas period falling below expectations. This represents poor stock management by Wal-Mart standards. The business, however, expects to get back on track and to ensure that stocks grow by less than half the rate of sales revenue in the future.

Source: Information taken from *Financial Times*, Lex column, 19 February 2003.

These budgets should deal with each product that the business makes and/or sells. It is important that every attempt is made to ensure the budgets' accuracy, as they will determine future ordering and production levels. The budgets may be derived in various ways. They may be developed using statistical techniques such as time series analysis, or they may be based on the judgement of the sales and marketing staff. We considered stock budgets, and their link to sales and production budgets, in Chapter 12.

Financial ratios

One ratio that can be used to help monitor stock levels is the average stock turnover period, which we examined in Chapter 7. As we should recall, this ratio is calculated as follows:

$$\text{Average stock turnover period} = \frac{\text{Average stock held}}{\text{Cost of sales}} \times 365$$

This will provide a picture of the average period for which stocks are held, and can be useful as a basis for comparison. It is possible to calculate the stock turnover period for individual product lines as well as for stocks as a whole.

Recording and reordering systems

The management of stocks in a business of any size requires a sound system of recording stock movements. There must be proper procedures for recording stock purchases and sales. Periodic stock checks may be required to ensure that the amount of physical stocks held is consistent with the stock records.

There should also be clear procedures for the reordering of stocks. Authorisation for both the purchase and the issue of stocks should be confined to a few senior staff. This should avoid problems of duplication and lack of co-ordination. To determine the point at which stock should be reordered, information will be required concerning the **lead time** (that is, the time between the placing of an order and the receipt of the goods) and the likely level of demand.

ACTIVITY 16.3

An electrical retailer keeps a particular type of light switch in stock. The annual demand for the light switch is 10,400 units, and the lead time for orders is four weeks. Demand for the stock is steady throughout the year. At what level of stock should the business reorder, assuming that it is confident of the information given above?

The average weekly demand for the stock item is 10,400/52 = 200 units. During the time between ordering the stock and receiving it, the stock sold will be 4 × 200 units = 800 units. So the business should reorder no later than when the stock level reaches 800 units, in order to avoid a 'stockout'.

In most businesses, there will be some uncertainty surrounding the above factors and so a buffer or safety stock level may be maintained in case problems occur. The amount of buffer stock to be held is really a matter of judgement. This judgement will depend on:

- the degree of uncertainty concerning the above factors;
- the likely costs of running out of stock; and
- the cost of holding the buffer stock.

REAL WORLD 16.4

Taking on the big boys

The use of technology in stock recording and reordering may be of vital importance to the survival of small businesses that are being threatened by larger rivals. One such example is that of small independent bookshops. Technology can come to their rescue in two ways. First, electronic point-of-sale (EPOS) systems can record books as they are sold and can constantly update stocks held. Thus, books that need to be reordered can be quickly and easily identified. Second, the reordering process can be improved by using web-based technology, which allows books to be ordered in real time. Many large book wholesalers provide free web-based software to their customers for this purpose and try to deliver books ordered during the next working day. This means that a small bookseller, with limited shelf space, may keep only one copy of a particular book, but maintain a range of books that competes with that of a large bookseller.

Source: Information taken from 'Small stores keep up with the big boys', FT.com, 5 February 2003.

Levels of control
. . . .

Senior managers must make a commitment to the management of stocks. However, the cost of controlling stocks must be weighed against the potential benefits. It may be possible to have different levels of control according to the nature of the stocks held. 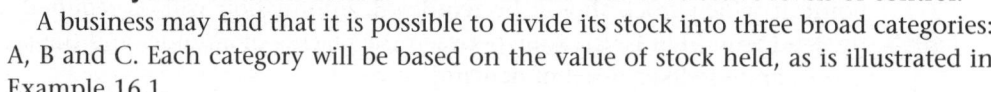 The **ABC system of stock control** is based on the idea of selective levels of control.

A business may find that it is possible to divide its stock into three broad categories: A, B and C. Each category will be based on the value of stock held, as is illustrated in Example 16.1.

Example 16.1

Alascan Products plc makes door handles and door fittings. It makes them in brass, in steel and in plastic. The business finds that brass fittings account for 10 per cent of the physical volume of the finished stock that it holds, but these represent 65 per cent of its total value. This is treated as Category A stock. There are sophisticated recording procedures, tight control is exerted over stock movements and there is a high level of security at the stock's location. This is economic because the stock represents a relatively small proportion of the total volume.

The business finds that steel fittings account for 30 per cent of the total volume of finished stock and represent 25 per cent of its total value. This is treated as Category B stock, with a lower level of recording and management control being applied.

The remaining 60 per cent of the volume of stock is plastic fittings, which represent the least valuable items that account for only 10 per cent of the total value of finished stock held. This is treated as Category C stock, so the level of recording and management control would be lower still. Applying to this stock, the level of control that is applied to Category A or even Category B stock would be uneconomic.

Categorising stock in this way seeks to direct management effort to the most important areas, and tries to ensure that the costs of controlling stock are appropriate to its importance.

Figure 16.2 shows the logic of the ABC approach to stock (inventory) control.

Figure 16.2 **ABC method of analysing and controlling stock**

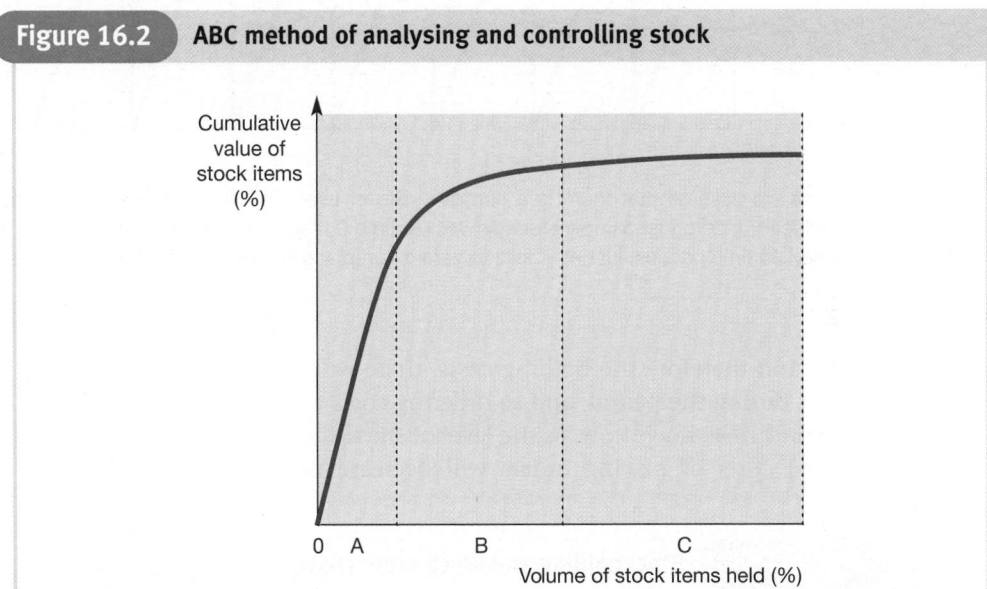

Category A contains stock that, though relatively few in quantity, accounts for a large proportion of the total value. Category B stock consists of those items that are less valuable but more numerous. Category C comprises those stock items that are very numerous but relatively low in value. Different stock control rules would be applied to each category. For example, only Category A stock would attract the more expensive and sophisticated controls.

Stock (inventory) management models

It is possible to use decision models to help manage stock. The **economic order quantity (EOQ)** model is concerned with answering the question 'How much stock should be ordered?' In its simplest form, the EOQ model assumes that demand is constant, so that stocks will be depleted evenly over time, and replenished just at the point that the stock runs out. These assumptions would lead to a 'saw tooth' pattern to represent stock movements within a business, as shown in Figure 16.3.

The EOQ model recognises that the key costs associated with stock management are the costs of holding it and the cost of ordering it. The model can be used to calculate the optimum size of a purchase order by taking account of both of these cost elements. The cost of holding stock can be substantial, and so management may try to minimise the average amount of stock held. However, by reducing the level of stock

Figure 16.3 **Patterns of stock movements over time**

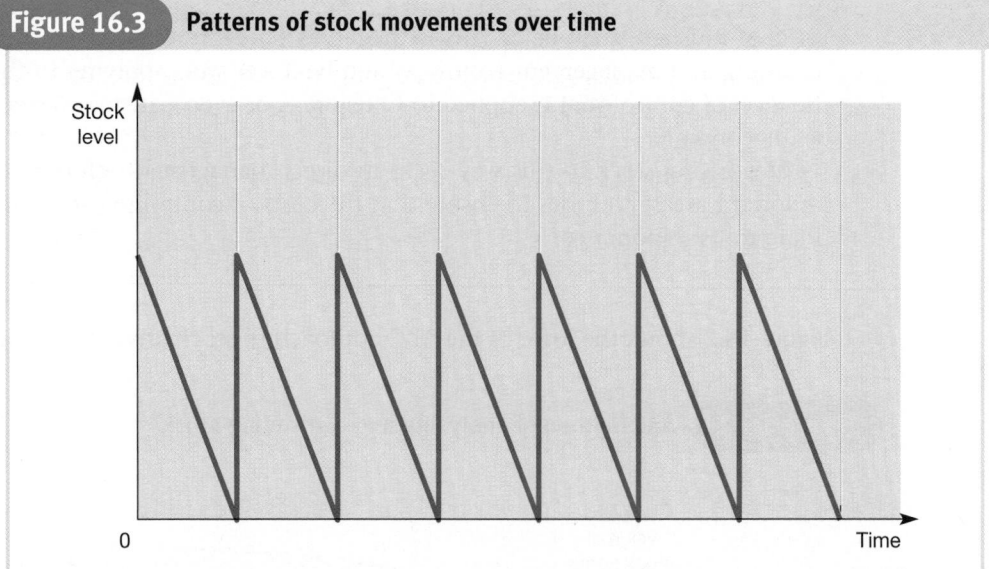

Here we assume that there is a constant rate of usage of the stock item, and that stock is reduced to zero just as new stock arrives. At time 0 there is a full level of stock. This is steadily used as time passes; just as it falls to zero it is replaced. This pattern is then repeated.

held, and therefore the holding costs, there will be a need to increase the number of orders during the period, and so ordering costs will rise.

Figure 16.4 shows how, as the level of stock and the size of stock orders increase, the annual costs of placing orders will decrease because fewer orders will be placed.

Figure 16.4 **Stockholding and stock order costs**

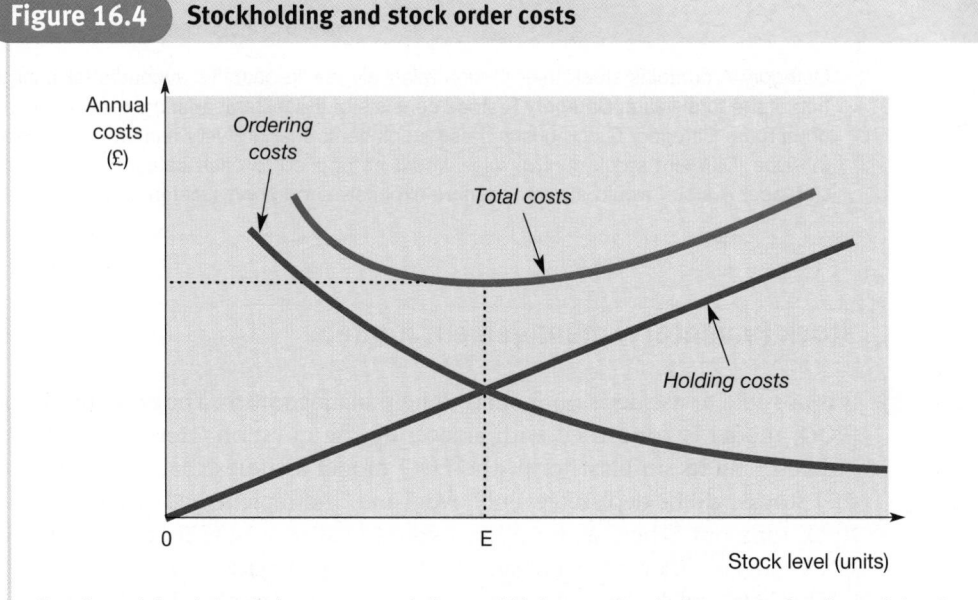

Small stock levels imply frequent reordering and high annual ordering costs. Small stock levels also imply relatively low stockholding costs. High stock levels imply exactly the opposite. There is, in theory, an optimum order size that will lead to the sum of ordering and stockholding costs (total costs) being at a minimum.

However, the cost of holding stock will increase, as there will be higher average stock levels. The total costs curve, which is based on the sum of holding costs and ordering costs, will fall until the point E, which represents the minimum total cost. Thereafter, total costs begin to rise. The EOQ model seeks to identify point E at which total costs are minimised. This will represent half of the optimum amount that should be ordered on each occasion. Assuming, as we are doing, that stock is used evenly over time and falls to zero before being replaced, the average stock level equals half of the order size.

The EOQ model, which can be used to derive the most economic order quantity, is:

$$\text{EOQ} = \sqrt{\frac{2DC}{H}}$$

where:

D = the annual demand for the item of stock (expressed in units of the stock)
C = the cost of placing an order
H = the cost of holding one unit of stock for one year.

ACTIVITY 16.4

HLA Ltd sells 2,000 bags of cement each year. It has been estimated that the cost of holding one bag of cement for a year is £4. The cost of placing an order for stock is estimated at £250.

Calculate the EOQ for bags of cement.

Your answer to this activity should be as follows:

$$\text{EOQ} = \sqrt{\frac{2 \times 2,000 \times 250}{4}}$$

$$= 500 \text{ units}$$

This will mean that the business will have to order bags of cement four times each year so that sales demand can be met.

Note that the cost of the stock concerned, that is the price paid to the supplier, does not directly impact on the EOQ model. The EOQ model is only concerned with the administrative costs of placing each order and the costs of looking after the stock. Where the business operates an ABC system of stock control, however, more expensive stock items will have greater stock holding costs. So the cost of the stock may have an indirect effect on the economic order size that the model recommends.

The basic EOQ model has a number of limiting assumptions. In particular, it assumes that:

● demand for the product can be predicted with accuracy;
● demand is constant over the period and does not fluctuate through seasonality or for other reasons;
● no 'buffer' stock is required; and
● there are no discounts for bulk purchasing.

However, the model can be developed to accommodate the problems of each of these limiting assumptions. Many businesses use this model (or a development of it) to help in the management of stocks.

Materials requirement planning systems

 A **materials requirement planning (MRP) system** takes planned sales demand as its starting point. It then uses a computer package to help schedule the timing of deliveries of bought-in parts and materials to coincide with production requirements. It is a co-ordinated approach that links materials and parts deliveries to the scheduled time of their input to the production process. By ordering only those items that are necessary to ensure the flow of production, stock levels are likely to be reduced. MRP is really a 'top-down' approach to stock management, which recognises that stock ordering decisions cannot be viewed as being independent from production decisions. In recent years, this approach has been extended so as to provide a fully integrated approach to production planning. The approach also takes account of other manufacturing resources such as labour and machine capacity.

Just-in-time stock (inventory) management

In recent years, many businesses have tried to eliminate the need to hold stocks by adopting **'just-in-time' (JIT) stock management**. This approach was first used in the US defence industry during World War II, but in more recent times it has been widely used. It was first used on a wide scale commercially by Japanese manufacturing businesses. The essence of JIT is, as the name suggests, to have supplies delivered to a business just in time for them to be used in the production process or in a sale. By adopting this approach the stockholding costs rest with suppliers rather than with the business itself. On the other hand, a failure by a particular supplier to deliver on time could cause enormous problems and costs to the business. Thus JIT can save cost, but it tends to increase risk.

For JIT to be successful, it is important that the business informs suppliers of its stock requirements in advance, and that suppliers, in their turn, deliver materials of the right quality at the agreed times. Failure to do so could lead to a dislocation of production or supply to customers and could be very costly. Thus a close relationship is required between the business and its suppliers.

Though a business that applies JIT will not have to hold stocks, there may be other costs associated with this approach. As the suppliers will be required to hold stocks for the business, they may try to recoup this additional cost through increased prices. The close relationship necessary between the business and its suppliers may also prevent the business from taking advantage of cheaper sources of supply if they become available.

Many people view JIT as more than simply a stock control system. The philosophy underpinning this approach is concerned with eliminating waste and striving for excellence. There is an expectation that suppliers will always deliver stock on time and that there will be no defects in the items supplied. There is also an expectation that, for manufacturers, the production process will operate at maximum efficiency. This means there will be no production breakdowns and the queuing and storage times of products manufactured will be eliminated, as only that time spent directly on processing the products is seen as adding value. (We should recall value chain analysis in Chapter 11.) While these expectations may be impossible to achieve, they do help to create a culture that is dedicated to the pursuit of excellence and quality.

Real Worlds 16.5 and **16.6** show how two very well-known businesses operating in the UK (one a retailer, the other a manufacturer) use JIT to advantage.

REAL WORLD 16.5

JIT at Boots

The Boots Company plc, the UK's largest health-care retailer, has recently improved the stock management at its stores. The business is working towards a JIT system where a stock delivery from its one central warehouse in Nottingham will be made every day to each retail branch, with nearly all of the stock lines being placed directly onto the sales shelves, not into a branch stock room. The business says that this will bring significant savings of stores staff time and lead to significantly lower levels of stock being held, without any lessening of the service offered to customers. The new system is expected to lead to major economic benefits for the business.

Source: Information taken from The Boots Company plc annual report and accounts for 2003.

REAL WORLD 16.6

JIT at Nissan

Nissan Motors UK Limited, the UK manufacturing arm of the world famous Japanese car business, has a plant in Sunderland in the north east of England. Here it operates a well-developed JIT system. Sommer supplies carpets and soft interior trim from a factory close to the Nissan plant. It makes deliveries to Nissan once every 20 minutes on average, so as to arrive exactly as they are needed in production. This is fairly typical of all of the 200 suppliers of components and materials to the Nissan plant.

Source: Information taken from Partnership Sourcing Best Practice Case Study (www.pslcbi.com/studies/docnissan.hmt).

Managing debtors (receivables)

Selling goods or services on credit results in costs being incurred by a business. These costs include credit administration costs, bad debts, and opportunities forgone in using the funds for more profitable purposes. However, these costs must be weighed against the benefits of increased sales resulting from the opportunity for customers to delay payment.

Selling on credit is very widespread, and appears to be the norm outside the retail trade. When a business offers to sell its goods or services on credit, it must have clear policies concerning:

● which customers it is prepared to offer credit to;
● what length of credit it is prepared to offer;
● whether discounts will be offered for prompt payment; and
● what collection policies should be adopted.

In this section, we shall consider each of these issues.

Which customers should receive credit?

A business offering credit runs the risk of not receiving payment for goods or services supplied. Thus, care must be taken over the type of customer to whom credit facilities are offered. When considering a proposal from a customer for the supply of goods or services on credit, the business must take a number of factors into account. The following **five Cs of credit** provide a business with a useful checklist.

- *Capital.* The customer must appear to be financially sound before any credit is extended. Where the customer is a business, its financial statements should be examined. Particular regard should be given to the customer's likely future profitability and liquidity.

- *Capacity.* The customer must appear to have the capacity to pay amounts owing. Where possible, the payment record of the customer to date should be examined. If the customer is a business, the type of business operated and the physical resources of the business will be relevant. The value of goods that the customer wishes to buy on credit must be related to the customer's total financial resources.

- *Collateral.* On occasions, it may be necessary to ask for some kind of security for goods supplied on credit. When this occurs, the business must be convinced that the customer is able to offer a satisfactory form of security.

- *Conditions.* The state of the industry in which the customer operates, and the general economic conditions of the particular region or country, may have an important influence on the ability of a customer to pay the amounts outstanding on the due date.

- *Character.* It is important for a business to make some assessment of the customer's character. The willingness to pay will depend on the honesty and integrity of the individual with whom the business is dealing. Where the customer is a limited company this will mean assessing the characters of its directors. The business must feel satisfied that the customer will make every effort to pay any amounts owing.

Once a customer has been considered creditworthy, credit limits for the customer should be established, and procedures should be laid down to ensure that these are adhered to.

ACTIVITY 16.5

Assume that you are the credit manager of a business and that a limited company approaches you with a view to buying goods on credit. What sources of information might you decide to use to help assess the financial health of the potential customer?

There are various possibilities. You may have thought of some of the following:

- *Trade references.* Some businesses ask potential customers to supply them with references from other suppliers who have made sales on credit to them. This may be extremely useful, provided that the references supplied are truly representative of the opinions of a customer's suppliers. There is a danger that a potential customer will attempt to be selective when giving details of other suppliers, in order to gain a more favourable impression than is deserved.

- *Bank references.* It is possible to ask the potential customer for a bank reference. Though banks are usually prepared to supply references, the contents of such references are not always very informative. If customers are in financial difficulties, the bank may be unwilling to add to their problems by supplying poor references.

- *Published financial statements*. A limited company is obliged by law to file a copy of its annual financial statements with the Registrar of Companies. These financial statements are available for public inspection and provide a useful source of information.
- *The customer*. You may wish to interview the directors of the customer business and visit its premises in an attempt to gain some impression about the way that the customer conducts its business. Where a significant amount of credit is required, the business may ask the customer for access to internal budgets and other unpublished financial information to help assess the level of risk involved.
- *Credit agencies*. Specialist agencies exist to provide information that can be used to assess the creditworthiness of a potential customer. The information that a credit agency supplies may be gleaned from various sources, including the financial statements of the customer, court judgments and news items relating to the customer from both published and unpublished sources.

Length of credit period

A business must determine what credit terms it is prepared to offer its customers. The length of credit offered to customers can vary significantly between businesses, and may be influenced by such factors as:

- the typical credit terms operating within the industry;
- the degree of competition within the industry;
- the bargaining power of particular customers;
- the risk of non-payment;
- the capacity of the business to offer credit; and
- the marketing strategy of the business.

The last point identified may require some explanation. The marketing strategy of a business may have an important influence on the length of credit allowed. For example, if a business wishes to increase its market share it may decide to be more generous in its credit policy in an attempt to stimulate sales. Potential customers may be attracted by the offer of a longer credit period. However, any such change in policy must take account of the likely costs and benefits arising.

To illustrate this point, consider Example 16.2.

Example 16.2

Torrance Ltd produces a new type of golf putter. The business sells the putter to wholesalers and retailers and has an annual turnover of £600,000. The following data relate to each putter produced.

	£	£
Selling price		40
Variable costs	20	
Fixed cost apportionment	6	26
Net profit		14

The business's cost of capital is estimated at 10 per cent a year.

Torrance Ltd wishes to expand the sales volume of the new putter. It believes that offering a longer credit period can achieve this. The business's average collection

→

period is currently 30 days. It is considering three options in an attempt to increase sales revenue. These are as follows:

	Option		
	1	*2*	*3*
Increase in average collection period (days)	10	20	30
Increase in sales revenue (£)	30,000	45,000	50,000

To enable the business to decide on the best option to adopt, it must weigh the benefits of the options against their respective costs. The benefits arising will be represented by the increase in profit from the sale of additional putters. From the cost data supplied we can see that the contribution (that is, selling price (£40) less variable costs (£20)) is £20 a putter, that is, 50 per cent of the selling price. So, whatever increase there may be in sales revenue, the additional contributions will be half of that figure. The fixed costs can be ignored in our calculations, as they will remain the same whichever option is chosen.

The increase in contribution under each option will therefore be:

	Option		
	1	*2*	*3*
50% of the increase in sales revenue (£)	15,000	22,500	25,000

The increase in debtors under each option will be as follows:

	Option		
	1	*2*	*3*
Projected level of debtors	£	£	£
40 × £630,000/365 (Note 1)	69,041		
50 × £645,000/365		88,356	
60 × £650,000/365			106,849
Less Current level of debtors			
30 × £600,000/365	49,315	49,315	49,315
Increase in debtors	19,726	39,041	57,534

The increase in debtors that results from each option will mean an additional finance cost to the business.

The net increase in the business's profit arising from the projected change is:

	Option		
	1	*2*	*3*
	£	£	£
Increase in contribution (see above)	15,000	22,500	25,000
Less Increase in finance cost (Note 2)	1,973	3,904	5,753
Net increase in profits	13,027	18,596	19,247

The calculations show that Option 3 will be the most profitable one.

Notes:
1 If the annual sales revenue total £630,000 and 40 days' credit are allowed (both of which will apply under Option 1), the average amount that will be owed to the business by its customers, at any point during the year, will be the daily sales revenue (that is, £630,000/365) multiplied by the number of days that the customers take to pay (that is, 40).

   Exactly the same logic applies to Options 2 and 3 and to the current level of debtors.
2 The increase in the finance cost for Option 1 will be the increase in debtors (£19,726 × 10%). The equivalent figures for the other options are derived in a similar way.

Example 16.2 illustrates the way in which a business should assess changes in credit terms. However, if there is a risk that, by extending the length of credit, there will be an increase in bad debts, this should also be taken into account in the calculations, as should any additional collection costs that will be incurred.

Real World 16.7 provides some insight to the typical length of credit taken by UK businesses.

REAL WORLD 16.7

Length of credit taken by UK businesses

In their annual reports, UK limited companies are legally obliged to disclose the average length of trade credit that they take from their suppliers. For a random sample of 21 listed UK businesses, the following applied:

Shortest period taken by any business	9 days
Longest period taken by any business	60 days
Mean (simple average) period for all of the businesses	33 days
Median (middle ranking) period of all of the businesses	32 days

Source: Information taken from the 2002 and 2003 annual reports of a random sample of UK Stock Exchange listed businesses.

Cash discounts

A business may decide to offer a **cash discount** in an attempt to encourage prompt payment from its credit customers. The size of any discount will be an important influence on whether a customer decides to pay promptly.

From the business's viewpoint, the cost of offering discounts must be weighed against the likely benefits in the form of a reduction both in the cost of financing debtors and in the amount of bad debts.

In practice, there is always the danger that a customer may be slow to pay and yet may still take the discount offered. Where the customer is important to the business it may be difficult to insist on full payment.

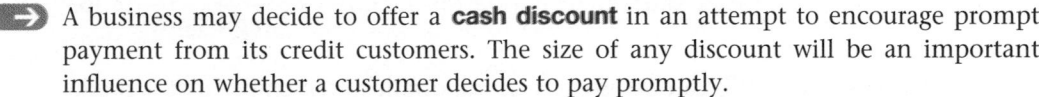

SELF-ASSESSMENT QUESTION 16.1

Williams Wholesalers Ltd at present requires payment from its customers by the end of the month after the month of delivery. On average, customers take 70 days to pay. Sales revenue amounts to £4m a year and bad debts to £20,000 a year.

It is planned to offer customers a cash discount of 2 per cent for payment within 30 days. Williams estimates that 50 per cent of customers will accept this facility but that the remaining customers, who tend to be slow payers, will not pay until 80 days after the sale. At present the business has an overdraft facility at an interest rate of 13 per cent a year. If the plan goes ahead, bad debts will be reduced to £10,000 a year and there will be savings in credit administration expenses of £6,000 a year.

Should Williams Wholesalers Ltd offer the new credit terms to customers? You should support your answer with any calculations and explanations that you consider necessary.

Debt factoring and invoice discounting

We saw on page 542 in Chapter 15 that trade debts can, in effect, be turned into cash by either factoring them or having sales invoices discounted. These both seem to be fairly popular approaches to managing trade debtors.

Collection policies

A business offering credit must ensure that amounts owing are collected as quickly as possible. An efficient collection policy requires an efficient accounting system. Invoices (bills) must be sent out promptly to customers, as must regular monthly statements. Reminders must also be despatched promptly to customers who are late in paying.

It is almost inevitably the case that a business making significant sales on credit will sometimes be faced with customers who do not pay. When this occurs, there should be agreed procedures for dealing with the situation. However, the cost of any action to be taken against delinquent debtors must be weighed against the likely returns. For example, there is little point in taking legal action against a customer, incurring large legal expenses, if there is evidence that the customer does not have the necessary resources to pay. Where possible, an estimate of the cost of bad debts should be taken into account when setting prices for products or services.

Management can monitor the effectiveness of collection policies in a number of ways. One method is to calculate the **average settlement period for debtors** ratio, which we dealt with in Chapter 7. This ratio, we should recall, is calculated as follows:

$$\text{Average settlement period for debtors} = \frac{\text{Trade debtors}}{\text{Credit sales}} \times 365$$

Though this ratio can be useful, it is important to remember that it produces an *average* figure for the number of days for which debts are outstanding. This average may be badly distorted by a few large customers who are very slow or very fast payers.

A more detailed and informative approach to monitoring debtors may be to produce an **ageing schedule of debtors**. Debts are divided into categories according to the length of time the debt has been outstanding. An ageing schedule can be produced, on a regular basis, to help managers see the pattern of outstanding debts. An example of an ageing schedule is set out in Example 16.3.

Example 16.3

Ageing schedule of debtors at 31 December

Customer	Days outstanding				Total
	1 to 30 days	31 to 60 days	61 to 90 days	More than 90 days	
	£	£	£	£	£
A Ltd	20,000	10,000	–	–	30,000
B Ltd	–	24,000	–	–	24,000
C Ltd	12,000	13,000	14,000	18,000	57,000
Total	32,000	47,000	14,000	18,000	111,000

This shows a business's trade debtor figure at 31 December, which totals £111,000. Each customer's balance is analysed according to how long the debt has been outstanding.

Thus we can see from the schedule that A Ltd has £20,000 outstanding for 30 days or less (that is, arising from sales during December) and £10,000 outstanding for between 31 and 60 days (arising from November sales). This information can be very useful for credit control purposes.

Many accounting software packages now include this ageing schedule as one of the routine reports available to managers. Such packages often have the facility to put customers on 'hold' when they reach their credit limits. Putting a customer 'on hold' means that no further credit sales will be made to that customer, until debts arising from past sales have been settled.

ACTIVITY 16.6

What kind of corrective action might the managers of a business decide to take if they find that debtors are paying more slowly than anticipated?

Managers might decide to do one or more of the following:

- offer cash discounts to encourage prompt payment;
- inform customers that debts are to be paid more promptly;
- improve the accounting system to ensure that customers are billed more promptly, reminders are sent out promptly and so on; and
- change the eligibility criteria for customers who receive credit.

As a footnote to our consideration of managing debtors, **Real World 16.8** outlines some of the excuses that long-suffering credit managers must listen to when chasing payment for outstanding debt.

REAL WORLD 16.8

It's in the post

Accountants' noses should be growing, if we're to believe a new survey listing the bizarre excuses given by businesses that fail to pay their debts.

'The director's been shot' and 'I'll pay you when God tells me to' are just two of the most outrageous excuses listed in a survey published by the Credit Services Association, the debt collection industry body.

The commercial sector tends to blame financial problems, and excuses such as 'you'll get paid when we do' and 'the finance director is off sick' are common. However, those in the consumer sector apparently feel no shame in citing personal relationship problems as the reason for not paying the bill.

Source: Accountancy, April 2000, p. 18.

Managing cash

Why hold cash?

Most businesses hold a certain amount of cash. The amount of cash held tends to vary considerably between businesses.

ACTIVITY 16.7

Why do you think a business may decide to hold at least some of its assets in the form of cash? (*Hint*: There are broadly three reasons.)

They are:

1 To meet day-to-day commitments, a business requires a certain amount of cash. Payments for wages, overhead expenses, goods purchased and so on must be made at the due dates.

2 If future cash flows are uncertain for any reason, it would be prudent to hold a balance of cash. For example, a major customer that owes a large sum to the business may be in financial difficulties. Given this situation, the business can retain its capacity to meet its obligations by holding a cash balance. Similarly, if there is some uncertainty concerning future outlays, a cash balance will be required.

3 A business may decide to hold cash to put itself in a position to exploit profitable opportunities as and when they arise. For example, by holding cash, a business may be able to acquire a competitor business that suddenly becomes available at an attractive price.

How much cash should be held?

Though cash can be held for each of the reasons identified, this may not always be necessary. If a business is able to borrow quickly, the amount of cash it needs to hold can be reduced. Similarly, if the business holds assets that can easily be converted to cash (for example, marketable securities such as shares in Stock Exchange listed businesses or government bonds), the amount of cash held can be reduced.

The decision as to how much cash a particular business should hold is a difficult one. Different businesses will have different views on the subject.

ACTIVITY 16.8

What do you think are the major factors that influence how much cash a business will hold? See if you can think of five possible factors.

You may have thought of the following:

- *The nature of the business*. Some businesses such as utilities (for example, water, electricity and gas suppliers) may have cash flows that are both predictable and reasonably certain. This will enable them to hold lower cash balances. For some businesses, cash balances may vary greatly according to the time of year. A seasonal business may accumulate cash during the high season to enable it to meet commitments during the low season.
- *The opportunity cost of holding cash*. Where there are profitable opportunities it may not be wise to hold a large cash balance.
- *The level of inflation*. Holding cash during a period of rising prices will lead to a loss of purchasing power. The higher the level of inflation, the greater will be this loss.
- *The availability of near-liquid assets*. If a business has marketable securities or stocks that may easily be liquidated, the amount of cash held may be reduced.
- *The availability of borrowing*. If a business can borrow easily (and quickly) there is less need to hold cash.
- *The cost of borrowing*. When interest rates are high, the option of borrowing becomes less attractive.
- *Economic conditions*. When the economy is in recession, businesses may prefer to hold cash so that they can be well placed to invest when the economy improves. In addition, during a recession, businesses may experience difficulties in collecting debts. They may therefore hold higher cash balances than usual in order to meet commitments.
- *Relationships with suppliers*. Too little cash may hinder the ability of the business to pay suppliers promptly. This can lead to a loss of goodwill. It may also lead to discounts being forgone.

Controlling the cash balance

Several models have been developed to help control the cash balance of the business. One such model proposes the use of upper and lower control limits for cash balances and the use of a target cash balance. The model assumes that the business will invest in marketable investments that can easily be liquidated. These investments will be purchased or sold, as necessary, in order to keep the cash balance within the control limits.

The model proposes two upper and two lower control limits (see Figure 16.5). If the business exceeds an *outer* limit, the managers must decide whether or not the cash balance is likely to return to a point within the *inner* control limits set, over the next few days. If this seems likely, then no action is required. If, on the other hand, it does not seem likely, management must change the cash position of the business by either lending or borrowing (or possibly by buying or selling marketable securities).

In Figure 16.5 we can see that the lower outer control limit has been breached for four days. If a four-day period is unacceptable, managers must sell marketable securities to replenish the cash balance.

The model relies heavily on management judgement to determine where the control limits are set and the time period within which breaches of the control limits are acceptable. Past experience may be useful in helping managers decide on these issues. There are other models, however, that do not rely on management judgement. Instead, these use quantitative techniques to determine an optimal cash policy.

| Figure 16.5 | Controlling the cash balance |

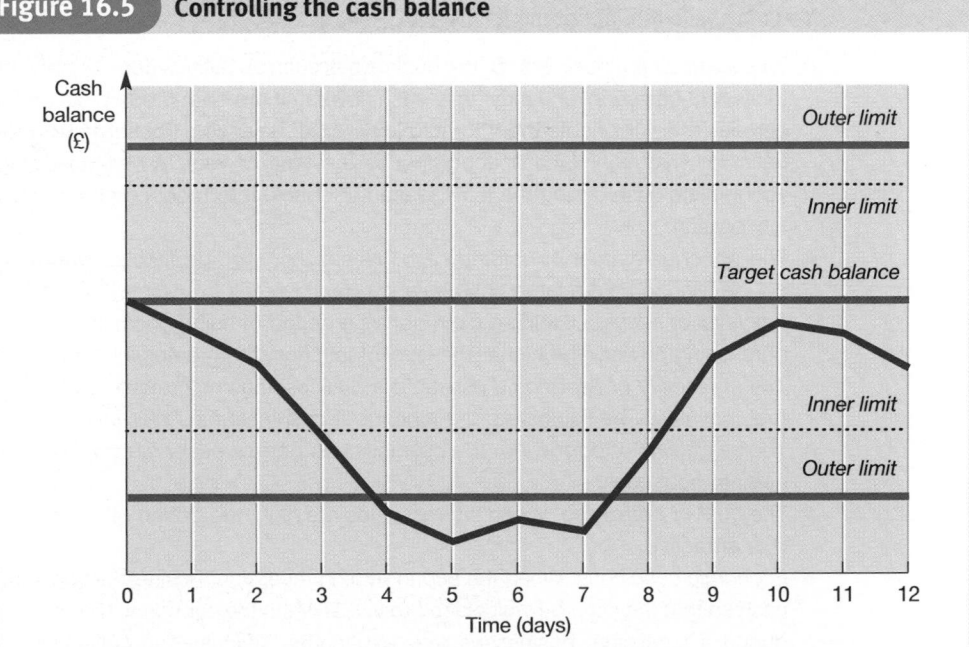

Management sets the upper and lower limits for the business's cash balance. When the balance goes beyond either of these limits, unless it is clear that the balance will return fairly quickly to within the limit, action will need to be taken. If the upper limit is breached, some cash will be placed on deposit or used to buy some marketable securities. If the lower limit is breached, the business will need to borrow some cash or sell some securities.

Cash budgets and managing cash

To manage cash effectively, it is useful for a business to prepare a cash budget. This is a very important tool for both planning and control purposes. Cash budgets were considered in Chapter 12, and so we shall not consider them again in detail. However, it is worth repeating the point that these statements enable managers to see the expected outcome of planned events on the cash balance. The cash budget will identify periods when cash surpluses and cash deficits are expected.

When a cash surplus is expected to arise, managers must decide on the best use of the surplus funds. When a cash deficit is expected, managers must make adequate provision by borrowing, liquidating assets or rescheduling cash payments or receipts to deal with this. Cash budgets are useful in helping to control the cash held. The actual cash flows can be compared with the budgeted cash flows for the period. If there is a significant divergence between the budgeted cash flows and the actual cash flows, explanations must be sought and corrective action taken where necessary.

It would probably be helpful to look back at Chapter 12, p. 407 to refresh your memory on cash budgets.

Though cash budgets are prepared primarily for internal management purposes, prospective lenders sometimes require them when a loan to a business is being considered.

Operating cash cycle

·······························

When managing cash, it is important to be aware of the **operating cash cycle (OCC)** of the business. For a retailer, for example, this may be defined as the time period between the outlay of cash necessary for the purchase of stocks and the ultimate receipt of cash from the sale of the goods. In the case of a business, for example a wholesaler, that purchases goods on credit for subsequent resale on credit, the OCC is as shown in Figure 16.6.

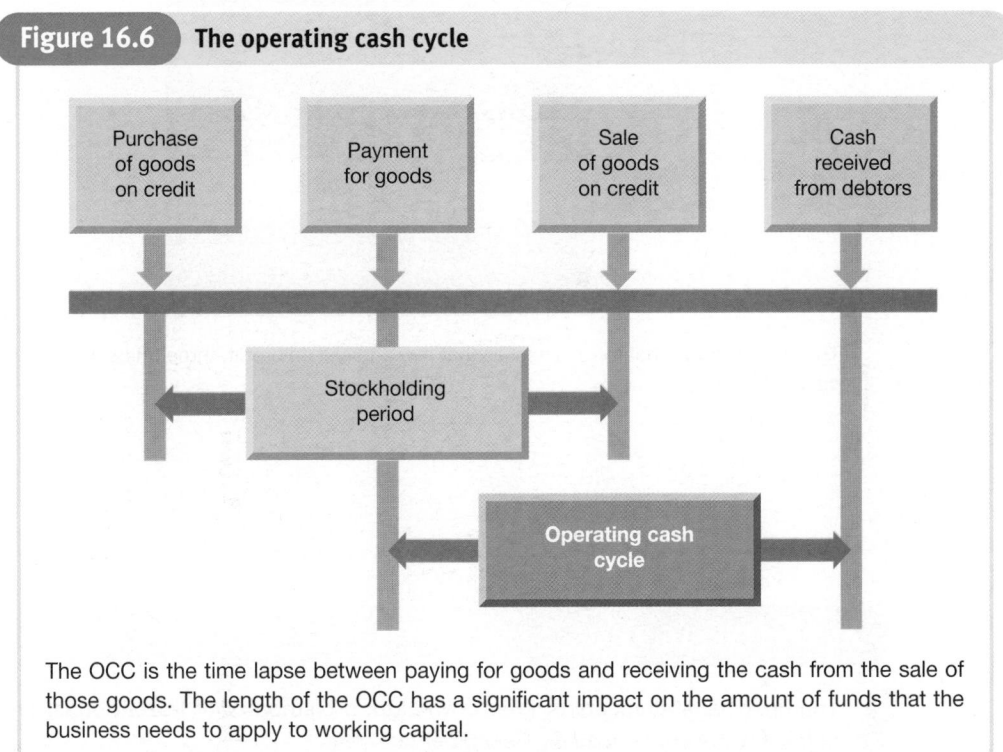

Figure 16.6   **The operating cash cycle**

The OCC is the time lapse between paying for goods and receiving the cash from the sale of those goods. The length of the OCC has a significant impact on the amount of funds that the business needs to apply to working capital.

Figure 16.6 shows that payment for goods acquired on credit occurs some time after the goods have been purchased, and therefore no immediate cash outflow arises from the purchase. Similarly, cash receipts from debtors will occur some time after the sale is made, and so there will be no immediate cash inflow as a result of the sale. The OCC is the time period between the payment made to the creditor for goods supplied and the cash received from the debtor. Though Figure 16.6 depicts the position for a retailing or wholesaling business, the precise definition of the OCC can easily be adapted for both service and manufacturing businesses.

The OCC is important because it has a significant influence on the financing requirements of the business: the longer the cycle, the greater the financing requirements of the business and the greater the financial risks. For this reason, a business is likely to want to reduce the OCC to the minimum possible period.

For the type of business mentioned above, which buys and sells on credit, the OCC can be calculated from the financial statements by the use of certain ratios. It is calculated as shown in Figure 16.7 on p. 582 (see also Activity 16.9).

| Figure 16.7 | Calculating the operating cash cycle |

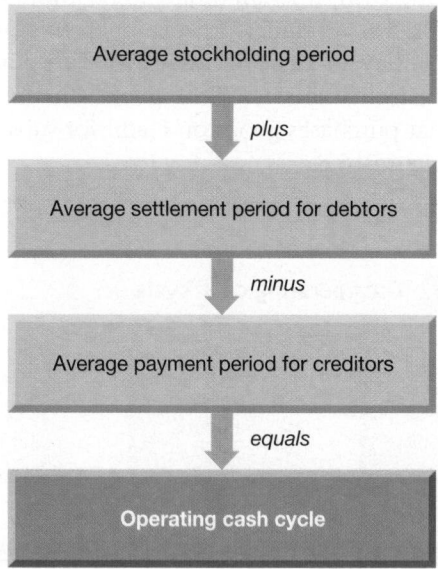

This figure shows that for businesses that buy and sell on credit, three ratios are required to calculate the OCC.

ACTIVITY 16.9

The financial statements of Freezeqwik Ltd, a distributor of frozen foods, are set out below for the year ended 31 December last year.

Profit and loss account (income statement) for the year ended 31 December last year

	£000	£000
Sales revenue		820
Less Cost of sales		
Opening stock	142	
Purchases	568	
	710	
Less Closing stock	166	544
Gross profit		276
Administration expenses	(120)	
Selling and distribution expenses	(95)	
Financial expenses	(32)	(247)
Net profit		29
Corporation tax		(7)
Net profit after tax		22

Balance sheet as at 31 December last year

Non-current assets	£000	£000	£000
Property, plant and equipment			
Freehold premises at valuation			180
Fixtures and fittings at written-down value			82
Motor vans at written-down value			102
			364
Current assets			
Stock		166	
Trade debtors		264	
Cash		24	
		454	
Less **Current liabilities**			
Trade creditors	159		
Corporation tax	7	166	288
			652
Equity			
Ordinary share capital			300
Preference share capital			200
Retained profit			152
			652

All purchases and sales are on credit.

Calculate the length of the OCC for the business and go on to suggest how the business may seek to reduce this period.

....

The OCC may be calculated as follows:

	No. of days
Average stockholding period:	

$$\frac{\text{(Opening stock + Closing stock)}/2}{\text{Cost of sales}} \times 365 = \frac{(142 + 166)/2}{544} \times 365 \qquad\qquad 103$$

Average settlement period for debtors:

$$\frac{\text{Trade debtors}}{\text{Credit sales}} \times 365 = \frac{264}{820} \times 365 \qquad\qquad\qquad 118$$

$$221$$

Less
Average settlement period for creditors:

$$\frac{\text{Trade creditors}}{\text{Credit purchases}} \times 365 = \frac{159}{568} \times 365 \qquad\qquad\qquad 102$$

OCC   119

The business can reduce the length of the OCC in a number of ways. The average stockholding period seems quite long. At present, average stocks held represent more than three months' sales. Lowering the level of stocks held will reduce this. Similarly, the average settlement period for debtors seems long, at nearly four months' sales. Imposing tighter credit control, offering discounts, charging interest on overdue accounts and so on, may reduce this. However, any policy decisions concerning stocks and debtors must take account of current trading conditions.

Extending the period of credit taken to pay suppliers could also reduce the OCC. However, for reasons that will be explained later, this option must be given careful consideration.

Cash transmission

A business will normally wish to benefit from receipts from customers at the earliest opportunity. The benefit is immediate where payment is made in cash. However, when payment is made by cheque, there is normally a delay of three to four working days before the cheque can be cleared through the banking system. The business must therefore wait for this period before it can benefit from the amount paid in. In the case of a business that receives large amounts in the form of cheques, the opportunity cost of this delay can be very significant.

To avoid this, a business could require payments to be made in cash. This is not usually very practical, mainly because of the risk of theft and/or the expense of conveying cash securely. Another option is to ask for payment to be made by standing order or by direct debit from the customer's bank account. This should ensure that the amount owing is always transferred from the bank account of the customer to the bank account of the business on the day that has been agreed.

It is also possible for funds to be transferred directly to a business's bank account. As a result of developments in computer technology, customers can pay for items by using debit cards, which results in the appropriate account being instantly debited and seller's bank account being instantly credited with the required amount. This method of payment is widely used by large retail businesses, and may well extend to other types of business.

Bank overdrafts

Bank overdrafts are simply bank current accounts that contain a negative amount of cash. They are a type of bank loan. We looked at these in Chapter 15, p. 542, in the context of short-term bank lending. They can be a useful tool in managing the business's cash flow requirements.

Managing trade creditors (payables)

Trade credit arises from the fact that most businesses buy their goods and service requirements on credit. In effect, suppliers are lending the business money, interest free, on a short-term basis. Trade creditors are the other side of the coin from trade debtors. One business's trade creditor is another one's trade debtor, in respect of a particular transaction. Trade creditors are an important source of finance for most businesses. It has been described as a 'spontaneous' source, as it tends to increase in line with the increase in the level of activity achieved by a business. Trade credit is widely regarded as a 'free' source of finance and, therefore, a good thing for a business to use. There may be real costs associated with taking trade credit, however.

Firstly, customers who take credit may not be as well treated as those who pay immediately. For example, when goods are in short supply, credit customers may receive lower priority when allocating the stock available. In addition, credit customers may be less favoured in terms of delivery dates or the provision of technical support services. Sometimes, the goods or services provided may be more costly if credit is required. However, in most industries trade credit is the norm. As a result, the above costs will not apply except, perhaps, to customers that abuse the credit facilities. A business purchasing supplies on credit may also have to incur additional administration and accounting costs in dealing with the scrutiny and payment of invoices, maintaining and updating creditors' accounts and so on.

REAL WORLD 16.9

Can't pay; won't pay

In some cases, delaying payment to creditors can be a sign of impending financial failure. One such example occurred in 2001 when Kmart, a large US retailer, suffered a cash crisis. This was largely as a result of one manager ordering $850m worth of stocks, which was later described in an internal report as 'excessive'. To conserve cash, the business implemented Project Slow It Down. This involved systematically delaying or reducing payments to trade creditors. The project also involved denying creditors access to records of the amounts owed by Kmart and giving false reasons as to why they had not been paid on time.

Source: Information taken from 'Kmart's fall is tale of poor governance', *Financial Times*, 29 January 2003.

Where a supplier offers a discount for prompt payment, the business should give careful consideration to the possibility of paying within the discount period. Example 16.4 illustrates the cost of forgoing possible discounts.

Example 16.4

Hassan Ltd takes 70 days to pay for goods from its supplier. To encourage prompt payment, the supplier has offered the business a 2 per cent discount if payment for goods is made within 30 days.

Hassan Ltd is not sure whether it is worth taking the discount offered.

If the discount is taken, payment could be made on the last day of the discount period (that is, the 30th day). However, if the discount is not taken, payment will be made after 70 days. This means that by not taking the discount the business will receive an extra 40 days' (that is, 70 minus 30) credit. The cost of this extra credit to the business will be the 2 per cent discount forgone. If we annualise the cost of this discount forgone, we have:

$$365/40 \times 2\% = 18.3\%*$$

We can see that the annual cost of forgoing the discount is very high, and it may be profitable for the business to pay the supplier within the discount period, even if it means that it will have to borrow to enable it to do so.

* This is an approximate annual rate. For the more mathematically minded, the precise rate is:

$$(((1 + 2/98)^{9.125}) - 1) \times 100\% = 20.2\%$$

The above points are not meant to imply that taking credit is a burden to a business. There are of course real benefits that can accrue. Provided that trade credit is not abused, it can represent a form of interest-free loan. It can be a much more convenient method of paying for goods and services than paying by cash, and during a period of inflation there will be an economic gain by paying later rather than sooner for goods and services purchased. For most businesses, these benefits will exceed the costs involved.

Controlling trade creditors (payables)

➜ To help monitor the level of trade credit taken, management can calculate the **average settlement period for creditors**. As we saw in Chapter 7, this ratio was as follows:

$$\text{Average settlement period} = \frac{\text{Trade creditors}}{\text{Credit purchases}} \times 365$$

Once again this provides an average figure, which could be misleading. A more informative approach would be to produce an ageing schedule for creditors. This would look much the same as the ageing schedule for debtors described earlier.

Since, as was pointed out earlier in this section, one business's trade creditor is another one's trade debtor, the information contained in **Real World 16.7** (p. 575) provides some indication of typical lengths of trade credit taken by UK businesses.

Working capital problems of the small business

We saw earlier (**Real World 16.1**, p. 562) that the amounts invested by businesses in working capital are often high in proportion to the total assets employed. It is, therefore, important that these amounts are properly managed. Although this point applies to businesses of all sizes, it may be of particular importance to small businesses. It is often claimed that many small businesses suffer from a lack of capital and, where this is the case, tight control over working capital investment becomes critical. There is evidence, however, that small businesses are not very good at managing their working capital and this has been cited as a major cause of their high failure rate compared with that of large businesses. In this section, we consider the working capital management problems associated with small businesses.

Credit management

Small businesses often lack the resources to manage their trade debtors (receivables) effectively. It is not unusual for a small business to operate without a separate credit control department. This tends to mean that both the expertise and the information required to make sound judgements concerning terms of sale and so on may not be available. A small business may also lack proper debt collection procedures, such as prompt invoicing and sending out regular statements. This will increase the risks of late payment and defaulting debtors.

These risks probably tend to increase where there is an excessive concern for growth. In an attempt to increase sales, small businesses may be too willing to extend credit to customers that are poor credit risks. Whilst this kind of problem can occur in businesses of all sizes, small businesses seem particularly susceptible.

Another problem faced by small businesses is their lack of market power. They will often find themselves in a weak position when negotiating credit terms with larger businesses. Moreover, when a large customer exceeds the terms of credit, the small supplier may feel inhibited from pressing the customer for payment in case future sales are lost.

It seems that small businesses have a much greater proportion of overdue debts than large businesses. **Real World 16.10** refers to evidence of this.

REAL WORLD 16.10

Small businesses wait longer

A survey undertaken by the Credit Management Research Centre (CMRC) during April and June 2003, indicates that small businesses (that is, those with annual sales turnover of less than £5m) are likely to have to wait an average of 60 days for their trade debtors to pay. This contrasts with the average of 32 to 33 days for the large businesses mentioned earlier (see Real World 16.7).

Source: Information taken from 'Small firms still have to wait for their money' by Doug Morrison, *Sunday Telegraph*, 14 September 2003. The article discussed the CMRC research.

The reason for the delay suffered by small businesses probably relates to one of the factors mentioned above, namely the bargaining power of customers. The customers of small businesses may well be larger ones, which can use a threat, perhaps implied, of withdrawing custom, to force small businesses to accept later trade debtor settlement.

In the UK, the government has intervened to help deal with this problem and the law now permits small businesses to charge interest on overdue accounts. In addition, large companies are now required to disclose the payment policy adopted towards suppliers in their published financial statements in the hope that this will improve the behaviour of those that delay payments. However, it is unlikely that legislation alone will make a significant improvement. Whilst small businesses may be able to charge interest on overdue accounts, they will often avoid doing so because they fear thatlarge customers would view this as a provocative act. What is really needed to help small businesses is a change in the payment culture.

We saw in Chapter 15 that one way of dealing with the credit management problem is to factor the outstanding debts. Under this kind of arrangement, the factor will take over the sales records of the business and will take responsibility for the prompt collection of debts. However, some businesses are too small to take advantage of this facility. The set-up costs of a factoring arrangement often make businesses with a small turnover (say, £100,000 a year or less) an uneconomic proposition for the factor.

Managing stock (inventory)

A lack of financial management skills within a small business often creates problems in managing stock in an efficient and effective way. The owners of small businesses are not always aware that there are costs involved in holding too much stock and that there are also costs involved in holding too little. These costs, which were discussed earlier, may be very high in certain industries such as manufacturing and wholesaling, where stock accounts for a significant proportion of the total assets held.

It was mentioned earlier in the chapter that the starting point for an effective stock management system is good planning and budgeting systems (see p. 564). In particular, there should be reliable sales forecasts, or budgets, available for stock ordering purposes. However, it seems that not all small businesses prepare these forecasts or budgets. A survey by Chittenden *et al.* (see reference 1 at the end of the chapter) of small and medium-sized businesses indicated that only 78 per cent of those replying prepare a sales budget. Stock management can also benefit from good reporting systems and the application of quantitative techniques (for example, the economic order quantity model) to try to optimise stock levels. However, the same survey found that more than one-third of small businesses rely on manual methods of stock control and the majority do not use stock optimisation techniques.

Managing cash

The management of cash raises similar issues to those relating to the management of stocks. There are costs involved in holding both too much and too little cash. Thus, there is a need for careful planning and monitoring of cash flows over time. The Chittenden survey found, however, that only 63 per cent of those replying prepared a cash budget. It was also found that cash balances are generally proportionately higher for smaller businesses than for larger ones. More than half of those in the survey held surplus cash balances on a regular basis (see reference 1 at the end of the chapter). Though this may reflect a more conservative approach to liquidity among the owners of smaller businesses, it may suggest a failure to recognise the opportunity costs of cash balances.

Managing credit suppliers

In practice, small businesses often try to cope with the late payment of credit customers by delaying payments to their credit suppliers. We saw earlier in the chapter, however, that this can be an expensive option. Where discounts are forgone, the annual cost of this financing option compares unfavourably with most other forms of short-term financing. Nevertheless, the vast majority of small and medium-sized businesses are unaware of the very high cost of delaying payment, according to the Chittenden survey (see reference 1 at the end of the chapter).

SUMMARY

The main points of this chapter may be summarised as follows:

Working capital (WC) = stock + debtors + cash − creditors − bank overdrafts

● An investment in WC cannot be avoided in practice – typically large amounts are involved.

Stock-in-trade (inventories)

● Costs of holding stock include:
  – Lost interest.
  – Storage cost.
  – Insurance cost.
  – Obsolescence.
● Costs of not holding sufficient stock include:
  – Loss of sales and customer goodwill.
  – Production dislocation.
  – Loss of flexibility – cannot take advantage of opportunities.
  – Reorder costs – low stock implies more frequent ordering.

- Practical points on stock management include:
  - Identify optimum order size – models can help with this.
  - Set stock reorder levels.
  - Use budgets.
  - Keep reliable stock records.
  - Use accounting ratios (for example, stock turnover period ratio).
  - Establish systems for security of stock and authorisation.
  - Consider just-in-time (JIT) stock management.

Trade debtors (receivables)

- Five Cs of credit:
  - Capital.
  - Capacity.
  - Collateral.
  - Conditions.
  - Character.

- Costs of allowing credit:
  - Lost interest.
  - Lost purchasing power.
  - Costs of assessing customer creditworthiness.
  - Administration cost.
  - Bad debts.
  - Cash discounts (for prompt payment).

- Costs of denying credit:
  - Loss of customer goodwill.

- Practical points on debtor management:
  - Establish a policy.
  - Assess and monitor customer creditworthiness.
  - Establish effective administration of debtors.
  - Establish a policy on bad debts.
  - Consider cash discounts.
  - Use accounting ratios (for example, average settlement period for debtors ratio).
  - Use ageing summaries.

Cash

- Costs of holding cash:
  - Lost interest.
  - Lost purchasing power.

- Costs of holding insufficient cash:
  - Loss of supplier goodwill if unable to meet commitments on time.
  - Loss of opportunities.
  - Inability to claim cash discounts.
  - Costs of borrowing (should an obligation need to be met at short notice).

- Practical points on cash management:
  - Establish a policy.
  - Plan cash flows.

- Make judicious use of bank overdraft finance – it can be cheap and flexible.
- Use short-term cash surpluses profitably.
- Bank frequently.
- Operating cash cycle (for a retailer) = length of time from buying stock to receiving cash from debtors less creditors' payment period (in days).
- Transmit cash promptly.

● An objective of WC management is to limit the length of the OCC, subject to any risks that this may cause.

Trade creditors (payables)

● Costs of taking credit:
  - Higher price than purchases for immediate cash settlement.
  - Administrative costs.
  - Restrictions imposed by seller.

● Costs of not taking credit:
  - Lost interest-free borrowing.
  - Lost purchasing power.
  - Inconvenience – paying at the time of purchase can be inconvenient.

● Practical points on creditor management:
  - Establish a policy.
  - Exploit free credit as far as possible.
  - Use accounting ratios (for example, average settlement period ratio).

● Working capital and the small business:
  - Small businesses often lack the skills and resources to manage working capital effectively.
  - Small businesses often suffer from large businessses delaying payments for goods supplied.
  - Changes in the law designed to help small businesses have had limited success.

→ Key terms

working capital   p. 560
lead time   p. 565
ABC system of stock control   p. 566
economic order quantity
  (EOQ)   p. 567
materials requirement planning (MRP)
  system   p. 570
just-in-time (JIT) stock management
  p. 570

five Cs of credit   p. 572
cash discount   p. 575
average settlement period for
  debtors   p. 576
ageing schedule of debtors   p. 576
operating cash cycle (OCC)   p. 581
average settlement period for
  creditors   p. 586

Further reading

If you would like to explore the topics covered in this chapter in more depth, we recommend the following books:

Corporate Financial Management, *Arnold G.*, 2nd edn Financial Times Prentice Hall, 1998, chapter 13.

Business Finance: Theory and practice, *McLaney E.*, 6th edn, Financial Times Prentice Hall, 2003, chapter 13.

Corporate Finance and Investment, *Pike R. and Neale B.*, 4th edn, Prentice Hall International, 2002, chapters 14 and 15.

Financial Management and Decision Making, *Samuels J., Wilkes F. and Brayshaw R.*, International Thomson Business Press, 1999, chapter 18.

Reference

1 **Financial Management and Working Capital Practices in UK SMEs**, *Chittenden F., Poutziouris P. and Michaelis N.*, Manchester Business School, 1998.

REVIEW QUESTIONS

Answers to these questions can be found on the students' side of the Companion Website at www.pearsoned.co.uk/atrillmclaney.

16.1 Tariq is the credit manager of Heltex plc. He is concerned that the pattern of monthly sales receipts shows that credit collection is poor compared with budget. Heltex's sales director believes that Tariq is to blame for this situation, but Tariq insists that he is not. Why might Tariq not be to blame for the deterioration in the credit collection period?

16.2 How might each of the following affect the level of stocks held by a business?
- An increase in the number of production bottlenecks experienced by the business.
- A rise in the level of interest rates.
- A decision to offer customers a narrower range of products in the future.
- A switch of suppliers from an overseas business to a local business.
- A deterioration in the quality and reliability of bought-in components.

16.3 What are the reasons for holding stocks? Are these reasons different from the reasons for holding cash?

16.4 Identify the costs of holding:
(a) too little cash, and
(b) too much cash.

EXERCISES

Exercises 16.4 to 16.8 are more advanced than 16.1 to 16.3. Those with a coloured number have an answer at the back of the book.

16.1 Hercules Wholesalers Ltd has been particularly concerned with its liquidity position in recent months. The most recent profit and loss account and balance sheet of the business are as follows:

Profit and loss account for the year ended 31 December last year

	£000	£000
Sales revenue		452
Less Cost of sales		
Opening stock	125	
Add Purchases	341	
	466	
Less Closing stock	143	323
Gross profit		129
Expenses		132
Net loss for the period		(3)

Balance sheet as at 31 December last year

	£000	£000	£000
Non-current assets			
Property, plant and equipment			
Freehold premises at valuation			280
Fixtures and fittings at cost less depreciation			25
Motor vehicles at cost less depreciation			52
			357
Current assets			
Stock		143	
Debtors		163	
		306	
Less **Current liabilities**			
Trade creditors	145		
Bank overdraft	140	285	21
			378
Less **Non-current liabilities**			
Loans			120
			258
Equity			
Ordinary share capital			100
Retained profit			158
			258

The debtors and creditors were maintained at a constant level throughout the year.

Required:
(a) Explain why Hercules Wholesalers Ltd is concerned about its liquidity position.
(b) Calculate the operating cash cycle for Hercules Wholesalers Ltd based on the information above. (Assume a 360-day year.)
(c) State what steps may be taken to improve the operating cash cycle of the business.

16.2 International Electric plc at present offers its customers 30 days' credit. Half the customers, by value, pay on time. The other half takes an average of 70 days to pay. The business is considering offering a cash discount of 2% to its customers for payment within 30 days.

The credit controller anticipates that half of the customers who now take an average of 70 days to pay (that is, a quarter of all customers) will pay in 30 days. The other half (the final quarter) will still take an average of 70 days to pay. The scheme will also reduce bad debts by £300,000 a year.

Annual sales revenue of £365 million is made evenly throughout the year. At present the business has a large overdraft (£60 million) with its bank at 12% a year.

Required:
(a) Calculate the approximate equivalent annual percentage cost of a discount of 2%, which reduces the time taken by debtors to pay from 70 days to 30 days. (*Hint*: This part can be answered without reference to the narrative above.)
(b) Calculate debtors outstanding under both the old and new schemes.
(c) How much will the scheme cost the business in discounts?
(d) Should the business go ahead with the scheme? State what other factors, if any, should be taken into account.
(e) Outline the controls and procedures that a business should adopt to manage the level of its debtors.

16.3 The managing director of Sparkrite Ltd, a trading business, has just received summary sets of statements for last year and this year:

Sparkrite Ltd
Profit and loss accounts for years ended 30 September last year and this year

	Last year		This year	
	£000	£000	£000	£000
Sales revenue		1,800		1,920
Less Cost of sales				
Opening stock	160		200	
Purchases	1,120		1,175	
	1,280		1,375	
Less Closing stock	200		250	
		1,080		1,125
Gross profit		720		795
Less Expenses		680		750
Net profit		40		45

Balance sheets as at 30 September last year and this year

	Last year		This year	
	£000	£000	£000	£000
Non-current assets		950		930
Current assets				
Stock	200		250	
Debtors	375		480	
Bank	4		2	
	579		732	
Less Current liabilities	195		225	
		384		507
		1,334		1,437
Equity				
Fully paid £1 ordinary shares		825		883
Reserves		509		554
		1,334		1,437

The finance director has expressed concern at the increase in stock and debtors levels.

Required:
(a) Show, by using the data given, how you would calculate ratios that could be used to measure stock and debtor levels during last year and this year.
(b) Discuss the ways in which the management of Sparkrite Ltd could exercise control over:
   (i) stock levels;
   (ii) debtor levels.

16.4 Your superior, the general manager of Plastics Manufacturers Limited, has recently been talking to the chief buyer of Plastic Toys Limited, which manufactures a wide range of toys for young children. At present, Plastic Toys is considering changing its supplier of plastic granules and has offered to buy its entire requirement of 2,000 kg a month from you at the going market rate, provided that you will grant it three months' credit on its purchases. The following information is available:

1 Plastic granules sell for £10 a kg, variable costs are £7 a kg, and fixed costs £2 a kg.
2 Your own business is financially strong, and has sales revenue of £15 million a year. For the foreseeable future it will have surplus capacity, and it is actively looking for new outlets.

3 Extracts from Plastic Toys' financial statements:

Year	1	2	3
	£000	£000	£000
Sales revenue	800	980	640
Profit before interest and tax	100	110	(150)
Capital employed	600	650	575

Year	1	2	3
	£000	£000	£000
Current assets			
Stocks	200	220	320
Debtors	140	160	160
	340	380	480
Current liabilities			
Creditors	180	190	220
Overdraft	100	150	310
	280	340	530
Net current assets	60	40	(50)

Required:

(a) Write some short notes suggesting sources of information that you would use to assess the creditworthiness of potential customers who are unknown to you. You should critically evaluate each source of information.

(b) Describe the accounting controls that you would use to monitor the level of your business's trade debtors.

(c) Advise your general manager on the acceptability of the proposal. You should give your reasons and do any calculations you consider necessary. (*Hint*: To answer this question you must weigh the costs of administration and cash discounts against the savings in bad debts and interest charges.)

16.5 Mayo Computers Ltd has an annual turnover of £20m before taking into account bad debts of £0.1m. All sales made by the business are on credit, and, at present, credit terms are negotiable by the customer. On average, the settlement period for trade debtors is 60 days. Trade debtors are financed by an overdraft bearing a 14% a year interest rate. The business is currently reviewing its credit policies to see whether more efficient and profitable methods could be employed. Only one proposal has so far been put forward concerning the management of trade credit.

The credit control department has proposed that customers should be given a $2^{1}/_{2}$% discount if they pay within 30 days. For those who do not pay within this period, a maximum of 50 days' credit should be given. The credit department believes that 60% of customers will take advantage of the discount by paying at the end of the discount period, and the remainder will pay at the end of 50 days. The credit department believes that bad debts can be effectively eliminated by adopting the above policies and by employing stricter credit investigation procedures, which will cost an additional £20,000 a year. The credit department is confident that these new policies will not result in any reduction in sales revenue.

Required:

Calculate the net annual cost (savings) to the business of abandoning its existing credit policies and adopting the proposals of the credit control department. (*Hint*: To answer this question you must weigh the costs of administration and cash discounts against the savings in bad debts and interest charges.)

16.6 Boswell Enterprises Ltd is reviewing its trade credit policy. The business, which sells all of its goods on credit, has estimated that sales revenue for the forthcoming year will be £3 million under the existing policy. Thirty per cent of trade debtors are expected to pay one month after being invoiced and 70% are expected to pay two months after being invoiced. These estimates are in line with previous years' figures.

At present, no cash discounts are offered to customers. However, to encourage prompt payment, the business is considering giving a $2^1/_2$% cash discount to debtors who pay in one month or less. Given this incentive, the business expects 60% of trade debtors to pay one month after being invoiced and 40% of debtors to pay two months after being invoiced. The business believes that the introduction of a cash discount policy will prove attractive to some customers and will lead to a 5% increase in total sales revenue.

Irrespective of the trade credit policy adopted, the gross profit margin of the business will be 20% for the forthcoming year and three months' stock will be held. Fixed monthly expenses of £15,000 and variable expenses (excluding discounts), equivalent to 10% of sales revenue, will be incurred and will be paid one month in arrears. Trade creditors will be paid in arrears and will be equal to two months' cost of sales. The business will hold a fixed cash balance of £140,000 throughout the year, whichever trade credit policy is adopted. No dividends will be proposed or paid during the year. Ignore taxation.

Required:

(a) Calculate the investment in working capital at the end of the forthcoming year under:
  – The existing policy
  – The proposed policy.

(b) Calculate the expected net profit for the forthcoming year under:
  – The existing policy
  – The proposed policy.

(c) Advise the business as to whether it should implement the proposed policy.

(*Hint*: The investment in working capital will be made up of stock, debtors and cash, *less* trade creditors and any unpaid expenses at the year end.)

16.7 Delphi plc has recently decided to enter the expanding market for minidisc players. The business will manufacture the players and sell them to small TV and hi-fi specialists, medium-sized music stores and large retail chain stores. The new product will be launched next February and predicted sales revenue for the product from each customer group for February and the expected rate of growth for subsequent months are as follows:

Customer type	February sales revenue (£000)	Monthly compound sales revenue growth (%)	Credit sales (months)
TV and hi-fi specialists	20	4	1
Music stores	30	6	2
Retail chain stores	40	8	3

The business is concerned about the financing implications of launching the new product, as it is already experiencing liquidity problems. In addition, it is concerned that the credit control department will find it difficult to cope. This is a new market for the business and there are likely to be many new customers who will have to be investigated for creditworthiness.

Workings should be in £000 and calculations made to one decimal point only.

Required:

(a) Prepare an ageing schedule of the monthly debtors' balance relating to the new product for each of the first four months of the new product's life, and comment on the results. The schedule should analyse the debts outstanding according to customer type. It should also indicate, for each customer type, the relevant percentage outstanding in relation to the total amount outstanding for each month.

(b) Identify and discuss the factors that should be taken into account when evaluating the creditworthiness of the new business customers.

16.8   Goliath plc is a retail business operating in Ireland. The most recent financial statements of the business are as follows:

Profit and loss account for the year to 31 May

	£000	£000
Sales revenue		2,400.0
Less Cost of sales		
Opening stock	550.0	
Add Purchases	1,450.0	
	2,000.0	
Less Closing stock	560.0	1,440.0
Gross profit		960.0
Administration expenses	(300.0)	
Selling expenses	(436.0)	
Interest payable	(40.0)	(776.0)
Net profit before taxation		184.0
Less Corporation tax (25%)		46.0
Net profit after taxation		138.0

Balance sheet as at 31 May

	£000	£000	£000
Non-current assets			
Property, plant and equipment			
Machinery and equipment at cost		424.4	
Less Accumulated depreciation		140.8	283.6
Motor vehicles at cost		308.4	
Less Accumulated depreciation		135.6	172.8
			456.4
Current assets			
Stock at cost		560.0	
Trade debtors		565.0	
Cash at bank		36.4	
		1,161.4	
Current liabilities			
Trade creditors	(451.0)		
Corporation tax due	(46.0)	(497.0)	664.4
			1,120.8
Non-current liabilities			
Loan capital			(400.0)
			720.8
Equity			
£1 ordinary shares			200.0
Retained profit			520.8
			720.8

All sales and purchases are made on credit.

The business is considering whether to grant extended credit facilities to its customers. It has been estimated that increasing the settlement period for debtors by a further 20 days will increase the turnover of the business by 10 per cent. However, stocks will have to be increased by 15 per cent to cope with the increased demand. It is estimated that purchases will have to rise to £1,668,000 during the next year as a result of these changes. To finance the increase in stocks and debtors, the business will increase the settlement period taken for suppliers by 15 days and utilise a loan facility bearing a 10 per cent rate of interest for the remaining balance.

If the policy is implemented, bad debts are likely to increase by £120,000 and administration costs will rise by 15 per cent.

Required:

(a) Calculate the increase or decrease to each of the following that will occur in the forthcoming year if the proposed policy is implemented:
   (i)   operating cash cycle (based on year-end figures)
   (ii) net investment in stock, debtors and creditors
   (iii) net profit after taxation.

(b) Should the business implement the proposed policy? Give reasons for your conclusion.

PART 4

Supplementary information

Part 4 provides information that is supplementary to the main text of the book.

Appendix A takes the format of a normal textual chapter and describes the way in which financial transactions are recorded in books of account. Generally, this is by means of the 'double entry' system, described in basic terms in the Appendix.

Appendix B gives definitions of the key terms highlighted throughout the main text and summarised at the end of each chapter. The aim of the Appendix is to provide a single location to check on the meanings of the major accounting terms used in this book and in the world of finance.

Appendices C and D give answers to some of the questions set in the course of the main text. Appendix C gives answers to the self-assessment questions, and Appendix D to those of the exercises that are marked as having their answers provided in the book.

Appendix E is a table of present value factors that can be used to discount future cash flows.

Appendix A
Recording financial transactions

OBJECTIVES

When you have completed this Appendix, you should be able to:

- Explain the basic principles of double-entry bookkeeping.

- Write up a series of business transactions and balance the accounts.

- Extract a trial balance and explain its purpose.

- Prepare a set of financial statements from the underlying double-entry accounts.

INTRODUCTION

In Chapters 2 and 3, we saw how the financial transactions of a business may be recorded by making a series of entries on the balance sheet and/or profit and loss account (income statement). Each of these entries had its corresponding 'double', meaning that both sides of the transaction were recorded. However, adjusting the financial statements, by hand, for each transaction can be very messy and confusing. With a reasonably large number of transactions it is pretty certain to result in mistakes.

For businesses whose accounting systems are on a computer, this problem is overcome because suitable software can deal with a series of 'plus' and 'minus' entries very reliably. Where the accounting system is not computerised, however, it would be helpful to have some more practical way of keeping accounting records. Such a system not only exists but, before the advent of the computer, was the routine way of keeping accounts. It is this system that is explained in this Appendix. We should be clear that the system we are going to consider follows exactly the same rules as those that we have already met. Its distinguishing feature is its ability to provide those keeping accounting records by hand, a methodical approach that allows each transaction to be clearly identified and errors to be minimised.

The basics of double-entry bookkeeping

When we record accounting transactions by hand, we use a recording system known as **double-entry bookkeeping**. This system does not use plus and minus entries on the face of a balance sheet and profit and loss account to record a particular transaction, in the way described in Chapters 2 and 3. Instead, these are recorded in accounts. An **account** is simply a record of one or more transactions relating to a particular item, such as cash, fixtures and fittings, loans outstanding, sales revenue, rent payable and capital. A business may keep few or many accounts, depending on the size and complexity of its operations. Broadly, businesses tend to keep a separate account for each item that appears in either the profit and loss account or the balance sheet.

An example of an account, in this case the cash account, is as follows:

We can see that an account has three main features:

- A title indicating the item to which it relates
- A left-hand side, known as the **debit** side
- A right-hand side, known as the **credit** side

One side of an account will record increases in the particular item and other will record decreases. This, of course, is slightly different to the approach we used when adjusting the financial statements. When adjusting the balance sheet, for example, we put a reduction in an asset or claim in the same column as any increases, but with a minus sign against it. However, when accounts are used, a reduction is shown on the opposite side of the account.

The side on which an increase or decrease is shown will depend on the nature of the item to which the account relates. For example, an account for an asset, such as cash, will show increases on the left-hand (debit) side of the account and decreases on the right-hand (credit) side. However, for claims (that is, capital and liabilities) it is the other way around. An increase in the account for capital or for a liability will be shown on the right-hand (credit) side and a decrease will be shown on the left-hand (debit) side.

To understand why this difference exists, we should recall from Chapter 2 that the balance sheet equation is:

$$\text{Assets} = \text{Capital} + \text{Liabilities}$$

We can see that assets appear on one side of the equation and capital and liabilities appear on the other. Recording transactions in accounts simply expresses this difference in the recording process. Increases in assets are shown on the left-hand side of an account and increases in capital and liabilities are shown on the right-hand side of the account. We should recall the point made in Chapter 2 that each transaction has two aspects. Thus, when we record a particular transaction, two separate accounts will be affected. Recording transactions in this way is known as double-entry bookkeeping.

It is worth going through a simple example to see how transactions affecting balance sheet items would be recorded under the double-entry bookkeeping system. Suppose a new business started on 1 January with the owner putting £5,000 into a newly-opened business bank account, as initial capital. This entry would appear in the cash account as follows:

Cash

	£		£
1 January Capital	5,000		

The corresponding entry would be made in the capital account as follows:

Capital

	£		£
		1 January Cash	5,000

It is usual to show, in each account by way of note, where the other side of the entry will be found. Thus, someone looking at the capital account will know that the £5,000 arose from a receipt of cash. This provides potentially useful information, partly because it establishes a 'trail' that can be followed when checking for errors. Including the date of the transaction provides additional information to the reader of the accounts.

Now suppose that, on 2 January, £600 of the cash is used to buy some stock. This would affect the cash account as follows:

Cash

	£		£
1 January Capital	5,000	2 January Stock	600

This cash account, in effect, shows 'positive' cash of £5,000 and 'negative' cash of £600, a net amount of £4,400.

ACTIVITY A.1

As you know, we must somehow record the other side of the transaction involving the acquisition of the stock for £600. See if you can work out what to do in respect of the stock.

....

We must open an account for stock. Since stock is an asset, an increase in it will appear on the left-hand side of the account, as follows:

Stock

	£		£
2 January Cash	600		

What we have seen so far highlights the key rule of double-entry bookkeeping: each left-hand entry must have a right-hand entry of equal size. Using the jargon, we can say that *every debit must have a credit*.

It might be helpful at this point to make clear that the words 'debit' and 'credit' are no more than accounting jargon for left and right, respectively. It general English (that is when not referring to accounting), people tend to use credit to imply something good and debit something undesirable. Debit and credit have no such implication in accounting. Each transaction requires both a debit and a credit entry. This is equally true whether the transaction is a 'good' one, like being paid by a debtor, or a 'bad' one like having to treat a debtor's balance as worthless because the debtor has gone bankrupt.

Recording trading transactions

The rules of double entry also extend to 'trading' transactions – that is, making revenue (sales and so on) and incurring expenses. To understand how these transactions are recorded, we should recall that in Chapter 3 the extended balance sheet equation was set out as follows:

$$\text{Assets} = \text{Capital} + (\text{Revenues} - \text{Expenses}) + \text{Liabilities}$$

This equation can be rearranged so that:

$$\text{Assets} + \text{Expenses} = \text{Capital} + \text{Revenues} + \text{Liabilities}$$

We can see that increases in expenses are shown on the same side as assets and this means that they will be dealt with in the same way for recording purposes. Thus, an increase in an expense, such as wages, will be shown on the left-hand (debit) side of the wages account and a decrease will be shown on the right-hand (credit) side. Increases in revenues are shown on the same side as capital and liabilities and so will be dealt with in the same way. Thus, an increase in revenue, such as sales, will be shown on the right-hand (credit) side and a decrease will be shown on the left hand (debit) side.

To summarise, therefore, we can say that:

● **Debits (left-hand entries) represent increases in assets and expenses and decreases in claims and revenues.**
● **Credits (right-hand entries) represent increases in claims and revenues and decreases in assets and expenses.**

Let us continue with our example by assuming that on 3 January, the business paid £900 to rent business premises for the three months to 31 March. To record this transaction, we should normally open a 'rent account' and make entries in this account and in the cash account as follows:

Rent

		£		£
3 January	Cash	900		

Cash

		£			£
1 January	Capital	5,000	2 January	Stock	600
			3 January	Rent	900

The fact that assets and expenses are dealt with in the same way should not be altogether surprising since assets and expenses are closely linked. Assets actually transform into expenses as they are 'used up'. Rent, which, as here, is usually paid in advance, is an asset when it is first paid. It represents the value to the business of being entitled to occupy the premises for the forthcoming period (until 31 March in this case). As the three months progress, this asset becomes an expense; it is 'used up'. We need to remember that the debit entry in the rent account does not necessarily represent either an asset or an expense; it could be a mixture of the two. Strictly, by the end of the day on which it was paid (3 January), £30 would have represented an expense for the three days; the remaining £270 would have been an asset. As each day passes, an additional £10 (that is, £900/90 (there are 90 days in January, February and March altogether)) will transform from an asset into an expense. As we have already seen, it is not necessary for us to make any adjustment to the rent account as the days pass.

Assume, now, that on 5 January the business sold stock costing £200 for £300 on credit. As usual, when we are able to identify the cost of the goods sold at the time of sale, we need to deal with the sale and the cost of the stock sold as two separate issues, each having its own set of debits and credits.

Firstly, let us deal with the sale. We now need to open accounts for both 'sales revenue' and 'trade debtors' – which do not, as yet, exist. The sale is an increase in revenue and so there is a credit entry in the sales revenue account. The sale also creates an asset of trade debtors and so there is debit entry in trade debtors:

Sales revenue

	£			£
		5 January	Trade debtors	300

Trade debtors

		£		£
5 January	Sales revenue	300		

Let us now deal with the stock sold. Since the stock sold has become the expense 'cost of sales', we need to reduce the figure on the stock account by making a credit entry and to make the corresponding debit in a 'cost of sales' account, opened for the purpose:

Stock

		£			£
2 January	Cash	600	5 January	Cost of sales	200

Cost of sales

		£		£
5 January	Stock	200		

We shall now look at the other transactions for our hypothetical business for the remainder of January. These can be taken to be as follows:

8 January	Bought some stock on credit costing £800
11 January	Bought some office furniture for £600, paying by cheque
15 January	Sold stock costing £600 for £900, on credit
18 January	Received £800 from trade debtors
21 January	Paid trade creditors £500
24 January	Paid wages for the month £400
25 January	Bought stock on credit for £800
31 January	Borrowed £2,000 from the Commercial Finance Company

Naturally, we shall have to open several additional accounts to enable us to record all of these transactions in any meaningful way. By the end of January, the set of accounts would appear as follows:

Cash

		£			£
1 January	Capital	5,000	2 January	Stock	600
18 January	Trade debtors	800	3 January	Rent	900
31 January	Comm. Fin Co	2,000	11 January	Office furniture	600
			21 January	Trade creditors	500
			24 January	Wages	400

Capital

		£			£
			1 January	Cash	5,000

Stock

		£			£
2 January	Cash	600	5 January	Cost of sales	200
8 January	Trade creditors	800	15 January	Cost of sales	600
27 January	Trade creditors	800			

Rent

		£		£
3 January	Cash	900		

Sales revenue

	£			£
		5 January	Trade debtors	300
		15 January	Trade debtors	900

Trade debtors

		£			£
5 January	Sales revenue	300	18 January	Cash	800
15 January	Sales revenue	900			

Cost of sales

		£		£
5 January	Stock	200		
15 January	Stock	600		

Trade creditors

		£			£
21 January	Cash	500	8 January	Stock	800
			27 January	Stock	800

Office furniture

	£		£
11 January Cash	600		

Wages

	£		£
24 January Cash	400		

Loan creditor – Commercial Finance Company

	£		£
		31 January Cash	2,000

All of the transactions from 8 January onwards are quite similar in nature to those up to that date, which we discussed in detail, and so we should be able to follow them using the date references as a guide.

Balancing accounts and the trial balance

Businesses keeping their accounts in the way shown would find it helpful to summarise their individual accounts periodically – perhaps weekly or monthly – for two reasons:

- To be able to see at a glance how much is in each account (for example, to see how much cash the business has left).
- To help to check the accuracy of the bookkeeping so far.

Let us look at the cash account again:

Cash

		£			£
1 January	Capital	5,000	2 January	Stock	600
18 January	Trade debtors	800	3 January	Rent	900
31 January	Comm. Fin. Co.	2,000	11 January	Office furniture	600
			21 January	Trade creditors	500
			24 January	Wages	400

Does this account tell us how much cash the business has at 31 January? The answer is partly yes and partly no!

We do not have a single figure showing the cash balance but we can fairly easily deduce this by adding up the debit (receipts) column and deducting the sum of the credit (payments) column. However, it would be better if a cash balance were provided for us.

To summarise or **balance** this account, we add up the column with the largest amount (in this case, the debit side) and put this total on *both* sides of the account. We then put in, on the credit side, the figure that will make that side add up to the total that appears in the account. We cannot put in this balancing figure only once as the double-entry rule would be broken. Thus, to preserve the double entry, we also put it in on the other side of the same account below the totals, as follows:

Cash

		£			£
1 January	Capital	5,000	2 January	Stock	600
18 January	Trade debtors	800	3 January	Rent	900
31 January	Comm. Fin Co	2,000	11 January	Office furniture	600
			21 January	Trade creditors	500
			24 January	Wages	400
			31 January		
				Balance carried down	4,800
		7,800			7,800
1 February					
	Balance brought down	4,800			

Note that the balance carried down (usually abbreviated to 'c/d') at the end of one period becomes the balance brought down ('b/d') at the beginning of the next. Now we can see at a glance what the present cash position is, without having to do any mental arithmetic.

ACTIVITY A.2

Try balancing the stock account and then say what we know about the stock position at the end of January.

The stock account will be balanced as follows:

Stock

		£			£
2 January	Cash	600	5 January	Cost of sales	200
8 January	Trade creditors	800	15 January	Cost of sales	600
27 January	Trade creditors	800	31 January	Balance c/d	1,400
		2,200			2,200
1 February	Balance b/d	1,400			

We can see at a glance that the business held stock that had cost £1,400 at the end of January. We can also see quite easily how this situation arose.

We can balance all of the other accounts in similar fashion. However, there is no point in formally balancing accounts that have only one entry at the moment (for example, the capital account) because we cannot summarise one figure; it is already in as summarised a form as it can be. After balancing them, the remaining accounts will be as follows:

Capital

	£			£
		1 January	Cash	5,000

Rent

		£			£
3 January	Cash	900			

Sales revenue

		£			£
31 January	Balance c/d	1,200	5 January	Trade debtors	300
			15 January	Trade debtors	900
		1,200			1,200
			1 February	Balance b/d	1,200

Trade debtors

		£			£
5 January	Sales revenue	300	18 January	Cash	800
15 January	Sales revenue	900	31 January	Balance c/d	400
		1,200			1,200
1 February	Balance b/d	400			

Cost of sales

		£			£
5 January	Stock	200	31 January	Balance c/d	800
15 January	Stock	600			
		800			800
1 February	Balance b/d	800			

Trade creditors

		£			£
21 January	Cash	500	8 January	Stock	800
31 January	Balance c/d	1,100	27 January	Stock	800
		1,600			1,600
			1 February	Balance b/d	1,100

Office furniture

		£			£
11 January	Cash	600			

Wages

		£			£
24 January	Cash	400			

Loan creditor – Commercial Finance Company

	£			£
		31 January	Cash	2,000

ACTIVITY A.3

If we now separately total the debit balances and the credit balances, for each of the above accounts, what should we expect to find?

We should expect to find that these two totals are equal. This must, in theory be true since every debit entry was matched by an equally-sized credit entry.

Let us see if our expectation in Activity A.3 works in our example, by listing the debit and credit balances as follows:

	Debits £	Credits £
Cash	4,800	
Stock	1,400	
Capital		5,000
Rent	900	
Sales revenue		1,200
Trade debtors	400	
Cost of sales	800	
Trade creditors		1,100
Office furniture	600	
Wages	400	
Loan creditor		2,000
	9,300	9,300

This statement is known as a **trial balance**. The fact that it agrees gives us *some* indication that we have not made bookkeeping errors.

This situation, does not, however, give us total confidence that no error could have occurred. Consider the transaction that took place on 3 January (paid rent for the month of £900). In each of the following cases, all of which would be wrong, the trial balance would still have agreed:

- The transaction was completely omitted from the accounts; that is, no entries were made at all.
- The amount was misread as £9,000 but then (correctly) debited to the rent account and credited to cash.
- The correct amount was (incorrectly) debited to cash and credited to rent.

Nevertheless, a trial balance that agrees does give some confidence that accounts have been correctly written up.

ACTIVITY A.4

Why do you think the words 'debtor' and 'creditor' are used to describe those who owe money or are owed money by a business?

The answer simply is that debtors have a debit balance in the books of the business, whereas creditors have a credit balance.

Preparing the financial statements (final accounts)

If the trial balance agrees and we are confident that there are no errors in recording, the next stage is to prepare the profit and loss account (income statement) and balance sheet. Preparing the profit and loss account is simply a matter of going through the individual accounts, identifying those amounts that represent revenue and expenses of the period, and transferring them to a profit and loss account, which is itself part of the double-entry system.

We shall now do this for the example we have been using. The situation is complicated slightly for three reasons:

1 As we know, the £900 rent paid during January relates to the three months January, February and March.
2 The business's owner estimates that the electricity used during January is about £110. There is no bill yet from the electricity supply business because it normally only bills customers at the end of each three-month period.
3 The business's owner believes that the office furniture should be depreciated by 20 per cent each year (straight-line).

These three factors need to be taken into account. As we shall see, however, the end-of-period adjustments of these types are very easily handled in double-entry accounts. Let us deal with these three areas first.

The rent account will appear as follow, after we have completed the transfer to the profit and loss account:

Rent

		£			£
3 January	Cash	900	31 January	Profit and loss	300
				Balance c/d	600
		900			900
1 February	Balance b/d	600			

At 31 January, because two months' rent is still an asset, this is carried down as a debit balance. The remainder (representing January's rent) is credited to the rent account and debited to a newly opened profit and loss account. As we shall shortly see, the £600 debit balance remaining will appear in the 31 January balance sheet.

Now let us deal with the electricity. The electricity account will be as follows after the transfer to the profit and loss account:

Electricity

	£			£
		31 January	Profit and loss	110

Because there has been no cash payment or other transaction recorded so far for electricity, we do not already have an account for it. It is necessary to open one. We need to debit the profit and loss account with the £110 of electricity used during January and credit the electricity account with the same amount. At 31 January, this credit balance reflects the amount owed by this business to the electricity supplier. Once again, we shall shortly see that this balance at the year end will appear on the balance sheet.

Next we shall consider what is necessary regarding the office furniture. The depreciation for the month will be $20\% \times £600 \times \frac{1}{12}$, that is £10. Normal accounting practice is to charge (debit) this to the profit and loss account, with the corresponding credit going to a 'provision for depreciation of office furniture' account. The latter entry will appear as follows:

Provision for depreciation of office furniture account

		£			£
			31 January	Profit and loss	10

This £10 balance will be reflected in the balance sheet at 31 January by being deducted from the office furniture itself, as we shall see.

The balances on the following accounts represent straightforward revenue or expenses for the month of January:

- Sales revenue
- Cost of sales
- Wages.

The balances on these accounts will simply be transferred to the profit and loss account.

To transfer balances to the profit and loss account, we simply debit or credit the account concerned, such that any balance amount is eliminated, and make the corresponding credit or debit in the profit and loss account. Take sales revenue, for example. This has a credit balance (because the balance represents a revenue). We must debit the sales revenue account with £1,200 and credit the profit and loss account with the same amount. So a credit balance on the sales revenue account becomes a credit entry in the profit and loss account. For the three accounts, then, we have the following:

Sales revenue

		£			£
31 January	Balance c/d	1,200	5 January	Trade debtors	300
			15 January	Trade debtors	900
		1,200			1,200
31 January	Profit and loss	1,200	1 February	Balance b/d	1,200

Cost of Sales

		£			£
5 January	Stock	200	31 January	Balance c/d	800
15 January	Stock	600			
		800			800
1 February	Balance b/d	800	31 January	Profit and loss	800

Wages

		£			£
24 January	Cash	400	31 January	Profit and loss	400

The profit and loss account will now look as follows

Profit and loss account

		£			£
31 January	Cost of sales	800	31 January	Sales revenue	1,200
31 January	Rent	300			
31 January	Wages	400			
31 January	Electricity	110			
31 January	Depreciation	10			

We must now transfer the balance on the profit and loss account (a debit balance of £420).

ACTIVITY A.5

What does the balance on the profit and loss account represent, and to where should it be transferred?

....

The balance is either the profit or the loss for the period. In this case it is a loss as the total expenses exceed the total revenue. This loss must be borne by the owner, and it must therefore be transferred to the capital account.

The two accounts would now appear as follows:

Profit and loss account

		£			£
31 January	Cost of sales	800	31 January	Sales revenue	1,200
31 January	Rent	300			
31 January	Wages	400			
31 January	Electricity	110			
31 January	Depreciation	10	31 January	Capital (net loss)	420
		1,620			1,620

Capital

		£			£
31 January	Profit and loss (net loss)	420	1 January	Cash	5,000
31 January	Balance c/d	4,580			
		5,000			5,000
			1 February	Balance b/d	4,580

The last thing done was to balance the capital account.

Now all of the balances remaining on accounts represent either assets or claims as at 31 January. These balances can now be used to produce a balance sheet, as follows:

Balance sheet as at 31 January

	£	£
Non-current assets		
Property, plant and equipment		
Office furniture: cost		600
depreciation		(10)
		590
Current assets		
Stock	1,400	
Prepaid expense	600	
Trade debtors	400	
Cash	4,800	
	7,200	
Current liabilities		
Accrued expense	(110)	
Trade creditors	(1,100)	
	(1,210)	5,990
		6,580
Less **Non-current liability**		
Loan creditor		2,000
		4,580
Capital		4,580

The profit and loss account could be written in a more stylish manner, for reporting to users, as follows:

Profit and loss account for the month ended 31 January

	£	£
Sales revenue		1,200
Cost of sales		800
Gross profit		400
Less Rent	300	
Wages	400	
Electricity	110	
Depreciation	10	
		820
Net loss for the month		(420)

The ledger and its division

The book in which the accounts are traditionally kept is known as the ledger and 'accounts' are sometimes referred to as 'ledger accounts', even where they are computerised.

In a handwritten accounting system, the ledger is often divided into various sections. This tends to be for two main reasons:

1 Having all of the accounts in one book means that it is only possible for one person at a time to use the accounts, either to make entries or to extract useful information.
2 Dividing the ledger along logical grounds can allow specialisation, so that various individual members of the accounts staff can look after their own part of the system.

This can lead to more efficient record keeping. It can also lead to greater security, that is less risk of error and fraud by limiting an individual's access to only part of the entire set of accounts.

There are no clear, universal rules on the division of the ledger, but the following division is fairly common:

- *The cash book.* This tends to be all of the accounts relating to cash either loose or in the bank.
- *The sales (or trade debtors) ledger.* This contains the accounts of all of the business's individual trade debtors.
- *The purchases (or trade creditors) ledger.* This consists of the accounts of all of the business's individual trade creditors.
- *The nominal ledger.* These accounts tend to be those of expenses and revenue, for example sales revenue, wages, rent, and so on.
- *The general ledger.* This contains the remainder of the business's accounts, mainly those to do with non-current assets and long-term finance.

SUMMARY

The main points in this Appendix may be summarised as follows:

Double-entry bookkeeping = a system for keeping accounting records by hand, such that a relatively large volume of transactions can be handled effectively and accurately

- A separate account for each asset, claim, expense and liability that needs to be separately identified.
- Each account looks like a letter T.
- Left-hand (debit) side of the account records increases in assets and expenses and decreases in revenues and claims.
- Right-hand (credit) side records increases in revenues and claims and decreases in assets and expenses.
- There is an equal credit entry in one account for a debit entry in another.
- Double-entry bookkeeping can be used to record day-to-day transactions.
- It can also follow through to generate the profit and loss account.
- Balance sheet is a list of the net figure (the 'balance') on each of the accounts after appropriate transfers have been made to the profit and loss account.
- The accounts are traditionally kept in a 'ledger', a term that persists even with computerised accounting.
- The ledger is traditionally broken down into several sections, each containing particular types of account.

→ Key terms

double-entry bookkeeping p. 602
account p. 602
debit p. 602
credit p. 602
balance p. 607
trial balance p. 610

Further reading

If you would like to explore the topics covered in this appendix in more depth, we recommend the following books:

Foundations of Business Accounting, *Dodge R.*, 2nd edn, Thomson Business Press, 1997, chapter 3.

An Introduction to Financial Accounting, *Thomas A.*, 4th edn, McGraw-Hill, 2001, chapters 3, 4, 5 and 6.

Practical Accounting, *Benedict A. and Elliott B.*, Financial Times Prentice Hall, 2001, chapters 2–5.

Financial Accounting, *Bebbington J., Gray R. and Laughlin R.*, 3rd edn, Thomson Learning, 2001, chapters 2–7.

EXERCISES

All three exercises have answers at the back of the book.

A.1 In respect of each of the following transactions, state in which two accounts must an entry be made and whether the entry is a debit or a credit. (For example, if the transaction were purchase of stock for cash, the answer would be debit the stock account and credit the cash account.)

(a) Purchased stock on credit.
(b) Owner made cash drawings.
(c) Paid interest on a business loan.
(d) Purchased stock for cash.
(e) Received cash from a credit customer.
(f) Paid wages to employees.
(g) The owner received some cash from a credit customer, which was taken as drawings rather than being paid into the business's bank account.
(h) Paid a credit supplier.
(i) Paid electricity bill.
(j) Made cash sales.

A.2 (a) Record the following transactions in a set of double-entry accounts:

1 February	Lee (the owner) put £6,000 into a newly opened business bank account to start a new business
3 February	Purchased stock for £2,600 for cash
5 February	Purchased some equipment (non-current asset) for cash for £800
6 February	Purchased stock costing £3,000 on credit
9 February	Paid rent for the month of £250
10 February	Paid fuel and electricity for the month of £240
11 February	Paid general expenses of £200
15 February	Sold stock for £4,000 in cash; the stock had cost £2,400
19 February	Sold stock for £3,800 on credit; the stock had cost £2,300
21 February	Lee withdrew £1,000 in cash for personal use
25 February	Paid £2,000 to trade creditors
28 February	Received £2,500 from trade debtors

(b) Balance the relevant accounts and prepare a trial balance (making sure that it agrees).
(c) Prepare a profit and loss account for the month and a balance sheet at the month end. Assume that there are no prepaid or accrued expenses at the end of the month and ignore any possible depreciation.

A.3 The following is the balance sheet of David's business at 1 January of last year.

	£			£
Non-current assets			**Capital**	25,050
Property, plant and equipment				
Buildings		25,000	**Non-current liability**	
Fittings: cost	10,000		Loan	12,000
dep'n	(2,000)			
		8,000	**Current liabilities**	
Current assets			Trade creditors	1,690
Stock of stationery		140	Accrued electricity	270
Stock-in-trade		1,350		
Prepaid in rent		500		
Trade debtors		1,840		
Cash		2,180		
		39,010		39,010

The following is a summary of the transactions that took place during the year:

1 Stock was purchased on credit for £17,220.
2 Stock was purchased for £3,760 cash.
3 Credit sales revenue amounted to £33,100 (cost £15,220).
4 Cash sales revenue amounted to £10,360 (cost £4,900).
5 Wages of £3,770 were paid.
6 Rent of £3,000 was paid. The annual rental amounts to £3,000.
7 Electricity of £1,070 was paid.
8 General expenses of £580 were paid.
9 Additional fittings were purchased on 1 January for £2,000, The cash for this was raised from an additional loan of this amount. The interest rate is 10% a year, the same as for the existing loan.
10 £1,000 of the loan was repaid on 30 June.
11 Cash received from debtors amounted to £32,810.
12 Cash paid to creditors amounted to £18,150.
13 The owner withdrew £10,400 cash and £560 stock.

At the end of the year it was found that:

(a) The electricity bill for the last quarter of the year for £290 had not been paid.
(b) It was also found that trade debts amounting to £260 were unlikely to be received.
(c) The value of stationery remaining was estimated at £150. Stationery is included in general expenses.
(d) Depreciation to be taken at 20% on the cost of the fittings owned at the year end. Buildings are not depreciated.

Required:
(1) Open ledger accounts and bring down all of the balances in the opening balance sheet.
(2) Make entries to record the transactions 1 to 13 (above), opening any additional accounts as necessary.
(3) Open a profit and loss account (part of the double entry, remember). Make the necessary entries for the items a to d (above) and the appropriate transfers to the profit and loss account.
(4) List the remaining balances in the same form as the opening balance sheet (above).

ABC system of stock control   A method of applying different levels of stock control, based on the value of each category of stock. *p. 566*

Account   A section of a double-entry bookkeeping system that deals with one particular asset, claim, expense or revenue. *p. 602*

Accounting   The process of identifying, measuring and communicating information to permit informed judgements and decisions by users of the information. *p. 2*

Accounting conventions   Accounting rules that have evolved over time in order to deal with practical problems rather than to reflect some theoretical ideal. *p. 46*

Accounting information system   The system used within a business to identify, record, analyse and report accounting information. *p. 12*

Accounting rate of return (ARR)   The average profit from an investment, expressed as a percentage of the average investment made. *p. 467*

Accounting (financial reporting) standards   Rules, which should be followed by pre-parers of the annual accounts of companies. *p. 148*

Accruals accounting   The system of accounting that follows the accruals convention. This is the system followed in drawing up the balance sheet and profit and loss account. *p. 76*

Accruals convention   The convention of accounting that asserts that profit is the excess of revenue over expenses, not the excess of cash receipts over cash payments. *p. 76*

Accrued expense   An expense that is outstanding at the end of an accounting period. *p. 72*

Acid test ratio   A liquidity ratio that relates the current assets (less stocks) to the current liabilities. *p. 225*

Activity-based budgeting (ABB)   A system of budgeting based on the philosophy of activity-based costing (ABC). *p. 415*

Activity-based costing (ABC)   A technique for more accurately relating overheads to specific production or provision of a service. It is based on acceptance of the fact that overheads do not just occur but are caused by activities, such as holding products in stores, which 'drive' the costs. *p. 350*

Adverse variance   A difference between planned and actual performance, usually where the difference will cause the actual profit to be lower than the budgeted one. *p. 435*

Ageing schedule of debtors   A report dividing debtors into categories, depending on the length of time outstanding. *p. 567*

Allotted share capital   *See* Issued share capital. *p. 122*

Asset   A resource held by a business, that has certain characteristics. *p. 32*

Asset-based financing   A form of financing where assets are used as security for cash advances to the business. Factoring and invoice discounting, where the security is trade debtors, are examples of asset-based financing. *p. 544*

Auditor   A professional whose main duty is to make a report as to whether, in his or her opinion, the accounting statements of a company do that which they are supposed to do, namely show a true and fair view and comply with statutory, and accounting standard, requirements. *p. 157*

Authorised share capital   The maximum amount of share capital that directors are authorised by the shareholders to issue. *p. 122*

Average settlement period for creditors   The average time taken for a business to pay its creditors. *pp. 219, 586*

Average settlement period for debtors   The average time taken for debtors to pay the amounts owing. *pp. 218, 576*

Average stock turnover period   An efficiency ratio that measures the average period for which stocks are held by a business. *p. 218*

Bad debt   An amount owed to the business that is considered to be irrecoverable. *p. 91*

Balance   The net of the debit and credit totals in an account in a double-entry book-keeping system. *p. 607*

Balance sheet   A statement of financial position that shows the assets of a business and the claims on those assets. *p. 28*

Balanced Scorecard   A framework for translating the aims and objectives of a business into a series of key performance measures and targets. *p. 375*

Bank overdraft   A flexible form of borrowing that allows an individual or business to have a negative current-account balance. *p. 542*

Batch costing   A technique for identifying full cost, where the production of many types of goods and services – particularly goods – involves producing in a batch of identical or nearly identical units of output, but where each batch is distinctly different from other batches. *p. 336*

Behavioural aspects of budgetary control   The effect on people's attitudes and behaviour of the various aspects of using budgets as the basis of exercising control over performance. *p. 453*

Benchmarking   Identifying a successful business, or part of a business, and measuring the effectiveness of one's own business by comparison with this standard. *p. 372*

Bonus issue   Reserves that are converted into shares and given 'free' to shareholders. *p. 120*

Bonus shares   *See* Bonus issue. *p. 120*

Break-even analysis   The activity of deducing the break-even point of some activity through analysing costs and revenue. *p. 286*

Break-even chart   A graphical representation of the costs and revenue of some activity, at various levels, that enables the break-even point to be identified. *p. 287*

Break-even point   A level of activity where revenue will exactly equal total cost, so there is neither profit nor loss. *p. 287*

Budget   A financial plan for the short term, typically one year. *p. 393*

Budget committee A group of managers formed to supervise and take responsibility for the budget-setting process. *p. 402*

Budget holder An individual responsible for a particular budget. *p. 406*

Budget officer An individual, often an accountant, appointed to carry out, or take immediate responsibility for having carried out, the tasks of the budget committee. *p. 402*

Budgetary control Using the budget as a yardstick against which the effectiveness of actual performance may be assessed. *p. 450*

Business angel An individual who supplies finance (usually equity finance) and advice to a small business. Usually the amount of finance supplied falls between £10,000 and £100,000. *p. 549*

Business entity convention The convention that holds that, for accounting purposes, the business and its owner(s) are treated as quite separate and distinct. *p. 46*

Called-up share capital That part of a company's share capital for which the shareholders have been asked to pay the agreed amount. Part of the claim of the owners against the business. *p. 122*

Capital The owner's claim on the assets of the business. *p. 35*

Capital expenditure The outlay of funds on non-current assets. *p. xxx*

Capital rationing A situation where a business has insufficient funds to undertake all of the investments that it judges to be beneficial. *p. 502*

Capital reserve A reserve that arises from an unrealised 'capital' profit or gain rather than from normal trading activities. *p. 118*

Cash discount A reduction in the amount due for goods or services sold on credit in return for prompt payment. *p. 575*

Cash flow The movement of cash. *p. xxx*

Cash flow statement A statement that shows the sources and uses of cash for a period. *p. 28*

Cash generated from operations per ordinary share An investment ratio that relates the cash generated from operations and available to ordinary shareholders to the number of ordinary shares. *p. 235*

Cash generated from operations to maturing obligations ratio A liquidity ratio that compares the cash generated from operations to the current liabilities of the business. *p. 226*

Claim An obligation on the part of a business to provide cash or some other benefit to an outside party. *p. 32*

Combined Code A code of practice for companies listed on the London Stock Exchange that deals with corporate governance matters. *p. 112*

Committed cost A cost that has not yet been incurred but that must, under some contract or obligation, be incurred. *p. 270*

Common costs Costs that relate to more than one business segment. *p. 316*

Comparability The requirement that items that are basically the same should be treated in the same manner for measurement and reporting purposes. Lack of comparability will limit the usefulness of accounting information. *p. 8*

Compensating variances The situation that exists when two variances, one adverse the other favourable, are of equal size and therefore cancel each other out. *p. 449*

Consistency convention   The accounting convention that holds that, when a particular method of accounting is selected to deal with a transaction, this method should be applied consistently over time. *p. 90*

Consolidated financial statements   *See* Group financial statements. *p. 132*

Consolidating   Reducing the number of shares by increasing their nominal value. *p. 119*

Continual budget   A budgeting system that continually updates budgets so that there is always a budget for a full planning period. (Also known as a *rolling budget*.) *p. 396*

Contribution (per unit)   Sales revenue per unit less variable costs per unit. *p. 291*

Convertible loan stocks   Loan capital that can be converted into equity share capital at the option of the holders. *p. 523*

Corporate governance   Systems for directing and controlling a company. *p. 110*

Corporation tax   Taxation that a limited company is liable to pay on its profits. *p. 109*

Cost   The amount of resources, usually measured in monetary terms, sacrificed to achieve a particular objective. *p. 264*

Cost allocation   Dividing costs between cost centres according to the amount of cost that has been incurred in them. *p. 329*

Cost apportionment   The dividing of costs between cost centres according to the amount of cost that is seen as being fair. *p. 330*

Cost behaviour   The manner in which costs alter with changes in the level of activity. *p. 318*

Cost centre   Some area, object, person or activity for which costs are separately collected. *p. 328*

Cost driver   An activity that causes costs. *p. 350*

Cost of sales   The cost of the goods sold during a period. Cost of sales can be derived by adding the opening stock held to the stock purchases for the period and then deducting the closing stocks held. *p. 65*

Cost pool   The sum of the overhead costs that are seen as being caused by the same cost driver. *p. 350*

Cost-plus pricing   An approach to pricing output that is based on full cost, plus a percentage profit loading. *p. 337*

Cost unit   The objective for which the cost is being deduced, usually a product or service. *p. 319*

Creative accounting   Adopting accounting polices to achieve a particular view of performance and position that preparers would like users to see rather than what is a true and fair view. *p. 169*

Credit   An entry made in the right-hand side of an account in double-entry bookkeeping. *p. 602*

Current asset   An asset that is not held on a continuing basis. Current assets include cash itself and other assets that are expected to be converted to cash at some point in the future. *p. 40*

Current liabilities   A claim against the business which is expect to be settled within the normal course of the business's operating cycle or within 12 months of the balance sheet date or they are held primarily for trading purposes; and the business does not have the right to defer settlement beyond 12 months after the balance sheet date. *p. 42*

Current ratio   A liquidity ratio that relates the current assets of the business to the current liabilities. *p. 224*

Debenture   A long-term loan, usually made to a company, evidenced by a trust deed. *pp. 123, 522*

Debit   An entry made in the left-hand side of an account in double-entry bookkeeping. *p. 602*

Debt factoring   A service offered by a financial institution (a factor) that involves the factor taking over the management of the trade debtors of the business. The factor is often prepared to make an advance to the business, based on the amount of trade debtors outstanding. *p. 542*

Deep discount bond   Redeemable loan capital offering a rate of interest below the market rate and issued at a discount to its redeemable value. *p. 523*

Depreciation   A measure of that portion of the cost of a non-current asset that has been consumed during an accounting period. *p. 76*

Direct costs   Costs that can be identified with specific cost units, to the extent that the effect of the cost can be measured in respect of each particular unit of output. *p. 316*

Direct method   An approach to deducing the cash flows from operating activities, in a cash flow statement, by analysing the business's cash records. *p. 186*

Director   An individual who is elected to act as the most senior level of management of a company. *p. 110*

Directors' report   A report containing information of a financial and non-financial nature that the directors must produce as part of the annual financial report to shareholders. *p. 157*

Discount factor   The rate applied to future cash flows to derive the present value of those cash flows. *p. 480*

Discretionary budget   A budget based on a sum allocated at the discretion of top management. *p. 406*

Discriminate function   A boundary line, produced by multiple discriminate analysis, that identifies those businesses that are likely to suffer financial distress and those that are not. *p. 246*

Dividend   The transfer of assets (usually cash) made by a company to its shareholders. *p. 116*

Dividend cover ratio   An investment ratio that relates the earnings available for dividends to the dividend announced, to indicate how many times the former covers the latter. *p. 233*

Dividend payout ratio   An investment ratio that relates the dividends announced for the period to the earnings available for dividends that were generated in that period. *p. 232*

Dividend per share   An investment ratio that relates the dividends announced for a period to the number of shares in issue. *p. 234*

Dividend yield ratio   An investment ratio that relates the cash return from a share to its current market value. *p. 233*

Double-entry bookkeeping   A system for recording financial transactions where each transaction is recorded twice, once as a debit and once as a credit. *p. 602*

Dual aspect convention   The accounting convention that holds that each transaction has two aspects and that each aspect must be recorded in the financial statements. *p. 49*

Earnings per share An investment ratio that relates the earnings generated by the business during a period, and available to shareholders, to the number of shares in issue. *p. 234*

Economic order quantity (EOQ) The quantity of stock that should be purchased in order to minimise total stock costs. *p. 567*

Economic value added (EVA®) A measure of business performance that concentrates on wealth generation. It is based on the conventional accounting profit figure, but adjusted for distorting factors. *p. 380*

Economies of scale Cost savings per unit that result from undertaking a large volume of activities; they are due to factors such as division and specialisation of labour. *p. 295*

Elasticity of demand The manner in which the level of demand alters with changes in price. *p. 357*

Equity Ordinary shares and reserves of a company. *p. 115*

Eurobond A bond issued by a listed company where the finance is raised on an international basis. The bond is issued in a currency that is different from the currency in which the company raising the finance is based. *p. 522*

Expected net present value (ENPV) A weighted average of the possible present value outcomes, where the probabilities associated with each outcome are used as weights. *p. 494*

Expense A measure of the outflow of assets (or increase in liabilities) incurred as a result of generating revenue. *p. 62*

Fair value The value ascribed to an asset as an alternative to historic cost. It is usually the current market value (that is, the exchange values in an arms-length transaction). *p. 52*

Favourable variance A difference between planned and actual performance, usually where the difference will cause the actual profit to be higher than the budgeted one. *p. 435*

Feedback control A control device where actual performance is compared with planned and where action is taken to deal with future divergences between these. *p. 432*

Feedforward control A control device where forecast future performance is compared with planned and where action is taken to deal with divergences between these. *p. 433*

Final accounts The profit and loss account, cash flow statement and balance sheet taken together. *p. 31*

Finance The study of how businesses raise funds and select appropriate investments. *p. 3*

Finance lease A financial arrangement where the asset title remains with the owner (the lessor) but the lease agreement transfers virtually all the rewards and risks to the business (the lessee). *p. 528*

Financial accounting The measuring and reporting of accounting information for external users (those users other than the managers of the business). *p. 12*

Financial derivative Any form of financial instrument, based on share or loan capital, that can be used by investors either to increase their returns or to decrease their exposure to risk. *p. 526*

Financial gearing   The existence of fixed payment-bearing securities (for example, loans) in the capital structure of a business. *p. 227*

Financial management   A subject area concerned with the financing and investing decisions of businesses. *p. 14*

First in, first out (FIFO)   A method of stock valuation that assumes that the earlier stocks are to be sold first. *p. 86*

Five Cs of credit   A checklist of factors to be taken into account when assessing the creditworthiness of a customer. *p. 572*

Fixed cost   A cost that stays the same when changes occur to the volume of activity. *p. 281*

Flexible budget   A budget that is adjusted to reflect the actual level of output achieved. *p. 435*

Flexing (the budget)   Revising the budget to what it would have been had the planned level of output been different. *p. 434*

Forecast   A prediction of future outcomes or of the future state of the environment. *p. 396*

Framework of principles   The main principles that underpin accounting, which can help in identifying best practice and in developing accounting rules. *p. 158*

Full cost   The total amount of resources, usually measured in monetary terms, sacrificed to achieve a particular objective. *p. 314*

Full cost (cost-plus) pricing   Pricing output on the basis of its full cost, normally with a loading for profit. *p. 363*

Full costing   Deducing the total direct and indirect (overhead) costs of pursuing some activity or objective. *p. 314*

Fully paid shares   Shares on which the shareholders have paid the full issue price. *p. 122*

Gearing ratio   A ratio that relates the contribution of long-term lenders to the total long-term capital of the business. *p. 230*

Going concern convention   The accounting convention that holds that it is assumed that the business will continue operations for the foreseeable future, unless there is reason to believe otherwise. In other words, there is no intention, or need, to liquidate the business. *p. 49*

Gross profit   The amount remaining (if positive) after trading expenses (for example, cost of sales) have been deducted from trading revenue (for example, sales revenue). *p. 64*

Gross profit margin   A profitability ratio relating the gross profit for the period to the sales revenue for the period. *p. 215*

Group financial statements   Sets of financial accounting statements that combine the performance and position of a group of companies that are under common control. *p. 132*

Historic cost   What an asset cost when it was originally acquired. *p. 264*

Historic cost convention   The accounting convention that holds that assets should be recorded at their historic (acquisition) cost. *p. 48*

Income statement   See profit and loss account. *pp. 28, 64*

Incremental budgeting Constructing budgets on the basis of what happened in the previous period, with some adjustment for expected changes in the forthcoming budget period. *p. 406*

Indirect costs (or overheads) All costs except direct costs; that is, those that cannot be directly measured in respect of each particular unit of output. *p. 316*

Indirect method An approach to deducing the cash flows from operating activities, in a cash flow statement, by analysing the business's final accounts. *p. 187*

Inflation The increase in money prices of goods or services. *p. 477*

Intangible assets Assets that do not have a physical substance (for example, patents, goodwill and debtors). *p. 34*

Interest cover ratio A gearing ratio that divides the net profit before interest and taxation by the interest payable for a period. *p. 230*

Internal rate of return (IRR) The discount rate for a project that will have the effect of producing a zero NPV. *p. 482*

International accounting (financial reporting) standards Transnational accounting rules that have been adopted, or developed, by the International Accounting Standards Board and which should be followed in preparing the published financial statements of limited companies. *p. 149*

Investigating variances The act of looking into the practical causes of budget variances, once those variances have been identified. *p. 446*

Invoice discounting A loan provided by a financial institution based on a proportion of the face value of credit sales outstanding. *p. 543*

Irrelevant cost A cost that is not relevant to a particular decision. *p. 265*

Issued share capital That part of the authorised share capital which has been issued to shareholders. Also known as allotted share capital. *p. 122*

Job costing A technique for identifying the full cost per unit of output, where that output is not similar to other units of output. *p. 317*

Just-in-time (JIT) stock management A system of stock management that aims to have supplies delivered to production just in time for their required use. *p. 570*

***Kaizen* costing** An approach to cost control where an attempt is made to control costs by trying continually to make cost savings, often only small ones, from one time period to the next. *p. 371*

Last in, first out (LIFO) A method of stock valuation that assumes that the latest stocks are the first to be sold. *p. 86*

Lead time The time lag between placing an order for goods or services and their deliery. *p. 565*

Learning curve The tendency for people to carry out tasks more quickly as they become more experienced in doing so. *p. 444*

Liabilities Claims of individuals and organisations, apart from the owner, that have arisen from past transactions or events such as supplying goods or lending money to the business. *p. 35*

Limited company An artificial legal person that has an identity separate from that of those who own and manage it. *pp. 19, 105*

Limited liability The restriction of the legal obligation of shareholders to meet all of the company's debts. *p. 108*

Limiting factor   Some aspect of the business (for example, lack of sales demand) that will prevent it achieving its objectives to the maximum extent. *p. 403*

Loan stock   *See* Debenture. *pp. 123, 522*

Loan convenant   A condition contained within a loan agreement that is designed to help protect the lenders. *p. 526*

Management accounting   The measuring and reporting of accounting information for the managers of a business. *p. 12*

Management by exception   A system of control, based on a comparison of planned and actual performance, that allows managers to focus on areas of poor performance rather than dealing with areas where performance is satisfactory. *p. 399*

Margin of safety   The extent to which the planned level of output or sales revenue lies above the break-even point. *pp. 127, 291*

Marginal analysis   The activity of decision making through analysing variable costs and revenue, ignoring fixed costs. *p. 298*

Marginal cost   The addition to total cost that will be incurred by making/providing one more unit of output. *p. 298*

Marginal cost pricing   Pricing output on the basis of its marginal cost, normally with a loading for profit. *p. 365*

Master budgets   A summary of the individual budgets, usually consisting of a budgeted profit and loss account, a budgeted balance sheet and a budgeted cash flow statement. *p. 397*

Matching convention   The accounting convention that holds that, in measuring income, expenses should be matched to revenue, which they helped generate in the same accounting period as that revenue was realised. *p. 72*

Materiality   The requirement that material information should be disclosed to users of financial reports. *p. 9*

Materiality convention   The accounting convention that states that, where the amounts involved are immaterial, only what is expedient should be considered. *p. 75*

Materials requirement planning (MRP) system   A computer-based system of stock control that schedules the timing of deliveries of bought-in parts and materials to coincide with production requirements to meet demand. *p. 570*

Mission statement   A brief statement setting out the aims of the business. *p. 391*

Money measurement convention   The accounting convention that holds that accounting should deal only with those items which are capable of being expressed in monetary terms. *p. 47*

Mortgage   A loan secured on property. *p. 526*

Multiple discriminate analysis   A statistical technique used to predict financial distress, which involves using an index based on a combination of financial ratios. *p. 246*

Net present value (NPV)   A method of investment appraisal based on the present value of all relevant cash flows associated with the project. *p. 475*

Net profit   The amount remaining (if positive) after the total expenses for a period have been deducted from total revenue. *p. 65*

Net profit margin   A profitability ratio relating the net profit for the period to the sales revenue for the period. *p. 215*

Nominal value   The face value of a share in a company. (Also called *par value*.) *p. 115*

Non-current asset   An asset held with the intention of being used to generate wealth rather than being held for resale. Non-current assets can be seen as the tools of the business and are held on a continuing basis. (Also known as *fixed asset.*) *p. 41*

Non-current liability   A claim against the business that is not within the definition of a current liability. *p. 42*

Non-operating profit variances   Differences between budgeted and actual performance that do not lead directly to differences between budgeted and actual operating profit. *p. 446*

Objective probabilities   Probabilities based on information gathered from past experience. *p. 497*

Objectivity convention   The convention that holds that, in so far as is possible, the financial statements prepared should be based on objective verifiable evidence rather than matters of opinion. *p. 50*

Offer for sale   An issue of shares that involves a public limited company (or its shareholders) selling the shares to a financial institution which will, in turn, sell the shares to the public. *p. 537*

Operating and financial review   A narrative report that helps users to understand the operating and financial results of a business for a period. *p. 164*

Operating cash cycle (OCC)   The period between the outlay of cash to purchase supplies and the ultimate receipt of cash from the sale of goods. *p. 581*

Operating gearing   The relationship between the total fixed and the total variable costs for some activity. *p. 291*

Operating lease   A short-term arrangement where one business hires an asset for a short time. Hiring an asset under an operating lease tends to be an operating, rather than a financing, decision. *p. 528*

Operating profit   The profit achieved from business operations before any financing expenses are taken into account. *p. 130*

Opportunity cost   The cost incurred when one course of action prevents an opportunity to derive some benefit from another course of action. *p. 264*

Ordinary shares   Shares of a company owned by those who are due the benefits of the company's activities after all other stakeholders have been satisfied. *p. 116*

Outlay cost   A cost that involves the spending of money or some other transfer of assets. *p. 266*

Outsourcing   Subcontracting activities to (sourcing goods or services from) outside organisations. *p. 302*

Overheads (or indirect costs)   Any cost except a direct cost; a cost which cannot be directly measured in respect of each particular unit of output. *p. 316*

Overhead absorption (recovery) rate   The rate at which overheads are charged to cost units (jobs), usually in a job costing system. *p. 320*

Overtrading   The situation arising when a business is operating at a level of activity which cannot be supported by the amount of finance which has been committed. *p. 241*

Paid-up share capital   That part of the share capital of a company that has been called and paid. *p. 122*

Parent/holding company   A company that has a controlling interest in another company. *p. 132*

Partnership A form of business unit where there are at least two individuals, but usually no more than twenty, carrying on a business with the intention of making a profit. *p. 18*

Past cost A cost that has been incurred in the past. *p. 266*

Payback period (PP) The time taken for the initial investment in a project to be repaid from the net cash inflows of the project. *p. 472*

Penetration pricing Setting prices at a level low enough to encourage wide market acceptance of a product or service. *p. 367*

Periodic budget A budget developed on a one-off basis to cover a particular planning period. *p. 396*

Post-completion audit A review of the performance of an investment project to see whether actual performance matched planned performance and whether any lessons can be drawn from the way in which the investment was carried out. *p. 504*

Preference shares Shares of a company owned by those who are entitled to the first part of any dividend which the company may pay. *p. 116*

Prepaid expenses Expenses that have been paid in advance at the end of the accounting period. *p. 75*

Price/earnings ratio An investment ratio that relates the market value of a share to the earnings per share. *p. 235*

Price skimming Setting prices at a high level to make the maximum profit from the product or service before the price is lowered to attract the next segment of the market. *p. 367*

Private company A limited company for which the directors can restrict the ownership of its shares. *p. 108*

Private placing An issue of shares that involves the company 'placing' the shares with selected investors such as large financial institutions. *p. 538*

Process costing A technique for deriving the full cost per unit of output, where the units of output are exactly similar or it is reasonable to treat them as being so. *p. 315*

Product cost centre Some area, object, person or activity for which costs are separately collected, in which cost units have costs added. *p. 328*

Profit The increase in wealth attributable to the owners of a business that arises through business operations. *p. 62*

Profit and loss account A financial statement (also known as *income statement*) that measures and reports the profit (or loss) the business has generated during a period. It is derived by deducting from total revenue for a period, the total expenses associated with that revenue. *pp. 28, 64*

Profit–volume (PV) chart A graphical representation of the contributions (revenue less variable costs) of some activity, at various levels, which enables the break-even point, and the profit at various activity levels, to be identified. *p. 294*

Provision for doubtful debts An amount set aside out of profits to provide for anticipated losses arising from debts that may prove irrecoverable. *p. 91*

Prudence convention The accounting convention that holds that financial statements should err on the side of caution. *p. 49*

Public company A limited company for which the directors cannot restrict the ownership of its shares. *p. 108*

Public issue A method of issuing shares that involves a public limited company (plc) making a direct invitation to the public to purchase shares in the company. *p. 538*

Realisation convention The accounting convention that holds that revenue should be recognised only when it has been realised. *p. 68*

Reducing-balance method A method of calculating depreciation that applies a fixed percentage rate of depreciation to the written-down value of an asset in each period. *p. 79*

Relevance The ability of accounting information to influence decisions; regarded as a key characteristic of useful accounting information. *p. 7*

Relevant cost A cost that is relevant to a particular decision. *p. 265*

Relevant range The range of volume of activities that a particular business is expected to operate. *p. 296*

Reliability The requirement that accounting should be free from material error or bias. Reliability is regarded as a key characteristic of useful accounting information. *p. 8*

Reserves Part of the owners' claim on a limited company that has arisen from profits and gains, to the extent that these have not been distributed to the shareholders. *p. 115*

Residual value The amount for which a non-current asset is sold when the business has no further use for it. *p. 78*

Return on capital employed (ROCE) A profitability ratio expressing the relationship between the net profit (before interest and taxation) and the long-term capital invested in the business. *p. 214*

Return on ordinary shareholders' funds (ROSF) A profitability ratio that compares the amount of profit for the period available to the ordinary shareholders with their stake in the business. *p. 213*

Revenue A measure of the inflow of assets (for example, cash or amounts owed to a business by debtors), or a reduction in liabilities, that arise as a result of trading operations. *p. 62*

Revenue reserve Part of the owners' claim on a company that arises from realised profits and gains, including after-tax trading profits and gains from disposals of non-current assets. These profits and gains have been reinvested in the company rather than distributed to the owners. *p. 116*

Rights issue An issue of shares for cash to existing shareholders on the basis of the number of shares already held. *p. 535*

Risk The extent and likelihood that what is estimated to occur will not actually occur. *p. 476*

Risk-adjusted discount rate A discount rate applied to investment projects that is increased (decreased) in the face of increased (decreased) risk. *p. 501*

Risk premium An extra amount of return required from an investment, owing to a perceived level of risk. The greater the perceived risk, the larger the required risk premium. *p. 477*

Sale and leaseback An agreement to sell an asset (usually property) to another party and simultaneously to lease the asset back in order to continue using the asset. *p. 529*

Sales revenue per employee An efficiency ratio that relates the sales revenue generated during a period to the average number of employees of the business. *p. 221*

Sales revenue to capital employed An efficiency ratio that relates the sales revenue generated during a period to the capital employed. *p. 220*

Scenario building Creating a model of a business decision, usually on a computer spreadsheet, enabling the decision maker to look at the effect of different assumptions on the decision outcome. *p. 493*

Segmental financial reports Reports that break down the operating results of a business according to its business or geographical segments. *p. 161*

Semi-fixed (semi-variable) cost A cost that has an element of both fixed and variable cost. *p. 284*

Sensitivity analysis An examination of the key variables affecting a project, to see how changes in each input might influence the outcome. *p. 491*

Service cost centre Some area, object, person or activity for which costs are collected separately, in which cost units do not have cost added, because service cost centres only render services to product cost services and to other service cost centres. *p. 328*

Share A portion of the ownership, or equity, of a company. *pp. 7, 105*

Share premium account A capital reserve reflecting any amount, above the nominal value of shares, that is paid for those shares when issued by a company. *p. 119*

Sole proprietorship An individual in business on his or her own account. *p. 17*

Stable monetary unit convention The accounting convention that assumes that money, which is the unit of measurement in accounting, will not change in value over time. *p. 50*

Standard quantities and costs Planned quantities and costs (or revenue) for individual units of input or output. Standards are the building blocks used to produce the budget. *p. 443*

Statement of changes to equity A financial statement, required by IAS 1, which shows the effect of gains/losses and capital injections/withdrawals on the equity base of a company. *p. 155*

Stepped fixed cost A fixed cost that does not remain fixed over all levels of output but which changes in steps as a threshold level of output is reached. *p. 283*

Stock Exchange A market where 'second-hand' shares may be bought and sold and new capital raised. *p. 539*

Straight-line method A method of accounting for depreciation that allocates the amount to be depreciated evenly over the useful life of the asset. *p. 78*

Subjective probabilities Probabilities based on opinion rather than past data. *p. 498*

Summary financial statement A summarised version of the complete annual financial statements, which shareholders may receive as an alternative to the complete statements. *p. 168*

Sunk cost A cost which has been incurred in the past; the same as a past cost. *p. 270*

Takeover The acquisition of control of one company by another, usually as a result of acquiring a majority of the ordinary shares of the former. *p. 133*

Tangible assets Those assets that have a physical substance (for example, plant and machinery, motor vehicles.) *p. 34*

Target costing Where the business starts with the projected selling price and from it deduces the target cost per unit which must be met to enable the company to meet its profit objectives. *p. 370*

Tender issue A public issue of shares or loan stocks where potential investors are invited to place bids for the securities concerned. *p. 538*

Term loan A loan, usually from a bank, which is tailored specifically to the needs of the borrower. The loan contract usually specifies the repayment date, interest rate and so on. *p. 521*

Total life-cycle costing Paying attention to all of the costs that will be incurred during the entire life of a product or service. *p. 369*

Transfer price The price at which goods or services are sold, or transferred, between divisions of the same business. *p. 162*

Trial balance A totalled list of the of the balances on each of the accounts in a double-entry bookkeeping system. *p. 610*

Understandability The requirement that accounting information should be understood by those for whom the information is primarily compiled. Lack of understandability will limit the usefulness of accounting information. *p. 8*

Univariate analysis A method used to help predict financial distress, which involves the use of a single ratio as a predictor. *p. 244*

Value chain analysis Analysing each activity undertaken by a business to identify any that do not add value to the output of goods or services. *p. 371*

Value driver A factor that creates wealth, such as employee satisfaction, customer loyalty and level of product innovation. *p. 373*

Variable cost A cost that varies according to the volume of activity. *p. 281*

Variance The financial effect, usually on the budgeted profit, of the particular factor under consideration being more or less than budgeted. *p. 435*

Variance analysis Carrying out calculations to find the area of the business's operations that has caused the budgets not to have been met. *p. 442*

Venture capital Long-term capital provided by certain institutions to small and medium-sized businesses to exploit relatively high-risk opportunities. *p. 546*

Warrant A document giving the holder the right, but not the obligation, to acquire ordinary shares in a company at an agreed price. *p. 524*

Weighted average cost (AVCO) A method of valuing stocks that assumes that stocks entering the business lose their separate identity and any issues of stock reflect the weighted average cost of the stocks held. *p. 86*

Working capital Current assets less current liabilities. *p. 560*

Written-down value (WDV) The difference between the cost (or revalued amount) of a non-current asset and the accumulated depreciation relating to the asset. The written down-value is also referred to as the net book value (NBV). *p. 79*

Zero-base budgeting (ZBB) An approach to budgeting, based on the philosophy that all spending needs to be justified annually and that each budget should start as a clean sheet. *p. 406*

Appendix C
Solutions to self-assessment questions

Chapter 2

2.1   The balance sheet you prepare should be set out as follows:

Simonson Engineering
Balance sheet as at 30 September 2005

	£	£	£
Non-current assets			
Freehold premises			72,000
Plant and machinery			25,000
Motor vehicles			15,000
Fixtures and fittings			9,000
			121,000
Current assets			
Stock-in-trade		45,000	
Trade debtors		48,000	
Cash in hand		1,500	
		94,500	
Current liabilities			
Trade creditors	(18,000)		
Bank overdraft	(26,000)		
		(44,000)	
			50,500
Total assets less current liabilities			171,500
Non-current liabilities			
Loan			(51,000)
Net assets			120,500
Capital			
Opening balance			117,500
Add Profit			18,000
			135,500
Less Drawings			15,000
			120,500

Chapter 3

3.1 TT and Co

Balance sheet as at 31 December 2004

Assets	£	Claims	£
Delivery van		Capital	
(12,000 − 2,500)	9,500	(50,000 + 26,900)	76,900
Stock-in-trade (143,000 +			
12,000 − 74,000 − 16,000)	65,000	Trade creditors	
		(143,000 − 121,000)	22,000
Trade debtors			
(152,000 − 132,000 − 400)	19,600	Accrued expenses	
		(630 + 620)	1,250
Cash at bank (50,000 − 25,000			
− 500 − 1,200 − 12,000 −			
33,500 − 1,650 − 12,000			
+ 35,000 − 9,400 + 132,000			
− 121,000)	750		
Prepaid expenses			
(5,000 + 300)	5,300		
	100,150		100,150

Profit and loss account for the year ended 31 December 2004

	£	£
Sales revenue (152,000 + 35,000)		187,000
Less Cost of stock sold		
(74,000 + 16,000)		90,000
Gross profit		97,000
Less		
Rent	20,000	
Rates (500 + 900)	1,400	
Wages (33,500 + 630)	34,130	
Electricity (1,650 + 620)	2,270	
Bad debts	400	
Van depreciation [(12,000 − 2,000)/4]	2,500	
Van expenses	9,400	
		70,100
Net profit for the year		£26,900

The balance sheet could now be rewritten in a more stylish form as follows:

Balance sheet as at 31 December 2004

	£	£	£
Non-current assets			
Motor van			9,500
Current assets			
Stock in trade	65,000		
Trade debtors	19,600		
Prepaid expenses	5,300		
Cash	750		
		90,650	
Less **Current liabilities**			
Trade creditors	22,000		
Accrued expenses	1,250		
		23,250	
			67,400
			76,900
Capital			
Original			50,000
Retained profit			26,900
			76,900

Chapter 4

4.1   Dev Ltd

(a) The summarised balance sheet of Dev Ltd, immediately following the rights and bonus issue, is as follows:

Balance sheet as at 31 December 2005

	£
Net assets [235 + 40 (cash from the rights issue)]	275,000
Equity	
Share capital: 100,000 shares @ £1 [(100 + 20) + 60]	180,000
Share premium account (30 + 20 − 50)	–
Revaluation reserve (37 − 10)	27,000
Profit and loss account balance	68,000
	275,000

Note that the bonus issue of £60,000 is taken from capital reserves (reserves unavailable for dividends) as follows:

	£
Share premium account	50,000
Revaluation reserve	10,000
	60,000

More could have been taken from the revaluation reserve and less from the share premium account without making any difference to dividend payment possibilities.

(b) There may be pressure from a potential creditor for the business to limit its ability to pay dividends. This would place creditors in a more secure position because the maximum buffer or safety margin between the value of the assets and the amount owed by the business is maintained. It is not unusual for potential creditors to insist on some measure to lock up shareholders' funds in this way as a condition of granting the loan.

(c) The summarised balance sheet of Dev Ltd, immediately following the rights and bonus issue, assuming a minimum dividend potential objective, is as follows:

Balance sheet as at 31 December 2005

	£
Net assets [235 + 40 (cash from the rights issue)]	275,000
Equity	
Share capital: 100,000 shares @ £1 ((100 + 20) + 60)	180,000
Share premium account (30 + 20)	50,000
Revaluation reserve	37,000
Profit and loss account balance (68 − 60)	8,000
	275,000

(d) Before the bonus issue, the maximum dividend was £68,000. Now it is £8,000. Thus the bonus issue has had the effect of locking up an additional £60,000 of the business's assets in terms of the business's ability to pay dividends.

(e) Before the issues, Lee had 100 shares worth £2.35 (£235,000/100,000) each or £235 in total. Lee would be offered 20 shares in the rights issue at £2 each or £40 in total. After the rights issue, Lee would have 120 shares worth £2.2917 (£275,000/120,000) each or £275 in total.

   The bonus issue would give Lee 60 additional shares. After the bonus issue, Lee would have 180 shares worth £1.5278 (£275,000/180,000) each or £275 in total.

   None of this affects Lee's wealth. Before the issues, Lee had £235 worth of shares and £40 more in cash. After the issues, Lee has the same total wealth but all £275 is in the value of the shares.

(f) The things that we know about the company are as follows:

   (i) It is a private (as opposed to a public) limited company, for it has 'Ltd' (limited) as part of its name, rather than plc (public limited company).

   (ii) It has made an issue of shares at a premium, almost certainly after it had traded successfully for a period. (There is a share premium account. It would be very unlikely that the original shares, issued when the company was first formed, would have been issued at a premium.)

   (iii) Certain of the assets in the balance sheet have been upwardly revalued by at least £37,000. (There is a revaluation reserve of £37,000. This may just be what is left after a previous bonus issue had taken part of the balance.)

   (iv) The company has traded at an aggregate profit (though there could have been losses in some years), net of tax and any dividends paid. (There is a positive balance on the profit and loss account.)

Chapter 5

5.1 J Baxter plc

We can see from the table below that the Italian segment generates the highest revenue, but also generates the lowest profit. We shall be considering financial ratios in detail in Chapter 7, however, it is helpful to compare the profit generated with the sales for each geographical segment. We can see from the table below that the French segment generates the most profit in relation to sales revenue. Fifteen per cent or £0.15 in every £1, of profit is derived from the sales revenue generated. However, for the Italian segment, only 2.1%, or £0.02 in every £1, of profit is derived from the sales revenue generated.

We can also compare the profit generated with the net assets employed (that is, total assets – total liabilities) for each segment. We can see from the table below that the UK segment produces the best return on net assets employed: £0.36 for every £1 invested. Once again, the Italian segment produces the worst results.

The reasons for the relatively poor results from the Italian segment need further investigation. There may be valid reasons; for example, this segment may have deliberately engaged in low pricing during the period in an attempt to increase market share. However, it may suggest that the business needs to re-evaluate its presence in this geographical region.

It is interesting to note that the Italian segment benefited most from capital expenditure during the period. The reasons for such a large investment in such a poorly-performing segment needs to be justified. It is possible that the business will reap rewards for the investment in the future; however, we do not have enough information to understand the reasons for the investment decision.

The reasons why the depreciation charges in the Italian segment are significantly lower than in the other geographical segments should also be investigated. The depreciation charge as a percentage of total assets is much lower. It is possible that the mix of assets is different in the Italian segment from that in the other two segments. If, however, this is not the case and a higher depreciation charge is really warranted, the profitability of this segment would be even worse.

Table of key results

	UK	France	Italy
Total revenue	270	200	390
Segment result	34	30	8
Net assets	94	122	94
Segment result as a percentage of sales revenue	12.6%	15.0%	2.1%
Segment result as a percentage of net assets employed	36.2%	24.6%	8.5%
Capital expenditure	£20m	£15m	£35m
Depreciation as a percentage of total assets	21.7%	23.3%	9.5%

Chapter 6

6.1 Touchstone plc

Touchstone plc
Cash flow statement for the year ended 31 December 2005

	£m	£m
Cash flows from operating activities		
Net profit, after interest, before taxation		
(see Note 1 below)	60	
Adjustments for:		
Depreciation	16	
Interest expense (Note 2)	4	
	80	
Increase in trade debtors (26 – 16)	(10)	
Decrease in trade creditors (38 – 37)	(1)	
Decrease in stocks (25 – 24)	1	
Cash generated from operations	70	
Interest paid	(4)	
Corporation tax paid (Note 3)	(12)	
Dividend paid	(18)	
Net cash from operating activities		36
Cash flows from investing activities		
Payments to acquire tangible non-current assets (Note 4)	(41)	
Net cash used in investing activities		(41)
Cash flows from financing activities		
Issue of debenture stock (40 – 20)	20	
Net cash used in financing activities		20
Net increase in cash and cash equivalents		15
Cash and cash equivalents at 1 January 2005		
Cash		4
Cash and cash equivalents at 31 December 2005		
Cash		4
Treasury bills		15
		19

To see how this relates to the cash of the business at the beginning and end of the year it can be useful to provide a reconciliation as follows:

Analysis of cash and cash equivalents during the year ended 31 December 2005

	£m
Cash and cash equivalents at 1 January 2005	4
Net cash inflow	15
Cash and cash equivalents at 31 December 2005	19

Notes:

1 This is simply taken from the profit and loss account for the year.

2 Interest payable expense must be taken out, by adding it back to the profit figure. We subsequently deduct the cash paid for interest payable during the year. In this case the two figures are identical.

3 Companies pay tax of 50% during their accounting year and the other 50% in the following year. Thus the 2005 payment would have been half the tax on the 2004 profit (that is, the figure that would have appeared in the current liabilities at the end of 2004), plus half of the 2005 tax charge (that is, $4 + (1/2 \times 16) = 12$).

4   Since there were no disposals, the depreciation charges must be the difference between the start and end of the year's non-current asset values, adjusted by the cost of any additions.

	£m
Book value, at 1 January 2005	147
Add Additions (balancing figure)	41
	188
Less Depreciation (6 + 10)	16
Book value, at 31 December 2005	172

Chapter 7

7.1   Financial ratios

In order to answer this question you may have used the following ratios:

	Ali plc	Bhaskar plc
Current ratio	$\dfrac{853.0}{422.4} = 2.0$	$\dfrac{816.5}{293.1} = 2.8$
Acid test ratio	$\dfrac{(853.0 - 592.0)}{422.4} = 0.6$	$\dfrac{(816.5 - 403.0)}{293.1} = 1.4$
Gearing ratio	$\dfrac{190}{(687.6 + 190)} \times 100 = 21.6\%$	$\dfrac{250}{(874.6 + 250)} \times 100 = 22.2\%$
Interest cover ratio	$\dfrac{(131.9 + 19.4)}{19.4} = 7.8$ times	$\dfrac{(139.4 + 27.5)}{27.5} = 6.1$ times
Dividend payout ratio	$\dfrac{135.0}{99.9} \times 100 = 135\%$	$\dfrac{95.0}{104.6} \times 100 = 91\%$
Price/earnings ratio	$\dfrac{£6.50}{31.2p} = 20.8$ times	$\dfrac{£8.20}{41.8p} = 19.6$ times

Ali plc has a much lower current ratio and acid test ratio than Bhaskar plc. The reasons for this may be partly due to the fact that Ali plc has a lower average settlement period for debtors. The acid test ratio of Ali plc is substantially below 1.0: this may suggest a liquidity problem.

The gearing ratio of each business is quite similar. Neither business has excessive borrowing. The interest cover ratio for each business is also similar. The respective ratios indicate that both businesses have good profit coverage for their interest charges.

The dividend payout ratio for each business seems very high. In the case of Ali plc, the dividends announced for the year are considerably higher than the earnings generated during the year that are available for dividend. As a result, part of the dividend was paid out of retained profits from previous years. This is an unusual occurrence; although it is quite legitimate, such action may nevertheless suggest a lack of prudence on the part of the directors.

The P/E ratio for both businesses is high, which indicates market confidence in their future prospects.

Chapter 8

8.1   JB Limited

(a)

	£	
Material M1		
1,200 @ £5.50	6,600	The original cost is irrelevant since any stock used will need to be replaced
Material P2		
800 @ £2.00 (that is, £3.60 – £1.60)	1,600	The best alternative use of this material is as a substitute for P4 – an effective opportunity cost of £2.00/kg
Part no. 678		
400 @ £50	20,000	
Labour		
Skilled 2,000 @ £6	12,000	The effective cost is £6/hour
Unskilled 2,000 @ £5	10,000	
Overheads	3,200	It is only the additional cost which is relevant, the method of apportioning total overheads is not relevant
Total relevant cost	53,400	
Potential revenue		
400 @ £150	60,000	

Clearly, on the basis of the information available it would be beneficial for the business to undertake the contract.

(b) There is an almost infinite number of possible answers to this part of the question, including:

- If material P2 had not been in stock, it may be that it would not be possible to buy it in and still leave the contract as a beneficial one. In this case the business may be unhappy about accepting a price under the particular conditions that apply, which could not be accepted under other conditions.
- Will the replacement for the skilled worker be able to do the normal work of that person to the necessary standard?
- Is JB Limited confident that the additional unskilled employee can be made redundant at the end of this contract without cost to itself?

Chapter 9

9.1   Khan Ltd

(a) The break-even point if only the Alpha service were rendered would be:

$$\frac{\text{Fixed costs}}{\text{Sales revenue per unit} - \text{Variable cost per unit}} = \frac{£40,000}{£30 - (15 + 6)} = 4,445 \text{ units (a year)}$$

(Strictly it is 4,444.44 but 4,445 is the smallest number of units of the service that must be rendered to avoid a loss.)

(b)

	Alpha £/unit	Beta £/unit	Gamma £/unit
Selling price	30	39	20
Variable materials	(15)	(18)	(10)
Variable production costs	(6)	(10)	(5)
Contribution	9	11	5
Staff time (hr/unit)	2	3	1
Contribution/staff-hour	£4.50	£3.67	£5.00
Order of priority	2nd	3rd	1st

(c)

Render:	Hours		Contribution £
5,000 Gamma using	5,000	generating (that is, 5,000 × £5 =)	25,000
2,500 Alpha using	5,000	generating (that is, 2,500 × £9 =)	22,500
	10,000		47,500
		Less Fixed costs	40,000
		Profit	7,500

Leaving a demand for 500 units of Alpha and 2,000 units of Beta unsatisfied.

Chapter 10

10.1 Hector and Co. Ltd

Job costing basis

			£
Materials:	Metal wire	1,000 × 2 × £2.20*	4,400
	Fabric	1,000 × 0.5 × £1.00*	500
Labour:	Skilled	1,000 × (10/60) × £7.50	1,250
	Unskilled	1,000 × (5/60) × £5.00	417
Overheads		1,000 × (15/60) × (50,000/12,500)	1,000
Total cost			7,567
Add Profit loading		12.5% thereof	946
Total tender price			8,513

* In the traditional approach to full costing, historic costs of materials tend to be used. It would not necessarily have been incorrect to have used the 'relevant' (opportunity) costs here.

Minimum contract price (relevant cost basis)

			£
Materials:	Metal wire	1,000 × 2 × £2.50 (replacement cost)	5,000
	Fabric	1,000 × 0.5 × £0.40 (scrap value)	200
Labour:	Skilled	(there is no effective cost of skilled staff)	–
	Unskilled	1,000 × 5/60 × £5.00	417
Minimum tender price			5,617

The difference between the two prices is partly that the relevant costing approach tends to look to the future, partly that it considers opportunity costs, and partly that the job-costing basis total has a profit loading.

Chapter 11

11.1 Psilis Ltd

(a) *Full cost (present basis)*

	Basic		Super	
	£		£	
Direct labour (all £5/hour)	20.00	(4 hours)	30.00	(6 hours)
Direct material	15.00		20.00	
Overheads	18.20	(£4.55* × 4)	27.30	(£4.55* × 6)
	53.20		77.30	

* Total direct-labour-hours worked = (40,000 × 4) + (10,000 × 6) = 220,000 hours. Overhead recovery rate = £1,000,000/220,000 = £4.55 per direct-labour-hour.

Thus the selling prices are currently:

Basic: £53.20 + 25% = £66.50
Super: £77.30 + 25% = £96.63

(b) *Full cost (activity basis)*

Here, the cost of each cost-driving activity is apportioned between total production of the two products.

Activity	Cost £000	Basis of apportionment	Basic £000		Super £000	
Machine set-ups	280	Number of set-ups	56	(20/100)	224	(80/100)
Quality inspection	220	Number of inspections	55	(500/2,000)	165	(1,500/2,000)
Sales order processing	240	Number of orders processed	72	(1,500/5,000)	168	(3,500/5,000)
General production	260	Machine-hours	182	(350/500)	78	(150/500)
Total	1,000		365		635	

The overheads per unit are:

$$\text{Basic:} \quad \frac{£365,000}{40,000} = £9.13$$

$$\text{Super:} \quad \frac{£635,000}{10,000} = £63.50$$

Thus, on an activity basis the full costs are as follows:

	Basic		Super	
	£		£	
Direct labour (all £5/hour)	20.00	(4 hours)	30.00	(6 hours)
Direct material	15.00		20.00	
Overheads	9.13		63.50	
Full cost	44.13		113.50	
Current selling price	£66.50		£96.63	

(c) It seems that the Supers are being sold for less than they cost to produce. If the price cannot be increased, there is a very strong case for abandoning this product. At the same time, the Basics are very profitable to the extent that it may be worth considering lowering the price to attract more revenue.

The fact that the overhead costs can be related to activities and, more specifically, to products does not mean that abandoning Super production would lead to immediate overhead cost savings. For example, it may not be possible or desirable to dismiss machine-setting staff overnight. It would certainly rarely be possible to release factory space occupied by machine setters and make immediate cost savings. Nevertheless, in the medium term these costs can be avoided and it may be sensible to do so.

Chapter 12

12.1 **Antonio Ltd**

(a) (i) Raw materials stock budget for the six months ending 31 December (physical quantities):

	July units	Aug units	Sept units	Oct units	Nov units	Dec units
Opening stock (Current month's production)	500	600	600	700	750	750
Purchases (Balance figure)	600	600	700	750	750	750
	1,100	1,200	1,300	1,450	1,500	1,500
Less Issues to prod'n (From question)	500	600	600	700	750	750
Closing stock (Next month's production)	600	600	700	750	750	750

Raw materials' stock budget for the six months ending 31 December (in financial terms), that is, the physical quantities × £8:

	July £	Aug £	Sept £	Oct £	Nov £	Dec £
Opening stock	4,000	4,800	4,800	5,600	6,000	6,000
Purchases	4,800	4,800	5,600	6,000	6,000	6,000
	8,800	9,600	10,400	11,600	12,000	12,000
Less Issues to prod'n	4,000	4,800	4,800	5,600	6,000	6,000
Closing stock	4,800	4,800	5,600	6,000	6,000	6,000

(ii) Creditors budget for the six months ending 31 December:

	July £	Aug £	Sept £	Oct £	Nov £	Dec £
Opening balance (Current month's payment)	4,000	4,800	4,800	5,600	6,000	6,000
Purchases (From raw materials stock budget)	4,800	4,800	5,600	6,000	6,000	6,000
	8,800	9,600	10,400	11,600	12,000	12,000
Less Payments	4,000	4,800	4,800	5,600	6,000	6,000
Closing balance (Next month's payment)	4,800	4,800	5,600	6,000	6,000	6,000

(iii) Cash budget for the six months ending 31 December:

	July £	Aug £	Sept £	Oct £	Nov £	Dec £
Inflows						
Receipts:						
Debtors (40% of sales revenue of two months previous)	2,800	3,200	3,200	4,000	4,800	5,200
Cash sales revenue (60% of current month's sales)	4,800	6,000	7,200	7,800	8,400	9,600
Total inflows	7,600	9,200	10,400	11,800	13,200	14,800
Outflows						
Creditors (from creditors budget)	(4,000)	(4,800)	(4,800)	(5,600)	(6,000)	(6,000)
Direct costs	(3,000)	(3,600)	(3,600)	(4,200)	(4,500)	(4,500)
Advertising	(1,000)	–	–	(1,500)	–	–
Overheads: 80%	(1,280)	(1,280)	(1,280)	(1,280)	(1,600)	(1,600)
20%	(280)	(320)	(320)	(320)	(320)	(400)
New plant			(2,200)	(2,200)	(2,200)	
Total outflows	(9,560)	(10,000)	(12,200)	(15,100)	(14,620)	(12,500)
Net inflows (outflows)	(1,960)	(800)	(1,800)	(3,300)	(1,420)	2,300
Balance c/f	5,540	4,740	2,940	(360)	(1,780)	520

The balances carried forward are deduced by deducting the deficit (net outflows) for the month from (or adding the surplus for the month to) the previous month's balance.

Note how budgets are linked; in this case the stock budget to the creditors budget and the creditors budget to the cash budget.

(b) The following are possible means of relieving the cash shortages revealed by the budget:

- Make a higher proportion of sales on a cash basis.
- Collect the money from debtors more promptly, for example during the month following the sale.
- Hold lower stocks, both of raw materials and of finished goods.
- Increase the creditor payment period.
- Delay the payments for advertising.
- Obtain more credit for the overhead costs; at present only 20% are on credit.
- Delay the payments for the new plant.

Chapter 13

13.1 Toscanini Ltd

(a) and (b)

	Budget			Actual	
	Original	Flexed		Actual	
Output (units) (prod'n and sales)	4,000	3,500		3,500	
	£	£		£	
Sales revenue	16,000	14,000		13,820	
Raw materials	(3,840)	(3,360)	(1,400 kg)	(3,420)	(1,425 kg)
Labour	(3,200)	(2,800)	(350 hr)	(2,690)	(345 hr)
Fixed overheads	(4,800)	(4,800)		(4,900)	
Operating profit	4,160	3,040		2,810	

	£		Manager accountable
Sales volume variance (4,160 – 3,040)	(1,120)	(A)	Sales
Sales price variance (14,000 – 13,820)	(180)	(A)	Sales
Materials price variance (1,425 × 2.40) – 3,420	0		–
Materials usage variance [(3,500 × 0.4) – 1,425] × £2.40	(60)	(A)	Production
Labour rate variance (345 × £8) – 2,690	70	(F)	Personnel
Labour efficiency variance [(3,500 × 0.10) – 345] × £8	40	(F)	Production
Fixed overhead spending (4,800 – 4,900)	(100)	(A)	Various depending on the nature of the overheads
Total net variances	(1,350)	(A)	
Budgeted profit	4,160		
Less Total net variance	1,350		
Actual profit	2,810		

(c) Feasible explanations include the following:

- Sales volume – unanticipated fall in world demand would account for $400 \times £2.24 = £896$ of this variance (£2.24 is the budgeted contribution per unit). The remainder is probably caused by ineffective marketing, though a lack of availability of stock to sell may be a reason.
- Sales price – ineffective selling seems the only logical reason.
- Materials usage – inefficient usage of material, perhaps because of poor performance by labour or substandard materials.
- Labour rate – less overtime worked or lower production bonuses paid as a result of lower volume of activity.
- Labour efficiency – more effective working.
- Overheads – ineffective control of overheads.

(d) Clearly, not all of the sales volume variance can be attributed to poor marketing, given a 10% reduction in demand.

It will probably be useful to distinguish between that part of the variance that arose from the shortfall in general demand (a planning variance) and a volume variance, which is more fairly attributable to the manager concerned. Thus accountability will be more fairly imposed.

	£
Planning variance (10% × 4,000) × £2.24	896
'New' sales volume variance	
[4,000 − (10% × 4,000) − 3,500] × £2.24	224
Original sales volume variance	1,120

Chapter 14

14.1   Beacon Chemicals plc

(a) Relevant cash flows are as follows:

	Year 0 £000	Year 1 £000	Year 2 £000	Year 3 £000	Year 4 £000	Year 5 £000
Sales revenue	–	80	120	144	100	64
Loss of contribution		(15)	(15)	(15)	(15)	(15)
Variable costs		(40)	(50)	(48)	(30)	(32)
Fixed costs (Note 1)		(8)	(8)	(8)	(8)	(8)
Operating cash flows		17	47	73	47	9
Working capital	(30)					30
Capital cost	(100)					
Net relevant cash flows	(130)	17	47	73	47	39

Notes:
1 Only the fixed costs that are incremental to the project (only existing because of the project) are relevant. Depreciation is irrelevant because it is not a cash flow.
2 The research and development cost is irrelevant since it has been spent irrespective of the decision on X14 production.

(b) The payback period is as follows:

	Year 0 £000	Year 1 £000	Year 2 £000	Year 3 £000
Cumulative cash flows	(130)	(113)	(66)	7

Thus the equipment will have repaid the initial investment by the end of the third year of operations.

(c) The net present value is as follows:

	Year 0 £000	Year 1 £000	Year 2 £000	Year 3 £000	Year 4 £000	Year 5 £000
Discount factor	1.00	0.926	0.857	0.794	0.735	0.681
Present value	(130)	15.74	40.28	57.96	34.55	26.56
Net present value	45.09	(That is, the sum of the present values for years 0 to 5.)				

Chapter 15

15.1   Helsim Ltd

(a) The liquidity position may be assessed by using the liquidity ratios discussed in Chapter 7:

$$\text{Current ratio} = \frac{\text{Current assets}}{\text{Current liabilities (Creditors due within one year)}}$$

$$= \frac{£7.5m}{£5.4m}$$

$$= 1.4$$

$$\text{Acid test ratio} = \frac{\text{Current assets (excluding stock)}}{\text{Current liabilities (Creditors due within one year)}}$$

$$= \frac{£3.7m}{£5.4m}$$

$$= 0.7$$

These ratios reveal a fairly weak liquidity position. The current ratio seems quite low and the acid test ratio very low. This latter ratio suggests that the business does not have sufficient liquid assets to meet its maturing obligations. It would, however, be useful to have details of the liquidity ratios of similar businesses in the same industry in order to make a more informed judgement. The bank overdraft represents 67% of the short-term liabilities and 40% of the total liabilities of the business. The continuing support of the bank is therefore important to the ability of the business to meet its commitments.

(b) The finance required to reduce trade creditors to an average of 40 days outstanding is calculated as follows:

	£m	
Trade creditors at balance sheet date	1.80	
Trade creditors outstanding based on 40 days' credit		
40/365 × £8.4m (that is, credit purchases)	(0.92)	
Finance required	0.88	(say £0.9m)

(c) The bank may not wish to provide further finance to the business. The increase in overdraft will reduce the level of trade creditors but will increase the exposure of the bank. The additional finance invested by the bank will not generate further funds and will not therefore be self-liquidating. The question does not make it clear whether the business has sufficient security to offer the bank for the increase in overdraft facility. The profits of the business will be reduced and the interest cover ratio, based on the profits generated to the year ended 31 May 2001, would reduce to less than 2.0* times if the additional overdraft was granted (based on interest charged at 10% each year). This is very low and means that only a small decline in profits would leave interest charges uncovered.

* Existing bank overdraft (3.6) + extension of overdraft to cover reduction in trade creditors (0.9) + debentures (3.5) = £8.0m. Assuming a 10% interest rate means a yearly interest payment of £0.8m. Before interest, the profit was £1.3m (that is, 6.4 − 3.0 − 2.1). Interest cover would be 1.63 (that is, 1.3/0.8).

(d) A number of possible sources of finance might be considered. Four possible sources are as follows:

- *Issue equity shares.* This option may be unattractive to investors. The return on equity is fairly low at 7.9% (that is, net profit after tax (0.3)/share capital and reserves (3.8)) and there is no evidence that the profitability of the business will improve. If profits remain at their current level the effect of issuing more equity will be to reduce further the returns to equity.

- *Issue loans.* This option may also prove unattractive to investors. The effect of issuing further loans will have a similar effect to that of increasing the overdraft. The profits of the business will be reduced and the interest cover ratio will decrease to a low level. The gearing ratio of the business is already quite high at 48% (that is, debentures (3.5)/(debentures + capital and reserves (3.5 + 3.8)) and it is not clear what security would be available for the loan. The gearing ratio would be much higher if the overdraft were to be included.

- *Chase debtors.* It may be possible to improve cash flows by reducing the level of credit outstanding from debtors. At present, the average settlement period is 93 days (that is, (debtors (3.6)/sales revenue (14.2)) × 365), which seems quite high. A reduction in the average settlement period by approximately one-quarter would generate the funds required. However, it is not clear what effect this would have on sales.

- *Reduce stock.* This appears to be the most attractive of the four options. At present, the average stockholding period is 178 days (that is, (closing stock (3.8)/cost of sales (7.8)) × 365), which seems very high. A reduction in this period by less than one-quarter would generate the funds required. However, if the business holds a large amount of slow-moving and obsolete stock, it may be difficult to reduce stock levels.

Chapter 16

16.1 Williams Wholesalers Ltd

	£	£
Existing level of debtors (£4m × 70/365)		767,123
New level of debtors: £2m × 80/365	438,356	
£2m × 30/365	164,384	602,740
Reduction in debtors		164,383
Costs and benefits of policy		
Cost of discount (£2m × 2%)		40,000
Less Savings		
Interest payable (£164,383 × 13%)	21,370	
Administration costs	6,000	
Bad debts (20,000 − 10,000)	10,000	37,370
Net cost of policy		2,630

The above calculations reveal that the business will be worse off by offering the discounts.

Appendix D
Solutions to selected exercises

Chapter 2

2.1

Cash flow statement for day 4

	£
Opening balance (from day 3)	59
Cash from sale of wrapping paper	47
	106
Cash paid to purchase wrapping paper	(53)
Closing balance	53

Profit and loss account for day 4

	£
Sales revenue	47
Cost of goods sold	(33)
Profit	14

Balance sheet at the end of day 4

	£
Cash	53
Stock of goods for resale (23 + 53 − 33)	43
Total business wealth	96

2.2

	£
Cash introduced by Paul on day 1	40
Profit of day 1	15
Profit of day 2	18
Profit of day 3	9
Profit of day 4	14
	96

Thus the wealth of the business, all of which belongs to Paul as sole owner, consists of the cash he put in to start the business plus the profit earned each day.

2.3

Profit and loss account for day 1

	£
Sales revenue (70 × £0.80)	56
Cost of sales (70 × £0.50)	(35)
Profit	21

Cash flow statement for day 1

	£
Opening balance	40
Add Cash from sales	56
	96
Less Cash for purchases (80 × £0.50)	40
Closing balance	56

Balance sheet as at end of day 1

	£
Cash balance	56
Stock of unsold goods (10 × £0.50)	5
Helen's business wealth	61

Profit and loss account for day 2

	£
Sales revenue (65 × £0.80)	52.0
Cost of sales (65 × £0.50)	(32.5)
Profit	19.5

Cash flow statement for day 2

	£
Opening balance	56.0
Add Cash from sales	52.0
	108.0
Less Cash for purchases (60 × £0.50)	30.0
Closing balance	78.0

Balance sheet as at end of day 2

	£
Cash balance	78.0
Stock of unsold goods (5 × £0.50)	2.5
Helen's business wealth	80.5

Profit and loss account for day 3

	£
Sales revenue (20 × £0.80) + (45 × £0.40)	34.0
Cost of sales (65 × £0.50)	(32.5)
Profit	1.5

Cash flow statement for day 3

	£
Opening balance	78.0
Add Cash from sales	34.0
	112.0
Less Cash for purchases (60 × £0.50)	30.0
Closing balance	82.0

Balance sheet as at end of day 3

	£
Cash balance	82.0
Stock of unsold goods	–
Helen's business wealth	82.0

3.5
(a) Rent payable – expense for period   £9,000
(b) Rates and insurance – expense for period   £6,000
(c) General expenses – paid in period   £7,000
(d) Loan interest payable – prepaid   £500
(e) Salaries – paid in period   £6,000
(f) Rent receivable – received during period   £3,000

3.7

WW Limited
Balance sheet as at 31 December 2005

Assets	£	Claims	£
Machinery		Capital	
(+25,300 + 6,000 + 9,000 − 13,000 + 3,900 − 9,360)	21,840*	(+48,900 − 23,000 + 26,480)	52,380
Stock-in-trade			
(+12,200 + 143,000 + 12,000 − 127,000 − 25,000)	15,200		
		Trade creditors	
		(+16,900 + 143,000 − 156,000)	3,900
Trade debtors	34,300	Accrued expenses	860
(+21,300 + 211,000 − 198,000)		(+1,700 − 1,700 + 860)	
Cash at bank (overdraft)	−19,700		
(+8,300 − 23,000 − 25,000 − 2,000 − 6,000 − 23,800 − 2,700 − 12,000 + 42,000 + 198,000 − 156,000 − 17,500)			
Prepaid expenses	5,500		
(+400 − 400 + 500 + 5,000)			
	57,140		57,140

	£
*	
Cost less accumulated depreciation at 31 December 2004	25,300
Less Book value of machine disposed of (£13,000 − £3,900)	9,100
	16,200
Add Cost of new machine	15,000
	31,200
Depreciation for 2005 (£31,200 × 30%)	9,360
Net book value of machine at 31 December 2005	21,840

Profit and loss account for the year ended 31 December 2005

	£	£
Sales revenue (+211,000 + 42,000)		253,000
Less Cost of stock sold (+127,000 + 25,000)		152,000
Gross profit		101,000
Less		
Rent (+20,000)	20,000	
Rates (+400 + 1,500)	1,900	
Wages (−1,700 + 23,800 + 860)	22,960	
Electricity (+2,700)	2,700	
Machinery depreciation (+9,360)	9,360	
Loss on disposal of the old machinery (+13,000 − 3,900 − 9,000)	100	
Van expenses (+17,500)	17,500	
		74,520
Net profit for the year		26,480

The loss on disposal of the old machinery is the book value (cost less depreciation) less the disposal proceeds. Since the machinery had only been owned for one year, with a depreciation rate of 30%, the depreciation on it so far is £3,900 (that is, £13,000 × 30%). The effective disposal proceeds were £9,000 because, as a result of trading it in, the business saved £9,000 on the new asset.

The depreciation expense for 2005 is based on the cost less accumulated depreciation of the assets owned at the end of 2005. Accumulated depreciation must be taken into account because the business uses the reducing-balance method.

The balance sheet could now be rewritten in a more stylish form as follows:

WW Limited
Balance sheet as at 31 December 2005

	£	£	£
Non-current assets			
Machinery			21,840
Current assets			
Stock-in-trade	15,200		
Trade debtors	34,300		
Prepaid expenses	5,500		
		55,000	
Less **Current liabilities**			
Trade creditors	3,900		
Accrued expenses	860		
Bank overdraft	19,700		
		24,460	30,540
			52,380
Capital			
Original			48,900
Profit			26,480
			75,380
Less Drawings			23,000
			52,380

3.8 An examination of the trading and profit and loss accounts for the two years reveals a number of interesting points, which include:

- An increase in sales value and gross profit of 9.9% in 2005.
- The gross profit expressed as a percentage of sales revenue remaining at 70%.
- An increase in salaries of 7.2%.
- An increase in selling and distribution costs of 31.2%.
- An increase in bad debts of 392.5%.
- A decline in net profit of 39.3%.
- A decline in the net profit as a percentage of sales revenue from 13.3% to 7.4%.

Thus, the business has enjoyed an increase in sales revenue and gross profits, but this has failed to translate to an increase in net profit because of the significant rise in overheads. The increase in selling costs during 2005 suggests that the increase in sales revenue was achieved by greater marketing effort, and the huge increase in bad debts suggests that the increase in sales revenue may be attributable to selling to less creditworthy customers or to a weak debt-collection policy. There appears to have been a change of policy in 2005 towards sales, and this has not been successful overall as the net profit has shown a dramatic decline.

Chapter 4

4.1 Limited companies can no more set a limit on the amount of debts they will meet than can human beings. They must meet their debts up to the limit of their assets, just as we as individuals must. In the context of owners' claim, 'reserves' mean part of the owners' claim against the assets of the company. These assets may or may not include cash. The legal ability of the company to pay dividends is not related to the amount of cash that it has.

Preference shares do not carry a guaranteed dividend. They simply guarantee that the preference shareholders have a right to the first slice of any dividend that is paid. Shares of many companies can, in effect, be bought by one investor from another through the Stock Exchange. Such a transaction has no direct effect on the company, however. These are not new shares being offered by the company, but existing shares that are being sold 'second-hand'.

4.2 (a) The first part of the quote is incorrect. Bonus shares should not, of themselves, increase the value of the shareholders' wealth. This is because reserves, belonging to the shareholders, are used to create bonus shares. Thus, each shareholder's stake in the company has not increased.

Share splits should not increase the wealth of the shareholder, and so that part of the quote is correct.

(b) This statement is incorrect. Shares can be issued at any price, provided that it is not below the nominal value of the shares. Once the company has been trading profitably for a period, the shares will not be worth the same as they were (the nominal value) when the company was first formed. In such circumstances, issuing shares at above their nominal value would not only be legal, but essential to preserve the wealth of the existing shareholders relative to any new ones.

(c) This statement is incorrect. From a legal perspective, the company is limited to a maximum dividend of the current extent of its revenue reserves. This amounts to any after-tax profits or gains realised that have not been eroded through, for example, payments of previous dividends. Legally, cash is not an issue; it would be perfectly legal for a company to borrow the funds to pay a dividend – although whether such an action would be commercially prudent is another question.

(d) This statement is partly incorrect. Companies do indeed have to pay tax on their profits. Depending on their circumstances, shareholders might also have to pay tax on their dividends.

4.4 **Iqbal Ltd**

Year	Maximum dividend £	
2002	0	No profit exists out of which to pay a dividend
2003	0	There remains a cumulative loss of £7,000. Since the revaluation represents a gain that has not been realised, it cannot be used to justify a dividend
2004	13,000	The cumulative net realised gains are derived as (−£15,000 + £8,000 + £15,000 + £5,000)
2005	14,000	The net realised profits and gains for the year
2006	22,000	The net realised profits and gains for the year

4.6   Pear Limited

Balance sheet as at 30 September 2005

	£000	£000
Non-current assets		
Property, plant and equipment		
Cost (1,570 + 30)	1,600	
Depreciation (690 + 12)	702	
		898
Current assets		
Stock	207	
Debtors (182 + 18 – 4)	196	
Cash at bank	21	
	424	
Less **Current liabilities**		
Trade creditors	88	
Other creditors (20 + 30 + 15 + 2)	67	
Taxation	17	
Dividend approved	25	
Bank overdraft	105	
	302	
Net current assets		122
Less **Non-current liabilities**		
10% debenture – repayable 2008		(300)
		720
Equity		
Shares capital		300
Share premium account		300
Retained profit at beginning of year	104	
Retained profit for year	16	120
		720

Profit and loss account for the year ended 30 September 2005

	£000	£000
Revenue (1,456 + 18)		1,474
Cost of sales		(768)
Gross profit		706
Less Salaries	220	
Depreciation (249 + 12)	261	
Other operating costs [131 + (2% × 200) + 2]	137	
		(618)
Operating profit		88
Interest payable (15 + 15)		(30)
Profit before taxation		58
Taxation (58 × 30%)		(17)
Profit after taxation		41
Dividend approved		(25)
Retained profit for the year		16

4.7   Chips Limited

Balance sheet as at 30 June 2005

	Cost £000	Depreciation £000	£000
Non-current assets			
Property, plant and equipment			
Buildings	800	(112)	688
Plant and equipment	650	(367)	283
Motor vehicles (102 – 8); (53 – 5 + 19)	94	(67)	27
	1,544	(546)	998
Current assets			
Stock		950	
Trade debtors (420 – 16)		404	
Cash at bank (16 + 2)		18	
		1,372	
Less **Current liabilities**			
Trade creditors (361 + 23)		(384)	
Other creditors (117 + 35)		(152)	
Taxation		(26)	
		(562)	
Net current assets			810
Less **Non-current liabilities**			
Secured 10% loan			(700)
			1,108
Equity			
Ordinary shares of £1, fully paid			800
Reserves at 1 July 2000		248	
Retained profit for year		60	308
			1,108

Profit and loss account for the year ended 30 June 2005

	£000	£000
Revenue (1,850 – 16)		1,834
Cost of sales (1,040 + 23)		1,063
Gross profit		771
Less Depreciation [220 – 2 – 5 + 8 + (94 × 20%)]	(240)	
Other operating costs	(375)	
		(615)
Operating profit		156
Interest payable (35 + 35)		(70)
Profit before taxation		86
Taxation (86 × 30%)		(26)
Profit after taxation		60

Chapter 5

5.1   Many believe that the annual reports of companies are becoming too long and contain too much information. To illustrate this point, a few examples of the length of the 2003 accounts of large companies are as follows:

Rolls-Royce plc	76 pages
The Boots Company plc	68 pages
Cadbury Schweppes plc	148 pages
Vodafone Group plc	152 pages

There is a danger that users will suffer from 'information overload' if they are confronted with an excessive amount of information and that they will be unable to cope with it. This may, in turn, lead them to:

● Fail to distinguish between important and less important information.
● Fail to approach the analysis of information in a logical and systematic manner.
● Feel a sense of confusion and avoid the task of analysing the information.

Lengthy annual reports are likely to be a problem for the less sophisticated user. This problem has been recognised and many companies publish abridged accounts for private investors, which include only the key points. However, for sophisticated users the problem may be that the annual reports are still not long enough. They often wish to glean as much information as possible from the company in order to make investment decisions.

5.3

I. Ching (Booksellers) plc
Profit and loss account for the year ended 31 December 2005

	£000
Revenue	943
Cost of sales	(460)
	483
Other income	42
	525
Distribution costs	(110)
Administrative expenses	(314)
Other expenses	(25)
Finance costs	(40)
Total expenses	(489)
Profit before tax	36
Corporation tax	(9)
Profit for the period	27

5.4

Manet plc
Statement of changes in equity for the year ended 30 June 2005

	Share Capital £m	Share premium £m	Reval. reserve £m	Translat. reserve £m	Retained earnings £m	Total £m
Balance as at 30 June 2004	250	50	120	15	380	815
Changes in equity for the year ended 30 June 2005						
Gain on revaluation of properties			30			30
Exchange differences on translation of foreign operations				(5)		(5)
Net income recognised directly to equity			30	(5)		25
Profit for the period					160	160
Total recognised income and expense for the period			30	(5)	160	185
Dividends					(80)	(80)
Balance at 30 June 2005	250	50	150	10	460	920

5.5   Here are some points that might be made concerning accounting regulation and accounting measurement:

For

- It seems reasonable that companies, particularly given their limited liability, should be required to account to their members and to the general public and that the law should prescribe how this should be done – including how particular items should be measured. It also seems sensible that accounting standards should amplify these rules, to try to establish some uniformity of practice. Investors could be misled if the same item appeared in the financial statements of two separate companies but had been measured in different ways.

- Companies would find it difficult to attract finance, credit and possibly employees without publishing credible information about themselves. An important measure of performance is profit, and investors often need to make judgements concerning relative performance within an industry sector. Without clear benchmarks by which to judge performance, investors may not invest in a company.

Against

- Some would argue that it is up to the companies to decide whether or not they can survive and prosper without publishing information about themselves. If they can, then so much the better for them as they will have saved large amounts of money by not doing so. If it is necessary for a company to provide financial information in order to be able to attract investment finance and other necessary factors, then the company can make the necessary judgement of how much information is necessary and what forms of measurement are required.

- Not all company managements view matters in the same way. Allowing companies to select their own approaches to financial reporting enables them to reflect their personalities. Thus, a conservative management will adopt conservative accounting policies such as writing off research and development expenditure quickly, whereas more adventurous management may adopt less conservative accounting policies such as writing off research and development expenditure over several years. The impact of these different views will have an effect on profit and will give the reader an insight to the approach adopted by the management team.

5.8   Unilever plc

(a) We can see from the first table that the Personal Care segment has the both the highest sales revenue (turnover) and the highest profit. Revenue is approximately three times higher and profit is approximately four times higher that of the smallest segment: the Health and Wellness and Beverages segment.

The Personal Care segment also generates the highest profit when expressed as a percentage of sales revenue. It is almost twice that of the Home Care and Professional Cleaning segment, which produces the lowest return in relation to sales revenue (excluding other operations). This wide difference in returns between the segments may reflect factors such as differences in the competitive environment, differences in pricing policies and so on. The Personal Care segment also produces the highest profit when expressed as a percentage of the assets employed. It is more than twice the return of the next best segment, the Spreads and Cooking Products segment. Personal Care seems to be the 'star' segment.

The Savoury and Dressings segment has substantially more assets employed than other segments and the return on assets employed is very low in relation to other segments (excluding other operations). The reasons for this should be established, as it seems that assets are not being used as productively in this segment as in the others. The capital expenditure as a percentage of sales revenue is fairly low for all of the business segments.

The geographical analysis shown in the second table is not very helpful as around two-thirds of both assets and revenue have been lumped together under the heading of 'other'. We can see, however, that the US segment is significantly larger than the UK segment in terms of both revenue and assets employed.

Tables of key results

	Business segments						
	Savoury and dressings	Spreads and cooking products	Health & wellness and beverages	Ice cream and frozen foods	Home care & professional cleaning	Personal care	Other operations
Group revenue (turnover)	9,272	6,145	4,064	7,456	8,565	12,236	532
Trading result	1,362	834	504	704	725	1,976	27
Capital expenditure	202	166	167	270	215	251	27
Total assets by operation	19,717	3,610	4,095	3,851	3,581	4,066	2,662
Segment result as a percentage of revenue (turnover)	14.7%	13.6%	12.4%	9.4%	8.5%	16.1%	5.1%
Segment result as percentage of total assets	6.9%	23.1%	12.3%	18.3%	20.2%	48.6%	1.0%
Capital expenditure as a percentage of revenue (turnover)	2.2%	2.7%	4.1%	3.6%	2.5%	2.1%	5.1%

Geographical segments

	UK	US	Other	Total
Revenue (turnover) as a percentage of total revenue	11.2%	23.7%	65.1%	100.0%
Property, plant and equipment as a percentage of total property, plant and equipment	13.2%	21.0%	65.8%	100.0%

(b) Information on the liabilities relating to each business segment would be helpful. This information is a requirement under IAS 14 *Segment Reporting*. In addition, a more detailed breakdown of geographical segments would be helpful, along with information relating to the profits generated by each segment.

Chapter 6

6.1 (a) An increase in the level of stock in trade (inventory) would, ultimately, have an adverse effect on cash.

(b) A rights issue of ordinary shares will give rise to a positive cash flow, which will be included in the 'financing' section of the cash flow statement.

(c) A bonus issue of ordinary shares has no cash flow effect.

(d) Writing off some of the value of the stock (inventory) has no cash flow effect.

(e) A disposal for cash of a large number of shares by a major shareholder has no cash flow effect as far as the business is concerned.

(f) Depreciation does not involve cash at all. Using the indirect method of deducing cash flows from operating activities involves the depreciation expense in the calculation, but this is simply because we are trying to find out from the profit (after depreciation) figure what the profit before depreciation must have been.

6.3

Torrent plc
Cash flow statement for the year ended 31 December 2005

	£m	£m
Cash flows from operating activities		
Net profit, after interest, before taxation (see Note 1 below)	170	
Adjustments for:		
Depreciation (Note 2)	78	
Interest expense (Note 3)	26	
	274	
Decrease in stock (41 – 35)	6	
Increase in trade debtors (145 – 139)	(6)	
Decrease in trade creditors (54 – 41)	(13)	
Cash generated from operations	261	
Interest paid	(26)	
Corporation tax paid (Note 4)	(41)	
Dividend paid	(60)	
Net cash from operating activities		134
Cash flows from investing activities		
Payments to acquire plant and machinery	(67)	
Net cash used in investing activities		(67)
Cash flows from financing activities		
Redemption of debenture stock (250 – 150) (Note 5)	(100)	
Net cash used in financing activities		(100)
Net decrease in cash and cash equivalents		(33)
Cash and cash equivalents at 1 January 2005		
Bank overdraft		(56)
Cash and cash equivalents at 31 December 2005		
Bank overdraft		(89)

To see how this relates to the cash of the business at the beginning and end of the year it can be useful to provide a reconciliation as follows:

Analysis of cash and cash equivalents during the year ended 31 December 2005

	£m
Cash and cash equivalents at 1 January 2005	(56)
Net cash outflow	(33)
Cash and cash equivalents at 31 December 2005	(89)

Notes:

1 This is simply taken from the profit and loss account for the year.
2 Since there were no disposals, the depreciation charges must be the difference between the start and end of the year's plant and machinery values, adjusted by the cost of any additions.

	£m
Book value, at 1 January 2005	325
Add Additions	67
	392
Less Depreciation (balancing figure)	78
Book value, at 31 December 2005	314

3 Interest payable expense must be taken out, by adding it back to the profit figure. We subsequently deduct the cash paid for interest payable during the year. In this case the two figures are identical.

4 Companies pay 50% tax during their accounting year and 50% in the following year. Thus the 2005 payment would have been half the tax on the 2004 profit (that is, the figure that would have appeared in the current liabilities at the end of 2004), plus half of the 2005 tax charge (that is, $23 + (^1/_2 \times 36) = 41$).

5 It is assumed that the cash payment to redeem the debentures was simply the difference between the two balance sheet figures.

It seems that there was a bonus issue of ordinary shares during the year. These increased by £100m. At the same time, the share premium account balance reduced by £40m (to zero) and the revaluation reserve balance fell by £60m.

6.6

Blackstone plc
Cash flow statement for the year ended 31 March 2005

	£m	£m
Cash flows from operating activities		
Net profit, after interest, before taxation		
(see Note 1 below)	1,853	
Adjustments for:		
Depreciation (Note 2)	1,289	
Interest expense (Note 3)	456	
	3,598	
Increase in stocks (2,410 – 1,209)	(1,201)	
Increase in trade debtors (1,173 – 641)	(532)	
Increase in trade creditors (1,507 – 931)	576	
Cash generated from operations	2,441	
Interest paid	(456)	
Corporation tax paid (Note 4)	(300)	
Dividend paid	(400)	
Net cash from operating activities		1,285
Cash flows from investing activities		
Proceeds of disposals	54	
Payment to acquire intangible non-current asset	(700)	
Payments to acquire property, plant and equipment	(4,578)	
Net cash used in investing activities		(5,224)
Cash flows from financing activities		
Bank loan	2,000	
Net cash from financing activities		2,000
Net decrease in cash and cash equivalents		(1,939)
Cash and cash equivalents at 1 April 2004		
Cash at bank		123
Cash and cash equivalents at 31 March 2005		
Bank overdraft		(1,816)

To see how this relates to the cash of the business at the beginning and end of the year it can be useful to provide a reconciliation as follows:

Analysis of cash and cash equivalents during the year ended 31 March 2005

	£m
Cash and cash equivalents at 1 April 2004	123
Net cash outflow	(1,939)
Cash and cash equivalents at 31 March 2005	1,816

Notes:

1 This is simply taken from the profit and loss account for the year.

2 The full depreciation charge was that stated in Note 1 to the question (£1,251m), plus the deficit on disposal of the non-current assets. According to the table in Note 4 to the question, these non-current assets had originally cost £581m and had been depreciated by £489m, that is a net book value of £92m. They were sold for £54m, leading to a deficit on disposal of £38m. Thus the full depreciation expense for the year was £1,289m (that is, £1,251m + £38m).

3 Interest payable expense must be taken out, by adding it back to the profit figure. We subsequently deduct the cash paid for interest payable during the year. In this case the two figures are identical.

4 Companies pay tax at 50% during their accounting year and the other 50% in the following year. Thus the 2005 payment would have been half the tax on the 2004 profit (that is, the figure that would have appeared in the current liabilities at 31 March 2004), plus half of the 2005 tax charge (that is, $105 + (^1/_2 \times 390) = 300$).

6.7

York plc

Cash flow statement for the year ended 30 September 2005

	£m	£m
Cash flows from operating activities		
Net profit, after interest, before taxation		
(see Note 1 below)	10.0	
Adjustments for:		
Depreciation (Note 2)	9.8	
Interest expense (Note 3)	<u>3.0</u>	
	22.8	
Increase in stock and debtors (122.1 − 119.8)	(2.3)	
Increase in creditors (82.5 − 80.0)	<u>2.5</u>	
Cash generated from operations	23.0	
Interest paid	(3.0)	
Corporation tax paid (Note 4)	(2.3)	
Dividend paid	<u>(3.5)</u>	
Net cash from operating activities		14.2
Cash flows from investing activities		
Proceeds of disposals (Note 2)	5.2	
Payments to acquire non-current assets	<u>(20.0)</u>	
Net cash used in investing activities		(14.8)
Cash flows from financing activities		
Increase in long-term loan	3.0	
Share issue (Note 5)	<u>5.0</u>	
Net cash from financing activities		<u>8.0</u>
Net increase in cash and cash equivalents		<u>7.4</u>
Cash and cash equivalents at 1 October 2004		
Cash at bank		<u>9.2</u>
Cash and cash equivalents at 30 September 2005		
Cash at bank		<u>16.6</u>

To see how this relates to the cash of the business at the beginning and end of the year it can be useful to provide a reconciliation as follows:

Analysis of cash and cash equivalents during the year ended 30 September 2005

	£m
Cash and cash equivalents at 1 October 2004	9.2
Net cash inflow	<u>7.4</u>
Cash and cash equivalents at 30 September 2005	<u>16.6</u>

Notes:

1 This is simply taken from the profit and loss account for the year.

2 The full depreciation charge was the £13.0m, less the surplus on disposal (£3.2m), both stated in Note 1 to the question.

   According to the table in Note 3 to the question, the non-current assets disposed of had a net book value of £2.0m. To produce a surplus of £3.2m, they must have been sold for £5.2m.

3 Interest payable expense must be taken out, by adding it back to the profit figure. We subsequently deduct the cash paid for interest payable during the year. In this case the two figures are identical.

4 Companies pay 50% tax during their accounting year and the other 50% in the following year. Thus the 2005 payment would have been half the tax on the 2004 profit (that is, the figure that would have appeared in the current liabilities at 30 September 2004), plus half of the 2005 tax charge (that is, $1.0 + (^1/_2 \times 2.6) = 2.3$).

5 This issue must have been for cash since it could not have been a bonus issue – the share premium is untouched and the 'Reserves' had only altered over the year by the amount of the 2005 retained profit. The shares seem to have been issued at par (that is, at their nominal value). This is a little surprising since the business has assets that seem to be above that value. On the other hand, were this a rights issue, the low issue price would not have disadvantaged the existing shareholders since they were also the beneficiaries of the advantage of the low issue price.

6.8

Axis plc
Cash flow statement for the year ended 31 December 2005

	£m	£m
Cash flows from operating activities		
Net profit, after interest, before taxation (see Note 1 below)	34	
Adjustments for:		
Depreciation (Note 2)	19	
Interest expense (Note 3)	2	
	55	
Decrease in stock (25 – 24)	1	
Increase in debtors (26 – 16)	(10)	
Increase in creditors (36 – 31)	5	
Cash generated from operations	51	
Interest paid	(2)	
Corporation tax paid (Note 4)	(15)	
Dividend paid	(14)	
Net cash from operating activities		20
Cash flows from investing activities		
Proceeds of disposals (Note 2)	4	
Payments to acquire non-current assets	(25)	
Net cash used in investing activities		(21)
Cash flows from financing activities		
Issue of debentures	20	
Net cash from financing activities		20
Net increase in cash and cash equivalents		19
Cash and cash equivalents at 1 January 2005		
Cash at bank		nil
Short-term investments		nil
		nil
Cash and cash equivalents at 31 December 2005		
Cash at bank		7
Short-term investments		12
		19

To see how this relates to the cash of the business at the beginning and end of the year it can be useful to provide a reconciliation as follows:

Analysis of cash and cash equivalents during the year ended 31 December 2005

	£m
Cash and cash equivalents at 1 January 2005	nil
Net cash inflow	19
Cash and cash equivalents at 31 December 2005	19

Notes:
1 This is simply taken from the profit and loss account for the year.
2 The full depreciation charge for the year is the sum of two figures labelled 'depreciation' and the deficit on disposal of non-current assets (that is, £2m + £16m + £1m = £19m). These were detailed in the profit and loss account (income statement).

According to the note in the question, the non-current assets disposed of had a net book value of £5.0m (that is, £15m − £10m). To produce a deficit of £1m, they must have been sold for £4m.
3 Interest payable expense must be taken out, by adding it back to the profit figure. We subsequently deduct the cash paid for interest payable during the year. In this case the two figures are identical.
4 Companies pay 50% tax during their accounting year and the other 50% in the following year. Thus the 2005 payment would have been half the tax on the 2004 profit (that is, the figure that would have appeared in the current liabilities at 31 December 2004), plus half of the 2005 tax charge (that is, $7 + (1/2 \times 16) = 15$).

Chapter 7

7.1 I. Jiang (Western) Ltd

The effect of each of the changes on ROCE is not always easy to predict.

(i) On the face of it, an increase in the gross profit margin would tend to lead to an increase in ROCE. An increase in the gross profit margin *may*, however, lead to a decrease in ROCE in particular circumstances. If the increase in the margin resulted from an increase in price, which in turn led to a decrease in sales revenue, a fall in ROCE can occur. A fall in sales revenue can reduce the net profit (the numerator (top part of the fraction) in ROCE) if the overheads of the business did not decrease correspondingly.
(ii) A reduction in sales revenue can reduce ROCE for the reasons mentioned above.
(iii) An increase in overhead expenses will reduce the net profit and this in turn will result in a reduction in ROCE.
(iv) An increase in stocks held would increase the amount of capital employed by the business (the denominator (bottom part of the fraction) in ROCE) where long-term funds are employed to finance the stocks. This will, in turn, reduce ROCE.
(v) Repayment of the loan at the year end will reduce the capital employed and this will increase the ROCE, assuming that the year-end capital employed figure has been used in the calculation. Since the net profit was earned during a period in which the loan existed, there is a strong argument for basing the capital employed figure on what was the position during the year, rather than at the end of it.
(vi) An increase in the time taken for debtors to pay will result in an increase in capital employed if long-term funds are employed to finance the debtors. This increase in long-term funds will, in turn, reduce ROCE.

7.2 The ratios for Amsterdam Ltd and Berlin Ltd reveal that the debtors turnover ratio for Amsterdam Ltd is three times that for Berlin Ltd. Berlin Ltd is therefore much quicker in collecting amounts outstanding from customers. On the other hand, there is not much difference between the two businesses in the time taken to pay trade creditors.

It is interesting to compare the difference in the debtor and creditor collection periods for each business. As Amsterdam Ltd allows an average of 63 days' credit to its customers, yet pays creditors within 50 days, it will require greater investment in working capital than Berlin Ltd, which allows an average of only 21 days to its debtors but takes 45 days to pay its creditors.

Amsterdam Ltd has a much higher gross profit percentage than Berlin Ltd. However, the net profit percentage for the two businesses is identical. This suggests that Amsterdam Ltd has much higher overheads (as a percentage of sales revenue) than Berlin Ltd. The stock turnover period for Amsterdam Ltd is more than twice that of Berlin Ltd. This may be due to the fact that Amsterdam Ltd maintains a wider range of goods in stock in an attempt to meet customer requirements. The evidence therefore suggests that Amsterdam Ltd is the one that prides itself on personal service. The higher average settlement period for debtors is consistent with a more relaxed attitude to credit collection (thereby maintaining customer goodwill) and the high overheads are consistent with incurring the additional costs of satisfying customers' requirements. Amsterdam Ltd's high stock levels are consistent with maintaining a wide range of stock, with the aim of satisfying a range of customer needs.

Berlin Ltd has the characteristics of a more price-competitive business. Its gross profit percentage is much lower than that of Amsterdam Ltd, that is, a much lower gross profit for each £1 of sales revenue. However, overheads have been kept low, the effect being that the net profit percentage is the same as Amsterdam Ltd's. The low stock turnover period and average collection period for debtors are consistent with a business that wishes to minimise investment in current assets, thereby reducing costs.

7.6   **Bradbury Ltd**

(a)

	2004	2005
(i) Net profit margin		
914/9,482 × 100%	9.6%	
1,042/11,365 × 100%		9.2%
(ii) ROCE		
914/11,033 × 100%	8.3%	
1,042/13,943 × 100%		7.5%
(iii) Current ratio		
4,926/1,508	3.3:1	
7,700/5,174		1.5:1
(iv) Gearing ratio		
1,220/11,033 × 100%	11.1%	
3,674/13,943 × 100%		26.4%
(v) Days debtors		
(2,540/9,482) × 365	98 days	
(4,280/11,365) × 365		137 days
(vi) Sales revenue to capital employed		
9,482/(9,813+1,220)	0.9 times	
11,365/(10,269 + 3,674)		0.8 times

(b) The net profit margin was slightly lower in 2005 than in 2004. Though there was an increase in sales revenue in 2005, this could not prevent a slight fall in ROCE in 2005. The lower net profit margin and increases in sales revenue may well be due to the new contract. The capital employed of the company increased in 2005 by a larger percentage than the increase in revenue. Hence, the sales revenue to capital employed ratio decreased over the period. The increase in capital during 2005 is largely due to an increase in borrowing. However, the gearing ratio is probably still low in comparison with other businesses. Comparison of the freehold premises and loans figures indicates possible unused debt capacity.

The major cause for concern has been the dramatic decline in liquidity during 2005. The current ratio has more than halved during the period. There has also been a similar decrease in the acid test ratio, from 1.7:1 in 2004 to 0.8:1 in 2005. The balance sheet shows that the business now has a large overdraft and the trade creditors outstanding have nearly doubled in 2005.

The trade debtors outstanding and stocks have increased much more than appears to be warranted by the increase in sales revenue. This may be due to the terms of the contract that has been negotiated and may be difficult to influence. If this is the case, the business should consider whether it is overtrading. If the conclusion is that it is, increasing its long-term funding may be a sensible policy.

7.7 Harridges Ltd

(a)

	2004	2005
ROCE	$\frac{310}{1,600} = 19.4\%$	$\frac{350}{1,700} = 20.6\%$
ROSF	$\frac{155}{1,100} = 14.1\%$	$\frac{175}{1,200} = 14.6\%$
Gross profit margin	$\frac{1,040}{2,600} = 40\%$	$\frac{1,150}{3,500} = 32.9\%$
Net profit margin	$\frac{310}{2,600} = 11.9\%$	$\frac{350}{3,500} = 10\%$
Current ratio	$\frac{735}{400} = 1.8$	$\frac{660}{485} = 1.4$
Acid test ratio	$\frac{485}{400} = 1.2$	$\frac{260}{485} = 0.5$
Days debtors	$\frac{105}{2,600} \times 365 = 15$ days	$\frac{145}{3,500} \times 365 = 15$ days
Days creditors	$\frac{235}{1,560} \times 365 = 55$ days	$\frac{300}{2,350^*} \times 365 = 47$ days
Stock turnover period	$\frac{250}{1,560} \times 365 = 58$ days	$\frac{400}{2,350} \times 365 = 62$ days
Gearing ratio	$\frac{500}{1,600} = 31.3\%$	$\frac{500}{1,700} = 29.4\%$
EPS	$\frac{155}{490} = 31.6$p	$\frac{175}{490} = 35.7$p

* Used because the credit purchases figure is not available.

(b) There has been a considerable decline in the gross profit margin during 2005. This fact, combined with the increase in sales revenue by more than one-third, suggests that a price-cutting policy has been adopted in an attempt to stimulate sales. The resulting increase in sales revenue, however, has led to only a small improvement in ROCE and ROSF. Similarly, there has only been a small improvement in EPS.

Despite a large cut in the gross profit margin, the net profit margin has fallen by less than 2%. This suggests that overheads have been tightly controlled during 2005. Certainly, overheads have not risen in proportion to sales revenue.

The current ratio has fallen and the acid test ratio has fallen by more than half. Even though liquidity ratios are lower in retailing than in manufacturing, the liquidity of the business should now be a cause for concern. However, this may be a passing problem. The business is investing heavily in non-current assets and is relying on internal funds to finance this growth. When this investment ends, the liquidity position may improve quickly.

The debtors period has remained unchanged over the two years, and there has been no significant change in the stock turnover period in 2005. The gearing ratio is quite low and provides no cause for concern given the profitability of the business.

Overall, the business appears to be financially sound. Though there has been rapid growth during 2005, there is no real cause for alarm provided that the liquidity of the business can be improved in the near future. In the absence of information concerning share price, it is not possible to say whether or not an investment should be made.

7.8 **Genesis Ltd**

(a) and (b)
These parts have been answered in the text of the chapter and you are referred to it for a discussion on overtrading and its consequences.

(c)

$$\text{Current ratio} = \frac{232}{550} = 0.42$$

$$\text{Acid test ratio} = \frac{104}{550} = 0.19$$

$$\text{Stock turnover period} = \frac{128}{1,248} \times 365 = 37 \text{ days}$$

$$\text{Average settlement period for debtors} = \frac{104}{1,640} \times 365 = 23 \text{ days}$$

$$\text{Average settlement period for creditors} = \frac{184}{1,260} \times 365 = 53 \text{ days}$$

(d) Overtrading must be dealt with either by increasing the level of funding to match the level of activity, or by reducing the level of activity to match the funds available. The latter option may result in a reduction in profits in the short term but may be necessary to ensure long-term survival.

Chapter 8

8.1 Lombard Ltd

Relevant costs of undertaking the contract are:

	£
Equipment costs	200,000
Component X (20,000 × 4 × £5)	400,000
Component Y (20,000 × 3 × £8)	480,000
Additional costs (20,000 × £8)	160,000
	1,240,000
Revenue from the contract (20,000 × £80)	1,600,000

Thus, from a purely financial point of view the project is acceptable. (Note that there is no relevant labour cost since the staff concerned will be paid irrespective of whether the contract is undertaken.)

8.2 The local authority

(a) *Net benefit of accepting the touring company proposal*

	£
Net reduction in ticket revenue (see workings below)	(10,000)
Savings on: Costumes	2,800
Scenery	1,650
Casual staff	1,760
Net deficit	3,790

Since there is a net deficit, on financial grounds, the touring company's proposal should be rejected.

Note that all of the following are irrelevant, because they will occur irrespective of the decision:
- full-time staff salaries
- artistes' salaries
- heating and lighting
- administration costs
- refreshment revenue and costs
- programme advertising.

Workings

Normal ticket sales revenue:		£
	200 @ £12 =	2,400
	500 @ £8 =	4,000
	300 @ £6 =	1,800
		8,200

Ticket revenue at 50% capacity for 20 performances (£8,200 × 50% × 20)	82,000

Touring company ticket sales revenue:

Total revenue for each performance for a full house:

	£
200 @ £11 =	2,200
500 @ £7 =	3,500
300 @ £5 =	1,500
	7,200

Ticket revenue	(£7,200 × 10 × 50%)	36,000
	(£7,200 × 15 × $^2/_3$ × 50%)	36,000
		72,000
Net loss of revenue (£82,000 − £72,000)		10,000

(b) Other possible factors to consider include:

- The reliability of the estimations, including the assumption that programme and refreshment sales will not be altered by the level of occupancy.
- A desire to offer theatregoers the opportunity to see another group of players.
- Dangers of loss of morale of staff not employed, or employed to do other than their usual work.

8.3 Andrews and Co. Ltd

Minimum contract price

			£
Materials	Steel core:	$10,000 \times £2.10$	21,000
	Plastic:	$10,000 \times 0.10 \times £0.10$	100
Labour	Skilled:		–
	Unskilled:	$10,000 \times 5/60 \times £5$	4,167
Minimum tender price			25,267

8.6 The local education authority

(a) *One-off financial net benefits of closing:*

	D only	A and B	A and C
Capacity reduction	800	700	800
	£m	£m	£m
Property developer (A)	–	14.0	14.0
Shopping complex (B)	–	8.0	–
Property developer (D)	9.0	–	–
Safety (C)	–	–	3.0
Adapt facilities	(1.8)	–	–
Total	7.2	22.0	17.0
Ranking based on total one-off benefits	3	1	2

(Note that all past costs of buying and improving the schools are irrelevant.)

Recurrent financial net benefits of closing:

	D only £m	A and B £m	A and C £m
Rent (C)	–	–	0.3
Administrators	0.2	0.4	0.4
Total	0.2	0.4	0.7
Ranking based on total of recurrent benefits	3	2	1

On the basis of the financial figures alone, closure of either A and B or A and C looks best. It is not possible to add the one-off and the recurring costs directly, but the large one-off cost-saving associated with closing schools A and B makes this option look attractive. (In Chapter 14 we shall see that it is possible to add one-off and recurring costs in a way that should lead to sensible conclusions.)

(b) The costs of acquiring and improving the schools in the past are past costs or sunk costs and, therefore, irrelevant. The costs of employing the chief education officer is a future cost, but irrelevant because it is not dependent on outcomes, it is a common cost.

(c) There are many other factors, some of a non-quantifiable nature. These include:
- Accuracy of projections of capacity requirements.
- Locality of existing schools relative to where potential pupils live.
- Political acceptability of selling schools to property developers.
- Importance of purely financial issues in making the final decision.
- The quality of the replacement sporting facilities compared with those at school D.
- Political acceptability of staff redundancies.
- Possible savings/costs of employing fewer teachers, which might be relevant if economies of scale are available by having fewer schools.
- Staff morale.

8.7   Rob Otics Ltd

(a) The minimum price for the proposed contract would be:

	£
Materials	
Component X (2 × 8 × £180)	2,880
Component Y	0
Component Z [(75 + 32) × £20] – (75 × £25)	265
Other miscellaneous items	250
Labour	
Assembly (25 + 24 + 23 + 22 + 21 + 20 + 19 + 18) × £48*	8,256
Inspection (8 × 6 × £18)	864
Total	12,515

* £60 – £12 = £48.

The assembly labour cost is irrelevant here because it will be incurred irrespective of which work the members of staff do. The historic cost of the stock of component X and the fact that it is not yet paid for are both irrelevant. The historic cost and the £1,500 relating to component Y are also irrelevant. Thus the minimum price is £12,515.

(b) Other factors include:
- Competitive state of the market.
- The fact that the above figure is unique to the particular circumstances at the time – for example, having component Y in stock but having no use for it. Any subsequent order might have to take account of an outlay cost.
- Breaking even (that is, just covering the costs) on a contract will not fulfil the business's objective.
- Charging a low price may cause marketing problems. Other customers may resent the low price for this contract. The current enquirer may expect a similar price in future.

Chapter 9

9.4   Motormusic Ltd

(a) Break-even point = Fixed costs/(contribution per unit)
= (80,000 + 60,000)/[60 – (20 + 14 + 12 + 3)] = 12,727 radios.
These would have a sales value of £763,620 (that is, 12,727 × £60)
(b) The margin of safety is 7,273 radios (that is, 20,000 – 12,727).
This margin would have a sales value of £436,380 (that is, 7,273 × £60)

9.5   **Products A, B and C**

(a)   Total time required on cutting machines is:

$$(2,500 \times 1.0) + (3,400 \times 1.0) + (5,100 \times 0.5) = 8,450 \text{ hours}$$

Total time available on cutting machines is 5,000 hours. Therefore, this is a limiting factor.

Total time required on assembling machines is:

$$(2,500 \times 0.5) + (3,400 \times 1.0) + (5,100 \times 0.5) = 7,200 \text{ hours}$$

Total time available on assembling machines is 8,000 hours. Therefore, this is not a limiting factor.

	A (per unit) £	B (per unit) £	C (per unit) £
Selling price	25	30	18
Variable materials	(12)	(13)	(10)
Variable production costs	(7)	(4)	(3)
Contribution	6	13	5
Time on cutting machines	1.0 hour	1.0 hour	0.5 hour
Contribution per hour on cutting machines	£6	£13	£10
Order of priority	3rd	1st	2nd

Therefore, produce:

3,400 product B using	3,400 hours
3,200 product C using	1,600 hours
	5,000 hours

(b)   Assuming that the business would make no saving in variable production costs by subcontracting, it would be worth paying up to the contribution per unit (£5) for product C, which would therefore be £5 × (5,100 − 3,200) = £9,500 in total.

Similarly it would be worth paying up to £6 per unit for product A – that is, £6 × 2,500 = £15,000 in total.

9.6   **Darmor Ltd**

(a)   Contribution per hour of skilled labour of product X is:

$$\frac{(£30 - 6 - 2 - 12 - 3)}{6/6} = £7$$

Given the scarcity of skilled labour, if the management is to be indifferent between the products, the contribution per skilled labour hour must be the same. Thus for product Y the selling price must be:

$$(£7 \times (9/6)) + 9 + 4 + 25 + 7 = £55.50$$

(that is, the contribution plus the variable costs), and for product Z the selling price must be:

$$(£7 \times (3/6)) + 3 + 10 + 14 + 7 = £37.50$$

(b) The business could pay up to £13 an hour (£6 + £7) for additional hours of skilled labour. This is the potential contribution per hour, before taking account of the labour rate of £6 an hour.

9.7 Intermediate Products Ltd

(a)

	A £	B £	C £	D £
Total costs per unit	(65)	(41)	(36)	(46)
Less Fixed costs	20	8	8	12
Variable cost per unit	(45)	(33)	(28)	(34)
Buying/selling price per unit	70	45	40	55
Contribution per unit	25	12	12	21
Hours on special machine	0.5	0.4	0.5	0.3
Contribution per hour	50	30	24	70
Order of preference	2	3	4	1

Optimum use of hours on special machine	*Balance of hours*
D 3,000 × 0.3 = 900	5,100 (that is, 6000 – 900)
A 5,000 × 0.5 = 2,500	2,600 (that is, 5,100 – 2,500)
B 6,000 × 0.4 = 2,400	200 (that is, 2,600 – 2,400)
C 400 × 0.5 = 200	–
6,000	

Therefore, make all of the demand for Ds, As and Bs plus 400 (of 4,000) Cs.

(b) The contribution per hour from Cs is £24, and so this is the maximum amount per hour that it would be worth paying to rent the machine, for a maximum of 1,800 hours (that is, 3,600 × 0.5, the time necessary to make the remaining demand for Cs).

(c) Other possible actions to overcome the shortage of machine time include the following:
- Alter the design of the products to avoid the use of the special machine.
- Increase the selling price of the product so that the demand will fall, making the available machine-time sufficient but making production more profitable.

9.8 Gandhi Ltd

(a) Given that the spare capacity could not be used by other services, the standard service should continue to be offered. This is because it renders a positive contribution.

(b) The standard service renders a contribution per unit of £15 (that is, £80 – £65), or £30 during the time it would take to render one unit of the nova service. The nova service would provide a contribution of only £25 (that is, £75 – £50).

    The nova service should, therefore, not replace the standard service.

(c) Under the original plans, the following contributions would be rendered by the basic and standard services:

		£
Basic	11,000 × (£50 – 25) =	275,000
Standard	6,000 × (£80 – 65) =	90,000
		365,000

If the basic were to take the standard's place, 17,000 units (that is, 11,000 + 6,000) of them could be produced in total. To generate the same total contribution, each unit of the standard service would need to provide £21.47 (that is, £365,000/17,000) of contribution. Given the basic's variable cost of £25, this would mean a selling price of £46.47 each (that is £21.47 + 25.00).

Chapter 10

10.4   Promptprint Ltd

(a) The budget may be summarised as:

	£	
Sales revenue	196,000	
Direct materials	(38,000)	
Direct labour	(32,000)	
Total overheads	(77,000)	(2,400 + 3,000 + 27,600 + 36,000 + 8,000)
Profit	49,000	

The job may be priced on the basis that both overheads and profit should be apportioned to it on the basis of direct labour cost, as follows:

	£	
Direct materials	4,000	
Direct labour	3,600	
Overheads	8,663	(£77,000 × 3,600/32,000)
Profit	5,513	(£49,000 × 3,600/32,000)
	21,776	

This answer assumes that variable overheads vary in proportion to direct labour cost.

Various other bases of charging overheads and profit loading the job could have been adopted. For example, materials cost could have been included (with direct labour) as the basis for profit-loading, or even apportioning overheads.

(b) This part of the question is, in effect, asking for comments on the validity of 'full cost-plus' pricing. This approach can be useful as an indicator of the effective long-run cost of doing the job. On the other hand, it fails to take account of relevant opportunity costs as well as the state of the market and other external factors. For example, it ignores the price that a competitor printing business may quote.

(c) Revised estimates of material direct costs for the job:

	£	
Paper grade 1	1,500	(£1,200 × 125%) This stock needs to be replaced
Paper grade 2	0	It has no opportunity cost value
Card	510	(£640 – 130: using the card on another job would save £640, but cost £130 to achieve that saving)
Inks and so on	300	This stock needs to be replaced
	2,310	

10.5 Bookdon plc

(a) To answer this question, we need first to allocate and apportion the overheads to product cost centres, as follows:

Cost	Basis of apportionment	Total	Department			
			Machine shop	Fitting section	Canteen	Machine main'ce section
		£	£	£	£	£
Allocated items:	Specific	90,380	27,660	19,470	16,600	26,650
Rent, rates, heat, light	Floor area	17,000	9,000 *(3,600/ 6,800)*	3,500 *(1,400/ 6,800)*	2,500 *(1,000/ 6,800)*	2,000 *(800/ 6,800)*
Dep'n and insurance	Book value	25,000	12,500 *(150/300)*	6,250 *(75/300)*	2,500 *(30/300)*	3,750 *(45/300)*
		132,380	49,160	29,220	21,600	32,400
Canteen	Number of employees	–	10,800 *(18/36)*	8,400 *(14/36)*	(21,600)	2,400 *(4/36)*
		132,380	59,960	37,620	–	34,800
Machine maintenance section	Specified %	–	24,360 *(70%)*	10,440 *(30%)*	–	(34,800)
		132,380	84,320	48,060	–	–

Note that the canteen overheads were reapportioned to the other cost centres first because the canteen renders a service to the machine maintenance section but does not receive a service from it.

Calculation of the overhead absorption (recovery) rates can now proceed:

(i) Total budgeted machine-hours are:

	Hours
Product X (4,200 × 6)	25,200
Product Y (6,900 × 3)	20,700
Product Z (1,700 × 4)	6,800
	52,700

Overhead absorption rate for the machine shop is:

$$\frac{£84,320}{52,700} = £1.60/\text{machine-hour}$$

(ii) Total budgeted direct labour cost for the fitting section is:

	£
Product X (4,200 × £12)	50,400
Product Y (6,900 × £3)	20,700
Product Z (1,700 × £21)	35,700
	106,800

Overhead absorption rate for the fitting section is:

$$\frac{£48,060}{£106,800} \times 100\% = 45\% \text{ or } £0.45 \text{ per } £ \text{ of direct labour cost.}$$

(b) The cost of one unit of product X is calculated as follows:

		£
Direct materials		11.00
Direct labour		
Machine shop		6.00
Fitting section		12.00
Overheads		
Machine shop (6 × £1.60)		9.60
Fitting section (£12 × 45%)		5.40
		44.00

Therefore, the cost of one unit of product X is £44.00.

10.6   Products A, B and C

Allocation and apportionment of overheads to product cost centres

	Basis of apportionment	Department				
		Cutting £	Machining £	Pressing £	Engineering £	Personnel £
Total		154,482	64,316	58,452	56,000	34,000
Personnel	specified	18,700 (55%)	3,400 (10%)	6,800 (20%)	5,100 (15%)	(34,000)
		173,182	67,716	65,252	61,100	–
Engineering	specified	12,220 (20%)	27,495 (45%)	21,385 (35%)	(61,100)	
		185,402	95,211	86,637	–	–

Note that the personnel overheads were reapportioned to the other cost centres first because the canteen renders a service to the engineering department section, but does not receive a service from it.

Calculation of the overhead absorption (recovery) rates
In both the cutting and pressing departments, no machines seem to be used, and so a direct-labour-hour basis of overhead absorption seems reasonable.

In the machining department, machine hours are far in excess of labour hours and the overheads are probably machine related. In this department, machine-hours seem a fair basis for cost units to absorb overheads.

Total planned direct-labour-hours for the cutting department are thus:

Product A	4,000 × (3 + 6) =	36,000
Product B	3,000 × (5 + 1) =	18,000
Product C	6,000 × (2 + 3) =	30,000
		84,000

The overhead absorption rate for the cutting department = £185,402/84,000 = £2.21 per direct-labour-hour.

Total planned machine-hours for the machining department are thus:

Product A	4,000 × 2.0 =	8,000
Product B	3,000 × 1.5 =	4,500
Product C	6,000 × 2.5 =	15,000
		27,500

The overhead absorption rate for the machining department = £95,211/27,500 = £3.46 per machine-hour.

Total planned direct-labour-hours for the pressing department

Product A	4,000 × 2 =	8,000
Product B	3,000 × 3 =	9,000
Product C	6,000 × 4 =	24,000
		41,000

The overhead absorption rate for the cutting department = £86,637/41,000 = £2.11 per direct-labour-hour.

(a) *Cost of one completed unit of product A*

		£
Direct materials		7.00
Direct labour		
cutting department: skilled	(3 × £8)	24.00
unskilled	(6 × £5)	30.00
machining department	(0.5 × £6)	3.00
pressing department	(2 × £6)	12.00
Overheads		
cutting department	(9 × £2.21)	19.89
machining department	(2 × £3.46)	6.92
pressing department	(2 × £2.11)	4.22
		107.03

(b) *Cost of one uncompleted unit of product B*

		£
Direct materials		4.00*
Direct labour		
cutting department: skilled	(5 × £8)	40.00
unskilled	(1 × £5)	5.00
machining department	(0.25 × £6)	1.50
Overheads		
cutting department	(6 × £2.21)	13.26
machining department	(1.5 × £3.46)	5.19
		68.95

* This assumes that all of the materials are added in the cutting or machining departments.

10.7

Offending phrase	Explanation
'Necessary to divide the business up into departments'	This can be done but it will not always be of much benefit. Only in quite restricted circumstances will it give significantly different job costs.
'Fixed costs (or overheads)'	This implies that fixed costs and overheads are the same thing. They are not really connected with one another. 'Fixed' is to do with how costs behave as the level of output is raised or lowered; 'overheads' are to do with the extent to which costs can be directly measured in respect of a particular unit of output. Though it is true that many overheads are fixed, not all are. Also, direct labour is usually a fixed cost.
	All of the other references to fixed and variable costs are wrong. The person should have referred to indirect and direct costs.
'Usually this is done on the basis of area'	Where overheads are apportioned to departments, they will be apportioned on some logical basis. For certain costs – for example, rent, the floor area may be the most logical; for others, such as machine maintenance costs, the floor area would be totally inappropriate.
'When the total fixed costs for each department have been identified, this will be divided by the number of hours that were worked'	Where overheads are dealt with on a departmental basis, they may be divided by the number of direct-labour-hours to deduce a recovery rate. However, this is only one basis of applying overheads to jobs. For example, machine-hours or some other basis may be more appropriate to the particular circumstances involved.
'It is essential that this approach is taken in order to deduce a selling price'	It is relatively unusual for the 'job cost' to be able to dictate the price at which the manufacturer can price its output. For many businesses, the market dictates the price.

10.8   (a) Charging overheads to jobs on a departmental basis means that overheads are collected 'product' cost centre (department) by 'product' cost centre. This involves picking up the overheads that are direct to each department and adding to them a share of overheads that are general to the business as a whole. The overheads of 'service' cost centres must then be apportioned to the product cost centres. At this point, all of the overheads for the whole business are divided between the 'product' cost centres, such that the sum of the 'product'-cost-centre overheads equals those for the whole business.

Dealing with overheads departmentally is believed to provide more fair and useful information to decision makers, because different departments may have rather different overheads, and applying overheads departmentally can take account of that and reflect it in job costs.

In theory, dealing with overheads on a departmental basis is more costly than on a business-wide basis. In practice, it possibly does not make too much difference to the cost of collecting the information. Normally, businesses are divided into departments, and the costs are collected departmentally, as part of the normal routine for exercising control over the business.

(b) In order to make any difference to the job cost that will emerge as a result of dealing with overheads departmentally, as compared with a business-wide basis, the following *both* need to be the case:

- The overheads per unit of the basis of charging (for example direct-labour-hours) need to be different from one department to the next.
- The proportion (but not the actual amounts) of total overheads that are charged to jobs must differ from one job to the next.

Assume for the sake of argument that direct-labour-hours are used as the basis of charging overheads in all departments. Also assume that there are three departments, A, B and C.

There will be no difference to the overheads charged to a job if the rate of overheads per direct-labour-hour is the same for all departments. Obviously, if the charging rate is the same in all departments, that same rate must also apply to the business taken as a whole.

Also, even where overheads per direct-labour-hour differ significantly from one department to another – if all jobs spend, say, about 20% of their time in Department A, 50% in Department B and 30% in Department C – it will not make any difference whether overheads are charged departmentally or overall.

These conclusions are not in any way dependent on the basis of charging overheads or even that overheads are charged on the same basis in each department.

The statements above combine to mean that, probably in many cases in practice, departmentalising overheads is not providing information that is significantly different from that which would be provided by charging overheads to jobs on a business-wide basis.

Chapter 11

11.1 Woodner Ltd

A Output	B Sales price per unit	C Total sales revenue (A × B)	D Marginal unit sales revenue	E Total variable cost (A × £20)	F Total cost (variable cost (£2,500)	G Marginal cost per unit	H Profit/(loss)
units	£	£	£	£	£	£	£
0	0	0	0	0	2,500	–	(2,500)
10	95	950*	95†	200	2,700	20	(1,750)
20	90	1,800	85	400	2,900	20	(1,100)
30	85	2,550	75	600	3,100	20	(550)
40	80	3,200	65	800	3,300	20	(100)
50	75	3,750	55	1,000	3,500	20	250
60	70	4,200	45	1,200	3,700	20	500
70	65	4,550	35	1,400	3,900	20	650
80	60	4,800	25	1,600	4,100	20	700
90	55	4,950	15	1,800	4,300	20	650
100	50	5,000	5	2,000	4,500	20	500

* (10 × £95)
† ((950 − 0)/(10 − 0))

An output of 80 units each week will maximise profit at £700 a week. This is the nearest, given the nature of the input data, to the level of output where marginal cost per unit equals marginal revenue per unit. (For the mathematically minded, this question could have been solved by using calculus to find the point at which slopes of the total sales revenue and total costs lines were equal.)

11.2 Cost-plus pricing means that prices are based on calculations/assessments of how much it costs to produce the good or service, and includes a margin for profit. 'Cost' in this context might mean relevant cost, variable cost, direct cost or full cost. Usually cost-plus prices are based on full costs.

If a business charges the full cost of its output as a selling price, it will in theory break even. This is because the sales revenue will exactly cover all of the costs. Charging something above full cost will yield a profit. Thus, in theory, cost-plus pricing is logical.

If a cost-plus approach to pricing is to be taken, the question that must be addressed is the level of profit required from each unit sold. This must logically be based on the total profit that is required for the period. Normally, businesses seek to enhance their wealth through trading. The extent to which they expect to do this is normally related to the amount of wealth that is invested to promote wealth enhancement. Businesses tend to seek to produce a particular percentage increase in wealth. In other words, they seek to generate a particular return on capital employed. It seems logical, therefore, that the profit loading on full cost should reflect the business's target profit and that the target should itself be based on a target return on capital employed.

An obvious problem with cost-plus pricing is that the market may not agree with the price. Put another way, cost-plus pricing takes no account of the market demand function (the relationship between price and quantity demanded). A business may fairly deduce the full cost of some product and then add what might be regarded as a reasonable level of profit, only to find that a rival producer is offering a similar product for a much lower price, or that the market simply will not buy at the cost-plus price.

Most suppliers are not strong enough in the market to dictate pricing; most are 'price takers', not 'price makers'. They must accept the price offered by the market or they do not sell any of their wares. Cost-plus pricing may be appropriate for price makers, but it has less relevance for price takers.

The cost-plus price is not entirely useless to price takers. When contemplating entering a market, knowing the cost-plus price will tell the price taker whether it can profitably enter the market or not. As has been said above, the full cost can be seen as a long-run break-even selling price. If entering a market means that this break-even price, plus an acceptable profit, cannot be achieved, then the business should probably stay out. Having a breakdown of the full cost may put the business in a position to examine where costs might be capable of being cut in order to bring the full cost-plus profit to within a figure acceptable to the market.

Being a price maker does not always imply that the business dominates a particular market. Many small businesses are, to some extent, price makers. This tends to be where buyers find it difficult to make clear distinctions between the prices offered by various suppliers. An example of this might be a car repair. Though it may be possible to obtain a series of binding estimates for the work from various garages, most people would not normally do so. As a result, garages normally charge cost-plus prices for car repairs.

11.3 **Kaplan plc**

(a) At present, the business makes each model of suitcase in a batch. The direct materials and labour costs will be recorded for each batch. To these costs will be added a share of the overheads of the business for the period in which production of the batch takes place. The basis of the batch absorbing overheads is a matter of managerial judgement.

Direct-labour-hours spent working on the batch, relative to total direct-labour-hours worked during the period, is a popular method. This is not the 'correct' way, however. There is no correct way. If the activity is capital intensive, some machine-hour basis of dealing with overheads might be more appropriate, though still not 'correct'. Overheads might be collected, department by department, and charged to the batch as it passes through each department. Alternatively, all of the overheads for the entire production facility might be totalled and the overheads dealt with more globally. It is only in restricted circumstances that overheads charged to batches will be affected by a decision to deal with them departmentally, rather than globally.

Once the 'full cost' (direct costs plus a share of indirect costs) has been ascertained for the batch, the cost per suitcase can be established by dividing the batch cost by the number in the batch.

(b) The uses to which full cost information can be put have been identified as:

● *For pricing purposes.*   In some industries and circumstances, full costs are used as the basis of pricing. Here the full cost is deduced and a percentage is added on for profit. This is known as cost-plus pricing. A solicitor handling a case for a client probably provides an example of this.

In many circumstances, however, suppliers are not in a position to deduce prices on a cost-plus basis. Where there is a competitive market, a supplier will probably need to accept the price that the market offers – that is, most suppliers are 'price takers' not 'price makers'.

● *For income-measurement purposes.*   To provide a valid means of measuring a business's income, it is necessary to match expenses with the revenue realised in the same accounting period. Where manufactured stock is made or partially made in one period but sold in the next, or where a service is partially rendered in one accounting period but the revenue is realised in the next, the full cost (including an appropriate share of overheads) must be carried from one accounting period to the next. Unless we are able to identify the full cost of work done in one period, which is the subject of a sale in the next, the profit figures of the periods concerned will become meaningless.

Unless all related production costs are charged in the same accounting period as the sale is recognised in the profit and loss account, distortions will occur that will render the profit and loss account much less useful. Thus it is necessary to deduce the full cost of any production undertaken completely or partially in one accounting period but sold in a subsequent one.

(c) Whereas the traditional approach to dealing with overheads is just to accept that they exist and deal with them in a fairly broad manner, ABC takes a much more enquiring approach. ABC takes the view that overheads do not just 'occur', but that they are caused or 'driven' by 'activities'. It is a matter of finding out which activities are driving the costs and how much cost they are driving.

For example, a significant part of the costs of making suitcases of different sizes might be resetting machinery to cope with a batch of a different size from its predecessor batch. Where a particular model is made in very small batches, because it has only a small market, ABC would advocate that this model is charged directly with its machine-setting costs. The traditional approach would be to treat machine setting as a general overhead that the individual suitcases (irrespective of the model) might bear equally. ABC, it is claimed, leads to more accurate costing and thus to more accurate assessment of profitability.

(d) The other advantage of pursuing an ABC philosophy and identifying cost drivers is that, once the drivers have been identified, they are likely to become much more susceptible to being controlled. Thus the ability of management to assess the benefit of certain activities against their cost becomes more feasible.

11.6 **GB Company – the International Industries (II) enquiry**

(a) The minimum acceptable price of 120,000 motors to be supplied over the next four months is:

	£000	
Direct materials	600	(120,000 × £5.00)
Direct labour	720	(120,000 × £6.00)
Variable manufacturing overheads	360	(120,000 × £3.00 (that is, £3.00 for half an hour))
Fixed manufacturing overheads	60	(4 × £15,000)
Total	1,740	

The offer price is:

$$120,000 \times £19.00 = £2,280,000$$

On this basis, the price of £19 per machine could be accepted, subject to a number of factors identified in (b) below.

(b) The assumptions on which the above analysis and decision in (a) are based include the following:

● That the contract can be accommodated within the 30% spare capacity of GB. If this is not so, then there will be an opportunity cost relating to lost 'normal' production, which must be taken account of in the decision.
● That sales commission and freight costs will not be affected by the contract.
● It is unlikely that work more remunerative to GB than the contract will be available during the period of the contract.

There are also some strategic issues involved in the decision, including:

● The possibility that the contract could lead to other and better remunerated work from II.
● A problem of selling similar products in the same market at different prices. Other customers, knowing that GB is selling at marginal prices, may make it difficult for the business to resist demand from other customers for similarly priced output.

11.7 **Sillycon Ltd**

(a) **Overhead analysis**

	Electronics £000	Testing £000	Service £000
Variable overheads	1,200	600	700
Apportionment of service dept (800:600)	400	300	(700)
	1,600	900	–
Direct-labour-hours ('000)	800	600	
Variable overheads per direct-labour-hour	£2.00	£1.50	

	Electronics £000	Testing £000	Service £000
Fixed overheads	2,000	500	800
Apportionment of service dept (equally)	400	400	(800)
	2,400	900	–
Direct-labour-hours	800	600	
Fixed overheads per direct-labour-hour	£3.00	£1.50	

Product cost (per unit)

		£	
Direct materials		7.00	
Direct labour:	electronics	40.00	(4 × £10.00)
	testing	18.00	(3 × £6.00)
Variable overheads:	electronics	8.00	(4 × £2.00)
	testing	4.50	(3 × £1.50)
Total variable cost		77.50	(assuming direct labour to be variable)
Fixed overheads:	electronics	12.00	(4 × £3.00)
	testing	4.50	(3 × £1.50)
Total 'full' cost		94.00	
Add Mark-up, say 30%		28.20	
		122.20	

On the basis of the above, the business could hope to compete in the market at a price that reflects normal pricing practice.

(b) At this price, and only taking account of incremental fixed overheads, the break-even point (BEP) would be given by:

$$\text{BEP} = \frac{\text{Fixed costs}}{\text{Contribution per unit}} = \frac{£150,000^*}{£122.20 - £77.50} = 3,356 \text{ units}$$

* (£13,000 + £100,000 + £37,000) namely the costs specifically incurred.

As the potential market for the business is around 5,000 to 6,000 units a year, the new product looks viable.

Chapter 12

12.3 Nursing Home

(a) The rates per patient for the variable overheads, on the basis of experience during months 1 to 6, are as follows:

Expense	Amount for 2,700 patients	Amount per patient
	£	£
Staffing	59,400	22
Power	27,000	10
Supplies	54,000	20
Other	8,100	3
	148,500	55

Since the expected level of activity for the full year is 6,000, 3,300 (that is, 6,000 − 2,700) is the expected level of activity for the second six months.

Thus the budget for the second six months will be:

Variable element:	£
Staffing	72,600 (3,300 × £22)
Power	33,000 (3,300 × £10)
Supplies	66,000 (3,300 × £20)
Other	9,900 (3,300 × £3)
	181,500 (3,300 × £55)

Fixed element:

Supervision	60,000	⎫
Depreciation/finance	93,600	⎬ 6/12 of the values given in the question
Other	32,400	⎭
	186,000	(per patient = £ 56.36 (£186,000/3,300))
Total (second six months)	367,500	(per patient = £111.36 (£56.36 + 55.00))

(b) For the second six months the actual activity was 3,800 patients. For a valid comparison with the actual outcome, the budget will need to be revised to reflect this activity.

	Actual costs	Budget (3,800 patients)	Difference
	£	£	£
Variable element	203,300	209,000 (3,800 × £55)	5,700 (saving)
Fixed element	190,000	186,000	4,000 (overspend)
Total	393,300	395,000	1,700 (saving)

(c) Relative to the budget, there was a saving of nearly 3% on the variable element and an overspend of about 2% on fixed costs. Without further information, it is impossible to deduce much more than this.

   The differences between the budget and the actual may be caused by some assumptions made in framing the budget for 3,800 patients in the second part of the year. There may be some element of economies of scale in the variable costs; that is, the costs may not be strictly linear. If this were the case, basing a relatively large activity budget on the experience of a relatively small activity period would tend to overstate the large activity budget. The fixed-cost budget was deduced by dividing the budget for twelve months by two. In fact, there could be seasonal factors or inflationary pressures at work that might make such a crude division of the fixed cost element unfair.

12.4 Linpet Ltd

(a) Cash budgets are extremely useful for decision-making purposes. They allow managers to see the likely effect on the cash balance of the plans that they have set in place. Cash is an important asset and it is necessary to ensure that it is properly managed. Failure to do so can have disastrous consequences for the business. Where the cash budget indicates a surplus balance, managers must decide whether this balance should be reinvested in the business or distributed to the owners. Where the cash budget indicates a deficit balance, managers must decide how this deficit should be financed or how it might be avoided.

(b) Cash budget to 30 November

	June £	July £	Aug £	Sept £	Oct £	Nov £
Receipts						
Cash sales revenue (note 1)	4,000	5,500	7,000	8,500	11,000	11,000
Credit sales revenue (note 2)	–	–	4,000	5,500	7,000	8,500
	4,000	5,500	11,000	14,000	18,000	19,500
Payments						
Purchases (note 3)	–	29,000	9,250	11,500	13,750	17,500
Overheads	500	500	500	500	650	650
Wages	900	900	900	900	900	900
Commission (note 4)	–	320	440	560	680	880
Equipment	10,000					7,000
Motor vehicle	6,000					
Leasehold	40,000					
	57,400	30,720	11,090	13,460	15,980	26,930
Cash flow	(53,400)	(25,220)	(90)	540	2,020	(7,430)
Opening bal.	60,000	6,600	(18,620)	(18,710)	(18,170)	(16,150)
Closing bal.	6,600	(18,620)	(18,710)	(18,170)	(16,150)	(23,580)

Notes:

1 50% of the current month's sales.
2 50% of sales of two months previous.
3 To have sufficient stock to meet each month's sales will require purchases of 75% of the month's sales figures (25% is profit). In addition, each month the business will buy £1,000 more stock than it will sell. In June, the business will also buy its initial stock of £22,000. This will be paid for in the following month. For example, June's purchases will be (75% × £8,000) + £1,000 + £22,000 = £29,000, paid for in July.
4 This is 5% of 80% of the month's sales, paid in the following month. For example, June's commission will be 5% × 80% × £8,000 = £320, payable in July.

12.5 **Lewisham Ltd**

(a) The finished goods stock budget for the three months ending 30 September (in units of production) is:

	July '000 units	Aug '000 units	Sept '000 units
Opening stock (note 1)	40	48	40
Production (note 2)	188	232	196
	228	280	236
Less Sales (note 3)	180	240	200
Closing stock	48	40	36

(b) The raw materials stock budget for the two months ending 31 August (in kg) is:

	July '000 kg	Aug '000 kg
Opening stock (note 1)	40	58
Purchases (note 2)	112	107
	152	165
Less Production (note 4)	94	116
Closing stock	58	49

(c) The cash budget for the two months ending 30 September is:

	Aug £	Sept £
Inflows		
Debtors – Current month (note 5)	493,920	411,600
Preceding month (note 6)	151,200	201,600
Total inflows	645,120	613,200
Outflows		
Payments to creditors (note 7)	168,000	160,500
Labour and overheads (note 4)	185,600	156,800
Fixed overheads	22,000	22,000
Total outflows	375,600	339,300
Net inflows/(outflows)	269,520	273,900
Balance c/f	289,520	563,420

Notes:

1 The opening balance is the same as the closing balance from the previous month.
2 This is a balancing figure.
3 This figure is given in the question.
4 This figure derives from the finished stock budget.
5 This is 98% of 70% of the current month's sales revenue.
6 This is 28% of the previous month's sales.
7 This figure derives from the raw materials stock budget.

12.6   Newtake records

(a) The cash budget for the period to 30 November is:

	June £000	July £000	Aug £000	Sept £000	Oct £000	Nov £000
Cash receipts						
Sales (Note 1)	227	315	246	138	118	108
Cash payments						
Administration (Note 2)	(40)	(41)	(38)	(33)	(31)	(30)
Goods purchased	(135)	(180)	(142)	(94)	(75)	(66)
Loan repayments	(5)	(5)	(5)	(5)	(5)	(5)
Selling expenses	(22)	(24)	(28)	(26)	(21)	(19)
Tax paid				(22)		
Shop refurbishment		(14)	(18)	(6)		
	(202)	(264)	(253)	(164)	(132)	(120)
Cash surplus (deficit)	25	51	(7)	(26)	(14)	(12)
Opening balance	(35)	(10)	41	34	8	(6)
Closing balance	(10)	41	34	8	(6)	(18)

Notes:

1   (50% of the current month's sales revenue) + (97% × 50% of that sales revenue). For example, the June cash receipts = (50% × £230,000) + (97% × 50% × £230,000) = £226,550.

2   The administration expenses figure for the month, *less* £15,000 for depreciation (a non-cash expense).

(b) The stock budget for the six months to 30 November is:

	June £000	July £000	Aug £000	Sept £000	Oct £000	Nov £000
Opening balance	112	154	104	48	39	33
Stock purchased	180	142	94	75	66	57
	292	296	198	123	105	90
Cost of stocks sold (60% sales revenue)	(138)	(192)	(150)	(84)	(72)	(66)
Closing balance	154	104	48	39	33	24

(c) The budgeted profit and loss account for the six months ending 30 November is:

	£000	£000
Sales revenue		1,170
Less Cost of goods sold		702
Gross profit		468
Selling expenses	(136)	
Admin. expenses	(303)	
Credit card charges	(18)	
Interest charges	(6)	(463)
Net profit for the period		5

(d) We are told that the business is required to eliminate the bank overdraft by the end of November. However, the cash budget reveals that this will not be achieved. There is a decline in the overdraft of nearly 50% over the period, but this is not enough and ways must be found to comply with the bank's requirements. It may be possible to delay the refurbishment programme that is included in the forecasts or to obtain an injection of funds from the owners or other investors. It may also be possible to stimulate sales in some way. However, there has been a decline in the sales revenue since the end of July and the November sales are approximately one-third of the July sales revenue. The reasons for this decline should be sought.

The stock levels will fall below the preferred minimum level for each of the last three months. However, to rectify this situation it will be necessary to purchase more stock, which will, in turn, exacerbate the cash flow problems of the business.

The budgeted profit and loss account reveals a very low net profit for the period. For every £1 of sales, the business is only managing to generate 0.4p in profit. The business should look carefully at its pricing policies and its overhead expenses. The administration expenses, for example, absorb more than one-quarter of the total sales revenue. Any reduction in overhead expenses will have a beneficial effect on cash flows.

12.7 Prolog Ltd

(a) Cash budget for the six months to 30 June

	Jan £000	Feb £000	Mar £000	Apr £000	May £000	June £000
Receipts						
Credit sales (Note 1)	100	100	140	180	220	260
Payments						
Trade creditors (Note 2)	112	144	176	208	240	272
Operating expenses	4	6	8	10	10	10
Shelving				12		
Taxation			25			
	116	150	209	230	250	282
Cash flow	(16)	(50)	(69)	(50)	(30)	(22)
Opening balance	(68)	(84)	(134)	(203)	(253)	(283)
Closing balance	(84)	(134)	(203)	(253)	(283)	(305)

Notes:

1 Sales receipts will equal the month's sales revenue, but be received two months later. For example, the January sales revenue = £2,000 × (50 + 20) = £140,000, to be received in March.
2 Creditor payments will equal the next month's sales requirements, payable the next month. For example, January purchases = £1,600 × (50 + 40) = £144,000, payable in February.

(b) A banker may require various pieces of information before granting additional overdraft facilities. These may include:
 ● Security available for the loan.
 ● Details of past profit performance.
 ● Profit projections for the next 12 months.
 ● Cash projections beyond the next six months to help assess the prospects of repayment.
 ● Details of the assumptions underlying projected figures supplied.
 ● Details of the contractual commitment between Prolog Ltd and its supplier.
 ● Details of management expertise. Can they manage the expansion programme?
 ● Details of new machine and its performance in relation to competing models.
 ● Details of funds available from owners to finance the expansion.

Chapter 13

13.1 (a) A favourable direct labour rate variance can only be caused by something that leads to the rate per hour paid being less than standard. Normally, this would not be linked to efficient working. Where, however, the standard envisaged some overtime working, at premium rates, the actual labour rate may be below standard if efficiency has removed the need for the overtime.

(b) The statement is true. The action will lead to an adverse sales price variance and may well lead to problems elsewhere, but the sales volume variance must be favourable.

(c) It is true that below-standard material could lead to adverse materials usage variances because there may be more than a standard amount of scrap. This could also cause adverse labour efficiency variances because working on materials that would not form part of the output would waste labour time.

(d) Higher-than-budgeted sales could well lead to an adverse labour-rate variance because producing the additional work may require overtime working at premium rates.

(e) The statement is true. Nothing else could cause such a variance.

13.2 Pilot Ltd

(a) and (b)

	Budget			Actual	
	Original	Flexed			
Output (units) (production and sales)	5,000	5,400		5,400	
	£	£		£	
Sales revenue	25,000	27,000		26,460	
Raw materials	(7,500)	(8,100)	(2,700 kg)	(8,770)	(2,830 kg)
Labour	(6,250)	(6,750)	(1,350 hr)	(6,885)	(1,300 hr)
Fixed overheads	(6,000)	(6,000)		(6,350)	
Operating profit	5,250	6,150		4,455	

	£		Manager accountable
Sales volume variance (5,250 − 6,150)	900	(F)	Sales
Sales price variance (27,000 − 26,460)	(540)	(A)	Sales
Materials price variance (2,830 × 3) − 8,770	(280)	(A)	Buyer
Materials usage variance [(5,400 × 0.5) − 2,830] × £3	(390)	(A)	Production
Labour rate variance (1,300 × £5) − 6,885	(385)	(A)	Personnel
Labour efficiency variance [(5,400 × 0.25) − 1,300] × £5	250	(F)	Production
Fixed overhead spending (6,000 − 6,350)	(350)	(A)	Various − depends on the nature of the overheads
Total net variances	£795	(A)	

Budgeted profit	£5,250
Less Total net variance	795
Actual profit	£4,455

13.4 (a) Flexing the budget identifies what the profit would have been, had the only difference between the original budget and the actual figures been concerned with the difference in volume of output. Comparing this profit figure with that in the original budget reveals the profit difference (variance) arising solely from the volume difference (sales volume variance). Thus, flexing the budget does not mean at all that volume differences do not matter. Flexing the budget is the means of discovering the effect on profit of the volume difference.

In one sense, all variances are 'water under the bridge', to the extent that the past cannot be undone, and so it is impossible to go back to the last control period and put in a better performance. Identifying variances can, however, be useful in identifying where things went wrong, which should enable management to take steps to ensure that the same things do not to go wrong in the future.

(b) Variances will not tell you what went wrong. They should, however, be a great help in identifying the manager within whose sphere of responsibility things went wrong. That manager should know why it went wrong. In this sense, variances identify relevant questions, but not answers.

(c) Identifying the reason for variances may well cost money, usually in terms of staff time. It is a matter of judgement in any particular situation, of balancing the cost of investigation against the potential benefits. As is usual in such judgements, it is difficult, before undertaking the investigation, to know either the cost or the likely benefit.

In general, significant variances, particularly adverse ones, should be investigated. Persistent (over a period of months) smaller variances should also be investigated. It should not automatically be assumed that favourable variances can be ignored. They indicate that things are not going according to plan, possibly because the plans (budgets) are flawed.

(d) Research evidence does not show this. It seems to show that managers tend to be most motivated by having as a target the most difficult goals that they find acceptable.

(e) Budgets normally provide the basis of feedforward and feedback control. During a budget preparation period, potential problems (for example a potential stock shortage) might be revealed. Steps can then be taken to revise the plans in order to avoid the potential problem. This is an example of a feedforward control: potential problems are anticipated and eliminated before they can occur.

Budgetary control is a very good example of feedback control, where a signal that something is going wrong triggers steps to take corrective action for the future.

13.5 Bradley-Allen Ltd

(a)

	Original	Flexed		Actual	
		Budget			
Output (units) (production and sales)	800	950		950	
	£	£		£	
Sales revenue	64,000	76,000		73,000	
Raw materials – A	(12,000)	(14,250)	(285 kg)	(15,200)	(310 kg)
– B	(16,000)	(19,000)	(950 m)	(18,900)	(920 m)
Labour – skilled	(4,000)	(4,750)	(475 hr)	(4,628)	(445 hr)
– unskilled	(10,000)	(11,875)	(1,484.375 hr)	(11,275)	(1,375 hr)
Fixed overheads	(12,000)	(12,000)		(11,960)	
Operating profit	10,000	14,125		11,037	

Sales variances

Volume:	$10,000 - 14,125 = £4,125$	(F)
Price:	$76,000 - 73,000 = £3,000$	(A)

Direct materials A variances

Usage:	$[(950 \times 0.3) - 310] \times £50 = £1,250$	(A)
Price:	$(310 \times £50) - £15,200 = £300$	(F)

Direct materials B variances

Usage:	$[(950 \times 1) - 920] \times £20 = £600$	(F)
Price:	$(920 \times £20) - £18,900 = £500$	(A)

Skilled direct labour variances

Efficiency:	$[(950 \times 0.5) - 445] \times £10 = £300$	(F)
Rate:	$(445 \times £10) - £4,628 = £178$	(A)

Unskilled direct labour variances

Efficiency:	$[(950 \times 1.5625) - 1,375] \times £8 = £875$	(F)
Rate:	$(1,375 \times £8) - £11,275 = £275$	(A)

Fixed overhead variances

Spending:	$(12,000 - 11,960) = £40$	(F)

Budgeted profit				£10,000
Sales:	Volume	4,125	(F)	
	Price	(3,000)	(A)	1,125
Direct material A:	Usage	(1,250)	(A)	
	Price	300	(F)	(950)
Direct material B:	Usage	600	(F)	
	Price	(500)	(A)	100
Skilled labour:	Efficiency	300	(F)	
	Rate	(178)	(A)	122
Unskilled labour:	Efficiency	875	(F)	
	Rate	(275)	(A)	600
Fixed overheads:	Expenditure			40
Actual profit				**£11,037**

(b) The statement in (a) is useful to management because it enables them to see where there have been failures to meet the original budget and to be able to quantify the extent of such failures. This means that junior managers can be held accountable for the performance of their particular area of responsibility.

13.7 Varne Chemprocessors

(a) The standard usage rate of UK194 (per litre of Varnelyne) is $200/5,000 = 0.04$.

The standard price = $£392/200 = £1.96$ per litre of UK194.

Materials usage variance (UK194) is

$$[(637,500 \times 0.04) - 28,100] \times £1.96 = £5,096 \text{ (A)}$$

Materials price variance is

$$(28,100 \times £1.96) - £51,704 = £3,372 \text{ (F)}$$

(b) The net variance on UK194 was, from the calculations in (a), £1,724 (A) (that is £5,096 − 3,372). This seems to have led directly to savings elsewhere of £4,900, giving a net cost saving of over £3,000 for the month.

Unfortunately things may not be quite as simple as the numbers suggest. Will the non-standard mix to make the Varnelyne lead to a substandard product, which could have very wide-ranging ramifications in terms of potential loss of market goodwill?

There is also the possibility that the material for which the UK194 was used as a substitute was already in stock. If this were the case, is there any danger that this material may deteriorate and, ultimately, prove to be unusable?

Other possible adverse outcomes of the non-standard mix could also arise.

The question is raised by the analysis in part (a) (and by the production manager's comment) of why the cost standard for UK194 had not been revised to take account of the lower price prevailing in the market.

(c) The variances, period by period and cumulatively, for each of the two materials are given as follows:

		UK500		UK800	
		Period £	Cumulative £	Period £	Cumulative £
Period	1	301 (F)	301 (F)	298 (F)	298 (F)
	2	(251) (A)	50 (F)	203 (F)	501 (F)
	3	102 (F)	152 (F)	(52) (A)	449 (F)
	4	(202) (A)	(50) (A)	(98) (A)	351 (F)
	5	153 (F)	103 (F)	(150) (A)	201 (F)
	6	(103) (A)	zero	(201) (A)	zero

Without knowing the scale of these variances relative to the actual costs involved, it is not possible to be too dogmatic about how to interpret the above information.

UK500 appears to show a fairly random set of data, with the period variances fluctuating from positive to negative and giving a net variance of zero. This is what would be expected from a situation that is basically in control.

UK800 also shows a zero cumulative figure over the six periods, *but* there seems to be a more systematic train of events, particularly the four consecutive adverse variances from period 3 onwards. This looks as if it may be out of control and worthy of investigation.

Chapter 14

14.1 Mylo Ltd

(a) The annual depreciation of the two projects is:

$$\text{Project 1: } \frac{(£100{,}000 - £7{,}000)}{3} = £31{,}000$$

$$\text{Project 2: } \frac{(£60{,}000 - £6{,}000)}{3} = £18{,}000$$

Project 1

(i)

	Year 0 £000	Year 1 £000	Year 2 £000	Year 3 £000
Net profit(loss)		29	(1)	2
Depreciation		31	31	31
Capital cost	(100)			
Residual value				7
Net cash flows	(100)	60	30	40
10% discount factor	1.000	0.909	0.826	0.751
Present value	(100.00)	54.54	24.78	30.04
Net present value	**9.36**			

(ii) Clearly the IRR lies above 10%; try 15%:

15% discount factor	1.000	0.870	0.756	0.658
Present value	(100.00)	52.20	22.68	26.32
Net present value	**1.20**			

Thus the IRR lies a little above 15%, perhaps around 16%.

(iii) To find the payback period, the cumulative cash flows are calculated:

Cumulative cash flows	(100)	(40)	(10)	30

Thus the payback will occur after 3 years if we assume year-end cash flows.

Project 2

(i)

	Year 0 £000	Year 1 £000	Year 2 £000	Year 3 £000
Net profit (loss)		18	(2)	4
Depreciation		18	18	18
Capital cost	(60)			
Residual value				6
Net cash flows	(60)	36	16	28
10% discount factor	1.000	0.909	0.826	0.751
Present value	(60.00)	32.72	13.22	21.03
Net present value	6.97			

(ii) Clearly the IRR lies above 10%; try 15%:

15% discount factor	1.000	0.870	0.756	0.658
Present value	(60.00)	31.32	12.10	18.42
Net present value	1.84			

Thus the IRR lies a little above 15%; perhaps around 17%.

(iii) The cumulative cash flows are:

Cumulative cash flows	(60)	(24)	(8)	20

Thus, the payback will occur after 3 years (assuming year-end cash flows).

(b) Presuming that Mylo Ltd is pursuing a wealth-maximisation objective, project 1 is preferable since it has the higher NPV. The difference between the two NPVs is not significant, however.

(c) NPV is the preferred method of assessing investment opportunities because it fully addresses each of the following:

- *The timing of the cash flows.* Discounting the various cash flows associated with each project, according to when they are expected to arise, takes account of the fact that cash flows do not all occur simultaneously. Associated with this is the fact that by discounting, using the opportunity cost of finance (namely the return that the next-best alternative opportunity would generate), the net benefit, after financing costs have been met, is identified (as the NPV).

- *The whole of the relevant cash flows.* NPV includes all of the relevant cash flows irrespective of when they are expected to occur. It treats them differently according to their date of occurrence, but they are all taken into account in the calculation of the NPV and they all have, or can have, an influence on the decision.

- *The objectives of the business.* NPV is the only method of appraisal where the output of the analysis has a direct bearing on the wealth of the business. (Positive NPVs enhance wealth; negative NPVs reduce it.) Since most private-sector businesses seek to increase their value and wealth, NPV clearly is the best approach to use.

14.5 Newton Electronics Ltd

(a) **Option 1**

	Year 0 £m	Year 1 £m	Year 2 £m	Year 3 £m	Year 4 £m	Year 5 £m
Plant and equipment	(9.0)					1.0
Sales revenue		24.0	30.8	39.6	26.4	10.0
Variable costs		(11.2)	(19.6)	(25.2)	(16.8)	(7.0)
Fixed costs (ex. dep'n)		(0.8)	(0.8)	(0.8)	(0.8)	(0.8)
Working capital	(3.0)					3.0
Marketing costs		(2.0)	(2.0)	(2.0)	(2.0)	(2.0)
Opportunity costs		(0.1)	(0.1)	(0.1)	(0.1)	(0.1)
	(12.0)	9.9	8.3	11.5	6.7	4.1
Discount factor 10%	1.000	0.909	0.826	0.751	0.683	0.621
Present value	(12.0)	9.0	6.9	8.6	4.6	2.5
NPV	19.6					

Option 2

	Year 0 £m	Year 1 £m	Year 2 £m	Year 3 £m	Year 4 £m	Year 5 £m
Royalties	–	4.4	7.7	9.9	6.6	2.8
Discount factor 10%	1.000	0.909	0.826	0.751	0.683	0.621
Present value	–	4.0	6.4	7.4	4.5	1.7
NPV	24.0					

Option 3

	Year 0	Year 2
Instalments	12.0	12.0
Discount factor 10%	1.000	0.826
Present value	12.0	9.9
NPV	21.9	

(b) Before making a final decision, the board should consider the following factors:
  ● The long-term competitiveness of the business may be affected by the sale of the patents.
  ● At present, the business is not involved in manufacturing and marketing products. Would a change in direction be desirable?
  ● The business will probably have to buy in the skills necessary to produce the product itself. This will involve costs, and problems will be incurred. Has this been taken into account?
  ● How accurate are the forecasts made and how valid are the assumptions on which they are based?
(c) Option 2 has the highest NPV and is therefore the most attractive to shareholders. However, the accuracy of the forecasts should be checked before a final decision is made.

14.6 Chesterfield Wanderers

(a) and (b)

Player option

	0 £000	1 £000	2 £000	3 £000	4 £000	5 £000
Sale of player	2,200					1,000
Purchase of Bazza	(10,000)					
Sponsorship and so on.		1,200	1,200	1,200	1,200	1,200
Gate receipts		2,500	1,300	1,300	1,300	1,300
Salaries paid		(800)	(800)	(800)	(800)	(1,200)
Salaries saved		400	400	400	400	600
Net cash received (paid)	(7,800)	3,300	2,100	2,100	2,100	2,900
Discount factor 10%	1.000	0.909	0.826	0.751	0.683	0.621
Present values	(7,800)	3,000	1,735	1,577	1,434	1,801
NPV	1,747					

Ground improvement option

	1 £000	2 £000	3 £000	4 £000	5 £000
Ground improvements	(10,000)				
Increased gate receipts	(1,800)	4,400	4,400	4,400	4,400
	(11,800)	4,400	4,400	4,400	4,400
Discount factor 10%	0.909	0.826	0.751	0.683	0.621
Present values	(10,726)	3,634	3,304	3,005	2,732
NPV	1,949				

(c) The ground improvement option provides the higher NPV and is therefore the preferable option, based on the objective of shareholder wealth maximisation.

(d) A professional football club may not wish to pursue an objective of shareholder wealth maximisation. It may prefer to invest in quality players in an attempt to enjoy future sporting success. If this is the case, the NPV approach will be less appropriate because the club is not pursuing a strict wealth-maximisation objective.

14.7   Simtex Ltd

(a) Net operating cash flows each year will be:

	£000	£000
Sales revenue (160 × £6)		960
Less		
Variable costs (160 × £4)	640	
Relevant fixed costs	170	810
		150

The estimated NPV of the new product can then be calculated:

	£000
Annual cash flows (150 × 3.038*)	456
Residual value of equipment (100 × 0.636)	64
	520
Less Initial outlay	480
Net present value	40

* This is the sum of the discount rates over four years. Where the cash flows are constant, it is a quicker procedure than working out the present value of cash flows for each year and then adding them together.

(b) (i)   Assume the discount rate is 18%. The net present value of the project would be:

	£000
Annual cash flows (150 × 2.690)	404
Residual value of equipment (100 × 0.516)	52
	456
Less Initial outlay	480
NPV	(24)

Thus an increase of 6%, from 12% to 18% in the discount rate causes a fall from +40 to –24 in the NPV, a fall of 64 or 10.67 (that is, 64/6) for each 1% rise in the discount rate. So a zero NPV will occur with a discount rate approximately equal to 12 + (40/11.67) = 15.4%. (This is, of course, the IRR.)

This higher discount rate represents an increase of about 28% on the existing cost of capital figure.

(ii) The initial outlay on equipment is already expressed in present-value terms and so, to make the project no longer viable, the outlay will have to increase by an amount equal to the NPV of the project (that is, £40,000) – an increase of 8.3% on the stated initial outlay.

(iii) The change necessary in the annual net cash flows to make the project no longer profitable can be calculated as follows:

Let Y = change in the annual operating cash flows. Then (Y × cumulative discount rates for a four-year period) – NPV = 0

This can be rearranged as: Y × cumulative discount rates for a four-year period = NPV

$$Y \times 3.038 = £40,000$$
$$Y = £40,000/3.038$$
$$Y = \underline{£13,167}$$

In percentage terms, this is a decrease of 8.8% on the estimated cash flows.

(iv) The change in the residual value required to make the new product no longer profitable can be calculated as follows:

Let V = change in the residual value:

(V × discount factor at end of four years) – NPV of product = 0

This can be rearranged as follows:

$$V \times \text{discount factor at end of four years} = \text{NPV of product}$$
$$V \times 0.636 = £40,000$$
$$V = £40,000/0.636$$
$$V = \underline{£62,893}$$

This is a decrease of 63.9% in the residual value of the equipment.

(c) The NPV of the product is positive and so it will increase shareholder wealth. Thus, it should be produced. The sensitivity analysis suggests the initial outlay and the annual cash flows are the most sensitive variables for managers to consider.

14.8 Kernow Cleaning Services Ltd

(a) The first step is to calculate the expected annual cash flows:

Year 1	£	Year 2	£
£ 80,000 × 0.3	24,000	£140,000 × 0.4	56,000
£160,000 × 0.5	80,000	£220,000 × 0.4	88.000
£200,000 × 0.2	40,000	£250,000 × 0.2	50,000
	144,000		194,000
Year 3		Year 4	
£140,000 × 0.4	56,000	£100,000 × 0.3	30,000
£200,000 × 0.3	60,000	£170,000 × 0.6	102,000
£230,000 × 0.3	69,000	£200,000 × 0.1	20,000
	185,000		152,000

698 APPENDIX D SOLUTIONS TO SELECTED EXERCISES

The *expected net present value (ENPV)* can now be calculated as follows:

Period	Expected cash flow £	Discount rate 10%	Expected PV £
0	(540,000)	1.000	(540,000)
1	144,000	0.909	130,896
2	194,000	0.826	160,244
3	185,000	0.751	138,935
4	152,000	0.683	103,816
ENPV			(6,109)

(b) The *worst possible outcome* can be calculated by taking the lowest values of savings each year, as follows:

Period	Cash flow £	Discount rate 10%	PV £
0	(540,000)	1.000	(540,000)
1	80,000	0.909	72,720
2	140,000	0.826	115,640
3	140,000	0.751	105,140
4	100,000	0.683	68,300
NPV			(178,200)

The probability of occurrence can be obtained by multiplying together the probability of *each* of the worst outcomes above, that is $0.3 \times 0.4 \times 0.4 \times 0.3 = \underline{0.014}$.

Thus, the probability of occurrence is 1.4%, which is very low.

Chapter 15

15.1 H. Brown (Portsmouth) Ltd

(a) The main factors to take into account are:
- *Risk.* If a business borrows, there is a risk that at the maturity date of the loan the business will not have the funds to repay the amount owing and will be unable to find a suitable form of replacement borrowing. With short-term loans, the maturity dates will arrive more quickly and the type of risk outlined will occur at more frequent intervals.
- *Matching.* A business may wish to match the life of an asset with the maturity date of the borrowing. In other words, long-term assets will be purchased with long-term loan funds. A certain level of current assets, which form part of the long-term asset base of the business, may also be funded by long-term borrowing. Those current assets that fluctuate owing to seasonality and so on will be funded by short-term borrowing. This approach to funding assets will help reduce risks for the business.
- *Cost.* Interest rates for long-term loans may be higher than for short-term loans as investors may seek extra compensation for having their funds locked up for a long period. However, issue costs may be higher for short-term loans as there will be a need to refund at more frequent intervals.
- *Flexibility.* Short-term loans may be more flexible. It may be difficult to repay long-term loans before the maturity period.

(b) When deciding to grant a loan, a lender should consider the following factors:
- Security.
- Purpose of the loan.
- Ability of the borrower to repay.
- Loan period.
- Availability of funds.
- Character and integrity of the senior managers.

(c) Loan conditions may include:
- The need to obtain permission before issuing further loans.
- The need to maintain a certain level of liquidity during the loan period.
- A restriction on the level of dividends and directors pay.

15.2 Devonian plc

(a) (i) *Ex rights price*

	£
5 original shares @ £2.10 per share	10.50
1 rights share @ £1.80	1.80
	12.30
Theoretical ex-rights price (£12.30/6)	£2.05

(ii) *Value of rights*

	£
Value of a share after the rights issue	2.05
Cost of a rights share	1.80
Value of rights	0.25
Value of rights attached to each original share	£0.25/5
	£0.05

(b) (i) *Share price in one year's time*
Rights issue
We must first calculate the existing P/E ratio in order to determine the share price in one year's time. This can be done as follows:

	£m
Net profit before interest and taxation (Year 4)	40.0
Less Corporation tax (30%)	12.0
Profit available to shareholders	28.0

Earnings per share (EPS) (£28.0m/200m) = £0.14

$$\text{P/E ratio} = \frac{\text{Share price}}{\text{EPS}} = £2.10/£0.14 = 15 \text{ times}$$

	£m
Net profit before interest and taxation (Year 5)	50.0
Less corporation tax (30%)	15.0
Profit available to ordinary shareholders	35.0

Earnings per share (£35m/240m) = £0.146
Share price (Year 5) = EPS × P/E ratio = £0.146 × 15 = £2.19

(ii) *Loan issue*

	£m
Net profit before interest and taxation profit (Year 5)	50.0
Less Loan interest payable (£72m @ 10%)	7.2
	42.8
Less Corporation tax (30%)	12.8
Profit available to ordinary shareholders	30.0

Earnings per share (£30m/200m)	= £0.15
Share price (Year 5)	= EPS × P/E ratio
	= £0.15 × 13.5
	= £2.03

These calculations reveal that in one year's time the share price is expected to rise by more than 4% above the current share price if a rights issue is made, whereas the share price will fall by more than 3% if a loan issue is made. Given the additional financial risks attached to a loan issue, it seems that a rights issue offers the better alternative – at least in the short term.

(c) By issuing shares at a discount in a rights issue, pressure is put on the shareholders either to take up the shares or sell the right to someone that will. Failure to do one of these will lead to a loss of wealth for the shareholder.

(d) The price at which rights issues are made is not critical. It needs to be sufficiently low to put pressure on shareholders to take them up or sell the rights. It also needs to be low enough to make it unlikely that, between setting the issue price and the date of the issue, the current market price of the existing share will not have fallen below the rights issue price. Since the discount does not represent a real bonus to the shareholders, it can be quite large.

15.3 Brocmar plc

(a) (i) EPS = £1.8m/10m   = £0.180

    (ii) Rights price = £1.80 – (20% × £1.80)   = £1.44

    (iii) No. of shares issued = £2.88m/£1.44   = 2m

    (iv) EPS for next year = (£1.8m + £0.4m)/(10m + 2m) = £0.183

    (v) Ex-rights price: 5 shares @ £1.80   = £9.00

                        1 share @ £1.44   = £1.44

                         6   £10.44

    Theoretical ex-rights price per share = £10.44/6   = £1.74

(b) Additional information should include:
- future cash flows from the project
- the degree of risk associated with the project
- the cost of capital required to undertake the project
- the NPV of the project
- the extent to which the project fits with the strategy of the business.

15.4 Raphael Ltd

The existing credit policies have the following costs:

	£
Cost of investment in trade debtors [(50/365) × £2.4m × 12%]	39,452
Cost of bad debts (1.5% × £2.4m)	36,000
Total cost	75,452

Employing a factor will result in the following costs and savings:

	£
Charges of the factor (2% × £2.4m)	48,000
Interest charges on advance [(30/365) × (80% × £2.4m) × 11%]	17,359
Interest charges on overdraft [(30/365) × (20% × £2.4m) × 12%]	4,734
Total cost	70,093
Less Credit control savings	(18,000)
Net cost	52,093

We can see the net cost of factoring is lower than the existing costs, and so there would be a benefit gained from entering into an agreement with the factor.

15.6 Carpets Direct plc

(a) The earnings per share (EPS) is:

$$\frac{\text{Profit after taxation}}{\text{Number of ordinary shares}} = \frac{£4.5m}{120m} = £0.0375$$

The current market value per share is:

$$\text{Earnings per share} \times \text{P/E} = £0.0375 \times 22 = £0.825$$

The rights issue price will be £0.825, less 20% discount = £0.66.
  The theoretical ex-rights price is:

	£
Original shares (4 @ £0.825)	3.30
Rights share (1 @ £0.66)	0.66
Value of five shares following rights issue	3.96

Therefore, the value of one share following the rights issue is:

$$\frac{£3.96}{5} = 79.2p$$

(b)

Value of one share after rights issue	79.2p
Cost of a rights share	(66.0p)
Value of rights to shareholder	13.2p

(c) (i) *Taking up rights issue*

	£
Shareholding following rights issue [(4,000 + 1,000) × 79.2p]	3,960
Less Cost of rights shares (1,000 × 66p)	(660)
Shareholder wealth	3,300

(ii) *Selling the rights*

Shareholding following rights issue (4,000 × 79.2p)	3,168
Add Proceeds from sale of rights (1,000 × 13.2p)	132
Shareholder wealth	3,300

(iii) *Doing nothing*

As the rights are neither purchased nor sold, the shareholder wealth following the rights issue will be:

Shareholding (4,000 × 79.2p)	3,168

We can see that the investor will have the same wealth under the first two options. However, by the investor doing nothing, the rights offer will lapse and so the investor will lose the value of the rights and will be worse off.

Chapter 16

16.1 **Hercules Wholesalers Ltd**

(a) The liquidity ratios of the business 1:0.6 seem low. The current ratio is only 1:1.1 (that is, 306/285) and its acid test ratio is 1:0.6 (that is, 163/285). This latter ratio suggests that the business has insufficient liquid assets to pay its short-term obligations. A cash flow projection for the next period would provide a better insight to the liquidity position of the business. The bank overdraft seems high and it would be useful to know whether the bank is pressing for a reduction and what overdraft limit has been established for the business.

(b) The operating cash cycle can be calculated as follows:

No. of days

Average stockholding period:

$$\frac{[(\text{Opening stock} + \text{Closing stock})/2] \times 360}{\text{Cost of sales}} = \frac{[(125 + 143)/2] \times 360}{323} = 149$$

Add Average settlement period for debtors:

$$\frac{\text{Trade debtors} \times 360}{\text{Credit sales}} = \frac{163}{452} \times 360 \qquad = \underline{130}$$

$$= 279$$

Less Average settlement period for creditors:

$$\frac{\text{Trade creditor} \times 360}{\text{Credit purchases}} = \frac{145}{341} \times 360 \qquad = \underline{153}$$

$$= \underline{126}$$

(c) The business can reduce the operating cash cycle in a number of ways. The average stockholding period seems quite long. At present, average stocks held represent almost five months' sales. This period can be reduced by reducing the level of stocks held. Similarly, the average settlement period for debtors seems long at more than four months' sales revenue. This may be reduced by imposing tighter credit control, offering discounts, charging interest on overdue accounts, and so on. However, any policy decisions concerning stocks and debtors must take account of current trading conditions.

The operating cash cycle would also be reduced by extending the period of credit taken to pay suppliers. However, for the reasons mentioned in the chapter, this option must be given careful consideration.

16.5

Mayo Computers Ltd
New proposals from credit control department

	£000	£000
Current level of investment in debtors		
(£20m × (60/365))		3,288
Proposed level of investment in debtors		
((£20m × 60%) × (30/365))	(986)	
((£20m × 40%) × (50/365))	(1,096)	(2,082)
Reduction in level of investment		1,206

The reduction in overdraft interest as a result of the reduction in the level of investment will be £1,206,000 × 14% = £169,000.

	£000	£000
Cost of cash discounts offered (£20m × 60% × 2½%)		300
Additional cost of credit administration		20
		320
Bad debt savings	(100)	
Interest charge savings (see above)	(169)	(269)
Net cost of policy each year		51

These calculations show that the business would incur additional annual costs if it implemented this proposal. It would therefore be cheaper to stay with the existing credit policy.

16.6 Boswell Enterprises Ltd

(a)

	Current policy		New policy	
	£000	£000	£000	£000
Debtors				
[(£3m × 1/12 × 30%) + (£3m × 2/12 × 70%)]		425.0		
[(£3.15m × 1/12 × 60%) + (£3.15m × 2/12 × 40%)]				367.5
Stocks				
[£3m − (£3m × 20%)] × 3/12]		600.0		
{[£3.15m − (£3.15m × 20%)] × 3/12}				630.0
Cash (fixed)		140.0		140.0
		1,165.0		1,137.5
Creditors				
[£3m − (£3m × 20%)] × 2/12]	(400.0)			
{[£3.15m − (£3.15m × 20%)] × 2/12}			(420.0)	
Accrued variable expenses				
[£3m × 1/12 × 10%]	(25.0)			
[£3.15m × 1/12 × 10%]			(26.3)	
Accrued fixed expenses	(15.0)	(440.0)	(15.0)	(461.3)
Investment in working capital		725.0		676.2

(b) The forecast net profit for the year

	Current policy		New policy	
	£000	£000	£000	£000
Sales revenue		3,000.0		3,150.0
Cost of goods sold		(2,400.0)		(2,520.0)
Gross profit (20%)		600.0		630.0
Variable expenses (10%)	(300.0)		(315.0)	
Fixed expenses	(180.0)		(180.0)	
Discounts	–	(480.0)	(47.3)	542.3
Net profit		120.0		87.7

(c) Under the proposed policy we can see that the investment in working capital will be slightly lower than under the current policy. However, profits will be substantially lower as a result of offering discounts. The increase in sales revenue resulting from the discounts will not be sufficient to offset the additional costs of making the discounts to customers. It seems that the business should, therefore, stick with its current policy.

16.7 **Delphi plc**

(a) The debtors ageing schedule is:

	1 month or less £000	%	1 to 2 months £000	%	2 to 3 months £000	%	Total debtors £000	%
				Number of months outstanding				
February								
TV and hi-fi	20.0	(22.2)					20.0	(22.2)
Music	30.0	(33.3)					30.0	(33.3)
Retail	40.0	(44.5)					40.0	(44.5)
	90.0	(100.0)					90.0	(100.0)
March								
TV and hi-fi	20.8	(12.5)					20.8	(12.5)
Music	31.8	(19.2)	30.0	(18.1)			61.8	(37.3)
Retail	43.2	(26.1)	40.0	(24.1)			83.2	(50.2)
	95.8	(57.8)	70.0	(42.2)			165.8	(100.0)
April								
TV and hi-fi	21.6	(10.0)					21.6	(10.0)
Music	33.7	(15.6)	31.8	(14.7)			65.5	(30.3)
Retail	46.7	(21.4)	43.2	(19.9)	40.0	(18.4)	129.9	(59.7)
	102.0	(47.0)	75.0	(34.6)	40.0	(18.4)	217.0	(100.0)
May								
TV and hi-fi	22.5	(9.6)					22.5	(9.6)
Music	35.7	(15.4)	33.7	(14.6)			69.6	(30.0)
Retail	50.4	(21.7)	46.7	(20.1)	43.2	(18.6)	140.2	(60.4)
	108.6	(46.7)	80.4	(34.7)	43.2	(18.6)	232.3	(100.0)

We can see that the debtors figure will increase substantially in the first four months. The retail chains will account for about 60% of the total debtors outstanding by May as this group has the fastest rate of growth. There is also a significant decline in the proportion of total debts outstanding from TV and hi-fi shops over this period.

(b) In answering this part of the question, you should refer to the 'five Cs of credit' that were discussed in detail in the chapter.

16.8   Goliath plc

(a) (i)   The existing operating cash cycle can be calculated as follows:

	Number of days
Stockholding period $= \dfrac{\text{Stock at year end}}{\text{Cost of sales}} \times 365$	
$= \dfrac{560}{1{,}440} \times 365 =$	142
Add Debtors settlement period $= \dfrac{\text{Debtors at year end}}{\text{Sales}} \times 365$	
$= \dfrac{565}{2{,}400} \times 365 =$	86
	228
Less Creditors settlement period $= \dfrac{\text{Creditors at year end}}{\text{Purchases}} \times 365$	
$= \dfrac{451}{1{,}450} \times 365 =$	(114)
Operating cash cycle	114

The new operating cash cycle is:

	Number of days
Stockholding period $= \dfrac{(560 \times 1.15)}{(2{,}400 \times 1.10) \times 0.60} \times 365 =$	148
Debtors settlement period $= 86 + 20$	106
	254
Less Creditors settlement period $= 114 + 15$	(129)
	125
New operating cash cycle	125
Existing operating cash cycle	(114)
Increase in operating cash cycle (days)	11

(ii)

	£000
Increase (decrease) in stock held [(560 × 1.15) − 560]	84.0
Increase (decrease) in debtors {[(2,400 × 1.1) × (106/365)] − 565}	201.7
	285.7
(Increase) decrease in creditors [1,668 × (129/365) − 451]	(138.6)
Increase (decrease) in net investment	147.1

(iii)

	£000	£000
Gross profit increase [(2,400 × 0.1) × 0.40]		96.0
Adjust for		
Admin. expenses increase (15%)	(45.0)	
Bad debts increase	(120.0)	
Interest (10%) on borrowing for increased net investment in working capital (147.1)	(14.7)	(179.7)
Increase (decrease) in net profit before tax		(83.7)
Decrease in tax charge for the period (25% × 83.7)		20.9
Increase (decrease) in net profit after tax		(62.8)

(b) There would be an increase in the operating cash cycle and this will have an adverse effect on liquidity. The existing debtors and stockholding periods already appear to be quite high. Any increase in either of these must be justified. The planned increase in the creditors period must also be justified because it may risk the loss of goodwill from suppliers. Though there is an expected increase in revenue of £240,000 from adopting the new policy, the net profit after taxation will decrease by £62,800. This represents a substantial decrease when compared with the previous year. (The increase in bad debts is a major reason why the net profit is adversely affected.) There is also a substantial increase in the net investment in stocks, debtors and creditors, which seem high in relation to the expected increase in sales revenue. The new policy requires a significant increase in investment and is expected to generate lower profits than are currently being enjoyed. It should, therefore, be rejected.

Appendix A

A.1

	Account to be debited	*Account to be credited*
(a)	Stock	Trade creditors
(b)	Capital (or a separate drawings account)	Cash
(c)	Loan interest	Cash
(d)	Stock	Cash
(e)	Cash	Trade debtors
(f)	Wages	Cash
(g)	Capital (or a separate drawings account)	Trade debtors
(h)	Trade creditors	Cash
(i)	Electricity (or heat and light)	Cash
(j)	Cash	Sales revenue

Note that the precise name given to an account is not crucial so long as those who are using the information are clear as to what each account deals with.

A.2   (a) and (b)

Cash

		£			£
1 Feb	Capital	6,000	3 Feb	Stock	2,600
15 Feb	Sales revenue	4,000	5 Feb	Equipment	800
28 Feb	Trade debtors	2,500	9 Feb	Rent	250
			10 Feb	Fuel and electricity	240
			11 Feb	General expenses	200
			21 Feb	Capital	1,000
			25 Feb	Trade creditors	2,000
			28 Feb	Balance c/d	5,410
		12,500			12,500
1 Mar	Balance b/d	5,410			

Capital

		£			£
21 Feb	Cash	1,000	1 Feb	Cash	6,000
28 Feb	Balance c/d	5,000			
		6,000			6,000
			1 Mar	Balance b/d	5,000
28 Feb	Balance c/d	7,410	28 Feb	Profit and loss	2,410
		7,410			7,410
			1 Mar	Balance b/d	7,410

Stock

		£			£
3 Feb	Cash	2,600	15 Feb	Cost of sales	2,400
6 Feb	Trade creditors	3,000	19 Feb	Cost of sales	2,300
			31 Jan	Balance c/d	900
		5,600			5,600
1 Mar	Balance b/d	900			

Equipment

		£			£
5 Feb	Cash	800			

Trade creditors

		£			£
25 Feb	Cash	2,000	6 Feb	Stock	3,000
28 Feb	Balance c/d	1,000			
		3,000			3,000
			1 Feb	Balance b/d	1,000

Rent

		£			£
9 Feb	Cash	250	28 Feb	Profit and loss	250

Fuel and electricity

		£			£
10 Feb	Cash	240	28 Feb	Profit and loss	240

General expenses

		£			£
11 Feb	Cash	200	28 Feb	Profit and loss	200

Sales revenue

		£			£
28 Feb	Balance c/d	7,800	15 Feb	Cash	4,000
			19 Feb	Trade debtors	3,800
		7,800			7,800
28 Feb	Profit and loss	7,800	28 Feb	Balance b/d	7,800

Cost of sales

		£			£
15 Feb	Stock	2,400	28 Feb	Balance c/d	4,700
19 Feb	Stock	2,300			
		4,700			4,700
28 Feb	Balance b/d	4,700	28 Feb	Profit and loss	4,700

Trade debtors

		£			£
19 Feb	Sales revenue	3,800	28 Feb	Cash	2,500
			28 Feb	Balance c/d	1,300
		3,800			3,800
1 Mar	Balance b/d	1,300			

(b) Trial balance as at 28 February

	Debits £	Credits £
Cash	5,410	
Capital		5,000
Stock	900	
Equipment	800	
Trade creditors		1,000
Rent	250	
Fuel and electricity	240	
General expenses	200	
Sales revenue		7,800
Cost of sales	4,700	
Trade debtors	1,300	
	13,800	13,800

(c)

Profit and loss account

			£			£
28 Feb	Cost of sales		4,700	28 February	Sales revenue	7,800
28 Feb	Rent		250			
28 Feb	Fuel and electricity		240			
28 Feb	General expenses		200			
28 Feb	Capital (net profit)		2,410			
			7,800			7,800

Balance sheet as at 28 February

	£	£
Non-current assets:		
Equipment		800
Current assets:		
Stock	900	
Trade debtors	1,300	
Cash	5,410	
	7,610	
Current liabilities		
Trade creditors	1,000	
		6,610
		7,410
Capital		7,410

Profit and loss account for the month ended 28 February

	£	£
Sales revenue		7,800
Cost of sales		4,700
Gross profit		3,100
Less Rent	250	
Fuel and electricity	240	
General expenses	200	
		690
Net profit for the month		2,410

A.3

Buildings

		£			£
1 Jan	Balance brought down	25,000			

Fittings – cost

		£			£
1 Jan	Balance brought down	10,000	31 Dec	Balance carried down	12,000
	Cash	2,000			
		12,000			12,000
1 Jan	Balance brought down	12,000			

Fittings – depreciation

		£			£
31 Dec	Balance carried down	4,400	1 Jan	Balance brought down	2,000
			31 Dec	Profit and loss	
				(£12,000 × 20%)	2,400
		4,400			4,400
			1 Jan	Balance brought down	4,400

General expenses

		£			£
1 Jan	Balance brought down	140	31 Dec	Profit and loss	570
	Cash	580		Balance carried down	150
		720			720
1 Jan	Balance brought down	150			

Stock-in-trade

		£			£
1 Jan	Balance brought down	1,350	31 Dec	Cost of sales	15,220
31 Dec	Trade creditors	17,220		Cost of sales	4,900
	Cash	3,760		Capital	560
				Balance carried down	1,650
		22,330			22,330
1 Jan	Balance brought down	1,650			

Cost of sales

		£			£
31 Dec	Stock-in-trade	15,220	31 Dec	Profit and loss	20,120
	Stock-in-trade	4,900			
		20,120			20,120

Rent

		£			£
1 Jan	Balance brought down	500	31 Dec	Profit and loss	3,000
31 Dec	Cash	3,000		Balance carried down	500
		3,500			3,500
1 Jan	Balance brought down	500			

Trade debtors

		£			£
1 Jan	Balance brought down	1,840	31 Dec	Cash	32,810
31 Dec	Sales revenue	33,100		Profit and loss (bad debt)	260
				Balance carried down	1,870
		34,940			34,940
1 Jan	Balance brought down	1,870			

Cash

		£			£
1 Jan	Balance brought down	2,180	31 Dec	Stock-in-trade	3,760
31 Dec	Sales revenue	10,360		Wages	3,770
	Loan	2,000		Rent	3,000
	Trade debtors	32,810		Electricity	1,070
				General expenses	580
				Fittings	2,000
				Loan	1,000
				Trade creditors	18,150
				Capital	10,400
				Balance carried down	3,620
		47,350			47,350
1 Jan	Balance brought down	3,620			

Capital

		£			£
31 Dec	Stock-in-trade	560	1 Jan	Balance brought down	25,050
	Cash	10,400		Profit and loss (profit)	10,900
	Balance carried down	24,990			
		35,950			35,950
			1 Jan	Balance brought down	24,990

Loan

		£			£
30 June	Cash	1,000	1 Jan	Balance brought down	12,000
31 Dec	Balance carried down	13,000		Cash	2,000
		14,000			14,000
			1 Jan	Balance brought down	13,000

Trade creditors

		£			£
30 June	Cash	18,150	1 Jan	Balance brought down	1,690
31 Dec	Balance carried down	760	31 Dec	Stock-in-trade	17,220
		18,910			18,910
			1 Jan	Balance brought down	760

Electricity

		£			£
31 Dec	Cash	1,070	1 Jan	Balance brought down	270
31 Dec	Balance carried down	290	31 Dec	Profit and loss	1,090
		1,360			1,360
			1 Jan	Balance brought down	290

Sales revenue

		£			£
31 Dec	Profit and loss	43,460	31 Dec	Trade debtors	33,100
				Cash	10,360
		43,460			43,460

Wages

		£			£
31 Dec	Cash	3,770	31 Dec	Profit and loss	3,770

Loan interest

	£			£
		31 Dec	Profit and loss	1,350
			[(6/12 × 14,000) +	
			(6/12 × 13,000)] × 10%	

Profit and loss

		£			£
31 Dec	Cost of sales	20,120	31 Dec	Sales revenue	43,460
	Depreciation	2,400			
	General expenses	570			
	Rent	3,000			
	Bad debts (Trade debtors)	260			
	Electricity	1,090			
	Wages	3,770			
	Loan interest	1,350			
	Profit (Capital)	10,900			
		43,460			43,460

Balance sheet as at 31 December last year

	£			£
Non-current assets			Capital	24,990
Property, plant and equipment				
Buildings		25,000		
Fittings: cost	12,000		**Non-current liabilities**	
depreciation	(4,400)	7,600	Loan	13,000
Current assets			**Current liabilities**	
Stock of stationery		150	Trade creditors	760
Stock-in-trade		1,650	Accrued electricity	290
Prepaid rent		500	Accrued loan interest	1,350
Trade debtors		1,870		
Cash		3,620		
		40,390		40,390

Appendix E
Present Value Table

Present value of £1, that is, $1/(1 + r)^n$

where r = discount rate
n = number of periods until payment

Periods (n)					Discount rates (r)						
	1%	2%	3%	4%	5%	6%	7%	8%	9%	10%	
1	0.990	0.980	0.971	0.962	0.952	0.943	0.935	0.926	0.917	0.909	1
2	0.980	0.961	0.943	0.925	0.907	0.890	0.873	0.857	0.842	0.826	2
3	0.971	0.942	0.915	0.889	0.864	0.840	0.816	0.794	0.772	0.751	3
4	0.961	0.924	0.888	0.855	0.823	0.792	0.763	0.735	0.708	0.683	4
5	0.951	0.906	0.863	0.822	0.784	0.747	0.713	0.681	0.650	0.621	5
6	0.942	0.888	0.837	0.790	0.746	0.705	0.666	0.630	0.596	0.564	6
7	0.933	0.871	0.813	0.760	0.711	0.665	0.623	0.583	0.547	0.513	7
8	0.923	0.853	0.789	0.731	0.677	0.627	0.582	0.540	0.502	0.467	8
9	0.914	0.837	0.766	0.703	0.645	0.592	0.544	0.500	0.460	0.424	9
10	0.905	0.820	0.744	0.676	0.614	0.558	0.508	0.463	0.422	0.386	10
11	0.896	0.804	0.722	0.650	0.585	0.527	0.475	0.429	0.388	0.350	11
12	0.887	0.788	0.701	0.625	0.557	0.497	0.444	0.397	0.356	0.319	12
13	0.879	0.773	0.681	0.601	0.530	0.469	0.415	0.368	0.326	0.290	13
14	0.870	0.758	0.661	0.577	0.505	0.442	0.388	0.340	0.299	0.263	14
15	0.561	0.743	0.642	0.555	0.481	0.417	0.362	0.315	0.275	0.239	15

(continued over)

Periods (n)	Discount rates (r)										
	11%	12%	13%	14%	15%	16%	17%	18%	19%	20%	
1	0.901	0.893	0.885	0.877	0.870	0.862	0.855	0.847	0.840	0.833	1
2	0.812	0.797	0.783	0.769	0.756	0.743	0.731	0.718	0.706	0.694	2
3	0.731	0.712	0.693	0.675	0.658	0.641	0.624	0.609	0.593	0.579	3
4	0.659	0.636	0.613	0.592	0.572	0.552	0.534	0.516	0.499	0.482	4
5	0.593	0.567	0.543	0.519	0.497	0.476	0.456	0.437	0.419	0.402	5
6	0.535	0.507	0.480	0.456	0.432	0.410	0.390	0.370	0.352	0.335	6
7	0.482	0.452	0.425	0.400	0.376	0.354	0.333	0.314	0.296	0.279	7
8	0.434	0.404	0.376	0.351	0.327	0.305	0.285	0.266	0.249	0.233	8
9	0.391	0.361	0.333	0.308	0.284	0.263	0.243	0.225	0.209	0.194	9
10	0.352	0.322	0.295	0.270	0.247	0.227	0.208	0.191	0.176	0.162	10
11	0.317	0.287	0.261	0.237	0.215	0.195	0.178	0.162	0.148	0.135	11
12	0.286	0.257	0.231	0.208	0.187	0.168	0.152	0.137	0.124	0.112	12
13	0.258	0.229	0.204	0.182	0.163	0.145	0.130	0.116	0.104	0.093	13
14	0.232	0.205	0.181	0.160	0.141	0.125	0.111	0.099	0.088	0.078	14
15	0.209	0.183	0.160	0.140	0.123	0.108	0.095	0.084	0.074	0.065	15

Index